The Somme Battlefields

A Guide to the
Cemeteries and Memorials
of the Battlefields of the Somme

1914-18

by

Michael Scott

The Naval & Military Press Ltd

Published by

The Naval & Military Press Ltd
Unit 5 Riverside, Brambleside,
Bellbrook Industrial Estate,
Uckfield, East Sussex,
TN22 1QQ England

Tel: +44 (0) 1825 749494
Fax: +44 (0) 1825 765701

www.naval-military-press.com
www.nmarchive.com

CONTENTS

Introduction	2
Cemeteries	3
Commonwealth War Graves Commission	316
The Battles on the Somme	317
Orders of Battle	321
Cemetery Dead	349
Victoria Cross Winners	364
Terms and Abbreviations	368
Bibliography	370
Index	372

INTRODUCTION

A war that ended in 1918 and in which the men who fought are now dead is today of great historical interest for many British people. The Centenary Celebrations have brought a renewed level of interest in a conflict that is still 'touchable' in that almost all of us know someone at one or two, or even three, generations distance from us. We feel they are our family though time has brought separation. When we make our journeys to the battlefields, we take part in a pilgrimage of sorts, one that remembers those who took part in the battles, the day to day trudge of existence, the familial brotherhood of survival, the occasional laughter and pleasure of simple things, but also honours those who will not get to do what we do, which is return to our families and live our lives to a hopefully old and fulfilled age.

Each year I lead groups to the battlefields of World War One. In trying to provide these groups with as much insight as well as information. But always the question to be answered as we stop at, or more often pass, a cemetery is "Why is this cemetery here?", then of course "Who is buried here?". It was important to me to be able to have answers that showed that every cemetery, and every headstone, (or name on a memorial) has a story. It is easy, especially in somewhere like Serre Road No. 2 Cemetery, to forget that every grave is a life lived, with relatives, experiences and aspirations. This book aims to tell some of the stories, while only scratching the surface. But, importantly, every burial, and every cemetery no matter how isolated or small, call tell us something of our social history.

Defining the area to be covered by the book is a personal decision and quite arbitrary. First, I decided what is the battlefield of the Somme? That means to me 1916 and 1918. Consequently, a much larger area that may be considered the 'Battle of the Somme', which is often only the area involved on 1 July 1916. But in wanting to include the battlefields of 1916 and 1918 I had also to include areas involved in the Retreat to the Hindenburg Line and parts of the Battles of Arras and Cambrai, all in 1917. I know that men who were involved in the battles, and died of a result of their wounds, are not here. Some died months later in Britain. I took one family to follow the footsteps of a relative wounded at Luke Copse near Serre on 1 July 1916 who died of his wounds five days late at a Base Hospital in Rouen and is buried in St Sever Cemetery.

I had to draw lines somewhere and I am satisfied that my boundaries allowed me to validly cover as much of the battlefields of the Somme as made sense.

So, those boundaries are
- The southern boundary of the Department of the Somme from the N1 in the west to the boundary with the Department of the Oise just east of Ham.
- The D930 Ham to St Quentin road
- The A26 from the D930 just west of St Quentin to the D939 Cambrai to Arras road
- The D939 Cambrai to Arras road to the south-western boundary of Arras
- The southern perimeter of Arras from the D939 to the N25 Arras to Doullens road
- The N25 Arras to Doullens, southern bypass of Doullens and N25 Doullens to Amiens road
- A line north south through Amiens
- The N25 south of Amiens to the border of the Department of the Somme.

There is a 'sister' book to this on the cemeteries of the Ypres Salient. It was written in 1991 some 25 years ago. It took some criticism for not being a weighty analysis of the battles of substantial piece of research. Both criticism were valid, but the book was never intended to be either analytic or in-depth research. I did not claim it to be either and did not represent the book as anything other than it was. Similarly, with this book on the cemeteries of the Somme. Nonetheless, I have valued that criticism and kept it in mind as I worked on this book. While there is research into the stories, it is limited and I only want to create something that opens doors. I intend to, as I have said earlier, show that every cemetery is made up of burials that are real people with stores to tell. Some of the stories are easy to include, the Victoria Cross winners, senior officers, those 'Shot at Dawn', the sportsmen, the 'great and the good'. But all of the entries are equally important, as are those that have not found their way here. To use a phrase I use often – 'it is what it is'. However, I firmly believe this is a much better book than the original version of that on the Ypres Salient. I would hope my skills and knowledge base are better after 25 years. Consequently, an improved book on the Salient will be available soon. And my in-depth research, a book on one of the Divisions that has not had a book written about it before will also be competed in the future.

All the burial grounds are accessible though it is not possible to get a car right up to the entrance of each one and sometimes great care will have to be taken when using/driving larger vehicles.

I have included each British cemetery alphabetically using the names as spelt by the Commonwealth War Graves Commission. Following these are the French and German cemeteries.

So, I hope you find the book useful and have as much enjoyment reading it as I did in writing it.

ACHEUX BRITISH CEMETERY

HISTORY

The cemetery was opened in July 1916 and was used during the early battles of 1916. Most of the remaining graves date from the German offensive of 1918.

INFORMATION

The cemetery was begun at the VIII Corps Collecting Station which had been placed in the village as preparations were made for the 1916 offensives. Rows A and B represent the men of 1916. The other rows are mostly men of 1918.

One of the men buried here is Private Frank Joseph Wolfe of the 10th West Yorkshires. He had survived his battalion's disaster at Fricourt on the first day of the Somme, been wounded twice, torpedoed on returning to France and rescued before his death in June 1918 aged 22.

Also buried here is Private William Barry Nelson, 14th Durham Light Infantry. He was a Kitchener volunteer who had absconded from duty twice. At his first court martial he received a sentence of one year's imprisonment followed by penal servitude for life. His third desertion brought a death sentence carried out in Acheux on 11 August 1916.

Another here is Private Harry Walker, 'A' Company, 10th Sherwood Foresters (Notts and Derby Regiment), killed on 6 May 1918 aged 24 years. His brother, Private Arthur Walker, 8th York and Lancasters died on 9 April 1917 aged 21 years and is commemorated on the Menin Gate at Ieper. Another brother, Private Fred Walker, 2/6th West Yorkshires died on 15 February 1917 aged 27 years and is buried in Serre Road Cemetery No. 1.

East of the village is a memorial to the 'Picardy Martyrs of the Resistance 1940-45'.

UK – 179   Can - 1

LOCATION

Acheux-en-Amienois lies between Doullens and Albert on the main road. The cemetery is south-west of the village on the north side of the road to Lealvillers. The cemetery is about 50m from the road and reached by a path. This is a peaceful setting on the edge of a valley with good views.

ACHIET-LE-GRAND COMMUNAL CEMETERY EXTENSION

HISTORY

The cemetery was opened in April 1917 and used by the 45th and 49th Casualty Clearing Stations until March 1918. Then the Germans occupied the area and used the cemetery briefly before the Allies returned in August 1918. The Extension was expanded by the concentration of 645 graves after the war.

INFORMATION

The town was occupied by the 7th Bedfordshires in March 1917 when the Germans withdrew to the Hindenburg Line. The Germans re-took the village from the 1/6th Manchesters on 25 March 1918 and lost it again on 23 August 1918. The station in the village was a British railhead while they were here.

One man buried here is Private Arthur Mitchel, 1/6th Lancashire Fusiliers who was executed in the village on 20 August 1917 for desertion. He had served in Gallipoli but gone absent just before being sent into the trenches again having only spent six months in the Western Front. He was arrested working in a field behind the lines wearing blue trousers and a policeman's hat.

Buried here is Bombardier E. Watmough, Royal Field Artillery, killed on 31 August 1918 aged 27 years. His brother, 2nd Lieutenant John Cyril Watmough, 2nd Northumberland Fusiliers died on 10 July 1915, aged 26 years is buried in Ridge Wood Cemetery near Ieper. Another brother, Private Victor Watmough, 15th Royal Scots, died on 22 October 1917 aged 19 years and is commemorated on the Tyne Cot Memorial.

Also buried here is Lieutenant Colonel Philip Vaughan Holberton. He was five times Mentioned in Despatches and held the Order of the White Eagle (Serbia). He was Brevet Major and Brevet Colonel with the 2nd Manchesters. He died on 26 March 1918 aged 38 years.

Concentrated here:

Achiet-Le-Grand German Cemetery - on the road to Bihucourt about 500m south-east of here, in which were one British soldier buried by the Germans, and five buried by the British in August 1918.

Achiet-Le-Petit Communal Cemetery - on the east side of the village about 1.5km south-west of here. It contained the graves of three British soldiers and one from New Zealand, buried by the Germans.

Achiet-Le-Petit Communal Cemetery German Extension – east of the communal cemetery. It was begun by the Germans, carried on by the Allies in August 1918, and completed after the war by the concentration of 360 German Graves. It contained the graves of 50 British soldiers, 39 from New Zealand and 1147 Germans.

Beaumetz-Les-Cambrai Communal Cemetery – about 10km east of here south of the Bapaume-Cambrai road. Six

British soldiers, three from Australia and one from Canada, all buried by the Germans, were among 201 Germans.

Beaumetz-Les-Cambrai Communal Cemetery German Extension – located next to the Communal Cemetery containing the grave of one British soldier among 298 Germans.

Behagnies Churchyard – about 3km east of here. It was used by the Germans in 1916 for the burial of 86 German soldiers and one British soldier.

Behagnies German Cemetery - on the main road through the village. It was used in 1918 for the burial of 100 German, four French and one British soldiers.

Beugnatre Communal Cemetery German Extension – located about 5km east of here. It contained 200 German graves and those of two British soldiers (one of whom is now buried in Bancourt British Cemetery while the other is here).

Beugny Churchyard and German Extension – located about 10km east of here on the Bapaume-Cambrai road. Buried here were 46 British soldiers, of whom 34 belonged to the Royal Garrison Artillery, six from Australia, 19 French and 183 German soldiers.

Beugny German Cemetery (Heldenfriedhof) - located in the north-west area of the village It contained the graves of five Australian and four British soldiers among 831 Germans.

Boursies Communal Cemetery German Extension - located about 15km east of here on the Bapaume-Cambrai road. It contained the graves of 173 German soldiers, one RAF officer, and one Canadian soldier.

Doignies German Cemetery - located about 15km east of here and south of the Bapaume-Cambrai road, on the south side of the village. It contained the graves of 15 British soldiers, one from Australia, and 150 German men.

Hermies Communal Cemetery – found about 20km east of here south of the Bapaume-Cambrai road. Buried here were six British men and two Australian soldiers buried by the Germans.

Louverval German Cemetery, Doignies - located about 15km east of here and north of the Bapaume-Cambrai road just outside Louverval Château grounds. It contained the burials of seven unidentified Highlanders and 138 German soldiers.

Queant Communal Cemetery – located about 15km north-east of here. Among 180 German burials were three British soldiers who died in March 1918.

Queant Communal Cemetery German Extension – it contained ten British men, with 660 Germans and four Russians.

Velu German Cemetery – located about 12km east of here south of the Bapaume-Cambrai road, on the east side of the village. Buried with 850 Germans were five British, two Newfoundland, one Australian, one Indian and one French soldiers.

Villers-au-Flos-German Cemetery – on the north side of the village which is about 8km south-east of here. Three Australian and three British graves of men who died in 1916 were removed from here.

Vraucourt Churchyard – located about 6km east of here. It contained the graves of two Australian men who died in 1917

UK – 1259	Aust – 61	NZ – 95 Can – 4
NF – 1	SAfr – 4	Ger – 42
Unnamed – 200		Area – 3506 sq mts

Special Memorials to eight men known or believed to be buried among the unnamed.

Special Memorials for ten men buried in other cemeteries whose graves could not be found at the time of concentration.

LOCATION
Achiet-le-Grand can be found about 3km north-west of Bapaume. It is on the main Amiens-Arras railway and has a small station. The cemetery is on the north-west edge of the village on the west side of the Communal Cemetery. The road upon which it stands is a dead-end and the cemetery can be difficult to locate.

ADANAC MILITARY CEMETERY, MIRAUMONT AND PYS

HISTORY
This is a concentration cemetery made entirely after the war.

INFORMATION
Miraumont and Pys were taken by the Germans in 1914. They were objectives on the first day of the Battle of the Somme on 1 July 1916, but were never captured. They were lost by the Germans in February 1917 when they withdrew to the Hindenburg Line. The villages were captured by the Germans on 25 March 1918 but recaptured, by the 42nd Division, on 24 August 1918.

The concentrations came from a wide area, many from an area bounded by Le Sars, Martinpuich and Flers where there are no cemeteries. It is designated a Canadian Cemetery. Adanac is Canada spelt backwards. The register is bi-lingual and there is a Maple Leaf on the entrance gate. The battlefields at Courcelette were fought over by many Canadian units so many of the graves brought in were of Canadians and hence the name of the cemetery. The cemetery was built up around one grave, that of Private A Edwards, 5th Battalion Machine Gun Corps who was killed on 21 August 1918 when British troops re-took the area and now lies in Plot IV, Row D, Grave 30.

Buried here is Sergeant Samuel Forsyth, VC, No. 3 Field Company, New Zealand Engineers attached 2nd Auckland Infantry Regiment, NZEF. He won a posthumous Victoria Cross on 24 August 1918 at Grevillers. His citation reads 'For most conspicuous bravery and devotion to duty in attack. On nearing the objective, his company came under heavy machine-gun fire. Through Serjt. Forsyth's dashing leadership and total disregard of danger, three machine-gun positions were rushed and the crews taken prisoner before they could inflict many casualties on our troops. During subsequent advance his company came under heavy fire from several machine guns, two of which he located by a daring reconnaissance. In his endeavour to gain support from a Tank, he was wounded, but after having the wound bandaged, he again got in touch with the Tank, which in the face of very heavy fire from machine guns and anti-Tank guns, he endeavoured to lead with magnificent coolness to a favourable position. The Tank, however, was put out of action. Serjt. Forsyth then organised the Tank crew and several of his men into a section, and led them to a position where the machine guns could be outflanked. Always under heavy fire, he directed them into positions which brought about a retirement of the enemy machine guns and enabled the advance to continue. This gallant N.C.O. was at that moment killed by a sniper. From the commencement of the attack until the time of his death Serjt. Forsyth's courage and coolness, combined with great power of initiative proved an invaluable incentive to all who were with him and he undoubtedly saved many casualties among his comrades.'

Another holder of the Victoria Cross buried here is Private (Piper) James Clelland Richardson, VC, 16th (Manitoba Regt) Canadian Infantry, killed on 9 October 1916 aged 20 years. The citation reads 'For most conspicuous bravery and devotion to duty when, prior to attack, he obtained permission from his Commanding Officer to play his company "over the top". As the Company approached the objective, it was held up by very strong wire and came under intense fire, which caused heavy casualties and demoralised the formation for the moment. Realising the situation, Piper Richardson strode up and down outside the wire, playing his pipes with the greatest coolness. The effect was instantaneous. Inspired by his splendid example, the company rushed the wire with such fury and determination that the obstacle was overcome and the position captured. Later, after participating in bombing operations, he was detailed to take back a wounded comrade and prisoners. After proceeding about 200 yards Piper Richardson remembered that he had left his pipes behind. Although strongly urged not to do so, he insisted on returning to recover his pipes. He has never been seen since, and death has been presumed accordingly owing to lapse of time.'

Another man buried here is Private Thomas Alexander Jackson of 11th Argyll & Sutherland Highlanders, killed on 9 October 1916 aged 39. Thomas was an international football player who made six appearances for Scotland between 1904 and 1907. He was considered a stylish right back who spent most of his career until 1909 at St. Mirren. Three boys aged 16 years at the time of their death are here. Private Russell Lewis Collingridge, 3rd Canadian Infantry, from Ontario was killed in action on 8 October 1916. Private Joseph Lorne Dewart, 87th Canadian Infantry, from Ottawa was killed in action between 21 and 22 October 1916. Private Thomas Ethelbert Tombs, 50th Canadian Infantry was killed on 19 November 1916.

Concentrated here:

Pys British Cemetery - situated about 1km south of Pys and 2km north of Courcelette near the road between the villages. It contained the graves of 22 Canadian, two British and five unidentified soldiers. There was also a memorial to 33 men of the 72nd Canadian Infantry (Seaforth Highlanders).

Pys New British Cemetery - situated in the village. It was made by the 42nd Division in August and September 1918. It contained 35 British soldiers and a New Zealander.

Aqueduct Road Cemetery, Pys - near the road between Pys and Le Sars. It was made by the 6th and 99th Infantry Brigades in March 1917. It contained eleven British soldiers.

New Zealand Cemetery, Grevillers - situated close to Grevillers churchyard. It contained the graves of 19 New Zealand soldiers who died in August and September 1918.

Shrine Cemetery, Grevillers - situated about 1km west of the village on the road to Irles. It contained the graves of thirteen New Zealand and two British soldiers who died in August 1918.

UK – 1973	Can – 1071	NZ – 70
Aust – 53	KUG – 5	Ger – 1
Unnamed – 1711		Area – 8697 sq mts

Special Memorials to thirteen British soldiers known, or believed, to be buried among the unnamed graves.

LOCATION

Miraumont and Pys are villages to the west of the main Albert-Bapaume road about 15km north-east of Albert and 5km south-west of Bapaume. The cemetery lies across the border of the two villages on the east side of the road from Miraumont to Courcelette on a ridge, in open fields, midway between the two villages. It has very good views of the battlefield.

ADELAIDE CEMETERY, VILLERS-BRETONNEUX

HISTORY

The cemetery was begun in June 1918 during the defence of Amiens and was used until 8 August 1918 when the fighting moved away from here. It was used after the war for the concentration of over 850 graves from small graveyards and the surrounding battlefields.

INFORMATION

Villers-Bretonneux was the point at which the German advance of 1918 was halted. (See Villers-Bretonneux Military Cemetery) German tanks and infantry captured the village on 23 April 1918. It was retaken by the 13th and 15th Australian Brigades, with help from the British 8th and 18th Divisions, on the following day and overnight into 25 April, the third anniversary of the first ANZAC Day. Hence, this can be seen to be the limit of the German advance in the 'Great Gamble' of 1918.

Adelaide Cemetery was begun by the 2nd and 3rd Australian Divisions. Most of Plot I was completed by August when the cemetery, then comprising about 80 graves, was closed.

The concentrations after the war were almost exclusively those of men who fell between March and September 1918. Plot II was made up almost entirely of British graves and Plot III of Australian graves. This shows the Australian policy of concentrating graves into large cemeteries after the war.

The 13th Australian Infantry Brigade, the 49th, 50th, 51st and 52nd Australian Infantry Battalions and the 22nd Durham Light Infantry erected memorials to their dead but these have now been removed. There is an empty space in front of the Cross of Sacrifice where the memorials were situated.

Buried here is Lieutenant Colonel Stephen Grey Latham, DSO, MC and Bar commanding the 2nd Northamptonshires who was killed in a night counter-attack on 24 April 1918 aged 46 years. He is buried next to a Private from his battalion killed in the same attack. His Distinguished Service Order was awarded posthumously in July 1918 for managing his battalion well rather than a single act.

Among those here are brothers Lieutenant Ronald Grahame Henderson, MC, 18th Australian Infantry, killed in action on 9 April 1918 aged 25 years and Private Hugh Grahame Henderson, 35th Australian Infantry, died of wounds on 4 April 1918 aged 18 years. Ronald was the intelligence officer for the 5th Brigade and won the Military Cross at Ieper in September 1917. He was killed by a German shell.

On 11 November 1993 the remains of an unidentified Australian soldier were removed from the cemetery in Plot III, Row M, taken to Canberra and reburied in the Australian War Memorial.

Concentrated here :

Embankment Cemetery, Villers-Bretonneux - located about 200m west of Adelaide Cemetery, by the railway and next to a Dressing Station. It was used by the 2nd and 4th Australian Divisions from April to July 1918. It contained 37 Australian soldiers and a British airman.

Chalk Lane Cemetery, Villers-Bretonneux - 100m north-west of Adelaide Cemetery. It was used in April and May 1918 for the burial of fourteen British and ten Australian soldiers.

White Chateau Cemetery, Cachy - located 1.5km west of Adelaide Cemetery between the wood and the railway. It was used from April to August 1918 for the burial of 23 Australian, nine British and two Canadian soldiers.

Cachy British Cemetery - situated on the north-western edge of the village. It was used for the burial of two British soldiers who died in March 1918 and for ten Canadians who died in August 1918.

UK – 365   Aust – 519   Can – 22
KUG – 48   Unnamed – 260   Area – 4373 sq mts

Special memorials to four Australians known, or believed, to be buried among the unnamed graves.

LOCATION

Villers-Bretonneux lies on the main Amiens-St. Quentin road about 15km east of the centre of Amiens. The cemetery also lies on the main road, on the north side, and on the western edge of the village next to the railway crossing as the road enters a valley. It is at the rear of an old quarry.

AGNY MILITARY CEMETERY

HISTORY

The cemetery was begun by the French when they occupied the sector in 1914. The British began to make burials here in March 1916 and it remained in use until June 1917. Two further burials were made in September 1918 and the cemetery was enlarged after the war.

INFORMATION

The village was always behind the British front-line though the fighting came close on several occasions. There were several burial grounds in the village. For example, north of the village was a British burial ground called the 'Railway Arch' which has been removed to Douchy-les-Ayette British Cemetery.

At the end of the war the Cemetery contained 311 graves but the 40 French graves have been removed as has a German Cemetery containing over 1000 graves. In 1923-24, 137 graves were concentrated here from the battlefields east of Arras.

Among those here is 2nd Lieutenant Gordon Amhurst Forsyth, 8th Royal Fusiliers, killed in action on 27 August 1916 aged 28 years. He was educated in London and Switzerland. His father was in the Stock Exchange, he joined in 1911 and married the daughter of a member of the Stock Exchange. He joined the 12th Royal Fusiliers as a Private in 1914, rising to the rank of Sergeant before they went to France in September 1915. He fought first at Loos and stayed with the battalion until June 1916. He was commissioned and transferred to 8th Royal Fusiliers with whom he served for a few weeks on the Somme until killed by a mortar shell.

Also here is 2nd Lieutenant Philip Edward Thomas, 244th Siege Battery, Royal Garrison Artillery who died on 9 April 1917 aged 39 years. A member of the Dymock group of poets, he was a friend of Rupert Brooke and initially enlisted with the 1/28th (Artists Rifles) Londons in July 1915. He was commissioned into the artillery in August 1916 and went to France with his Battery in February 1917. He was killed when a shell exploded near to him while he was on observation duties.

Also of note is 2nd Lieutenant Robert Henry Hose, 2nd Bedfordshires, killed in action on 18 March 1917 with Private Thomas Pearson from his battalion. They were killed by a German booby trap left as the Germans retreated to the Hindenburg Line. Hose had been at the Front for three days.

UK – 407   Aust – 1   Ger – 5
Unnamed – 118   Area – 2498 sq mts

LOCATION

Agny is situated about 3km south of Arras in the valley of the River Crinchon. The Military Cemetery is north-west of the village on the east side of the Achicourt-Wailly road. It is north of the old chateau grounds in a small clearing in the woods behind new housing. It is a very pleasant and surprisingly peaceful location.

A.I.F. BURIAL GROUND, GRASS LANE, FLERS

HISTORY

The Cemetery was begun by Australian medical units, posted in the nearby caves, in November 1916 and used until February 1917. It was very greatly enlarged after the war by the concentration of 3842 British and French graves from the battlefields of the Somme, and afterwards from a wider area. Most of these graves date from the autumn of 1916, but one is of 1914, and others date from the spring of 1917 and the spring and summer of 1918.

INFORMATION

Flers was in German hands until it was captured on 15 September 1916 in the Battle of Flers-Courcelette. It was entered by the New Zealand and 41st Divisions when tanks were used for the first time. It was lost in the German advance in March 1918 and retaken at the end of the following August.

The nearby village of Gueudecourt was an objective for the tanks on 15 September 1916. Three tanks almost reached the village but they were stopped by German artillery and the 41st Division infantry did not get to them. Most of the men killed in tanks on that day suffered their fate south of Gueudecourt. The village was captured on 29 September 1916 after a co-ordinated attack by infantry, tanks and the Royal Flying Corps – quite a feat for that time. The first men in the village were from the 19th Lancers of the Indian Army and South Irish Horse followed by the 6th Leicesters of the 21st Division.

The original cemetery had only 32 graves, now Plot I, Rows A and B. The post war concentration came in two phases. Plots 1 to 6 including the French graves were made first. Plots 7 to 16 were added later. This was probably done when Thiepval was being cleared to make way for the Memorial to the Missing. Many graves are unidentified but those that are identified show men from units that were involved in fighting at Thiepval in 1916 and 1918 – notably the 36th (Ulster) Division on 1 July 1916. When completed, the cemetery was one of the largest on the 1916 battlefield.

North of Gueudecourt, on a ridge between Gueudecourt and Beaulencourt, on the line of the furthest 1916 advance is a Newfoundland Memorial. It is a copy of the Caribou at Newfoundland Park, Beaumont-Hamel. There is also a preserved section of trench in a small enclosure. Although the Newfoundlanders suffered heavily on 1 July 1916 they were in action again on 12 October 1916 attacking the German Hilt Trench north of Gueudecourt. The Germans counter-attacked and pushed the 1st Essex, who had attacked with the Newfoundlanders, out of their section of the trench, but the Newfoundlanders re-took the line holding off repeated attacks throughout the day and night. The trench preserved with the memorial is actually part of Mild Trench rather than Hilt Trench.

Buried here is Sergeant Harold Jackson of 'C' Company, 7th East Yorkshires, killed on 24 August 1918 aged 26 years. He won the Victoria Cross at Hermies on 22 March 1918 but was later killed and his body was concentrated here into Plot 15. His citation reads 'For most conspicuous bravery and devotion to duty. Sgt. Jackson volunteered and went out through the hostile barrage and brought back valuable information regarding the enemy's movements. Later, when the enemy had established themselves in our line, this N.C.O. rushed at them and, single-handed, bombed them out into the open. Shortly afterwards, again single-handed, he stalked an enemy machine-gun, threw Mills bombs at the detachment, and put the gun out of action. On a subsequent occasion, when all his officers had become casualties, this very gallant N.C.O. led his company in the attack, and, when ordered to retire, he withdrew the company successfully under heavy fire. He then went out repeatedly under heavy fire and carried in wounded.'

Also buried here is Lieutenant Colonel Charles William Reginald Duncombe though his surname is recorded as Feversham. He was the 2nd Earl of Feversham, a title he inherited from his grandfather in 1915. He was killed, on his first day in action, while commanding 21st (Yeoman Rifles) King's Royal Rifle Corps, though he had previously commanded the Yorkshire Hussars. He had been an MP until 1915. Originally his grave had been located about 1km north-east of Flers near the Ligny-Thilloy road. The body was moved the 200m to the cemetery after WW2.

Among the Australians buried here is Private Edward Claude Perkins, 17th Australian Infantry, a carpenter from Sydney, who claimed to be 21 years old when he enlisted in January 1916. He was killed by shell fire near High Wood on 8 November 1916 aged 16 years 8 months.

The most senior Australian officer buried here is Major George Matson Nicholas, DSO, MiD, 25th Australian Infantry. He won the Distinguished Service Order as a Captain at Pozieres in 1916 leading an assault on a German machine-gun. He was married to Hilda Rix, a renowned Australian artist who was living in France at the outbreak of the war. She was advised to evacuate from her studio in Etaples so she abandoned all her artwork and, with her widowed mother and sister, hastily left France to England. Hilda's sister contracted enteric fever and died soon after arriving in England. Her mother also passed away two years later. By this time, her former studio was used by members of the 24th Australian Infantry. Major Nicholas, found her artwork and admired it so greatly that when he was on leave in England he found Hilda. A whirlwind romance led to marriage. A few days after the ceremony, Major Nicholas returned to France where he was killed at Flers six weeks later on 14 November 1916.

Another Australian is 2nd Lieutenant Frederick William Hordern Matthews, DCM, 6th Company, Australian Machine Gun Corps, killed in action at Flers on 8 November 1916 aged 26 years. On 4 July 1916 at Armentieres he and his two brothers, Arthur aged 23 years, and Henry aged 20 years, were manning a machine gun when attacked by a German raiding party. In the fighting his brothers were killed. They are buried at Ration Farm Military Cemetery near Armentieres. At Pozieres in July he manned a machine gun holding back a German attack and later, while still under fire, rescued men buried by shell-fire. For these acts he was awarded the Distinguished Conduct Medal.

Concentrated here:

Factory Corner, Flers - a little west of the crossing of the roads from Eaucourt-l'Abbaye to Gueudecourt and from Flers to Ligny-Thilloy. This location had been a German Headquarters for Artillery and Engineers and had a German Cemetery. It was taken by the 1st Canterbury Infantry, NZEF on 25 September 1916, and again by the 7th East Yorkshires on the 27 August 1918. Fifteen British and thirteen Australian soldiers were buried there between October 1916 to March 1917, and in August 1918.

North Road Cemetery, Flers - north-west of the village at the crossing of the Eaucourt-l'Abbaye road with 'North Road' (to Factory Corner). Here were buried in the winter of 1916-17 thirteen Australian and seven British soldiers.

UK – 2815	Aust – 417	NZ – 89
Can – 67	SAfr – 27	Fr – 164
Ger – 3	Unnamed – 2262	
KUG – 60	Area – 9827 sq mts	

Special Memorials are erected to fifteen Australian, five British and three New Zealand men, known or believed to be buried here among the unnamed graves.

Special Memorials record the names of three British soldiers buried in a cemetery at Flers, who graves could not be found.

LOCATION

Flers is about 7km north-east of Albert and 5km south of Bapaume. The cemetery is about 2km north-east of Flers, on a track known to the Army as Grass Lane. The local name of the site is 'Aux Cavées'. It is 200m east of the Bapaume-Flers road and 50m south of the Le Sars-Gueudecourt road.

ALBERT COMMUNAL CEMETERY EXTENSION

HISTORY

The Extension was begun in August 1915 when British troops took over this area from the French. Battalions from 1915 to November 1916 buried men, by bringing casualties in from the front line, in what had been part of the Communal Cemetery and was later separated from it. Field Ambulances stationed in and near the town used the burial ground particularly in, and after, September 1916. From November 1916, the 5th Casualty Clearing Station used it for two months. From March 1917 to March 1918 it was only used for four burials. Finally, at the end of August 1918, Plot II was added by the 18th Division in a raised area by the entrance. This raised area was also used for the WW2 burials.

INFORMATION

Albert was held by the French during the German advance in 1914. Although the town fell to the Germans they only held it for a short time before the French recaptured the town. The British took over this sector in the summer of 1915. The front lines were only 2km north of the town from 1914 to July 1916. The town played an important role as a significant logistics centre during the Battles of the Somme in 1916. The first major fighting in the area involving the British was 1 July 1916, during which the British suffered their worst ever casualties for a single day. The town was captured by the Germans on 26 March 1918 when the 7th Suffolks were the last to leave before German Marines entered Albert. Before its recapture by the 8th East Surreys on 22 August it had been completely destroyed by artillery fire. A plaque on the Hotel de Ville says 'There remained only the name, the glory and the ruins'.

The town has a long history as a centre of pilgrimage. This began in the Middle Ages when a shepherd found a statue of the Virgin Mary, the Black Madonna, near what is now Bapaume Post Cemetery. From that time there was an annual animal pilgrimage to the Basilica of Notre Dame de Brebieres.

The Basilica was completed in 1897 with a golden statue of the Virgin Mary and child on the top of the tower. The soldiers claimed that should the virgin fall from the tower the war would end. French Engineers propped up the statue after heavy shelling by the Germans struck the basilica on 15 January 1915. Meanwhile the tower had been used by artillery observers and the church used as a Dressing Station during the start of the Somme offensive in 1916. The statue finally fell after British shelling on 16 April 1918 during the period of German occupation and the war ended soon after. Today's statue is a modern replacement. Today you will find the Somme 1916 Museum in a tunnel beneath the Basilica in the centre of the town.

Once the German marines had captured Albert in March 1918 they were ordered to press on their attack. They did not because of British machine guns on the road to Amiens and the Marines, who had been without food for two days or more, had discovered the food supplies that the British had abandoned.

There was an attempt after the war to declare Albert a 'Zone Rouge' like Verdun. Some argued it was too dangerous to rebuild after the war. Fortunately, that argument was lost.

In WW2 the village fell to German Panzers on 20 May 1940. Thirteen men of the 7th Queen's Own Royal West Kents were killed in the town square and buried here. The Germans set up an HQ in the town and took over the aircraft factory. Albert was liberated on 1 September 1944 after a short battle when the Guards Armoured Division, on its way north, met unexpected resistance in the town. Three of their casualties are buried here. The 50th Division finally cleared the town.

The first burial here was Private H Mason of the 1/4th Kings Own attached 179th Tunnelling Company, Royal Engineers who died on 31 August 1915 when he was overcome by gas after he fell down a mine shaft. He is buried in the corner of the Extension furthest from the Cross of Sacrifice. Major Thomas Charles Richardson, MC and 2nd Lieutenant Arthur James Latham of the 185th Company, Royal Engineers were killed with eighteen of their men when gas filled the tunnels near La Boiselle following an explosion of a German mine in February 1916.

There is a communal grave for thirteen men of 10th Essex killed in November 1915 when the Germans exploded a mine under them at the Glory Hole at La Boiselle. Another communal grave contains eleven men of 41st (Durham) Siege Battery and an Army Service Corps driver killed on 14 July 1916 when a German shell hit them.

Brigadier-General Henry Frederick Hugh Clifford, DSO, commanding 149th Brigade is buried here. He was killed on 11 September 1916 when he was shot through the heart by a German sniper while he was inspecting newly dug trenches near Mametz Wood. He was attempting to cross open land from one trench to another rather than use the sensible and safe route. His father had won a Victoria Cross at the Battle of Inkerman. Clifford was commissioned in 1888 and had seen service in the South African Wars. His Distinguished Service Order was awarded in February 1915 'for services in connection with operations in the field.'

There is also a Special Memorial to Brigadier-General Randle Barnett-Barker, DSO & Bar, five times MiD, who was killed while commanding 99th Brigade on 24 March 1918. He had retired from the army in 1913 and was re-commissioned at the outbreak of war. He was killed by shell-fire near Gueudecourt and carried to Albert by his men. His grave was subsequently destroyed by shell-fire. He gained the Distinguished Service Order during fighting at Delville Wood in late July/early August 1916, and the Bar to the DSO for leadership and bravery at Arras in 1917. His Staff-Captain Edward Inkerman Jordan Bell, MC, is beside him and also commemorated by a Special Memorial.

Also buried here is an IWGC worker who died in 1921.

Private Henry Palmer of 1/5th Northumberland Fusiliers was executed in Albert for desertion on 27 October 1916 and buried here aged 21 years. He deserted in an attack at Le Sars on 1 October 1916 although he was seen going over the top. He had tried to change his story several times and also claimed to be injured but no-one could see any marks.

Also executed in Albert and buried here is Pioneer or Sapper Ernest Beeby of 212th Company, Royal Engineers, executed for desertion on 9 December 1916. He was the first member of the Royal Engineers to be executed for a military offence in the war. He had managed to reach the coast and was about to board a ship before being captured.

Among those buried here are Samuel Hamer and James Street, both 16th (2nd Salford Pals) Lancashire Fusiliers who were killed on 19 December 1915 when the Germans exploded mines during the Salford Pals' first familiarisation tour of the front-line. They are the Salford Pals first casualties.

Among those buried here are three officers of the 13th Canadian Infantry, who were killed when their dugout at Courcelette was destroyed on 26 September 1916. Lieutenant Colonel Victor Carl Buchanan, DSO, aged 47 years; Captain Carleton Carroll Green, aged 27 years and Major Wilfred Ferrier Petermann, MiD, aged 28 years.

Also here is Lieutenant Colonel Roland Playfair Campbell, commanding 6th Field Ambulance, Canadian Army Medical Corps, killed in action in the main street of Courcelette on 16 September 1916.

There are some graves in the Communal Cemetery on the east side of the Extension that have headstones that are very similar to GCWG headstones. However, they are not CWGC graves. Do not be deceived.

UK – 618	Aust – 39	Can – 202
BWI – 2	Others – 1	Unnamed – 12
India – 3	KUG – 1	WW2 – 17

Area – 3491 sq mts

Special Memorials to five men whose graves were destroyed by shellfire but who are buried here.

LOCATION

Albert is a large town of over 10000 people and is the third largest on the Somme. It lies on the River Ancre in the heart of the area covered by this book. Albert Communal Cemetery is on the south-east side of the town, on the road to Fricourt and Peronne. The Extension is entirely enclosed by the Communal Cemetery except for the frontage to the Fricourt road. The Extension is near the east end of the Communal Cemetery on the north side.

ALLONVILLE COMMUNAL CEMETERY

HISTORY

The Communal Cemetery was begun by the 39th Casualty Clearing Station in August 1916 when it was stationed here. They continued to use it until February 1917. Australian battalions used it from April to July 1918.

INFORMATION

Most men who died in the CCS died from illness rather than wounds. Buried here are the crew of a FE2b 6366 plane of No. 22 Squadron, Royal Flying Corps, on a mission with four other planes from the squadron to take photographs escorted by two DH2s of No. 24 Squadron on 9 September 1916. It was last seen going down in flames and crashing near Contalmaison, where the dead crewmen were pulled from wreckage. The crew were pilot Lieutenant Hamish Strathy Mackay, No. 22 Squadron, Royal Flying Corps and 1st Hampshire Heavy Battery, Royal Garrison Artillery, aged 22 years, and observer Lieutenant Arthur James Bowerman, 8th Somerset Light Infantry, aged 20 years.

| UK – 38 | Aust – 40 | WW2 - 1 |

LOCATION

Allonville is situated about 8km north-east of Amiens. The cemetery is on the western edge of the village on the south side of the road from the church to Querrieu. Fourteen graves are along the western edge of the cemetery. The others are in two rows in a Plot on the eastern edge.

ANCRE BRITISH CEMETERY, BEAUMONT-HAMEL

HISTORY

The cemetery was created in the spring of 1917 when the Germans withdrew to the Hindenburg Line. The V Corps made a number of cemeteries in the old no-man's land to bury the men who had lain dead, some since July 1916, between the two front-lines. The cemetery was only used during the war for this purpose. However, it was enlarged after the war.

INFORMATION

Beaumont-Hamel was an objective for the morning of 1 July 1916 and was attacked by the 29th Division flanked by the 4th Division to its right and the 36th (Ulster) Division to its left. The attacked failed with the loss of very heavy casualties. A further attempt was made on 3 September which also failed. In some of the final acts of the Battles of the Somme in 1916 another attack was made in November. From 13-14 November the 51st, 63rd, 39th and 19th Divisions captured a number local objectives.

The V Corps made several cemeteries, most of which have since been concentrated or given other names, from February to April 1917 to bury the dead of the battles of 1916. This cemetery was then named Ancre River No. 1 British Cemetery or V Corps Cemetery No. 26. Most of the 517 graves made here at that time, in what are now Plots 3 and 4, were men of the 36th, 63rd and 39th Divisions. The men in this section come from attacks by two battalions of the 36th (Ulster) Division on 1 July 1916; five battalions of the 39th Division on 3 September 1916 when some men reached the German line before being pushed back incurring 1850 casualties; and the 63rd (Royal Naval) Division on 13 November 1916 who left a front-line that was close to the edge of this cemetery (though the cemetery was not here) and took all their objectives in a morning but suffered 3500 casualties.

Nearly 2000 men, mostly from the three battles for Beaumont-Hamel in 1916, were concentrated here after the war from seven small battlefield cemeteries. There are many Royal Navy men buried here. The Honourable Artillery Company is also notable.

Buried here is Captain Eric S Ayre of the Royal Newfoundland Regiment who was killed in the slaughter of the battalion on 1 July 1916. He was one of four cousins, all officers, including Eric's brother, killed on 1 July 1916, three within yards of each other. One cousin Wilfred is in Knightsbridge Cemetery while the other, Gerald, has no known grave and is commemorated on the Newfoundland Memorial in Newfoundland Park at Beaumont-Hamel. Eric's brother, Bernard, was in England when war broke out and was commissioned into the Norfolk Regiment in 1914. He is buried in Carnoy Military Cemetery.

Also buried here is Lieutenant The Honourable Vere Sidney Tudor Harmsworth, son of the 1st Viscount Rothermere who was owner of Associated Newspapers including the Daily Mail and who later became a strong supporter of appeasement to Hitler in the 1930's. Harmsworth was killed in the attack by the 63rd (Royal Naval) Division on 13 November 1916 aged 21 years. His elder brother, Captain The Honourable Harold Vyvyan Alfred St. George Harmsworth, MC, 2nd Irish Guards, died of wounds received in December 1917 on 12 February 1918 aged 23 years and is buried in Hampstead Cemetery in London. He was posthumously awarded the Military Cross.

You will find two brothers here both serving with 1st Royal Inniskilling Fusiliers when they were killed on 1 July 1916. Privates James Ford aged 21 and Martin Ford aged 22 years.

The Royal Naval Division Memorial can be found north of the Cemetery on the west side of the road to Albert, south of Beaucourt village. The memorial commemorates the battle of 13 November 1916.

Bernard Cyril Freyburg, (later 1st Baron Freyburg), VC, GCMG, KCB, KBE, DSO & 3 Bars, Temporary Lieutenant Colonel (later Lieutenant General) of Hood Battalion, 63rd (Royal Naval) Division, won a Victoria Cross nearby at Beaucourt in the attack on 13 November 1916. Freyburg's battalion had attacked and captured an enemy line. By then they were in confusion so Freyburg reorganised the situation with men from another unit and attacked and captured the second objective. He was twice wounded but remained in charge throughout the day and night. On the next day he attacked and captured the fortified village of Beaucourt, taking 500 prisoners. He was wounded twice more but refused to leave the line until he had issued instructions. During WW2 he commanded the New Zealand Expeditionary Force and became the Governor General of New Zealand after WW2.

Concentrated here:

Ancre River British Cemetery No. 2 (V Corps Cemetery No. 27) - situated about 400m east of here and made at the same time as the Ancre Cemetery. It contained the graves of 64 British soldiers who fell in September and November 1916. Most of the dead were from the 1st Honourable Artillery Company, 11th Royal Sussex or the Hood Battalion.

Beaucourt Station Cemetery - situated in the valley of the Ancre between the villages of Hamel and Beaucourt near the site of the old railway station. It was begun in late 1916 after Beaucourt had been captured by the 63rd Division in November. It contained 85 British men who died from November 1916 to March 1917 when the front-line moved away from here.

Green Dump Cemetery - situated south-east of Beaumont on the road that the Army called 'Station Road'. It was opened in November 1916 once the area had been captured from the Germans. It remained in use until March 1917 for the burial of 46 British soldiers.

Royal Naval Division Cemetery (V Corps Cemetery No. 21) - situated in the open fields between Beaumont and Hamel close to the present Newfoundland Park. Made during the spring of 1917 it contained the graves of 336 British men mostly from the Royal Naval Division.

Sherwood Cemetery (V Corps Cemetery No. 20) - situated about 700m north-west of the Royal Naval Division Cemetery. Made at the same time as this cemetery it contained the graves of 176 British soldiers, mostly men of the 36th or 63rd Divisions, the 17th Sherwood Foresters or the 17th King's Royal Rifle Corps.

Station Road Cemetery - situated on the south side of Station Road about 500m west of the railway line. The

cemetery was opened in November 1916. It remained in use until March 1917 for the burial of 82 British soldiers.
'Y' Ravine Cemetery No. 2 (V Corps Cemetery No. 18) - situated about 300m south-east of the present 'Y' Ravine Cemetery which is in Newfoundland Park. Made during the spring of 1917 it contained the graves of 140 British soldiers, with two men from Newfoundland, who died during the three battles for Beaumont-Hamel in 1916.

UK – 2446   Newf – 32   NZ – 2   SAfr – 1
Ger – 1   Unnamed – 1335
Area – 7374 sq mts

Special Memorials are erected to 33 British soldiers and ten Newfoundlanders who are known, or believed, to be buried among the unnamed graves.

Special Memorials are erected to sixteen British soldiers who were buried in Green Dump and Grandcourt Station cemeteries whose graves could not be identified at the time of concentration.

LOCATION
Beaumont-Hamel is a commune in the valley of the River Ancre about 8km north of Albert. The cemetery is about 2km south of Hamel and 7km north of Albert. It lies on the west side of the Albert-Miraumont road in the valley of the Ancre between Hamel and Beaucourt. The cemetery is high above the road in a valley running west to Newfoundland Park. It is a very striking cemetery and very memorable.

ASSEVILLERS NEW BRITISH CEMETERY

HISTORY
The cemetery was made after the war by the concentration of graves from the battlefields of the Somme and from other burial grounds. Those buried here were killed mostly in 1915, 1917 and from March and August of 1918.

INFORMATION
The village was taken back from the Germans, who had held it since 1914, by the French in the autumn of 1916. It was lost by the Fifth Army on 26 March 1918, and retaken by the 5th Australian Division on 28 August 1918.

Buried here is 2nd Lieutenant Oliver Chetwode Stokes, 2nd Royal Munster Fusiliers killed in action on 5 March 1917. In his Memoirs "The Storm of Steel" Ernst Junger describes an incident 'On the 5 March a patrol approached our trench in the early morning and began to cut our wire. Lieutenant Eisen with a few men hurried off to warn the nearest post, and threw bombs. The enemy patrol then took flight leaving two men behind them. One, a young lieutenant, died immediately; the other a sergeant was severely wounded in the arm and leg. It appeared from papers found on the officer that he belonged to the Royal Munster Fusiliers. He was very well clothed, and his features though distorted in death were intelligent and energetic. It affected me to find the addresses of several London girls in his pocket-book. We buried him behind our trench and put a simple cross at his head. I saw from this that all patrols need not end so fortunately as mine had done in days past.'
Ernst Junger's Regiment was in the line near the ruins of Villers-Carbonnel and it is believed Stokes was the officer referred to in this extract.

Also here is Private John Hawkins, 2nd Company, Machine Gun Corps (Infantry), died on 24 February 1917 aged 21 years. One brother, Private Fred Hawkins, 700th Motor Transport Company, Army Service Corps, died on 18 January 1918 after an accident aged 29 years and is buried in Croughton (All Saints) Churchyard. Another brother, Private George Hawkins, 6th Oxford and Bucks Light Infantry, was killed on 3 September 1916 aged 31 years and is commemorated on the Thiepval Memorial.

The nearby Belloy-en-Santerre church contains a memorial to an American soldier-poet, Alan Seegar from New York, who was living in Paris when the war began. He joined the French Foreign Legion with forty other Americans and served on the Western Front until killed on 4 July 1916. He was buried in a communal battlefield grave and thought lost. Recent research discovered his body in a mass grave, Ossuaire No. 1, at Lihons National Cemetery. Below the plaque is another listing local men who died in WW1 and volunteers from Barcelona, probably in the French Foreign Legion. Seegar's family provided bells for the church after the war.

Also nearby at Estrees-Deniecourt is a memorial at the junction with the Fay road. The memorial is to men of the French 329th Infantry Regt who died on 4 July 1916 when they were led into an impossible attack by Lieutenant Colonel Puntons, one of eight officers killed in the attack. The regiment took the village on 5 July 1916.

Concentrated here:

Barleux German Cemetery - about 400m north-east of Barleux, in which ten Australian soldiers were buried by their comrades in August and September 1918.

Bouchavesnes (or Peronne Road) German Cemetery - between Marrieres Wood and Bouchavesnes, in which seven South African and three British soldiers were buried by Germans in March 1918. They were probably killed during the disastrous fight at Marrieres Wood on 24 March 1918.

Estrees-Deniecourt German Cemetery - between Estrees and Fay, where two Australian soldiers were buried by the Germans.

Foucaucourt French Military Cemetery - at the south-west corner of the village. Four British soldiers were buried in 1915 and 1917.

Highway Cemetery, Cappy - a French Military Cemetery midway between Cappy and Herbécourt, where six men of the Royal Horse Artillery and one Australian soldier were buried in August and September 1918.

Hyencourt-Le-Grand 'German Cemetery - made by the 61st Infantry Regiment on the Chaulnes-Marchélepot road, where two RAF officers were buried in May 1918.

Kiboko Wood Cemetery, Biaches – between Biaches and Flaucourt. Thirty British soldiers were buried by the 40th Division in February and March 1917. Twenty nine were from the Royal Warwickshires of which twenty were men from the 1/6th Battalion.

Misery Chateau German Cemetery – sixteen British men were buried by a German Field Hospital in March 1918.

P.C. Hedevaux French Military Cemetery (P.C. means Poste de Commandement) – 600m south of Belloy-en-Santerre. Ten British men were buried by their comrades in February and March 1917.

Plantation Cemetery - a French Military Cemetery about 1km east of Cappy. One British soldier was buried in February 1917 and four Australians in August and September 1918.

Vauvillers Communal Cemetery - Four British soldiers who died in March 1918 were reburied here from isolated graves before concentration to Assevillers.

Vermandovillers French Military Cemetery - at the west end of the village. Two British soldiers were buried in March 1917.

Several cemeteries were made by French troops at Assevillers, and in one, at the west end of the village, thirteen British soldiers, now moved to Fouquescourt British Cemetery, were buried by Field Ambulances in February and March 1917.

UK – 647   Aust – 111   Can – 3
SAfr – 16   French - 1   Unnamed - 332
Area – 2656 sq mts

Special memorials are erected to 26 British men, 25 from the 2nd Middlesex who were killed holding a bridge over the Somme helping men to withdraw in March 1918, known or believed to be buried among the unnamed soldiers.

Special memorials record the names of eleven British men, buried in other cemeteries, whose graves were destroyed by shell fire. These cemeteries include Misery Chateau German Cemetery, Foucaucourt Military Cemetery, Hyencourt-le-Grand German Cemetery and Vermandovillers German Cemetery.

LOCATION
Assevillers is located about 10km south-west of Peronne. This is about 1km north of Junction 13 on the A1 Autoroute. Assevillers New British Cemetery is east of the village, just west of the A1 and the new rail link to the UK on the north side of the road to Peronne.

AUBIGNY BRITISH CEMETERY

HISTORY
The cemetery was created between April and August 1918.

INFORMATION
The cemetery was made by Australian units, mostly 54th to 57th Infantry Battalions. Most of the burials are Australians with seven British gunners. One grave of an American soldier has been removed.

Buried here is Captain Norman Beresford Lovett, MC & Bar, Croix de Guerre, 54th Australian Infantry, killed in action on 9 April 1918. He was a teacher before enlisting in the 1st Light Horse Regiment and went overseas as a Sergeant. He fought at Gallipoli, where he was slightly wounded in May 1915. Upon recovery he returned to Gallipoli and remained with the Light Horse until the evacuation. He was then commissioned and transferred as a 2nd Lieutenant in the 53rd Australian Infantry. At Fromelles in July 1916 Lovett led his platoon during an assault on German trenches when he was wounded but continued through a night of very heavy fighting, taking charge of the captured enemy position. He returned to the Australian front line at daylight to have his wounds dressed, but a counter-attack by the Germans caused Lovett to take command of a disorganised group of men to repulse the German attack. For this he was awarded the Military Cross. On the night of 4-5 February 1917, while attached to 13th Australian Infantry, he was in an attack which took a German position after which the Germans counter-attacked. The Officer Commanding the 13th Battalion needed mortar cover and Lovett became the runner to get the support needed. For this courage under fire he received a Bar to his MC. Lovett was promoted to Captain and became Adjutant to the 54th Australian Infantry in the Villers-Bretonneux area. He was killed when the battalion HQ dugout was shelled, killing the Commanding Officer, Lieutenant-Colonel McConaghy, Captain Lovett and Lieutenant Staples.

Aust – 88   UK – 7   Unnamed – 1
Area – 506 sq mts

LOCATION
Aubigny is about 5km east of Amiens on the south bank of the River Somme. The cemetery is on the southern edge of the village about 100m north of the D1 from Amiens to Corbie on the west side of the road north into Aubigny.

AUCHONVILLERS COMMUNAL CEMETERY

HISTORY
The cemetery was used to bury thirteen men in April 1916, one man in 1915 and one in 1918.

INFORMATION
From 1914 to summer 1915 this front was held by French troops, so French casualties were buried here but they have been removed. It was only just behind the front-line and fortified by the French. It was completely destroyed by shelling during the war. The village was called 'Ocean Villas' by the Tommies. And there is a B&B and tea rooms in the village called 'Ocean Villas' that is a great place for lunch or a break.

The British burials of 1915 and 1918 were originally away from the others but regrouped in 1923, so there is now a single row of 15 graves. Thirteen men of the 1st Borders were killed on 6 April 1916 when German artillery shelled a communication trench. Among them is Company Serjeant Major Albert Herbert Cormack, 1st Border Regiment aged 37 Years. He held the Long Service and Good Conduct Medals.

UK – 15   Area – 506 sq mts

LOCATION
Auchonvillers is about 10km north of Albert and 15km west of Bapaume. The Communal Cemetery is south-east of the village, on the north side of the road to the Newfoundland Park and Hamel at the junction of the roads to Hamel and Engelbelmer. The British burials are on the northern edge of the cemetery.

AUCHONVILLERS MILITARY CEMETERY

HISTORY
The Military Cemetery was begun by French troops in June 1915 and burials practically ceased with the German retreat in February 1917. It saw 90 burials in July 1916, mostly men of the 29th Division. The 24 New Zealand burials date from early 1918.

INFORMATION
One row of graves (Plot II, row M, graves 4-18) was concentrated here after the war from scattered positions east of the Cemetery.

Buried here is Private Richard Dale Lovett who left his plantation in India at the start of the war and joined the 16th (Public Schools Battalion) Middlesex. He was killed in the attack on Hawthorn Ridge on 1 July 1916, aged 46 years.

Buried here is Serjeant William Edward Lynn, 1st Royal Irish Fusiliers who died on 17 July 1916 aged 21 years. Three of his brothers also died in the war. Driver Robert Lynn, 87th Battery, Royal Field Artillery, died on 6 August 1915 aged 30 years and is buried in Hop Store Cemetery near Ieper. Private John Lynn, 1st Royal Inniskilling Fusiliers, died of wounds on 9 August 1916 aged 26 years. He is buried in Lijssenthoek Military Cemetery near Ieper. Serjeant James Lynn, 906th Company, Royal Army Service Corps died on 7 August 1920 aged 37 years and is buried in Haifa War Cemetery.

You will find here Corporal Tommy Farrell, 1st Lancashire Fusiliers, killed in action near the Sunken Road at Beaumont Hamel on 1 July 1916. Tommy had briefly played for Manchester City before the war.

UK – 496   NZ – 24   NF – 8
Fr – 6   Unnamed - 44

LOCATION
The Military Cemetery is about 300m from the church on the south-west corner of the village on the road to Mailly. It is 30m from the road reached by a short path. It has an attractive entrance.

AUTHUILE MILITARY CEMETERY

HISTORY
This cemetery was used from August 1915 to December 1916. In late 1917 and 1918 Indian Labour Companies created a few burials. Most graves date from the period of preparation for 1 July 1916.

INFORMATION

This is an attractive cemetery on valley slopes above the River Ancre. The graves are laid out to follow the contours of the valley which makes it very inviting. But, as it is hidden from the main road, it is not often visited.

The village was held by the French until the British troops occupied it from the summer of 1915 to March 1918, when it was captured in the German offensive. The village was destroyed by shell fire.

The earliest burials are at the bottom of the slope nearest the river. Men of the same units are buried together here. A small plot of Indian cavalry burials dating from 1915 is higher up the slope. There is a communal grave for twelve men of the 1st Dorsets alongside their officer, 2nd Lieutenant Vere Talbot Bayly, aged 19, killed on 8 May 1916 when the Germans raided their trench near Thiepval.

UK – 451   SAfr – 3   India – 18
Ger – 1   Unnamed – 38   Area – 2662 sq mts

Special Memorials are erected to eighteen British soldiers known or believed to be buried among the unnamed graves

LOCATION

Authuile is located about 5km north of Albert. This Cemetery is on the south-west edge of the village, between the road to Albert and the River Ancre. There are CWGC signs from the road and it can also be accessed from the church. The last 20m is by a path.

AVELUY COMMUNAL CEMETERY EXTENSION

HISTORY

The Extension was opened by the French when they held the front-line here in early 1915. The British continued to use it from August 1915 to March 1917. It was used again in August 1918.

INFORMATION

The British came to the area in July 1915 and remained until 26 March 1918 when the village fell to the German spring offensive. They held the village until it was retaken in August 1918.

The first British burials, dating from August 1915, are in the row closest to the Communal Cemetery. The Extension was used by medical units until 1917. The 3rd and 9th Casualty Clearing Stations were stationed here from March to November 1917when 49 burials were made including 40 Australians wounded during the German retreat to the Hindenburg Line. Two graves were made when the village was retaken from the Germans in August 1918.

Also buried here during the German retreat to the Hindenburg Line is Lieutenant Colonel Henry May Henderson, who was senior Royal Engineers officer of the 18th Division when he died on 10 March 1917 aged 38 years. With him when he was killed, and buried here, is Major Archibald Alderman Chase, DSO and 3 times MiD, Royal Engineers, attached and commanding 8th Royal Sussex who died of wounds on 11 March 1917. They had been inspecting a road at Grandcourt when hit by a German shell.

Another burial here is that of Captain The Honourable Roland Erasmus Philipps, MC, 9th Royal Fusiliers, killed in action on 7 July 1916 aged 26. He was a writer and a leading member of the Scouting movement. He was son of the 1st Viscount Davids. His elder brother, a Captain in the Horse Guards, was killed in 1915 and is commemorated on the Menin Gate.

Also here is Private Henry A Styles, 2nd Middlesex, killed in action on 18 May 1916. His two brothers died in action on the same day in 1915 with the same battalion. Sydney and William Styles, 1st Grenadier Guards are buried in adjacent graves in Ypres Reservoir Cemetery.

The cemetery also contained 30 French and eight German graves but these have been removed.

UK - 549   Aust – 54   Can – 7
KUG – 27   Indian Labour Corps - 2
South African Native Labour Corps – 1
Area – 3513 sq mts

Special Memorials to three British men who are believed to be buried in the Extension.

LOCATION

Aveluy is on the northern edge of Albert and can now almost be considered to be a suburb. The Communal Cemetery is in the north side of the village on a dead end road, Rue du Cimetiere, leading from the centre of the village. The Extension is on the south side of the Communal Cemetery.

AVELUY WOOD CEMETERY (LANCASHIRE DUMP), MESNIL-MARTINSART

HISTORY
The cemetery was opened in June 1916 in preparation for the Battle of the Somme. It remained in use until February 1917 when the Germans withdrew to the Hindenburg Line. It was used again in September 1918 after the Germans had held the wood from March to August. After the war it was enlarged by the concentration of graves from the wood and the surrounding area.

INFORMATION
In the German spring offensive of 1918 the Germans reached the wood on 27 March. The 12th, 47th and 63rd Divisions held the wood but were finally pushed out by 5 April. The wood was not retaken, despite many attacks by several Divisions, until the end of August 1918 when the 38th (Welsh) Division captured it. The V Corps Burial Officer then made graves of men who fell from April to September 1918 in Plot I, Row H.

After the war Plots II and III were added by the concentration of 100 graves from the wood. In 1923, 124 graves were concentrated from a wide area into Plot I, Rows I to M.

Buried here is Captain Edward Roy Pallett, 7th Royal Fusiliers, killed in action on 6 April 1918 aged 23 years. He had played Minor Counties cricket for Essex Second XI and for Essex Young Amateurs in 1914. He had also played six matches for Ipswich Town FC between 1912 and 1914.

The cemetery lies in an attractive clearing in Aveluy Wood. The wood is the largest one on or near the 1916 battlefield. It is still possible to make out some of the trench lines within the wood.

UK – 365   Aust – 26   Unnamed – 172
Area – 1896 sq mts
Special memorials to twenty British men known to be buried among the unnamed.

LOCATION
Aveluy Wood lies north of Albert on the west bank of the Ancre between Mesnil, Martinsart and Aveluy. 'Lancashire Dump' was made during the war on the northern edge of the wood. The cemetery now lies on the site of that 'Dump' on the west side of the road from Albert to Hamel. It is 100m south of the crossroads of the Mesnil-Authuille road.

AYETTE BRITISH CEMETERY

HISTORY
The cemetery was used from March to June 1918.

INFORMATION
The village was in British hands once they took over from the French in March 1916. They held it until 27 March 1918. The Guards Division tried to recapture the village on 28 March but it fell to the 32nd Division on 3 April 1918. The majority of burials here are men from Guards units. Among those here is Lieutenant William Brett St. Leger, MC, 2nd Coldstream Guards, killed in action on 27 April 1918 aged 23 years. He was a volunteer in the Cape Town Highlanders whilst at college, and worked at the Wynberg Detention Barracks until April 1915, before joining the 6th South African Infantry as a Corporal. He was in German South West Africa at the end of 1915. He sailed to England in May 1916 where, after training, he was commissioned into the 2nd Coldstream Guards, and was sent to France where he took part in the Somme offensive from September 1916. He was slightly wounded at Passendale in July 1917, and it was here, in a raid near Proven, that he won the Military Cross 'for conspicuous gallantry and devotion to duty. Whilst leading his platoon with great gallantry through hostile barrage to their final objective he was severely wounded in the leg. He carried on, however, until his company commander ordered him to withdraw. Refusing the aid of stretcher bearers, he was struggling back on foot when he came across a wounded stretcher bearer. He placed him on the stretcher and carried him back for a distance of two and a half miles, showing splendid pluck and determination.' He fought at Cambrai in 1917 and the Arras offensive from January to March 1918. His father was also a Major in the South African Medical Corps.

Also here is Captain Edward Budd, MC and two Bars, 1st Irish Guards, killed in action on 8 May 1918 aged 24 years. He was commissioned into the Irish Guards in August 1914 but did not join his Battalion in France until 1916. He was awarded the Military Cross in May 1917. The citation reads 'For conspicuous gallantry and devotion to duty. He carried out a dangerous reconnaissance under heavy fire, and brought back most valuable information. He has on many occasions done fine work.' He took command of 4th Company in August 1917 and in the same month received a Bar to his MC for an act the previous month. The citation reads 'conspicuous gallantry and devotion to duty. After a personal reconnaissance of an enemy blockhouse which was harassing his front line, he made sound and skilful disposition for its capture which was effectively carried out. The capture of the blockhouse not only relieved the front line from annoyance and loss, but enabled the whole line in this vicinity to be advanced about 200 yards. He showed very great initiative and military skill.' In July 1918 he received a second Bar for another daring reconnaissance when all communications had been broken. The citation reads 'For conspicuous gallantry and devotion to duty. He led his company with great skill and judgment, and during the subsequent consolidation displayed marked ability and disregard of danger, reorganising his own company and rendering great assistance to neighbouring company commanders. Later, when, during an enemy attack, all communications were cut, he volunteered to go up to the front line and clear up the situation. He successfully accomplished this task, in spite of continuous sniping and machine-gun fire. Throughout the operations his coolness was most marked, and his sound judgement was of the greatest help to his battalion commander.' He was killed by mortar fire when the only direct hit on their line exploded in his command dug-out.

UK – 53   Chinese – 1   Area – 328 sq mts
Special Memorials are for three men whose graves were destroyed by shell-fire.

LOCATION
Ayette is a village about 14km south of Arras. The cemetery is in the north-west edge of the village, about 100m west of the D919 Arras-Amiens road. From the centre of the village, follow the CWGC sign onto the Rue du 11 Novembre. Then take the farm track to the cemetery. The CWGC site says 'It should be noted that vehicle access is difficult along the farm track during wet conditions.'

AYETTE INDIAN AND CHINESE CEMETERY

HISTORY
The cemetery was begun in September 1917 and used until November 1918. After the war 43 graves were concentrated here from isolated burials and other cemeteries.

INFORMATION
Most of the Chinese buried here died after the war in 1918-19 whereas the Indians died during the war. It is to be remembered that the Indians were mainly military personnel while the Chinese were here, though subject to military law, as civilian labourers under fixed contracts.

Among those buried here is Jemadar Ram Singh, IDSM, 39th King George's Own Central India Horse, killed on 1 December 1917. He was killed by a direct hit from a shell while his unit were attacking Villers-Guislain and Gauche Wood near Cambrai, when four Sowars were also killed & several wounded. He received his medal in February 1917.

Indian – 52   Chinese – 33   Ger – 1
Unnamed – 17   Area – 869 sq mts

LOCATION
The cemetery is on the south-east side of the village on a hill above the village. It is reached from the D7 Ayette-Bapaume road. The cemetery is on a track from the road that joins two parts of Ayette village.

BAC-DU-SUD BRITISH CEMETERY, BAILLEUVAL

HISTORY
The cemetery was opened in March 1918. It remained in use throughout 1918 until it was closed in September.

INFORMATION
The 7th, 20th and 43rd Casualty Clearing Stations were here when the cemetery was begun but they were replaced by Field Ambulances, particularly those of the 31st Division and Canadian Corps, during the German offensive in April 1918. In August and September the 45th and 46th CCS were located here. There is a group of 55 Germans buried here who died as Prisoners of War. The German plot is closest to the road. The French ex-soldiers of Bailleulval erected a shield at the left of the entrance as a Memorial to their allies.

Buried here is Captain John Herbert Towne Letts, MC, No. 87 Squadron, Royal Air Force and Lincolnshire Regiment, died of wounds on 11 October 1918 aged 21 years. He is recorded with thirteen victories making him an 'ace'. He was commissioned as a 2nd Lieutenant in the Lincolnshire Regiment in January 1916. He was immediately seconded to the Royal Flying Corps, and posted to No. 1 Reserve Squadron to begin his flying training. He was made a Flying

Officer in May 1916, posted to No. 27 Squadron in France in June but was back in England injured from August to February 1917. He returned to France with No. 48 Squadron and had his first victory on 9 April which was followed by several more with the reward of a Military Cross for his acts on 24 May. The citation reads 'For conspicuous gallantry and devotion to duty. He attacked four large two seaters, driving two down out of control and forcing the remaining two down. He has helped to destroy eight machines, and throughout has set a splendid example.' More victories led to a transfer as instructor to the School of Air Fighting from October 1917. He went back to France on 10 October 1918 at his own request and was posted to No. 64 Squadron, but on arrival he was as ordered to join No. 87 Squadron. The following day Letts borrowed a plane from No. 32 Squadron, but shortly after taking off the aircraft rolled, then plunged to earth killing him.

UK – 640   Can – 48   Ger – 55
Unnamed – 4   Area – 2380 sq mts

LOCATION
Le Bac-du-Sud is a suburb of Bailleuval which is a village about 12km south-west of Arras. The cemetery is on the north side of the main Arras-Doullens road about 1km west of the hamlet of Bac-du-Sud.

BAILLEULMONT COMMUNAL CEMETERY

HISTORY
The graves in the British plot were made by Field Ambulances and fighting units in 1916-18.

INFORMATION
The headstones are made of red Locharbriggs sandstone rather than the more usual Portland stone.

Buried here are four men who were executed. Private William G Hunt, 18th (3rd Manchester Pals) Manchesters, was executed for desertion on 14 November 1916 aged 20 years. He had served with the 2nd Manchesters since 1914 joining the 18th battalion in late 1916. He had missed an attack with his battalion that had failed, though there is evidence that he went over the top with a unit of the South Lancashires. He was executed to make an example despite his officers' recommendation of leniency. He refused to get drunk before the execution, refused to walk to the place of execution and refused a blindfold. Men of his own unit made up the uncooperative firing squad. He was still alive after the squad had failed to do their job so he was executed by the officer in charge.

Nearby are two other men of the 18th Manchesters executed in 1916. Private Alfred Longshaw, aged 21 and married, and Private Albert Ingham, aged 24, had known each other before the war working for the Lancashire and Yorkshire Railways as clerks in Salford. They served together in 'C' Company and had both been made part of the Brigade's Machine Gun Company. When the unit was ordered to prepare for an attack they decided to desert and made it as far as the coast. They even managed to board a ship at Dieppe. At the execution on 1 December a witness recalls hearing Longshaw bid farewell to his friend. They are buried together. As with other men executed the deaths were reported at home as 'died of gunshot' or 'died of wounds'. However, Ingham's father learnt of the truth of the execution at some point and insisted that the words 'Shot at Dawn' be placed on his son's headstone. To my knowledge this is unique.

Finally, Private Benjamin O'Connell of 1st Irish Guards was executed in the village on 8 August 1918. This was his third conviction for desertion having been sentenced to two years and ten years imprisonment for the previous offenses. He is buried next to Captain George Claud Lathom Insole, MC, MiD, 1st Welsh Guards killed in April 1918.

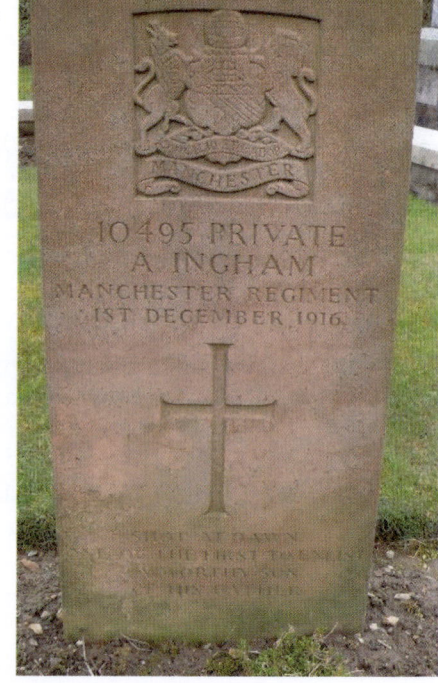

The grave of a Canadian Chaplain, The Reverend Georges Etienne R. Crochetiere, killed in 1918 is buried away from the other graves.

UK – 33   Can – 1

LOCATION
Bailleulmont is a village located about 500m south of the Doullens-Arras road. The village is on the D1 about 10km south-west of Arras. The cemetery is south-west of the village south of the D1 in a small valley next to a stream. The graves are in the north-east corner of the communal cemetery.

BANCOURT BRITISH CEMETERY

HISTORY
The cemetery was opened and closed in September 1918. It was used again after the war for the concentration of graves from isolated positions and smaller British and German cemeteries on the battlefields to the east and south of the village.

INFORMATION
The village was in German hands from 1914 and was occupied by the British Army when the Germans withdrew to the Hindenburg Line in March 1917. The Germans took the village again in March 1918 but it was taken for the final time, by the New Zealand Division, largely the 2nd Auckland Battalion, on 30 August 1918.

The New Zealand Division then opened this cemetery. The wartime cemetery now makes up Plot I, Rows A and B and contains the bodies of 94 men from New Zealand and one British soldier. The main part of the cemetery was made after the war when 2341 graves were concentrated here. Most of the concentrations were of men who died during the winter of 1916-1917, the German spring offensive in March 1918 or the final advance in August and September 1918.

Buried here is Private Wilfred Clarke, 2nd Durham Light Infantry, executed on 9 February 1918 aged 23 years for desertion. He was under a suspended sentence of death for an earlier desertion.

Also buried here is Sergeant David Jones, VC, 12th Kings (Liverpools), killed in action at Bancourt on 7 October 1916 aged 25 years. He had been awarded the Victoria Cross posthumously for his actions at Guillemont on 3 September 1916. The citation says 'For most conspicuous bravery, devotion to duty, and ability displayed in the handling of his platoon. The platoon to which he belonged was ordered to a forward position, and during the advance came under heavy machine gun fire, the officer being killed and the platoon suffering heavy losses Serjt. Jones led-forward the remainder, occupied the position, and held it for two days and two nights without food or water, until relieved. On the second day he drove back three counter-attacks, inflicting heavy losses. His coolness was most praiseworthy. It was due entirely to his resource and example that his men retained confidence and held their post.'

The remains of one man buried here were moved to Combles Communal Cemetery Extension.

Concentrated here:

Bapaume Reservoir German Cemetery - on the southern edge of the town on the Bapaume-Beaulencourt road. It contained the graves of nineteen British soldiers, twelve who died in March and April 1918 whereas the others died in August 1918. There were also three men from New Zealand who were killed in August 1918.

Bapaume Road Cemetery, Beaulencourt - situated about 400m south-west of the village close to the present Autoroute. It was made by the 5th Australian Division in April 1917 for the burial of 20 British soldiers who died in October 1916.

Beaulencourt Road Cemeteries - these three cemeteries, situated on the north-east edge of Gueudecourt, were made by the 5th Australian Division in April 1917. They contained the graves of 88 British soldiers who died either in autumn 1916 or April 1917.

Cloudy Trench Cemetery, Gueudecourt - made in April 1917 by the 5th Australian Division. It contained 40 British soldiers who were killed in October and November 1916.

Fremicourt Communal Cemetery Extension - situated on the southern edge of the village. The Extension was begun by the Germans during the summer of 1918. They buried 136 British soldiers among the 1346 German graves. When the British captured the village in September 1918 they took over the Extension and added a further 94 British graves. All the burials have now been removed.

Sunken Road Cemetery, Lesboeufs - situated between Gueudecourt and Le Transloy near the present Autoroute. It was made by the 5th Australian Division in April 1917 for the burial of 49 British soldiers with an Australian who died in October 1916.

UK – 1999   Aust – 248   NZ – 176
Newf – 13   Unnamed – 1463   Area – 7402 sq mts

Special Memorials to 40 British, two Australian and one New Zealand soldiers who are known, or believed, to be buried among the unnamed graves.

Special Memorial to a British soldier, buried in Bapaume Reservoir German Cemetery, whose grave could not be identified at the time of concentration.

LOCATION
Bancourt is located about 4km east of Bapaume. The British cemetery is situated on the eastern edge of the village opposite the Communal Cemetery. Both are found on a road that runs from the D7 Bapaume-Haplincourt road to D930 Bapaume-Cambrai road. This small road is easy to miss.

BAPAUME AUSTRALIAN CEMETERY

HISTORY
The cemetery was begun in March 1917 by the 3rd Australian Casualty Clearing Station. It remained in use until June 1918.

INFORMATION
The Germans occupied Bapaume on 26 September 1914. The town was one of the key objectives on 1 July 1916 but it was not taken by the British until 17 March 1917 when the Germans retreated to the Hindenburg Line and the 2nd Australian Division occupied the town. They discovered the Germans had mined many buildings including the Town Hall which blew up a few days after the Australians' arrival. The Germans captured Bapaume in March 1918. The town fell for the final time on 29 August 1918 when the New Zealand Division captured the area.

Among the dead is Major William Ingham Macauley, twice MiD, Assistant Director of Veterinary Services, Army Veterinary Corps, died on 14 May 1917 aged 38 years. From Northern Ireland he graduated from the London Veterinary College in 1905 and joined the Army Veterinary Corps as a Lieutenant in February 1906. He became a Captain in 1911 while serving in Egypt, India and Burma. In 1914 he went to France with the 2nd (Queen's Bays) Dragoon Guards taking part in the retreat from Mons and being Mentioned in Despatches. He was for some time in charge of No. 20 Veterinary Hospital. In February 1916 he was appointed Assistant Director of Veterinary Services on the staff of a Division, and was promoted to Major. He was again Mentioned in Despatches in January 1917. On 14 May 1917, his body was found behind the front lines with a single gunshot wound, believed to be self-inflicted. It was recorded that he had been deeply disturbed by what he had seen on the battlefield and had been in an unstable state of mind in the days before his death, but newspapers reported he had been killed in action.

The group of German graves were created during April and May 1918. A larger German cemetery on the east side of this cemetery, which contained 168 graves, has been removed and the burials concentrated into Villers-au-Flos German Cemetery.

The Germans swept through the town on their way to the coast in May 1940. Bapaume was also the sight of a battle in the Franco-Prussian war of 1870-71. There is a memorial by the side of the road to Arras about 1km north of the town.

| UK – 12 | Aust – 74 | India – 1 |
| Ger – 23 | KUG – 1 | Area - 542 sq mts |

LOCATION
Bapaume is situated about 15km south of Arras at a strategic crossroads. The cemetery is on the south-east edge of the town behind a modern housing area and on the edge of fields. It is possible to follow signs from the Bapaume-Peronne road.

BAPAUME COMMUNAL CEMETERY

HISTORY
The cemetery was begun in March 1917 by the Australians who continued to bury their dead until May 1917. Four men from New Zealand were buried here on 26 August 1918. One man was buried here in 1944.

INFORMATION
British graves made here by the Germans have all been removed. Among those here is Warrant Officer Thomas William Wilkinson, 7th Company, Australian Army Service Corps, died of wounds on 7 April 1918 aged 37 years. He enlisted in October 1915 as an Acting Sergeant and left Australia on 12 November 1915.

There is a memorial to the French Commander at the Battle of Bapaume in 1870, General Faidherbe, in this cemetery. There is also a monument to the German dead of their XIV Reserve Corps, many of whom were buried here late in the war.

| UK – 2 | Aust – 20 | NZ – 4 |
| Unnamed – 2 | WW2 - 1 | |

LOCATION
The cemetery is on the north side of the town on the east side of the D917 to Arras. The graves are in five clusters, three at the rear on the south side of the main path. Two clusters are on the north side of the main path.

BAPAUME POST MILITARY CEMETERY, ALBERT

HISTORY
The cemetery was begun on 1 July 1916 to bury the dead from the failed attack on La Boiselle. The wartime burials were completed in January 1917. It was enlarged after the war when over 250 graves were concentrated here from the battlefields west and east of the cemetery.

INFORMATION
The village of Albert was the main forward base for British troops in this sector. It fell to the Germans on 26 March 1918 for the only time but was recaptured during the Battle of Albert from 21 to 23 August 1918.

On 1 July 1916 the front-line ran across the Bapaume road between this cemetery and La Boiselle. The 34th Division was to attack the German line in front of the village of La Boiselle. The 101st Brigade on the right was to advance towards Sausage Valley the 102nd (Tyneside Scottish) Brigade, made up of 20th – 23rd Northumberland Fusiliers, towards the village itself. Both Brigades were to attack at zero hour. The 20th and 23rd Northumberland Fusiliers had to cross 800m of open ground facing an alert enemy hence suffering enormous casualties. The reserve brigade, the 103rd (Tyneside Irish), made up of 24th – 27th Northumberland Fusiliers, left their position at 7.40am and by the time some units of this brigade had arrived at the British front line they had suffered 70% casualties on the slopes behind their own front line. This area saw some of the greatest losses at Brigade and Divisional level on the whole battlefield of 1 July. La Boiselle did not fall for several days during which time the 34th Division had swapped two Brigades with the 37th Division so that it could fight on.

The cemetery lies on the west side of Tara Hill and South-West of Usna Hill, named by the Tyneside Irish Brigade after a line of hills in Ireland. It was sometimes known as either the Tara Hill Cemetery or the Usna Hill Cemetery.

Most of Plot I of the Cemetery was completed by January 1917 when the cemetery, containing 152 graves, was closed. This cemetery was one of the first to be completed by the IWGC after the war when it was finished in 1924.

After the war 257 bodies were concentrated here from the surrounding battlefields. Many of the bodies were men of the 34th Division who had fallen on 1 July 1916. Buried here are 105 Northumberland Fusiliers of which 78 are unnamed. Many others buried here were men of the 38th Division who had recaptured Usna Hill on 23 August 1918.

Buried here side by side are Lieutenant Colonel William Lyle commanding 23rd (4th Tyneside Scottish) Northumberland Fusiliers and Lieutenant Colonel Charles Cecil Archibald Sillery commanding 20th (1st Tyneside Scottish) Northumberland Fusiliers. Both were killed on 1 July leading their men into attack. The other two commanding officers of battalions who made up the Tyneside Scottish Brigade in the 34th Division were also killed on 1 July 1916. Lieutenant Colonel Frederick Christian Heneker, commanding 21st (2nd Tyneside Scottish) Northumberland Fusiliers is buried in Ovillers Military Cemetery. Lieutenant Colonel Arthur Percy Archibald Elphinstone of the 22nd Northumberland Fusiliers has no known grave and is commemorated on the Thiepval Memorial to the Missing. He was first commissioned into the Army, with the Warwickshires, on 2 June 1884. He transferred to the Indian Army with the 107th Pioneers, and later 106th Pioneers. He served in the Burma (1885-9) Campaign and Somaliland (1902-4) Campaign and retired from the Indian Army on 1 September 1911. He re-joined on 16 December 1914. He was known as Baronet Elphinstone though this was not an official title.

Also buried here is Major Sir Foster Hugh Egerton Cunliffe, 13th Rifle Brigade who died of wounds on 10 July 1916 aged 41 years. He was the second in command of the battalion and was shot in the leg in front of Contalmaison, lying out in the open for days before being found. He was 6th Baronet and was an English historian and cricketer who played first class cricket for Oxford University from 1895 to 1898, for Middlesex from 1897 to 1903 and for MCC from 1899 to 1903.

Another here is Captain Henry 'Harry' Hutton Scott, 87th Canadian Infantry, killed in action at the capture of Regina Trench on 21 October 1916 aged 24 years. Harry's father, Frederick George Scott served as a senior chaplain with the 1st Canadian Division. After the Canadians later took and held the Trench, Canon Scott's duties brought him to the front lines where Harry died. He searched for his son's remains among the "hastily made graves" on the front lines. When he found his son, he carried him back to bury him behind the lines. Nearby is Scott's brother officer, Lieutenant James William Williams, 87th Canadian Infantry, killed in the attack on Desire Trench on 18 November 1916 aged 28 years. He was son of the Bishop of Quebec. Two other officers of 87th Canadian Infantry, Major Franklin Edward Hall, aged 39 years and Major John Simon Lewis aged 42 years, who died in the attack on Desire Trench are here.

UK – 327   Can – 64   Aust – 18
SAfr – 1   Unnamed – 181   Area - 2078 sq mts

Special Memorials to three British soldiers who died in August 1918 who are believed to be buried among the unnamed.

LOCATION
The cemetery lies on the east side of the Albert-Bapaume road, an old Roman road, on the northern edge of Albert as the road climbs away from the town.

BARASTRE COMMUNAL CEMETERY

HISTORY
The cemetery was used by the Allies in 1918 once the village had finally been taken from the Germans. One grave was made in August 1916 by the Germans.

INFORMATION
The village was occupied by British troops when the Germans withdrew to the Hindenburg Line in March 1917. The Germans retook it in their advance in March 1918. The village was finally taken by the Allies on 5 September 1918 when the 42nd (East Lancashire) Division took the area.

A German extension has been removed. In addition 225 German and four French graves have been removed from the Communal Cemetery.

Buried here is Lieutenant Colonel Frederick Hoysted Bradley, DSO, MiD, Royal Army Medical Corps attached 15th Field Ambulance. He is buried alongside his second in command, Major Campbell McNeill McCormack, MC & two Bars, RAMC. The unit had set up the Main Dressing Station at Bus-en-Artois when a high velocity shell landed directly on a small shelter where Bradley and McCormack were sleeping killing them on 22 September 1918.

UK – 11   NZ - 4

LOCATION
Barastre is about 3km south-east of Bapaume. The cemetery is on the north side of the village on the east side of the road to Haplincourt. The graves are on the south side of the cemetery near the east end.

BAVELINCOURT COMMUNAL CEMETERY

HISTORY
The Communal Cemetery was used by the Allies between April and August of 1918.

INFORMATION
The cemetery was made by the men and medical units of the 47th (London) and 58th (London) Divisions. The grave of an American soldier has been removed.

Buried here is Lieutenant G W Cranmore, 2/10th (Hackney) Londons, killed in action on 19 July 1918 aged 32 years. He was married and a member of the Masons. The Battalion was in a support line when Cranmore and one man were killed, with three men wounded, by a shell. He is buried with two other soldiers of the 2/10th Londons.

UK – 51   Aust – 3   Area – 305 sq mts

LOCATION
Bavelincourt is about 10km west of Albert and 15km north-east of Amiens. The cemetery is on the eastern edge of the village. To get to the cemetery take the road east from the church in the village centre. This leads to the cemetery which is about 400m from the church in open fields. The British graves are in the northern corner of the cemetery.

BAZENTIN-LE-PETIT COMMUNAL CEMETERY EXTENSION

HISTORY
The Extension was opened on 15 July 1916 and it remained in use, as a front-line cemetery, until December 1916. It was enlarged after the war by the concentration of graves from isolated positions on the battlefields of Bazentin and Contalmaison.

INFORMATION
The village was in German hands from 1914. Bazentin and the Bazentin Ridge were first-day objectives on 1 July 1916 but they were not taken by the British until two weeks later. The 3rd and 7th Divisions captured the Ridge and the villages of Bazentin-le-Grand and Bazentin-le-Petit on 14 July 1916 but did not press on with the advantage they had at that time. The 21st Division captured Bazentin Wood at the same time. In April 1918 during the German spring offensive the Germans recaptured the ground but it was taken by the 38th Division for the final time on 25 August. The village, and its counterpart, Bazentin-le-Grand, were destroyed during the war. They never really recovered. They are now little more than a hamlet with Bazentin-le-Grand significantly smaller than Bazentin-le-Petit.

10th Gloucestershires, killed in action on 18 August 1916 aged 41 years. He was an accountant before the war, a prominent member of Dundee society, a mountaineer, skilled cricketer and all round sportsmen. He had been with the Gloucestershires for about six weeks before his death at Contalmaison when he and another officer were killed by a shell as they left battalion HQ.

UK -179　　　　Can – 5　　　　Aust – 1
Unnamed – 53　　　　Area - 740 sq mts

Special Memorials erected to 58 British soldiers, mainly men of the 1st Northamptonshires, whose graves were destroyed by shell-fire. The battalion were fighting between Bazentin and High Wood in August 1916. They used the cemetery to bury five officers and 42 men. The markers for the officers were identified after the war but not those of the men.

LOCATION
Bazentin-le-Petit is situated about 8km north-east of Albert and 10km south of Bapaume. The Communal Cemetery is on the east side of the village in a valley and the Extension is on the north side of the Communal Cemetery.

At the end of the war the Extension contained 135 graves, 50 were concentrated here after the war. At that time six German graves were removed. Later a British soldier was concentrated here from Sailly-Laurette German Cemetery, 15km south of here, at the same time as the 556 German graves were moved elsewhere.

Among those here is Captain Thomas Handyside Baxter Rorie, 1/4th Black Watch (Royal Highlanders) attached

BAZENTIN-LE-PETIT MILITARY CEMETERY

HISTORY
The cemetery was opened at the end of July 1916 and it remained in use, as a front-line cemetery, until May 1917.

INFORMATION
The cemetery's main period of use was from October 1916 until spring 1917 during the period that an advanced Dressing Station was located in the village.

Among those here is 2nd Lieutenant Wynnum Groom McDonald Hennessey, 6th Australian Infantry, killed in action on 10 February 1917 aged 21 years. He was an officer in the 55th Collingwood Infantry when the war started and enlisted immediately. He was utilised to train men to go overseas, then spent a short period in Egypt before transfer to England where again he trained men for the front-line. He wanted to join his two brothers at the front so he transferred to the 6th Australian Infantry. A short spell in hospital for bronchitis happened just five weeks before his death. Whilst the adjacent 5th Battalion was conducting trench raids on the Germans, the 6th Battalion was subject to shelling in which the battalion lost three men including Hennessey.

The graves of 33 German soldiers were removed from the Military Cemetery in 1923. This has left gaps in the rows.

At the north end of the village is the 'Nine Brave Men' Memorial. On the night of 27 July 1916 No. 3 Section of 82nd Field Company, Royal Engineers was detailed to build several strongpoints north of the village. The work was completed but every man became a casualty. The memorial was made by the Royal Engineers with bricks taken from the ruined village. It has recently been renovated. There are nine names recorded though only one, Sapper John Higgins from Newcastle, has a known grave. He is buried in Becourt Military Cemetery. Another man, Sapper Charles Douglas Ellisson is buried in Caterpillar Valley Cemetery but his grave is marked by a Special Memorial as the exact position has been lost. They both died of wounds.

UK – 116　　　　Aust – 55　　　　SAfr – 10
Unnamed – 15　　　　Area - 1532 sq mts

LOCATION
The Military Cemetery is situated on the western edge of the village, on the north-west corner of Bazentin Wood, behind a group of cottages. It is reached by a path from the road.

BEACON CEMETERY, SAILLY-LAURETTE

HISTORY
The cemetery was opened on 15 August 1918 and used in the following weeks until it was closed as the fighting moved away. It was greatly enlarged after the war by the concentration of graves from the surrounding area.

INFORMATION
For most of the war this was a quiet area in the rear of the British front-line. The first fighting took place here on 26 March 1918 when the British Third Army withdrew to a line nearby between Albert and Sailly-le-Sec. On 4 July the line was advanced to a position close to this village and the village found itself behind the lines again as the front-line moved west from 8 August.

The cemetery gained its name from the tall chimney 'Brick Beacon' that has now gone but was on the summit of the nearby ridge to the south-east. The cemetery was begun by the 18th Division. They buried the dead of the attack by the 12th, 18th and 58th Divisions who advanced from a line between the Somme near here and the Ancre near Albert on 8 August. The early burials are near the centre of the cemetery.

At the end of the war the cemetery contained 109 graves, mostly of the 12th Division, now in Plot III, Rows C, E, G and I. After the war 660 graves were concentrated from isolated positions and smaller graveyards on the surrounding battlefields. Most of these were men from London and Eastern Counties regiments or Australians.

Among those here is Company Serjeant Major H Betts, MC, DCM & Bar, 1/1st Cambridgeshire Regiment, killed in action on 22 August 1918 aged 22 years. His Military Cross citation from 1 February 1919 reads 'During the attack on Morlancourt on 9th August, 1918, the right flank was held up by a nest of machine guns. This Warrant Officer immediately went forward alone, and, with great gallantry and disregard of danger, killed three and captured thirty of the enemy and four machine guns, thereby clearing the way for his company and disposing of an obstruction which might have upset the whole operation. He did magnificent work.' He was recommended for a Victoria Cross for his actions, but awarded the MC.

The Distinguished Conduct Medal citation, dated 6 February 1918, for actions in September 1917 reads 'For conspicuous gallantry and devotion to duty. Whilst in charge of a platoon he held a position which was very heavily shelled and enfiladed by snipers. Locating two of the latter he crawled out in front of the trench, and from a very exposed position, shot them both with his rifle. On the following evening, under very heavy concentrated shelling, he walked up and down the parados of his trench encouraging his men and setting them a magnificent example. Throughout the whole operations his conduct was distinguished by courageous and soldier like qualities.'

The citation for the Bar to the DCM, dated 3 September 1918, for actions in March 1918 at which time he was Acting Regimental Sergeant Major reads 'For conspicuous gallantry and devotion to duty. During ten days very hard fighting this warrant officer, who had taken over the duties of regimental sergeant major early in the operations, showed an impressive example of courage and coolness under heavy fire on all occasions. On one occasion the battalion, which had been very much reduced in numbers, both officers and men, delivered a successful counter-attack, driving back the enemy a considerable distance, and capturing men and machine guns. Company Sergeant Major Betts was conspicuous for the fearless manner in which he attacked the machine gun positions, and his behaviour had a marked effect on the men.'

The 25th Australian Battalion had erected a memorial nearby to their comrades who had fallen in this area on 10 June 1918 which was re-erected in this cemetery. However, it has since been removed.

Concentrated here:

Croydon Cemetery, Glisy - situated between the N29 and D934 roads to the east of Amiens about 15km south-west of here. It contained fourteen British and thirteen Australian soldiers who died from May to August 1918.

Sussex Cemetery, Sailly-Laurette - situated about 1km south-east of here. It was used from 16-21 August 1918 for the burial of 43 British soldiers, mostly of the 7th Royal Sussex, and an Australian soldier, all of whom died on 8 August.

Taille Wood Cemetery, Etinehem - situated about 3km west of Bray on the edge of Taille Wood which is south of the road and about 8km east of here. It contained the graves of sixteen Australian and two British soldiers who died from 13-23 August 1918.

UK – 575   Aust – 195   SAfr – 1
Can – 1   Unnamed – 257   Area – 2563 sq mts

Special Memorials to four British soldiers known, or believed, to be buried among the unnamed graves.

LOCATION
Sailly-Laurette is a village on the north bank of the Somme about 10km south of Albert and 15km east of Amiens. The cemetery can be found north of the village and south of the D1 Bray-Corbie road and a little west of the Morlancourt road. It is on a high ridge north of the Somme with excellent views of the area to the north.

BEAUCOURT BRITISH CEMETERY

HISTORY
The cemetery was made in August 1918 after the capture of the village.

INFORMATION
The village was in Allied hands for most of the war but lost to the Germans in March 1918. It was retaken by the 3rd Cavalry Division on 8 August 1918.

The beautiful small cemetery was also known as Beaucourt Church Cemetery. Two of the three rows are mass graves for men from Canada killed on 8 and 9 August 1918. Most are from Central Ontario. The British are mostly from 1st Tank Battalion. Three artillery men who died in March 1918 and who were buried in the churchyard were moved here. Among those here is Captain Richard Philip Bawden, 9th Brigade, Canadian Field Artillery, killed in action on 10 August 1918 aged 31 years. He went to England with 20th Battery, 2nd Canadian Division but when the Canadian Force was reorganised he was transferred to 3rd Canadian Division and promoted to Captain. He was killed by a bomb dropped from a plane.

UK – 10   Can – 77   Unnamed - 1
Area – 239 sq mts

Special Memorials to two British men whose graves could not be identified when three graves were moved from the churchyard.

LOCATION
The village of Beaucourt-en-Santerre is about 18km south-east of Amiens and 5km east of Moreuil. The cemetery is on a small road to Le Quesnel and can be reached from the centre of the village opposite the church. It is high on a bank on a bend in the road about 300m from the centre of the village. There are steps to enter.

BEAULENCOURT BRITISH CEMETERY

HISTORY
The cemetery was opened in September 1918 and used until the end of the war. The cemetery was greatly enlarged after the war by the concentration of nearly 600 graves from the neighbouring battlefields and cemeteries.

INFORMATION
The cemetery was made originally by the 3rd, 4th, 43rd and 58th Casualty Clearing Stations. The first three were stationed in the village in September and October 1918. The 58th CCS was here from 11 December until 1919. The original burials from these are in Plot I, Rows A to D. Most of the Chinese and the Indians buried here died in 1919.

Among those buried here is Captain Alfred Spencer Mason summers, MiD, No. 60 Squadron, Royal Flying Corps and 19th (Queen Alexandra's Own Royal) Hussars, killed in action on 15 September 1916 aged 30 years. He had been a pre-war officer with the Hussars and gone to war with them. He trained with the RFC in 1915 gaining aviators licence number 2095. He was shot down, having destroyed a Kite Balloon near Bapaume, while flying a Nieuport 16. He was probably a victim of Lieutenant Wilhelm Frankl of Jasta 4, the 11th of his eventual 20 victories. His father had been a Liberal MP though had died in 1913.

Concentrated here:

Beaulencourt Churchyard - two British soldiers were buried by the Germans in 1918.

Beaulencourt German Cemeteries - one a little north of the village, and another at the southern end of the village, both were on what is now the D917. These were used by the Germans in 1916 and 1918. Among the German burials there were about 50 British and New Zealand soldiers who have been removed partly to Beaulencourt British Cemetery, and partly to Favreuil.

Grevillers German Cemetery - on the road from Grevillers to Bihucourt. It contained 500 German soldiers among whom were twelve British and eleven New Zealand soldiers buried by the Germans. There was also one British man buried by the British in August 1918.

UK – 599   Aust – 51   NZ – 81
Can – 3   SAfr – 1   India – 1
Chinese – 14   Unnamed – 309   Area – 2917 sq mts

Special Memorials are erected to 21 British soldiers known or believed to be buried among the unnamed.

LOCATION
Beaulencourt is a village located about 1km south of Bapaume on the D917 to Peronne. The cemetery is about 1km west of the village on the road from Beaulencourt to Ligny-Thilloy. While it is on the road to Thilloy the cemetery called Thilloy Road cemetery is not and that cemetery is closer to Beaulencourt than this. Nonetheless, it is in an attractive location in open fields and has a pretty little entrance.

BEAUMETZ CROSSROADS CEMETERY

HISTORY
The cemetery was begun in March 1917 during the German withdrawal to the Hindenburg Line. It remained in use until February 1918. Further British burials were made in September and October 1918 during fighting in this area. The cemetery was increased in size after the war by the concentration of burials from the surrounding battlefields.

INFORMATION
The village was in Allied hands for most of the war but was captured by the Germans on 22 March 1918 taking it from the 51st (Highland) and 25th Divisions. It was retaken in the middle of September 1918. The original burials make up Row D while the burials of late 1918 are now Rows E and F. The Germans called it No. 6 (English Military) Cemetery. After the war the body of one United States soldier was removed.

Buried here is Brigadier General Gilbert Burrell Spencer Follett, DSO, MVO, Croix de Guerre, commanding 3rd Brigade of Guards who was killed in action at Flesquieres on 27 September 1918 aged 40 years. He was killed by machine gun fire as he was moving his brigade headquarters forward to a new position. He was made a Member of the Victorian Order in 1907. He was awarded the Distinguished Service Order in January 1917 for inspecting front-line trenches under heavy fire and while wounded as well as for his leadership skills.

UK – 207   Aust – 56   NZ – 12
Unnamed – 99   Ger - 4   Area - 1405 sq mts

Special Memorials are erected to four British and three Australian soldiers known or believed to be buried among the unnamed.

LOCATION
Beaumetz-les-Cambrai is situated about 10km east of Bapaume and 1km south of the Bapaume-Cambrai road. The cemetery is south of the village on the road to Hermies. It is on a ridge above the village on the east side of the road about 300m from the junction of the Hermies and Bertincourt roads.

BEAUMETZ-LES-CAMBRAI MILITARY CEMETERY No. 1

HISTORY
The cemetery was begun by Germans in March 1918 after they had captured the area. It was used only briefly for Allied burials.

INFORMATION
The Cemetery was called No. 9 Military Cemetery by the Germans. After the war 307 German graves were removed and the British graves regrouped. The cemetery is mostly men of the 51st (Highland), 25th, 6th and 19th Divisions, mainly buried in collective graves. Almost all of the identified graves are of men killed defending the area between 21-26 March 1918 during the German advance. And with one exception, there are no known officers buried here.

Among those here is Corporal Thomas James Dinwoddie, DCM, 7th Black Watch (Royal Highlanders), killed in action on 26 March 1918 aged 28 years. The act for which he was awarded the Distinguished Conduct Medal took place when he was a Lance Corporal and was gazetted in February 1917. He held the Germans back, alone with a machine gun, saving lives of men in his platoon while they were digging in.

UK – 257   Unnamed – 182   Area - 819 sq mts

LOCATION
Beaumetz-les-Cambrai is located about 6km north-east of Bapaume and 10km south-west of Cambrai. The cemetery is north of the village very close to the Bapaume-Cambrai road.

BEAUMONT-HAMEL BRITISH CEMETERY

HISTORY
This cemetery was begun in November 1916 after the village had been captured from the Germans. It remained in use until February 1917 and was enlarged after the war by the concentration of graves from the surrounding battlefields.

INFORMATION
Beaumont-Hamel was in German hands from 1914 and was an objective on 1 July 1916. It was reached but could not be held. The village was not taken until 13 November when it was captured by 51st (Highland) and 63rd (Royal Navy) Divisions. The cemetery was begun soon after for the burial of men who fell in the November attack and in subsequent actions until the Germans withdrew to the Hindenburg Line.

This cemetery was originally titled 'V Corps Cemetery No. 23'. It is located in the area of no-man's land attacked by 1st Lancashire Fusiliers on 1 July 1916.

Buried here is Lieutenant Frederic Baron Tanqueray, 'B' Company, 16th (Public Schools) Middlesex, killed in action on 1 July 1916 aged 24 years. He was a solicitor in his father's firm before the war. At the beginning of the war he enlisted in the Public Schools battalion of the Middlesex Regiment and was soon promoted to Sergeant. Early in 1915 he took a commission in the same battalion and went to France in November. His battalion attacked the Hawthorn Ridge and Crater that had been blown early to allow footage to be taken to add to the 'official' film of the battle. Hence, the Germans had been ready for the attack. As many of the men in the 16th Middlesex were from Public Schools what talent was lost for a few seconds of film footage? Most of his fellow officers were killed or wounded early in the day, and it is merely known that he went over with his platoon and was seen going forward at mid-day, when he called out "Good Luck" to a wounded friend as he passed him. He was officially reported as 'Missing', after the attack.

There are many cemeteries in the area and several memorials. The Newfoundland Memorial Park, with several Cemeteries and Memorials, is on the ridge opposite Beaumont. Nearby to the west of this cemetery near the road to Auchonvillers is the Memorial to the 8th Argyll and Sutherland Highlanders who suffered many casualties during the capture of Beaumont in November 1916. To the east of Beaumont and just south of Beaucourt is the Memorial to the 63rd Division who took heavy casualties in attacks in the valley of the Ancre in November 1916. There used to be a large German cemetery nearby made by concentration after the war, one of the few on the Somme, but this has also been removed.

UK – 111   Can – 1   Newf – 1
KUG – 63   Ger – 2   Unnamed – 81
Area – 986 sq mts

Special Memorials to two British soldiers known to be buried among the unidentified graves.

LOCATION
Beaumont is a village about 12km north of Albert on the ridge to the west side of the River Ancre. The cemetery is 1km west of the village on the north side of the road to Auchonvillers. The cemetery is on the edge of a valley about 100m from the road.

BECOURT MILITARY CEMETERY

HISTORY
The Cemetery was begun in August 1915 by the 51st (Highland) Division and was used until the Battles of the Somme in 1916. It continued in use, chiefly by Field Ambulances, until April 1917. Plot II was made by the 18th Division at the end of August 1918.

INFORMATION
The hamlet of Becourt is now tiny as many people did not return after the war. The chateau is a replacement of the one that was here before the war. The original was used as a Brigade HQ in 1915-16.

The first burials are furthest from the entrance where nine highlanders of the 51st Division were buried soon after the Division took over this sector from the French in 1915. The Canadians buried here are nearly all artillerymen. Three German graves have been removed.

Buried here are 16 men of 185th Tunnelling Company, Royal Engineers, killed by a mine on 4 February 1916. The officers are buried in Albert while the other men are buried together here in a communal grave. Also buried together here are ten men of the 11th Royal Warwickshires who were killed when their small camp in Becourt Wood was shelled by the Germans on 1 August 1916.

There are three battalion commanders buried here. Lieutenant Colonel Jasper Fitzgerald Radcliffe, DSO, twice MiD, Devonshire Regiment attached 10th Essex was killed on 31 January 1916 aged 48 years. He was awarded the Distinguished Service Order for his service in the South African wars 1900-02. He was killed when he went into the telephonists' dugout as it received a direct hit causing a beam to collapse which hit Radcliffe on the head and killed him instantly. His son, Lieutenant Dering John Jasper Radcliffe, also died on the Western Front, as a Lieutenant with 5th Grenadier Guards, on 31 October 1917 aged 22 years and is buried in Gosnay Communal Cemetery. He transferred from the Devonshires in 1916 and seems to have been at an Army Corps School so temporarily attached to the 5th Grenadier Guards, who never left England, when he died.

Lieutenant Colonel John Plunkett Verney Hawksley, DSO, three times MiD, Order of the Osmanieh (4th Class - awarded while attached to the Egyptian Army), killed in action when shot by a sniper on 8 August 1916 aged 38 years. He was a career soldier, and had served in the South African and Sudan Campaigns, before being awarded the temporary rank of Major at the outbreak of the war. After seeing action with the 32nd Brigade, Royal Field Artillery in 1914, he fought through 1915, and in March 1916 was promoted to Lieutenant-Colonel in command of 110th Brigade, Royal Field Artillery, attached to 25th Division. He was awarded the Distinguished Service Order for his actions in the Retreat from Mons in 1914. Interestingly, he sent letters home in December 1914 describing the events of the 'Christmas Truce' near Ieper in which he talks of a football match between the two sides.

Lieutenant Colonel Arthur Joseph Berkeley Addison, twice MiD, commanding 9th York and Lancasters formerly Royal Irish Rifles was killed leading his men into attack at 'The Nab' on the extreme left of 70th Brigade's assault north of Ovillers on 1 July 1916. The battalion were tasked to attack the German line north of Ovillers from Authuille Wood. They took machine gun fire from the Thiepval Spur and did not reach the German line. It was the first time in battle for this New Army battalion who lost over 400 men. All four battalion commanders in the Brigade became casualties.

Also here is Captain Thomas Sowerby 'Tom' Rowlandson, MC, 1/4th Yorkshires, killed in action on 15 September 1916 whilst leading his men over the parapet of a German trench where he was hit by a German bomb. He was a footballer who briefly played for Sunderland and Newcastle United, where he was described as being a 'lithesome' goalkeeper who possessed a 'splendid moustache', before moving to Old Carthusians. He had been educated at Charterhouse and Cambridge University. At the start of the war he gave his house to the Red Cross before joining up.

In the village you can find a memorial in the form of a Crucifix to Lieutenant Josephe de Valicourt, killed in Champagne in 1917.

UK – 606   Aust – 72   Can – 31
Unnamed – 8   SAfr - 3   Area – 4,327 sq mts
Special memorial to one British soldier known to be buried among the unnamed.

LOCATION
The village of Bécordel-Bécourt and the hamlet of Bécourt, about 2km east of Albert, are separated by Bécourt Wood. The Military Cemetery is on the west side of Bécourt Wood, and on the south side of the road to Albert midway between Becourt and Becordel. It is at the head of a valley that leads from Becordel to Becourt. This is an attractive, quiet wooded area on the valley's edge.

BELLACOURT MILITARY CEMETERY, RIVIERE

HISTORY
The cemetery was begun by the French in October 1914 who used it until the British took over the sector in the summer of 1915. The British began to make burials here in February 1916. It remained in use until September 1918.

INFORMATION
British burials were made by the Divisions that held the line nearby. In turn these were the 46th, 55th, 58th and 49th Divisions. Later the Canadian Corps made burials here. In 1923 the French Plot was increased by the concentration of graves from other smaller cemeteries. In addition the sixteen American graves were removed. They were graves of men who fell in July and August 1918, all but one were men from the 320th Regiment.

Buried here is Private Leopold Delisle, 22nd (Canadien Francais, Quebec Regiment) Canadian Infantry, who was executed for desertion on 21 May 1918 aged 25 years. He had gained a bad record due to several acts that broke army regulations. He had already spent one year at No. 3 Military Prison in Le Havre for striking an officer being released on 22 March 1917. He avoided any dangers, including involvement in the assault on Passendale in October-November 1917, until deserting on 29 March 1918. It was for this act that he was sentenced to death.

Two men who held the rank of Major are buried here, both killed on 22 August 1918. Major Bernard Charles Tennant, MC, served in the Royal Army Medical Corps with the 7th Field Ambulance. He was awarded the Military Cross in August 1917. Major Bertie Christopher Butler Tower, MC and Bar, three times MiD, was commanding 4th Royal Fusiliers. He was awarded the MC in January 1916 and the Bar in September 1918. They are almost buried side by side in Plot III, Row F. Between them is a Captain of the Royal Field Artillery who died on the same day.

Also buried here is Private Wilfred John Martin, 2nd South Staffordshires, killed in action on 10 May 1918 aged 19 years. His brother, Lance Corporal Herbert William Martin, 1/23rd Londons was killed in action on 26 May 1915 and is commemorated on the Le Touret Memorial. Another brother, 2nd Corporal Alan Stewart Martin, 29th Divisional Signal Company, Royal Engineers, died of wounds on 11 May 1918 aged 22 years and is buried in Boulogne Eastern Cemetery.

UK – 259 Can – 173 Fr 117
Ger – 1 Unnamed – 1 Area – 3560 sq mts

LOCATION
The cemetery is on the edge of the valley of the River Crinchon that lies between Riviere and the Arras-Doullens road. Bellacourt is now part of a series of villages that have merged into one so can be seen as a suburb of Riviere and has almost no individual identity. The cemetery is 50m north-east of the Beaumetz-les-Loges to Ayette road. The cemetery is on the north side of Riviere.

BERLES-AU-BOIS CHURCHYARD EXTENSION

HISTORY
The Extension was begun by the French when they held this sector before the British arrived in 1915. The British 46th Division began to make burials here in September 1915 and it remained in use until January 1917. It was also used during the German advance in 1918.

INFORMATION
The village was in Allied hands throughout the war, first under the French and from the summer of 1915 under the British. It was severely damaged by shell-fire. Fourteen French burials and the grave of one German soldier have been removed though some still remain. There are eight German burials made in WW2.

Among those here is Major Charles Francis Simonds, MiD, 13th King's Royal Rifle Corps, killed in action on 29 June 1916 aged 38 years. He was part of a well-known banking family in Reading, though their bank had been taken over by Barclays by 1914. He served in the South African Wars as a member of the Berkshire Mounted Infantry, then retired, re-joined the army in September 1914 being commissioned into the Kings Royal Rifle Corps in February 1915 and reaching the Front in July 1915. He was a keen sportsman which included rowing for Oxford University. He was killed shortly after leading a trench raid when the Germans shelled his HQ burying him and several other officers.

UK – 144 Fr – 44
Ger – 1 (+ 8 WW2) Unnamed - 2
Area – 1066 sq mts

Special Memorial erected to one British soldier whose grave has been destroyed by shell-fire.

LOCATION
Berles-au-Bois is a village located 25km north of Albert and about 3km south of the Arras-Doullens road. The churchyard is at the north end of the village though the Church is now gone. The Extension is on the north side of the churchyard and can only be reached through it. It is behind a red brick wall.

BERLES NEW MILITARY CEMETERY, BERLES-AU-BOIS

HISTORY
The New Military Cemetery was begun in January 1917 when the space in the Churchyard Extension had been filled. It remained in use until April 1917 and some further burials were added from April to August 1918.

INFORMATION
Fifteen French graves have been removed while the eleven that remain are at the rear of the cemetery.

Buried here is Brigadier General Frederick William Lumsden, VC, CB, DSO and three Bars, four times MiD, Croix de Guerre (France), Croix de Guerre (Belgium), General Staff, Commanding 14th Brigade, 32nd Division (late Royal Marine Artillery), killed at Blairville near Arras on 4 June 1918, aged 45 years. His Victoria Cross was awarded for actions that took place between 3 and 4 April 1917 in Francilly, France. The citation reads 'For most conspicuous bravery, determination and devotion to duty. Six enemy field guns having been captured, it was necessary to leave them in dug-in positions, 300 yards in advance of the position held by our troops. The enemy kept the captured guns under heavy fire. Major Lumsden undertook the duty of bringing the guns into our lines. In order to effect this, he personally led four artillery teams and a party of infantry through the hostile barrage. As one of these teams' sustained casualties, he left the remaining teams in a covered position, and, through very heavy rifle, machine gun and shrapnel fire, led the infantry to the guns. By force of example and inspiring energy he succeeded in sending back two teams with guns, going through the barrage with the teams of the third gun. He then returned to the guns to await further teams, and these he succeeded in attaching to two of the three remaining guns, despite rifle fire, which had become intense at short range, and removed the guns to safety. By this time the enemy, in considerable strength, had driven through the infantry covering points, and blown up the breach of the remaining gun. Major Lumsden then returned, drove off the enemy, attached the gun to a team and got it away.' He was born in India and served abroad until the start of the war. He was awarded the Distinguished Service Order in the New Year's Honours List in January 1917. Unusually he was awarded two bars to his DSO in the same gazette in May 1917. He was the first person to receive a third Bar when it was awarded in April 1918. He had given up a staff post to take command of 14th Highland Light Infantry in April 1917 but was then given 14th Brigade just a few days later. It was in that period with his battalion that he was involved in the action for which he gained his Victoria Cross. He was made a Commander of the Order of the Bath just before he was killed as he went to the front line when an alarm had gone up. One report says he was shot through the head while another says he was killed by a shell splinter.

Also here is Captain John Ernest Vivian Rathbone, 3rd attached 1st Dorsets, died on 4 June 1918 aged 20 years. He was a Sergeant Major in the Inns of Court Officer Training Corps so he was easily accepted in June 1915 for a commission in the 3rd Dorsets. He was seriously wounded on the Somme in July 1916 but returned to the Front in 1918 to join the 1st Dorsets. He was the younger brother of Basil Rathbone who became a famous actor after the war, notably for playing Sherlock Holmes. The death of his younger brother John is thought to be the main reason that long term American resident Rathbone remained a British subject. Captain Basil Rathbone was, at one stage, the Intelligence Officer for the 2/10th (Liverpool Scottish) King's (Liverpools).

UK – 167   Fr – 11   Unnamed – 1
Area – 972 sq mts

LOCATION
The New Military Cemetery is at the north end of the village at the junction of the roads to Bailleulmont and La Cauchie. It is on a ridge above the village.

BERLES POSITION MILITARY CEMETERY

INFORMATION
Most of the burials here were made by the 46th Division. It was also known as 'The Ravine Cemetery' or as 'Nobs Walk Cemetery'. Four German graves have been removed.
Almost all burials come from a few regiments – Royal Engineers, The Kings (Liverpools), Bedfordshires, South Staffordshires and Lincolnshires.
Among those here is 2nd Lieutenant Gavin Boyd, 4th Royal Engineers, killed in action on 13 July 1916. He went to Glasgow University for his scientific training. He received a commission in the 14th Argyll and Sutherland Highlanders before transfer to the Royal Engineers.

UK – 52   Unnamed – 1   Area – 379 sq mts

LOCATION
This cemetery is about 1km south-east of the village and lies in fields in a small valley that is to the south of the road to Monchy-au-Bois. It is reached from the road by a small path. It is very peaceful and tranquil.

HISTORY
The cemetery was opened by the 46th Division in July 1916 and remained in use until February 1917.

BERNAFAY WOOD BRITISH CEMETERY, MONTAUBAN

HISTORY
The cemetery was begun in August 1916 and remained in use until April 1917 when the fighting moved away from here. It was greatly enlarged after the war.

INFORMATION
Montauban was captured by the 30th and 18th Divisions on 1 July 1916 and was one of the few successes of the day. However, the British failed to press home their advantage. The wood was taken on 3 and 4 July 1916 by the 9th Division at the cost of five casualties. It was not an objective in the great attack of 1 July 1916, through it could have been taken. Lack of British success elsewhere meant that the only British troops to enter the wood were a small patrol who found a few Germans, took them prisoner, and withdrew.

The Germans retook Montauban and Bernafay Wood during their spring offensive on 25 March 1918. The village fell to the 7th Buffs and 11th Royal Fusiliers of the 18th Division on 25 August and the wood on 27 August 1918.

The cemetery was begun by a Dressing Station established here in the latter part of the 1916 battles. At the end of the war it contained 284 graves. After the war 638 graves were concentrated here. Of these, 417 are unidentified which is over 45% of the burials. The original burials are mostly identified as they came from the Dressing Station.

This is the only cemetery in this area on or near the line reached on 1 July 1916. It lies on the reverse side of Montauban Ridge.

Among those buried here is Lieutenant Alain Percy Mark Chawner, MiD, 3rd attached 1st Essex Regiment, killed in action on 21 October 1916 aged 22 years. He joined the East Surreys at the start of the war. His younger brother, Meredith Andre Chawner, a Captain in the 2nd Essex was killed in action on 21 May 1917 aged 21 years. He is buried in Orange Trench Cemetery, Monchy-le-Preux.

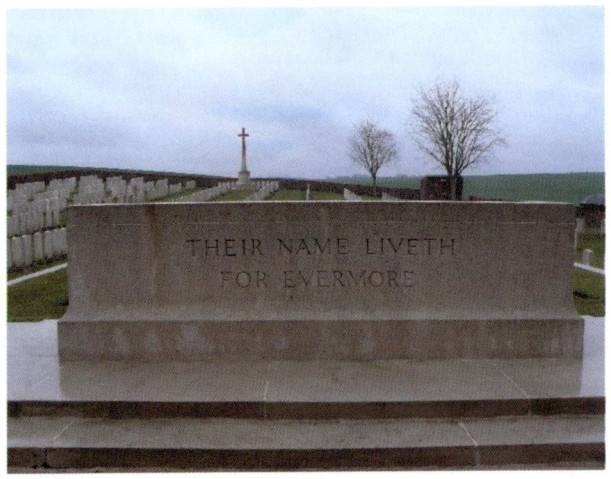

Concentrated here:
Bernafay Wood North Cemetery - situated just north of the wood on the east side of the road. It was begun at an advanced Dressing Station in July 1916 and remained in use until October. It contained the graves of 80 British soldiers and one German prisoner who was removed elsewhere.

| UK – 793 | Aust -122 | SAfr – 4 |
| NZ – 2 | India – 1 | Unnamed – 417 |

Area – 3409 sq mts

Special Memorials to ten British and two Australian soldiers known, or believed, to be buried among the unnamed graves.

Special Memorials erected to twenty British soldiers, buried in Bernafay Wood North Cemetery whose graves could not be identified at the time of concentration.

LOCATION
Montauban is situated 10km east of Albert. This cemetery is on the west side of the Longueval-Maricourt road, opposite the wood, about 1km north-east of the village.

BERTHAUCOURT COMMUNAL CEMETERY

HISTORY
The cemetery was only used between 9 September and 7 October 1918 during the advance that led to the end of the war.

INFORMATION
Those buried here are mostly from 2nd King's Royal Rifle Corps killed on 18 September, or 1st Northamptonshires and 2nd Royal Sussex killed on 24 September 1918. There are also a group of artillerymen, killed on 5 October 1918, from 'O' Battery, Royal Horse Artillery and 113th and 115th Batteries, 25th Brigade, Royal Field Artillery.

Buried here is Captain Geoffrey Sunderland, 'C' Company, 2nd Royal Sussex, killed in action 24 September 1918 aged 29 years. He was born in New Zealand but moved to the United Kingdom in 1896. He went to Cambridge University in 1910. He joined the King Edward's Horse (The King's Oversea Dominions Regiment), a unit mainly made up of men who had settled or seen service in the colonies, as a Corporal in June 1915. He rose to the rank of Sergeant and was then commissioned in March 1916, joining the 2nd Royal Sussex. He became a Captain after Third Ypres, but was killed in an attack at Gricourt about 1km south-east of here.

UK – 71   Unnamed - 4

LOCATION
Pontru is about 8km north-west of St. Quentin. Berthaucourt is a small settlement just east of Pontru. The cemetery is on the south-west edge of Pontru. It is on the east side of the road to Maissemy 250m from the fork to Le Verguier as the road rises. The British plot is at the rear of the cemetery.

BERTINCOURT CHATEAU BRITISH CEMETERY

HISTORY
The cemetery was first used when the village was captured in March 1917 and used again when the village was finally taken in 1918.

INFORMATION
The village was in German hands for much of the war until taken by the Allies in March 1917. It was evacuated on 24 March 1918 during the German advance, and re-occupied by the 1st Canterbury Infantry Battalion on 3 September 1918.

The chateau was at the north-east end of the village, and the cemetery is next to where it once stood. The 7th King's Own Yorkshire Light Infantry buried their dead here at the end of March 1917, and other units (mainly from the 37th and 42nd Divisions) used it again in September 1918.

Among those buried here is Major Reginald Harry Cade, 1/7th Lancashire Fusiliers, killed in action on 27 September 1918 aged 27 years. He was a lawyer and a Territorial before the war. He was wounded in Gallipoli in 1915, in France in 1917, and was gassed in early 1918.

UK – 47   Unnamed – 2   Area – 278 sq mts

LOCATION
Bertincourt is about 5km south of the main Bapaume-Cambrai road. The cemetery is on the north side of the road to Hermies on the east side of the village. It is a small and pretty little cemetery – a tranquil oasis

BERTRANCOURT MILITARY CEMETERY

HISTORY
The cemetery was begun on 31 July 1915 but was used mainly by Dressing Stations during the battles of 1916. Many of these burials were from Pals Battalions of the 31st Division who had been involved in the attack at Serre on 1 July 1916. Some burials were made in 1917 but the second wave of burials date from the German offensive of 1918 and are mostly men of the 42nd (East Lancashire) Division.

INFORMATION
The earliest burials can be found in Plot I which contains graves dating from July 1915 to November 1916. Plot II contains graves of autumn 1916 and of those of 1918. The cemetery was used by Field Ambulances, and by Corps and Divisional Burial Officers. There are also three German Prisoners of War in Plot II. There is no War Stone here which is unusual for a cemetery of this size.

There are four men buried here who were executed. Private Alfred Thomas Ansted, 4th Royal Fusiliers was executed for desertion on 15 November 1916 aged 29 years. He absconded for the second time, while under a suspended sentence of death, at Guillemont in August 1916. He gave himself up at Corbie and was court martialled on 5 November.

Private John Taylor, 15th (1st Salford Pals) Lancashire Fusiliers was executed for desertion on 27 January 1917. He was also under a suspended sentence, this time five years imprisonment for quitting his post.

Private Alexander Reid, 16th (2nd Glasgow Pals) Highland Light Infantry, was executed for murder on 31 January 1917. He was wounded in August 1916 and returned to his unit in December. A fight broke out in his barracks with Private James Henry Kean after an evening's drinking and gambling on 5 January 1917. Kean was shot and killed during the fight. Kean is buried in Rubempre Communal Cemetery.

Rifleman William Murphey, 5/6th Royal Scots, had never been in the front line, had only been with the battalion for a week, and disappeared while marching at La Vicogne in January 1917. He was executed for desertion on 7 February 1917.

Also here is Gunner Lionel Reginald Wills, 112th Siege Battery, Royal Garrison Artillery, died 1 July 1916 aged 16 years.

UK - 416   Ger – 3
Unnamed – 2   KUG - 2

LOCATION
Bertrancourt is situated about 5km north-west of Albert. The cemetery can be found in open fields 400m south-west of the village between the road to Acheux and Louvencourt. It is about 70m north of the road to Acheux and reached by a path from the road.

BIENVILLERS MILITARY CEMETERY

INFORMATION
The cemetery was opened by the 37th Division. Its twenty-one Plots show a contrast of original burials in regimental or Divisional groups and other groups of post-war concentrated graves. The graves of nine German soldiers have been removed to Maison-Blanche German Cemetery. Among those here is Lieutenant Colonel Walter Lorraine Brodie, VC, MC, 2nd Highland Light Infantry, killed in action near Moeuvres on 23 August 1918. He won the Victoria Cross as a Captain on 11 November 1914 near Becelaere in Belgium and was one of the 'Old Contemptibles'. His citation says 'For conspicuous gallantry near Becelaere on the 11th November, in clearing the enemy out of a portion of our trenches which they had succeeded in occupying. Heading the charge, he bayoneted several of the enemy, and thereby relieved a dangerous situation. As a result of Lieutenant Brodie's promptitude, 80 of the enemy were killed and 51 taken prisoners.'

There are seven other men of the rank of Lieutenant Colonel including battalion commanders killed in 1918 buried here.

HISTORY
The cemetery was begun in September 1915 and continued in use until March 1917. It came in to use again from March to September 1918. The cemetery was used in 1922-24 for the concentration of 480 graves, mainly deaths of 1916, from the battlefields of the Ancre.

	Death	Age	Unit	Awards	Grave
Oswyn St. Leger Davies	05/04/1918	44	6th Manchesters Commanding 8th Lancashire Fusiliers		XVII. A. 4
Claud Frederick Pilkington Parry	20/08/1918	48	34th Bde. Royal Field Artillery	DSO, MiD	XIX. E. 3.
Thomas William Bullock	11/04/1918	43	1st Dorsetshires		I. A. 33.
John Hay Maitland Hardyman	24/08/1918	23	8th Somerset Light Infantry	DSO, MC, Twice MiD	XIX. F. 11.
Charles Kenneth James	19/05/1918	26	6th Borders	DSO and Bar	XVI. D. 7.
Archibald Hugh James	26/03/1918	40	8th Northumberland Fusiliers attached 8th West Yorkshires	DSO	I. A. 24.
Ronald Beaumont Wood	21/08/1918	36	12th (Prince of Wales's Royal) Lancers attached 6th Tank Corps	MiD	XIX. E. 2.

UK – 1567   Aust – 25   NZ – 9
Can – 3   SAfr – 1   Ger – 1
Unnamed – 427   WW2 – 16
Area – 7154 sq mts

Special memorials are erected to two British soldiers known or believed to be buried among the unnamed.

LOCATION
Bienvillers-Au-Bois is about 15km south-west of Arras. The cemetery is south of the village on the west side of the road to Souastre.

BLANGY-TRONVILLE COMMUNAL CEMETERY

HISTORY
This cemetery was used in 1918 from March to July during the German advance and the period in which that advance was halted before the Allies began the final push to victory.

INFORMATION
The British and French used the cemetery. Two large extensions, on the north side of the cemetery, have been removed. Of those buried here over 50% are artillerymen. Among those buried here is Captain John Edward Wallace Bushelle, MC, 36th Australian Infantry, killed in action on 6 April 1918. He was an original member of the Battalion as

a 2nd Lieutenant. Shortly after his marriage he left Australia on 13 May 1916 arriving, via time in England, in France on 22 November. He was promoted to Lieutenant on 21 March 1917. On return from leave in July 1917 he was promoted to Captain and command of a Company. He survived the Third Battle of Ypres that saw 60 Officers and 1322 other ranks lose their lives. He received the Military Cross in the First Battle of Villers-Bretonneux. His citation reads 'On the 4th of April 1918, when his Battalion counter-attacked, he led his company with exceptional dash and determination, and succeeded in recapturing a position which had been lost earlier in the afternoon. Throughout the operation and in the face of heavy machine gun fire and sniper fire, he showed an utter disregard of danger and by his fearless leadership and personal greatly assisted in the success of the operation of his Battalion. Later while under heavy and close machine gun fire he moved in the open supervising and directing the work of his company in consolidating the position captured.' At this time his battalion was made up of the remaining twelve officers and 132 men partly as Australia refused to introduce conscription so battalions continued with company strength numbers. Two days later he was shot by a sniper. It is interesting to note that in his file in Australia, there are a series of letters dealing with the fact that the original War Graves Commission records and registers omitted the Military Cross. This was finally corrected in 1930.

UK – 26   Aust – 16   Fr - 1
Area – 292 sq mts

There is one special memorial to a soldier whose grave was destroyed by shell-fire.

LOCATION
Blangy-Tronville is a small village on the eastern edge of Amiens. It is now almost a suburb. It lies on the south side of the River Somme close to the D167. The cemetery is on the southern edge of the village, south of the railway, on a ridge at the end of a road. There are excellent views across the valley from here. The graves are in several areas – two along the western edge of the cemetery and at the northern edge near the Cross of Sacrifice as well as some burials near the entrance.

BLIGHTY VALLEY CEMETERY

HISTORY
Blighty Valley Cemetery was begun in July 1916 soon after the front-line had moved away from this area. It remained in use until November 1916 at the close of the Battles of the Somme. After the war it was enlarged by over 300%.

INFORMATION
Blighty Valley was the name given by the British to part of a valley running south-west through Authuille Wood to the River Ancre. During the early months of the Battles of the Somme it carried a light railway along the dangerous valley. At this time, the upper part of the valley was called Nab Valley though as many men gained their 'Blighty' wound (one that could take them back across the Channel) in the area it gained its present name.

When closed at the end of war the cemetery contained 212 graves in what is now Plot I. After the war 784 graves were concentrated from isolated cemeteries and smaller graveyards east of the cemetery as the battlefields were cleared. Most of the graves concentrated were of men who died on 1 July 1916. Many were from the 8th Division.

The 70th Brigade contained many men from mining areas in Yorkshire and Nottinghamshire. Their attack on 1 July 1916 was a disaster as, among other factors, the German stronghold at Mouquet Farm, which was their objective, had good links to reserve lines. The Brigade has been told to walk across no-man's land and that their lunch would be brought to them at the Farm. Only a few reached the German wire as the Brigade suffered nearly 2000 casualties or more than 70% of those involved in the attack. Of the unnamed buried here, the majority probably come from 70th Brigade.

Two battalion commanding officers were among the dead, and two others were wounded. One is buried here, Lieutenant Colonel B L Maddison, 2nd attached and commanding 8th York and Lancasters. The battalion, as part of 70th Brigade, was to attack the German line north of Ovillers in the area of The Nab. 8th Kings Own Yorkshire Light Infantry were on the right, and two leading waves of both battalions managed to cross no man's land and the front trench moving onto the second trench. Very few of the third and fourth waves got across. At the second trench opposition stiffened and further progress of the first waves became slow although some men entered the third trench 200m beyond. No reinforcements appeared. The two battalions in support lost heavily from machine gun fire from the Thiepval Spur. The 8th lost 21 officers including Maddison and his Adjutant Lieutenant Sydney Dawson, and 576 other ranks, the heaviest in the 8th Division. The other commanding officer who was killed is in Becourt Military Cemetery.

Also buried here is Lieutenant Colonel Cusack Grant Forsyth, 2nd Yorkshires attached 6th Wiltshires, DSO, Legion of Honour, killed on 14 September 1916, aged 29 years. He is on the CWGC register as 2nd Northumberland Fusiliers attached 6th Yorkshires. He was awarded the Distinguished Service Order in the New Year's Honours List in January 1916. He was one of five brothers, three of whom were killed in the war and one who died before the war. Lieutenant and Adjutant John C. Forsyth, 23rd Brigade, Royal Field Artillery, killed on 22 September 1914 and commemorated by a Special Memorial in Braine Communal Cemetery. Lieutenant Samuel S. Forsyth, Royal Field Artillery, killed on 25 September 1915 and commemorated on the Menin Gate Memorial in Ieper. One other brother survived the war, Captain and Brevet Major Frederick Richard Gerard Forsyth, MC, twice MiD, Seaforth Highlanders, attached Royal Engineers.

Another commanding officer buried here is Lieutenant Colonel William Beresford Gibbs, 3rd Worcestershires, who died of wounds on 3 September 1916. His battalion was to attack the western side of the Leipzig Salient. At 5.10am the British guns opened fire on the Thiepval Ridge and the battalion advanced. The leading companies advanced behind the barrage into the German trenches overwhelming the defenders. They then attempted to secure the ground but the trenches had been destroyed. The Germans, realising the situation, opened a bombardment. Both Company commanders were killed and then Gibbs was hit. The young adjutant took command and tried to hold but as casualties mounted he decided to withdraw.

Concentrated here:

Quarry Post Cemetery, Authuille Wood - situated on the south-east edge of the wood near Aveluy. It was used from July 1916 to February 1917, mostly by the 12th Division, for the burial of 50 British soldiers.

UK – 993   Aust – 2   Can – 1
Unnamed – 532   Area - 4236 sq mts

Special Memorials to 24 British soldiers known, or believed, to be buried among the unidentified graves.

Special Memorials to five British soldiers, buried by the Germans in Becourt German Cemetery in spring 1918, whose graves could not be found upon concentration.

LOCATION
Authuille and Aveluy lie in the valley of the River Ancre about 4km north-east of the town of Albert. Blighty Valley is on the east side of the road between the two villages about 1km South of Authuille. The cemetery is in a valley half way between these two villages about 300m from the road and reached by a clearly distinguishable GWGC path. This is a very peaceful cemetery as it is so isolated.

BONNAY COMMUNAL CEMETERY EXTENSION

HISTORY
The Extension was opened on 1 April 1918 and remained in use until 24 August 1918.

INFORMATION
The earlier burials are mainly of men who fell in the Battles of Villers-Bretonneux when the 13th and 15th Australian Brigades with the British 18th Division recaptured and then held the village. (For a fuller description see entry on Villers-Bretonneux Military Cemetery) Other burials are of men who fell in the defence of Amiens. Of the British who are buried here, 24 belonged to the 47th Division.

The Great Cross was unveiled by the Prime Minister of Australia in 1921.

Among those buried here is Captain Albert Edward Halstead, MC, 42nd Australian Infantry, killed in action on 16 April 1918 aged 30 years. He was son of Lieutenant Colonel William Henry Halstead, VD, CMF. He was originally commissioned into the 31st Australian Infantry but fell ill and was transferred to the 42nd once he had recovered. He won the Military Cross at Broodseinde Ridge near Ieper in October 1917 for capturing seven Germans from a pill-box. He was killed by a shell at Shrapnel Gully near Sailly-le-Sec.

UK – 31   Aust – 75   Area – 591 sq mts

LOCATION
Bonnay lies on the north-west bank of the River Ancre about 10km east of Amiens and 15km south-west of Albert. The Communal Cemetery is about 200m north-west of the village on the road to Franvillers overlooking the village. The cemetery is in open countryside next to the Communal Cemetery.

BOOTHAM CEMETERY

HISTORY
The cemetery was made in April 1917 by the 56th (London) Division.

INFORMATION
The village of Heninel was in German hands for much of the war. It was taken by the 56th (London) Division and the 21st Division on 12 April 1917 during the German retreat to the Hindenburg Line.

The cemetery is one row of graves in an attractive triangular shaped area. The cemetery was named after a trench, which was itself named after Bootham School. Of those buried here, 71 were from the 2nd Royal Scots Fusiliers killed on 23 April 1917 while attacking the high ground overlooking Cherisy, and 44 from 1/16th (Queens Westminster Rifles) Londons killed on 14 April 1917 by enfilading fire from Guemappe on their exposed flank. They were among more than 300 casualties in the battalion during the attack. This accounts for all the identified burials. One German grave has been removed.

Among those here is Lance Corporal Horace Kingsley Stedeford, 1/16th (Queen's Westminster Rifles) Londons, killed in action on 14 April 1917 aged 23 years. He was married and had been a Civil Service clerk before the war.

UK – 186   Unnamed – 71   Area – 1006 sq mts

LOCATION
The cemetery is about 1km east of the village of Heninel. This is about 10km south-east of Arras and 1km east of the A1 Autoroute. It lies on a ridge in open farmland on the south side of a small road between Heninel and Cherisy. It gives excellent views of the battlefields.

BOUCHOIR NEW BRITISH CEMETERY

HISTORY
This is a concentration cemetery and was made entirely after the war. Bodies, mostly of men who died during the battles here in 1918, were concentrated from isolated positions on the battlefields or from small British cemeteries to the south and surrounding the village.

INFORMATION
Bouchoir was behind the British and French lines for much of the war. It played a minor role as a support town during the Battles of 1916. However, during the German spring advance in 1918 it came into the front-line when it was defended by the 30th Division on 27 March. It fell to the Germans for a brief period before recapture by the 8th Canadian Infantry Brigade in August 1918.

An unusual feature of this cemetery is the numbering of graves. Those in Plots I, II, III and IV are numbered consecutively whereas those in Plots V and VI are numbered by Row in the usual manner for CWGC cemeteries.

Most of the unnamed died during the German advance in early 1918 while the majority of the identified are from the Allied advance later in 1918. Most of the Canadian burials date from August 1918. Many of the men buried here are from the 32nd Division who met fierce resistance nearby during attacks on 10 and 11 August 1918.

Among those buried here is Lieutenant Colonel Harold Echalez Welch, DSO and Bar, 6th King's Shropshire Light Infantry, killed in action on 29 March 1918 aged 39 years. He served with the Middlesex Regiment in the Boer War. In 1914 he re-joined the army going to France in July 1915 as a Major commanding 'D' Company of 6th King's Shropshire Light Infantry. He saw action at the Battle of Loos on 25 September 1915 and shortly after became second-in-command of the battalion. In September 1916 he took command while on the Somme. In September 1917, during the Third Battle of Ypres, Welch was promoted to Acting Lieutenant Colonel. He led the Battalion in the Battle of the Menin Road and was awarded the Distinguished Service Order. In November, in the Battle of Cambrai, the battalion was held up by machine gun fire. Welch was awarded a Bar to the DSO. The citation reads 'During the hours which elapsed before the advance could continue [Welch] moved about under fire regardless of danger, reconnoitring the situation, visiting his companies, and issuing orders. Owing to his efforts his battalion was eventually able to continue the advance successfully. His leadership and courage set a magnificent example to all ranks.' During the German offensive in March 1918, the battalion was in reserve when it came under shell-fire.

Welch was hit by a piece of shrapnel and died shortly afterwards.

Concentrated here:

Bois-De-Gentelles British Cemetery, Gentelles - situated about 25km north-west of here on the north side of the Amiens-Roye road directly south of the village. It was used in August 1918 for the burial of nineteen Canadian and eleven British soldiers with a body that was unidentified and a French soldier who has been removed elsewhere.

Bouchoir British Cemetery - situated directly opposite this New Cemetery. It was made in August 1918 by the Canadian Corps for the burial of 47 men of the 2nd Canadian Mounted Rifles and three British soldiers.

Bouchoir French Military Cemetery - situated on the north-western edge of the village near the road to Folies. The French soldiers have been removed to Montdidier French National Cemetery. Four British and two Canadian soldiers were brought here.

Damery British Cemetery, Parvillers - situated about 5km east of here in the fields north-west of Damery and south-west of Parvillers. It was made in August 1918 for the burial of 37 British soldiers, mostly of the 1st Dorsets or 5th/6th Royal Scots, with two men from Canada.

Folies Churchyard - situated in the centre of the village which is 1km north of here. It contained the graves of six Canadian soldiers and a British serviceman who died in August 1918.

Folies Communal Cemetery Extension - the Communal Cemetery is situated at the western edge of the village about 1km north-west of here. The Extension contained the graves of 23 Canadian and four British soldiers who were killed in August 1918. The Communal Cemetery had been used by French and German troops and still contains the graves of a Canadian and British soldier dating from August 1918.

Laboissiere German Cemetery - the village is situated about 10km directly south of here and the cemetery was on the north side of the village near the Chateau. Two British RAF officers were buried among the Germans who have been removed to Montdidier German Cemetery.

Parvillers British Cemeteries - three cemeteries, No. 1, No. 2 and No. 3 were all situated north-west of the village in the fields between it and Rouvroy about 4km to the north-east of here. The village was taken back from the Germans, who held it for about a week, by the 3rd Canadian Division on 15 August 1918. No. 1 Cemetery contained 28 British men of the 5th/6th Royal Scots who had been killed on 11 August 1918. No. 2 Cemetery contained 60 British soldiers, 54 of the 5th/6th Royal Scots, who were also killed on 11 August. No. 3 Cemetery contained the graves of 16 British and four Canadian soldiers who died in August 1918.

UK – 541   Can – 216   Aust – 6
Unnamed – 231   Area – 3486 sq mts

Special Memorials to five British soldiers who are known, or believed, to be buried among the unidentified graves.

Special Memorial to a British airman, buried in Laboissiere German Cemetery, whose grave could not be located at the time of concentration. This was Lieutenant William Cecil Cutmore, naval pilot of No. 206 Squadron, RAF, shot down aged 18 years in his Airco DH9 bomber in June 1918.

LOCATION

Bouchoir is situated on the main road from Amiens to Roye. It lies about 30km south-east of Amiens and 8km north-west of Roye. The cemetery is on the north side of the road about 1km south-west of the village. The cemetery cannot be accessed directly from the D934. I cannot advise parking on the dangerous dual carriageway D934. About 100m north-west of the cemetery is a junction with the old road, now a farm road, on the side of the westbound carriageway. Use this side road to get to the cemetery.

BOUZINCOURT COMMUNAL CEMETERY

HISTORY

The Communal Cemetery was used by the British for burials from March to February 1917, though very few burials were made after July 1916, and from April to June 1918.

INFORMATION

The cemetery was used by Field Ambulances from early 1916 until the Germans withdrew to the Hindenburg Line and the British left the area of the River Ancre. This location fell into German possession for a brief period in April 1918. The 1916 burials were made in Rows A and B which are to the right of the central path. The 1918 burials are in Rows C and D which are near the entrance to the churchyard.

An Irish Catholic Chaplain was buried here in 1916. He lies near the crucifix. He was originally among some French soldiers but they have been removed. He is Father The Reverend Donal Vincent O'Sullivan, killed in action on 5 July 1916 age 26 years. He was from Killarney in Ireland and had been a Professor at St. Brendan's Seminary, Killarney. At the time of his death he was Chaplain to the Loyal North Lancashire Regiment.

UK - 33

LOCATION

Bouzincourt lies about 3km north-west of Albert. The Communal Cemetery is at the north-west corner of the village on the north side of the road to Engelbelmer.

BOUZINCOURT COMMUNAL CEMETERY EXTENSION

HISTORY
The Communal Cemetery Extension was opened in March 1916 and remained in use until February 1917 when the Germans withdrew to the Hindenburg Line. It was used again during the German offensive in 1918 from March to September. After the war the Extension was enlarged by the concentration of graves from the surrounding battlefields.

INFORMATION
The cemetery was used in 1916 but during the battles of July some bodies were brought straight from the front-line for burial. Nearly forty men died of wounds here on 1 July 1916 and a further ninety in the first week of the Battle of the Somme. There are several men from artillery units buried here who were killed during the bombardment that led up to 1 July 1916. The Dressing Stations here on 1 July dealt with many men of 32nd Division who had attacked Thiepval. The burials of 1918 were mainly of men of the 38th Division.

In 1919 20 graves were brought from isolated positions in, and around, the village. They are in what is now Plot III, Row A. In 1924-25 a further 108 graves were concentrated from various parts of the battlefields on the Somme, and from Framerville Churchyard, into Plots I, III and IV.

Buried here is Major Harris Laurance Stocks, DSO, 15th Royal Scots, killed in action in Sausage Valley on 1 July 1916. His body was brought back by his men from the battlefield when the remnants of the 34th Division was withdrawn to this village on the evening of 1 July. He had been Captain of the 4th (Kirkauldy) Company Boys Brigade. His father was a Provost and steamship owner.

A senior officer buried here is Lieutenant-Colonel Robert Lowndes Aspinall, DSO, 11th Cheshires, formerly Yorkshire Regiment, and 15th Hussars, killed in action near Thiepval in an attack on the Leipzig Salient on 3 July 1916 aged 47 years. He was gazetted to the 15th Hussars in 1888 and promoted to Captain before retiring from the Hussars in 1899. He went to South Africa in the Boer War with the Yorkshire Regiment, where he served on Sir John French's staff as ADC, (Lady French being his aunt) where he was awarded his Distinguished Service Order. In 1914 Aspinall commanded the 3rd Yorkshires on their mobilization, and later commanded troops of the South Garrison, Redcar. He then raised the 11th (Darlington Pals) Yorkshires, before being transferred to the Cheshire Regiment, with whom he went to France. He was killed leading his men into attack when he was shot in the right shoulder.

Also here are two brothers, Lieutenant Archibald Lyall and Lieutenant James Thomson Lyall. Both were with the 15th (1st Glasgow Pals or Glasgow Tramways) Highland Light Infantry, Archibald with 'B' Company and James with 'D' Company. Both were killed on 3 July 1916 and are buried together. Only two companies of the Highland Light Infantry attacked at the Leipzig Salient that day.

Among those buried here is Private Arthur Grove Earp, 1/5th Royal Warwickshires who was executed on 22 July 1916 for the two charges of quitting his post and for conduct to the prejudice of good order and military discipline. He was the first soldier to be executed for an action during the Battle of the Somme. He had left the front line during the barrage before 1 July 1916 when he was in the line near Hebuterne. The officers at his trial argued for mercy, which was the tone taken at every level until the papers reached Rawlinson.

Concentrated here:
Framerville Churchyard - the village is situated about 15 km south-east of here on the Amiens-St. Quentin road. It fell to the 2nd Australian Division on 9 August 1918. They then buried two of their dead at the south end of the Churchyard.

UK – 561	Aust – 8	Can – 7
SAfr – 2	NZ – 1	Ger - 2
KUG – 8	Unnamed – 107	Area – 1851 sq mts

Special Memorials to two British soldiers believed, or known, to be buried among the unnamed graves.

LOCATION
The Extension is behind the Communal Cemetery.

BOUZINCOURT RIDGE CEMETERY

HISTORY
The cemetery was begun in early September 1918. The majority of burials date from after the war as the cemetery was increased in size by the concentration of bodies from the local area.

INFORMATION
The Bouzincourt Ridge was, for most of the war, in Allied hands. Parts of it were taken by the Germans after March 1918, though their advance was halted by the 12th and 38th (Welsh) Divisions. The eastern section of the ridge was attacked by 12th and 18th Divisions in June 1918 and the rest was cleared in August 1918 by the 38th Division. Hence, there are a lot of Welsh burials here.

This cemetery was begun by V Corps in the first few days of September 1918. These burials now make up Plot I. The rest of the cemetery is made of concentration burials.

Buried here is Acting Lieutenant-Colonel John Stanhope Collings-Wells, VC, DSO, MiD, commanding 4th

Bedfordshires, killed in action on 27 March 1918. He won the Victoria Cross for his actions between 22-27 March 1918 during a fighting retreat from Marcoign to Albert. His citation reads 'For most conspicuous bravery, skillful leading and handling of his battalion in very critical situations during a withdrawal. When the rearguard was almost surrounded and in great danger of being captured, Lieutenant Colonel Collings-Wells, realising the situation, called for volunteers to remain behind and hold up the enemy whilst the remainder of the rearguard withdrew, and with his small body of volunteers held them up for one and half hours until they had expended every round of ammunition. During this time he moved freely amongst his men guiding and encouraging them, and by his great courage undoubtedly saved the situation. On a subsequent occasion, when his battalion was ordered to carry out a counter-attack, he showed the greatest bravery. Knowing that his men were extremely tired after six days' fighting, he placed himself in front and led the attack, and even when twice wounded refused to leave them but continued to lead and encourage his men until he was killed at the moment of gaining their objective. The successful results of the operations were, without doubt, due to the undaunted courage exhibited by this officer.'

UK – 667   Aust – 35   Can – 6
Unnamed – 313   Area – 2481 sq mts

Special Memorial to an officer of the 38th Division who lies among the unnamed graves.

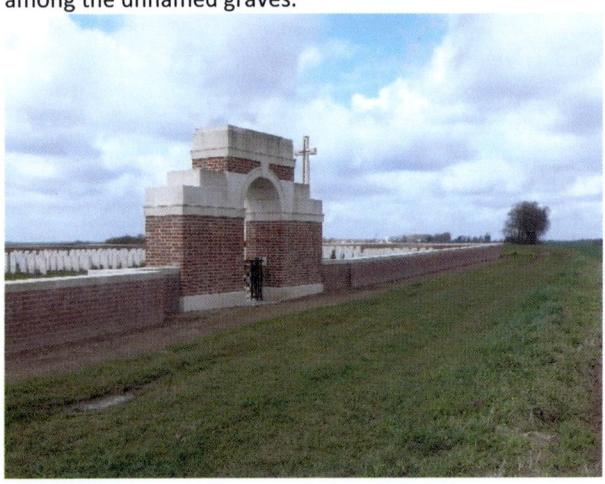

LOCATION
The cemetery is situated on the ridge near the Aveluy-Bouzincourt road. It is midway between the villages, 100m south of the road in open fields. The 250m track to the cemetery is rough, so the cemetery is isolated and not often visited. Do not take a car, unless it is a 4x4 or you feel adventurous, down the track as it deteriorates. There are excellent views from the cemetery which make the walk worth the effort.

BOVES EAST COMMUNAL CEMETERY

HISTORY
Burials were made here in April and August 1918.

INFORMATION
Boves has two communal cemeteries, one on either side of the river. The 49th Casualty Clearing Station was at Boves from 23 April to the end of August 1918 and the 1st and 4th Canadian CCS's during August 1918. The burials in the two communal cemeteries and the extension to the West Cemetery are mainly those of soldiers who died in the three hospitals.

Buried here is Private Walter Edward Medhurst, 30th Australian Infantry, killed in action on 7 April 1918 aged 33 years. He was killed, with a Corporal Burgess, while on pack guard in Gentelles Wood about 10km behind the lines, by a bomb from a plane at about 11.00am. He and Burgess are side by side.

There is a German officer buried here who died during the Franco-Prussian War of 1870-71. There are also five French soldiers nearby.

Henry V's army crossed the rivers here in 1415. One man stole Pyx, a container in which the Blessed Sacrament was kept. Henry had the man hanged.

UK- 8   Can – 4   Aust – 3
Fr - 5

LOCATION
Boves is a village on the south-eastern edge of Amiens. It is in the valley of the Avre and Noye rivers. This communal cemetery is at the north end of the east part of the village, sometimes called St. Nicholas. The Allied graves are in the west corner of the cemetery at the rear near the main path.

BOVES WEST COMMUNAL CEMETERY

HISTORY
Burials were made here in late March, April and August 1918.

INFORMATION
See Boves East Communal Cemetery.
An American soldier is buried in this cemetery away from the Allied graves.

Buried here is Major Thomas Anthony Stewart Swinburne, DSO, three times MiD, Legion of Honour (France), 2nd Field Squadron, Royal Engineers, killed in action on 1 April 1918 aged 31 years. He went to Woolwich, where he gained his commission with the Royal Engineers, and then served in India and the Persian Gulf before returning home. He was based in Ireland when war began and he was in France with the first units. He was promoted to Captain in October 1914, and Major and Commanding Officer of his Squadron in November 1916. He received the Distinguished Service Order on 15 March 1916. The citation reads 'For conspicuous gallantry and continuous good work in action, notably when a mine was exploded by us in close proximity to the enemy. Directly our bombers had made good the near edge of the crater, Captain Swinburne organised and controlled the digging parties to consolidate it. Later he explored the far edge of the crater and descended the main shaft, as it appeared that some of the enemy had been entombed by the explosion.' He also received the Legion d'Honour, and was Mentioned in Despatches on 31 May 1915, 30 November 1915, and on 30 April 1916. He was killed by a shell in Moreuil Wood. A detachment of the French Chasseurs d'Afrique attended his funeral as a mark of respect as he held the Legion d'Honour.

UK – 45   Aust – 5   Can – 1
Fr – 12   Others - 1

LOCATION
This communal cemetery is on the south side of the road to Sains-en-Amienois on a ridge climbing out of the town. The cemetery is on a bend and easily missed. The Allied graves are in the south-west corner.

BOVES WEST COMMUNAL CEMETERY EXTENSION

The Extension consists of one row rising up the hill to the Cross of Sacrifice. The cemetery includes the grave of one unidentified airman killed in WW2. The graves of 82 French and eight German soldiers have been removed.

Among those buried here is Captain Herbert Ellery Turner, Croix de Guerre, Order of the Crown (Belgium), 169th Siege Battery, Royal Garrison Artillery, killed in action on 15 April 1918 aged 38 years. Before the war he was an Electrical Engineer employed at the Hull Corporation. He joined the Hull Royal Garrison Artillery territorials in 1909. He started the war as a Corporal and was commissioned in July 1915. He went to France in October 1916, became a Lieutenant in June 1917 and Captain in February 1918.

UK – 38   Aust – 4   Can – 48
BWI – 1   Unnamed – 1   WW2 - 1
Area – 1037 sq mts

LOCATION
The Extension is to the right hand side of the Communal Cemetery. It has a separate entrance but can be accessed through the Communal Cemetery.

HISTORY
Burials were made here in late March, April and August 1918.

INFORMATION
See Boves East Communal Cemetery for other information.

BOYELLES COMMUNAL CEMETERY EXTENSION

HISTORY
The cemetery was used from March 1917 to March 1918 and again in August and September 1918.

INFORMATION
The village was in German hands for much of the war. It was given up in the German withdrawal to the Hindenburg Line when it was occupied by the 7th Division on 19 March 1917. The Germans recaptured the village in March 1918. The Allies captured it for a final time on 23 August 1918.

Many of the burials are men of 21st, 33rd and 56th (London) Divisions.

Buried here is Lieutenant Robert Ward Shepherd Robertson, 4th Queen's (Royal West Surreys) attached 19th Company, Machine Gun Corps (Infantry), killed in action on 27 May 1917. He was from Canada, had enlisted with the Royal Montreal Regiment, and had served as a Private with the machine gun section of the 14th Canadian Infantry until commissioned in January 1916. At that time he was transferred to the Queens to fight with their machine gun company. His brother was wounded at Courcelette in 1916.

Also of note is 2nd Lieutenant Ronal Henry Sampson, 123rd Siege Battery, Royal Garrison Artillery, killed in action on 30 August 1918 aged 20 years. He had intended to join the clergy before the war intervened in his plans. His brother, Christopher Bolckow Sampson, did join the clergy and became chaplain to the Queen in 1958.

UK – 142   Ger – 4   Unnamed - 5

Area – 803 sq mts

LOCATION
Boyelles is a village found about 10km south of Arras midway between Bapaume and Arras. This cemetery is on the north side of the village, a little east of the Arras-Bapaume road, and on the south-west side of the Communal Cemetery. Access is by a path around the Communal Cemetery.

BRAY HILL BRITISH CEMETERY, BRAY-SUR-SOMME

HISTORY
The cemetery was begun on 31 August 1918. No further wartime burials were made but the cemetery was enlarged after the war.

INFORMATION
Bray was behind the British and French lines for much of the war and became an important base town. Bray was one of the focal points for troops to stop in camps before heading out to the 1916 front-line. Hence, it was always busy with everything you would expect in army camps – from pay clerks to barbers. As such, it also contained Field Ambulances (1916) and Casualty Clearing Stations (1917). It fell to the Germans in March 1918 but was recaptured by the 40th Australian Infantry on 24 August. Despite its involvement in various actions the village survived the war relatively undamaged.

The 58th Division, who had taken part in the attacks here, began this cemetery soon after the village had been recaptured in August 1918. The British graves include 65 men of the 58th (London) Division. The original cemetery contained 41 graves but 63 graves were concentrated here after the war. The dead came from the battlefields between Bray and Fricourt and had been killed in March and August 1918. The graves of twelve German soldiers have been removed elsewhere.

Buried here is 2nd Lieutenant Arthur Darley Morton, 21st (First Surrey Rifles) London Regiment, killed in action on 24 August 1918 aged 38 years. He was a member of Blackheath Harriers, Surrey Walking Club and the Inter-Banks Athletic Association.

UK – 102   Aust – 2   Unnamed – 32

Area - 423 sq mts

LOCATION
Bray lies in the valley of the River Somme, on the north side of the river, 8km south-east of Albert. Bray Hill Cemetery is about 2km north of the village, on a ridge, on the west side of the road to Fricourt. It has excellent views.

BRAY MILITARY CEMETERY

HISTORY
The cemetery was begun in April 1916 by fighting units and Field Ambulances situated nearby. It remained in use until March 1918 when the village fell to the Germans. The cemetery was used again briefly in August 1918. After the war the cemetery was enlarged by the concentration of graves from isolated positions in the surrounding battlefields.

INFORMATION
In September 1916 the XIV Corps Main Dressing Station was located here and it used the cemetery. In 1917 it was used by the 5th, 48th and 38th Casualty Clearing Stations which cared for men of the British and French armies.

The 40th Australian Infantry used the cemetery for a few days having captured the village on 24 August 1918. A small Plot for Indians and Egyptians was created towards the rear of the cemetery.

Soon after the war 97 graves were concentrated here. In 1924 a further 106 graves were concentrated into Plot III. Many of the headstones record more than one burial.

Buried here is Sergeant Michael Healy, AM, DCM, MM & Bar, 2nd Royal Munster Fusiliers who died of wounds here on 2 March 1917. He was awarded the Albert Medal (later George Cross), one of only two buried on the Somme, though it is not shown on his headstone. A War Office letter records 'On 1 March 1917, this non-commissioned officer, with a total disregard for his own personal safety and solely prompted by the desire to save his comrades, rushed to pick up a live bomb which had been thrown by a Private and which struck the parapet and rolled back into the trench near Lieutenant Roe and the Private. Sergeant Healy, fearing the party could not escape in time, made a most gallant attempt to seize and hurl the bomb from the trench. It exploded, however, and mortally wounded him. This was the last of Sergeant Healy's many acts of gallantry and devotion to duty. He was previously awarded the Distinguished Conduct Medal and the Military Medal and later a bar to his Military Medal.' It is known that Healy gained his Distinguished Conduct Medal on 17 July 1916 during an attack by the 2nd Munsters on a German position north of Contalmaison in which he captured a machine gun and five prisoners. He gained his first Military Medal on 10 August 1916 and his second in the following month.

Sergeant Malcolm McArthur, 2nd Argyll and Sutherland Highlanders, DCM, MM & Bar who died of wounds on 7 March 1917 aged 21 years is buried here. His Distinguished Conduct Medal citation reads 'For conspicuous gallantry in action. He went out under heavy fire during an attack and brought into safety a badly wounded man. Later he went out to his company commander three times to dress his wounds and take him water. After dark, with a stretcher, he brought him in.' The award of the DCM was during the course of the Battle of the Somme, probably in the attack on High Wood around 15 July 1916.

Also buried here is Corporal Jesse Wilton of 15th Sherwood Forresters who was executed on 17 August 1916 aged 40 years for quitting his post. He and his squad of seven men had been manning an exposed Observation Post between Trones Wood and Guillemont for 48 hours without food or water. They had recently been involved in failed attacks and the entire battalion had been short on rations for days. Officers had drawn pistols to prevent a panicked retreat from the line by others in the battalion. Under heavy fire he ordered his team to evacuate the stressful post six hours early which is the act for which he was court-martialled.

You will also find Lieutenant-Colonel John Norman Sinclair, DSO, Royal Field Artillery, killed on 24 March 1918 in front of Peronne during the German spring offensive while directing the fire of his batteries. He joined the army as a 2nd Lieutenant, RFA in May 1900 and was promoted to Lieutenant in June 1901. From 1906 to 1909 he served with 'D' Battery, Royal Horse Artillery in India and was made Captain, RFA in May 1910. From April 1912 to September 1914 he was Adjutant of the Honorable Artillery Company. He went to Egypt with the HAC and served as Staff Captain from September 1914 to August 1915, though he became a Major in October 1914. He was Deputy Assistant Adjutant and Quartermaster to 2nd Mounted Division at Sulva Bay, Gallipoli from 10-19 August 1915 and Assistant Adjutant and Quarter Master General from 20 August to 28 December 1915 before he was then invalided home. He went to France and served as a Battery Commander and then Brigade Major, Royal Artillery to November 1917 when he became Acting Lieutenant Colonel, RFA. He was Officer Commanding a Field Artillery Brigade from December 1917 to his death. He was Mentioned in Despatches on 15 June 1916 and was gazetted for the Distinguished Service Order on 3 June 1916 in the Birthday Honours List.

Another man buried here is Gunner Albert Maurice Derrez, 8th Brigade, Australian Field Artillery, who died on 28 August 1918 aged 29 years. He was a native of France who had emigrated to Australia and married. He was accidentally killed when an ammunition wagon ran over him in the latter stages of the war.

UK – 739	Aust – 31	Can – 3
SAfr – 2	India – 4	KUG-79

Indian Labour Corps – 9
Egyptian Labour Corps – 8
Unnamed - 127 (43 UK, 2 Aust, 1 SAfr, 1 India and 1 Egypt)
Area – 3074 sq mts

LOCATION
The Military Cemetery lies on the west side of the road to Maricourt on the northern edge of the village. It is past the Communal Cemetery and French National Cemetery as the road dips into a valley. The cemetery is about 50m from the road and on a farm track.

BRAY VALE BRITISH CEMETERY, BRAY-SUR-SOMME

HISTORY
The cemetery was used in August 1918. The cemetery was enlarged after the war.

INFORMATION
The original cemetery consisted of 25 graves of men who died in August 1918 and now makes up Plot II, Row A. After the war 89 British graves were concentrated here by the French Army. They also concentrated 33 German graves next to Plot II but they have since been removed. In 1923 a further 165 graves were concentrated here, mainly from Thiepval and Courcellette, filling the space now called Plots III and IV between the original cemetery and the road. The

cemetery was previously known as Bray No. 2 British Cemetery.

The cemetery is on two levels. The rear is the wartime and immediate post-war burials, mainly men of the 58th Division buried here in August 1918. The lower section is the concentration burials – men brought in from the 1916 battlefield. Most of these later burials are unnamed. Many are from Thiepval when it was cleared to make way for the memorial.

North of this cemetery is a valley called 'Happy Valley'. While there were many such named valleys on the Western Front this is the only one officially named on military maps of the time.

Buried here is Major George Horner Gaffikin, MiD, 'B' Company, 9th Royal Irish Rifles, killed on 1 July 1916 aged 30 years. He led his men into attack at the Schwaben Redoubt near Thiepval waving an orange sash from his position in the Ulster Volunteer Force when he was killed. Notably, the first day of the Battle of the Somme is also the anniversary of the Battle of the Boyne so a special day for all Unionists.

UK – 258   Aust – 17   Newf – 3
Can – 1   KUG – 2   Unnamed – 172
Area - 1199 sq mts

LOCATION
Bray Vale Cemetery is about 2km north-west of the village on the east side of the road to Albert.

BRIE BRITISH CEMETERY

HISTORY
The cemetery was opened by the British in early September 1918 when the area had fallen to the British. It was closed during October when the fighting moved to the east and north. The cemetery was enlarged after the war when graves were concentrated from the surrounding battlefields.

INFORMATION
The village was behind the German lines for much of the war. It was occupied by the British on 20 March 1917 after they had spent three days repairing the bridge over the River Somme following the German withdrawal to the Hindenburg Line. The Germans quickly retook the village on 23 March 1918 but it fell to the British again when the 32nd Division entered the village on 5 September 1918.

The cemetery was opened soon after. It served the 5th, 47th and 48th Casualty Clearing Stations throughout September and October until they were moved closer to St. Quentin and the cemetery was closed. After the war 85 graves were concentrated from St. Cren British and German cemeteries and from the battlefields to the south and east.

Buried here are Lieutenant Cecil Frederick Witt, No. 35 Squadron, Royal Flying Corps and King's Royal Rifle Corps aged 18 years when he died and 2nd Lieutenant George Alexander Malcolm Webster, No. 35 Squadron, Royal Flying Corps and South Lancashire Regiment aged 20 years when he died. They were killed in a flying accident on 28 February 1918. Witt was the observer and Webster the pilot.

Concentrated here:
St. Cren British And German Cemeteries - situated together at the north-western edge of the hamlet which is 7km to the east of Brie. Among the German graves were 23 British and four Australian soldiers who died in March, April, September and October 1918.

UK – 365   Aust – 27   Can – 1
Ger – 36   Unnamed – 49   KUG – 1
Area – 1401 sq mts

Special Memorials to fifteen British soldiers known, or believed, to be buried among the unnamed graves.

LOCATION
Brie is situated on the Amiens-St. Quentin road directly south of Peronne on the east bank of the River Somme. The cemetery is about 1km south of the village on the east side of the road to Ham just as the road descends into the valley of the River Omignon.

BRONFAY FARM MILITARY CEMETERY, BRAY-SUR-SOMME

HISTORY
The cemetery was begun by the French in 1914 when they occupied this sector, but they made only a few burials. The British began to make burials in August 1915 and it remained in use until February 1917 when the Germans withdrew to the east and the front-line moved away. Further British burials were made during the fighting here in 1918. It was enlarged after the war.

INFORMATION
Bronfay Farm still exists opposite the cemetery on the road from Bray to Maricourt. Most of the British burials were made from the XIV Corps Main Dressing Station that was stationed at the farm, from which the cemetery gets its name, during the Battles of the Somme in 1916.

A few French burials were made here in September 1916. Some German Prisoners of War were also buried here but the nineteen French and 26 German graves have been removed. After the war 42 graves were concentrated here from isolated positions in the fields between the cemetery and Bray. They were men who had been killed in the fighting of August and September 1918.

Nearby, on what is now a track between Bray and Mametz, is an area known as 'The Loop'. A pre-1914 narrow gauge railway north from Bray made a loop here. British troops added a link from the main line at Dernancourt to bring supplies to the front-line. The first tanks were brought here on 26 August 1916 for a demonstration to Haig to show how they could be used with infantry.

Buried here is Lieutenant-Colonel Hubert Pulteney Dalzell-Walton, MiD, 8th Royal Inniskilling Fusiliers who was killed in action in the attack at Ginchy on 9 September 1916 aged 50 years. He was the son of Hubert Izaak Walton, Director General of Telegraphs, Bombay and Persian Gulf. He joined the army after a year with the Royal Navy where he failed his exams. He had served in the Bechuanaland Expedition 1884-5, the Burma Campaign 1886-89, where he was twice wounded, as Assistant Superintendent Burma Military Police and in the South African War 1899-1902 as a Major with the South African Constabulary. He volunteered his services soon after the outbreak of war and was made a Major with the 8th Royal Inniskilling Fusiliers on 6 October 1914. He was promoted to Lieutenant Colonel in command of the battalion on 2 April 1916. He was killed when shot through the heart whilst encouraging his men under heavy shell-fire just as they were about to attack for which he was also Mentioned in Despatches in November.

Also here is Captain The Honourable Reginald Nicholas Barnewall, 5th attached 2nd Leinsters Regiment, killed on 24 March 1918 aged 18 years. He was son the 18th Baron Trimlestown.

| UK – 516 | Aust – 15 | SAfr – 1 |
| India – 2 | KUG – 1 | Unnamed – 13 |

Area - 2637 sq mts

Special Memorials to two British soldiers believed to be buried among the unnamed graves.

LOCATION
Bray-sur-Somme is located in the valley of the Somme on the north side of the river about 8km south-east of Albert and to the east of Amiens. Bronfay Farm can be found 3km north-east of the village on the road to Maricourt. The cemetery is on the south-east side of the road, opposite the farm. It is in open fields midway between Carnoy and Bray almost on top of a ridge north of the River Somme.

BUCQUOY COMMUNAL CEMETERY EXTENSION

HISTORY
The burials were made in September 1918 when men who had died from 23-28 August were buried.

INFORMATION
The village was a German base area until the withdrawal to the Hindenburg Line in March 1917 when the 7th Division occupied the village. It fell to the Germans briefly in March 1918 but was soon retaken. It is from this village that British Whippet tanks first went into action in March 1918. The cemetery was created by the Royal Naval Division at the beginning of September 1918. Most of the men buried here fought with the 37th Division or with the Royal Naval Division.

There are a group of twelve men of the 1/1st Hertfordshires buried here. They were among two officers and 26 men killed in an attack by the battalion on 23

August 1918 when they captured a railway cutting at Achiet-le-Grand. The others are buried in Fonquevillers Military Cemetery.

Also here is the last commanding officer of the Nelson Battalion of the Royal Naval Division, Commander Stuart Gale Jones, VD, Royal Naval Volunteer Reserve. He was killed in action while commanding Hawke Battalion, Royal Naval Division of whom he had taken command in April 1918, leading them in action at Thilloy on 25 August 1918 aged 37 years. He had received the Volunteer Officers Decoration before 1908.

UK – 68   Unnamed – 2   Area – 299sq mts

LOCATION

Bucquoy is located about 10km south of Arras and 7km west of Bapaume. The Communal Cemetery and Extension are north-east of the village. The extension is to the west of the Communal Cemetery.

BUCQUOY ROAD CEMETERY, FICHEUX

HISTORY

The cemetery was begun in April 1917 following the German withdrawal to the Hindenburg Line. It remained in use until March 1918 when the area fell to the Germans. It was used again in September and October 1918. After the war the cemetery was enlarged by the concentration of 690 burials from the surrounding area.

INFORMATION

The village of Ficheux had been behind the German lines for most of the war until the start of 1917 though it had been an objective of the Battle of the Somme in 1916. The German retreat to the Hindenburg Line gave up the village. In April and May 1917 the VII Corps Main Dressing Station was posted near the village on the main road and used this cemetery. The 20th and 43rd Casualty Clearing Stations followed and were posted to Boisleux-au-Mont until March 1918 so also used this cemetery. In April 1918 the Germans captured the area though it was retaken in August. The 22nd, 30th and 33rd CCS's were then posted to Boisleux-au-Mont and they extended the cemetery until the end of the war when it contained 1166 graves.

The cemetery was used again in May 1940 for the burial of 136 troops killed during the German advance. Of these, 26 are unidentified and special memorials commemorate 39 soldiers whose graves in the cemetery could not be specifically located. Many of the burials of these are men of the Durham Light Infantry or of the Black Watch (Tyneside Scottish). The large WW2 Plot is close to the Cross of Sacrifice.

Buried here is Brigadier General John Arthur Tanner CB, CMG, DSO, Royal Engineers who was killed on 23 July 1917 aged 58 years when he was the senior officer of the RE in VII Corps. He had served overseas with the army since joining in 1877. Having been in Waziristan, the Sudan in 1885, Burma and the North-West Frontier he retired in April 1914. In October he volunteered and was appointed Commander of Royal Engineers (CRE) of 22nd Division and became Chief Engineer (CE) to VII Corps in October 1915. He was killed by a shell behind Wancourt whilst on his way to inspect the defences at Cavalry Farm.

Of note buried here is Private Joseph Standing Buffalo, 78th (Manitoba Regiment) Canadian Infantry who died on 29 September 1918 aged 20 years. He was the grandson of Sitting Bull of the Lakota Sioux Nation who led his people at the Battle of the Little Big Horn in 1876 in which General Custer and his men were killed.

Also of note is Captain John Arthur Gascoyne-Cecil, MC, 75th Brigade, Royal Field Artillery, died on 27 August 1918 aged 25 years. His brother, Lieutenant Randle William Gascoyne-Cecil, Royal Horse Artillery and Royal Field Artillery, was killed on 1 December 1917 aged 28 years and is commemorated on the Cambrai Memorial. Another brother, Lieutenant Rupert Edward Gascoyne-Cecil, 1st Bedfordshires, died on 11 July 1915 and is buried in Railway Dugouts Burial Ground (Transport Farm) near Ieper. Their father was later the Bishop of Exeter. Their grandfather was Lord Salisbury, three time Prime Minister of the United Kingdom.

Also here are two men who were executed. Private John B Milburn, 24/27th Northumberland Fusiliers, a Tyneside Irish volunteer, was shot for desertion on 8 November 1917. He was already under a sentence of death for desertion. On 17 February 1918 Private Ernest Horler, 12th West Yorkshires, was shot for desertion aged 26 years. He was described as mentally weak but, when his case was raised in Parliament, assurances were given that he had been examined and found to be mentally sound. However, he was caught as he had been traced through letters sent to his mother during his period of absence.

Concentrated here:

Boiry-Ste. Rictrude British Cemetery - situated on the west side of the village which is about 2km south of here. It contained sixteen British soldiers, mainly of the 56th Division, who died in March and April 1917.

Boisleux-St. Marc British Cemetery - situated between Boisleux-St. Marc and Boyelles on the Arras-Bapaume road about 5km south-east of here. It contained ten British soldiers, nine of the 2/1st Londons, who died in March and May 1917.

Boisleux-St. Marc Military Cemetery - about 900m south of Mercatel on the road to Boisleux-St. Marc and about 2km east of here. It was also known as Mercatel Road Cemetery. It contained eleven British soldiers who died in March and April 1917.

Crossroads Cemetery, Boisleux-St. Marc - on the Boiry road a little east of the village. It contained 25 British soldiers, eighteen of the 1/14th (London Scottish) Londons, who died in August and September 1918.

Bushes Cemetery, Boisleux-St. Marc - situated a little south of the village which is about 5km south-east of here. It contained seventeen British soldiers of the 1st Grenadier Guards who died in March and April 1918.

Hamelincourt British Cemetery - between Hamelincourt and Courcelles about 6km south-east of here. It contained eight British soldiers of the 3rd Grenadier Guards who died on 22-24 August 1918.

Hemelincourt Communal Cemetery Extension - situated in the heart of the village. It contained 20 British soldiers who died in March, August and September 1918.

Monchy-Au-Bois British Cemetery - situated on the north-east edge of the village which is about 10km south-west of here. It contained fourteen British soldiers, twelve of the 42nd Division, who died in March 1918.

Henin-Sur-Cojeul German Cemetery - situated in the south-west part of the village which is about 18km east of here. It contained 28 British soldiers, buried in April and May 1917, among the German graves.

UK – 1453   Can – 447   India – 1
KUG – 91   Unnamed – 169   WW2 – 136
Area – 5244 sq mts

Special Memorials to 23 British soldiers who are known, or believed, to be buried among the unnamed graves.

Special Memorials to 21 British soldiers buried in Henin-sur- Cojeul German Cemetery whose graves could not be found upon concentration.

LOCATION

Ficheux is about 10km south of Arras to the west of the road to Amiens. The cemetery is about 1km east of the village on the west side of the Arras-Amiens road. It lies in a bend in the road so can be missed.

BULLS ROAD CEMETERY, FLERS

HISTORY

The cemetery was begun on 19 September 1916 and remained in use until March 1917 when the Germans withdrew to the Hindenburg Line. The cemetery was used again, briefly, in September 1918. The majority of the cemetery was made after the war.

INFORMATION

The village of Flers, and the site of this cemetery, was held by the Germans for much of the war. The area was captured on 15 September 1916 during the Battle of Flers-Courcelette. The attack by the 41st and New Zealand Divisions was the first attack to be supported by tanks. The 41st Division was the last of Kitchener's New Army Divisions. They had only been on the Western Front since May 1916 and this was their first attack.

Thirteen tanks of 'D' Company, Machine Gun Corps (Heavy Branch), later 4th Tank Battalion, started out from a position near Delville Wood on 15 September 1916. Twelve reached the German line and eleven reached a German trench that ran level with the southern edge of the village. Six reached the north edge of the village and three nearly reached Gueudecourt, about 4km miles from their start.

Tank D16 advanced through the village centre commanded by Lieutenant Arthur Edmund Arnold who, when returning to his tank to help a wounded man, was hit by a German machine-gun. His gunner took command. Arnold received the Military Cross and Gunner Glaister the Military Medal. These were the first decorations recognised as being for the Tank Corps. Arnold was subsequently wounded and taken prisoner at Ieper in August 1917. He met his brother in captivity in 1918. He survived the war to farm in southern Africa. Glaister remained with the unit and was awarded the Distinguished Conduct Medal for his actions later in 1916. He was wounded in this action and returned to England where he remained to survive the war.

Flers fell to the Germans again in March 1918 but was retaken on 27 August by the 10th West Yorkshires and 6th Dorsets of the 17th Division.

The cemetery name probably derives from the fact that it is situated on the road from Flers to Lesboeufs which can be incorrectly translated into English as 'The Bulls'.

Most of the original burials in the cemetery are of Australian men who were part of the attempts to take the surrounding areas in 1916. The burials of 1916 now make up the 154 graves in Plot I and were made after Flers had been captured. A further seventeen graves were added by the 17th Division in Row A of Plot II in September 1918. The remaining graves were made after the war by the concentration of graves from isolated positions on the battlefields between Flers and Longueval though a few were brought from as far away as Serre. Most of the concentrated graves are of men who fell in September 1916 or August 1918. There are about 120 New Zealanders who were killed in fighting west of Flers in September 1916. There are also 148 Australians killed north of Flers in September and October 1916.

Buried here is Lieutenant Frederick William Woods, 'B' Company, 4th Dorsets, Territorial Efficiency Medal, killed in action on 28 August 1918 aged 37 years. He was a pre-war territorial becoming Regimental Sergeant Major with the 1/6th Hampshires who had served in India from 1914-16. He was commissioned in August 1916 into the Dorsets and fought on the Western Front until November 1917. He had then gone to the USA to help train the Americans as they joined the war. He returned to France with the Dorsets in August 1918 but only survived a few weeks.

The 41st Division Memorial can be found on Flers village green in the middle of the village. The memorial features on the cover of Rose Coombes book 'Before Endeavours Fade', and has inspired many journeys across the battlefields of World War One.

South of the village is a memorial to the French 17th and 18th Infantry Regiments of the 82nd Territorial Division which fought here in September 1914.

UK – 493   Aust – 155   NZ – 122
KUG – 2   Unnamed – 296
Area – 3288 sq mts

Special Memorials to eight Australian, five British and two New Zealand soldiers known, or believed, to be buried among the unnamed graves.

LOCATION
Flers can be found about 12km north-west of Albert and 5km south of Bapaume. Bulls Road Cemetery is 100m east of the village on the south side of the old road to Lesboeufs though this is now little more than a farm track. The valley in which it stands leads north to the A.I.F. Burial Ground. The original Plot is nearest the entrance above the rest of the cemetery on the east side.

2nd CANADIAN CEMETERY, SUNKEN ROAD, CONTALMAISON

HISTORY
The cemetery was created in September and October 1916.

INFORMATION
The 'Sunken Road' is part of a road between Pozieres and Contalmaison. The site was formerly a wood known as the Vallee du Bois Derrieux. The cemetery is close to the Sunken Road Cemetery.

All the men here are from the 2nd (Eastern Ontario) Canadian Infantry, which makes it unique as the only cemetery on the 1916 battlefield to contain men from only one battalion. They arrived on the Somme on 1 September 1916, with the first burial made on 3 September, and remained until 13 October 1916.

Among the men buried here is Private William Howard Curtis, MM, killed in action at Regina Trench on 8 October 1916 aged 24 years. He had served before the war with 57th (Peterborough Rangers) Regiment militia unit and joined the 9th Canadian Infantry, as part of the volunteers from Edmonton's 101st Regiment, in September 1914. The 9th Canadian Infantry was used as reinforcements for other battalions which is how Curtis came to the 2nd Canadian Infantry in February 1915. He was wounded twice and the Military Medal was awarded posthumously for his actions on the Somme.

Can – 44   Area 383 sq mts

LOCATION
Contalmaison is a small village about 6km north-east of Albert. It can be reached by the road from Pozieres off the main Albert-Bapaume road, or from Fricourt off the Albert-Peronne road. The cemetery is in fields north of the village and north of the Contalmaison-Pozieres road. It is at the head of a valley running north-east from the road. A rough track leads 300m to the cemetery which is on the west side of the track. The track can be impassable in winter, there is no turning area for vehicles and it will be necessary to reverse back up the track, so walking is best from the road.

CAGNICOURT BRITISH CEMETERY

HISTORY
The cemetery was opened just after the Battle of the Drocourt-Queant Line that took place nearby in early September 1918. It remained in use until the middle of October 1918. The cemetery was further enlarged after the war by the concentration of graves from the surrounding area which trebled the size of the cemetery.

INFORMATION
The village fell to the British on 2 September 1918 during the Battle of the Drocourt-Queant Line. The cemetery was next to a German cemetery that has been removed. The cemetery also contains the grave of one soldier killed in fighting nearby in April 1940 – he is at the rear of the cemetery. The identified burials with dates of death before 2 September 1918 are those of men concentrated here after the war.

Among those buried here is Captain Sidney Edward Cowan, MC and two Bars, No. 29 Squadron, Royal Flying Corps, killed on 17 November 1916 aged 19 years. Cowan was one of the Royal Flying Corps' first 'aces', as he scored seven victories in 1916, six with No. 24 Squadron and one with No. 29 Squadron, in his DH2. He was wounded in action on 9 August 1916. Cowan was killed in a crash following a mid-air collision with another British aircraft having brought down one German plane and turning to attack another. He was reported as missing in action and was buried by the Germans at Ablainzeville, his grave being discovered in April 1917 and moved here after the war. The citation for his Military Cross, won as a 2nd Lieutenant in May 1916, reads 'He dived on to an enemy machine in the enemy's lines and drove it to the ground, where it was smashed, and then circled round and fired at the pilot and observer as they ran for shelter. Although forced to land through his engine stopping he contrived to restart it and got back under heavy fire.' The citation for the Bar in October 1916 reads 'For conspicuous gallantry and skill. He has done fine work in aerial combats, and has shot down four enemy machines.' The citation for the second Bar, won as an acting Captain in November 1916 reads 'For conspicuous gallantry in action. He fought a long contest with seven enemy machines, finally bringing one down in flames. He has displayed great skill and gallantry throughout.' His brother, Captain Philip Chalmers Cowan, No. 56 Squadron, Royal Flying Corps was killed in action on 8 November 1917 and is commemorated on the Arras Flying Services Memorial.

UK – 248	Aust – 5	NZ – 1
Can – 24	NF – 4	Unnamed - 180
WW2 – 1	Others – 1	Area – 1116 sq mts

LOCATION
Cagnicourt is about 15km south-east of Arras and 10km north-west of Cambrai. It lies south of the Arras–Cambrai road. The cemetery is on the north-east corner of the village on the east side of the road to Villers-les-Cagnicourt. It is next to the road on the village side of the Communal Cemetery.

CAIX BRITISH CEMETERY

HISTORY
The cemetery was opened after the war as a concentration cemetery.

INFORMATION
The village was in German hands for much of the war but was taken by British troops in March 1917. The Germans re-captured the village a year later. The Canadian Corps finally re-took the village on 8 August 1918.
The cemetery was first known as Caix New British Cemetery. Most of the burials here are of men who fell in March and August 1918. All were brought here from solitary burials or small battlefield cemeteries in the area. This is a good example of a small concentration cemetery. The battlefield graves would have been very difficult to maintain so one cemetery made things easier and created a better final resting place.
Buried here is Lieutenant Colonel Arthur John Alexander Menzies, DSO, MiD, commanding officer of 3rd Cavalry Field Ambulance, who was killed in an air raid on 9 August 1918. He was awarded the Distinguished Service Order 'For conspicuous gallantry and devotion to duty from 26 to 29 September in Loos. Capt Menzies was unremitting in his attention to the wounded of all units. He was twice seen carrying wounded on a stretcher under rifle fire, and for 55 hours he was continually exposing himself to heavy shell fire while carrying out his duties' when he was attached as medical officer to the 1st Royal Dragoons.
Also here is Major Sidney Smith Burnham, DSO, MiD, Regimental Depot, (Central Ontario), seconded to 2nd Canadian Division HQ, killed on 9 August 1918 aged 28 years. His Distinguished Service Order was awarded in October 1917. The citation reads 'For conspicuous gallantry and devotion to duty. Previous to an attack he displayed exceptional initiative and forethought in personally supervising the placing of observation posts in the forward area, thus securing that at no time during the battle was there any lack of communication from the front to rear. On at least two occasions he made daring personal reconnaissances under very heavy machine-gun and shell fire, and brought back very valuable information. His cheerfulness and coolness throughout this period were a wonderful example to the men in the front line.' A pre-war militia officer he enlisted in 1914, went to France commanding 19th Canadian Infantry in September 1915, was Mentioned in Despatches in June 1916 and was wounded in September 1916. He returned to his battalion in November 1916 before joining 2nd Canadian Infantry Brigade HQ and then 2nd Canadian Division HQ.
Concentrated here:
Beaucourt Chateau German Cemetery – in the chateau at Beaucourt-en-Santerre. It contained four British men who died in March and April 1918.

Beaufort German Cemetery – in an orchard near the village church. It contained four British soldiers killed in April 1918, three were brought here and one was taken to Hangard Communal Cemetery Extension.

Caix (Old) British Cemetery – close to a farmhouse on the east side of the village. It was made by the Canadian Corps and contained the graves of 91 men from Canada and nineteen British men who died in August 1918.

Cayeux Chateau German Cemetery – at Cayeux-en-Santerre. It contained fourteen British men with one Canadian. Two men had been buried by the Germans while the rest had been buried by the 3rd Cavalry Division, with which most had served, in August 1918.

De Luce British Cemetery, Caix – close to the north bank of the river. It contained the graves of seventeen British, eight Canadian and five Australian men, all killed in August 1918.

Le Quesnel German Cemetery – a little east of the village church. It contained four men of the Canadian Mounted Rifles buried by the regiment in August 1918.

Ridge Cemetery, Hangard – about 1km west of the village overlooking the River Luce. It contained the graves of 20 Canadian men killed on 8 August 1918.

UK – 133   Aust – 13   Can – 219
Unnamed – 70   Area – 1243 sq mts

LOCATION
The village of Caix is situated about 28km south-east of Amiens, midway between the Amiens-St. Quentin road (N29), and the Amiens-Roye road (D934). The Cemetery is south of the village near to, and accessed from, the road to Le Quesnel. Turn left just before the Communal Cemetery and follow the side road where the British Cemetery will be found on the right on the top of the ridge about 150m past the German Cemetery.

CAIX COMMUNAL CEMETERY

HISTORY
The cemetery was used for the burial of one British soldier in 1918 who lies near a burial ground of 140 French men who were killed in the war.

INFORMATION
The French plot contains men who died of wounds in 1916. The French Plot is at the rear of the cemetery.

Four of the men originally buried here have been moved to Caix British Cemetery. This leaves the grave of Lieutenant Alexander Revel Tod, MC, 5th East Surreys, died of wounds in German hands on 18 April 1918. He had been commissioned from the ranks in September 1915 having joined up as a Private with the 1/14th (London Scottish) Londons. The citation for his Military Cross reads 'He organised and successfully led two separate bombing parties against the German, who had gained a footing in the trench. Though wounded in the head, he continued to drive them back while bombs lasted. He showed fine dash and determination' which probably is the cause of his death some weeks later.

UK – 1   Fr – 140

LOCATION
See Caix British Cemetery. The Communal Cemetery is closer to the road to Le Quesnel and is passed to reach the British Cemetery. There is easy access from the entrance opposite the German cemetery.

CAMON COMMUNAL CEMETERY

HISTORY
The cemetery was used from April to August 1918.

INFORMATION
The village, on the edge of Amiens, was in Allied hands throughout the war.

The burials include one Anglo-French artillery officer, an Australian Machine Gunner drowned while swimming in the Somme and six men of the Australian Ordnance Corps killed on 2 May 1918. Among these is Sub-Conductor Herbert Lindsay Watson, Australian Army Ordnance Corps, died 2 May 1918. He enlisted in 1916 with the 47th Australian Infantry transferring to the Ordnance Corps in March 1917. He was promoted to Sub-Conductor in March 1918.

The WW2 graves are men from a plane shot down on 17 April 1943. It was Lancaster ED441 of No. 49 Squadron, RAF who had attacked Pilzen on its twelfth operation. Six men were killed with one being captured. The oldest member of the crew was aged 26 years.

UK – 9 Aust – 8 Unnamed – 1
WW2 - 6

LOCATION
Camon is now a suburb of Amiens on the eastern side of the town. The Communal Cemetery is on the north side of the village on the east side of a road to the N25. The British graves are on the north edge of the cemetery opposite each other. The WW2 graves are together further from the entrance.

CARNOY MILITARY CEMETERY

HISTORY
The cemetery was opened in August 1915 and remained in use until March 1917. When the Germans occupied the area in 1918 they made a few burials.

INFORMATION
The village was in Allied hands for most of the war. The cemetery was begun by the 2nd King's Own Scottish Borderers and 2nd King's Own Yorkshire Light Infantry when they were first posted to the area in 1915. The village was just behind the front line at that time. During the Battle of the Somme in 1916 Field Ambulances were stationed here on higher ground just north of the village and they made a large number of burials here.

When the Germans attacked in 1918 and took the village, they made burials in the cemetery and created a German cemetery. All German graves were removed in 1924.

Buried here is Captain Bernard Ayre of the 8th Norfolks. A Newfoundlander, he was in England when war broke out and was commissioned into the Norfolk Regiment in 1914. He is one of four members of his family, all officers, to be killed on 1 July 1916, three within yards of each other. One cousin Wilfred is in Knightsbridge Cemetery while the other, Gerald, has no known grave and is commemorated on the Newfoundland Memorial in the Newfoundland Park at Beaumont-Hamel. Bernard's brother, Captain Eric Stanley Ayre, Royal Newfoundland Regiment is buried in Ancre British Cemetery.

Also buried here are seven officers of the 8th East Surreys who were killed on 1 July 1916. The battalion is famous for crossing no man's land kicking footballs, though it is only 'B' Company who actually did so. The commanding officer of 'B' Company, Captain Wilfred Percy Nevill, had purchased the balls in London to help his men cope with the experience of going over the top. Two footballs were printed with the messages 'The Great European Cup-Tie Final. East Surreys V Bavarians. Kick off at zero' and 'No Referee'. Nevill was killed in front of the German wire. Nevill's second in command Lieutenant Robert Eley Soames is also here. Their bodies were recovered from the battlefield and were buried together in the cemetery on the afternoon of 3 July. Only Nevill has his own headstone - which bears the cap badge of his original unit, the East Yorkshires, and not the East Surreys, because he was still officially only attached to the battalion. The officers are buried together. They lost 446 men killed, wounded or taken prisoner that day, though the battalion won two Distinguished Service Orders, two Military Crosses, two Distinguished Conduct Medals and nine Military Medals. Importantly, and unusually for the day, their objectives were secured.

The road from Carnoy to Montauban reaches the old front line on a small crest which had been an objective for both sides in 1915 and 1916. Any small rise was important to have and hold. The area had been mined several times during that period but a large mine was detonated by the 6th Royal Berkshires west of the road just before the attack on 1 July 1916. This position was known as Casino Point. It is in approximately this area, west of the road, that Nevill led his men into battle with footballs.

Four battalion commanders are also buried here. They were all killed in 1916 leading their battalions in action. They are

- Lieutenant Colonel Hubert Lionel Budge, 12th Royal Scots, killed on 13 July 1916. He had served in the Boer War.
- Lieutenant Colonel Ronald James Walter Carden, 17th Lancers attached 16th Royal Welsh Fusiliers, killed at Mametz Wood on 10 July 1916 aged 40 years.
- Lieutenant Colonel Fitzroy Edmund Penn Curzon, Royal Irish Rifles attached 6th Royal Irish Regt. He was Mentioned in Despatches by Haig on 13 November 1916. He was killed on 9 September 1916 aged 57 years.
- Lieutenant Colonel John Staples Holesworth Lenox-Conyngham, 6th Connaught Rangers, killed at Guillemont on 3 September 1916. He had served with 1st and 2nd Connaught Rangers 1881-1911 and had been recalled to raise and train his current unit.

Others buried here are Private Ernest W Harris, 'C' Company, 10th Lancashire Fusiliers and Driver Robert Murray, 'A' Battery, 147th Brigade, Royal Field Artillery executed side by side on 3rd February 1917 for desertion. Private Harris was 20 years old and was under two suspended sentences, the latter having been a sentence of death. Murray landed in France in September 1915 but, after only nine months service, surprisingly was granted home leave. Following his return to his unit, Murray absconded and travelled to the south of France taking up residence with a prostitute who, following a quarrel, reported him to the French Police.

In March 1917 a camp was established here as the Germans retreated to the Hindenburg Line. An abandoned mine exploded killing one officer of the 5th Borders and two officers and ten men of the 12th King's (Liverpools). Eleven are buried in this cemetery but the remains of two men could not be found. Fifty other men were injured in the explosion.

UK – 845   Aust – 1   NZ – 5
Can – 3   SAfr – 1   Unnamed – 29
Area – 4441 sq mts

Special Memorials to eighteen men known or believed to be buried among the unnamed.

LOCATION
Carnoy is situated about 5km east of Albert just north of the road between Albert and Peronne. The cemetery is in a valley on the south side of the village on the road to Suzanne. It is an attractive oval shaped cemetery with an interesting entrance.

CATERPILLAR VALLEY CEMETERY, LONGUEVAL

HISTORY
The cemetery was opened and closed in September 1918 after the fighting in this area. After the war the cemetery was greatly enlarged.

INFORMATION
This area was behind German lines until the middle of July 1916 when it fell to the British after heavy fighting. It was lost in March 1918 but recaptured by the 38th (Welsh) Division on 28 August.

At that time this cemetery was begun. It was closed soon after containing the graves, now in Plot I, of 25 men of the 38th Division and 6th Dragoon Guards. This Plot of 1918 burials is set at an angle to the remaining concentrated burials, near the road, so is easily identified. After the war 31 Plots were added. They contained the graves of 5511 men concentrated here from isolated positions or smaller cemeteries on the battlefields of the Somme. Most of the men fell during the fighting of late 1916 or in the battles of 1918. This is now one of the largest British cemeteries on the Western Front, but over 65% of the graves are unnamed.

The cemetery was mis-named when it was created in 1918 in that Caterpillar Valley is 2km south of this location. However, the name was retained after the war.

The rear wall is the approximate position of the main German trench captured by the 12th Royal Scots and 9th Scots Rifles on 14 July 1916. Just to the west of the cemetery is the scene of one of the last cavalry charges by the British army in WW1 which took place on 14 July 1916 as they attacked High Wood. It is also possible to see the area near Delville Wood from which tanks went into action in September 1916 for the first time. Hence, this is one of those places where we can see the world change – from the use of horses as power to the use of horsepower.

On 6 November 2004, the remains of an unidentified New Zealand soldier were removed from this cemetery from Plot XIV, Row A, Grave 27 and laid to rest at the National War Memorial, Wellington, New Zealand.

Among those buried here is Private Frederick Chick, Royal West Kent Hussars attached 13th Middlesex, who was killed in action on 31 August 1916. He was a footballer before the war playing for Charlton Athletic.

Also here is Rifleman Horace Twigger, 3rd New Zealand Rifle Brigade who died on 29 September 1916 aged 16 years. He had been at the Front for just a few weeks when he was killed.

Another here is 2nd Lieutenant Sir Arthur MacNaghten, Douglas, 8th Rifle Brigade, died on 15 September 1916 aged 19 years when attacking the line north of Delville Wood with tank support early in the morning. He was the 7th Baronet MacNaghten of Dundarave succeeding to the title on the death of his brother, the 6th Baronet, 2nd Lieutenant Sir Edward Harry Macnaghten of Dundarave, Black Watch attached to the 12th Royal Irish Rifles who was killed on 1 July 1916 aged 20 years with the 36th (Ulster) Division near Thiepval. He in turn had held the title only since the death of his father on 31 December 1914. Arthur was succeeded by his uncle.

Also here is Private George Frederick Chapman, 1/22nd (The Queen's) Londons, died on 6 October 1916 aged 30 years. His brother, Rifleman Walter Raymond Chapman, 'A'

Company, 2/5th (London Rifle Brigade) Londons, died on 18 May 1917 aged 21 years and is commemorated on the Arras Memorial. Another brother, Private Archibald Gordon Chapman, 10th Royal Fusiliers, died on 29 August 1918 aged 31 years and is buried in Wimereux Communal Cemetery.

Concentrated here:

Clark's Dump Cemetery, Bazentin - situated about 1km north of here a little west of High Wood. It contained the graves of 26 British and two South African soldiers who were killed between August and December 1916.

Ginchy German Cemetery - situated about 1km north of the village that is about 5km east of here. Now removed, it was in fields midway between the roads from Ginchy to Flers and Lesboeufs. Among the Germans two unidentified British soldiers were buried.

McCormick's Post Cemetery, Flers - situated about 3km north of here and 1km west of Flers. It contained the graves of nineteen British, nine Australian and nine New Zealand men who were killed from September to November 1916.

Martinpuich Road Cemetery, Bazentin - situated about 3km north-west of here on the road from Bazentin to Martinpuich. It contained the graves of 41 British soldiers killed in July and August 1916.

Snowdon Cemetery, Bazentin - situated about 1km west of here in Bazentin-le-Grand village. It contained the graves of 24 British soldiers of the 38th Division, who died in August and September 1918.

Welsh Cemetery, Longueval - situated about 2km north of here in the fields between Flers and High Wood. It contained the graves of seventeen British soldiers of the 38th Division, who were killed in August and September 1918.

UK – 5229	NZ – 214	Aust – 100
SAfr – 18	Can – 6	Newf – 2
Rhodesia – 1		Unnamed – 3798

Area – 14835 sq mts

Special Memorials erected to 33 British and two Australian soldiers known, or believed, to be buried among the unnamed graves.

Special Memorials erected to three British soldiers buried in McCormick's Post Cemetery whose graves were destroyed by shell-fire.

New Zealand Memorial to the Missing

This forms part of the east wall of the cemetery. New Zealand decided after the war that its missing soldiers should be commemorated on small memorials near the battlefields on which they died. Therefore, this Memorial covers the New Zealand troop's actions to the north and north-east of here in September and October 1916 when 1560 men were killed. Of these, 1205 are on this memorial. Nearly all died between 15 September and 2 October. It is possible to see, to the north of here, a memorial to all New Zealand troops involved in action on the Somme.

Nearby, at the junction with the road to Martinpuich and High Wood, is the memorial erected to the 12th Gloucesters who made a successful attack nearby on 27 July 1916. They were a 'Pals' battalion known as 'Bristol's Own'.

LOCATION

Longueval is a village situated about 8km east of Albert on the ridges north of the Albert-Peronne road. The cemetery is on a ridge 1km west of the village on the south side of the road to Bazentin and Contalmaison. This is a huge and impressive cemetery on the Longueval Ridge. The view from the back of the cemetery covers Waterlot Farm, Trones Wood, Bernafay Wood, Mametz Wood, Montauban village, and the Montauban Ridge captured on 1 July 1916. From the front of the cemetery you can see High Wood.

CAYEUX MILITARY CEMETERY

HISTORY

The cemetery was begun by French troops. The British used it from March to May 1917 and again for a few burials in March and August 1918. After the war the cemetery was enlarged by the concentration of isolated burials from the battlefields to the north of this cemetery.

INFORMATION

Cayeux village, which had been in the hands of Allied forces for most of the war, was lost on 27 March 1918, but recaptured by the Canadian Corps on the following 8 August.

The earliest of the burials here were made by the 36th Casualty Clearing Station when it was here in March-May 1917. They now form Plot 1, Rows A-E. The cemetery is different from others in the area in that is has no significant links to the fighting here in 1918. 634 French and 223 German burials have been removed when the concentration burials, most of whom were killed on 1 July 1916 and include Ulstermen from Thiepval and Tynesiders from La Boiselle, were made.

Among those here is Lieutenant William Wilson Cowan, No. 7 Squadron, Royal Flying Corps and 8th Royal Scots, killed on 14 April 1917 aged 24 years. He joined the Royal Scots in July 1915 and was made Officer in Charge of quarrying in November-December 1915. In May 1916 he went to the Divisional Bomb School, but shortly after applied for the RFC and was transferred in July 1916.

One British soldier was brought here from Marcelcave French Military Cemetery not to be confused with the present Marcelcave French National Cemetery. The military cemetery was at the north-west corner of the village and was removed at the end of the war.

UK – 207	Can – 5	SAfr – 2
Aust - 1	India – 1	Unnamed - 114

Area – 992 sq mts

LOCATION
Cayeux-en-Santerre is situated about 15km east of Amiens, north of the Amiens-Roye road. This cemetery is about 1km south of the village at a place known as 'Le Ceriselet'. It is a pretty cemetery with difficult access. It is not an easy cemetery to find. A sign in the centre of the village leads to a narrow road running south that seems to go nowhere. Stick with it as the narrow road winds south through a typical Somme dry chalk valley. After 2km a bend reveals another CWGC sign. Park here as the rough track is not designed for cars and there is no good spot to turn. Climb up onto the ridge and you can see the cemetery, about 400m away on a path through the trees. This is not an easy climb, especially in winter.

CERISY-GAILLY FRENCH NATIONAL CEMETERY

HISTORY
The cemetery was created next to the village Communal Cemetery by a French Tenth Army casualty clearing hospital in February 1916. Most of the casualties buried here died during the Battles of the Somme in the summer of 1916.

INFORMATION
The area was also the location for the 39th and 13th Casualty Clearing Stations during the early part of 1917, and of the 41st Stationary Hospital from May 1917 to March 1918. The villages were then captured by the Germans, but were retaken by the Australian Corps in August 1918. Men who died in those medical units were buried here between February 1917 and March 1918. This Plot was extended after the war when graves were brought in from the battlefields of the Somme and from Buire Communal Cemetery Extension. 158 French and 35 German graves were removed from the British section after the war.

Fr – 990	UK – 342	Canada – 4
Australia – 44	NZ – 1	RGLI – 1
Unnamed – 296		Area - 5122 sq mts

LOCATION
Cerisy is found in the valley of the River Somme about 10km south of Albert. The cemetery is near the British Military Cemetery. It lies on the west side of the village at the end of Rue du Cimetiere which leads to the Communal Cemetery. It is about 150m north of the road to Hamel and next to the Communal Cemetery on its south side. The British Plot is at the western end of the French National Cemetery. Easiest access to the British plots are through the French National Military Cemetery.

CERISY-GAILLY MILITARY CEMETERY

HISTORY
The cemetery was opened in February 1917. It remained in use until March 1918 and again from August 1918. It was used again after the war for the concentration of graves from the surrounding battlefields.

INFORMATION
The cemetery was begun by the 39th and 13th Casualty Clearing Stations when stationed here in early 1917. They were replaced by 41st Stationary Hospital which was here from May 1917 to March 1918. At that time, the village fell to the Germans. It was retaken by the Australian Corps in August 1918. The cemetery was originally called the New French Military Cemetery.

The first two rows of Plot 2 are mostly Canadians. There are several decorated men. For example, Captain David McAndie, MC, DCM, MM, MiD, 10th Canadian Infantry was killed on 15 August 1918. The remainder of Plot 2 are graves concentrated from Maricourt. Plot 1 is the original cemetery. Plot 3 is made up of concentrated graves including men of 1 July 1916 from Thiepval moved to make way for the memorial. When the British graves were being concentrated here 158 French and 35 German graves were moved elsewhere.

Wilfred Owen is known to have spent time in the CCS here in March 1917 and later in May 1917. He wrote a poem called 'Hospital Barge at Cerisy' while here.

Among those buried here is 2nd Lieutenant Eric Clowes Pashley, MiD, No. 24 Squadron, Royal Flying Corps, died on 17 March 1917 aged 24 years. He is credited with eight victories making him an air 'ace'. He was killed in a flying accident when he spun from 2000 feet during target practice.

Buried here is Private Wilson Ling, 2nd (Eastern Ontario Regt) Canadian Infantry, who was executed for desertion on 12 August 1918 aged 22 years. He was sentenced to death for desertion in 1915 but the sentence was commuted. He deserted again on 21 June 1917 and stayed at large until 1918. He was tried on 8 July and was the last Canadian to be executed in the war.

West of Cerisy on the banks of the River Somme in a hamlet called Bouzencourt opposite Sailly-le-Sec, you will find a British memorial. The inscription in French is to Captain Francis L Mond and Lieutenant Edgar M Martyn who died here on 15 May 1918. Both were with the RAF and were shot down in a DH4 bomber of No. 57 Squadron after attacking Bapaume. They crashed close to the British trenches. Both are buried in Doullens Cemetery Extension No. 2.

Concentrated here:

Beaufort British Cemetery - about 300m north of Beaufort Church. It was made in August 1918, after the capture of the village by the 1st Canadian Division, next to the German Cemetery. It contained the graves of 56 Canadian and two British soldiers.

Buigny-Les-Gamaches Communal Cemetery - contained the grave of one British soldier buried in July 1918 by the 26th Field Ambulance.

Buire Communal Cemetery Extension - on the north side of the Communal Cemetery. It contained three German plots and one British. In the British plot were buried 36 Australian and four British soldiers. These men died in September 1918 except three who were buried by the Germans in March.

Maricourt Military Cemetery - at the south-east corner of the village, on the road to Clery. It was begun by French troops in December 1914, and was known to the French as 'Ferme Caudron'. It was taken over by British troops in August 1915 and used until July 1916. It contained the graves of 887 French, 260 British and six German men.

Ste. Helene British Cemetery, Pontruet - on the east side of the hamlet. It was made in September and October 1918 during the capture of Ste. Helene by the 46th (North Midland) Division. It contained the graves of 89 British men, the majority of whom belonged to the 46th Division or the 1st Dorsets.

UK – 597   Can – 65   Aust – 81
SAfr – 2   Unnamed – 114   Others - 1
Area – 2748 sq mts

Special Memorials to five soldiers, buried at Maricourt Military Cemetery and Ste. Helene British Cemetery, whose graves could not be identified at the time of concentration.

LOCATION

Cerisy is found about 10km south of Albert on the River Somme. The cemetery is near the French National Cemetery. It lies on the west side of the village, about 70m north of the road to Hamel and close to the Communal Cemetery.

CHAPELLE BRITISH CEMETERY, HOLNON

HISTORY

This is a concentration cemetery made after the war.

INFORMATION

The cemetery was named after a small shrine at the roadside. The burials here came from the battlefields west of St. Quentin. Graves were brought from Holnon Communal Cemetery and local French Military Cemeteries. The village and Holnon Wood were the scene of heavy fighting from 14-19 September 1918 when the 6th Division attacked the Germans.

Among those here is 2nd Lieutenant Charles Arthur Smith, DCM, 1/2nd Leicestershires, killed in action on 19 September 1918, aged 27 years. He enlisted in the Northumberland Fusiliers on the outbreak of war and rose to the rank of Sergeant Major. In June 1917 he was awarded the Distinguished Conduct Medal for his actions in the fighting at the Messines Ridge. Following this he was commissioned into the Leicesters. He was killed near St. Quentin, buried nearby and brought here in 1919. One of his brothers was killed at the Schwaben Redoubt near Thiepval in 1916.

North-east of the cemetery, about 500m away and next to the E44 autoroute is the position of a British redoubt known as Engien. It is possibly named after a former French fortification in turn named after a French Marshal. He first employed the great 16th and 17th Century builder of fortifications, Vauban, when he was just a soldier under Enghien during the rebellion of 1648-52 against King Louis XIV known as the 'Fronde'. The redoubt, held by 2/8th Worcestershires, fell on 21 March 1918, as did the neighbouring Ellis Redoubt held by 2/4th Oxford & Bucks Light Infantry. The Germans had an advantage caused by the heavy fog. Hence, the enfilading machine gun fire from each redoubt was useless as they could not see the Germans.

UK – 621   Unnamed – 260   Area – 2073 sq mts

Special memorials to seventeen British men known to be buried among the unnamed.

Special memorials to four British men, buried in Holnon Communal Cemetery, whose graves were destroyed by shell-fire and could not be found.

LOCATION

Holnon is about 4km north-west of St. Quentin. The village is 50m south of the Amiens–St. Quentin road. The cemetery is on the north-west edge of the village. Access is from the centre of the village, not the N29, and the cemetery is found on the edge of a housing estate.

CHERISY ROAD EAST CEMETERY, HENINEL

The burials include seven men of 1/6th Durham Light Infantry killed on 14 April 1917. Also here are fifteen men of the Manchester Regiment, mostly 16th battalion but also 17th, 18th and 19th Battalions (the first four City of Manchester Pals battalions) alongside ten men of 2nd Royal Scots Fusiliers all killed on 23 April 1917. There are also eighteen men of the King's (Liverpool) Regiment killed in late April 1917. The only officer is 2nd Lieutenant Lawrence Band, 17th King's (Liverpools), killed in action with his men on 28 April 1917 aged 31 years.

UK – 82   Unnamed – 19   Area – 268 sq mts

LOCATION

Heninel is about 7km south-east of Arras and 10km north of Bapaume. The village is less than 1km east of the A1 Autoroute. The cemetery is on a ridge overlooking the battlefields by a small copse. It is about 100m east of the village between the roads to Cherisy and Fontaine-les-Croisilles. It is on the old road to Fontaine near the fork with the road to Cherisy.

HISTORY

The cemetery was only in use in April 1917.

INFORMATION

The village of Heninel was captured in a snowstorm on 12 April 1917 by the 56th (London) and 21st Divisions. The cemetery was then made by the 30th and 33rd Divisions.

CHIPILLY COMMUNAL CEMETERY

One of the first burials is of Rifleman Edward Fred Slade, 'C' Company, 1/9th (Queen Victoria's Rifles) Londons, who drowned on 12 August 1915 while swimming in the Somme.

The French made a few burials here, some have been removed leaving four graves. The Germans buried 21 men here while they occupied the village in 1918. They have all been removed.

In front of the church in the village is a memorial, erected by the locals, to the 58th Division, who captured the village in 1918.

UK – 55   Fr – 4   Unnamed - 2

LOCATION

Chipilly is found about 25km east of Amiens in the valley of the River Somme and lies on the north bank of the river. The cemetery is north of the village on a ridge overlooking the village and river. The cemetery is on the east side of the road to Etinehem. Access from vehicles is at the north end of the cemetery where there is a large parking area. The Extension is at the north end of the Communal Cemetery. It is difficult to distinguish between the Extension and the burials in the Communal Cemetery. However, the Communal Cemetery military burials include the four French graves.

HISTORY

Burials in the Communal Cemetery began in August 1915. It remained in use until March 1916 and was used again in July to October 1916. A final burial was made in April 1918.

INFORMATION

The cemetery was opened when the British took over the area from the French. The village was used by Field Ambulances in 1916. It was taken by the Germans in March 1918 and was recaptured in August 1918 when the 58th (London) Division took it after a fierce struggle.

CHIPILLY COMMUNAL CEMETERY EXTENSION

HISTORY
Burials in the Communal Cemetery Extension were made from March 1916 to February 1917. Three burials were added in late 1918.

INFORMATION
The Germans used the cemetery in April 1918. The graves of nine French and 22 German soldiers have been removed.

Buried here is Company Sergeant Major Gilbert Campbell Brodie, DCM, 11th Field Company, Australian Engineers, died of wounds on 26 August 1918 aged 25 years. He enlisted in January 1916 and served in France and Belgium being wounded twice. He was awarded the Distinguished Conduct Medal for leading his men in successfully building a strongpoint on Broodseinde Ridge at Ieper on 4 October 1917.

UK – 29   Aust - 2   Unnamed - 2

LOCATION
See Communal Cemetery.

CITADEL NEW MILITARY CEMETERY, FRICOURT

HISTORY
The cemetery was begun by the French Army in 1914 and they used it until the British took over the sector in 1915. The first British burials were made in August 1915 and it remained in use until November 1916. One burial was made in August 1918.

INFORMATION
Directly south of Fricourt, on the road to Bray, are two high points, 71m above sea-level, known to the British Army as 71 North and 71 South. Nearby is another hill known as 'The Citadel'. The cemetery was named after this, although it lies on the north side of what was called 'Happy Valley', and is near the road. It was called, during the war, 'Citadel Military Cemetery (Point 71)' and no-one now knows why the word 'New' was added later.

This was an area of Dressing Stations and artillery batteries before and during 1 July 1916. So, most of the men buried here died of wounds in the Dressing Stations nearby. The great majority of the burials were made before the Battle of the Somme in 1916. Later in 1916 the area became a large camp in the rear called 'Citadel Camp'. It was used mainly for units withdrawn from the front-line in October 1916. Thirty burials were made when the camp was here – most are officers who are buried together in Plot 2 near the entrance. The graves of six Germans and 27 French soldiers have been removed.

Among those buried here is Lieutenant Colonel The Honourable Guy Victor Baring, commanding 1st Coldstream Guards, twice MiD, killed on 15 September 1916 aged 43 years. He was a member of the family that owned Barings Bank and was a younger son of the 4th Baron Ashburton. He had fought in the Boer War and other African campaigns. Having retired from the army he became MP for Winchester, a seat he still held when killed in action. Baring's Battalion, with two other Coldstream battalions, were advancing along the Ginchy-Lesboeufs road. It was the first time that three Coldstream Guard battalions attacked together, but despite advancing 'as steadily as though they were walking down the Mall' the action took a heavy toll. Seventeen officers and 690 other ranks went into battle, but only three officers survived (one injured) along with 221 other ranks.

Also here is Captain Alfred Keith Smith Cuninghame, 6th Company, 2nd Grenadier Guards, MiD, killed in action at Lesboeufs on 25 September 1916 aged 25 years. He was the last surviving officer of the battalion who went to war in August 1914.

Buried here is Brigadier General Louis Murray Phillpotts, CMG, DSO, commanding Royal Artillery, 24th Division, who died on 8 September 1916 aged 46 years. He received his first commission in the Royal Artillery in February 1890, was promoted to Lieutenant in 1893, Captain in 1900, and Major in 1907. He served during the Second Boer War. He was promoted to Lieutenant Colonel in October 1914, and to Brigadier General in 1915. He received his Distinguished Service Order in 1901 for service in South Africa and made a Commander of the Order of St. Michael and St. George in 1916. He was killed near Maltz Horn Farm at Guillemont while reconnoitering with Captain H W Crippin, MC, of 56th Division HQ.

2nd Lieutenant John Howard Dothie, 2nd Borders, died on 27 June 1916 aged 21 years. He was employed as a stenographer and clerk at a gold mining company in London and joined the Honourable Artillery Company as a Private on 6 December 1914. He served on the Western Front from January 1915 and was invalided home in June 1915. After a period of training he was gazetted as 2nd Lieutenant in the 12th Borders in August 1915 and returned to France 13 June 1916. He was killed in action on the Somme on the 27 June 1916. His brother, 2nd Lieutenant E A Dothie was also killed and is commemorated on the Ploegsteert Memorial.

Also here is Corporal R O'Brien. He was in Siegfried Sassoon's company and regularly accompanied him on night raids into no man's land. He was killed on 25 May 1916 in one of those raids with Sassoon.

UK – 378		Unnamed – 15	Area - 3107 sq mts

LOCATION
Fricourt is situated about 5km directly east of Albert. The cemetery is about 2km south of the village 150m north-east of the road to Bray. The cemetery is 100m east of the Bray-Fricourt road about 2km south of Fricourt. It is reached by a farm road from a roundabout at the main road. It has interesting steps at the entrance up to the Cross of Sacrifice.

COJEUL BRITISH CEMETERY, ST. MARTIN-SUR-COJEUL

HISTORY
The cemetery was in use from April to October 1917.

INFORMATION
The village was in German hands for much of the war but was captured by the 30th Division on 9 April 1917. The Germans re-captured the village in March 1918 but lost it again in August 1918.

The cemetery was opened by the 21st Division and was damaged by shell-fire in later fighting. There is a memorial in the cemetery to the 64th Brigade who attacked the Hindenburg Line nearby.

Buried here is Captain Arthur Henderson, VC, MC, 4th Argyll & Sutherland Highlanders who was killed on 24 April 1917 aged 23 years. He was awarded the Victoria Cross for actions at Fontaine-les-Croisilles. His citation says 'For most conspicuous bravery. During an attack on the enemy trenches this officer, although almost immediately wounded in the left arm, led his Company through the front enemy line until he gained his final objective. He then proceeded to consolidate his position, which, owing to heavy gun and machine gun fire and bombing attacks, was in danger of being isolated. By his cheerful courage and coolness he was enabled to maintain the spirit of his men under most trying conditions. Captain Henderson was killed after he had successfully accomplished his task.' He was awarded the Military Cross for his leadership on the Somme in July 1916. His brother, Private George Henderson, 2nd Canadian Mounted Rifles was killed in action on 9 April 1917 and is commemorated on the Vimy Memorial.

Also here is Private Horace Waller, VC, 10th King's Own Yorkshire Light Infantry who was killed in action on 10 April 1917 aged 20 years. He was awarded the VC for his actions south of Heninel. His citation reads 'For most conspicuous bravery when with a bombing section forming a block in the enemy line. A very violent counter-attack was made by the enemy on this post, and although five of the garrison were killed, Pte. Waller continued for more than an hour to throw bombs, and finally repulsed the attack. In the evening the enemy again counter-attacked the post and all the garrison became casualties, except Pte. Waller, who, although wounded later, continued to throw bombs for another half an hour until he was killed. Throughout these attacks he showed the utmost valour, and it was due to his determination that the attacks on this important post were repulsed.' He had only been at the Front for a few months.

UK – 349		Unnamed – 35	Area – 1068 sq mts
Special Memorials to 31 graves destroyed by shell-fire.

LOCATION
St. Martin-sur-Cojeul is about 10km south-east of Arras just west of the A1 Autoroute. The cemetery is about 1km south-east of the village. It lies on a ridge south of the valley of the River Cojeul on the east side of the road to Fontaine-les-Croisilles. It is next to the railway with excellent views.

COMBLES COMMUNAL CEMETERY EXTENSION

HISTORY
The cemetery was begun in October 1916 by French troops. British burials began in December 1916 and they used it until March 1917. Further burials were made in August and September 1918. After the war this was used as a concentration cemetery bringing in remains from isolated graves and smaller cemeteries in the surrounding area.

INFORMATION
The village was in German hands for the first part of the war. It was captured in the early morning of the 26 August 1916 by units of the 56th (London) Division and of the

French Army. The Germans re-captured the village on 24 March 1918 after a stand by the South African Brigade at Marrieres Wood. On 29 August 1918 the 18th Division took the village.

The burials in 1918 were made by the 18th Division. The 94 French graves made in 1916 have been removed. From June to August 1918 194 German soldiers were buried in what was afterwards called Plot I but these graves have also been removed.

Plots II, V, VI and VII and most of Plot IV are the concentration burials. The majority came here in 1927 though some were added later. Most of these were men of the 18th Division who were killed near Mametz and Montauban on 1 July 1916. Some of the concentrated burials are men involved in the first attack made by tanks on 15 September 1916. Many of these men have Machine Gun Corps as the regimental emblem on their headstones. But Corporal Gerald Edmonds Pattison has 'C' Company, MGC (Heavy Branch) as the tank units were then known. His is the earliest dated Tank Corps headstone.

Also buried here is Private James Hollingworth, 2nd Manchesters, died of wounds on 15 August 1915. He was captured by the Germans from a forward sap on 15 August 1915 soon after the British took over this sector from the French and he is possibly the first British prisoner of war on the Somme. He was wounded in his capture and died at a German Dressing Station. He was buried by the Germans in the Communal Cemetery and later moved here in 1921 to now lie next to the Cross of Sacrifice.

Buried here is Captain Henry Sherard Osborn Ashington, 7th East Yorkshires, killed in action on 31 January 1917. Captain Ashington was wounded in Belgium in July 1916. After recovering from his injuries he was promoted to Captain and returned to the front line. On the last day of January 1917 he was struck by a sniper's bullet and never regained consciousness. He had represented Great Britain at the 1912 summer Olympics in Stockholm in the Long Jump and Standing Long Jump.

Another buried here is Gunner George Jarrett, Royal Garrison Artillery, died on 14 January 1917. One brother, Private Frank Jarrett, 2nd East Lancashires died on 9 May 1915 and is commemorated on the Ploegsteert Memorial. Another brother, Private John Jarrett, 10th Royal Fusiliers attached 111th Trench Mortar Battery, died on 27 April 1917 aged 20 years and is buried in Etaples Military Cemetery.

At the side of the road to Rancourt, near the autoroute, is a large private memorial to Sous-Lieutenant Charles Dansett from Armentieres who died here on 25 September 1916. This may also be his grave. South of the village on the road to Maurepas is a smaller memorial to Victor Hallarodittaeoez of 110th Tirailleurs Regiment who died on 12 September 1916. In the center of the village is a memorial to a Captain and Sous-Lieutenant of the French 27th Regiment of Artillery who were killed near Morval in October 1916.

Concentrated here:

Fregicourt Communal Cemetery - a hamlet between Combles and Sailly-Saillisel, in which four British soldiers were buried in the winter of 1916-17.

Leuze Wood Cemetery, Combles - at the north-east corner of Leuze Wood. It contained the graves of eleven British and five French soldiers who died in September 1916-January 1917.

Longtree Dump Military Cemetery, Sailly-Saillisel - a little south of the road from Morval to Sailly-Saillisel. It contained 20 French and twelve British soldiers who were buried in December 1916 and February 1917.

Maurepas Military Cemetery - on the south-west side of Maurepas village. In it were twelve French and nine British soldiers and one German prisoner buried in December 1916 to February 1917.

UK – 1462   Aust – 22   SAfr – 11
Can – 7   Unnamed – 973
Area – 5355 sq mts

Special Memorials to nine British men and one South African soldier known to be among the unnamed.

Special Memorials to three British men, known to have been buried in Maurapas and Longtree Dump cemeteries, whose graves were destroyed by shell-fire.

LOCATION

Combles is situated 13km south of Bapaume and 16km east of Albert. The cemetery is at the north end of the village between the roads to Sailly-Saillisel and Morval. Entry is from the end at the road to Sailly. The Extension is on the north-east side of the Communal Cemetery.

CONNAUGHT CEMETERY, THIEPVAL

HISTORY

Connaught Cemetery was begun at the end of September 1916 and was used until the end of the war. After the war it was enlarged by the concentration of graves from small cemeteries and isolated positions on the surrounding battlefields.

INFORMATION

The German trenches in this area were occupied by the 180th Regiment from Wurtemberg until the start of the Battles of the Somme in 1916. The attack from the British lines, which ran along the edge of Thiepval Wood behind the cemetery, on 1 July 1916, the anniversary of the Battle of the Boyne, was made by the 36th (Ulster) Division. At this location the 10th Royal Inniskilling Fusiliers went over the top. The Ulstermen walked and then charged from the edge of the wood to crest the ridge and beyond. They were the only men north of the Albert-Bapaume road to break the German lines. They took several sections of German trench in 30 minutes but, because the attacks on either flank were unsuccessful, they were unsupported so those who could were ordered to withdraw. Fourteen hours after the attack began, many were back where they had started. Those who could not withdraw fought to the death.

The Division won four Victoria Crosses in the action. They were for:

- Captain Eric Norman Frankland Bell, VC, 9th Royal Inniskilling Fusiliers. His citation reads 'For most conspicuous bravery. He was in command of a Trench Mortar Battery, and advanced with the Infantry in the attack. When our front line was hung up by enfilading machine gun fire Captain Bell crept forward and shot the machine gunner. Later, on no less than three occasions, when our bombing parties, which were clearing the enemy's trenches, were unable to advance, he went forward alone and threw Trench Mortar bombs among the enemy. When he had no more bombs available he stood on the parapet, under intense fire, and used a rifle with great coolness and effect on the enemy advancing to counter-attack. Finally he was killed rallying and reorganising infantry parties which had lost their officers. All this was outside the scope of his normal duties with his battery. He gave his life in his supreme devotion to duty.' His body was never found and he is commemorated on the Thiepval Memorial.
- Lieutenant Geoffrey St. George Shillington Cather, VC, 9th Royal Irish Fusiliers. He did not attack on 1 July 1916 as he was the battalion adjutant. But as his citation reads 'For most conspicuous bravery. From 7 p.m. till midnight he searched 'No Man's Land', and brought in three wounded men. Next morning at 8 a.m. he continued his search, brought in another wounded man, and gave water to others, arranging for their rescue later. Finally, at 10.30 a.m., he took out water to another man, and was proceeding further on when he was himself killed. All this was carried out in full view of the enemy, and under direct machine gun fire and intermittent artillery fire. He set a splendid example of courage and self sacrifice.' He was with a fellow officer when they were hit by a machine gun. His body was never found and he is commemorated on the Thiepval Memorial.
- Private William Frederick 'Billy' McFadzean, VC, 14th Royal Irish Rifles. His citation reads 'For most conspicuous bravery. While in a concentration trench and opening a box of bombs for distribution prior to an attack, the box slipped down into the trench, which was crowded with men, and two of the safety pins fell out. Private McFadzean, instantly realising the danger to his comrades, with heroic courage threw himself on the top of the Bombs. The bombs exploded blowing him to pieces, but only one other man was injured. He well knew his danger, being himself a bomber, but without a moment's hesitation he gave his life for his comrades.' He is commemorated on the Thiepval Memorial.
- Private (later Sergeant) Robert Quigg, VC, 12th Royal Irish Rifles. He received his award for repeatedly going out into no-man's land under enemy fire to search for wounded men on 2 July 1916, particularly that of his platoon commander, Lieutenant Harry MacNaghten (See Caterpillar Valley Cemetery). He never found him but rescued several others. He was ordered back with the remnants of his battalion and survived the war.

The Divisional Memorial, the Ulster Tower, which is a replica of Helen's Tower at Clandeboyne in Ireland on the estate of the Marquis of Dufferin and Ava, can now be found across the road in the old no-man's land. The estate at Clandeboyne was where the 36th Division had trained before leaving for the Western Front. The tower was re-dedicated in 1990 by Princess Alice, Duchess of Gloucester. Thiepval was attacked again by the British on 26 September 1916 when the 18th Division captured the village. The village was lost to the Germans on 25 March 1918 but was retaken, by the 17th and 38th Divisions, on 24 August 1918. At the end of the war the cemetery consisted of 228 graves in Plot I, all men who were killed here on 1 July or September 1916 – Ulstermen of 36th Division, Salford Pals, and West Riding Territorials. Over 1000 bodies, mostly men who fell in 1916, were concentrated here after the war.

A Memorial to the 1/5th West Yorkshires, who died at the Schwaben redoubt about 400m north of here on 28 September 1916, was erected in the cemetery but it was removed to the Battalion's Drill Hall in York before World War Two.

Among those here is Company Sergeant Major Edward Elisha Iredale, MM, of 'A' Company, 1/5th West Yorkshires, killed in action by shrapnel as he left his trench on 29 August 1916 aged 19 years. This is a young age to have become one of the senior NCO's in a battalion. His headstone credits him with a Distinguished Conduct Medal but I cannot find a citation or record of his having one though he was recommended for the award. His brother, Charles, died of pneumonia on 22 October 1918 with the Royal Army Medical Corps serving in the Salonika Campaign. He is buried in Bulgaria. Another brother served with the Royal Engineers and survived the war.

Burials are still being made here as excavation and archaeological work in the area, as well as the widening of the road, has led to recent discoveries of men killed in battle nearby. In fact, one body, that of Sergeant David Harkness Blakey, 11th Royal Inniskilling Fusiliers, killed in action on 1 July 1916 aged 26 years, was found at the roadside just to the north-west corner of the cemetery. Three men, including Blakey, were buried in October 2015. Concentrated here:

Battery Valley Cemetery, Grandcourt - situated about 1km south-west of the village near the road to St. Pierre-Divion. It contained 56 British graves dating from November and December 1916 with one from July 1917.

Bluff Cemetery, Authuille - situated about 1km north of the village near the road to Thiepval. It contained 43 British graves dating from July and September 1916.

Divion Road Cemetery No. 2, Thiepval - situated next to St. Pierre-Divion Cemetery No. 1. It contained 60 British graves dating from July to September 1916.

Gordon Castle Cemetery, Authuille - situated on the southern edge of Thiepval Wood. It contained 33 British graves, 26 of the 49th Division, dating from July to September 1916 with one French soldier who died in October 1914.

Paisley Hillside Cemetery, Authuille - situated on the south side of Thiepval Wood in the valley near the village. It was next to Paisley Avenue Cemetery, also removed, and both got their name from a trench of that name nearby. It contained 32 British graves, mainly men of the 49th Division, dating from July and August 1916.

Quarry Palace Cemetery, Thiepval - situated by the River Ancre a little north-east of St. Pierre-Divion which is about 500m north of here. It contained 23 British graves from late 1916 and early 1917.

Small Connaught Cemetery, Thiepval - on the other side of the road from Connaught Cemetery. It contained 41 British graves dating from 1 July 1916. The cemetery was made by the 11th Division in November 1916.

St. Pierre-Divion Cemetery No. 1, Thiepval - situated a little south-east of the village on the side of the ridge. It contained ten British graves dating from November 1916.

Thiepval Valley Cemetery - on the south-east side of Thiepval Wood near the road to Authuille. It contained eleven British graves.

Thiepval Village Cemetery - situated on the road to Grandcourt, north of the village, on the summit of the ridge. It contained 215 British soldiers most of whom who died in 1916 with a few from 1918.

UK – 1286   Unnamed – 642

Area - 4651 sq mts

Special Memorials to two British soldiers believed to be buried among the unnamed.

Special memorials to five soldiers formerly buried in Divion Wood Cemetery No. 2 whose graves could not be found at the time of concentration.

LOCATION

Thiepval is a village about 6km north of Albert. Thiepval Wood is between the village and the River Ancre to the west of the village. The cemetery is on the north side of the Wood between it and the road to Hamel. It is about 1km west of Thiepval just south of the Schwaben Redoubt.

CONTALMAISON CHATEAU CEMETERY

HISTORY

The Cemetery was begun on the evening of 14 July 1916. It remained in use until March 1917. A few burials were made in Plot I, Rows B and C, in August and September 1918 and some graves were concentrated here after the war.

INFORMATION

The village was in German hands for much of the war and was a primary objective on 1 July 1916, and is believed to have been entered by small parties of the Tyneside Irish Brigade of the 34th Division. It was stormed by the 23rd Division on 7 July, and some men of the Northumberland Fusiliers taken four days earlier, either here or nearby, were released. However, it was lost the same afternoon and not finally captured until the 8th and 9th Yorkshires cleared it on 10 July. The Germans re-took the village in March 1918. It was finally recaptured by the 38th (Welsh) Division on the evening of 24 August 1918.

The underground fortifications made by the Germans before 1916 played an important part in the defence of the village. The chateau housed a German HQ before the village fell. The cellars were later used as a Dressing Station.

The cemetery was opened by front-line units who were fighting locally. Field Ambulances in the area continued to use the cemetery. Forty seven graves were added after the war. Eighteen German graves and one French burial were removed.

Buried here is Private William Henry Short, VC, 'C' Company, 8th Yorkshires, who died of wounds on 7 August 1916 aged 31 years. He was awarded the Victoria Cross for his actions at Munster Alley, between Contalmaison and Pozieres, on 6 August 1916. His citation reads 'For most conspicuous bravery. He was foremost in the attack, bombing the enemy with great gallantry, when he was severely wounded in the foot. He was urged to go back, but refused and continued to throw bombs. Later his leg was shattered by a shell, and he was unable to stand, so he lay in the trench adjusting detonators and straightening the pins of bombs for his comrades. He died before he could be carried out of the trench. For the last eleven months he had always volunteered for dangerous enterprises, and has always set a magnificent example of bravery and devotion to duty.'

Also buried here is Lieutenant Colonel Dr Arthur Nimmo Walker, Royal Army Medical Corps, killed on 24 September 1916 aged 42 years. He was consultant eye surgeon at St. Paul's Eye and Ear Hospital, Liverpool, and is credited with raising the quality of care and work at the hospital to some of the best in the country.

In and around the village you can find several memorials. One is to the 12th Manchesters in the Communal Cemetery. The German trench on the southern boundary of the cemetery was attacked by the Manchesters on 7 July 1916 in the battalions' first major action. They took heavy casualties and the memorial is to 1039 men who died in the war.

At the church is a memorial to the 16th Royal Scots also known as 'McCrae's Battalion'. The battalion had a strong association with Heart of Midlothian Football Club, with 13 players from the club being among the first to join the battalion. Other professionals from Raith Rovers and Falkirk followed suit. Many supporters of Hearts also joined up, as did fans of Hibernians, the other main Edinburgh football club. But it was with Hearts that the battalion is most closely associated, and a smaller plaque on the memorial is in memory of the 'players, ticket-holders and supporters of Heart of Midlothian Football Club' who advanced on Contalmaison on the 1 July 1916.

One of the plaques on the memorial also commemorates the 15th Royal Scots, which was also known as the City of Edinburgh Battalion, raised in late 1914. It is worth noting that one company was unofficially known as the 'Manchester Scottish'. As well as all the other Pals battalions from Greater Manchester, an attempt was made to raise a 'Scottish' Pals battalion but only about a Company could be formed. This is no surprise as Manchester had already formed eight City Pals and four Salford Pals battalions with local towns such as Accrington also raising Pals battalions. Nearly 250 men from this battalion were killed on 1 July during the attack on Contalmaison.

South of the village is a memorial to 2nd Lieutenant Donald S Bell, VC, at a site known as Bell's Redoubt. Donald Bell served with the 9th Yorkshires (Green Howards), and is reported to be the first professional football player (he played for Bradford Park Avenue) to join up in 1914. He enlisted in the ranks with the West Yorkshires, but in 1915 was commissioned as an officer with the Green Howards. He won the Victoria Cross for his actions at Horseshoe Trench, which was about 1km west of here, when on the 5 July 1916 he attacked and destroyed a German machine-gun post. On the 10 July he undertook a similar action when he was killed. The bronze cross at the top of the memorial is a reproduction of the original wooden cross placed here by the men of his battalion in his memory. His body was moved in 1920 to Gordon Dump Cemetery, very near to where he won his VC.

There is also a memorial to Captain Francis Dodgson of the 8th Yorkshires at the spot where he was killed on 10 July 1916. It is on the village side of a track south of Bailiff Wood south-west of the village. He is buried in Serre Road No. 2 cemetery.

UK – 264   Aust – 21   Can – 4
Unnamed – 45   Area – 1355 sq mts

Special Memorial to one Australian soldier known to be among the unnamed.

LOCATION

Contalmaison is a small village about 6km north-east of Albert. It can be reached by the road from Pozieres off the main Albert-Bapaume road, or from Fricourt off the Albert-Peronne road. The Chateau Cemetery is within the chateau grounds on the north side of the main road through the village to Pozieres. There is a path from the road to the cemetery.

CONTAY BRITISH CEMETERY

HISTORY

The cemetery was opened in August 1916 and used until March 1917. It was used again during the German offensive from April to August 1918.

INFORMATION

The village was in Allied hands throughout the war. This is the largest British cemetery in the valley of the River Hallue, a tributary of the Somme.

Contay was conveniently located near a railway line which was used to bring casualties here and to evacuate men to Base Hospitals. The 49th Casualty Clearing Station made the first burials. It was joined by the 9th CCS in September 1916. These two made the majority of the burials during the period August 1916 to March 1917 forming Plots I to IV and most of Plots VII and VIII. The German withdrawal to the Hindenburg Line meant that the cemetery was not used again until 1918. When the Germans advanced to Albert in 1918 the 38th (Welsh) and a few other Divisions used the cemetery completing Plots VII and VIII and making Plot IX. A group of American graves were removed in 1920.

Among those buried here Sergeant John Macdonald, DCM, Princess Patricia's Canadian Light Infantry (Eastern Ontario Regiment), who died of wounds suffered near Courcelette on the Somme on 17 September 1916 aged 36 years. Originally from Scotland he was among the first to enlist in September 1914. He was awarded the Distinguished

Conduct Medal for actions on 5 May 1915 when he dug men out from a collapsed trench and rescued several others from no-man's land all under intense fire from the Germans.

| UK – 689 | Can - 414 | Aust – 29 |
| SAfr – 1 | Ger – 40 | Unnamed - 3 |

LOCATION
Contay is 8km west of Albert and 12km north-east of Amiens. The cemetery is on the southern edge of the village, close to the church, on the northern side of the road to Franvillers next to a quarry. It is located 200m from the Communal Cemetery just where the road dips into a valley. It is a peaceful location on the edge of the valley.

CORBIE COMMUNAL CEMETERY

HISTORY
The Communal Cemetery was first used by the British in July 1915 when British Third Army took over this sector and it remained in use until May 1916 when the available space was full.

INFORMATION
The town was a major base in the rear of the battlefield and served as a gateway for many units as they went to the Front. There is a statue in the town to the British honouring those who fought in 'The Great War 1914-18'.

5th Casualty Clearing Station was stationed in the town until October 1916. 21st CCS arrived in August 1915 and remained until April 1917. During the German advance of 1918, when the Germans came within 10km of Corbie, Field Ambulances of the 47th Division were stationed nearby. These were supplemented by the 12th Australian Field Ambulance in July 1918.

Buried here is 2nd Lieutenant Spenser Lort Mansel, 8th attached 9th Devonshires, who died of wounds received near Mametz on 24 February 1916. The copse that now contains Devonshire Cemetery was possibly named after him.

There is one person who worked for the IWGC buried here. The bridge over the River Somme was seized by the French Resistance and the Royal Horse Guards on 31 August 1944 to facilitate the dash from the Seine to Brussels.

| UK – 246 | Indian - 4 | Ger – 15 |
| Others - 1 | | |

LOCATION
Corbie is located about 10km east of Amiens in the valley of the river Somme. The cemetery lies north of the town, between the roads to Vaux and Bray.

CORBIE COMMUNAL CEMETERY EXTENSION

HISTORY
An extension to the Communal Cemetery was begun in May 1916, when the available space in the Communal Cemetery for British burials was full, and used throughout the Battles of 1916. It was used again during the German offensive of 1918.

INFORMATION
Plot I and most of Plot II of the Extension contain the graves of men who fell during the Battles of 1916. The close packed graves reflect the heavy use during those months. The remainder date from 1918. There is also a small plot, on the west side of the Communal Cemetery, containing the graves of German Prisoners of War who died in British hospitals.

Brevet Major William la Touche Congreve, VC, DSO, MC, MiD, Legion of Honour, Rifle Brigade, killed in action on 20 July 1916 aged 25 years is buried here. He was the son of Lieutenant General Sir Walter Congreve VC, KCB, MVO who was awarded the Victoria Cross during the Battle of Colenso in the South African Wars. They are one of only three father and son pairings to win a VC. William was awarded the VC for his actions from 6-14 July 1916 near Longueval where he was later killed. His body was brought back from the Front to be buried in a separate grave near the entrance and Cross of Sacrifice. His citation states 'For most conspicuous bravery during a period of fourteen days preceding his death in action. This officer constantly performed acts of gallantry and showed the greatest devotion to duty, and by his personal example inspired all those around him with confidence at critical periods of the operations. During preliminary preparations for the attack he carried out personal reconnaissances of the enemy lines, taking out parties of officers and non-commissioned officers for over 1,000 yards in front of our line, in order to acquaint them with the ground. All these preparations were made under fire. Later, by night, Major Congreve conducted a battalion to its position of employment, afterwards returning to it to ascertain the situation after assault. He established himself in an exposed forward position from where he successfully observed the enemy, and gave orders necessary to drive them from their position. Two days later, when Brigade Headquarters was heavily shelled and many casualties resulted, he went out and assisted the medical officer to remove the wounded to places of safety, although he was himself suffering severely from gas and other shell effects. He again on a subsequent occasion showed supreme courage in tending wounded under heavy shell fire. He finally returned to the front line to ascertain the situation after an unsuccessful attack, and whilst in the act of writing his report, was shot and killed instantly.' His brother, Commander Sir Geoffrey Cecil Congreve, DSO, MiD, won the Distinguished Service Order at sea and was killed in a raid on the French coast in 1941. Also buried here is Private Joseph Carey, 7th Royal Irish Fusiliers who was executed for desertion on 15 September 1916. He absconded for the third time to avoid service in the front line at Hulloch near Loos.

Captain William Stapleton De Courcy Stretton, 3rd attached 2nd Royal Warkwickshires, killed on 4 September 1916, is buried here. He was one of four brothers to die in the war. Captain Alexander Lynham de Courcy Stretton, MC, MiD, 1st South Lancashires, attached 1st Nigeria Regiment killed in action at Mahiwa, German East Africa, on 16 October 1917 aged 31 and commemorated on the Dar es Salaam British and Indian Memorial. He had been taken prisoner by the Germans in the Cameroons in September 1914 and released in January 1916. Able Seaman Conrad de Courcy Stretton, HMAS Australia, Royal Australian Navy, died of illness aboard ship on 12 March 1915 aged 24 years. He is buried at Queensferry alongside his father who had also served in the war. 2nd Lieutenant John de Courcy Stretton, MC, 3rd attached 1st Royal Warkwickshires died on 11 May 1918 aged 27 years and is buried in Le Vertannoy British Cemetery.

There are also four battalion commanders here. Lieutenant Colonel Humphrey Francis William Bircham, DSO, was killed leading the 2nd Kings Royal Rifle Corps on 23 July 1916 at Munster Alley near Pozieres.

Lieutenant Colonel Terence Patrick McSharry, CMG, DSO and Bar, MC, four times MiD was killed on 6 August 1918 with the 15th Australian Infantry. A pre-war Staff officer and officer in the Australian Intelligence Corps he had seen service at Gallipoli and taken command of his battalion in August 1916. He had temporarily taken command of a Brigade before returning to his battalion. He was awarded the Distinguished Service Order in the Birthday Honours Lists in June 1917 and was appointed Commander of the Order of St. Michael and St. George in the Birthday Honours List in June 1918. While helping a wounded man to shelter from a bombardment at Vaire-sous-Corbie, on the Somme, he was mortally wounded. He was posthumously awarded a Bar to his DSO.

Lieutenant Colonel William Alfred Smith, MiD, 18th Manchesters was killed on 9 July 1916 fighting with his men at Trones Wood. Lieutenant Colonel Joseph Leonard Swainson, DSO is recorded as with 6th Duke of Cornwall's Light Infantry. However, although he had joined the DCLI in 1908 with the rank of Captain after transferring from the Lancashire Fusiliers with whom he saw service in the Boer War, on 25 June 1916 he took over command of the 1/4th King's Own Royal Lancaster Regiment on the Somme. On 8 August 1916, the King's Own attacked Guillemont, only to find that the German wire had not been cut. In the face of severe casualties from shelling and machine gun fire only 50m of ground was captured. Swainson ordered the battalion to withdraw but was severely wounded whilst encouraging his men. 2nd Lieutenant Gabriel George Coury of 3rd attached 1/4th South Lancashires, who was on his way to the front line in order to dig a sap, gave what help he could in rallying the men. On hearing that Swainson had been wounded, Coury went out to look for him and bring him in. They brought him back to the new advanced trench over ground swept by machine gun fire. Swainson, however, died within a few minutes of being brought into the trench. For this action Coury was awarded the Victoria Cross.

UK – 831   Aust – 58   SAfr – 27
Ger – 1   Unnamed - 3

Special memorials to two men whose graves were destroyed by shell-fire and are known to be buried among the unnamed.

LOCATION
The Extension is to the east of the Communal Cemetery. There is a small wall between the Communal Cemetery and the Extension.

COUIN BRITISH CEMETERY

HISTORY
This cemetery was opened by Field Ambulances of the 48th Division in May 1916 and remained in use throughout the Battles of the Somme. It was closed at the end of January 1917 when the available space had been used and the New British Cemetery was opened.

INFORMATION
Couin Chateau, visible to the south from the high ground upon which this cemetery is situated, was used by the French Army early in the war. When the British arrived they used it as a Divisional Headquarters. Having stayed in the chateau I can attest that this is a beautiful old building now being restored as a hotel.

Buried here is Brigadier General Walter Long, CMG, DSO, Twice MiD, Order of St Stanislas (2nd Class with swords), Royal Scots Greys who was commanding 56th Brigade when he was killed by a shell at Hebuterne on 28 January 1917. He was one of a group of Staff officers from 19th Division who were taking part in a tour of the trenches close to what is now Gommecourt British Cemetery No. 2.

He was the only one to be killed. He was the son of Right Honourable Walter Hume Long, Secretary of State for the Colonies who became 1st Viscount Long of Wroxall, and was also grandson of the 9th Earl of Cork. His son became the 2nd Viscount. Long had seen service in the Boer War, where he won his Distinguished Service Order, taking part in the relief of Kimberley. He then became ADC to the Governor of Canada. He had served at Mons and taken command of the Brigade in November 1916.

Also buried here is Lieutenant Colonel Walter Robert Stewart, DSO, MC, 13th Rifle Brigade who was killed on 8 April 1918. He was son of a Major General and grandson of the 9th Earl of Galloway. Also here is Captain Basil Hallam Radford, No. 1 Army Kite Balloon Section, Royal Flying Corps, who died on 20 August 1916 when he fell from his observation balloon. He was better known as 'Basil Hallam' or 'Gilbert the Filbert' around the Music and Variety Halls of the day.

| UK – 397 | SAfr – 2 | Can – 1 |
| India – 1 | Ger – 3 | Area – 1651 sq mts |

LOCATION
Couin lies about 15km east of Doullens and 30km south-west of Arras in the valley of the River Authie. The British and New British Cemeteries can be found to the north of the village on either side of the road to Souastre at its junction with the road to Henu.

COUIN NEW BRITISH CEMETERY

HISTORY
The British Cemetery was closed at the end of January 1917 when the available space had been used. This cemetery was opened at that point and remained in use until the end of the war.

INFORMATION
The cemetery was opened by Field Ambulances in January 1917 and used by medical units until the end of the war. However, few burials were made in 1917 as the front-line moved to the east when the Germans withdrew to the Hindenburg Line.

Of the British buried here 159 came from Lancashire Regiments. One grave was concentrated here from a new cemetery that had just been begun at Coigneux to the east. Among those buried here is Sergeant Dickson Cornelius Savage (served as Richard Charles Travis), VC, DCM, MM, twice MiD, Croix de Guerre (Belgium), 2nd Battalion, Otago Regiment, NZEF, killed in action on 25 July 1918 at Rossignol Wood aged 34 years one day after the action for which he received his Victoria Cross. Known as 'Prince of Scouts' and 'King of No Man's Land', he had served in Gallipoli. His citation reads 'For most conspicuous bravery and devotion to duty. During 'surprise' operations it was necessary to destroy an impassable wire block. Serjt. Travis, regardless of personal danger, volunteered for this duty. Before zero hour, in broad daylight and in close proximity to enemy posts he crawled out and successfully destroyed the block with bombs, thus enabling the attacking parties to pass through. A few minutes later a bombing party on the right of the attack was held up by two enemy machine guns, and the success of the whole operation was in danger. Perceiving this Serjt. Travis with great gallantry and utter disregard of danger, rushed the position, killed the crews and captured the guns. An enemy officer and three men immediately rushed at him from a bend in the trench and attempted to retake the guns. These four he killed single handed, thus allowing the bombing party on which much depended to advance. The success of the operation was almost entirely due to the heroic work of this gallant NCO and the vigour with which he made and used opportunities for inflicting casualties on the enemy. He was killed 24 hours later when, in a most intense bombardment prior to an enemy counter-attack, he was going from post to post encouraging the men." The Distinguished Conduct Medal was awarded "For conspicuous gallantry in action. He went out by himself and accounted for several enemy snipers who were firing at a working party. He has on many previous occasions done very fine work.'

Also buried here is Lieutenant John Bernard Pye Adams, 1st Royal Welsh Fusiliers, died of wounds received the previous day leading his men in an attack near Serre on 27 February 1917 aged 26 years. The attack in which he was a part took heavy casualties. Adams was in his unit at the same time as Siegfried Sassoon and Robert Graves. Adams was the first of these three to publish his memoirs, 'Nothing of Importance – a record of 8 months at the Front with a Welsh Battalion October 1915 to June 1916' written whilst convalescing in England having been wounded in June 1916. His was the only record to be published in book form whilst the war was still being fought. He returned to the Front in January 1917.

Another here is Company Sergeant Major Richard McFadden, MM, 17th (Footballers) Middlesex, died of wounds on 23 October 1916 aged 27 years. He was a pre-war footballer who had been wounded at Delville Wood in July 1916.

UK – 344 NZ – 14 Can – 2
Ger – 2 Area – 1640 sq mts

LOCATION
See Couin British Cemetery.

COURCELETTE BRITISH CEMETERY

HISTORY
The cemetery was begun in November 1916 at the end of the Battles of the Somme to concentrate, during the war, the dead from the surrounding battlefields. However, the vast majority of the cemetery was made after the war as a concentration cemetery.

INFORMATION
Courcelette and the surrounding area were in German hands for much of the war. After fierce fighting it fell to the 2nd Canadian Division, supported by the first use of tanks, on 15 September 1916 during the Battle of Flers-Courcelette. The Canadians had taken over the sector from the Australians in early September 1916. The 4th and 6th Canadian Infantry Brigades captured the outer trenches while the 5th Brigade took the village. A German trench, the Fabeck Graben, ran along the farm track upon which the cemetery stands. It was captured on 15 September 1916 by the Princess Patricia's Canadian Light Infantry. In the period the Canadians were fighting in this area they suffered 17000 casualties.

The village was close to the front-line, and was destroyed by German artillery, until the Germans withdrew to the Hindenburg Line in March 1917. The Germans captured the village again on 25 March 1918 but it fell finally to the British on 24 August.

The cemetery began life called 'The Mouquet Road Cemetery' or the 'Sunken Road Cemetery'. At the end of the war it contained 74 graves, now in Plot I, Rows A to F. After the war 1882 graves were concentrated here mainly of men who fell in 1916 during the capture of Courcelette and Pozieres. The cemetery represents the Divisions which fought in this area including Australians from Pozieres and Mouquet Farm, Canadians who fell in September to November 1916 as well as the British.

One of the Special Memorials is to Lieutenant John Chilton Mewburn, 18th Canadian Infantry, killed nearby on 15 September 1916. He was son of the Canadian Minister of Militia and Defence. Also here is Private George Ritchie, Royal Canadian Regiment who died on 16 September 1916 aged 16 years. He had enlisted in April 1915.

Nearby on the west side of the Albert-Bapaume road, south of the village, is the Canadian Memorial that commemorates the Canadian dead of the Battles of the Somme who fell from 3 September to 18 November 1916. In the village, in the Communal Cemetery, you will find the grave of a man who worked for the IWGC in the 1920's and 1930's. Frank Hayward, who had fought in the war with the Royal Sussex Regiment, died on 20 December 1936.

Concentrated here:

Mouquet Farm Cemetery, Grandcourt - situated about 1km south of here at the farm which is on the north side of the Pozieres-Thiepval road midway between the villages. The farm was captured, after fierce fighting, by the 2nd Canadian Mounted Rifles on 16 September 1916. It fell to the Germans in March 1918 and was recaptured by the 17th Division on 24 August 1918. The cemetery was begun by the 111th Brigade Royal Field Artillery in October 1916 and contained 36 graves.

Red Chateau Cemetery, Courcelette - situated within the village. It was at the entrance to a ruined dug-out and was used from October to December 1916. It contained fifteen Canadian and two British soldiers.

UK – 673 Can – 783 Aust – 513
NZ – 1 KUG – 4 Unnamed – 1175
Area – 7052 sq mts

Special Memorials to five British and four Canadian soldiers who are believed to be buried among the unnamed.

LOCATION
Courcelette is situated about 10km north-east of Albert on the west side of the road to Bapaume. This cemetery is 1km south-west of the village on the old road to Thiepval which is now little more than a farm track. It is in open fields on a hillside facing the village with good views of the battlefield.

COURCELLES-AU-BOIS COMMUNAL CEMETERY EXTENSION

HISTORY
The Extension was opened in October 1916 when the space available in the Communal Cemetery had been filled. It was used until March 1917 when the Germans withdrew to the Hindenburg Line. A few burials were made during the German offensive in April 1918.

INFORMATION
The Extension was used by Field Ambulances and fighting units during the latter part of the Battles of the Somme and during the winter that followed. The last burials, in April 1918, were of five soldiers from New Zealand and a British artilleryman. Following this the village was occupied by the Germans for some months until recaptured by the Third Army.

Among those buried here is Captain Conrad Paul Taylor, 8th East Yorkshires, killed in action on 28 October 1916 aged 21 years. His father ran a company producing scientific instruments. He was at Cambridge briefly in 1914 before joining the army as a 2nd Lieutenant in November 1914. He went to France just before the Battle of Loos in September 1915. He was promoted Captain in July 1916. At Serre a shell hit his dug-out killing him. He was posthumously Mentioned in Despatches for his work on the Somme where, for a time, he was Second in Command of his battalion. His commanding officer recommended Taylor for a decoration for his actions at Waterlot Farm when in command of an attack of about 200 men.

The Communal Cemetery was used for the burial of five French soldiers and three British soldiers in September 1916. They were situated on the north side of the cemetery under a hedge. The British graves were concentrated in Row F of the Extension in October 1934 and are now situated next to the Cross of Sacrifice.

UK – 105   NZ – 5   SAfr – 3
Can – 2   Area – 722 sq mts

LOCATION
The village lies about 12km north of Albert and about 15km east of Doullens. The cemetery is on the north side of the village on the west side of the road to Sailly-au-Bois. It is on the north side of the Communal Cemetery. The cemetery is above the road level and reached by steps.

CROISILLES BRITISH CEMETERY

HISTORY
The cemetery was opened in April 1917 and remained in use until March 1918. It was extended after the war by the concentration of graves from the surrounding battlefields and small burial grounds.

INFORMATION
The village was in German hands for most of the war. It was attacked by the British 7th Division in March 1917 but did not fall until an attack on 2 April 1917 made in a blizzard. The Germans re-took the village on 21 March 1918. It fell for the final time, to the 56th (London) Division, on 28 August 1918 after heavy fighting. Most of the men buried here are from the Guards, 7th or 21st Divisions.

Among those buried here is Captain Charles Lindsay Murray Scott, No. 54 Squadron, Royal Flying Corps and North Staffordshire Regiment, killed in action on 15 February 1917 aged 24 years. He was killed flying a Sopwith Pup which left formation at 11.40am and is claimed to have been shot down by German Anti-aircraft artillery. His father was Lieutenant Colonel commanding the North Staffordshire battalion from which Scott had moved to the RFC after being wounded at Hill 60 near Ieper in April 1915. He was the nephew of General Sir Archibald Murray who was Chief of Staff to Sir John French and for a time commanded the Egyptian Expeditionary Force.

Also here is Serjeant Bertie Leopold Prince, 1st Royal Munster Fusiliers, killed in action on 20 November 1917. His brother, Private Reginald Luke Prince, DCM, 1st Somerset Light Infantry was killed in action on 1 July 1916 aged 30 years and is buried in Serre Road No. 2 Cemetery. Another brother, Lance Serjeant Joseph Ernest Prince, 1st Dorsetshires was killed in action on 30 September 1918 and is commemorated on the Vis-en-Artois Memorial.

The last 'WW1' burials here are two men of the 129th Company, Chinese Labour Corps who died in 1919. Both were concentrated here from H.A.C. British Cemetery which was about 500m south-west of Ecoust-St. Mein.

The WW2 burials are men of a Lancaster bomber of No. 514 Squadron, Royal Air Force shot down on 16 June 1944 while on a mission to bomb the railway yards at Valenciennes. Thiers was one of eleven planes from their mission to be lost, but one member of their crew, Flight Officer (Navigator) Arnold Hughes Morrison survived, evaded capture and escaped, with the help of the Resistance, back to England. He was awarded the Distinguished Flying Cross.

UK – 1165	Can – 3	Aust – 1
SAfr - 2	Chinese – 2	Ger – 18
Unnamed – 647		WW2 – 6
Area – 4487 sq mts		

Special Memorials to fourteen British soldiers known to be buried among the unnamed.

Special Memorials to two British soldiers, buried in Hendecourt-les-Cagnicourt Communal Cemetery in 1917, whose graves were destroyed by shell-fire.

LOCATION

Croisilles is located about 10km south-east of Arras and 7km north of Bapaume. It is on the east side of the A1 Autoroute. The cemetery is in a valley on the southern edge of the village. It has an imposing entrance. It is easy to confuse the CWGC signs in the village and end up at Croisilles Railway Cemetery – or is it just me?

CROISILLES RAILWAY CEMETERY

HISTORY

The cemetery was opened at the start of April 1917 and remained in use until January 1918. A further burial was made in September 1918.

INFORMATION

The cemetery was opened by the 21st Manchesters after their involvement in the capture of the village. The Germans buried 26 men here when they controlled the village in 1918.

Among those here is Lieutenant Richard Donaldson, MC, Anson Battalion attached 188th Trench Mortar Battery, Royal Naval Division, Royal Naval Volunteer Reserve, killed in action on 5 September 1918 aged 25 years. He had attended Glasgow University but left to join up as a 2nd Lieutenant in 1915. He became an Acting Lieutenant in July 1917 and Lieutenant in January 1918. He served first in Salonika and the Mediterranean before fighting with the Royal Naval Division on the Somme near Beaumont Hamel in November 1916 where he was wounded. He saw further action near Passendale in October 1917 for which he was awarded the Military Cross.

UK – 181   Ger – 26   Unnamed – 27

Special Memorial to one British soldier known to be buried among the unnamed.

LOCATION

The cemetery is in the same direction as the British cemetery. There is a CWGC sign from the British cemetery to this one. It is across the ridge to the south of the village upon which you find the British cemetery. There is a path from the road to the cemetery which is about 250m from the road. This is a very peaceful location.

CRUCIFIX CORNER CEMETERY, VILLERS-BRETONNEUX

HISTORY

The cemetery was used during the war only in August 1918. It was greatly enlarged after the war.

INFORMATION

See Villers-Bretonneux Military Cemetery.

The village was in Allied hands for most of the war. However during 1918 it was to mark the limit of the German advance and the start of their defeat. The Germans planned to capture Amiens and possibly, therefore, win the war. On 23 April German infantry and tanks reached, and captured, Villers-Bretonneux but also reached the final Allied defensive line in front of Amiens. On the following day the 13th and 15th Australian Brigades, assisted by parts of the British 8th and 18th Divisions, counter-attacked and recaptured the village at great cost. The Germans made no further gains in this sector and abandoned their plans to capture Amiens.

The cemetery was opened by the Canadian Corps and by the end of the war contained 90 burials, mainly Canadian, now in Plot I, Rows A to D. This was situated in what had been no-man's land over which the Canadian Corps had successfully attacked on 8 August 1918. The British Plots face towards the old German line. The concentration graves are mostly Australians.

The French burials made at that time are now in Plot II. After the war 700 graves were concentrated from the battlefields between the Rivers Somme and Luce. Since that time the graves of sixteen American, 241 French and ten German soldiers have been removed.

Among those buried here is Private George Wylie, 13th Australian Infantry, who was a school boy from Newtown, New South Wales. He was killed in action at Villers-Bretonneux on 2 May 1918, aged 16 years. George's brother-in-law Private Bruce Gough was awarded a Military Medal.

Also here is Private Herbert Jones, 20th Australian Infantry, who died on 9 July 1918 aged 28 years. He had represented Australia at Rugby Union on three occasions in 1913 while on tour in New Zealand.

Concentrated here:
Vaire Wood Cemetery, Vaire-Sur-Corbie - situated about 7km north of here, on the south bank of the Somme, on the eastern side of the village between the village and the wood. It contained the graves of 26 Australian soldiers with a British serviceman who were killed in July and August 1918.

UK – 288	Aust – 296	Can – 76
Fr – 141	Russia – 2	Unnamed – 191

Area – 3013 sq mts

Special Memorials erected to a British and an Australian soldier known, or believed, to be buried among the unnamed graves.

LOCATION
Villers-Bretonneux is situated on the main road from Amiens to St. Quentin about 10km east of Amiens. The cemetery is 1km south of the village in farming land on the west side of the road to Demuin, Moreuil and Montdidier. There is good parking and turning.

CUCKOO PASSAGE CEMETERY, HENINEL

HISTORY
The cemetery was in use from April-May 1917.

INFORMATION
The village of Heninel was captured in a snowstorm on 12 April 1917 by the 56th (London) and 21st Divisions.

The cemetery is named after a trench that ran beside the cemetery. This is a tranquil little 'Pals' cemetery of men mostly from Manchester. They are men of the 17th and 18th (3rd and 4th Manchester Pals) Manchesters killed on 23 April 1918. Their objective was the high ground overlooking Cherisy but the German barrage inflicted heavy casualties including all officers of the 18th Manchesters. The 19th battalion eventually captured the German trenches at great cost.

Among them is Private Bertram Denis Lemmon, 18th (3rd City Pals) Manchesters aged 23 years when he died. Before the war he was working for Cambridge University Press in the Art Department. He was originally from Levenshulme and enlisted in February 1916, going to France in January 1917, but is a good example to show that not all Pals were strictly located in the area from which the Pals Battalion was formed.

UK – 54   Unnamed – 1   Area – 283 sq mts

LOCATION
Heninel is about 7km south-east of Arras and 10km north of Bapaume. The village is less than 1km east of the A1 Autoroute. It is accessible from Heninel past the Communal Cemetery and Cherisy Road East Cemetery. The road ends at Rookery Cemetery and becomes a rough farm track. You can see the cemetery on the ridge to the right of the track. A steep path leads from the track through the fields to the cemetery which is very isolated and quiet.

DAMERY COMMUNAL CEMETERY

HISTORY
The Communal Cemetery was used for the burial of one British man in March 1918. A further group of Allied troops, who died in a few days in August 1918, were brought here by the French in August 1919.

INFORMATION
The village was captured by the 3rd Canadian Division on 15 August 1918 having been in German hands throughout most of the war.

The Communal Cemetery and an Extension across the road were used by the Germans. A burial made in March 1918 has been moved to Terlincthun British Cemetery so all the identified men here fell in August 1918. One of these is Private Nicholas Smith Drew Mutter, 52nd Canadian Infantry, died on 19 August 1918. He emigrated to Canada in 1911. When the French brought the bodies in 1919 his name had not yet been identified on the records.

UK – 1   Can – 10   Unnamed - 4

LOCATION

Damery is a small village about 4km north-west of Roye and 1km north of the Roye-Amiens road. The cemetery is about 300m south of the village in open fields on the edge of the road to Villers-les-Roye. The graves are in four plots at the rear of the cemetery. Three plots are to the right of the main path and the four men of the Fort Garry Horse are in one plot on the main path.

DANTZIG ALLEY BRITISH CEMETERY, MAMETZ

HISTORY

The cemetery was begun in July 1916 soon after this area had been captured from the Germans. It remained in use until November 1916 and a few further burials were made in August and September 1918. The cemetery was greatly enlarged after the war.

INFORMATION

Mametz was in German hands from 1914. It was an objective on 1 July 1916 which was taken by the 7th Division after fierce fighting near the village and here in one of the main German trench systems, Dantzig Alley. This marks one of the few British successes on the first day of the Battle of the Somme but the advantage was not pressed home. The area was lost during the German offensive in March 1918 but was retaken in August.

The cemetery is named after the large German trench, Dantzig Alley, between Mametz and Montauban. The cemetery was begun in the trench once the British Army had advanced to the north. The cemetery stands on the location where 2nd Queens and 22nd (7th Manchester Pals) Manchesters captured the trench.

At the end of the war it contained 183 graves, now in Plot I. After the war 1782 graves, mostly men who were killed in 1916, were concentrated here from the battlefields to the north and east of Mametz when most of the small battlefield cemeteries in this area were cleared after the war. At the same time seven German and five French graves were removed. Many of the men buried here were killed on 1 July 1916 fighting with 7th Division or with 18th and 30th Divisions at Montauban.

It is notable that the graves of men buried here who were serving with the King's (Liverpools) have the crest of Lord Derby rather than the regimental badge on the headstones. The 11th Earl of Derby was among the first to get permission to raise a city focussed battalion, meeting Kitchener on 24 August 1914 to offer to raise a battalion from the city's commercial class. He began to recruit on 31 August and had raised the first battalion by 10.00am. He provided four Liverpool Pals battalions, the 17th 18th, 19th and 20th King's (Liverpools), and was the first to use the term 'Pals Battalions' when he had the phrase 'a battalion of pals' on the signing up form.

Buried here is Lance Corporal Harry Greenfield, MM, killed in action on 1 July 1916 aged 26 years. He was the eldest of three brothers lost in the war. All served with 7th Queen's (Royal West Surreys). They died within two weeks of each other, two on the same day killed in the failed attack by the battalion from Longueval Alley towards Trones Wood. They are Company Sergeant Major Albert Frank Greenfield aged 22 years and Sergeant Percy Greenfield aged 20 years. Their bodies were not recovered and they are both commemorated on the Thiepval Memorial.

The commanding officer of the 20th (5th Manchester Pals) Manchesters, an Indian Army man, who attacked on the west side of Mametz is buried here. He is Lieutenant Colonel Harold Lewis, twice MiD, 37th Lancers (Baluch Horse) commanding 20th Manchesters, killed in action on 1 July 1916 aged 35 years. A film of the Battle of the Somme was made to be shown in cinema houses before the end of the Battle. One iconic image is the blowing of the Hawthorn Ridge mine. Several men have since been identified from the film, though we know significant scenes were filmed behind the lines to make the film more 'convincing'. But, it is believed that Lieutenant Colonel Lewis is shown in the film lying dead in no-man's land. He is identified by his dog lying beside him.

Also here is Private Charles Randall, 4th Coldstream Guards killed in action on 27 September 1916 aged 32 years. He was a footballer who had joined Arsenal from Newcastle United in September 1911. The centre forward made the first of his 44 starts for Arsenal in a 2-2 draw against Bolton in October of that year. Randall scored 12 times in his time at the club before transferring to North Shields in summer 1914. He had scored six goals in nineteen starts for Newcastle United from 1908 to 1911.

There are signs in the village which will lead you to the 38th (Welsh) Division Memorial in fields south of Mametz Wood. There is parking and turning at the memorial. The track can be followed through to Flatiron Copse Cemetery. On 7 July 1916 the 38th Division faced north from the ridge upon which this cemetery sits towards Mametz Wood. They were one of two Divisions making a pincer attack on the wood which was held by the Prussian Guard. The attack failed as machine guns in the wood caused heavy casualties upon the attackers crossing open ground. Battlefield communications failed and there was no smokescreen. On 10 July at 4.00am both Divisions attacked again. A frontal attack by the 38th Division was led by 13th (1st North Wales Pals), 14th and 16th Royal Welsh Fusiliers who entered the wood under heavy fire. There was very confused fighting in the trees with the whole Division committed to the attack. The fighting continued for two days until the Germans withdrew on the night of 11 July. The Division, which had been raised by Lloyd George, lost 4000 casualties including four pairs of brothers, one pair found in each other's arms. The Division contained men like Robert Graves and Siegfried Sassoon who provided a record of the battle. The Memorial was unveiled in 1987 on the anniversary of the battle. Near the entrance of the cemetery is a stone with an inscription in Welsh and English in memory of the Royal Welsh Fusiliers. At the rear of the cemetery is a memorial seat to the 14th Royal Welsh Fusiliers. This battalion, raised in Caernarvon and Anglesey, went into battle nearby for the first time in Mametz Wood. Concentrated here:

Aeroplane Cemetery, Fricourt - situated on the old German line, south of the village, near the present British cemetery. It contained the graves of 24 men of the 20th Manchesters who were killed on 1 July 1916.

Bottom Wood Cemetery, Fricourt - about 300m north of here on the southern edge of the small wood between Fricourt and Mametz Wood. The cemetery was opened in July 1916 and served a Field Ambulance stationed there. It remained in use until the end of 1916 and contained the graves of 98 British soldiers, five from New Zealand and an Australian.

Bulgar Alley Cemetery, Mametz - situated 100m south of here in the former German trench that ran from Dantzig Alley east to a position south of the village. It contained the graves of 24 British soldiers, 21 of the 22nd Manchesters, who were killed on 1 July 1916.

Hare Lane Cemetery, Fricourt - situated on the western edge of the village and named after a short trench. It contained the graves of 54 British soldiers, 49 of the 10th West Yorkshires, who were killed on 1 and 2 July 1916.

Mametz German Cemetery - situated 200m south of here next to the main Albert-Peronne road. Now removed, among the German graves, it contained the graves of twelve British soldiers buried by the British in July and August 1916.

Mansel Copse and Mansel Copse West Cemeteries, Mametz - situated on the south side of the Albert-Peronne road near the present Devonshire Cemetery. They contained the graves of 51 British soldiers from the 2nd Borders killed on 1 July 1916.

Montauban Road Cemetery, Carnoy - situated 1km south-east of here, on the edge of the road from Carnoy to Montauban. It contained the graves of 25 British soldiers, most of the 18th Division, who died on 1 July 1916.

Vernon Street Cemetery, Carnoy - situated about 2km south-east of here in the valley between Carnoy and Maricourt at a point known as 'Squeak Forward Position'. It contained the graves of 110 British soldiers, buried by the 21st Infantry Brigade, killed from July to October 1916.

UK – 2008	NZ – 18	Aust – 13
Can – 10	SAfr – 3	India – 1
Unnamed – 518		Area – 5722 sq mts

Special Memorials erected to seventeen British soldiers known, or believed, to be buried among the unnamed graves.

Special Memorials erected to 70 British soldiers, and one from New Zealand, buried in other cemeteries, whose graves were destroyed by shell-fire.

LOCATION

Mametz is situated 8km east of Albert about 1km north of the Albert-Peronne road. The cemetery is on the eastern edge of the village on the north side of the road to Montauban. It is on a ridge with good views of the battlefield.

DAOURS COMMUNAL CEMETERY EXTENSION

HISTORY

The Extension was opened in preparation for the Battles of the Somme and it remained in use until the German withdrawal to the Hindenburg Line in early 1917. The Extension was used again during the fighting of 1918 from April to September. It was also used for the burial of two men of the Chinese Labour Corps in November 1918.

INFORMATION

In June 1916 the 1/1st (South Midland), 21st, 34th, 45th and Lucknow Casualty Clearing Stations were all grouped in the village in readiness for the coming battles. They made the burials in Plots I and II, part of Plot III and the Indian Plot. When the Germans withdrew on 1917 the CCS's moved closer to the new front-line and the cemetery was temporarily closed. With the German attacks in March 1918 the Extension became almost a front-line cemetery. Throughout August and September 1918, as the Germans were pushed back, the 5th, 37th, 41st, 53rd, 55th and 61st CCS's moved to the village and then the cemetery closed once again at the end of September, except for two burials in November.

There is a small Plot of Chinese and Indian graves near the Cross of Sacrifice separated from the other burials. Both identified Chinese buried here died after the war in late

1918. A group of Germans were buried here who died as Prisoners of War, but they have been removed.

Among those buried here is Alfred Ernest England from Liverpool. He served with 272nd Mechanical Transport Company attached Heavy Artillery Australian Corps and died on 6 August 1918 aged 36 years. He was married on Boxing Day 1910 to Martha. He is one of 157 men who fulfilled Brooke's poem to the utmost extent in World War One by making a corner of a foreign field truly 'forever England'.

Also buried here are the Simmonds brothers, David John and Edward Ernest from Victoria, Australia. They both served with 55th Australian Infantry and died within two months of each other. They are buried side by side.

Captain Ludovic Heathcoat Amory, MiD, who died of wounds on 25 August 1918 aged 37 years is buried here. The family have provided several British Members of Parliament including a Chancellor of the Exchequer. He was the son of Sir John Heathcoat Heathcoat-Amory, 1st Baronet, of Knightshayes, Tiverton. He played cricket for Oxford University in 1902-03. In 1904 he undertook a tour of South Africa, India, Australia and New Zealand with his Oxford friend Edward Frederick Lindley Wood, later the 1st Earl of Halifax and Foreign Secretary at the start of WW2. He enters the war in October 1914, in the Royal 1st Devon Yeomanry, attached to the Royal Artillery and attached to the Headquarters of 32nd Division. He was promoted to Lieutenant on 31 December 1914, to Temporary Major on 29 August 1916, and to Staff-Captain RA on 15 January 1917. He had three children: Patrick Gerald Heathcoat-Amory born in 1912 and killed at El Alamein in 1942; Michael Ludovic Heathcoat-Amory born in 1914 and killed in an aeroplane accident in 1936; Edgar Fitzgerald Heathcoat-Amory born in 1917 and killed in Normandy in 1944.

Another here is Lieutenant Colonel Alfred St. Hill Gibbons, 13th King's (Liverpools), MiD, is buried here. His memorial at the church of St. Michael and All Angels, Budehaven, Cornwall states that he died of wounds, on 15 July 1916, received when leading his men into action at the Battle of the Somme when attacking Bazentin-le-Grand, aged 58 years. The Times printed an obituary on 20 July 1916 that stated that he was killed in action. He was best known as the explorer of the Upper Zambesi who completed the work which Livingstone had begun. He was, it is believed, the second white man to cross the continent from the Cape to Cairo. Although born in Liverpool, he obtained a commission in the Militia Battalion of the East Yorkshire Regiment, from which he retired with the honorary rank of Lieutenant-Colonel. In 1900 he volunteered for service in South Africa, and remained there until the end of that war, and afterwards took up farming in Northern Rhodesia, from which he returned in 1914 to join the war. He is named on the Northern Rhodesia WW1 Memorial near Victoria Falls.

Buried here is Lieutenant Colonel Montague Bruce Stow, 1st East Yorkshires, died of wounds received on 1 July 1916 north of the village of Fricourt. He was wounded early in the morning by shellfire and did not take part in the attack. Major Roland Elphinstone Gordon, MC and Bar, MiD, 'C' Battery, 251st Brigade, Royal Field Artillery, who died of wounds aged 25 on 30 August 1918 is buried here. He was a Scottish Rugby international representing his country at centre on three occasions. He played against France at Parc des Princes in 1913 in which he scored two tries on his debut with Scotland winning 21-3; against Wales at Inverleith which Wales won 8-0 and against Ireland, also at Inverleith, with Scotland winning 29-14. In 1911 he entered the Royal Military Academy at Woolwich where he was captain of the Rugby XV in 1912. He also represented the Royal Artillery, the Army and Blackheath. On 22 January 1913 he was commissioned as a 2nd Lieutenant in the Royal Artillery. On 5 March 1913 he sailed for India where he was attached to the 82nd Battery, Royal Field Artillery stationed at Kirki. In November 1914 he was posted to Mesopotamia where he was severely wounded in the summer of 1915 and returned to England. He returned to the Front and was awarded the Military Cross in June 1917, was wounded for a second time in November 1917 and for a third in May 1918. He was awarded a Bar to his Military Cross in the King's Birthday Honours List of June 1918. He was also Mentioned in Despatches. Following his wound in May he was offered a posting in England but refused it, preferring instead to return to the Front. In August 1918 he was wounded again, this time mortally.

Four Australians who won the Distinguished Conduct Medal are buried here. Lance Corporal Edward Brown Gibson, DCM, 59th Australian Infantry, killed in action on 18 August 1918 aged 32 years won his DCM at Harbonnieres for capturing a German post with 25 men and three machine guns. Corporal Charles Seaton Higginbotham, DCM, 5th Australian Infantry, killed in action on 23 August 1918 aged 20 years won his DCM at Lihons by capturing a machine gun post and killing six Germans. Private William Allan Irwin, DCM, 33rd Australian Infantry, died of wounds on 1 September 1918 won his DCM at Road Wood capturing three machine guns on his own before receiving the wounds from which he died. Company Sergeant Major Henry Todd, DCM, 9th Australian Infantry, killed in action on 11 August 1918 aged 23 years was awarded his DCM for his leadership qualities at Ieper in 1917.

UK - 760	Aust - 459	India – 8
Can - 2	NZ - 1	SAfr - 1
CLC - 2		Area – 4553 sq mts

Special Memorials to four men of the Chinese Labour Corps whose graves in White Chateau Cemetery, Cachy could not be located at the time of concentration.

LOCATION
Daours is a village about 10km east of Amiens lying on the north bank of the Somme. The Cemetery is about 300m north of the village on the west side of the road to La Neuville and Pont Noyelle. The Extension is on the south side of the Communal Cemetery and closer to the village.

DARTMOOR CEMETERY, BECORDEL-BECOURT

HISTORY
The cemetery was opened as a front-line cemetery in August 1915. It remained in use until March 1918, and for a few burials in August 1918, though it was infrequently used in 1917.

INFORMATION
The cemetery was begun by the 5th Division as Becordel-Becourt Military Cemetery in August 1915. The name was changed in May 1916 at the request of the 8th and 9th Devonshires who had many men buried here.
In September 1916 the XV Corps Main Dressing Station was established nearby and it made burials here until it moved east as the Germans withdrew to the Hindenburg Line. Hence, the cemetery was rarely used in 1917 as it was far from the fighting. The position was lost to the Germans on 26 March 1918 but was retaken by the 12th Division on 24 August 1918. At this time five burials were made.
A father and son, who served in the same artillery Battery and were killed together, are buried in this cemetery side by side. They are Sergeant George Lee, aged 44 years, and Corporal Robert Frederick Lee, aged 19 years, 'A' Battery, 156th Brigade Royal Field Artillery, both killed in action on 5 September 1916.
Also here is Lieutenant Henry Webber, 7th South Lancashires, MiD, who died of wounds received from shell-fire while talking to his battalion commanding officer at Mametz Wood on 21 July 1916. He was aged 68 years and is believed to be the oldest British soldier killed on the Western Front. He was the battalion Transport Officer and had lied about his age to be accepted into the army in 1915. He had three sons in the army who were all senior in rank to him.
Buried here is Private James Miller, VC, 7th King's Own Royal Lancashires, killed in action on 31 July 1916 aged 26 years. He was awarded the Victoria Cross for his actions at Bazentin-le-Petit. His citation reads 'For most conspicuous bravery. His Battalion was consolidating a position after its capture by assault. Private Miller was ordered to take an important message under heavy shell and rifle fire and to bring back a reply at all costs. He was compelled to cross the open, and on leaving the trench was shot almost immediately in the back, the bullet coming out through his abdomen. In spite of this, with heroic courage and self-sacrifice, he compressed with his hand the gaping wound in his abdomen, delivered his message, staggered back with the answer and fell at the feet of the officer to whom he delivered it. He gave his life with a supreme devotion to duty.'
Also buried here is Private John Joseph Sweeney, 1st Otago Battalion, NZEF. In October 1914, although an Australian, he enlisted in the NZEF as he was living in New Zealand. He served in Gallipoli as a tunneler and spent weeks in a hospital in Egypt after evacuation from Gallipoli and France. When sent to join his unit in France he deserted and was absent for five weeks. He was sentenced to be executed for desertion and the sentence was carried out at 6.40am on 2 October 1916. He was aged 37 years. His brother was killed in action in 1918 and his father committed suicide in 1925 when the news of the execution was about to be made public in New Zealand. He was one of five New Zealand soldiers who were executed (28 were sentenced to death) during the First World War and pardoned by the New Zealand Parliament in 2000.
Also here is Lieutenant Colonel H Allardice, 36th Jacob's Horse, Indian Army, attached and commanding 13th Northumberland Fusiliers, killed in action leading his men between Fricourt and La Boiselle on the afternoon of 1 July 1916. His headstone has the badge of his Indian Army unit.
You can also find Private Alfred Tufnell, 7th Bedfordshires, died on 4 November 1915 aged 33 years. One brother, Private Benjamin Tufnell, 1/5th Bedfordshires, was killed in action at Sulva Bay, Gallipoli on 15 August 1915 aged 28 years and is commemorated on the Helles Memorial. Another brother, Private H Tufnell, 1st Bedfordshires was killed in action at Hill 60 near Ieper on 21 April 1915 aged 35 years and is buried in Oosttaverne Wood Cemetery.
Another family to lose three sons, one of whom is buried here, are the Hogarth's from Australia. Buried here is Lieutenant Archie McDonald Hogarth, 'A' Battery, 104th Brigade, Royal Field Artillery, died on 9 July 1916 aged 36 years. One brother, Trooper Alexander Forbes Hogarth, 11th Australian Light Horse, died of pneumonia on 6 August 1915 aged 27 years and is buried in Cairo War Memorial Cemetery. Another brother, Driver Joseph Hogarth, 26th Australian Infantry, died at No. 1 Australian Auxiliary Hospital of sickness on 9 March 1918 aged 39 years and is buried in Harefield (St. Mary) Churchyard just to the west of London.

UK – 633   Aust – 71   NZ – 59
Can – 4   India – 1   KUG – 1
Unnamed – 6   Area – 4246 sq mts

LOCATION
Becordel is a small village, about 3km east of Albert on the south side of the Albert-Peronne road. Dartmoor Cemetery is on the northern edge of the village.

DAVENESCOURT COMMUNAL CEMETERY

HISTORY
The communal cemetery was used for burials in WW2.

INFORMATION
- Halifax Mk. III, serial LV880, No. 51 Squadron, Bomber Command exploded and crashed at Davenescourt on 11 April 1944 during a raid on Tergnier, France. Four men were killed and are buried here. Flying Officer F. G. Kirkwood, RAAF escaped, Sergeant P. W. Hegarty, RAF and Flight Sergeant M. J. Fairclough, RAAF were taken prisoner.
- Halifax Mk. III, serial HX350, No. 51 Squadron, Bomber Command crashed on 18 April 1944 at Davenescourt during a raid on Tergnier, France. There were no survivors out of the seven crew all of whom are buried here.

WW2 – 11 (UK – 8, Can – 1, Aust – 2)

LOCATION
Davenescourt is a village found 30km south-east of Amiens and 8km north of Montdidier. The Communal Cemetery is south-east of the village on the Marais du Parc at the bottom of a hill. The graves are to the left of the entrance.

DE CUSINE RAVINE BRITISH CEMETERY, BASSEUX

HISTORY
The cemetery was opened in February 1916 and used until March 1917. A further burial took place in September 1917.

INFORMATION
The ravine was called the 'Fosse de Berles', but known to the French troops, who had a field kitchen there, as the 'Ravin des Cuisines'. On the side of the ravine is the British Cemetery bearing a modified form of the French Army name. The cemetery was begun by the 13th King's Royal Rifle Corps. A French Military Cemetery close to it, also named from the ravine, has now been removed.

Two brothers are buried in Row C, graves 6 and 7. They are Privates J and W Critchley, 6th North Staffordshires. Both were killed on 26 September 1916 in a failed raid on the German trenches.

UK – 65   Ger – 3   Area – 615 sq mts

LOCATION
Basseux is a village located about 10km south-west of Arras and 1km south of the Doullens-Arras main road. The cemetery is about 1km south of the village in open fields. A farm road leads from the centre of the village which becomes a track on the northern edge of a small valley. It is best to walk the final part of the journey to the cemetery which you can see in a valley to the east of the track. The track takes a circuitous route to avoid private land, which is only for the very adventurous driver. I recommend the walk.

DELSAUX FARM CEMETERY, BEUGNY

HISTORY

The cemetery was begun by the Germans in March 1918. Further burials, by the British, were made in October and November 1918. A few graves were concentrated here shortly after the war.

INFORMATION

The cemetery was named after the farm here which had been made into an important defensive position by the Germans to which they withdrew in March 1917. The British attacked, and captured, the farm on 19 March 1917. The Germans recaptured the farm, and village, on 23 March 1918 at the start of their offensive. The 5th Division took Beugny on 2-3 September 1918.

The Germans began Beugny Military Cemetery No. 18 at the crossroads near Beugny in March 1918. They buried 103 British and 82 German dead here. The 29th and 46th Casualty Clearing Stations extended the cemetery in the last weeks of the war when they were stationed at the farm. At this time the cemetery gained its present name. Shortly after the war the German graves were removed and twelve British graves were concentrated here.

Among those buried here is Serjeant Miles John Sterry, DCM, MM & Bar, 7th Queen's Own (Royal West Kents), died of wounds on 27 October 1918. He was originally with the Gloucestershires. The citation for his Distinguished Conduct Medal reads 'During the operations on 23rd October 1918, east of Le Cateau, he displayed conspicuous gallantry in the attack, and handled his platoon with marked leadership. His coolness under heavy machinegun fire was most encouraging to the men, and when the objective was reached he went forward and cleared the ground of enemy snipers. He again showed conspicuous gallantry in a subsequent attack east of Bousies, and although wounded he continued to lead his platoon until the objective was reached and the line organised.' It, and his two Military Medals, were awarded posthumously.

UK – 482 NZ – 6 Can – 3
Aust – 2 BWI – 2 Unnamed – 61
Area – 1844 sq mts

Special Memorials erected to 32 British soldiers whose graves cannot now be located but who are known to be buried here.

LOCATION

Beugny is a village on the main Bapaume-Cambrai road about 5km north-east of Bapaume. The cemetery is about 1km south of the village at the crossroads of the Beugny-Haplincourt and Fremicourt-Lebuquiere roads. The farm is just to the north of the cemetery.

DELVILLE WOOD CEMETERY, LONGUEVAL

HISTORY

The cemetery was made after the war as a concentration cemetery for bodies buried in small cemeteries and isolated positions on the battlefields.

INFORMATION

Longueval was behind the German lines until July 1916. It stands on the eastern end of the ridge to which it gives its name. Across the fields to the south you can see a sugar beet factory. This is the location of what was known as Waterlot Farm, though never a real farm.

The village was mostly captured by the 9th Division on 14 July 1916 but the northern end, including the Wood and Waterlot Farm were still in German hands. Waterlot Farm was taken by a section of the South African Brigade and 5th Cameron Highlanders on 15 July. The South African Brigade captured most of Delville Wood on 15 July but was pushed back three days later. Despite heavy casualties, almost completely destroying the battalions involved, they managed to hold the wood until relieved by the 2nd Division on 20 July. This was the first significant action for the South African Brigade attached to the 9th (Scottish) Division. The Brigade went into action with 3153 men and left the wood with 778, though only 143 men departed unaided. Many men had been buried alive by shelling.

The wood was not cleared of Germans until the 14th Division completed the task on 29 August. It, and the village of Longueval, fell to the Germans again in April 1918 and was recaptured by the 38th Division on 28 August 1918.

Due to the bitter fighting the wood gained the name the 'Devil's Wood'. It was purchased by South Africa in 1920. The avenues in the park have stone markers recording the names of London, Edinburgh and Glasgow streets given to the avenues by the 9th Division in 1916. The wood outside of the paths has not been cleared of ordnance and straying from the avenues/paths is dangerous.

The cemetery is the third largest on the Somme. It includes the bodies of three unidentified men found in the wood during the building of the museum. Of the identified burials most fell between late July and September 1916. The cemetery represents many units that fought in this area. The South Africans buried here were all killed in the Wood. The graves of fifteen French soldiers have been removed.

Among those buried here is Sergeant Albert Gill, VC, 1st Kings Royal Rifle Corps, killed in action on 27 July 1916 in Delville Wood. His Victoria Cross citation reads 'For most conspicuous bravery. The enemy made a very strong counter-attack on the right flank of the battalion, and rushed the bombing post after killing all the company bombers. Serjeant Gill at once rallied the remnants of his platoon, none of whom were skilled bombers, and reorganised his defences, a most difficult and dangerous task, the trench being very shallow and much damaged. Soon afterwards the enemy nearly surrounded his men by creeping up through the thick undergrowth, and commenced sniping at about twenty yards' range. Although it was almost certain death, Serjeant Gill stood boldly up in order to direct the fire of his men. He was killed almost at once, but not before he had shown his men where the enemy were, and thus enabled them to hold up their advance. By his supreme devotion to duty and self-sacrifice he saved a very dangerous situation.'

Three other VCs were won by men in the Wood in July 1916. Corporal (later Staff Sergeant) Joseph John Davies, 10th Royal Welsh Fusiliers, VC, Order of St. George 1st Class (Russia) won his on 20 July 1916 when he and others were surrounded by a German attack. He halted the attack and led a counter-attack which pushed the Germans back. He survived the war.

From the same battalion and in the same attack on what is now Buchanan Street, which cost their unit 228 men, Private Albert Hill, VC, charged the enemy under heavy fire. Although cut off he again charged killing or wounding over twenty Germans. He went out again under fire to rescue men, but also brought in German prisoners.

Private (later Captain) William Frederick Faulds, VC, MC, 1st South African Infantry, was awarded his VC for actions on 18 and 20 July 1916 when rescuing men from no-man's land under fire. He served in WW2 and died in Rhodesia in 1950. He was the first South African serviceman to win the VC.

Buried here is Private James Rathband, 'C' Company, 9th Royal Dublin Fusiliers, who was killed in action on 9 September 1916 aged 16 years, one of 66 men of his battalion who fell in the attack on Ginchy. Another 16 year old buried here is Private James Walters, 9th Sherwood Foresters (Notts and Derby Regiment), killed on 9 August 1916. He had already seen service in Gallipoli and his mother was processing the papers for his discharge when he was killed.

Also here is Private Claude Newberry, 3rd South African Infantry, killed in action on 1 August 1916. He was a cricketer who had represented South Africa in four tests – all against England.

North of the village on the road to Flers is the New Zealand Memorial commemorating the part played by the New Zealand Division in 1916. Nearby is a memorial to the Footballers battalions. In the centre of the village is the Pipers Memorial.

THE SOUTH AFRICAN NATIONAL MEMORIAL

On 10 October 1926 the widow of General Louis Botha unveiled the national memorial to over 10000 South Africans killed in the war. South Africa provided 229,000 troops in the war. It has since become a memorial to all South African servicemen. It is not a memorial to the missing, and the memorial bears no names as 'missing'

South Africans are commemorated on the same memorials as British 'missing'.

It records actions such as the capture of German South West Africa in the first six months of the war; the capture of German East Africa; and the acts of the South African Brigade in France and Flanders, notably here at Delville Wood. At Arras and Passendale in April and September 1917 the Brigade made significant gains. In March 1918 the Brigade held up the German advance at Gauche Wood and performed a similar task at Kemmel in April. In October 1918 they forced the Germans from well-defended positions at Le Cateau and on 11 November 1918 the South Africans were furthest east of all Empire troops.

In 1987 the South African government completed a National Military Museum behind the memorial. The names of those who died on service are in the book of remembrance in the museum.

Concentrated here:

Angle Wood Cemetery, Ginchy - situated about 4km south-east of here in a small wood north-west of Maurepas. It contained 27 British soldiers buried in a shell-hole, mainly of the London Regiment, who were killed in August and September 1916.

Battery Copse Cemetery, Curlu - situated 5km south of here in a small copse between Curlu and Maurepas. It was called by the French 'Bois-Vieux No. 2 Mixed Cemetery'. It contained seventeen British graves among the French burials.

Bazentin-Le-Petit German Cemetery - situated 5km west of here at the south-east end of the village. It contained the graves of 2178 Germans, one French soldier and five British men who were killed in March and April 1918.

Courcelette Communal Cemetery German Extension - this contained the graves of three British soldiers and one from Canada among the 1040 German graves.

Ferme-Rouge French Military Cemetery, Curlu - situated close to Battery Copse Cemetery. It was called by the French 'Bois-Vieux 'B' Cemetery'. It contained a British soldier killed in March 1917 among the 138 French graves.

Guillemont German Cemetery No. 1 - situated 400m south-east of here at the west end of the village. It contained seven British graves of men who died in May and July 1918 among the 221 German graves.

Lone Ridge Cemetery, Longueval - situated 100m towards the centre of the village from here. It contained the graves of 52 British soldiers, men of the 38th Division and 6th Dragoon Guards, who were killed at the end of August 1918.

Maricourt (De La Cote) German Cemetery - situated 6km south of here on the south-west side of the village. It contained the graves of five British men among the Germans.

Martinpuich German Cemetery No. 1 - situated 5km north-west of here at the north-east end of the village. It contained the graves of seven British men, who were killed in March 1918, among the German graves.

Martinpuich German Cemetery No. 2 - situated 400m west of the No. 1 cemetery. It contained the grave of one British soldier.

UK – 5242	SAfr – 152	Aust – 81
Can – 29	NZ – 19	KUG – 3
Unnamed – 3587		Area – 14967 sq mts

Special Memorials erected to 26 British soldiers and one South African known, or believed, to be buried among the unnamed graves.

Special Memorials erected to three British soldiers buried in Courcelette Communal Cemetery German Extension whose graves could not be identified at the time of concentration.

LOCATION
Longueval is situated 10km north-east of Albert and a similar distance south of Bapaume. This cemetery is on the eastern edge of the village on the south side of the road to Ginchy. It is opposite Delville Wood and the South African Memorial and Museum. It is best to park at the visitor centre and walk to the cemetery and memorial.

DEMUIN BRITISH CEMETERY

HISTORY
The cemetery was made in August 1918 after the fighting to capture the area here during the final Allied advance to victory.

INFORMATION
Demuin was behind Allied lines for most of the war. However, it fell to the Germans on 30 March 1918, before brief recapture, and again on 31 March 1918. The 58th Canadian Infantry took the village on 8 August 1918.

The cemetery is on the battlefield over which the Canadians attacked on 8 August 1918 – the graves here reflect that attack including men of the 16th Canadian Infantry.

Among those buried here is Corporal George Hemstock, DCM, 16th Canadian Infantry, killed in action on 8 August 1918 at Aubercourt near Amiens. He was a farmer who enlisted in December 1915. He received his Distinguished Conduct Medal for taking control of his platoon when senior men were wounded or killed in a heavy bombardment. He encouraged and organised his men under fire.

UK – 2	Can – 40
Unnamed – 1	Area – 213 sq mts

LOCATION
Demuin is a small village on the north side of the main Amiens-Roye road about 15km south-east of Amiens. The British Cemetery is north of the village at a road junction on the west side of the road to Villers-Bretonneux as the road climbs the hill out of the village.

DERNANCOURT COMMUNAL CEMETERY

HISTORY
The Communal Cemetery was first used by the British for burials in September 1915 and remained in use until August 1916. It was used again in March 1918.

INFORMATION
Dernancourt was an important village in the rear during the Battle of the Somme in 1916. It had a pre-war main railway from which narrow gauge railways moved equipment and men to the front and back. It was a logical location for medical units who could evacuate men to the rear. The Communal Cemetery was used by Field Ambulances located near the village from the time that the British arrived. When the XV Corps Main Dressing Station was formed at Dernancourt in August 1916 the Extension was opened to take burials. Even so, when the need arose in March 1918, further burials were made in the Communal Cemetery.

Buried here is Lieutenant Colonel Bertrand Gorges Reginald Gordon, DSO, MiD commanding 2nd Gordon Highlanders. He had served in the Boer War and Africa with other regiments before joining the Highlanders. He was killed leading his men in an attack at High Wood on 20 July 1916. Having made good progress under a creeping barrage the Germans countered from the wood once the barrage ended catching the Gordons from the rear. The battalion withdrew to their start point having no success but taking many casualties. He received his Distinguished Service Order in the 1916 Birthday Honours List.

Buried in the British plot here is Mabel Jane Mills of Gloucester. She died in Dernancourt on 27 August 1943 while the village was under German occupation in WW2.

Nearby on the road to Buire is a memorial to Lieutenant Jacques Garnier and Sergeant Sagnes of 5th GRDI who were killed at Buire on 20 May 1940.

UK – 124   Aust – 3   Ger – 1   Fr - 133

LOCATION
Dernancourt is about 2km south of Albert in the valley of the Ancre. It can be reached easily from Albert and the road to Amiens from which it is well signed. The Communal Cemetery is on the western edge of the village near the railway. The graves in the Communal Cemetery are to the north side of the cemetery.

DERNANCOURT COMMUNAL CEMETERY EXTENSION

HISTORY
The Extension was opened in August 1916 during the Battles of the Somme and remained in use until 26 March 1918 when the Germans captured the village. The cemetery was used again in September 1918 when the village had been recaptured. It was enlarged after the war by the concentration of graves from small cemeteries and isolated positions in the surrounding battlefields.

INFORMATION
The 45th and 1/1st (South Midland) Casualty Clearing Stations arrived in September 1916 and remained until March 1917. They were followed by the 3rd Australian CCS in March and April 1917 and the 56th CCS from April 1917 to February 1918. The village was captured by the Germans on 26 March 1918, when the 3rd CCS was stationed here, but was retaken by the United States 33rd and British 12th Divisions on 9 August 1918. The 47th, 48th and 55th CCS's were then located here when the medical unit was given the name 'Edgehill'.

At the end of the war the Extension contained 1700 graves in Plots I to V. After the war 410 graves were concentrated into Plots VI to X. One official of the YMCA is buried here. Sergeant Thomas James Harris, VC, MM, 6th Queen's Own (Royal West Kents), killed in action on 9 August 1918 aged 26 years at Morlancourt in the act for which he was awarded his Victoria Cross is buried here. His citation reads 'For most conspicuous bravery and devotion to duty in attack when the advance was much impeded by hostile machine guns concealed in crops and shell-holes. Serjt. Harris led his section against one of these, capturing it and killing seven of the enemy. Later, on two successive occasions, he attacked single-handed two enemy machine-guns which were causing heavy casualties and holding up the advance. He captured the first gun and killed the crew, but was himself killed when attacking the second one. It was largely due to the great courage and initiative of this gallant N.C.O. that the advance of the battalion was continued without delay and undue casualties. Throughout the operations he showed a total disregard for his own personal safety, and set a magnificent example to all ranks.'

Also buried here is Driver G. S. Copland, 404th Field Company, Royal Engineers, died of wounds on 22 March 1918, aged 24 years. He was the eldest of three brothers who died in the war. The other brothers were Corporal C. Copland, 401st Field Company, Royal Engineers, died on 8 September 1917, aged 22 years and buried at Mendinghem Military Cemetery, Poperinge, Belgium; and Private W. S. Copland, 1/6th Black Watch (Royal Highlanders), died on 2 November 1918 aged 19 years and buried at Abbeville Communal Cemetery Extension.

Private William Lawrie, 11th Argyll & Sutherland Highlanders died of wounds on 12 October 1916, aged 23 years was the eldest of three brothers, all of whom died in the war. The other brothers were Lance Corporal Alexander Lawrie, 9th Black Watch (Royal Highlanders) who died on 31 July 1917 aged 20 and is commemorated on the Menin Gate Memorial; and Signalman John Gibb Lawrie, HM Trawler Dhoon, RNVR died on 24 November 1916, aged 21 years and who is commemorated on the Portsmouth Naval Memorial. HM Trawler "Dhoon" was lost on 24 November 1916 when it hit a mine whilst on patrol in the English Channel off the coast of Yarmouth, Isle of Wight.

Also here is a member of one of the families to lose five sons. Private Robert Smith, 1/6th Durham Light Infantry was killed on 19 September 1916 aged 22 years. Corporal George Henry Smith, 1/6th Durham Light Infantry was killed on 5 November 1916 aged 26 years and is commemorated on the Thiepval Memorial. A third brother, Private Frederick Smith, 20th Durham Light Infantry, was killed on 31 July 1917 aged 20 years and is commemorated on the Menin Gate Memorial at Ieper. Another brother, Private Alfred Smith, 1/9th Durham Light Infantry, died of wounds on 22 July 1918 aged 30 years and is buried in Terlincthun British Cemetery. The last sibling, a half brother John William Stout, 1/5th West Yorkshires, was killed in action on 9 October 1917 and is commemorated on the Tyne Cot Memorial near Ieper.

Another here is 2nd Lieutenant Frank Reginald Wilson, 1st Auckland Regiment, NZEF, killed on 19 September 1916 aged 31 years. An all-round sportsman he had represented his country at Rugby Union in 1910 but was injured and only played once for New Zealand.

Concentrated here:

Albert Road Cemetery, Buire-Sur-Ancre - this was on the main road from Albert to Amiens near the present section of dual carriageway just west of Buire. Created by Australian units and the British 58th and 12th Divisions, it contained the graves of 65 British and 33 Australian soldiers who died from April to August 1918.

Moor Cemetery, Edgehill, Dernancourt - about 1km west of this Extension near the top of the hill. It contained the graves of 42 British soldiers who were killed in defending this area from 23-25 March 1918.

UK – 1639   Aust – 425   NZ – 51
SAfr – 33   Can – 8   India – 6
Chinese – 3   BWI – 1   KUG – 112
Ger – 2   Unnamed – 177

Area - 5705 sq mts

Special Memorials to 29 officers and men known, or believed, to be buried among the unidentified graves.

Special Memorials to two Australians buried in Albert Road Cemetery whose graves were destroyed in later fighting.

LOCATION
The Communal Cemetery is on the western edge of the village near the railway and the Extension is next to it on the north-west side.

DEVONSHIRE CEMETERY, MAMETZ

HISTORY
The cemetery was created on 4 July 1916 for the burial of men who died on 1 July. It was immediately closed except for the burial of two men who died later in 1916.

INFORMATION
Mametz, and Mametz Wood to the north-east of the village, were an early objective of 1 July 1916. The village was captured by the 7th Division at the start of the battle but the wood was not taken until the middle of the month. The village marked the geographical beginning of British successes on 1 July. To the east the Germans were pushed back while to the west British victories were limited, or non-existant, and expensive.

The cemetery was made by men of the 8th and 9th Devonshires who buried their comrades in the trench from which they had attacked the village of Mametz on 1 July 1916. It is next to a small wood known as 'Mansel Copse'. This may have been named after 2nd Lieutenant Spenser Lort Mansel, 8th attached 9th Devonshires, wounded here on 24 February 1916 and buried in Corbie Communal Cemetery. The cemetery was subsequently given its name due to the composition of the regiments from which the men buried here came.

Of the men who lie here four officers and 34 men came from the 8th Devonshires while six officers and 116 men were from the 9th Devonshires. The two later burials were a Sergeant and Driver of B/92nd Brigade, Royal Field Artillery. There is now a stone at the entrance that says 'The Devonshires held this trench, the Devonshires hold it still.'

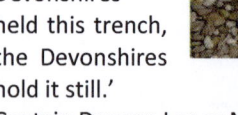

Captain Duncan Lenox Martin, 9th Devonshires, killed on 1 July 1916 is here. Before the attack he built a model of the battlefield in this area made of plasticine. He forecast that a German machine gun positioned at 'The Shrine', a crucifix in Mametz village cemetery, would cause heavy casualties on the right flank of the attack. He was proved correct even though the 8th and 9th Devonshires took their objectives. Also buried here is Lieutenant William Noel Hodgson, MC, 9th Devonshires who was killed on 1 July 1916. He was a war poet whose last poem, written near the trench in which he lies, prophetically contained the line 'Help me to die, O Lord'.

The 7th Division have erected a memorial nearby to commemorate their success here in 1916. The 14th and

16th Royal Welsh Fusiliers made memorials in the Wood as they were involved in its capture in 1916 but they have since been removed.

UK – 153   Unnamed – 10   Area - 558 sq mts

LOCATION
Mametz lies about 6km east of Albert just to the north of the Albert-Peronne road. The cemetery lies south of the village, within a small copse, on a hillside to the south of the Albert-Peronne road. There is now a small parking area off the road for cars and coaches. There are steps up to the cemetery.

DIVE COPSE BRITISH CEMETERY, SAILLY-LE-SEC

HISTORY
The cemetery was opened in June 1916 in preparation for the Battles of the Somme. Most of the burials were made during the first three months of the battles. The cemetery was used again during the offensive in August 1918. The final burials were made after the war when over 100 bodies were concentrated here from surrounding battlefields and smaller cemeteries.

INFORMATION
In June 1916 several Field Ambulances were posted to the area north of the cemetery. These became known as the XIV Corps Main Dressing Station. It was this Dressing Station that began the burials in the cemetery. Dive Copse was named after the Officer commanding the Dressing Station.

Plots I and II were made during the Battles in 1916. Plot III was begun during the fighting of August 1918 when 77 men were buried here. It was completed after the war with the concentration of 115 bodies.

The grave of 2nd Lieutenant George Helliwell Harding, No. 79 Squadron, Royal Flying Corps from Minneapolis, USA was added on 27 March 1918 at the back of Plot I. He was killed while flying a Sopwith Dolphin over German infantry during the German 1918 offensive.

Also here is Lieutenant Colonel William Digby Oswald, DSO, MiD, 5th Dragoon Guards (Princess Charlotte of Wales's) and commanding 12th West Yorkshires. He had served in South Africa with Kitchener and had returned to Britain in April 1914. On the outbreak of war he joined the Dragoons serving at Mons before being wounded near Ieper on 31 October 1914. He served with the artillery and General Staff through 1915 before joining the 12th West Yorkshires in December 1915 as second in command becoming commander in March 1916. On the 14 July 1916 the battalion was given orders to attack German positions on the following day at Caterpillar Valley on the ridge between Bazentin-le-Petit and Longueval. At 3.25am on 15 July the artillery barrage lifted from the German first line onto their second line and the West Yorkshires left their trenches, advancing briskly towards the enemy lines. At 4.30am Oswald sent a message back to Brigade HQ that his battalion had taken all its objectives in the German first line and had seized part of the second line as well. He reported that casualties had been heavy and that he needed reinforcements. At about 7.00pm Oswald, who had returned to Battalion HQ to rest, was hit in the chest by a shell band following a misfire from a British gun. He had earlier noted that the same gun was wrongly sighted and had issued orders that it should be corrected. Despite his injuries he appeared to be recovering but died of his wounds on the morning of the 16 July.

Concentrated here:

Essex Cemetery, Sailly-Le-Sec - situated 1km north of this cemetery on the edge of the Bray-Corbie road. Begun by the 10th Essex in August 1918, it contained the graves of 30 British soldiers and three Australians.

UK – 512   Aust – 59   SAfr – 18
KUG – 10   Unnamed – 20
Area – 2384 sq mts

Special Memorials to four men of the London Regiment and six Australians who are known to be buried among the unnamed graves.

LOCATION
Sailly-le-Sec lies on the north bank of the Somme about 20km east of Amiens. The cemetery is north of the village. It is in open ground with excellent views on a ridge north of the river.

DOINGT COMMUNAL CEMETERY EXTENSION

HISTORY
The cemetery was only used during September and October 1918 following the capture of the area.

INFORMATION
Doingt was captured by the 5th Australian Division on 5 September 1918, though the village was almost completely destroyed. The 20th, 41st and 55th Casualty Clearing

Stations soon arrived and began the cemetery. They made burials here until October when they left and the cemetery was closed. The cemetery had three distinct sections. Plot I contained graves of British and Empire troops. Plot II contained American troops and Plot III was mixed. The 115 American graves have since been removed. The two WW2 burials date from the retreat of 1940.

Among those here is Company Serjeant Major Ethan Edwin James, DCM, 25th Royal Welsh Fusiliers, killed in action on 19 September 1918 aged 36 years. Married and from Swansea, he was awarded the Distinguished Conduct Medal for attacking a German machine-gun on his own capturing it and its crew. Then, during the withdrawal, he organised covering positions to enable the wounded to be withdrawn safely.

UK – 342	Aust – 67	SAfr – 5
Can – 2	KUG – 1	WW2 – 2
Unnamed – 1		Area – 1613 sq mts

LOCATION
Doingt lies on the River Cologne on the south-eastern edge of Peronne. The Communal Cemetery is on the north-eastern side of the village and the Extension is to the north-east of the Communal Cemetery. A path leads around the Communal Cemetery to the Extension.

DOMINION CEMETERY

HISTORY
The cemetery was made by Canadian units in September 1918.

INFORMATION
The village of Hendecourt-Les-Cagnicourt was captured by the 57th (West Lancashire) and 52nd (Lowland) Divisions on the night of the 1-2 September 1918 during the Battle of the Drocourt-Quéant Line. The cemetery was made soon after by Canadian troops also involved in the battle. The grave of one Canadian airman was brought in after the war from an isolated position.

Acting Sergeant Arthur George Knight, VC, Croix de Guerre (France), 10th (Alberta Regiment) Canadian Infantry, is buried here. He was awarded the Victoria Cross for his actions on 2 September 1918 but died of his wounds the following day. His citation reads 'For most conspicuous bravery, initiative, and devotion to duty when, after an unsuccessful attack, Serjt. Knight led a bombing section forward, under very heavy fire of all descriptions, and engaged the enemy at close quarters. Seeing that his party continued to be held up, he dashed forward alone, bayoneting several of the enemy machine-gunners and trench-mortar crews, and forcing the remainder to retire in confusion. He then brought forward a Lewis gun and directed his fire on the retreating enemy, inflicting many casualties. In the subsequent advance of his platoon in pursuit, Serjt. Knight saw a party of about thirty of the enemy go into a deep tunnel which led off the trench. He again dashed forward alone, and, having killed one officer and two NCO's, captured twenty other ranks. Subsequently he routed, single-handed, another enemy party which was opposing the advance of his platoon. On each occasion he displayed the greatest valour under fire at very close range, and by his example of courage, gallantry and initiative was a wonderful inspiration to all. This very gallant NCO was subsequently fatally wounded.'

Buried here is Lieutenant Alex Campbell-Johnston, 16th Canadian Infantry, killed in action on 2 September 1918 aged 18 years, he had enlisted as a Private aged 16 years. His brother, Private Ronald Alfred Campbell-Johnston, 7th Canadian Infantry was killed on 3 September 1918 aged 29 years and is also buried here.

| UK – 17 | Can – 214 | Unnamed – 5 |

Special Memorial to a Canadian soldier believed to be buried among the unnamed.

LOCATION
Hendecourt-Les-Cagnicourt is a village about 15km south-east of Arras and 4km south of the Arras-Cambrai main road. The village is on the Bapaume-Douai road. The cemetery lies in open fields on the low rolling ridges in this area. It is about 1km north east of the road between Hendecourt-les-Cagnicourt and Cagnicourt. These are areas of mainly farm tracks though accessible. The cemetery lies 50m from the nearest track and is finally reached by a CWGC path.

DOMINO BRITISH CEMETERY

HISTORY
The cemetery was in use in October 1918 and for one concentrated burial after the war.

INFORMATION
The area was in German hands for most of the war. It was captured at the beginning of April 1917, lost on the 22 March 1918 and finally retaken, in the Battle of Epéhy, on the 18 September 1918 by the 12th (Eastern) Division.

The cemetery was made by the 33rd Division and named after the divisional sign.

Among those here is Lieutenant William Wood McLean, MC, 2nd Argyll and Sutherland Highlanders, killed in action on 23 September 1918. He was a former student of Glasgow University. On the day he died the battalion attacked the Hindenburg line at 9.30am. They were soon counter-attacked in force. They held out until 5.00pm when they ran out of ammunition and were forced to retire.

A Memorial has been erected to commemorate the 1/4th Loyal North Lancashires about 450m north-east of the cemetery at Vaucelette Farm.

UK – 51   Unnamed – 5   Area – 255 sq mts

LOCATION
Epehy is between Cambrai and Péronne, 15km and 20km from each. It is about 3km west of the A26 Autoroute. The cemetery is 2km north of the village near the road to Villers-Guislain, 70m east of the small road between Epéhy and Gouzeaucourt. It is close to the old railway line and accessible on farm tracks, small roads and finally by a CWGC path.

DOUCHY-LES-AYETTE BRITISH CEMETERY

HISTORY
The British Cemetery was begun in August and September 1918. It was enlarged after the war by the concentration of graves from the battlefields of Arras and the Ancre and from other burial grounds.

INFORMATION
The village was in German hands for most of the war. It fell to the British on 21 March 1917 during the German withdrawal to the Hindenburg Line. In March 1918, the Germans advanced as far as the Communal Cemetery, and held it for a few days until the British pushed them back in early April.

This cemetery was begun by the 3rd Division. The original burials are scattered among eight rows in what are now Plots II and IV. The Germans made a cemetery while they were here which had 380 graves. They have been removed. Corporal Thomas Woodcock, VC, 2nd Irish Guards, died on 27 March 1918 at Bullecourt aged 29 years is buried here.

He won his Victoria Cross on 12-13 September 1917 north of Broenbeek, Belgium 'For most conspicuous bravery and determination. He was one of a post commanded by Lce. Serjt. Moyney, which was surrounded. The post held out for 96 hours, but after that time was attacked from all sides in overwhelming numbers and was forced to retire. Pte. Woodcock covered the retirement with a Lewis gun, and only retired when the enemy had moved round and up to his post and were only a few yards away. He then crossed the river, but hearing cries for help behind him, returned and waded into the stream amid a shower of bombs from the enemy and rescued another member of the party. The latter he then carried across the open ground in broad daylight towards our front line regardless of machine gun fire that was opened on him.'

Also buried here is Captain Arthur Gerald Knight, DSO, MC, No. 29 Squadron, Royal Flying Corps, a British-born Canadian World War I 'ace' credited with eight victories. One claim was the German ace, Oswald Boelcke, who had 40 victories to his name. Knight's first success was with No. 24 Squadron on 22 June 1916. He gained the Military Cross in November 1916 and the Distinguished Service Order in December a week before he was shot down by Baron von Richthoffen on 20 December 1916 aged 21 years. The citation for his MC reads 'For conspicuous skill and gallantry. He has shown great pluck in fights with enemy machines, and has accounted for several. On one occasion, when a hostile machine was interfering with a reconnaissance, he attacked at very close range, and brought down the enemy machine in flames.' The citation for his DSO reads 'For conspicuous gallantry in action. He led four machines against 18 hostile machines. Choosing a good moment for attack he drove down five of them and dispersed the remainder. He has shown the utmost dash and judgment as a leader of offensive patrols.'

Concentrated here:

Brasserie Military Cemetery, Le Fermont, Riviere - on the Bretencourt-Wailly Road about 5km north of here. It was begun by French troops and contained the graves of ten British soldiers who died in April 1916, and one who died in January 1918.

Favreuil German Cemetery - at the north-east corner of the village about 7km south-east of here. It contained the graves of four British soldiers and one Canadian buried by the Germans in 1916 among their 389 German soldiers.

Fremicourt Communal Cemetery – located about 8km south-east of here in which 20 German soldiers and two Royal Flying Corps officers, who died in 1916 in a German hospital in the Church, were buried.

Gastineau Farm French Military Cemetery, Ransart - on the Bellacourt-Berles road about 5km north-west of here. It contained one British soldier who was buried in February 1916.

Gomiecourt German Cemetery - a little west of the village and about 3km south-east of here, in which 126 German and 27 British soldiers were buried in 1916-18.

Grosville Churchyard, Riviere – located about 5km north of here, in which two men of the 1/10th (Liverpool Scottish) King's (Liverpools) were buried in February 1916.

L'Alouette French Military Cemetery, Ransart - on the Bellacourt-Berles road about 5km north-west of here. It contained ten British soldiers who were buried in 1916.

Morchies Communal Cemetery German Extension – located about 10km east of here. Among the graves of 400 German soldiers were five Australians and one British soldier who died in 1916-17.

Moyenneville German Cemetery - in the south-west part of the village about 2km east of here. It contained eleven British men who were buried by the Germans in 1916-17.

Ransart Churchyard – located about 2km north of here, it contained the grave of one British soldier buried in March 1917.

Ransart MDS Cemetery - located about 2km north of here, twelve British soldiers were buried at the end of August 1918.

Sapignies German Cemetery - in the south-west corner of the village about 5km south-east of here. It contained the graves of 28 British soldiers who died in 1916-18 among 840 German graves.

Wailly Military Cemetery - at the north-east end of the village about 5km north of here. It contained 30 French graves and those of 23 men of the 55th Division who died in 1916.

Willow Road Cemetery, Boiry-Ste. Rictrude – located about 2km north of here and in which 25 British soldiers, largely of the Guards Division, were buried in 1918.

UK – 727 Can – 1 Aust – 5
SAfr – 2 Ger – 1 Unnamed – 242
Area - 2418 sq mts

Special Memorial is erected to an officer of the Lincolnshires believed to be buried among the unnamed.

LOCATION

The village is found about 10km north-west of Bapaume. The cemetery is on the eastern edge of the village on the north side of the road to Ayette. It is opposite the Communal Cemetery.

DOULLENS COMMUNAL CEMETERY EXTENSION No. 1

HISTORY

This Extension, originally called the 'French Extension (No. 1)', was opened by the French in the early part of the war. The British began to make burials here in February 1916 and it was used until April 1918 when the available space had been filled.

INFORMATION

Doullens was an important base for the French early in the war, when it had been Marshal Foch's Headquarters, and then for the British from February 1916 when the Arras Front was taken over by the British. From 1915 to March 1916 it had been a junction between the French Tenth Army and the British Third Army covering the Somme sector.

The Hotel de Ville was the scene of an important meeting on 26 March 1918 between British and French commanders and politicians to cope with the crisis caused by the German offensive. French and British armies were falling back under the German offensive and there was a fear that the two armies might become separated. Hence, the war could be lost without a unified command. Haig said he was willing to place the British Army under French control so the French took over part of the line near Amiens. They also supplied reserves the British did not have. The main result was an Allied Supreme Commander for the first time. The room where the meeting took place has been preserved as the Salle de Conference.

The Citadelle was first used as a French Military Hospital. Beginning in March 1916 the British 41st, 35th and 11th Casualty Clearing Stations had, in turn, been positioned in Doullens and these had made burials in the Extension. At the end of 1916 these had been replaced by the 3rd Canadian Stationary Hospital, which remained until June 1918, and the 2/1st Northumbrian CCS who continued to use the No. 1 Extension until the available space had been filled. The men here mostly died of wounds in the hospitals in the town. Most of the graves date from 1918 and they come from many units.

Buried here is Brigadier General Harry Townsend Fulton, CMG, DSO, commanding 3rd New Zealand (Rifle) Brigade, NZEF. He was an Indian born British Army officer who served with the Indian Army on the Northwest Frontier. He was also seconded to the New Zealand Military Forces during both the Boer War and First World War. Fulton was part of the Samoa Expeditionary Force before coming to the Western Front where he commanded the New Zealand Rifle Brigade during the Somme offensive and the Battle of Messines. He died on 29 March 1918 as a result of wounds received when his headquarters was shelled, and was one of three New Zealand Brigadier-Generals killed during the war.

Also buried here is Lieutenant Colonel Harry Fearnley Kirkpatrick, DSO & Bar, three times MiD, The Buffs (East Kents) attached and commanding Anson Battalion, Royal Naval Division, killed on 27 March 1918. He was awarded the Distinguished Service Order in the New Year's Honours List in January 1918. The Bar was awarded in July 1918 for leadership during the period in which he was killed. He was the second son of the 8th Baronet Kirkpatrick – a man who had played in the FA Cup Final in 1878. His younger brother, 2nd Lieutenant Athol Kirkpatrick, 3rd attached 6th Buffs (East Kents), died on 3 May 1917 and is commemorated on the Arras Memorial.

The cemetery now contains a large Plot of French soldiers and a small group of Germans who died as Prisoners of War. There is also a row of Moroccan and Indian graves.

In May 1940 the town was defended for 2½ hours by 6th Royal West Kents when they were attacked by the 6th Panzer Division and the Luftwaffe. Most of the WW2 burials here date from that defence on 20 May 1940. The WW2 burials are in the rear of the cemetery together.

South-west of the town is a small village called Bagneux which contains a British war cemetery. However, it is just outside the boundaries of this book. Nonetheless, it contains the graves, buried side by side, of three nurses killed in Doullens during a German air raid on 30 May 1918. They are Nursing Sisters D M Y Baldwin, Eden Lyal Pringle and A MacPherson of Canadian Army Nursing Service, 3rd Canadian Stationary Hospital. Also buried there is Brigadier General Lumley Owen Williams Jones, DSO, Chevalier of the Legion of Honour (France) and Officer of the Order of St. Maurice and St. Lazarus (Italy), commanding 13th Brigade, 5th Division late Essex Regiment who died of pneumonia 14 September 1918 aged 41 years. He was the last of twelve generals to die on the Somme.

UK – 1146	NZ – 78	Aust – 69
Can – 36	Newf – 4	SAfr – 3
RGLI – 1	Indian – 2	BWI – 2
UK Civ – 1	Ger – 13	Fr – 479
WW2 – 29	Unnamed - 16	

LOCATION

Doullens lies at the western edge of the area defined by this book as being within the battleground of the Battle of the Somme. It is 28km north of Amiens and a similar distance north-west of Albert. It is 36km south-west of Arras. The Communal Cemetery and the Extensions are on the eastern edge of the town next to the by-pass. About 100m north of the road to the hospital is a small road leading east to the cemetery behind high walls. There is parking by houses at the old and main entrance on the south side of the cemetery. You can identify how the cemetery has grown by studying the layout of the walls. This Extension is on the far side of the cemetery from the town. The British graves are found in two main groups.

DOULLENS COMMUNAL CEMETERY EXTENSION No. 2

HISTORY

This Extension was opened in April 1918 when the No. 1 Extension had been filled and as the Germans launched their 1918 offensive. It remained in use until the end of the war.

INFORMATION

The No. 2 Extension was opened by the Hospital in the Citadelle (see Doullens Communal Cemetery Extension No. 1), as new burial space was needed, on the opposite side of the Communal Cemetery. The cemetery now contains a group of Germans who died as Prisoners of War.

Among those buried here is Major Ralph Noel Vernon Montgomery, DSO, 'D' Battery, 88th Brigade, Royal Field Artillery, who died of pneumonia on 1 April 1919 aged 34 years.

Also buried here is Private Harry Victor Barnard, 17th (Empire) Royal Fusiliers who died on 9 June 1918 aged 19 years. His brother, Private William Barnard, 1st Norfolks, died on 24 August 1914 aged 24 years is commemorated on the La Ferte-Sous-Jouarre Memorial. Another brother, Private George Zachariah Barnard, 1/4th Norfolks, died on 19 April 1917 aged 25 years and is commemorated on the Jerusalem Memorial.

Also here is Major Francis Shuldham Watson, DSO, MC, twice MiD, 276th Siege Battery, Royal Garrison Artillery, died of wounds on 2 May 1918, his 38th birthday. He received his Distinguished Service Order posthumously in July 1918. His brother, Major George Edmund Borlase Watson, DSO, MC, Royal Horse Artillery, commanding 'O' Battery (The Rocket Troop), died on 29 August 1918, aged

33 years and is buried in Frise Communal Cemetery, the only CWGC burial there. He was awarded his Distinguished Service Order in the Birthday Honours List in June 1917 and his Military Cross in the 1916 Birthday Honours List. Another brother, Captain Charles Reginald Watson, 28th Punjabis, Indian Army, was killed in action on 6 April 1918 aged 28 years and is commemorated on the Basra Memorial.

| UK – 321 | NZ – 28 | Can – 24 |
| SAfr – 2 | Aust – 1 | CLC – 1 | Ger - 84 |

LOCATION
See Doullens Communal Cemetery Extension No. 1.

ECLUSIER COMMUNAL CEMETERY

HISTORY
The cemetery was used by the British in February and March 1917.

INFORMATION
The village was taken over from the French by the British in early 1917. The Germans then captured the village in March 1917 having held it for much of the war before it fell to the French in 1916. It fell, finally, to the Allies in summer 1918.

The 23 British graves are mostly men of the 48th Division or artillerymen, killed on 6 February 1917, from an anti-aircraft battery that was stationed here in early 1917. The French used the cemetery for many burials when they were here.

Among those buried here are brothers Gunners Geoffrey and Harry Nutter, 'P' Anti-Aircraft Battery, Royal Field Artillery, both killed in action 6 February 1917 and buried side by side. From Brierley near Burnley, Lancashire, they had enlisted in January 1916 and trained together before being sent to the Front together. Both had been teachers before the war. They were among five members of the Battery killed when a German shell burst close to them while they were loading the gun. Their younger brother Eric, a Driver in the Royal Horse Artillery, died on 3 November 1918 killed by a piece of shrapnel. Another brother, Sergeant James in the Royal Army Medical Corps, won the Military Medal and Bar. His Military Medal was for actions in October 1916 on the Somme while the Bar was won for his actions on 27 August 1918 at Belgian Battery Corner Advanced Dressing Station near Ieper.

UK – 23   French - 126

LOCATION
Eclusier-Vaux is a small settlement between Peronne and Albert in the valley of the River Somme on the south side of the river. It is about 10km west of Peronne. The cemetery is on the west side of the village on the south side of the road to Cappy. Nearby is an ancient church, the 12th Century Eglise St. Nicholas. Private Boon is buried among the French, all other British burials are in one plot on the east side of the cemetery.

ECOUST MILITARY CEMETERY

HISTORY
The cemetery was begun in April 1917 and remained in use by the Allies until March 1918. It was extended after the war by the concentration of burials from the surrounding area.

INFORMATION
The village was behind the German lines for much of the war. It fell to the British 7th Division, and was taken by the 8th and 9th Devonshires, in a blizzard, on 2 April 1917 when several local villages were captured. The Germans retook the village on 21 March 1918. The 3rd Division captured the village for the final time at the end of August 1918.

The village is close to the site of the two battles at Bullecourt in 1917. There are no WW1 cemeteries at Bullecourt so the Australians who fought and died in those battles are buried in cemeteries such as this at Ecoust-St. Mein.

The cemetery lies on the German defensive positions of April 1917. Several German graves were made here though most are unidentified.

The men concentrated here after the war were mostly of the 2/6th North Staffordshires. They are in Plot II, Row B and had previously been buried close to this cemetery. They were almost all killed on 21 March 1918 at the start of the German attack when the battalion was overwhelmed by the Germans. The battalion commanding officer, Lieutenant-Colonel Thomas Bezley Houghton Thorne, was killed and is buried here with his men. The regimental war diary entry says 'Enemy opened an exceptionally heavy barrage on the front [at 5.00am firing 3000 rounds per minute for five hours at the British lines], support and reserve lines, with shells of every calibre. The enemy attacked in large numbers [storm troopers who carried very little except their weapons which included panic-spreading flamethrowers] and broke through on the right flank of the battalion and reached Hogs Back, completely cutting off the battalion.'

The men would have fixed bayonets and engaged in hand to hand fighting trying to drive the Germans back. Once it was clear the position was lost, they tried to fight their way to the reserve trenches in the rear. At this point there were no rules to the fighting. The troops would have used everything at their disposal, entrenching tools, clubs with nails driven through, knuckle dusters, in fact anything was used, and finally, fingers were used to gouge at eyes or rip at throats. Eventually the order came to retreat, though most soldiers were cut off, as the enemy had broken through. The North Staffordshires belonged to the 59th (2nd North Midland) Division who were overrun in the attack suffering more losses than any other Division.

Only one officer, Lieutenant Colonel Thomas Bezley Houghton Thorne, and three other ranks were officially listed as killed in the immediate aftermath. However, another 22 officers and 586 men of other ranks were listed as missing, many as prisoners of war when several died in captivity.

UK – 147   Aust - 9   Ger – 71
Unnamed – 72   Area – 1861 sq mts
Special Memorial to one soldier known to be among the unnamed.

LOCATION
Ecoust-St. Mein is a small village found about 10km north of Bapaume, 15km south-east of Arras and about 2km east of the A1 Autoroute. The cemetery is on the northern edge of the village about 400m north east of the main crossroads in the village. The cemetery lies about 150m from the road with a CWGC path for access. It is on the edge of an old railway embankment, though the light railway from Boisleux to Cambrai is long gone. It is possible to see Ecoust St. Mein British cemetery nearby but there is no direct access.

ECOUST-ST. MEIN BRITISH CEMETERY

HISTORY
The cemetery was begun at the start of September 1918 after the village had been captured from the Germans during the final advance to victory. It was used for only a few days.

INFORMATION
Soon after the final capture of the village the cemetery was opened as an Extension to the German Extension on the edge of the Communal Cemetery. The German Extension has since been removed leaving this British Cemetery rather than a Communal Cemetery Extension. Most of the British burials were men of the 2nd Suffolks or 13th King's (Liverpools). Many of the headstones bear two names.

Among those here is 2nd Lieutenant Frank Hillridge Viner, MC & Bar, 23rd (Tyneside Scottish) Northumberland Fusiliers attached 2/7th King's (Liverpools) killed in action on 12 September 1918. The citation for the Military Cross reads 'For conspicuous gallantry and devotion to duty. During five days fighting, this officer, by his cheerfulness and initiative maintained a fine fighting spirit in his platoon, helping them to hold their section of the line against repeated attacks. When his company commander was wounded, he took command and continued his good work until he was sent to hospital through illness.' And that for his Bar 'He led his platoon forward in an attack with great gallantry under intense machine fire. He brought his men across 400 yards of open ground, and reached his objective, though his platoon was then reduced to ten men. He himself was severely wounded, but remained at his post. It was mainly due to his personal courage and fine example of leadership that he got his men so far in spite of the heavy casualties.'

Also buried here is Serjeant John Pearson Neal, 13th King's (Liverpools), killed in action on 31 August 1918 aged 36 years. The CWGC Register states that he 'Enlisted in the 1st City Battalion (Cotton Contingent) of The King's Liverpool Regt.' This refers to the fact that on the first day of recruitment, St. George's Hall in Liverpool was divided into four sections, one for the Cotton Association, and one each for the corn, sugar and timber trades. So, Neal had been a worker in the cotton industry before enlistment. At some point he was transferred from the 17th (1st Liverpool Pals) Kings (Liverpools) to the 13th battalion.

UK – 145   Can – 6   Unnamed – 7
Area – 377 sq mts

LOCATION
This cemetery is about 1km north-west of the village on the north side of the road to Croisilles and close to the Communal Cemetery. It is possible to see Ecoust Military Cemetery from here but there is no direct access. The cemetery is a few yards from the road at the end of a short CWGC grass path.

ENGLEBELMER COMMUNAL CEMETERY

INFORMATION
The village was in Allied hands during the whole of the war. It was used as a Field Ambulance station but was sometimes within range of shelling by the Germans. The French graves buried here were made in 1914 and 1915 before the British took over the sector.

Buried here is Lieutenant Lewis Thierry Seymour, 2nd York and Lancasters, killed in action on 13 August 1916 aged 23 years. He was a member of the Oxford University Officers' Training Corps, and joined King Edward's Horse in 1913. When the war began he was commissioned in the York & Lancasters and trained men for France until he went himself in 1916. He was killed in trenches at Beaumont Hamel when a trench mortar hit his section.

UK – 50   NZ – 1   Fr – 6   KUG - 1

LOCATION
Englebelmer is found about 7km north-west of Albert. The cemetery is on the south-west edge of the village on the road to Bouzincourt and Forceville. The graves in the Communal Cemetery are in two plots by the entrance.

HISTORY
The cemetery was used by the British from June to September 1916 and April to May 1918.

ENGLEBELMER COMMUNAL CEMETERY EXTENSION

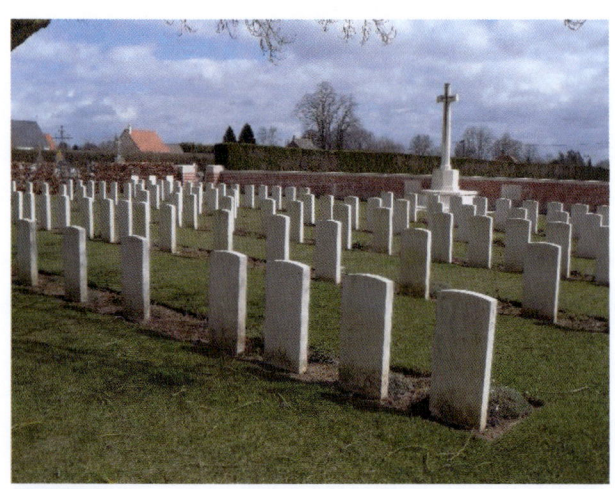

Among those here is Private James Cassidy, 1st Royal Inniskilling Fusiliers. He was executed for desertion on 23 July 1916 aged 39 years. Private Cassidy had enlisted in 1914, served at Gallipoli where he was wounded twice, and had a poor disciplinary record. He had returned from a period of punishment on 23 June and deserted on 24 June when he told another man he was going for food. On 1 July 1916 his battalion was attacking the German line in front of Beaumont-Hamel south of 'Y' Ravine where the losses were enormous. The battalion lost its commanding officer, Lieutenant Colonel Robert Campbell Pierce buried at Ancre British Cemetery, three other officers killed, eleven wounded and four missing. The battalion suffered 568 casualties, more than half of its strength. Cassidy was found by the French walking by a canal at Flexicourt on 30 June and executed 3 weeks later.

Five German graves were removed in 1923.

Concentrated here:

Beaussart Communal Cemetery Extension - in Mailly-Maillet. It was used from April 1916 to May 1918 and contained the graves of eighteen British soldiers and nine from New Zealand.

UK – 123   NZ – 27   Unnamed – 1
KUG – 1   Area – 714 sq mts

Special Memorials to two British men, buried at Beaussart, whose graves could not be found.

HISTORY
The cemetery was used by the British from October 1916 to March 1917. It came into use again in 1918. After the war 49 graves were concentrated here from small battlefield burial grounds and isolated locations to the north and east of this cemetery.

INFORMATION
See the Communal Cemetery.

One burial was made in 1919, Private Frederick Wookey who had served with 13th Devonshires but had transferred to No. 3 Area, Directorate of Graves Registration and Enquiries (D.G.R. and E.), Labour Corps. He died on 8 July while conducting the work of recording, identifying where possible, and caring for the fallen.

LOCATION
The Extension is at the south-west corner of the Communal Cemetery further from the road. Access is through the Communal Cemetery.

ENNEMAIN COMMUNAL CEMETERY EXTENSION

HISTORY
The Extension is a concentration cemetery made entirely in 1918 and 1919.

INFORMATION
The Extension was created by the concentration of graves from the battlefields west and east of Ennemain. Most of the dead were killed in this area during the German retreat to the Hindenburg Line in March 1917 and during the final advance to victory in September 1918.

Of the British soldiers buried here seventeen were men of the 1st Sherwood Foresters who were fighting here in March 1918. Some graves date to 15 April 1918 so the men died as Prisoners of War or they died of wounds in German hospitals.

Among those here is Private James Giffin (spelt on CWGC website as 'Griffin'), 15th Highland Light Infantry, killed in action on 30 August 1918 aged 24 years. The CWGC website shows him has being awarded the Military Cross which would be highly unusual for a soldier who was not an officer or Warrant Officer. However, the hard copy register does not show an MC so I think the transcription onto the website is an error in the same way that his named is incorrect on the website. He is an enigma.

UK – 72   Aust – 4   Can – 1
Unnamed – 40   Area – 451 sq mts

Special Memorials to one British and one Australian soldier who are known, or believed, to be buried among the unidentified graves.

LOCATION
Ennemain can be found about 10km south of Peronne on the south bank of the River Omignon about 3km east of the River Somme. The Communal Cemetery is to the east of the village on the south side of the road to Fourques. The Extension is on the south side of the Communal Cemetery. It is a pretty cemetery in open fields.

EPEHY WOOD FARM CEMETERY, EPEHY

HISTORY
The cemetery was begun in September 1918 after the capture of the village. It was enlarged after the war by the concentration of graves from smaller cemeteries and isolated positions on the surrounding battlefields.

INFORMATION
The village was behind German lines for most of the war. It fell to the British at the time of the German retreat in April 1917 and then found itself just behind the British front-line. The Germans recaptured the village at the start of their offensive on 21 March 1918 despite strong resistance by the Leicester Brigade of the 21st Division who held the German advance for a day at heavy cost as did the 2nd Royal Munster Fusiliers nearby at Malassise Farm. The village was captured for the last time, in the Battle of Epehy, on 18 September 1918 by the 7th Norfolks, 9th Essex and 1/1st Cambridgeshires of the 12th Division.

This cemetery was named after the nearby Ferme du Bois (Wood Farm) which was a little to the east of this position. Plots I and II contain the 404 wartime burials and were made by the 12th Division. Most of the men buried then were killed in the Battle of Epehy though some dated from earlier fighting in April 1917 and March 1918. Over 500 graves in Plots III-VI were made after the war. It is likely that many of the unnamed were men who fought in the area on 21 March 1918.

Buried here is Major Roland Damer Harrisson, DSO, MiD, Royal Field Artillery, died on 10 September 1917 aged 36 years. The original cross placed above his grave is now in St. Peter's Church, Sandwich, Kent, though it shows him as killed in action on 16 September. He joined the Royal Artillery in December 1900 and was promoted to Lieutenant three years later. He became a Captain in 1912 and began the war serving with 26th Divisional Ammunition Column. He was promoted to Major in May 1915 and was awarded the Distinguished Service Order for 'for gallantry at Guillemont from 20 July to 2 August 1916.' Nearby is the Communal Cemetery in the village where a British officer, attached to the Royal Flying Corps, is buried. On the road south-east from Epehy towards St. Quentin about 1km from the village is the 12th Division Memorial. The 12th Division twice fought major combats on the Somme in 1918, but as it captured Epehy in 1918, this was chosen as the location for its Memorial.

Concentrated here:

Deelish Valley Cemetery, Epehy - situated in a valley between the village and Pigeon Ravine Cemetery about 1km east of here. It contained the graves of 158 British soldiers, mostly of the 12th Division, who died in September 1918.

Epehy New British Cemetery - situated on the southern edge of the village near the road to Roisel. Created after the war, it contained the graves of 100 British soldiers who were killed from August 1917 to March 1918 and in September 1918.

Epehy R.E. Cemetery - situated about 150m north of the New British Cemetery on the southern edge of the village. It contained the graves of 31 British soldiers, eleven of the 429th Field Company, Royal Engineers, who were killed between April and December 1917.

UK – 996   Malta – 1   Unnamed – 235
Area – 3841 sq mts

Special Memorials are erected to 29 British soldiers known, or believed, to be buried among the unnamed graves.

Special Memorials are erected to two British soldiers, who were buried in Epehy New British Cemeteries, whose graves could not be located at the time of concentration.

LOCATION

Epehy is situated about 20km north-west of St. Quentin and a similar distance north-east of Peronne. It is now a little to the west of the A26 Autoroute. This cemetery is to the west of the village on the north side of the road to Saulcourt and is well signed from the northern end of the village. It has an interesting entrance building.

EPPEVILLE OLD CHURCHYARD

HISTORY

The cemetery was used in March 1918.

INFORMATION

The identified burials, and presumably the unnamed, are men who were killed in the retreat from the Germans in March 1918. Three are from the 14th Royal Irish Rifles. Some were in German hands when they died.

Buried here is 2nd Lieutenant Ralph Rowlands Galley, 'A' Company, 11th Durham Light Infantry, killed in action on 22 March 1918 aged 27 years. At the start of the war he joined the cavalry and was stationed at the Southern Cavalry Depot with the 14th Regiment of Reserve Cavalry. In June 1915 he was transferred to the 3rd Durham Light Infantry at South Shields, but was moved on to the 10th Battalion in France in August. On 26 September 1915 he was promoted to Lance Corporal, and Corporal in September 1916. In March 1917 he was sent back to England to train as an officer gaining his commission in September and joining this battalion on 9 December. He was reported missing presumed killed on 22 March 1918 in the first days of the German offensive. According to the war diary 'A' and 'B' Companies pushed forward to fill a gap between 60th and 61st Brigades at Tugny-L'Avesne. Captain Endean led 'A' Company holding the Germans until the battalion was ordered to retire through Ham to Offoy. Endean and two other officers with forty men fought their way through from a surrounded position. Galley was probably killed at this time. It took until 1919 'following much confusion' for his family to be formally informed that he was 'presumed' dead. In fact, his body had been brought back from the battlefield during the withdrawal but this information had been lost in the fog and confusion of the chaotic retreat of March 1918.

There is also a memorial here to the victims of bombing on 23 August 1944.

UK – 8   French – 3   Unnamed - 3

LOCATION

Eppeville is located at the southern end of the Department of the Somme and just within the boundary of this book. It is between Ham and Nesle just north of the road between the two towns about 1km east of Ham. It is west of a large sugar factory complex. The graves are near the bottom of a slope on the left from the entrance.

ERVILLERS MILITARY CEMETERY

HISTORY

The cemetery was first used by the Germans to bury two British soldiers, among German graves, in 1916. The British continued to use the cemetery in 1917.

INFORMATION

The village was in German hands for much of the war. It was occupied by the British in March 1917. The Germans re-took the village in March 1918 after a defence by the 42nd (East Lancashire) Division. It fell for the last time, to the 2nd Division, on 23 August.

Two cemeteries were made by the Germans at Ervillers. The first, now this Military Cemetery, contained the graves of two British prisoners who died in 1916. The British continued burials in 1917. The second, which contained over 100 German burials, was begun in the garden of the Mayor's house in March 1918, has been removed.

Buried here are brothers Bombardier Ben Whitaker and Driver Fred Whitaker from Otley, Yorks. They were both of 'D' Battery, 312th Brigade, Royal Field Artillery. They joined up on the same day, had consecutive service numbers and were killed together aged 25 and 27 years on 5 April 1917.

One of the men buried by the Germans is Private Denis Davies, 1/6th South Staffordshires, died 3 July 1916 aged 39 years. He was probably wounded and taken prisoner in the 'diversionary' attack at Gommecourt on 1 July 1916. He would then have been taken to a German hospital where he died.

The other man who died as a prisoner is Captain Herbert Spanner of No. 27 Squadron, Royal Flying Corps who was shot down near Beaumont-Hamel on 28 December 1916.

UK – 66   Aust – 1
Unnamed – 15   Area 442 sq mts

LOCATION
Ervillers is found between Arras and Bapaume almost 5km north of Bapaume. The cemetery is on the west edge of the village about 50m east of the church on the south side of the road to the sports stadium.

ETERPIGNY COMMUNAL CEMETERY EXTENSION

HISTORY
The cemetery was begun by the Germans in March 1918. It was used again for burials in August 1918.

INFORMATION
The village was in German hands for much of the war. It was taken during 1917 and fell to the Germans in March 1918 and was captured for the final time in August.

Many of the burials here are associated with the fighting in March 1918 especially by the 2nd Middlesex. One Company of the battalion fought at the bridge nearby in March 1918 fighting for two days to hold the position, losing and retaking the bridge six times, before the Germans crossed the river further north and cut off the men. This battalion had already lost a commanding officer who had committed suicide after the losses of 1 July 1916 on the Somme. The village fell to the British again in August 1918 and was the HQ for the Fourth Army in October 1918.

Buried here is Private James Frederick McDonald Harper, 26th Australian Infantry, killed in action on 29 August 1918. He was a hairdresser who enlisted in November 1916 and arrived in France in early 1917. His brother, Private Clyde McDonald Harper, 49th Australian Infantry was also killed in the war dying on 16 September 1918. He is commemorated on the Villers-Bretonneux Memorial.

The Germans buried twenty British soldiers beside fourteen Germans here in March 1918. The seven Australians were added in August 1918. The Germans graves were removed in 1924 leaving gaps as the British graves have not been moved.

UK – 20   Aust   7   Unnamed – 9
Area – 409 sq mts

LOCATION
Eterpigny is a small village about 3km south of Peronne in the valey of the River Somme on its east bank. The cemetery is on the eastern edge of the village, on a high bank above a road leading from the centre of the village to the Peronne-St. Quentin road. There is a steep climb through the entrance and Communal Cemetery to reach the Extension.

EUSTON ROAD CEMETERY, COLINCAMPS

HISTORY
The cemetery was opened on 1 July 1916 and used as a front-line cemetery for those killed in the attack on Serre at the start of the Battles of the Somme. It was mostly used before the German withdrawal to the Hindenburg Line in March 1917 though a few burials were made throughout 1917. Further burials were made in April and May 1918. The cemetery was enlarged after the war with the concentration of 758 graves from the surrounding battlefields and smaller graveyards.

INFORMATION
The village of Colincamps and the dump known as Euston were just behind the front-line before the start of the Battle of the Somme in 1916. The village and this cemetery fell to the Germans in March 1918 but the German advance was held nearby and the area was soon recaptured.

Hence, many of the men buried here date from three battles. The British attack upon Serre on 1 July 1916 and the British capture of Beaumont-Hamel on 13 November 1916. The third is the German attack on the 3rd New Zealand Rifle Brigade in front of Colincamps on 5 April 1918.

The original cemetery is now Plot I which contains men mostly of the 31st Division, a unit comprised of 'Pals' Battalions who attacked at Serre. For most, it was their first time over the top. It is worth spending time looking at the very moving inscriptions at the foot of the headstones – they are all paid for by the families when the cemeteries were formalised after the war. Families were asked to verify the information being placed upon headstones as the cemeteries were constructed. They were also asked if they wish to have an inscription or epitaph at the foot of the stone. They were allowed up to 66 letters at a cost of 3½d (old pence) or approximately 2p per letter when average wages were about £1.00-£2.00 per week.

One of the Special Memorials is to Sergeant John William 'Will' Streets of the 12th (Sheffield City Battalion) Yorks and Lancasters who had left school to become a miner as his family could not afford to send him to grammar school. He still managed to write, and have published, one book about mining and one of poetry – 'The Undying Splendour'. He was killed on the slope before Serre on 1 July 1916, aged 31 years, trying to rescue his men from no-man's land. His two brothers, a set of twins, were in the Albert Basilica on that day serving in the Royal Army Medical Corps. The inscription on his headstone is from one of his poems 'I fell, but yielded not my English soul, that lives out here beneath the battle's roll.'

Concentrated here:

Bayencourt Communal Cemetery Extension - on the edge of the Communal Cemetery which is on the western edge of the village. It was made by the 1st Essex in April 1918 for the burial of eleven British soldiers.

Colincamps British Cemetery - situated on the eastern edge of the village. It was used from March 1917 to September 1918 for the burial of 96 British and 23 New Zealand soldiers and one body who remains unidentified.

Colincamps Churchyard - on the site of the old church in the centre of the village. It was used for the burial of one British and fourteen New Zealand soldiers in March and April 1918.

Jean Bart British Cemetery, Sailly-Au-Bois - situated in the fields between Colincamps and Hebuterne near Jean Bart Trench. It was used for the burial of fifteen men of the 1st Battalion, 3rd New Zealand (Rifle) Brigade, who died on 5 April 1918.

John Copse British Cemeteries - John Copse was one of four small woods named after the four Gospels that lay on the British front-line of 1 July 1916. John Copse has since been removed and the others have merged into one wood that now contains a Memorial Park. In early 1917 V Corps made several cemeteries in the area to bury the dead that had lain in no-man's land for months. V Corps Cemetery No. 1 was made containing 38 British graves and V Corps Cemetery No. 2 contained 139 British graves almost all of the 12th (Hull Sportsmen) and 13th (Hull T'Others) East Yorkshires.

Lonely British Cemetery No. 2, Colincamps - situated about 1.5km north-east of the village close to Central Avenue Trench. It was used in March and May 1918 for the burial of seventeen New Zealand soldiers.

Southern Avenue Cemetery, Mailly-Maillet - about 1km east of this cemetery near to a trench known as Southern Avenue. It contained fourteen New Zealand graves dating from March and May 1918.

White City Cemetery, Auchonvillers - situated in the fields about 1km north-east of Auchonvillers. It contained 106 British, nine New Zealand and six Canadian soldiers buried in 1916 and 1918.

UK – 960	NZ – 302	Aust – 26
Can – 4	India – 1	KUG – 76
Unnamed – 170		Area – 3559 sq mts

Special Memorials to seventeen New Zealand, fourteen British and one Canadian soldiers known, or believed, to be buried among the unnamed graves.

Special Memorials to one British and one New Zealand soldier buried in other cemeteries but whose graves have been destroyed by shell-fire.

LOCATION

Colincamps is a village located about 8km north of Albert and 20km east of Doullens. Euston was a road junction and dump situated about 1.5km east of the village. The cemetery is on the Colincamps-Auchonvillers about 400m north of the Amiens-Arras road near the crossroads with that road..

FAVREUIL BRITISH CEMETERY

HISTORY
The cemetery was in use by the British from April 1917 to March 1918 and again in August and September 1918. It was increased in size after the war by the concentration of graves from small burial grounds and isolated locations in the surrounding battlefields.

INFORMATION
Favreuil village was in German hands for much of the war. It was occupied by British troops in March 1917 during the German withdrawal to the Hindenburg Line. It was lost in March 1918, and retaken by the 37th and New Zealand Divisions on 25 August 1918. The earliest burials contain many men of the 62nd (West Riding) Division.

The bodies of 45 German soldiers were removed after the war. There was also a German cemetery on the north-west side of this British cemetery. It contained 484 graves and has been removed.

Among the burials is Serjeant Harold Victor Evans, DCM, MM, 12th West Yorkshires, killed in action on 20 November 1917 aged 23 years. His Distinguished Conduct Medal was awarded posthumously for leadership and example rather than a specific act.

Concentrated here:
Beaulencourt Churchyard German Extension – it contained three South African and two British soldiers who were buried in July 1916.
Beugny German Cemetery No. 3 – located next to the present Red Cross Corner Cemetery. Among the 350 German soldiers were eight British men and one from New Zealand.
Velu Churchyard – it contained the graves of 39 German and five British soldiers.

UK – 347	Aust - 26	NZ – 19
Can - 1	SAfr - 3	Ger – 13
Unnamed - 11		Area – 1983 sq mts

Special Memorials to four British men known or believed to be buried among the unnamed.
Special Memorial to a British soldier, buried in Favreuil German Cemetery, whose grave could not be identified when the cemetery was removed.

LOCATION
Favreuil is a small village about 1km north of Bapaume. The cemetery is on the south-east edge of the village and on the west side of the road to Beugnatre at a bend before it joins the Bapaume-Ecoust-St. Mein road. The cemetery is 20m from the road and reached by a short grass CWGC path.

FEUCHY CHAPEL BRITISH CEMETERY

HISTORY
The cemetery was begun by the VI Corps Burial Officer in May 1917 and used until March 1918. Once the area had been recaptured from the Germans it was used again in August and September 1918. It was enlarged after the war.

INFORMATION
This area, including the Shrine at which a German redoubt was located from 1914, was taken from the Germans on 9 April 1917 after heavy fighting. It was lost in March 1918 and retaken by the Canadian Corps on 26 August 1918.

The cemetery contained 249 graves at the end of the war which now make up Plot I. After the war 834 graves of men, who mostly fell in April and May 1917, were brought in from isolated positions and small burials grounds on the battlefields of Fampoux, Roeux, Monchy and Wancourt.

Among those here is Acting Regimental Sergeant Major John Alexander Munro, MC, 7/8th King's Own Scottish Borderers, died of wounds, suffered earlier in the day, on 12 April 1917 at Arras. A pre-war regular as Corporal with 2nd Kings Own Scottish Borderers, he had received his Military Cross posthumously for actions three days before his death in rescuing a Private who later died. His brother, Sergeant William M. Munro, 1/5th (Sutherland and Caithness) Seaforth Highlanders was killed in action on 13 November 1916 aged 26 years at Beaumont Hamel and is buried in Mailly Wood Cemetery.

Also here is 2nd Lieutenant George Harry Pridmore, 21st West Yorkshires attached 1st Essex killed in action on 31 August 1918 aged 22 years. His brother Private John Thomas Pridmore, 2nd Kings Own Yorkshire Light Infantry was killed on 14 October 1914 and another brother Sergeant Arthur Edward Pridmore, also 2nd Kings Own Yorkshire Light Infantry was killed on 18 October 1918. They are commemorated on the Le Touret Memorial. A fourth brother, Private Albert Pridmore, 1/4th York and Lancasters, died on 22 June 1917 is commemorated in Sheffield (Burngreave) Cemetery.

Another family to suffer heavily in the war was that of Private James MacMillan, 'C' Company, 13th Royal Scots, killed in action on 28 March 1918 aged 32 years. His brother Private Gavin MacMillan, 1/9th Argyll and Sutherland Highlanders was killed in action on 10 May 1915 and is commemorated on the Menin Gate at Ieper. Another brother, Private John Murchie MacMillan, 1st King's Own Scottish Borderers, was killed in action on 11 April 1918 and is commemorated on the Ploegtseert Memorial near Ieper.

Similarly, Captain Roy Granville Kyrle Money, 3rd attached 6th Buffs (East Kents) was killed on 9 April 1917 aged 18 years. His brother, Sergeant Sydney Aubrey Kyrle Money, 1st Honourable Artillery Company was killed in action at Hooge near Ieper on 16 June 1915 and is commemorated on the Menin Gate at Ieper. Another brother, 2nd Lieutenant Gerald Hugh Kyrle Money, 18th Durham Light Infantry was killed in action on 27 July 1916 aged 19 years and is buried in St. Vaast Post Military Cemetery, Richebourg l'Avoue.

The 12th Division Memorial is near the cemetery.
Concentrated here:
Feuchy Chapel Quarry Cemetery, Feuchy – located about 200m north of 'Feuchy Chapel', containing the graves of seventeen British soldiers who died in April 1917.
Guildford Trench Cemetery, Tilloy-Les-Mofflaines – sited between St. Laurent Blangy and Tilloy, containing the graves of 24 British soldiers, mainly of the 12th Division, who died on 9 April 1917.

| UK – 1076 | Can - 26 | SAfr – 1 |
| Unnamed – 578 | | Area – 3498 sq mts |

Special Memorials to fourteen British men known or believed to be buried among the unnamed.
Special Memorials to six British soldiers, buried in Feuchy Chapel Quarry Cemetery, whose graves were destroyed by shell-fire.

LOCATION
The cemetery lies in the valley of the River Cojeul on the south side of the Arras-Cambrai road about 5km from the centre of Arras. It lies in a location 250m east of the original Chapel de Feuchy, a small shrine, and 250m west of the A1 Autoroute.

FIFTEEN RAVINE BRITISH CEMETERY, VILLERS-PLOUICH

HISTORY
The cemetery was begun in April 1917 following the German withdrawal and the battles for the nearby village. It remained in use until the German spring offensive in 1918 when the area fell to the Germans on 22 March. It was greatly enlarged after the war when graves were concentrated here from smaller cemeteries and isolated positions on the surrounding battlefields.

INFORMATION
The village was in German hands until captured by the 12th South Wales Borderers as part of the actions surrounding the German withdrawal to the Hindenburg Line. The area saw action during the Battle of Cambrai at the end of 1917. In March 1918 the ravine formed the boundary between the Third and Fifth Armies when the Germans began their offensive. It soon fell to the Germans and was not recaptured until September 1918.

This ravine was named by the British Army 'Farm Ravine', hence, the cemetery was for a time called 'Farm Ravine Cemetery'. 'Fifteen Ravine' was a shallow ravine, next to this valley and on the other side of the old railway. It was once bordered by fifteen trees about 1km south of the village.

The cemetery was begun by the 17th Welsh a few days after capture of the ravine by the South Wales Borderers. By March 1918 the cemetery contained 107 graves that now form Plot I. After the war 1105 graves were concentrated here, mostly of men who fell in the battles for the village in April 1917, in the Battle of Cambrai or in the local fighting in September and October 1918. One American soldier has been removed.

Nearly 60 seamen of the Royal Navy Division are buried here. Two Chaplains are also here. Also here is Acting Lieutenant Colonel William John Alderman, DSO, 6th Queen's Own (Royal West Kents), who was killed in action on 20 November 1917. He had started the war as a Quartermaster-Sergeant but was made a 2nd Lieutenant in August 1914 and Lieutenant before the end of the year. He was promoted to Captain on 1 January 1917 having held temporary posts up to that date. It was as a Captain that he took the role of temporary Major, Adjutant and acting Lieutenant Colonel in 1917. He was twice Mentioned in Despatches and awarded a Distinguished Service Order. The war diary for the date of his death shows 'Assembly position S.W. of GONNELIEU – Zero hour 6.20am. The Btn in conjunction with tanks and supported by a creeping barrage attacked the BROWN LINE including the highly important positions of LATEAU WOOD and LE QUENNET FARM. The enemy were taken completely by surprise and appeared utterly demoralised. Many prisoners, a battery of 5.9 [inch] howitzers and a MG were taken by the Btn in its successful advance. All objectives were captured in accordance with plan and time table and the work of consolidation commenced at once. This was continued throughout the night. The death of Major W J Alderman, DSO, who fell just as the battalion had achieved its object sent a shadow over an otherwise brilliant day's work. He led the battalion throughout the action and his death is greatly deplored by all ranks'. He is buried with four officers and three men of his unit who died in the attack.

Also here is Sergeant James Freeman, MM, 1/4th King's Shropshire Light Infantry, killed in action on 30 December 1917. James and his brother Corporal Charles Freeman, 1/4th King's Shropshire Light Infantry were both killed on the same day in the Battle of Cambrai. Charles is commemorated on the Thiepval Memorial. Their sister Mrs W Hawkins also lost her husband Private W H Hawkins, 1st King's Shropshire Light Infantry who died of wounds on 27 June 1915 while at home.

Another here is 2nd Lieutenant Gordon R Alexander, 2nd Royal Sussex attached 13th East Surreys, killed in action on 24 April 1917 aged 31 years. In an attack on Villers Plouich a soldier under his command was wounded by an artillery shell while digging a trench. Alexander was bandaging the soldier's wound when a further shell scored a direct hit on the two men killing them instantly. He was an excellent sailor and golfer but it was as a fencer that he became a British champion and represented Great Britain in foil and epee at the 1912 Olympics in Stockholm.

Concentrated here:

Argyle Road Cemetery, Beaucamp - the hamlet is situated about 1km north-west of Villers-Plouich and the cemetery was near the road to Ribecourt north of the hamlet. The cemetery contained the graves of 50 British soldiers. Eleven of the 14th Argyll and Sutherland Highlanders and 27 other men fell during the capture of Beaucamp on 24 April 1917 while the other twelve were killed in November and December 1917.

Bourlon German Cemetery - situated 10km north of here where the present motorway crosses the Bourlon-Marquion road. Next to the Communal Cemetery the Germans created a cemetery containing about 100 German, now removed, and 173 British soldiers most of whom are unidentified.

Marcoing Sunken Road Cemetery - situated about 1km north of here close to the present Communal Cemetery. It contained the graves of 75 British soldiers killed from December 1917 to April 1918. With them were four New Zealand men who died in September 1918.

UK – 1193   NZ – 60   SAfr – 10
Can – 1   Ger – 2   Unnamed – 740
Area – 4248 sq mts

Special Memorials erected to 44 British soldiers known, or believed, to be buried among the unnamed graves.

Special Memorials erected to ten men of the 14th Argyll and Sutherland Highlanders, buried in Argyle Road Cemetery, whose graves were destroyed by shell-fire.

LOCATION

Villers-Plouich is situated about 10km south-west of Cambrai and 2km west of the A26 motorway. The cemetery is south-east of the village off to the south of the road to Gonnelieu. A farm track leads 50m from the road to the cemetery entrance. It is accessible by car and sits in a pleasant little valley among the farmland.

FINS NEW BRITISH CEMETERY, SOREL-LE-GRAND

HISTORY

The cemetery was begun in July 1917 and remained in use until March 1918. Further burials were made by the British in September 1918. After the war the cemetery was enlarged.

INFORMATION

Fins and Sorel were behind the German lines for much of the war. They fell to the British in April 1917 in the actions that followed the German retreat to the Hindenburg Line. On 23 March 1918, despite stubborn defence by the 6th King's Own Scottish Borderers and the Staff of the South African Brigade Headquarters, the village was recaptured by the Germans. It fell for the final time to the British in September 1918.

The first burials in the village were made by the British in the Churchyard and the Churchyard Extension. When the available space was considered to be full the New Cemetery was begun. It was used by front-line units, notably the 40th, 61st and 9th Divisions, and Field Ambulances that were stationed in the village, during 1917. By March 1918, when the Germans entered the village, there were 590 graves in what are now Plots I to IV. During the German occupation in 1918 they added 255 burials in Plots IV to VI. This included 26 British soldiers cleared from the battlefields and some who died as prisoners of war. When the British returned in September a further 73 burials were made. After the war 591 graves were concentrated into Plots VII and VIII. Of the 276 German burials, 89 are unidentified.

Buried here is Private Harry J Knight of 1st Queen's (Royal West Surreys). He was executed on 6 October 1918 for desertion. He was a volunteer who had served since 1914 but had a poor record and had been wounded.

Also here is Major, Temporary Lieutenant-Colonel, Percy Balfour, DSO, 3rd Bedfordshires (Special Reserve), attached and commanding 2/7th Worcestershires who died on 12 December 1917, aged 42 years. He was a Clerk at the Stock Exchange before the war and was awarded the Distinguished Service Order in the Birthday's Honours List in June 1917 for his leadership including command of 2/5th Gloucestershires.

Another man here is Lieutenant-Colonel Charles Strangway Linton, DSO, MC, four times MiD, commanding 4th Worcestershires, killed in action on 20 November 1917 aged 36 years. He was commissioned in to the 3rd Battalion Welsh Regiment (Militia) as a 2nd Lieutenant on 10 April 1900. In 1901 he transferred to the regular army joining the 4th Worcestershires. He was promoted to Lieutenant in 1904 serving in Bermuda, Barbados, Malta and India. He was promoted to Captain in 1911 and became Adjutant. In 1914 he moved to the 1st Worcestershires and on 6 November 1914 arrived on the Western Front. He was wounded at Neuve Chapelle on 10 March 1915. After recovering from his wounds he was posted to Army HQ and was appointed Staff Captain at the Canadian Corps in April 1915. He was awarded the Military Cross for work on Staff during the battles of 1915. On 22 May 1916 he was promoted to Major and in June 1916 was awarded the Distinguished Service Order in the Birthday's Honours List. On 1 February 1917 he was appointed GSO2 (General Staff), but on 21 July 1917 he took over command of the 4th Worcestershires as acting Lieutenant-Colonel. During the Battle of Poelcappelle on 9 October 1917 he was awarded a Bar to his DSO for his able and fearless leadership. During the Battle of Cambrai, on 20 November 1917, the leading companies of his battalion pushed forward rapidly and soon reached their objective, the lock over the canal 1km south-east of Masnieres. The two companies crossed the lock, seized the trenches beyond it and organised their defence. At 2.00pm Linton went forward to see the situation for himself. On his way back, while crossing the lock, he was killed by a German sniper.

Concentrated here:

Equancourt Churchyard - situated in the village about 2km north-west of here. It contained the graves of three British soldiers buried in 1917 and 1918.

Fins Churchyard - situated on the north side of the village. It contained the graves of nine British soldiers buried in April 1917.

Fins Churchyard Extension - situated on the north side of the Churchyard within a garden. It contained the graves of 121 British soldiers and one Canadian who were killed from April to July 1917. There was also a German soldier killed in March 1918.

Sorel-Le-Grand German Cemetery - situated about 1km south of here on the west side of the village opposite the Communal Cemetery. The Germans buried seventeen British soldiers killed from 1916 to 1918 among the German graves.

UK – 1193	SAfr – 87	Can – 5
NZ – 3	Aust – 2	RGLI – 1
Ger – 276		Unnamed – 208

Area - 4524 sq mts

Special Memorials erected to nine British soldiers believed to be buried among the unnamed graves.

Special Memorial erected to a British soldier buried in Fins Churchyard Extension whose grave could not be identified at the time of concentration.

LOCATION

Fins is situated on the Peronne-Cambrai road about 14km north-east of Peronne and 20km south-west of Cambrai. The Cemetery is on the east side of the village on the south side of the road to Epehy. It lies on a ridge overlooking the village.

FIVE POINTS CEMETERY

HISTORY

The cemetery was used in September and October 1918.

INFORMATION

The village was in German hands for most of the war. It fell to the Allies in early 1917, was retaken by the Germans in March 1918, and captured again by the British in September 1918. The cemetery was created by the 53rd Field Ambulance and the 18th Casualty Clearing Station who were positioned nearby.

In 1934 the grave of an unidentified British soldier was concentrated into this cemetery from Lieramont Communal Cemetery.

Buried here is Brigadier General Arthur Richard Careless Sanders CMG, DSO & Bar, Legion d'Honour (France), Royal Engineers, commanding 50th Brigade, 17th Division. He was killed on 20 September 1918 aged 41 years when he was hit in the back by machine gun fire while in Gouzeaucourt as he returned from viewing the newly captured position of Quentin Redoubt. He had served most of the war on the General Staff having been in the army since 1877. He was appointed commander of his Brigade on 9 September 1918.

UK – 99	India – 1	Unnamed – 3

Area – 482 sq mts

LOCATION

The cemetery is located about 10km south-east of Bapaume in open countryside. The nearest village is Lechelle. The cemetery is about 1km east of the village on a ridge above the village. It is in fields 150m south of the Ytres-Etricourt road and reached by a CWGC path.

FLATIRON COPSE CEMETERY, MAMETZ

HISTORY

The cemetery was opened on 20 July 1916 following the fighting to capture Mametz Wood and Flatiron Copse. It remained in use until April 1917. After the war it was greatly enlarged.

INFORMATION

The cemetery was begun by the advanced Dressing Station that came to the copse in July 1916. It was used by Dressing Stations until late 1916 and then by Casualty Clearing Stations in 1917. Two burials were made in August 1918. At the end of the war the cemetery contained 374 graves which are now Plot I. After the war 1149 were concentrated here.

This copse was an objective for 1 July 1916 but it was not finally cleared, at great sacrifice, until 14 July when the 3rd and 7th Divisions pushed the last German troops back to the north. The copse is situated a short distance east of Mametz Wood which was an objective for a major attack. Flatiron Copse had to be captured first. Hence, the Germans put a crack Lehr Regiment in place recognising the importance of Flatiron Copse.

On 7 July 1916 the 38th (Welsh) Division faced north from the ridge upon which Dantzig Alley Cemetery sits towards Mametz Wood. They were one of two Divisions making a pincer attack on Mametz Wood which was held by the Prussian Guard. The Division was a creation of Lloyd George who had managed to get his choices in place as commanding officers. The attack on Mametz Wood and Flatiron Copse was the Welsh Pals Division's first time in action. The attack failed as machine guns in the wood caused heavy casualties upon the attackers crossing open ground. Battlefield communications failed and there was no smokescreen. As a consequence, the Divisional Commander was replaced. On 10 July at 4.00am they attacked again. A frontal attack by the 38th Division was led by 13th (1st North Wales), 14th and 16th Royal Welsh Fusiliers who entered the wood under heavy fire. There was very confused fighting in the trees with the whole Division committed to the attack. The fighting continued for two days until the Germans withdrew during the night of 11 July. The Division lost 4000 casualties.

The area fell to the Germans in March 1918 and was retaken in August during the final advance to victory.

A memorial, a glorious red dragon, was unveiled in 1987 on the anniversary of the battle. The track past the cemetery will lead you to the 38th (Welsh) Division Memorial in fields south of Mametz Wood. There is parking and turning at the memorial. The track can be followed through to Mametz and Fricourt.

About 600m south-west of the Memorial is the location called Queens Nullah at which Major-General Edward Charles Ingouville-Williams, CB, DSO (Inky-Bill to his men), the most senior officer to be killed on the Somme in 1916, was killed. His 34th Division had suffered tremendously at La Boiselle on 1 July 1916. He was not blamed as it was recognised that his Division had been asked to do the impossible. The Division was reformed with Brigades transferred from 37th Division and went into action again on 19 and 20 July. It was back in reserve when he was killed by shellfire on 22 July as he and his ADC, Guy Chapman, an officer from one of the Brigades transferred from 37th Division, and Lieutenant Grainger Stewart were reconnoitring. They were returning from Contalmaison past Mametz Wood when hit.

Buried here is Corporal Edward Dwyer, VC, Cross of St. George (Russia), 1st East Surreys, killed in action on 3 September 1916 at Wedge Wood and Valley Trench near Guillemont. The citation for his Victoria Cross won as a Private says 'For most conspicuous bravery and devotion to duty at "Hill 60" on the 20th April, 1915. When his trench was heavily attacked by German grenade throwers he climbed on to the parapet, and, although subjected to a hail of bombs at close quarters, succeeded in dispersing the enemy by the effective use of his hand grenades. Private Dwyer displayed great gallantry earlier on this day in leaving his trench, under heavy shell fire, to bandage his wounded comrades.'

Also here are three sets of brothers buried side by side. Privates Ernest and Herbert Philby of 1/8th Middlesex were buried here in the original cemetery. Lieutenants Arthur and Leonard Tregaskis of 16th (Cardiff City Battalion) Welsh and Corporal Thomas and Lance Corporal Henry Hardwidge of 15th Welsh were killed during the attack by the 38th Division on Mametz Wood. They were concentrated here after the war. Thomas Hardwidge was wounded by a sniper on 11 July, his brother went to take him water when they were shot and killed. Both of the brothers were married men with children and had been miners before the war. On Christmas Day 1916 another brother, Morgan, of 2nd Welsh, was killed on the Somme and his name is remembered on the Thiepval Memorial. The Tregaskis brothers had been killed in similar fashion on 7 July.

Also nearby is the final resting place of Lance Corporal Harry Fellowes, 12th Northumberland Fusiliers. This is located just within the northern side of Mametz Wood. A track leads from a gate near the point at which the track to this cemetery leaves the D20. The spot is marked by a headstone which is quite similar to those seen in CWGC cemeteries. The stone records that his ashes were buried here after he died in 1987, aged 91 years.

Concentrated here:

Caterpillar Cemetery, Montauban - situated in Caterpillar Wood about 4km south-east of here. It contained the graves of 21 British soldiers, twelve of the 6th and 7th Gordon Highlanders, who were killed in July 1916.

Cross Roads Cemetery, Bazentin - situated about 1km north-east of here where the road to Bazentin-le-Grand meets the Contalmaison-Longueval road. It contained the graves of fifteen British and four New Zealand soldiers who were killed in 1916 and 1917.

Mametz Wood Cemetery - situated about 1km west of here on the western edge of the wood. It contained the graves of eighteen British soldiers buried in 1916.

Quadrangle Cemetery, Bazentin - situated about 1km south-west of here in the direction of Fricourt between Mametz Wood and Bottom Wood at a place called the Quadrangle. It contained the graves of 32 British and three Australian soldiers buried in 1916. Of these, 22 were artillerymen.

Valley Cemetery, Montauban - situated about 2km south-east of here on the south-eastern edge of Montauban. It contained the graves of 72 British soldiers buried in August and September 1916.

Villa Wood Cemeteries No. 1 & No. 2, Contalmaison - situated about 2km north-west of here in a small copse that was north of the Contalmaison-Longueval road. It contained the graves of 62 British soldiers buried in 1916.

UK – 1520   NZ – 30   Aust – 17
SAfr – 1   Unnamed – 416

Area - 5221 sq mts

Special Memorials erected to 36 soldiers known, or believed, to be buried among the unnamed graves.

Special Memorials erected to nine British soldiers, buried in Mametz Wood Cemetery, whose graves were destroyed in later shell-fire.

LOCATION

Flatiron Copse is situated about 5km east of Albert. It is between Contalmaison and Longueval about 2km east of Contalmaison. The copse is 500m south of the Contalmaison-Longueval road and is reached by a track from the road.

FLESQUIERES HILL BRITISH CEMETERY

HISTORY

The cemetery was begun in late 1918 and used to the end of the war. It was greatly enlarged after the war.

INFORMATION

The village was attacked by the 51st (Highland) Division, with tanks, on 20 November 1917, in the Battle of Cambrai. Though the attack was held up for a time by a German officer with a few men, the village was captured on the following day. The attack was held up here for two reasons. First, General Harper, commanding 51st Division, did not use infantry-tank co-operation tactics properly because he did not use a 'V' formation or have the infantry advance behind the tanks in file. He used the tanks four abreast with infantry in line abreast. This led to heavier casualties. He also stopped the attack having captured the first line as he wanted time to re-organise which left his Division behind the continuing advance made by other Divisions and gave the Germans an opportunity to re-organise. Second, fire from Flesquieres Chateau hit many tanks. It is possible that Unteroffizier Kruger, who was killed in action, led this fire destroying between 7 and 16 tanks.

The village was lost in the later stages of the battle, and retaken by the 3rd Division on 27 September 1918.

The cemetery was begun by the 2nd Division, behind a German cemetery known as Flesquieres Soldiers Cemetery No. 2, but the German graves were removed after the war to Flesquieres Communal Cemetery German Extension, which in its turn was removed in 1924. The site of the German cemetery is now Plots III-VIII. Concentrated here were 688 British soldiers from the battlefields of Havrincourt, Flesquiéres, Marcoing and Masniéres.

Buried here is Captain Duncan Campbell, MC, Fort Garry Horse, who died on 20 November 1917. Captain Campbell led the initial charge by 'B' Squadron of the Fort Garry Horse during the opening day of the Battle of Cambrai in 1917. For this he was awarded the Military Cross. The citation reads 'for conspicuous gallantry and devotion to duty during an attack upon four lines of enemy defences. He was in command of the leading Squadron and seeing that the leading troops had lost direction owing to their leader and sergeant being wounded, he went forward and rallied them to their objective. This prompt action allowed many of dugouts to be cleared and a number of prisoners to be captured and very largely contributed to the success of the whole operation.'

Also here is Major Geoffrey de Bohun Devereux, MC, MiD, 1st Auckland Regiment, NZEF, killed on 1 October 1918 in the attempt to capture the village of Crevecouer. He was the grandson of the 15th Viscount Hereford and could trace his ancestry to the royal Plantagenets. He had been sent home already after winning the Military Cross in November 1917 before re-enlisting in 1918.

Another here is Captain Richard Aveline Maybery, MC & Bar, No. 56 Squadron, Royal Flying Corps, formerly 21st (Empress of India's) Lancers, died on 19 December 1917 aged 22 years. He was commissioned as a 2nd Lieutenant in the 21st (Empress of India's) Lancers in September 1913 and was serving in the North West Frontier Province when the war began. He was promoted to Lieutenant in October 1914. After being seriously wounded in action at Shabqadar in September 1915, Maybery was bored during his rehabilitation and became involved with a unit of the Royal Flying Corps who were based nearby. He was seconded to the RFC, and appointed a Flying Officer (observer) in October 1916. He then trained to be a pilot, becoming a Flying Officer (pilot) in April 1917 and was posted to France where he had 21 victories between 7 July and 19 December 1917. He was awarded the Military Cross on 26 September with a Bar to his MC in December. The citation for the MC reads 'For conspicuous gallantry and devotion to duty. After attacking two aerodromes in succession at very low altitudes, and inflicting considerable damage, he attacked and dispersed a number of mounted men and then attacked a goods train. He next attacked and shot down a hostile machine at 500 feet, and before returning attacked a passenger train. On numerous occasions he has attacked, single handed, large hostile formations and set a fine example by his gallantry and determination' and for the Bar reads 'For conspicuous gallantry and devotion to duty as leader of offensive patrols for three months, during which he personally destroyed nine enemy aeroplanes and drove down three out of control. On one occasion, having lost his patrol, he attacked a formation of eight enemy aeroplanes. One was seen to crash and two others went down, out of control, the formation being completely broken up.' Shortly after his final victory on 19 December over Bourlon Wood, he was either hit by an anti-aircraft battery or shot down by Vizefeldwebel Artur Weber of Jasta 5, and crashed near the village of Haynecourt. Maybery was buried in Haynecourt by the Germans, but after the war was moved here.

Buried here is Lieutenant Colonel Reginald Selby Walker, DSO, three times MiD, VI Corps HQ Royal Engineers. He died on 30 September 1918 aged 46 and was responsible for introducing the Army's first internal combustion engine whilst serving in the Boer War. He was awarded the Distinguished Service Order in the Birthday Honours List in June 1916.

Nearby, on 27 September 1918, a Victoria Cross was won by Field Marshal John Standish Surtees Prendergast Vereker, 6th Viscount Gort, VC, GCB, CBE, DSO & Two Bars, MVO, MC. On 5 August 1914, Gort was promoted to captain. He went to France with the British Expeditionary Force and fought on the Western Front taking part in the retreat from Mons. He became a staff officer with the First Army in December 1914 and then became Brigade Major of the 4th Guards Brigade in April 1915. He was awarded the Military Cross in June 1915. Promoted to the brevet rank of Major in June 1916, he became a staff officer at the Headquarters of the British Expeditionary Force and fought at the Battle of the Somme. He was given the acting rank of Lieutenant-Colonel in April 1917 on appointment as Commanding Officer of 4th Grenadier Guards and, having been awarded the Distinguished Service Order in June 1917, he led his battalion at the Battle of Passendale, earning a bar to his DSO in September 1917. The citation for his Victoria Cross reads 'For most conspicuous bravery, skilful leading and devotion to duty during the attack of the Guards Division on 27th September 1918, across the Canal du Nord, near Flesquieres, when in command of the 1st Grenadier Guards, the leading battalion of the 3rd Guards Brigade. Under heavy artillery and machine-gun fire he led his battalion with great skill and determination to the "forming-up" ground, where very severe fire from artillery and machine guns was again encountered. Although wounded, he quickly grasped the situation, directed a platoon to proceed down a sunken road to make a flanking attack, and, under terrific fire, went across open ground to obtain the assistance of a Tank, which he personally led and directed to the best possible advantage. While thus fearlessly exposing himself, he was again severely wounded by a shell. Notwithstanding considerable loss of blood, after lying on a stretcher for awhile [sic], he insisted on getting up and personally directing the further attack. By his magnificent example of devotion to duty and utter disregard of personal safety all ranks were inspired to exert themselves to the utmost, and the attack resulted in the capture of over 200 prisoners, two batteries of field guns and numerous machine guns. Lt.-Col. Viscount Gort then proceeded to organise the defence of the captured position until he collapsed; even then he refused to leave the field until he had seen the "success signal" go up on the final objective. The successful advance of the battalion was mainly due to the valour, devotion and leadership of this very gallant officer.' At the time he was Captain (Brevet Major, Acting Lieutenant-Colonel), 1st Grenadier Guards. During the 1930's he served as Chief of the Imperial General Staff, the professional head of the Army. He is most famous for commanding the British Expeditionary Force sent to France in the first year of World War II, which was evacuated from Dunkirk. Gort later served as Governor of Gibraltar and Malta, and as High Commissioner for Palestine.

Concentrated here:

Abancourt Communal Cemetery German Extension (Nord) – situated about 10km north-west of here and 5km north of Cambrai. Buried here in 1917-18 were 38 British soldiers and four men of the Chinese Labour Corps.

Havrincourt Communal Cemetery – located about 2km south-west of here from which four British soldiers were taken to Achiet-le-Grand Communal Cemetery Extension and three here.

Haynecourt German Cemetery – about 6km north of here and on the south side of the village, eight British graves were removed to Flesquieres and two to H.A.C. Cemetery,

Ecoust-St. Mein, while 138 German graves were moved to other German cemeteries.

Masnieres-Crevecoeur Road Cemetery, Crevecoeur-Sur-L'escaut – located about 5km east of here. Buried here in October 1918 were thirteen New Zealand soldiers and seven British men of the Devonshires.

Masnieres German Cemetery – located south of Masnieres and used by the New Zealand Division for eleven burials in October 1918.

63rd Division Cemetery - located between Marcoing and Villers-Plouich about 2km south-east of here, it was made by the Royal Naval Division at the end of 1917, and contained 41 graves.

UK – 810	Aust – 2	NZ – 63
Can – 10	NF – 22	RGLI – 4
Unnamed – 332		Area – 28882 sq mts

Special memorials are erected to five British men and two from New Zealand known or believed to be buried here.

Special memorials are erected to three men of the Royal Naval Division buried at the end of 1917 in the 63rd Division Cemetery, Marcoing, whose graves were destroyed by shell fire.

LOCATION

Flesquieres is 3km south of the Bapaume-Cambrai road. Flesquieres Hill Cemetery is a little north-east of the village, in the angle of the road to Cantaing and a track running south to the Flesquieres-Ribécourt road. There are CWGC signs from the centre of the village. The cemetery is on the south side of the road and stands above the level of the road. There are views from the cemetery over the ground across which 51st and 62nd Divisions attacked. Bourlon Wood is visible beyond Orival Wood and you can sometimes see the spires of Cambrai.

FONCQUEVILLERS MILITARY CEMETERY

HISTORY

The cemetery was begun by the French when they held the line here in 1914 and early 1915. It was first used by the British in late 1915 when they took over the area. It remained in use until the German withdrawal to the Hindenburg Line in March 1917. It was used again from March to August 1918 when the German offensive brought the front-line nearby. Some graves were concentrated here after the war.

INFORMATION

Before and during the Battles of the Somme the front-line ran between Foncquevillers and Gommecourt. The village was captured by the British in March 1917 and nearly fell to the Germans in 1918.

The first British burials here were made by the 10th Royal Fusiliers in September 1915. Plot 1, Row L is made up of men killed on 1 July 1916. After the war 74 graves were concentrated here from isolated positions east of the village. They are placed close to the road. At the same time 325 French military graves were moved to La Targette French National Cemetery near Arras.

The men buried here who died in WW2 are the crew of a Halifax Bomber of No. 427 Squadron, shot down during a raid on Arras.

Buried here is Captain John Leslie Green, VC, Royal Army Medical Corps, attached to 1/5th Sherwood Foresters who was awarded the Victoria Cross for his actions nearby on 1 July 1916 during which he was killed. His citation reads 'For most conspicuous devotion to duty. Although himself wounded, he went to the assistance of an officer who had been wounded and was hung up on the enemy's wire entanglements, and succeeded in dragging him to a shell hole, where he dressed his wounds, notwithstanding that bombs and rifle grenades were thrown at him the whole time. Captain Green then endeavoured to bring the wounded officer into safe cover, and had nearly succeeded in doing so when he himself was killed.'

Also here is Lieutenant Colonel Cecil Frederick George Humphries, DSO, MC and Bar, DCM, 1st Duke of Cornwall's Light Infantry attached 1st Norfolks, killed on 22 August 1918 aged 31 years. From New Zealand, he had served as a Private and rose through the ranks serving with the Army Service Corps, Manchesters, Highland Light Infantry, Duke of Cornwall's Light Infantry and Norfolks before he was killed in an attack on Achiet-le-Petit. His Adjutant, Captain Guy Cromwell Tyler, killed in the same attack, is buried next to him.

You will find Captain Gilbert Harding Fletcher of 1/5th North Staffordshires here. He was killed shortly after being told to retire on 1 July 1916 and saying 'The 1/5th never retire. Come on.'

Private George Thomas Palmer, 'B' Company, 1/4th Leicestershires is to be found here. He was killed in action on 28 February 1917, aged 21 years. His family had the following inscription engraved on their son's headstone, 'Will some kind hand in a foreign land place a flower on my son's grave'.

Captain Nigel Choveaux, 1/5th South Staffordshires, killed in action on 14 March 1917 aged 27 years lies here. Nigel Choveaux was born in 1890, educated in Jersey, and then gained employment with the Bombay and Burmah Trading Company. On the outbreak of the war, he was offered a commission in the Indian Army Reserve of Officers, but turned this down to be a 2nd Lieutenant in the 1/5th South Staffordshires. He was made Temporary-Lieutenant on 16 October 1915, following the attack on the Hohenzollern

Redoubt. He also served as Battalion Transport Officer and commanded the Brigade Pioneer Company. On 22 January 1917, Choveaux was appointed Acting Captain commanding 'A' Company. He was reported as missing following the fighting at Bucquoy on 14 March 1917, but a few days later his body was found and buried here.

UK – 625	NZ – 12	Aust – 6
Chinese Labour Corps – 2		Fr Civ – 1
Ger – 4	Unnamed – 53	WW2 - 5

Area – 3445 sq mts
Special Memorials to two British soldiers known to be buried among the unnamed graves.

LOCATION
Foncquevillers is situated about 20km north of Albert and 25km east of Doullens. This cemetery is on the western edge of the village on the road to Souastre. There are CWGC signs from the centre of the village.

FORCEVILLE COMMUNAL CEMETERY AND EXTENSION

HISTORY
The Communal Cemetery was used in 1915 for a burial of a British soldier. In August 1915 land to the south of the Communal Cemetery was taken for further military burials. The Extension was begun in September 1915 for the burial of men of the Third Army who died in trench warfare on the Somme. It remained in use at intervals throughout 1916 and it was used again during the German offensive of 1918. Two further burials were made in the Communal Cemetery, one in February 1916 and one in June 1918.

INFORMATION
The village was in Allied hands throughout the war. Field Ambulances were stationed here from February until the end of July 1916. These served the Fourth Army that occupied the area until 20 July 1916 when it was taken over by the Fifth Army. Plot I contains men who died from the opening of the cemetery to June 1916. The dead of the July and August battles are in Plot II while the dead of the autumn campaigns are in Plot III. Plot IV contains the dead of the German 1918 offensive which was halted just to the east of the cemetery.

There are seven German soldiers in Plot III. This includes the crew of a German plane shot down in September 1915. They are possibly the only German aircrew buried on the Somme battlefield.

The graves of two men buried in the Communal Cemetery, Rifleman J P K Tate, 13th Royal Irish Rifles, killed on 7 February 1916 and Private G Webber, 1st Somerset Light Infantry, killed on 5 August 1915, were enclosed by moving the boundary hedge of the Extension, so there are now no men within the current boundary of the Communal Cemetery. A third man, Corporal E Berry of 38th Battalion, Machine Gun Corps, killed on 19 June 1918, was originally buried in the Communal Cemetery but he has been moved into the Extension.

Buried here is Private John Lewis, 5th Dorsets, who was executed for desertion aged 21 years on 19 April 1917. He deserted with his friend on 1 January as they moved up to the front line. They escaped to England and were arrested in uniform near Lewis's home in Barking on 30 January. They were tried together but executed separately.

Also here is Major Ernest Frederick Powys Sketchley, DSO, three times MiD, General Staff, 63rd (Royal Naval) Division, Royal Marine Light Infantry, died of wounds on 12 October 1916 aged 35 years. He had been hit by shrapnel and died in the 1st (RN) Field Ambulance. His was awarded the Distinguished Service Order for actions on 13 July 1915 near Achi Baba at Gallipoli. The citation reads 'A retreat began and rapidly developed, which might have had very serious consequences. Major Sketchley, who was with the supports, assisted by a Corporal, prevented some of these men from retiring further. He then gathered together about 40 of them, reorganising them & leading them forward, reoccupied some of the trenches. He returned twice to gather more men & collecting in all about 100, retook further trenches, captured some 40 prisoners & secured the position. He exhibited great courage, presence of mind & powers of personal leadership in a moment of crisis.'

UK - 304	NZ – 2	Can – 1
Unnamed – 2		Ger - 7

LOCATION
The cemetery is situated to the west of the village which can be found between Doullens and Albert. It lies on the south side of the road to Acheux. The Extension is on the south side of the Communal Cemetery. Access is by a track on the east side of the cemeteries.

FORESTE COMMUNAL CEMETERY

HISTORY
The Communal Cemetery was used by the 92nd Field Ambulance in the spring of 1917, and later by the 61st (South Midland) Division in March 1918. In the summer of 1918 it fell into German hands and was used by German troops.

INFORMATION
Four French soldiers are buried in the cemetery, but the German graves have been removed.

Among those here is Private Thomas Harrison R McClean, 1st Royal Inniskilling Fusiliers, died of wounds on 2 April 1917 aged 19 years. He came from a farming family in Dungannon, Northern Ireland. Also here is Captain Stanley James Linzell, MC, Croix de Guerre (France), Royal Army Medical Corps, died on 3 April 1917. He was President of the Royal Medical Society at Edinburgh University and was posthumously awarded the Military Cross.

UK – 94   Fr – 4   Unnamed - 22

Special Memorials are erected to 23 men, buried by the Germans, whose graves cannot be traced.

LOCATION
Foreste is a village found about 8km north of Ham. The communal cemetery is on the south side of the village on the west side of the road to the D930 at Aubigny. The cemetery is next to a railway crossing. Parking is available. The graves are in several groups flanking the main path.

FOUILLOY COMMUNAL CEMETERY

HISTORY
The cemetery was used from March to October 1918.

INFORMATION
The village was in Allied hands throughout the war and was the location for 28th Casualty Clearing Station from September to November 1915. 53rd CCS and 41st Stationary Hospital were here in April 1918. The French used the cemetery before the British arrived. There is a Plot along the west wall. A Plot of German graves has been removed.

Buried here is Major Cyril Robert Seelenmeyer, MC, MiD, Australian Veterinary Corps, died of wounds on 8 August 1918. He was an Australian rules footballer who played for University in the Victorian Football League. For saving pack animals, which were crucial supplies, during World War I, he was awarded the Military Cross.

The last burial here was of Private W Montgomery, 103rd Auxiliary Petrol Company, Army Service Corps. He drowned in the River Somme on 16 September 1918 aged 20 years.

UK – 12   Aust – 25   Can – 1   Fr - 71

LOCATION
Fouilloy lies in the valley of the River Somme about 10km east of Amiens and 3km north of Villers-Bretonneux. The cemetery is on the western edge of the village on the north side of the road to Aubigny. It is close to a roundabout.

FOUQUESCOURT BRITISH CEMETERY

HISTORY
The cemetery was made after the war by the concentration of graves from other burial grounds and from the battlefields around the village.

INFORMATION
The village was in German hands from 1914 to early 1917. It fell to them again in March 1918 and was captured by the 10th Canadian Infantry Brigade on 10 August 1918.

The date of death in the great majority of those buried here is February or March 1917, when the British took over trenches north of the village from the French. Others are March, April or August 1918 when the German offensive followed by the British final advance to victory crossed this location. A few graves of 1915 are found in Plots I and III. Commemorated here is Lieutenant James Edward Tait, VC, MC, 78th (Winnipeg Grenadiers) Canadian Infantry. He was a Scottish Canadian and was killed leading his men into action on 11 August 1918 aged 31 years for which he received his Victoria Cross. His grave is marked by a Special Memorial as his original burial location has been lost. His citation reads 'For most conspicuous bravery and initiative in attack. The advance having been checked by intense machine-gun fire, Lt. Tait rallied his company and led it forward with consummate skill and dash under a hail of bullets. A concealed machine gun, however, continued to cause many casualties. Taking a rifle and bayonet, Lt. Tait dashed forward alone and killed the enemy gunner. Inspired by his example his men rushed the position, capturing twelve machine guns and twenty prisoners. His valorous action cleared the way for his battalion to advance. Later, when the enemy counter-attacked our positions under intense artillery bombardment, this gallant officer displayed outstanding courage and leadership, and, though mortally wounded by a shell, continued to aid and direct his men until his death.'

Also here is Captain Norman Charles Henry Macdonald Moreton, 3rd Kings Royal Rifle Corps, MC, MiD, grandson of the 1st Earl Ducie, who was killed in action on 13 October 1915.

And so is Lieutenant Colonel Henry Sidney Charles Peyton, commanding 2nd Rifle Brigade, died of wounds on 24 March 1918. His battalion was under constant orders to withdraw though each time with heavy casualties. He had taken command of his battalion in February 1918 and was one of the few Rifle Brigade men to have served in Gallipoli where he was on the HQ Staff following being invalided from France.

Concentrated here:

Arvillers Communal Cemetery – located about 6km south-west of here in which one unidentified British burial was made among the French graves. He was brought here in 1934.

Asseviller Military Cemetery – about 10km north of here and on the west side of the village. It was begun by the French who captured the area in 1916. It contained the graves of eleven British men, two soldiers from South Africa and one from Australia.

Beaufort Churchyard – located about 3km west of here. It contained one British burial, Private Thomas Guy Evans, 11th Durham Light Infantry, aged 19 years, made by the Germans on 30 March 1918 on the north side of the churchyard. The village contained a German cemetery on the north side of the churchyard which has also been removed.

Belloy-En-Santerre Communal Cemetery French Extensions – near Assevillers about 10km north of here. There were two extensions, containing respectively the graves of four and eleven British soldiers made in 1916 and 1917. The village was captured by the French Foreign Legion in July 1916.

Cappy French Military Cemetery – on the south bank of the River Somme about 12km north of here. This was an Extension of the Communal Cemetery north of the village used by both French and German troops. It contained the graves of 590 French soldiers, 213 German, as well as sixteen British and thirteen Australian burials. The British and Australian graves date from 1915 and 1918.

Chaulnes Communal Cemetery German Extension – located about 5km north of here. It was known as the 'New Military Cemetery by the Railway Station'. Among the 201 Germans it contained the graves of three British soldiers who died in April and May 1918.

Estrees-Deniecourt Military Cemetery - situated at the west end of the village which is 9km north of here. It contained the grave of one British soldier.

Meharicourt Communal Cemetery Extension – located about 3km north-west of here. The cemetery was on the north side of the Communal Cemetery. It contained the graves of nine British soldiers who died in February and March 1917, and 225 French soldiers.

UK – 139	Aust – 49	Can – 137
SAfr – 2	Unnamed – 130	KUG - 43

Area – 1222 sq mts

Special Memorial to one man believed to be buried here.
Special Memorials to five men buried by the Germans whose graves could not be found.

LOCATION

Fouquescourt is situated about 35km east of Amiens and 8km north of Roye. The cemetery is north of the village. Leave the village on the road to Maucourt. At a fork in the roads go right which will bring you towards the cemetery. You can see it from some distance.

FRANKFURT TRENCH BRITISH CEMETERY

HISTORY

The cemetery was made by V Corps in early 1917, after the German retreat to the Hindenburg Line, when their units cleared the Ancre battlefield.

INFORMATION

Beaumont-Hamel was in German hands from 1914. It was an early objective for the 29th Division on 1 July 1916 but their attack failed. It was attacked again, and taken, on 13 November 1916 by the 51st (Highland) and 63rd (Royal Naval) Divisions. Most of the dead buried here were killed in November 1916. Most are men of the Highland Light Infantry.

Frankfurt Trench British Cemetery is named from a German trench about 1.5km north-east of the village which was in

German hands until February 1917. The cemetery was also known as V Corps Cemetery No. 11.

The location is particularly remembered for an incident in the Battle of the Ancre, one of the last offensive actions of the Battle of the Somme. After the capture of Beaumont Hamel on 15 November, some of the day's objectives remained untaken. These included the German positions overlooking the village known as Munich Trench and Frankfurt Trench. On 18 November, the attack was renewed when units of the 32nd Division, including 16th (Glasgow Boys' Brigade) Highland Light Infantry, advanced in the early morning, through a driving snowstorm which later turned to sleet and then freezing rain. The attack failed and was called off, leaving 1387 men killed or wounded in front of Munich Trench. However, a small force of around 60 men of 'D' company from the 16th Highland Light Infantry, plus some men of the 11th Borders had managed to cross Munich Trench and had become surrounded and cut off in the next German position, Frankfurt Trench. No-one knew that this small force was there until some men managed to cross back to the British lines. Several rescue attempts were mounted, but they all failed with even further losses. The men in Frankfurt Trench managed to hold on for a week. The Germans stormed the trench on 25 November and found only 15 wounded men alive, three of whom died soon afterwards. General Sir Hubert Gough praised their stand under Army Order 193.

Buried here is Captain John Patrick Hamilton Wood, 22nd Manchesters, killed in action on 11 January 1917 aged 36 years. He had served in the South African Wars with Paget's Horse. His brother, Rifleman George Gilbert Beaton Wood, 1/9th (Queen Victoria's Rifles) Londons, was killed in action on 9 October 1916 and is commemorated on the Thiepval Memorial.

UK – 161   Unnamed – 34   Area – 427 sq mts

LOCATION

Beaumont-Hamel is a small village on the west side of the Ancre valley, about 8km north of Albert. The cemetery is on the ridge north of the village on the road to Miraumont. Signs lead from the village centre to the cemetery. At the top of the ridge a sign leads from the road along a farm track to the cemetery which is about 100m from the road. Only the brave should attempt this by vehicle in winter unless you have a good 4x4. But there is no turning place at the cemetery. It commands wide views in all directions over the battlefields of 1916-18, including Newfoundland Park, and the 36th (Ulster) Division Memorial near Thiepval and you can see many of the cemeteries created along the line of the 1 July 1916 battlefield from here..

FRANVILLERS COMMUNAL CEMETERY EXTENSION

HISTORY

The Extension was used from April to August 1918.

INFORMATION

The Extension was used by units involved in the defence of Amiens. The cemetery was made during the quiet months of 1918 between the German advance and the autumn battles. Australian units held the German advance nearby in April and remained through the summer. The later burials are men of the British 12th and 18th Divisions who attacked to the east of here in August.

Among those buried here is Lieutenant Colonel James Henry Paine, DSO, MiD, Commanding 76th Brigade, Royal Garrison Artillery, killed in action on 25 July 1918 aged 47 years. He joined the Royal Artillery as a 2nd Lieutenant in 1890, was promoted to Lieutenant three years later, to Captain in 1899 and Major in 1910. He was awarded the Distinguished Service Order for his work as a Lieutenant during the Mekran Campaign in 1898 in northwest India (now Pakistan). He was present at the action of Gok Parosh for which he was Mentioned in Despatches. He began the war with 26th Battery, Native Mountain Artillery, in India before going to France.

UK - 113   Aust – 134   NZ – 1
Ger – 5   Area – 1278 sq mts

LOCATION

Franvillers lies on the north side of the Albert-Amiens road midway between the two towns. The Communal Cemetery and the Extension are south-east of the village between it and the main road. The Extension is at the village end of the Communal Cemetery.

FRECHENCOURT COMMUNAL CEMETERY

HISTORY

The Communal Cemetery was used from April to August 1918.

INFORMATION

Of the dead, 50 are from artillery units. One of them is Captain Archibald Farquhar Martin, 11th Brigade, Australian Field Artillery, killed in action on 5 April 1918. He was born in New Zealand but grew up in Australia. He had served previously with the New South Wales Lancers as a Sergeant and 13th Battery, Australian Field Artillery. He joined the army in October 1915 as a Lieutenant and arrived in France as a Captain with 2nd Australian Division artillery. He was killed while commanding 41st Battery, Australian Field Artillery at Dernancourt as he was dressing the wounds of another officer of his Battery when a German shell exploded next to them killing both men.

UK – 8   Aust – 49   Area – 477 sq mts

LOCATION

Frechencourt is found just north of the Amiens-Albert road midway between the two towns and about 2km north of Querrieu. The cemetery is at the western end of the village about 100m from the church. There is a sign at the roadside to the entrance which is between houses. It is located behind the buildings and accessed by a narrow path. The pretty and peaceful CWGC plot is at the rear of the communal cemetery.

FRICOURT BRITISH CEMETERY (BRAY ROAD)

HISTORY

This cemetery was begun on 5 July 1916, by the 17th Division, shortly after the village of Fricourt had fallen during the opening days of the Battles of the Somme in 1916. It remained in use until October 1916. A further four burials were made in 1918.

INFORMATION

The village was in German hands from 1914. The plan for 1 July 1916 was to attack on either side of the village, encircling it, hoping for the Germans to retreat. Fricourt had been turned into a fortress and the attack by the 17th Division failed at great cost. 'A' Company of the 7th Yorkshires (Green Howards) attacked fifteen minutes after zero hour at 7.45am, due to some confusion or misunderstanding with the orders, and were cut to pieces by a single machine-gun as a result. They had orders to hold, but it seems the Company commanding officer attacked, without orders, and lost 108 out of 140 men. This cemetery still contains a stone memorial cross placed in memory of those Green Howards who died in that attack. A later attack by two companies of the 7th East Yorkshires was stopped at the British line taking 123 casualties. At the end of the day the Germans withdrew from the village which had been almost surrounded by troops of the 17th, 21st and 7th Divisions. The village was the major failure on the road to Peronne on 1 July 1916.

The Germans recaptured the village on 25 March 1918 during their offensive. It fell to the British for the final time on 26 August 1918.

The cemetery was started by the 7th East Yorkshires, in an area of no-man's land prior to 1 July 1916, to bury 89 of their comrades who had died in the unsuccessful attacks on Fricourt on 1 July 1916. They made most of the cemetery between 5 and 11 July placing 59 of their friends in two large graves in the middle of what is now Row A. The memorial to the battalion dead of 1 to 14 July 1916 is next to the burials.

Many of the names of those buried here can also be seen on the memorial cross to the Green Howards, for example that of 2nd Lieutenant Harold G. Hornsby killed on 1 July 1916. He was from London and before joining up had been on the Solicitor's staff of His Majesty's Customs and Excise. Also buried here is the Major Raper after whom the street in the village is named as he is considered the liberator of the village. Major Robert Raper, before the war a solicitor, served with the 8th South Staffordshires, and was killed on 2 July in Fricourt Wood. He was tasked to clear the village with bombing parties, which he did with some ease, taking 100 German prisoners until they met opposition in Fricourt Wood. He was originally buried in a field across the road from the cemetery, and stayed there as his parents bought the land on which his grave was located. This was maintained until the 1960's when his body was moved here. Rue Raper runs to the church. A plaque inside states that the Stations of the Cross are in memory of him.

There is also a memorial to the 17th Division commemorating the 494 officers and 8421 men who died in the war. Directly above is a statue of Joan of Arc who was burned by the English in 1431 at Rouen. Finally, the church has a memorial to a French soldier of the 125th Infantry Regiment who fell at Fricourt in 1914.

Fricourt British Cemetery has special significance for the Yorkshire Regiment, in that of the 132 identified casualties buried in the cemetery, 92 were from the Regiment. Of these 92 men, the large majority were killed on 1 July 1916 and almost all were from the 7th Battalion. The 7th Yorkshire Regiment suffered terribly at Fricourt on 1 July 1916, losing five officers killed and ten wounded, with 336 non-commissioned officers and men killed, wounded, or missing.

There is a commemorative stone in Fricourt British Cemetery which records the fact that 59 NCOs and men of the 7th Yorkshires are buried in a single place in the centre of the cemetery. Thus, there are 59 individual headstones which state that the soldier is "believed to be buried in this cemetery", in the communal grave as opposed to an individual grave.

The crossroads near this cemetery at the south of the village was one of the principal arteries of the 1916 battle after 1 July. A census of transport in the village in late July 1916 saw 26536 troops, 63 guns, 663 cars and buses, 617 motorcycles, 813 lorries, 1458 6-horse waggons, 568 4-horse waggons, 1215 2-horse waggons, 515 1-horse waggons, 5404 riding horses, 330 ambulances, 1043 bicycles and 10 caterpillars pass through the village.

Nearby is the spot from which Siegfried Sassoon watched the battle on 1 July. It is believed this is the start of his belief that the war was wrong. His path from here takes him to conflict with authorities, a letter to The Times condemning the war which is read out in Parliament as the Times refuses to print, throwing away his medal ribbons, meeting and developing poetry with Wilfred Owen in Craiglockhart hospital and his catalogue of work after the war.

Also in the village is Fricourt German Military Cemetery. It is the only German Military Cemetery within the area of the 1916 battles and contains over 15000 men.

UK – 131   NZ – 1   Area - 864 sq mts

Special Memorial erected to one British soldier who is known to be buried within the boundaries of the cemetery but whose grave cannot now be identified.

LOCATION

Fricourt is a village located about 5km east of Albert. The cemetery is in the valley just south of the village about 30m north of the crossroads with the Albert-Peronne road and south of the main part of the village.

FRICOURT NEW MILITARY CEMETERY

HISTORY

This cemetery was made in July 1916, by the 17th Division, shortly after the village of Fricourt had fallen during the opening days of the Battles of the Somme in 1916. Further burials were made in September 1916.

INFORMATION

This area is one of the worst tragedies in the 1 July 1916 attack in this sector, if not the whole front. The Tambour (French for drum) area was strongly held, opposing trenches were close together, and many mines were made. The bend in the line of trenches enabled the Germans to fire into and along the British trenches. The task of attacking here was given to the 10th West Yorkshires in their first action of the war. The Royal Engineers set three mines to provide cover for the attack but one mine did not explode. Added problems were caused by ineffective artillery shelling. The leading platoons took the German front line quickly but the rest of the battalion were held up by German machine-guns which were not shelled for another two hours. As they were attacking uphill, the battalion were pinned down in no-man's land for much of the day. They lost 396 dead and 314 wounded (710 casualties) which was the highest casualty figure for any single battalion on the day. The commanding officer, his second in command, the adjutant, two Company commanders, six Platoon commanders and two Company Sergeant Majors were all killed. Only one officer and 20 men survived the day. The Tambour mine craters can still be seen and the German line can be made out.

The cemetery was made by the 10th West Yorkshires to bury 159 of their comrades who were killed during the attack on Fricourt on 1 July 1916. The neat rows conceal the fact that these are four mass graves. Also here are 38 men of the 7th East Yorkshires as are a few men who were killed in later battles. The 10th West Yorkshires commanding officer, Lieutenant Colonel Arthur Dickson, is here with his men though his headstone has the badge of his original regiment, the 1st South Lancashires. His adjutant, Lieutenant John Webster Shann is here.

Major James Leadbitter Knott, DSO, second in command of the 10th West Yorkshires, was originally buried here. He was moved after the war to lay with his brother, Captain Henry Basil Knott, killed on 7 September 1915 serving with 9th Northumberland Fusiliers. They are now found in Ypres Reservoir Cemetery.

Also here is Private Albert Edward Barker, 7th East Yorkshires, killed in action on 1 July 1916 aged 16 years. He is the youngest soldier to be killed on the first day of the Battle of the Somme.

UK – 208   NZ – 2   Unnamed - 26

Area - 1240 sq mts

LOCATION

The cemetery is north-west of the village on the ridge overlooking the village and separating it from 'Sausage Valley'. It lies on the German front-line prior to 1 July 1916. It is reached by a farm track from the road to Contalmaison north of the village centre and is best visited on foot from the road rather than by car. A CWGC path leads south from the farm track to the cemetery.

GAUCHE WOOD CEMETERY, VILLERS-GUISLAIN

HISTORY
The cemetery was begun on 6 October 1918 and remained in use for only a few weeks.

INFORMATION
Villers-Guislain was behind the German lines for much of the war until it was attacked by the British in April 1917. The Germans recaptured the village in November during the Battle of Cambrai and held it against an attack by the Tank Corps and Guards Division. The British did not regain the village until 30 September 1918.

Gauche Wood was captured during the attack on the village on 1 December 1917. It was defended by the South African Brigade at the start of the German offensive on 21 March 1918 but fell after the Brigade had suffered very heavy casualties.

The cemetery was begun by the 21st Division Burial Officer. Among those buried here is Private George Draycott, 7th Lincolnshires, killed in action on 18 September 1918 aged 30 years. From Leicester, he represented Leicester Fosse FC as a centre-half on 44 occasions during the war. Before the war he had signed for Bradford Rovers from Gresley Rovers in March 1913, after playing a trial at Filbert Street, then Leicester City's ground, in a testimonial match. Before that, he had worked as a colliery horse driver and played for Newhall Swifts.

UK – 48   Unnamed – 5   Area – 232 sq mts

LOCATION
Villers-Guislain is located about 15km south of Cambrai, a similar distance north-east of Peronne and 2km west of the A26 motorway. The cemetery is about 2km south-east of the village, in a very isolated position, on a ridge overlooking the village next to the wood. It is reached by means of a farm track from the nearest road and I would not recommend anyone, except the most adventurous and well equipped, to take a car to the cemetery, though I have done it in my 4x4 in a bad winter.

GENTELLES COMMUNAL CEMETERY

HISTORY
The Communal Cemetery was used only in April 1918.

INFORMATION
The village was always behind the Allied front-line but came close to the line at the limit of the German advance in the spring of 1918. Hence, the cemetery was only used at that time.

The men buried here are mostly a mix of Infantry, Artillerymen and Engineers. But there are also an Australian Major, a Company Sergeant Major and an airman. Among those here is Private C E Andrews, DCM, 10th Essex, killed in action on 3 April 1918. His Distinguished Conduct Medal was gazetted on 28 March 1918 just before his death. He was in a group who were tasked with attacking a farm that had been turned into a blockhouse by the Germans. His Company Sergeant Major had gone forward and was under threat so Andrews ran forward and killed three German saving his CSM. He then bombed the German position allowing his pals to withdraw before doing so himself.

Nearby, on the Amiens-Roye road, is a memorial at the corner of Gentelles Wood. In August 1944, 27 men were executed at this location before the Germans withdrew. Only 19 of the men were identified.

UK – 17   Aust – 3   Unnamed - 2

Special Memorials to three men known to be buried here whose graves were destroyed by shellfire.

LOCATION
Gentelles is located about 5km south-east of Amiens. The cemetery is on the west edge of the village on the road to Boves. The graves are in one row along the west end of the cemetery.

GOMIECOURT SOUTH CEMETERY

HISTORY
The cemetery was made at the end of August 1918.

INFORMATION
The village was in German hands for most of the war and was captured by the 3rd Division on 23 August 1918. The cemetery was then made by the 62nd Division Burial Officer.

Buried here is Frederick William Watson, MC, DCM & Bar, 5th King's Own Yorkshire Light Infantry, killed in action on 27 August 1918 aged 38 years. He enlisted in the King's Own Yorkshire Light Infantry on 27 February 1897, aged 18 years, for seven years 'with the colours', with a further five years as a reservist. Within four years he had been promoted to Corporal and received two Good Conduct Awards. In 1901 he went to South Africa with 2nd Kings Own Yorkshire Light Infantry and was promoted to Sergeant. From South Africa he went to Malta and extended his service to twelve years and then to Crete before returning home in 1905 and again extending his service, this time to 21 years. He was seconded to the Nigeria Regiment for service in West Africa before returning home and marrying. He was, after a period in Ireland, posted to the 1/5th (Territorial Force) King's Own Yorkshire Light Infantry as a Drill Instructor in 1912. At the start of the war he was kept back from the front to train men and was promoted to Company Sergeant Major. Hence, he did not get to France until 1917 when he went with 2/5th King's Own Yorkshire Light Infantry in the 62nd Division. He was awarded the Distinguished Conduct Medal in March 1917. The War Diary of the 2/5th King's Own Yorkshire Light Infantry for 8 March describes how 2nd Lieutenant Atkin led a daylight patrol, an action for which he earned the Military Cross. The diary goes on 'CSM F W Watson established a post in Resurrection Trench to assist the 10th Essex to carry out a bombing attack. A previous attempt had failed. CSM Watson awarded the DCM.' The citation for the DCM reads 'For conspicuous gallantry and devotion to duty. He succeeded in establishing a post at a critical time under the most trying conditions. He has at all times set a splendid example of courage and determination.' Soon after he was made Regimental Sergeant Major but was reduced to Sergeant after being found drunk on duty. He was sent back to reserve to train men before returning, as a Company Sergeant Major in 'D' Company, to what was soon to become the 5th King's Own Yorkshire Light Infantry having merged with 1/5th battalion in the restructuring of early 1918. By now he had served his 21 years but enlisted again until the end of the war. He was wounded twice in July 1918 while 62nd Division were supporting the French on the Marne. He was killed in an attack by his Company near Mory when they were cut off and pinned down by machine gun fire and he was hit in the neck. It is not clear when the Bar to his DCM was awarded but he gained an unusual Military Cross in this action. The citation reads 'When the officers of two platoons became casualties he took command and led the men forward with great dash and skill. He was cut off with part of his platoon but fought his way back to his company. His courage and resolution were remarkable and his cheerfulness inspired all who were with him.' It is possible he was awarded a Bar to the DCM for the same actions.

UK – 206   Ger – 27   Unnamed - 10
Area – 677 sq mts

LOCATION
Gomiecourt is 16km south of Arras and 6km north-west of Bapaume. Gomiecourt South Cemetery is in open fields 200m south-east of the village, on the north side of the road to Ervillers. It is close to the civil cemetery. The German graves are along the west edge.

GOMMECOURT BRITISH No. 2 CEMETERY, HEBUTERNE

HISTORY
The cemetery was made in early 1917 and expanded after the war.

INFORMATION
Hebuterne village remained in British hands from March 1915 to the end of the war, although during the German advances of the summer of 1918 it was practically on the front line.

Gommecourt and Gommecourt Wood were attacked by the 56th (London) and 46th (North Midland) Divisions on 1 July 1916 as a 'diversion' with only temporary success, but the village was occupied by the 31st and 46th Divisions on the night of 27-28 February 1917, remaining in Allied hands until the end of the war.

Gommecourt British Cemeteries No. 1, No. 2, No. 3 and No. 4 were made in 1917 in what had been no-man's land, when the battlefields were cleared and the bodies of those who died on 1 July 1916, and lay in the fields for eight months, were collected. This is the only remaining one of the four. No. 2 originally contained 101 graves, almost all of the 56th Division, which form Plot I of the cemetery as it is today. After the war graves from the neighbouring battlefields were added.

Gommecourt British Cemetery No. 2 sits mid-way between the two front lines and is an excellent place from which to observe the battlefield. The sunken Hebuterne to Bucquoy road which leads to it is very much the same as it was in 1916 and gives a good example of what the Gommecourt-Puisieux road would have looked like at the time. From the rear wall of the cemetery, one looks over the fields across which the 169th Brigade attacked. 'Nameless Farm' has gone but this German position was located on the cemetery side of the Gommecourt-Puisieux road almost directly facing the cemetery wall. Look to the east and you can see the higher ground across which the 1/14th (London Scottish) Londons attacked.

Among those here are brothers Riflemen Henry Edward and Philip James Bassett, both of 1/9th (Queen Victoria's Rifles) Londons, killed on 1 July 1916.

Another to lose a brother buried here is Private Henry James Percy Peaceful, 1/2nd (Royal Fusiliers) Londons, killed in action on 1 July 1916, aged 24 years. His brother, Private Thomas Samuel Henry Peaceful, 4th Royal Fusiliers, who died on 4 June 1915 aged 21 years, seven months after arriving on the Western Front is buried in Bedford House Cemetery near Ieper. He is believed to be the inspiration for the Private Peaceful story by Michael Morpurgo.

Concentrated here:

Gommecourt British Cemetery No. 1 - was 100m north-west of here. It contained the graves of 107 British soldiers, mainly of the 56th Division, who died on 1 July 1916.

Gommecourt British Cemetery No. 3 - was at the south-west corner of the village. It contained the graves of 117 British soldiers, mainly of the 56th Division, who died on 1 July, and men who died on 12 November 1916.

Gommecourt British Cemetery No. 4 - was 50m south of No. 1. It contained the graves of 70 British soldiers, largely of the 56th Division, who died on 1 July and men who died on 12 November 1916, and at the end of February 1917.

UK – 1285   Aust – 26   NZ – 46
Unnamed – 682   Area – 3968 sq mts

Special Memorials to 33 men known or believed to be buried among the unnamed.

LOCATION

Hebuterne is located about 8km west of Bapaume and 20km south-west of Arras. The village is about 2km south-west of Gommecourt. The cemetery is on the north-eastern edge of Hebuterne in open fields about 1km from the village centre. This is about 2km south of Gommecourt. The cemetery is 50m north of the road from Hebuterne to Bucquoy and is reached by a path from the road. The headstones are very close together, with some bearing three names. It is very peaceful with good views.

GOMMECOURT WOOD NEW CEMETERY, FONCQUEVILLERS

HISTORY
The cemetery was made after the war.

INFORMATION
Foncquevillers was in British hands in 1915 and 1916. On 1 July 1916, Gommecourt Wood was attacked by the 46th (North Midland) Division, and the southern part of the village by the 56th (London) Division as a 'diversion'. The attack met with temporary success, but could not be sustained, and Gommecourt remained a salient in the German line until 27 February 1917, when it was evacuated. It was never retaken by the Germans so that at the end of their offensive of March 1918, it was just within the British lines.

Gommecourt Wood New Cemetery was made of graves brought in from the battlefields of July 1916, March 1917, and March, April and August 1918.

The cemetery is situated on a bank 'looking up' the no-man's land where the 46th (North Midland) Division attacked on 1 July 1916. Many of the unnamed are identified as being of that Division, mainly Sherwood Foresters or North and South Staffordshires. There is a memorial here to the men of the 46th Division.

Among those buried here is Lieutenant Colonel Charles Edward Boote, TD, commanding 1/5th North Staffordshires killed in action on 1 July 1916. He was one of three battalion commanders to die here in the attack, but the graves of the other commanding officers have not been identified. They may be here in unidentified graves.

Also here is Private E Whitlock of 1/4th Oxford and Bucks Light Infantry who, on 22 July 1915, was the first British soldier to be killed on the Somme. He was concentrated here from Hebuterne.

Concentrated here:-

Bastion Cemetery, Foncquevillers - in the old German line north of the Wood about 200m north-east of here, where

55 men, nearly all unidentified, of the 46th Division were buried.

Bretencourt French Military Cemetery - on the west side of the bridge between Bretencourt and Blamont Mill which is about 8km north-east of here. Buried in this cemetery were 233 French and 38 British soldiers, three men of the Indian Labour Corps, and one German prisoner.

Gommecourt Chateau Cemetery – located at the north-east corner of the chateau park 200m south of here. It was begun by the Germans. Here were buried 55 soldiers from New Zealand, who died in July and August 1918, and fourteen British men.

Gommecourt Wood Cemetery No. 1, or 'The Sap Cemetery, Foncquevillers' - between the old front lines about 200m north-east of here, in which were buried 111 men of the 46th Division, almost all unidentified.

Gommecourt Wood Cemetery No. 4 – also known as 'Little Z Cemetery', named after a strong point on the old German front line, it contained the graves of 23 British men, 22 of the 46th Division.

Gommecourt Wood Cemetery No. 5 - on the north-west side of the Wood about 300m north-east of here. It contained the graves of 27 men of the 46th Division.

Gommecourt Wood Cemetery No. 6 - close to No. 5, it contained the graves of 40 men, almost all of the 46th Division.

Gommecourt Wood Cemetery No. 8 - between the old front lines close to No. 6 cemetery. It contained the graves of 46 men of the 46th Division.

Point 75 British Cemetery, Foncquevillers – located on the old German front line, it contained the graves of 35 men of the 46th Division.

UK – 692   Aust – 1   NZ – 56
Unnamed – 465   Area – 2691 sq mts

Special Memorials for ten British men known or believed to be buried here among the unnamed.

LOCATION
Foncquevillers and Gommecourt are about 18km south-west of Arras. Gommecourt Wood New Cemetery is situated on the south side of the road between the two villages on the western edge of Gommecourt. It has good views of the battlefield.

GORDON CEMETERY, MAMETZ

HISTORY
The cemetery was created on 4 July 1916 for the burial of men who fell on 1 July. It was immediately closed except for the burial of three men who were buried later in the month.

INFORMATION
Mametz, and Mametz Wood to the north-east of the village, were an early objective of 1 July 1916 having been in German hands since 1914. The village was captured by the 7th Division at the start of the battle while the Wood was not taken until the middle of the month. The village marked the geographical beginning of noticeable British successes on 1 July. To the east the Germans were pushed back while to the west, British victories were limited and expensive.

The cemetery was made by the 2nd Gordon Highlanders to bury their comrades who died on the opening day of the Battles of the Somme. It contains men of the 2nd Gordon Highlanders who are buried in a support trench. Three artillerymen who fell on 9 July are buried with them. The headstones are arranged in two semi-circles around the Cross of Sacrifice.

Among those here is 2nd Lieutenant David Taylor King, 2nd Gordon Highlanders, killed in action on 1 July 1916 aged 21 years. He was from London and is one of six 2nd Lieutenants of the battalion killed on that day and buried side by side.

The 7th Division have erected a memorial nearby to commemorate their success here in 1916.

UK – 102   Unnamed – 5   Area - 351 sq mts

LOCATION
Mametz lies about 6km east of Albert just to the north of the Albert-Peronne road. The cemetery lies south of the village on the north side of the Albert-Peronne road.

GORDON DUMP CEMETERY, OVILLERS-LA BOISELLE

HISTORY
The cemetery was begun on 10 July 1916 and was used until September 1916. Most of the cemetery was made after the war when graves were concentrated from the battlefields nearby.

INFORMATION
On 1 July 1916 this area, having been in German hands since 1914, was attacked by units of the 34th Division. The villages of La Boiselle and Contalmaison were not captured and only a small amount of ground was taken. It is believed that some men of the Division may have got as far as this cemetery and to nearby Contalmaison. La Boiselle was

taken on 4 July by the 19th Division. The villages were lost in the German spring offensive in March 1918 and retaken in the following August.

The cemetery was called several names during the war. It was Gordon or Gordon's Dump Cemetery. It was also Sausage Valley Cemetery after the name given by the British Army to the valley on the east side of La Boiselle. The valley on the western side, between La Boiselle and Ovillers, was called Mash Valley. The burial ground was made next to a lane, now gone, that ran from La Boiselle to Contalmaison. The original plan that was designed when the lane existed no longer applies so a new entrance and path from the road has been created.

Plot I of the cemetery is the original part and was made during the summer of 1916 to contain the graves of 95 men, mainly Australian. After the war 1543 graves were concentrated from the battlefields at Ovillers and La Boiselle. Most of the men concentrated after the war had died in July 1916. There are also five graves dating from 1917 and 1918. The concentrated graves reflect the units that fought in this area in 1916 – many from the 34th Division at Lochnagar Crater and 21st Division at Fricourt. The Australians that fought at Pozieres and Canadians at Courcelette are also represented here. The graves of three French soldiers have been removed.

Nearby, and visible to the south, is the Lochnagar Crater which was created when 60,000lbs of ammonal was exploded under the German Line at the Schwaben Hohe two minutes before zero hour on 1 July 1916. It was one of seventeen mines used that morning. The name comes a nearby communication trench, Lochnagar Street, probably named by the 51st Division who were the first British troops here in 1915. The initial advance after the explosion seemed successful as the 2nd and 3rd Tyneside Scots (21st and 22nd Northumberland Fusiliers) attacked between the crater and the village while the 10th (Grimsby Chums) Lincolns and 11th (Cambridgeshire City Battalion) Suffolks attacked south-east of the crater. However, no significant ground beyond the German line was held. The tunnel dug by 185th Tunnelling Company used to create the mine was re-opened to get men to the new British front line. The crater gives excellent views of the local battlefield. Look south towards the Golden Virgin of Albert and you will see the Tara-Usna line from which the 34th Division attacked on 1 July 1916. The crater was purchased to preserve it in 1978. It is a war grave for Germans killed here.

Nearby memorials include the 19th Division Memorial, a blue granite cross in La Boiselle. The 34th Division Memorial, at the north-east end of La Boiselle, is on the site of the Divisional Headquarters in 1916. It is a white stone obelisk surmounted by the bronze figure of victory. The Tyneside (102nd and 103rd Brigades) Memorial, is a stone seat at the south end of the village on the old front-line position known as the 'Glory Hole'. It is in front of the destroyed communal cemetery.

I mention La Boiselle here as this is the nearest cemetery to the village that played an important role in 1916. The village is now larger than in 1914 with new houses on the main Albert-Bapaume road and an excellent tea-rooms called 'Old Blighty'. The British and German lines came within 50m of each other at the Albert end of the village.

This area was known as the 'Glory Hole'. There was a lot of tunnelling which is now being rediscovered. The village was not attacked frontally on 1 July 1916 but attacked on either side using Mash and Sausage Valleys. The first wave was the Brigade of Tyneside Scots followed by a wave of Tyneside Irish. They took parts of the German line though not the village but suffered the heaviest casualties of any Division on 1 July 1916. Over the next few days the 19th Division pressed forward led by the redoubtable one eyed, one armed, Lieutenant Colonel Adrian Carton de Wiart of the 8th Gloucestershires who won the Victoria Cross here on 2-3 July as did Private Thomas George Turrall, 10th Worcestershires who won the award for saving the life of an officer on 3 July near the village.

Buried here is 2nd Lieutenant Donald Simpson Bell, VC, 9th Yorkshires, killed in action on 10 July 1916. He was a former professional footballer with Bradford Park Avenue. His citation reads 'For most conspicuous bravery. During an attack a very heavy enfilade fire was opened on the attacking company by a hostile machine gun. 2nd Lt. Bell immediately, and on his own initiative, crept up a communication trench and then, followed by Cpl Colwill and Pte Batey, rushed across the open under very heavy fire and attacked the machine gun, shooting the firer with his revolver, and destroying gun and personnel with bombs. This very brave act saved many lives and ensured the success of the attack. Five days later this very gallant officer lost his life performing a very similar act of bravery.' Also here is Sergeant Harry Littlewood, 9th Kings Own Yorkshire Light Infantry, killed in action near Fricourt on 1 July 1916. Before the war he had won 100 boxing matches including taking the Pitman title in 1913 for boxers employed in mines. He had also won the 21st Division open heavyweight title in 1916.

UK – 1582 Aust – 91 Can – 2
India – 1 Unnamed – 1053
Area – 4753 sq mts

Special Memorials to 34 British soldiers and an Australian known, or believed, to be buried among the unidentified graves.

LOCATION
La Boiselle is a village on the Albert-Bapaume road about 2km north-east of Albert. The Cemetery can be found about 1km east of the village. It is some distance from the road and reached by a 100m path from the road.

GOUZEAUCOURT NEW BRITISH CEMETERY

HISTORY
The cemetery was begun in November 1917 and used by the British for a short period. Further British burials were made in September and October 1918. After the war the cemetery was greatly enlarged.

INFORMATION
The village was in German hands for much of the war. It was attacked and captured by the 8th Division on 12-13 April 1917. The Germans briefly re-entered the village on 30 November 1917 during the Battle of Cambrai but the 1st Irish Guards drove them out on the same day. The village fell to the Germans at the start of their offensive on 22 March 1918. The 38th Division attacked the village on 18 September 1918 but it did not fall to the British until it was captured by the 21st Division on 8 October.

The British wartime burials were infrequent and numbered only 55 at the end of the war. These are now in Plot III. The German made burials here when they occupied the village in 1918 but these have been removed. At the same time they buried two Russian Prisoners of War. After the war 1207 graves were concentrated here from the battlefields involved in the Battle of Cambrai.

It was at this time that the cemetery gained its present name when the original British Cemetery was concentrated here. To that point this cemetery was known as the Communal Cemetery Extension.

Among those here are Corporals Lewis and Sydney Garry, 2nd Battalion, 3rd New Zealand Rifle Brigade. Both are recorded as woodworkers when they joined up together. They were killed three days apart but Sydney's body could not be formally identfied at the time of concentration so his grave is marked by a Special Memorial as he is believed to be buried in this cemetery.

Concentrated here:

Arvon Cemetery, Heudicourt - situated about 2km west of here by the side of the road from Gouzeaucourt to Fins. It was begun by the 38th Division in September 1918 and contained the graves of 65 British soldiers.

Genin Well Copse Cemetery, Heudicourt - situated 3km south of here in the fields between Heudicourt and Villers-Guislain near 'Chapel Hill'. It contained the graves of twenty British soldiers who died in September and October 1918.

Gouzeaucourt British Cemetery - situated about 1km north-east of here next to the road to Villers-Guislain. It was next to the quarry and a little east of the railway crossing. Begun by the 2nd Rifle Brigade in April 1917 it remained in use until September 1917 and contained the graves of 29 British soldiers.

Gouzeaucourt Wood Cemetery, Metz-En-Couture - situated 3km north-west of here next to the wood between Gouzeaucourt and Metz-en-Couture. It contained the graves of 44 New Zealand men, mostly from the 3rd Rifle Brigade, and two British soldiers who died in September and October 1918.

UK – 1182	NZ – 85	SAfr – 24
Can – 2	Newf – 1	Russia – 2
Unnamed – 382		Area – 4784 sq mts

Special Memorials erected to 33 British and thirteen New Zealand soldiers known, or believed, to be buried among the unnamed graves.

Special Memorial erected to a British soldier buried in Gouzeaucourt Communal Cemetery in May 1917 whose grave was destroyed by shell-fire.

LOCATION
Gouzeaucourt is situated on the Peronne-Cambrai road midway between the two towns. The cemetery is on the south side of the village, opposite the Communal Cemetery, on the east side of the road to Heudicourt.

GRAND RAVINE CEMETERY, HAVRINCOURT

HISTORY
The cemetery was opened and used in December 1917 and again in October 1918.

INFORMATION
Havrincourt was well behind German lines for most of the war. It was captured by the 62nd Division on 20 November 1917 and then remained in British hands through the winter. On 23 March 1918 the Germans captured the village at the start of their offensive and it remained in German hands until the Allied final advance to victory when, on 12 September 1918, the 62nd Division again captured the village. The Division held the village during a counter-attack on the following day.

The cemetery was opened in 1917 by the 62nd Division when the burials that now make up Row B were made. The same Division added the burials in Rows A and C in October 1918. Both sets of burials were for men, mostly of the 62nd Division, who had been killed during the respective attacks upon the village by the 62nd Division in 1917 and 1918. The graves of thirteen German Prisoners of War have been removed. The Memorial to the 62nd Division is on the southern edge of the village.

One of those buried here is 2nd Lieutenant Joe Dines, 13th King's (Liverpools), who was killed on 27 September 1918 aged 32 years. He had been a pre-war footballer, amateur international and a participant in the 1912 Olympics winning the Gold Medal with the Great Britain football team.

UK – 139   Unnamed – 11   Area – 406 sq mts

LOCATION

Havrincourt is a village about 15km south-west of Cambrai and 25km directly east of Bapaume. It lies next to, and just south of, the A2/E19 Autoroute. Grand Ravine Cemetery is situated about 2km south-east of the village in farm land on the edge of Havrincourt Wood. It lies in a deep valley between Havrincourt and Fesmy and is reached by a rough track from the southern edge of the village. You need a good 4x4 in winter.

GRANDCOURT ROAD CEMETERY, GRANDCOURT

HISTORY

The cemetery was made in the spring of 1917 during the battlefield clearance following the German withdrawal to the Hindenburg Line.

INFORMATION

The village was in German hands from 1914 and was a first day objective on 1 July 1916. It was not captured and was abandoned by the Germans at the start of February 1917 when the 63rd Division found the village empty on the night of the 5-6 February. The village fell to the Germans again in April 1918 but was taken for the final time in August.

The cemetery is situated on what the soldiers called 'Stump Road'. 'Grandcourt Road' is to the east. The ground behind the cemetery rises to the German 'Stuff Redoubt', part of the German second line which was captured by the 10th Cheshires on 9 October 1916. Some of those who died in the attack are buried here.

It is almost certain that some men of the 36th (Ulster) Division reached this position on 1 July 1916, but were forced to retreat as other units did not make similar successes. Some men continued to fight through into 2 July as there are four men of the 8th Royal Irish Rifles buried here all killed on 2 July. Most of the graves are of the 19th Division which reflects the story of one of the last actions of the 1916 battles when men of the 19th Division tried to advance here in a blizzard on 18 and 19 November 1916.

Among those here is Major Fred Robert Fulford Warren, 14th Hampshires, killed in action on 22 October 1916. He led the first successful attack the battalion had made, but was killed in action near Thiepval. Major Warren was buried where he fell but in spring 1917 when the battlefields were cleared by V Corps his grave was moved to this cemetery. Subsequently the village was lost to German troops in March 1918 and the position of the grave was lost so he is among the unidentified graves and is commemorated by the special memorial placed near the wall by the entrance.

UK – 390   Can – 1   Unnamed – 108
Area - 498 sq mts

Special Memorial erected to a British soldier who is known to be buried among the unnamed graves.

LOCATION

Grandcourt is situated in the valley of the River Ancre about 10km north of Albert. The Cemetery is about 2km south of the village, in the fields between it and Thiepval and to the east of the road between the two villages. The road from which this cemetery is accessed is very narrow and there is no parking area. As the sides of the road are steep there is nowhere to leave a car in close proximity without blocking the road. It may be best to park at Stump Road Cemetery and walk from there to here. The cemetery, 500m on the southern side of the road, is in the middle of fields a fair walk from the road.

GREVILLERS BRITISH CEMETERY

HISTORY
The cemetery was created by Casualty Clearing Stations situated here from March 1917 to March 1918. It was also used by the British from August 1918 to the end of the war. After the war 200 graves were brought in from the battlefields to the south of the village, and 40 from the German Cemetery.

INFORMATION
The village was in German hands from 1914 until occupied by British troops on 14 March 1917. In April and May 1917 the 3rd, 29th and 3rd Australian Casualty Clearing Stations were posted nearby. On 25 March 1918 Grevillers was captured by the Germans who made a cemetery on the east side of the British burial ground. On 24 August the New Zealand Division recaptured Grevillers and in September the 34th, 49th and 56th Casualty Clearing Stations came to the village and resumed use of the British Cemetery.

The 927 German graves were removed. Some plots near the entrance give a dominant impression of Australian sunbursts on the stones. The French are buried near the Cross of Sacrifice.

Most of the WW2 graves are those of a bomber crew of No. 115 Squadron shot down in their Lancaster on 14 July 1943 after a raid on Aachen. With them is a pilot of No. 403 Squadron, Royal Canadian Airforce shot down on in his Spitfire on 13 May 1943.

Also here is Colonel Charles Christie Fleming, DSO. He had seen service with the Anglo–Egyptian Nile Expeditionary Force under General Kitchener, for which he received his Distinguished Service Order, and served in the South African Wars, Malta and Crete before retiring in 1910. In April 1915 he was made Assistant Director of Medical Services, Royal Army Medical Corps, in the 51st (Highland) Division. He died aged 53 years, on Christmas Eve, of wounds received from a bomb that exploded on 23 December 1917.

You can find the grave of Lieutenant Colonel George Bissett, DSO, MC and Bar, 1st Royal Scots Fusiliers who died on 10 October 1918 and that of Lieutenant Colonel William Scott Pennycook, 2nd Otago Regt, NZEF who died on 24 August 1918.

Another buried here is Captain Cecil Vernon Gardner, DFC, No. 19 Squadron, Royal Air Force, died on 30 September 1918 aged 29 years. He is credited with ten victories. Gardner enlisted in December 1915, transferring to the Royal Flying Corps as an Air Mechanic (2nd Class) in March 1917. Due to heavy losses Gardner was soon commissioned as a 2nd Lieutenant in July 1917. His final fight took place on 27 September, when he destroyed a German plane over Haynecourt, but he was then shot down and fatally injured. He died of his wounds three days later. He was posthumously awarded the Distinguished Flying Cross. The citation reads 'A bold and skilful leader, who has carried out many offensive patrols, proving himself at all times to be a brilliant fighting pilot. During recent operations he has accounted for eight enemy machines.'

Also buried here is Private John (Jack) Arnst, 1st Canterbury Regiment, NZEF, who died on 25 August 1918 aged 37 years. In the early 1900's he, and his brother Richard, had been champion cyclists in New Zealand and Australia with Jack becoming the Long Distance Road Champion of Australasia.

A young Australian buried here is Private Miller Mafaking Fergusson, 27th Australian Infantry, who was a labourer from South Australia. He joined the 27th on 9 April 1917, but only a month later, on 5 May 1917, he was wounded in action near Bapaume, and died later that day. He was 16 years 4 months old when he died. He had two brothers who also served in the war. Also here is Private Albert Charles Baden Govers, 1st Australian Infantry, from New South Wales, who had been a station-hand. He enlisted in February 1916 aged 15 and was killed in action at Flers on 5 November 1916 also aged 16 years 4 months.

UK – 1507	Aust - 428	NZ – 153
Can – 14	S Afr – 1	BWI – 1
India – 2	Fr – 18	Unnamed – 189
KUG – 4	WW2 - 7	Area - 5989 sq mts

Special Memorials are erected to fifteen Australian and three British soldiers known or believed to be buried among the unnamed.

Special Memorials record the names of two British soldiers, buried in Avesnes-les-Bapaume German Cemetery, whose graves could not be found.

New Zealand Memorial
The Memorial commemorates 446 officers and men of the New Zealand Division who died and who have no known grave in the fighting in this area from March to August 1918, and in the advance to Victory between 8 August and 11 November 1918. This is one of seven memorials in France and Belgium to those New Zealand soldiers who

died on the Western Front and whose graves are not known. The memorials are all in cemeteries chosen as appropriate to the fighting in which the men died.
Concentrated Here:
Avesnes-Les-Bapaume German Cemetery – it was about 1km east of here and contained the graves of two British soldiers who died in April 1918.

Bayonet Trench Cemetery, Gueudecourt – located about 4km south of here, it contained the graves of 19 soldiers of the 1st Australian Infantry who died on 5 November 1916.

LOCATION
Grevillers is found 3km west of Bapaume. The British Cemetery is a large cemetery on the eastern edge of the village on the north side of the road to Bapaume.

GROVE TOWN CEMETERY, MEAULTE

HISTORY
The cemetery was opened in September 1916 to deal with the casualties from the Battles of the Somme. It remained in use until April 1917 and, other than a few burials in late 1918, the cemetery was closed when the Germans withdrew to the Hindenburg Line.

INFORMATION
The 34th and 55th (2/2nd London) Casualty Clearing Stations were located here in September 1916 and they made the majority of the burials before April 1917. The location was known by the French as 'La Demie-lieue' though the British gave it the name 'Grove Town'. There is a group of Germans buried here who died as Prisoners of War.

The first burials followed the actions of 15 September 1916. Among those is Lieutenant George MacPherson, 4th Section, Machine Gun Corps who was the first tank officer to be killed. He was aged 20 years and his headstone bears the symbol of the Machine Gun Corps rather than Tank Corps. The Tank Corps began life as the Machine Gun Corps (Heavy Section).

Also here are Lieutenant Colonel Charles James Willoughby Hobbs, DSO, 2nd Sherwood Foresters, who died of wounds on 16 October 1916 aged 40 years and Major Edmund Rochfort Street, DSO, 2nd Sherwood Foresters who died of wounds on 15 October 1916 aged 40 years. Hobbs had seen action on the North-West Frontier and the South African Wars. His Distinguished Service Order was awarded in January 1916 for his leadership at Hooge in 1915 when his commanding officer had been wounded and he took charge. Street had served in India and the South African Campaign before resigning in 1906. He was made a Captain in the Sherwood Foresters in October 1914. His DSO was awarded for his actions under fire in May 1915 and for rescuing men from a mine when gas had affected them. They were commanding officer and his second in command who were both wounded as their unit attacked German gun pits at Cloudy Trench north-east of Gueudecourt.

Sergeant Leslie Coulson, 2/2nd Londons (Royal Fusiliers) attached 1/12th (The Rangers) Londons is buried here. He died of wounds on 8 October 1916 aged 27 years. He was a journalist and poet, who wrote 'From an Outpost and Other Poems'. He had served in Malta and Gallipoli with the 2/2nd Londons and on the Somme at Combles and Leuze Wood with the 1/12th Londons before being mortally wounded at Le Transloy on 7 October.

Buried here is Captain James Dacres Belgrave, MC & Bar, No. 60 Squadron, Royal Air Force and 2nd Oxford and Bucks Light Infantry, killed in action on 13 June 1918 aged 21 years. He is credited with eighteen victories making him an 'ace'. He was commissioned as a 2nd Lieutenant in the Oxford and Bucks Light Infantry in December 1914, but was wounded in action in November 1915. He was promoted to Lieutenant in February 1916 and joined the Royal Flying Corps in October 1916, serving in No. 45 Squadron. He was awarded the Military Cross in July 1917 for which the citation reads 'For conspicuous gallantry and devotion to duty. On at least five occasions he successfully engaged and shot down hostile aeroplanes, and has consistently shown great courage and determination to get to the closest range; an invaluable example in a fighting squadron.' He spent some time in England and returned to France in April 1918 moving to No. 60 Squadron. He was awarded a posthumous Bar to his MC, the citation reads 'For conspicuous gallantry and devotion to duty whilst leading offensive patrols. In four days he destroyed two enemy machines and drove down four others. The odds were heavy against him, and he did magnificent work.'

Also here is Private George Leonard Edwards, 11th Essex, who was killed in action on 24 September 1916 aged 15 years.

Finally the grave of Private Frank Hitchin, 59th Battalion, Machine Gun Corps, who died on 22 September 1916 aged 18 years has the inscription 'If this is Victory, then let God stop all wars – his loving mother'.

UK - 1365	Aust - 14	Newf – 12
NZ - 1	Fr - 1	Ger - 34
Unnamed – 2		Area – 3541 sq mts

LOCATION
Meaulte is now almost a suburb of Albert to the south-east of the town. This cemetery is on the southern side of the smaller of two roads leading from Albert to Bray-sur-Somme. It is about 3km from the centre of Albert. It is found in open fields on the south side of the airfield about 2km south-east of Meaulte. The last 200m is a farm track.

GUARDS' CEMETERY, COMBLES

HISTORY
It was begun by the Guards Division in September 1916, and used by other units until March 1917. It was used to a small extent in March, August and September 1918. At the end of the war it contained 96 graves, of which nineteen were those of officers and men of the Guards; and it was then increased by the concentration into Plot II of 56 graves from Priez Farm Cemetery. Six German graves of 1918 have been removed.

INFORMATION
The village was in German hands from 1914 until entered in the early morning of 26 September 1916 without a fight by units of the 56th (London) Division and of the French Army 73rd and 110th Infantry Regiments. It had been evacuated by the Germans overnight as it had almost been surrounded, though 500 men who failed to get away were captured. The village remained in Allied hands until 24 March 1918, when it was captured after a stubborn stand by the South African Brigade at Marrieres Wood. It was retaken on 29 August 1918 by the 18th Division.

Buried here is Lieutenant Colonel Alfred John Hamilton Bowen, 2nd Monmouthshires, DSO and Bar, three times MiD, killed on 2 March 1917 while commanding his men who were digging a new trench near Sailly-Saillisel. The citation for his Distinguished Service Order, awarded for actions near Ieper while he was a Captain, reads 'On the 13th May, 1915, east of Ieper, though wounded in two places in the head before dawn, he refused to leave his company, and continued to command it with conspicuous ability. After the action was over and the battalion returned to La Brique, he was found to be suffering from two other wounds in the body. He was then sent to hospital.'

Nearby is the farm known during the war as Falfemont Farm. The original farm, which is not to be confused with the one on the present site, was a German fortified strong point. It is on the road west from the cemetery and through the village. You will see the present Falfemont Farm and a track that leads to the site of the pre-war farm. There is a grave which contains three men of 1/2nd Londons. Captain R 'Dick' Heumann, CSM M B Mills and Sergeant A W Torrance, all killed by a shell on 10 September 1916 when discussing a forthcoming attack to stop a potential German counter-attack. There were buried in a shell hole. After the war, Heumann's family bought the ground and requested the grave be undisturbed. It is located in a field by the track leading from Combles to Falfemont Farm some 400m from Guards' Cemetery.

Concentrated here:

Priez Farm Cemetery, Combles - stood at the south-east corner of Le Priez Farm, on the north side of the road from Combles to Rancourt. The farm was taken by the 18th Division on 1 September 1918, after very heavy fighting. The cemetery contained the graves of 79 British soldiers who died in the winter of 1916-17 and in August and September 1918.

UK – 182   NF – 4   Unnamed - 15
Area - 989 sq mts

Special Memorials are erected to 30 British soldiers, buried in Priez Farm Cemetery and Combles German Cemetery, whose graves were destroyed by shell fire.

LOCATION
Combles is 16km east of Albert and 13km south of Bapaume. Guards' Cemetery is on the south-western outskirts of the village. There is a path leading 70m, from a by-road leading towards Maurepas, to the cemetery which is almost on top of a ridge overlooking the valley that runs south-west from the village.

GUARDS' CEMETERY, LESBOEUFS

HISTORY
The cemetery was begun in October 1916 to bury men of the Guards Division who died in the fighting in the area in September 1916. It was not used again during the war but it was greatly enlarged after the war by the concentration of graves from isolated positions and smaller cemeteries on the surrounding battlefields.

INFORMATION
The village was in German hands from 1914 and was captured by the Guards Division on 25 September 1916 after a previous unsuccessful attack by them from Ginchy towards Lesboeufs on 15 September. The Guards suffered heavily as the nine tanks allocated to them failed to materialise. Once the village had been captured the Guards had to hold the village. They were relieved having lost 7240 casualties in three weeks. This includes Captain Herbert Percy Meakin, Guards Trench Mortar Battery, who was killed at the spot at which his memorial can be found – on a ridge 400m south-west of the cemetery. His grave could not be identified after the war which is why his family bought this land for a memorial.

The Germans retook the village on 24 March 1918 despite resistance by the 63rd Battalion, Machine Gun Corps. The 10th South Wales Borderers recaptured the village on 29 August 1918.

The cemetery made during the war contained the graves of 40 soldiers, mostly officers, of the 2nd Grenadier Guards who had been killed during the attack on Lesboeufs on 25 September 1916. They are what is now Plot I. The cemetery was enlarged after the war as over 3000 bodies were concentrated here. At the same time the graves of 39 French soldiers were moved elsewhere.

Buried here is 2nd Lieutenant Thomas Percy Arthur Hervey, 21st (Yeoman Rifles) Kings Royal Rifle Corps, killed in action on 15 September 1916. He was the son of a Hampshire vicar and was in colonial service in Fiji when he volunteered.

Also here is Sergeant James Phillip Donnelly, DCM, MM, 1st East Yorkshires, killed on 25 September 1916, aged 44 years. He had been awarded the Distinguished Conduct Medal in the Boer War while a Private with 5th Mounted Infantry. He re-enlisted in 1914 and served in the depot as a Sergeant Instructor, but was posted to France in 1916 as a Private which is how he is recorded in the hard copy of the CWGC register. He was awarded the Military Medal in August 1916 soon after arriving. He was killed in front of Gueudecourt on the afternoon of the 25 September taking part in the 64th Brigade attack on Gird trench.

Memorials to the fighting of 1916 are situated nearby. The Grenadier Guards Memorial is situated about 200m south-west of the cemetery on the north-west side of the road to Ginchy. The Guards Division Memorial is a further 200m towards Ginchy almost on the line the Division reached. An important German position called 'The Triangle' is just south of the memorial. There is also a memorial north of the village to two French soldiers, Georges Lejoindre and Georges Pfister as well as their comrades in the 18th Territorial Infantry Regiment killed nearby in September 1914.

Concentrated here:

Flers Dressing Station Cemetery, Ginchy - situated about 1km west of here in the fields between Flers and Delville Wood. It contained the graves of 33 Australian and eight British soldiers who had been killed from September 1916 to March 1917.

Flers Road Cemetery, Flers - situated next to the Flers-Longueval road midway between the two villages. It was made in October 1916 for the burial of seventeen British soldiers, three men from New Zealand and one from Australia who died in action nearby.

Ginchy ADS Cemetery - situated about 1km south of here on the north side of Ginchy village. The cemetery was used from November 1916 until March 1917 for the burial of 77 British soldiers and an Australian who had died of wounds.

Ginchy Royal Field Artillery Cemetery - situated about 1km west of here in the fields between Ginchy and Flers. It contained the graves of sixteen British artillerymen and five Australian soldiers who died from October 1916 to February 1917.

Guards' Burial Ground, Lesboeufs - situated on the east side of the village. It was made in October 1916 for the burial of 21 soldiers of the Guards Division who had been killed on 15 September 1916.

Needle Dump Cemetery, Lesboeufs - situated next to the road from Flers to Lesboeufs midway between the two villages. It contained the graves of 23 Australian and four British soldiers who died from October 1916 to March 1917.

Needle Dump South Cemetery, Lesboeufs - situated about 50m south of Needle Dump Cemetery. It contained the graves of fourteen Australian and nine British soldiers who died between October 1916 and March 1917.

Switch Trench Cemetery, Flers - situated near Flers Road Cemetery but in the fields to the east of the road. It contained 102 Australian and eight British graves dating from 1916-1917. The New Zealand Memorial is nearby on another part of the former Switch Trench.

Windmill Trench Cemetery, Lesboeufs - situated about 1km north of here next to the road from Lesboeufs to Gueudecourt. It was made from September 1916 to March 1917 for the burial of 27 British and sixteen Australian soldiers.

UK – 2827	Aust – 202	NZ – 11
Newf – 4	Can – 1	Unnamed – 1643

Area – 8798 sq mts

Special Memorials are erected to 76 British and seven Australian soldiers who are known, or believed, to be buried among the unidentified graves.

Special Memorials are erected to five British soldiers, who were buried in Ginchy ADS Cemetery, but whose graves were destroyed by shell-fire.

Special Memorials to three officers of the 2nd Coldstream Guards who were buried near this cemetery at the crossroads of the Flers-Combles and Ginchy-Lesboeufs roads. They were killed together on 26 September 1916 but when the CWGC tried to find the graves for concentration they could not be located as the marker memorial was probably in the wrong place. The three are Major Harry Verelst, MC, Lieutenants Francis William Talbot Clerke and John Atholl.

LOCATION

Lesboeufs is situated about 11km east of Albert and just to the west of the A1 Autoroute. Guards' Cemetery is about 1km south-west of the village on the north side of the road to Ginchy. The cemetery is on a high bank as the road from Lesboeufs to Ginchy is a sunken road. It has an unusual central pathway with paving stones separated to allow flowers to grow between them.

GUÉMAPPE BRITISH CEMETERY, WANCOURT

HISTORY
It was begun by the 15th (Scottish) Division after the capture of Guémappe and used until January 1918.

INFORMATION
Guémappe was in German hands for most of the war. It captured by British troops on the 23 to 24 April 1917, lost on 23 March 1918, and retaken by the Canadian Corps on the following 26 August.

The cemetery was severely damaged by shell-fire in 1918. There are 112 men of the 8th Seaforth Highlanders and the 9th Black Watch buried here.

Also here is Pioneer Henry McGuire, 3rd Special Company, Royal Engineers, killed in action on 14 October 1917 aged 24 years. He was a self-employed plumber and decorator before the war. He had served at Gallipoli in the 4th Cheshires and was in the Suvla Bay landings but was sent home suffering from dysentery. Once well, even though he had served his time, he re-joined the Royal Engineers, and had been twelve months in France when killed by shell-fire. He had three brothers serving in the war and his elder brother, Company Sergeant Major J McGuire, 1/5th Kings (Liverpools) was the first territorial soldier to win the Distinguished Conduct Medal and Bar.

UK – 169   Unnamed – 6   Area – 584 sq mts

LOCATION
Guémappe is located 1km south-west of the main road from Arras to Cambrai. The cemetery is near the south side of the more northerly road to Wancourt, opposite the junction of the road to Monchy. It is set back from the road and reached by a path from the road.

GUILLEMONT ROAD CEMETERY, GUILLEMONT

HISTORY
The Cemetery was opened after the Battle of Guillemont in September 1916 and remained in use until March 1917. The cemetery was greatly enlarged after the war by the concentration of graves from the surrounding battlefields.

INFORMATION
Von Kluck's army had reached this village in 1914. So this is roughly where the actions of the French brought the Germans to a halt in this area and the front-lines began to solidify.

Guillemont was an important point in the German defences during the early part of the Battles of the Somme in 1916. It was occupied briefly by the 2nd Royal Scots Fusiliers on 30 July, as part of an attack by 30th Division, but they were forced to abandon the position. Most men were killed or captured in a German counter attack. However, the action by 30th Division had seen the 2nd Bedfordshires and the French 153rd Infantry Regiment capture the ruins of Maltz Horn Farm. There is now a memorial to this attack 2km south of this cemetery next to the road to Hardecourt-aux-Bois.

Units of the 55th Division entered the village again on 8 August, and the 2nd Division on 18 August, but on both occasions it was abandoned. It was not until the start of the Battle of Guillemont on 3 September that the village was captured and held by the 20th and 16th Divisions. The Germans took the village during their offensive in March 1918 but it was retaken for the final time by the 18th and 38th Divisions on 29 August.

Trones Wood was mis-named by military mapmakers during the war. The French name is Bois de Troncs, which means 'Trunks'. It was not an objective on 1 July 1916 but could have been taken. The British failure elsewhere along the front and the problem of co-operation with the French meant earlier success in the day in this area was not followed up. The Germans reinforced the wood so that units of 18th and 30th Divisions had a hard time from 8 to 14 July taking the wood. The final capture by 18th Division cost 4000 British casualties. The 18th Division also captured the wood in August 1918. They erected a memorial on the southern edge of the wood that reads 'The Greatest Thing in the World'.

The cemetery was sometimes known as Trones Wood Cemetery after the wood by which the cemetery stands. It was begun as a front-line cemetery by units of the Guards

Division and stands on ground across which many costly attacks were made.

An advanced Dressing Station of 16th Division was positioned here after the capture of Guillemont. Men who died in the ADS or whose remains were bought back from the battlefield were buried here until March 1917 making 121 graves just inside the modern entrance pavilion. The remainder of the cemetery is a concentration cemetery as 2139 graves, mostly men who died from July to September 1916, were moved here from the battlefields surrounding Guillemont. At the same time 39 French graves were moved elsewhere.

Among those here is 2nd Lieutenant William Stanhope Forbes, 1st Duke of Cornwall's Light Infantry, killed on 3 September 1916. He was an architecture student before the war, son of Stanhope Alexander Forbes of the Royal Academy. His inscription reads 'He saw beyond the filth of battle and thought death a fair price to pay to belong to the company of these fellows'.

Also here is Lieutenant Raymond Asquith, 3rd Grenadier Guards, son of the Prime Minister. He was shot in the chest during an attack on 15 September 1916 between Ginchy and Lesboeufs and died before reaching the ADS. His inscription reads 'Small time but in that small most greatly lived this star of England'.

Near to Asquith is Lieutenant the Honourable Edward Wyndham Tennant, 4th Grenadier Guards, killed on 22 September 1916 when his unit carried out a bombing attack towards Gird Trench. He was the son of Baron Glenconner and a cousin related by marriage to Asquith.

Two Lieutenant Colonels are here. Arthur Paston Mack, 9th Suffolks, killed leading his men in an attack on Straight Trench north-east of Ginchy on 15 September 1916 aged 53 years. John Colliers Stormouth-Darking, DSO, twice MiD, 1st Cameronians attached 9th Highland Light Infantry was killed on 1 November 1916 aged 38 years by a sniper near Le Transloy. In January 1900 he joined the 3rd Kings Own Scottish Borderers and was commissioned in the 2nd Scottish Rifles in August 1900. He served in South Africa and was Mentioned in Despatches. In 1914 he was Adjutant of the 1st Battalion, and with them took part in the retreat from Mons. Early in 1916 he was given command of a battalion of Highland Light Infantry. He was awarded the Distinguished Service Order posthumously for his leadership.

In the local fields, Captain Noel Chavasse, Royal Army Medical Corps, Medical Officer of the 1/10th (Liverpool Scottish) Kings (Liverpools) won the first of two Victoria Crosses on 9 August 1916. His second was awarded at Ieper in 1917. He is the only man to win the VC twice in WW1 – both for trying to save men in no-man's land armed with nothing more than his medical kit.

Several Memorials were erected in the cemetery but these have now been removed. However, nearby the 20th Division erected a Memorial at a crossroads 450m east of Guillemont, about 1km east of here, on the road to Combles. Next to the Church is a Memorial to the 16th Division. One casualty from the Division was the Irish economist, journalist, barrister, writer, poet, soldier and Home Rule politician, Lieutenant Thomas Michael 'Tom' Kettle, 9th Royal Dublin Fusiliers. He was killed leading a company of his men but has no known grave.

In fields about 1km north of the cemetery and south of the Guillemont-Longueval road is a memorial to 2nd Lieutenant George Marsden-Smedley, 3rd Rifle Brigade, killed aged 19 years on 18 August 1916 in his first attack. He had been in the battalion for 25 days. He was one of four 2nd Lieutenants from his unit killed on that day. The others are identified and buried in Delville Wood Cemetery. Marsden-Smedley was not and is commemorated on the Thiepval Memorial. Hence, his family had this memorial erected.

On the road from Guillemont to Combles is a well-marked track leading north to a place known as Dickens Cross. It is a personal memorial to Major Cedric Charles Dickens, grandson of the author. He had been in the army since 1915, wounded in 1915 and survived the attack at Gommecourt on 1 July 1916. He was killed on 9 September 1916 with the 1/13th (Kensington) Londons attacking Leuze Wood. His men put up a cross in 1917 where they believed he was buried but after the war, when the Dickens family tried to rebury their relative, no body could be found. The grave had been clearly marked so it is probable that it had been disturbed in 1918 and the original markers were put back out of position. In 1979 a farmer ploughed up some officer's equipment nearby. In the 1990's, the memorial cross was moved to a new and more accessible site nearer the road where you find it now. Dickens is commemorated on the Thiepval Memorial on the Addenda Panel.

Just north of Hardecourt-aux-Bois are two memorials. The closest to this cemetery is a memorial to two men of French 153rd Infantry Regiment, Marcel Boucher and Romeo Lapage, who died here on 28 July 1916. Nearby is a memorial to Captain Augustin Cochin, 4th Chausseurs, killed, at the site of the memorial, on 8 July 1916.

Concentrated here:

Hardecourt Village French Military Cemetery - situated on the edge of the village about 2km south of here though it has since been removed to larger French National Cemeteries. The village was captured by the French on 8 July 1916 but fell to the Germans in March 1917. It was taken by the British 58th and 12th Divisions on 28 August 1918. The cemetery was used in September 1916 for the burial of five British artillerymen. In September 1918 a further sixteen British soldiers, fourteen of the 9th Royal Fusiliers and two of the 7th Royal Sussex, were buried here by the 12th Division.

UK – 2259	Can – 1	Aust – 1
SAfr – 1	Newf – 1	Ger – 2
Unnamed – 1523		Area - 8344 sq mts

Special Memorials to eight British soldiers known, or believed, to be buried among the unnamed graves.

LOCATION

Guillemont can be found on the ridges north of the Somme, about 10km east of Albert and a similar distance north-west of Peronne. The cemetery lies on the north side of the road between Guillemont and Montauban about 1km west of Guillemont.

H.A.C. CEMETERY, ECOUST-ST. MEIN

HISTORY
This cemetery was begun by the 7th Division after the battles nearby in April 1917. After the war the remaining burials were made by the concentration of graves from local burial grounds

INFORMATION
The area was in German hands from 1914. The enemy line from Doignies to Hénin-sur-Cojeul, including the village of Ecoust-St. Mein, were captured on 2 April 1917 by the 4th Australian and 7th Divisions. It fell to the Germans in early 1918 and was taken back in the final push to victory.

The first part of the cemetery to be created was when 27 men of the 2nd Honourable Artillery Company who died, with one exception, on 31 March or 1 April 1917 were buried in what is now Plot I, Row A. After the German counter-attack near Lagnicourt on 15 April, twelve Australian gunners were buried in the same row. Rows B, C and part of D were made in August and September 1918, when the ground had been recaptured by the 3rd Division after five months in German hands. These 120 graves were the original H.A.C. Cemetery. After the war 1725 graves were added from the battlefields of Bullecourt and Ecoust-St. Mein and smaller burial grounds.

Among those buried here is Rifleman John Woodhouse, 12th Kings Royal Rifle Corps, who was executed for desertion on 4 October 1917. He had already been under a death sentence when he deserted during the Battle of Langemark. He was captured when found in a ditch near Calais after 16 days.

Also here are Lieutenant John Harold Pritchard and Private Christopher Douglas Elphick, both 2nd Honourable Artillery Company and both killed in action on 15 May 1917. Their remains were discovered by a farmer in 2009 and they were buried here, with several unidentified soldiers, on 23 April 2013.

Also of note is Private Arthur Frederick Cornwell, 1/13th (Kensington) Londons killed in action on 29 August 1918. His father, Private Eli Cornwell, died at home while serving with the 57th Protection Company, Royal Defence Corps on 25 October 1916 aged 64 years. Arthur's half-brother, Boy 1st Class John 'Jack' Travers Cornwell won the Victoria Cross in the Battle of Jutland aboard HMS Chester on 31 May 1916 and died on 2 June. He is one of the youngest winners of the VC being aged just 16 years and three months. Father and son are buried in Manor Park Cemetery, London.

Another here is Captain Auberon Thomas Herbert, No. 22 Squadron, Royal Flying Corps and Hampshire Yeomanry (Carabiniers), killed in action on 3 November 1916 aged 40 years. He was the 8th Baron Lucas and 11th Baron Dingwall. He had been a war correspondent for The Times during the South African Wars when he was wounded and lost his leg. He then held senior posts in the Civil Service before joining the Royal Flying Corps in 1915 and arriving in France in August 1916. He was buried by the Germans and moved here in 1925.

Buried here is Lieutenant Walter de Courcey Dodd, No. 11 Squadron, Royal Flying Corps, formerly 5th Royal Munster Fusiliers, killed in action on 31 October 1917 with his pilot 2nd Lieutenant Sidney Walter Randall, when they were shot down behind German lines. Dodd's brother, 2nd Lieutenant Francis Joseph Dodd, Machine Gun Corps, died of pneumonia, after being gassed, on 31 October 1918 and is buried in Grantham Cemetery, Lincolnshire. Another brother, Lieutenant John O'Connell Dodd, 6th Royal Munster Fusiliers, was killed in action on 7 November 1918 and is buried at Monceau-Saint-Waast Communal Cemetery.

Concentrated here:

Barastre Communal Cemetery German Extension – located about 6km south of here, it contained the graves of 284 Germans, 46 French, 39 British, four New Zealand men and one from Australia.

Bullecourt Churchyard – in the centre of the village 1km north-east of here and in which were buried two British airmen.

Bullecourt German Cemetery - south of the village in which 200 German and 30 British soldiers were buried.

Cagnicourt Communal Cemetery German Extension – located about 5km north-east of here, it contained 333 German and six Russian graves, and those of seventeen British soldiers and one from Australia.

Croisilles German Cemeteries – located about 2km north-west of here were two burial grounds on the road to Ecoust-St. Mein that contained 505 German, one French, and eleven British soldiers.

Epinoy Churchyard – located about 15km north-east of here and 5km north-west of Cambrai. It contained the graves of three British men and one from Canada as well as 136 Germans. The church was destroyed in the war.

Imperial Cemetery – 1km west of Hendecourt-Les-Cagnicourt which is about 3km north-east of here. It contained the graves of twelve British men and seven Canadian soldiers, who died in August and September 1918.

Inchy-En-Artois Churchyard - one British Royal Naval Air Service officer was buried here which is about 7km east of this location.

Lecluse Churchyard - one British Royal Flying Corps officer was buried here. It is located about 12km north-east of here in the valley of the River L'Hirondelle.

L'Homme Mort Cemetery No. 2, Ecoust-St. Mein – situated between L'Homme Mort and Vraucourt about 2km south-west of here. It contained the graves of nineteen British soldiers who died in August and September 1918.

Marquion German Cemetery – situated in the village of Marquion about 8km north-east of here. It contained the graves of 211 German, eight Russian, and seventeen British soldiers.

Mory-Ecoust Road Cemeteries No. 1 and No. 2, Ecoust-St. Mein - both located very near the road and about 1km south-west of here. They were made in March-May 1917 and contained the graves of 63 British soldiers, almost all 8th and 9th Devonshires and Royal Field Artillery, and one from Australia.

Queant German Cemetery – situated at the north-east end of the village which is about 4km east of here. Buried there were 22 British soldiers who died in March 1918.

Villers-Les-Cagnicourt Communal Cemetery – located about 8km north-east of here. Buried here were 25 German and two British soldiers.

UK – 1704   Aust – 176
NZ – 4   Can - 26
Unnamed – 1086   KUG – 145
Area – 5802 sq mts.

Special Memorials are erected to seventeen British soldiers and fourteen from Australia, known or believed to be buried here.

Special Memorials record the names of 34 British soldiers, buried in other cemeteries, whose graves were destroyed by shell fire.

LOCATION

Ecoust-St. Mein is situated between Arras, Cambrai and Bapaume. H.A.C. Cemetery is 1km south of the village, on the west side of the road to Bapaume.

HAM BRITISH CEMETERY, MUILLE-VILLETTE

HISTORY

The cemetery was created from January to March 1918 by the Casualty Clearing Station that was stationed nearby. Further graves were concentrated here after the war.

INFORMATION

This area was in German hands for most of the war. It was taken when the Germans withdrew to the Hindenburg Line in 1917. In January, February and March 1918, the 61st (South Midland) Casualty Clearing Station was posted at Ham, but on 23 March the Germans, in their advance towards Amiens, crossed the Somme at Ham capturing the town which saw the withdrawal of the CCS. The town remained in German hands until the French First Army re-took it from the Germans on 6 September 1918.

When the Fifth Army attempted to halt the German advance on 23-25 March 1918, the men of the 17th, 18th and 19th Kings (Liverpools) of 30th Division formed a defensive position on the north side of Ham. They believed the marshes of the River Somme on the south side of Ham would halt the Germans, but the Germans crossed the river east of Ham on 23 March 1918, captured the railway bridge over the canal which was held by the 21st Entrenching Battalion, and then moved to Ham. They fired on the Liverpool Battalions from the rear at the same time as other Germans launched a frontal attack. The Germans captured three bridges which allowed their continued advance. This was all achieved in just three hours.

The cemetery began in January 1918 as an extension of a German burial ground, one of several in the area. The present German Cemetery was not begun until they occupied the area in April 1918. In 1919 these graves were regrouped and others were added from the German Cemetery and from other burial grounds. You will see a few graves dating from periods other than early 1918 which have been concentrated from other cemeteries.

Among those here is Lance Serjeant E Proctor, DCM, 17th The King's (Liverpools), killed in action on 23 March 1918. His Distinguished Conduct Medal was awarded for continued high performance rather than a single act.

Also here are 2nd Lieutenants George Llewellyn Pitt, aged 28 years and Mark Head aged 30 years. Both are No. 8 Squadron, Royal Flying Corps and Pitt was also 10th York and Lancasters. They were killed on 28 December 1915 when shot down by a German Aviatik over Sancourt while flying a BE2c. They were buried in Douilly Communal Cemetery about 4km north of here and moved here in 1936.

Ham Communal Cemetery is found on the south side of the Cugny road. The Communal Cemetery contained three British graves made in 1914, of which one is unnamed. The others were Colonel Frank Ridley Farrer Boileau, 3rd Division Staff, who died of wounds on 28 August 1914 and Private W William, 18th Hussars who died of wounds on the following day. There were also nineteen French war graves. The British graves were moved to Terlincthun British Cemetery. The Communal Cemetery was also used by the Germans early in the war.

In March–August 1918, Ham Communal Cemetery German Extension (the Neuer Friedhof Chaunystrasse) was made. Three British soldiers were buried in the German burial ground until reburied here. Another German Cemetery was Ham Churchyard German Extension. There was also Muille-

Villette Communal Cemetery German Extension. The British Graves from these three have been moved here and to Roye New British Cemetery.

Ham (Muille-Villette) German Cemetery adjoins the west side of the British Cemetery. It contains the graves of 1113 identified and 420 unidentified German soldiers

Concentrated here:
- Croix-Molignaux German Cemetery (March and April 1918)
- Esmery-Hallon Churchyard
- Villers-St. Christophe Churchyard (March 1918)
- Eppeville Communal Cemetery German Extension (March 1918)
- St. Sulpice Communal Cemetery

Douilly Communal Cemetery – located about 4km north of here it contained four graves. Two officers in No. 8 Squadron, Royal Flying Corps killed while flying on 28 December 1915, one man of the 16th Lancashire Fusiliers who died on 1 April 1917 and a Driver in the Royal Field Artillery who died in an accident the following day.

Offoy Communal Cemetery – located about 4km north-west of here. It contained two graves of men buried on 14 May 1917. One of these is Private Thomas Hogan, 2nd Royal Inniskilling Fusiliers, who served as Murphy. He was executed for desertion and was the first Irishman to be executed in 1917.

Quivieres Communal Cemetery – located about 8km north of here with one grave of a British Corporal who died on 5 May 1917.

Ham Communal Cemetery German Extension – it contained three British soldiers killed in 1918.

Matigny Communal Cemetery – located about 6km north-west of here with one grave of a British Private killed on 27 August 1914.

UK – 485   Unnamed – 218

Area – 2212 sq mts

Special Memorials are erected to fourteen soldiers, believed to be buried in unnamed graves.

Special Memorials record the names of 53 British soldiers, buried in other cemeteries, whose graves were not found.

LOCATION

Ham is a small town in the valley of the Somme close to the southern boundary of the Department of the Somme and at the limit of the area covered by this book. It is about 20kms south west of St. Quentin at the crossroads of the D930 St. Quentin-Roye and the D937 Peronne-Chauny roads. The cemetery is in the neighbouring village of Muille-Villette. The British cemetery is at the rear of the German cemetery. There is a path at the side of the German cemetery as there is no access through the German cemetery.

HAMEL MILITARY CEMETERY, BEAUMONT-HAMEL

HISTORY

The cemetery was begun in August 1915 and remained in use until June 1917. A few burials were made in late 1918 and some graves were concentrated after the war.

INFORMATION

Beaumont was in German hands from 1914 until captured by British troops in November 1916, but Hamel was in British hands from the summer of 1915 until 27 March 1918. Hamel was a front line village for much of the war.

Many of the men here were killed in 1916. Following the main period of use a few further burials were made in Plot II, Row F, after the capture of the village in 1918. It was known at times by the names of 'Brook Street Trench Cemetery' and 'White City Cemetery'. It was enlarged after the war by the concentration of 48 graves from the immediate neighbourhood. There are also two men of the Labour Corps who died in 1919, possibly while clearing the battlefields.

Buried here is Lieutenant-Colonel Frederick John Saunders DSO, three times MiD, Royal Marine Light Infantry, commanding the Anson Battalion, Royal Naval Division killed by shellfire aged 40 years on the evening of 13 November 1916 as his battalion moved up for an attack on 14 November. He joined the RMLI in 1895, served in China and the South African Wars. It was noted that he was the tallest man in the Naval Brigade at the time. His clothing and equipment was hit five times, during the South African Wars, but his body not once. Nonetheless, he was invalided home with Enteric Fever, Mentioned in Despatches and awarded the Distinguished Service Order. Having been promoted to Major in July 1914, he served at Gallipoli where he was again Mentioned in Despatches. He received another 'Mention' posthumously.

Also here is Lieutenant-Colonel Norman Ormsby Burge, MiD, Royal Marine Light Infantry, of the Nelson Battalion killed in the attack on Beaucourt on 13 November 1916 aged 40 years. He had served in Gallipoli as commander of the Cyclist Corps before being given command of his battalion.

And you will also find from that Division Surgeon Godfrey Alan Walker, RN, 1st Field Ambulance, Royal Naval Division and Chaplain Ernest Wilberforce Trevor both killed on 14

November 1916 possibly when a Forward Dressing Station was shelled.

Private William Hawes, 15904, and Private Frederick Eames, 15903, both 1st Hampshires died on 31 July 1915 so some of the earliest burials are here side by side. They clearly joined up together and died on the same day. The headstone of Eames bears the inscription 'He laid down his life for his friend' but the battalion diary gives no hint of how the two friends died only recording 'a very quiet day in the trench.'

Another senior officer here is Lieutenant-Colonel Ernest Charles Patrick Boyle, DSO, MiD, 1st Honourable Artillery Company killed in action on 7 February 1917. He had enlisted in the HAC with his brother in 1886 and seen service in the South African Wars as Sergeant Major, 73rd Squadron, Imperial Yeomanry, Pagets Horse. He was a Captain in the HAC at the start of the war, received the Distinguished Service Order in the New Year's Honours List in January 1917 and was killed when he had received orders to attend a conference with the Brigadier, but when within two yards of the door of his dugout was mortally wounded and died at 2.35pm. He was Grandson of the fifth Earl of Cork and Orrery.

UK – 487   NZ – 1   Ger – 4
Unnamed – 80   Area - 2,246 sq mts

Special Memorials are erected to four British soldiers known or believed to be buried here.

LOCATION

Beaumont-Hamel is a commune in the Department of the Somme containing the two villages of Beaumont and Hamel. Hamel is in the valley of the River L'Ancre about 5km north of Albert. Hamel Military Cemetery is on the south side of the village, on the west side of the road to Albert.

HANCOURT BRITISH CEMETERY

HISTORY

The cemetery was created in September 1918. Some graves were concentrated here after the war.

INFORMATION

Hancourt was in German hands for much of the war. It fell to the Allies in April 1917 and was retaken by the Germans in March 1918. It was captured again, by the Australian Corps, in the middle of September 1918.

The cemetery was made by Australian units in September 1918 and these original graves are in Rows B, C and D. It was enlarged after the war by the concentration of 76 graves, mostly men of the 50th Division who fought here in March 1918. Many are of the 1/4th East Yorkshires. The new graves, mainly of March and September 1918, came from the battlefields in the immediate neighbourhood. One French grave has been removed.

Among those here is Lieutenant Colonel Arthur Stone, DSO, 16th Lancashire Fusiliers, killed in action on 2 October 1918 aged 41 years. He was awarded the Distinguished Service Order for leading a raid which did not go well. He then led his men back under heavy machine gun fire saving many lives by his calm leadership. His younger brother Captain Walter Napleton Stone won the Victoria Cross while with the 17th Royal Fusiliers at Bourlon Wood on 30 November 1917 in the Battle of Cambrai. He was presumed buried by the Germans near Moeuvres though his body was never identified and he is commemorated on the Cambrai Memorial to the Missing.

Buried here is Major Octavius Edward Fane, DSO, MC, 128th Heavy Battery, Royal Garrison Artillery died on 18 September 1918 aged 31 years. He received his Distinguished Service Order in the New Year's Honours List in January 1917. Grandson of the 6th Duke of Marlborough, he was one of three brothers killed in the war. Captain Horatio Alfred Fane, MC, Queen's Own Oxfordshire Hussars was killed on 11 August 1918 and is buried in Mezieres Communal Cemetery Extension about 25km north-east of here. Commander Robert Gerald Fane, Silver Medal for Military Valour (Italy), HMS Dartmouth, Royal Navy, died on 15 May 1917 aged 35 years and is buried in Bari War Cemetery. Originally, buried in Brindisi Communal Cemetery, he and several others were moved to Bari in 1981.

Concentrated here:

Estrees-En-Chaussee British Cemetery - was immediately south of Estrees village which is about 4km south-west of here. It contained the graves of 26 British soldiers and two from Australia who died in September 1918.

UK – 86   Aust – 31   Can – 1
Unnamed – 21   Area – 586 sq mts

Special memorials are erected to four men of the 7th Northamptonshires believed to be buried among the unidentified.

LOCATION

Hancourt is located 10km east of Peronne. The Cemetery is on the eastern edge of the village. It is on a farm track among farm buildings about 30m from the road.

HANGARD COMMUNAL CEMETERY EXTENSION

HISTORY

The cemetery was begun in August 1918 and used for just a few weeks. It was greatly enlarged after the war.

INFORMATION

The village was behind the Allied lines for much of the war but during the German advance in 1918 they reached the village at the end of March so the front-line ran through Hangard. At that time Hangard was at the military boundary of the French and Commonwealth forces defending Amiens. It was the scene of intense fighting when the German advance was halted here. The village and nearby wood were defended by the French and British from 4 to 25 April with the 18th Division notably active in the fighting. The line was fairly static for some months with neither side having an advantage, the village mostly lying in no-man's land, but on 8 August the 1st and 2nd Canadian Mounted Rifles pushed the Germans back from the village. The Extension was begun by the Canadian Corps who buried 32 men and at the end of the war it contained 51 graves that now make up Plot I. This included nineteen German graves but these have been removed. After the war 515 graves were concentrated here from smaller cemeteries and isolated positions surrounding Hangard and the Wood. Most of these are men who died in the April fighting, but some date from 1915.

Buried here is one of five sons of Mrs Julia Souls killed in the war. The family came from Great Rissington which is found between Oxford and Cheltenham. Lance Corporal Arthur William Souls, MM, 16th Cheshires attached 7th Queen's Own (Royal West Kents), killed in action on 25 April 1918 aged 31 years (twin of Alfred Souls) is buried here. His brothers are Private Alfred Souls, 11th Cheshires, killed in action on 20 April 1918 aged 31 years, buried in Strand Military Cemetery, Ploegsteert Wood; Private Albert Souls, Machine Gun Corps, killed in action on 14 March 1916 aged 20 years, buried at Bully-Grenay Communal Cemetery; Private Frederick George Souls, 16th Cheshires, killed in action on 19 July 1916 aged 30 years, commemorated on the Thiepval Memorial; Private Walter Davis Souls, Machine Gun Corps, died of wounds on 2 August 1916 aged 24 years, buried in St. Sever Cemetery, Rouen. We know of three families from the United Kingdom to lose five sons, the Souls, the Smiths (See Dernancourt Communal Cemetery Extension) and the Beecheys (see Villers-Bretonneux Memorial).

Concentrated here:

Andechy German Cemetery - the village is situated about 15km south-east of here just south of the main Amiens-Roye road. Now a permanent German Cemetery on the west side of the village an Irish soldier was buried among the over 2000 Germans graves.

Beaufort-En-Santerre German Cemetery - the village is on the north side of the Amiens-Roye road about 10km south-east of here. The cemetery contained a Scottish soldier buried among the German graves that have now been removed.

Belloy-En-Santerre Communal Cemetery German Extension - situated about 20km north-east of here near Peronne. The cemetery, now removed, contained a British and an Australian soldier among the German graves.

Fontaine-Les-Cappy Churchyard Extension - situated about 18km north-east of here 2km north of the Amiens-St. Quentin road. Now removed it contained the graves of 22 British soldiers dating from 1915 with Germans buried in 1918.

Gentelles French Military Cemetery, Cachy - situated 5km north-west of here on the road between Gentelles and Cachy. It contained the graves of 48 British soldiers who were killed in April 1918 among the over 200 French graves.

Hangard Military Cemetery - This was a French Extension to the Communal Cemetery on its east side. Now removed, among the French graves, it contained the graves of 38 British, eighteen Canadian and twelve Australian soldiers killed in April and August 1918.

Hangest German Cemetery - situated about 10km south-east of here on the north-east edge of the village of Hangest-en-Santerre opposite the Communal Cemetery. Now removed it contained the grave of a British soldier among the Germans.

Harbonnieres German Cemetery - situated 10km north-east of here on the eastern edge of the village. It contained the graves of six British soldiers and an Australian among the Germans that are also now removed.

Herleville German Cemetery - situated about 15km north-east of here and 1km south of the Amiens-St. Quentin road. It contained the graves of two British soldiers among the Germans graves that are now also removed.

Le Quesnel Chateau Cemetery - the village is about 7km south-east of here on the north side of the Amiens-Roye road. The cemetery was in the wood on the south side of the village north of the main road. It contained the graves of 100 Frenchmen and four Germans with one British soldier.

Saulchoy-Sur-Davesnescourt Communal Cemetery German Extension - this small hamlet is situated about 15km south-east of here and 7km west of Roye. The Extension, now removed, contained the graves of two British officers among the Germans.

Sourdon French Military Cemetery - situated about 15km south-west of here between the villages of Sourdon and Chirmont 20km south of Amiens. It contained the graves of 250 French soldiers and one Canadian airman.

Wiencourt-L'Equipee German Cemetery - situated about 5km north-east of here at the east end of the village. It contained the grave of a British soldier among the Germans that have also been removed.

UK – 444   Can – 72   Aust – 47
Ger – 1   Unnamed – 294
Area – 2860 sq mts

Special Memorials erected to eight British soldiers known to be buried among the unnamed graves.

Special Memorials erected to nine British soldiers buried in Fontaine-les-Cappy Churchyard Extension and Gentelles French Military Cemetery whose graves could not be located at the time of concentration.

LOCATION

Hangard is situated 1km north of the main Amiens-Roye road about 10km south-east of Amiens. The cemetery is on the eastern edge of the village on the north side of the road to Demuin and Aubercourt on the west side of the Communal Cemetery. It is separated from the Communal Cemetery by a line of small trees and is on a bank above the road.

HANGARD WOOD BRITISH CEMETERY

HISTORY

The cemetery was begun in late August 1918 after the bitter fighting in this area. Some graves were concentrated here after the war.

INFORMATION

The area was in Allied hands for most of the war. In July 1918 the wood was in German hands but after it was cleared by the Canadian Corps, their Burial Officer began the cemetery. He brought in a small number of graves dating from the defence of the village in April 1918 and made the rest of the cemetery from graves of men killed in retaking the village and wood in August 1918. After the war a further seven unidentified men in graves dating from April 1918 were concentrated here from the area around Villers-Bretonneux. In addition fifteen graves of men who were killed in October 1916 were concentrated from the Butte de Warlencourt.

One of these is 2nd Lieutenant William Nisbet Maxwell, 3rd attached 7th Seaforth Highlanders, killed in action on 12 October 1916 when the principal objective for the battalion was to clear the Butte de Warlencourt. The 7th Seaforth Highlanders were to attack 'Snag' and 'Tail' Trenches then the Butte itself, but suffered from intense machine-gun fire, and a heavy German barrage which cut off communications. They also experienced shelling from the British guns. The Battalion was relieved on 13 October but in the period 10-13 October had sustained 467 casualties.

The track that leads to this cemetery runs along no-man's land over which the 1st Canadian Division advanced on 8 August 1918. The cemetery is on a narrow strip of land between two woods just about on the line of the German front line that was attacked by 13th (Quebec) Canadian Infantry supported by 4th Tank Battalion.

A soldier of the 13th Canadian Infantry, Private John Bernard Croak, won the Victoria Cross here on 8 August but died of his wounds aged 26 years and is buried in this cemetery. His citation reads 'For most conspicuous bravery in attack when having become separated from his section he encountered a machine gun nest, which he bombed and silenced, taking the gun and crew prisoners. Shortly afterwards he was severely wounded, but refused to desist. Having rejoined his platoon, a very strong point, containing several machine guns, was encountered. Private Croak, however, seeing an opportunity, dashed forward alone and was almost immediately followed by the remainder of the platoon in a brilliant charge. He was the first to arrive at the trench line, into which he led his men, capturing three machine guns and bayonetting or capturing the entire garrison. The perseverance and valour of this gallant soldier, who was again severely wounded, and died of his wounds, were an inspiring example to all.'

UK – 58   Can – 61   Aust – 17
SAfr – 5   Fr – 20   Unnamed – 39
Area – 584 sq mts

LOCATION

The wood is north of the village and is reached by a small road by the church, marked by a CWGC sign, from the centre of the village. The road becomes a farm track as it nears the wood. This leads the final 400m to the cemetery which is on the south side of the wood and can be seen from some distance. It is possible to get to the cemetery in a car during the summer and carefully in winter.

HANNESCAMPS CHURCHYARD

HISTORY
The churchyard was first used by the French Army when they held the line here before the middle of 1915. It was used by the British from October 1915 to January 1916.

INFORMATION
The village was held by the French and British throughout the war though it was close to the front-line until June 1916 and again in 1918.

The British graves are twelve men of the 13th Royal Fusiliers, seven of the 13th Rifle Brigade and two of the 13th King's Royal Rifle Corps. There are no officers among them but there is Private William F Harries, 13th Royal Fusiliers, killed on 12 December 1915 aged 16 years. He went to France on 30 July 1915. There is no mention of his death in the battalion War Diary.

The ruins of the church are in the east corner of the churchyard and the British and remaining French graves are on the south-west side of the churchyard next to the New Military Cemetery. Most of the French military graves have been removed.

UK - 21

LOCATION
Hannescamps is situated about 25km north of Albert and a similar distance east of Doullens. The churchyard is on the south-west edge of the village on the road to Bienvillers. The graves are mostly in two plots.

HANNESCAMPS NEW MILITARY CEMETERY

HISTORY
The cemetery was begun in March 1916 when the space available in the churchyard had been used. It was used as an Extension to the churchyard until February 1917. It was used again in March 1918 and also after the war when 30 graves were concentrated from the surrounding battlefields.

INFORMATION
Buried here is 2nd Lieutenant Frank Cresswell, 9th Leicestershires, killed in action on 18 May 1916 aged 21 years. He was an only child and was about to enter Oxford University when the war began. Instead he joined the 1/4th Leicestershires, a Territorial Force battalion, as a Private. He became an officer in February 1915 joining the 9th Leicestershires and going to France in July. He died near Arras of the wounds he received an hour earlier, while bringing in one of his men who had been wounded when out with a wiring party.

UK – 100 Indian Labour Corps – 2
Unnamed – 19 Area – 614 sq mts

Special Memorial to a British soldier known to be buried among the unnamed graves.

LOCATION
The New Military Cemetery is, in effect, an Extension to the churchyard on its south-west side.

HARGICOURT BRITISH CEMETERY

HISTORY
The cemetery was begun in May 1917 and used until March 1918. A few burials were made in September and October 1918.

INFORMATION
Hargicourt was occupied by Germans in 1914 and by British troops in April 1917 during the actions surrounding the German withdrawal to the Hindenburg Line. It fell to the Germans again on 21 March 1918 and was recaptured by Australian troops on 18 September 1918.

The cemetery was mainly used by the 34th Division, when it was known as Hargicourt Quarry Cemetery, after the nearby quarry.

Among those buried here is Major Harold Graham Paris, MC & Bar, 138th Heavy Battery, Royal Garrison Artillery, killed in action on 6 October 1918 aged 31 years. He was commissioned in July 1907 and promoted to Lieutenant in

July 1910 and was stationed soon after in Hong Kong. He went to war in 1914 with the 35th Heavy Battery, Royal Garrison Artillery and took part in the retreat from Mons and the First Battle of Ypres. He was promoted to Captain and joined the newly formed 138th Heavy Brigade in July 1915. In February 1917, after being promoted to Major, Harold became Commanding Officer of his Brigade. His Military Cross was gazetted in August 1917. The citation reads 'For conspicuous gallantry and devotion to duty in keeping his men in action under very heavy hostile shell fire, during which he worked at a gun himself, setting a splendid example to his men. A few days later he most skilfully withdrew his guns under a heavy bombardment, and he has on many previous occasions displayed great courage and fine leadership.' The Bar was gazetted in September 1918. The citation reads 'For conspicuous gallantry and devotion to duty. This officer superintended the withdrawal of his guns under heavy fire, and largely owing to his efforts only one gun had to be abandoned. Earlier the same day he remained in the observation post, sending back information when his telephonists were severely wounded. Throughout the fighting he commanded his battery with skill and cheerfulness, keeping his men in good spirits.'

Concentrated here:
Hargicourt Communal Cemetery German Extension – three burials were brought from this cemetery after the war.

UK – 273   Aust – 15   India – 22
Ger – 2   Unnamed - 35
Area – 2151 sq mts
Special Memorial to one man known to be buried among the unnamed.

LOCATION
Hargicourt is located about 16km north-west of St. Quentin and about 3km west of the main road from St. Quentin to Cambrai. The Cemetery is at the western end of the village, on the south side of the road to Peronne.

HARGICOURT COMMUNAL CEMETERY EXTENSION

HISTORY
Burials were made here in August 1917 and January, September and October 1918.

INFORMATION
The Cemetery was made next to a German Extension of the Protestant Communal Cemetery. The 177 German graves have been removed, leaving a space between the civil cemetery and this one.

Among those here is 2nd Lieutenant George Henry Simons, DCM, 10th Lincolns, killed in action on 26 August 1917 aged 36 years. He worked for the Post Office before the war. His citation for the Distinguished Conduct Medal, gazetted in March 1916 when he was a Sergeant, reads 'For consistent gallantry, notably when, during operations, he laid wires and exposed himself to very heavy shell fire in order to establish and maintain communications.'

UK – 61   Australia - 12
Area – 348 sq mts

LOCATION
The cemetery is on the north side of the village. It is near, but not next to, the civil cemetery. It is best reached by taking the road towards Ronssoy north from the village centre, turn right onto the Rue du Cimetiere Protestant and then left in about 60m onto a track leading to the civil cemetery and this cemetery.

HARPONVILLE COMMUNAL CEMETERY

HISTORY
The Communal Cemetery in Harponville was only used during the fighting of 1918.

INFORMATION
The Communal Cemetery contains graves made during the German advance in April, May and June of 1918. Many of the graves in the Communal Cemetery are men of 38th Division while many of those in the Extension are from the 17th Division.

Among those buried here is Captain David Robertson Sillars, 12th Highland Light Infantry, killed in action on 4 June 1918. He joined the Territorial Force while still at school before the war entering the Royal Army Medical Corps as a Private. In August 1914, he was mobilised with the 4th Scottish General Hospital and in June 1915 transferred to the Cyclist Company of the 65th (Lowland) Division where he rapidly rose to the rank of Sergeant. In January 1917 he joined the Highland Light Infantry as a 2nd Lieutenant, and went to France fighting in the latter part of the Battle of the Somme. At the beginning of 1917 he was attached to the Intelligence Staff of the Fourth Army. Three months later he re-joined the Highland Light Infantry as Intelligence Officer but was wounded in the First Battle of Arras and sent home. On being passed fit for general service he re-joined his old battalion towards the close of 1917. In the German advance in 1918 he saw much heavy fighting, and was killed by a sniper's bullet.

UK - 34   Unnamed – 1   Area – 832 sq mts

LOCATION
Harponville lies about 10km west of Albert. The Communal Cemetery is on the north side of the village, on the road to Lealvillers, and the Extension is on the north side of the Communal Cemetery.

HARPONVILLE COMMUNAL CEMETERY EXTENSION

HISTORY
The cemetery was only used during the fighting of 1918 when it was created to take the dead of June, July and August.

INFORMATION
Among those buried in the Extension is Captain Leslie George Preston, 8th Queens Own (Royal West Kents), attached 6th Dorsetshires, who died of wounds on 10 July 1918, aged 27 years. He had started his war in the ranks and was commissioned in February 1917 upon transfer from the Machine Gun Corps and promotion from Sergeant. He became Captain in July 1917 and took command of 'A' Company in September. The citation for his Military Cross awarded on 26 September 1917 reads 'He led his platoon with magnificent dash, and with only twelve men left captured his objective. He then took out a bombing patrol, bombed dug-outs and took prisoners. Finding both flanks in the air, he formed his party into an advanced post until the remainder of his battalion was securely established.' The Bar to his MC was awarded posthumously on 24 September 1918.

Also here is Major Eric Brown Lees, Westmorland and Cumberland Yeomanry attached 10th Sherwood Foresters, killed in action on 31 July 1918. Major Lees was killed in action by a gas shell at 8.00pm, when serving in the Aveluy Wood Sector, near Albert. The Lees' were an old Lancashire family of landowners who owned collieries around Oldham. Eric, a JP, was the son of Lieutenant Colonel Edward Brown Lees, JP, DL and his wife Dorothy. The family home from the late 1800's was Thurland Castle near Carnforth. His wife erected a memorial window in his local church under which are the words of Owen's poem 'Dulce et Decorum Est Pro Patria Mori'.

UK - 138   Area – 832 sq mts

LOCATION
See Communal Cemetery

HAWTHORN RIDGE CEMETERY No. 1, AUCHONVILLERS

HISTORY
The cemetery was made as a battlefield clearance cemetery and only in use for a brief period in early 1917.

INFORMATION
The cemetery was made by the V Corps, who cleared the Ancre battlefields in the spring of 1917 after the German retreat to the Hindenburg Line, as V Corps Cemetery No. 9. The majority of burials belonged to the 29th Division, and 42 of these to the 16th (Public Schools) Middlesex. Almost all died on 1 July or 13 November 1916. There are just a few burials from June and July 1918.

This is one of series of small cemeteries which were not concentrated into larger cemeteries after the war. These burial grounds give us a poignant reminder of the failure in this area in July 1916 as the bodies could not be recovered until 1917. Most of the headstones bear two names.

This cemetery is situated very close to the Hawthorn Ridge Redoubt, under which the Hawthorn Ridge mine was exploded on 1 July 1916. The mine had 40,000lbs of explosive and was blown ten minutes early to allow a cameraman to get film of the explosion. This allowed the Germans to occupy the lip of the crater before the 16th

Middlesex attacked. Despite heavy casualties, the British captured part of the crater, the only brief success here, though it was lost later in the day. I always consider, with the death of so many public schoolboys, what potential was lost in the choice to get good camera footage? A further 30,000lbs of explosive were blown on 13 November 1916 to aid the successful attack by the 51st (Highland) Division.

Among those here is Captain George Henry Heslop, 16th Middlesex. He was a former student of Lancing College. He was described by Wisden as being 'the most promising young all-rounder who had yet to appear in a first class match'. He won a place at Trinity College Cambridge but did not take it, due to the outbreak of war, choosing to join the army. He had been recommended for Major, but was turned down as too young. He was killed in the first rush towards the Hawthorn Ridge crater. In a letter of 13 September 1916 his father wrote 'My boy was killed on the 1st of July in the first ten minutes of the great push. There is nothing to say. He had a duty to do and it was done.'

UK – 152   NF – 1   Unnamed - 71
Area – 432 sq mts

LOCATION
Auchonvillers is located 10km north of Albert. Hawthorn Ridge Cemetery No. 1 is 250m south of the Beaumont-Hamel—Auchonvillers road, on the north slope of the ridge. The cemetery is in fields west of the village, south of Beaumont and east of Newfoundland Park. It has excellent views of the battlefield. Access is from the Auchonvillers-Hamel road by a track and then a path across the fields, though the path is sometimes dug up by accident. The CWGC website says 'Access to this cemetery is by unmade, single track road. There is no turning point. Weather conditions can often render this track impassable for cars. Please do not proceed beyond the hardened surface.'

HAWTHORN RIDGE CEMETERY No. 2, AUCHONVILLERS

HISTORY
The cemetery was made as a battlefield clearance cemetery and only in use for a brief period in early 1917.

INFORMATION
It was made by the V Corps, as V Corps Cemetery No. 12, in the spring of 1917, and nine graves were brought in after the war, including several Newfoundlanders brought here to be with their comrades. Many of the graves are of men from the 29th Division who died on 1 July 1916. Just four of those here were killed on 13 November 1916.

Buried here is 2nd Lieutenant Arthur William Fraser, DSO, 1st Borders who led his Company into attack on 1 July 1916. He was leading as it was common practice for the Company commander to kept behind to form the core of reconstituted battalion if anything went badly for the attackers – as it did. Fraser was killed at the German wire, one of the few men to get near it, and was posthumously awarded the Distinguished Service Order for his actions.

Newfoundland Park
This is one of the more frequently visited places on the Western Front. It contains preserved trenches, monuments, three cemeteries, and a visitor centre with toilets. Newfoundland, an independent territory until it joined Canada in 1959, purchased the 84 acres in 1921. The park was opened by Haig on 7 June 1925.

The 29th Division Memorial, is near the entrance. The magnificent Caribou Memorial stands above the front-line of 1 July 1916. The 51st (Highland) Division, who captured the German line on 13 November 1916 and continued into Beaumont, have their Memorial situated on the German line near Y Ravine. It faces in the direction of the Division's attack and bears the Gaelic inscription 'Friends are good on the day of battle'.

The Newfoundlanders were one of the reserve units for the 29th Division on 1 July 1916. When called to move forward they felt the urgency of the situation and, as the communication trenches were in chaos, they moved from the reserve line to the front line by crossing the open ground between the lines. The 1st Essex were given the same order, but as 'regular' experienced soldiers, unlike the volunteer Newfoundlanders, they stuck to the communication trenches and took time to reach the front line. So, after the failure of the initial attack, the Newfoundlanders found themselves the only things moving on the horizon. It was said of them that 'The only visible sign that the men knew they were under this terrific fire, was that they all instinctively tucked their chins into an advanced shoulder as they had so often done when fighting their way home against a blizzard in some little outpost in far off Newfoundland'. Of the 801

Newfoundlanders who attacked that day, only 68 did not become casualties. This includes three men, two brothers and a cousin, of the Ayres family.

UK – 190   NF – 24   Unnamed – 65
Area – 1019 sq mts

LOCATION
Hawthorn Ridge Cemetery No. 2 is 500m south of No. 1, a little west of Y Ravine. It is in the north-west corner of Newfoundland Park and access is only through the park which is on the north side of the Auchonvillers-Hamel road. There is good parking available outside Newfoundland Park, but the car park closes at 5.00pm promptly. From here you cross the road and follow the paths through the park to the cemetery. It cannot be guaranteed that the paths through the park will be open at all times of the year. They are frequently closed in winter.

HEATH CEMETERY, HARBONNIERES

HISTORY
The cemetery is entirely a concentration cemetery with all the graves being brought here after the war.

INFORMATION
The village was in German hands from 1914 until captured by French troops in the summer of 1916. It was retaken by the Germans on 27 April 1918, and regained by the Australian Corps on 8 August 1918 when they attacked supported by armoured cars of the Tank Corps on the main road firing at German troops in the east. The 8th Brigade of 5th Australian Division captured hundreds of German reserves in the nearby Buchanan Wood on 8 August 1918.

Predominantly considered an Australian cemetery, Heath Cemetery is named after the wide open heathland upon which the cemetery stands. This is the second largest cemetery in the 1918 Somme battlefields. There are a few graves of British cavalry, Tank Corps, Royal Air Force and artillerymen, who were supporting the Australian advance in late 1918. Where you find British they are mostly men killed in the March retreat when remnants of the 8th, 39th, 50th and 66th Divisions were fighting nearby. So, this is very much a 1918 cemetery.

There was originally a French Military Cemetery here that contained 431 French and 1063 German graves. It had been started during the battles between the French and Germans in August 1914. It was removed and this cemetery replaced it as remains were brought in from battlefields and other smaller burial grounds. The earliest date of death is September 1915, the latest October 1918. However, the majority fell in March or August 1918.

Two men buried here won the Victoria Cross. Private Robert Matthew Beatham, VC, 8th Australian Infantry, killed in action on 11 August 1918, aged 24 years. His citation reads 'For most conspicuous bravery and self-sacrifice during the attack north of Rosieres, east of Amiens, on 9 August 1918. When the advance was held up by heavy machine gun fire, Pte. Beatham dashed forward, and, assisted by one man, bombed and fought the crews of four enemy machine guns, killing ten of them and capturing ten others, thus facilitating the advance and saving many casualties. When the final objective was reached, although previously wounded, he again dashed forward and bombed a machine gun, being riddled with bullets and killed in doing so. The valour displayed by this gallant soldier inspired all ranks in a wonderful manner.'

Lieutenant Alfred Edward Gaby, VC, 28th Australian Infantry, killed in action on 11 August 1918 aged 26 years. His citation reads 'For most conspicuous bravery and dash in attack, when, on reaching the wire in front of an enemy trench, strong opposition was encountered. The advance was at once checked, the enemy being in force about forty yards beyond the wire, and commanding the gap with machine guns and rifles. Lt. Gaby found another gap in the wire, and, single-handed, approached the strong point while machine guns and rifles were still being fired from it. Running along the parapet, still alone, and at point-blank range, he emptied his revolver into the garrison, drove the crews from their guns, and compelled the surrender of fifty of the enemy with four machine guns. He then quickly re-organised his men and led them on to his final objective, which he captured and consolidated. Three days later, during an attack, this officer again led his company with great dash to the objective. The enemy brought heavy rifle and machine-gun fire to bear upon the line, but in the face of this heavy fire Lt. Gaby walked along his line of posts, encouraging his men to quickly consolidate. While engaged on this duty he was killed by an enemy sniper.'

Also buried here is Captain Samuel James Paget, MiD, killed on 26 March 1918 aged 22 years. He had been Mentioned in Despatches and at the time of his death was serving as Brigade Major to 149th Brigade, 50th Division. Originally with the 5th Norfolks (The Sandringham Battalion) in 1914, he left them before they went to Gallipoli where they disappeared. For Staff officers to be caught up in the fighting gives us an insight into the conditions during the battle in March 1918. He was the son of the Rt. Reverend Henry Luke Paget, DD, Bishop of Chester.

The commanding officers of 36th and 37th Australian Infantry are both buried here. Lieutenant Colonel John Milne, DSO, commanding 36th Australian Infantry was killed on 12 April 1918 when a shell hit his battalion HQ. He won his Distinguished Service Order at Messines near Ieper in 1917. Lieutenant Colonel Ernest Knox-Knight, commanding 37th Australian Infantry was killed by a shell near Proyart on 10 August 1918.

Two other interesting men here are Corporal Harry Thorpe, MM, 7th Australian Infantry, who died of wounds received at Lihons on 9 August 1918 and Private William Reginald 'Bill' Rawlings, MM, 29th Australian Infantry, killed in action by machine gun fire at Vauvillers on 9 August 1918. Thorpe had received his Military Medal at Broodseinde Ridge near Ieper in 1917. Rawlings had received his at Morlancourt on 28-29 July 1918. Both were friends and aboriginal men who had joined up in defiance of rules prohibiting their enlistment.

Concentrated here:

Bayonvillers British Cemetery - at the north end of the village about 2km south-west of here. It contained the graves of 37 Australian and eleven British soldiers, one from Canada, and one French Interpreter, all of whom died in August 1918.

Bayonvillers French Military Cemetery - at the south end of the village where a British man was buried in March 1917.

Bayonvillers German Cemetery - near the Church, in which fourteen Australian and eleven British soldiers were buried in August 1918.

Cerisy-Gailly Communal Cemetery French Extension – about 5km north of here, it contained 157 French and 108 German graves. There were also three British soldiers who died in July 1916.

Clump Trench Cemetery, Rosieres-de-Picardie – 270m east of the road to Vauvillers and 6km south if here. It contained the graves of 20 Australian and three British soldiers who died in August 1918.

Copse Corner Cemetery, Vauvillers – the village is about 3km south-east of here while the cemetery was by a copse 820m north of Clump Trench Cemetery. It contained the graves of 22 men of the 7th Australian Infantry who died on 9 August 1918, and one British soldier who died three days later.

Davenescourt Churchyard – located about 12km south of here in the valley of the River L'Avre, in which five unidentified British soldiers were found.

Etinehem (or Cote 77) French Military Cemetery – situated near the crossing of the roads from Etinehem-Meaulte and Bray-Corbie which is about 8km north of here. There were 290 French soldiers, who are now reburied in Cote 80 French National Cemetery, with sixteen British men and one from Australia.

Framerville British Cemetery (or Quarry Cemetery) – located near the track leading to Herleville about 2km south-east of here, containing the graves of 23 British soldiers and three from Australia who died in August 1918.

Framerville French Military Cemetery - on the road to Proyart about 2km south-east of here. It contained the graves of two British soldiers who died in 1917.

Harbonnieres Communal Cemetery Extension – about 2km south of here in which 44 British soldiers and nineteen from Australia were buried in August 1918.

Lone Farm (or Lone House) Cemetery, Harbonnieres – situated about 900m east of Heath Cemetery. It contained 35 Australian and nine British soldiers most of whom died in August 1918. After the war 250 German soldiers who died near Harbonniéres were buried here but they have since been removed.

Louvrechy French Military Cemetery - at the west end of Louvrechy village which is 25km south-west of here. It contained the graves of 90 French soldiers and those of two British officers killed in July 1918.

Memorial Cemetery, Vauvillers - the village is about 3km south-east of here and the cemetery was a little south-east of the crossing of the Vauvillers-Rosieres and Harbonnieres-Lihons roads. Buried here were nineteen soldiers of the 9th Australian Infantry who died on 10 August 1918.

Mericourt-Sur-Somme Communal Cemetery – located about 3km north of here and in which one British officer was buried in September 1916.

Merignolles British Cemetery, Proyart – situated about half-way between Proyart and Chuignolles about 4km north-east of here, containing the graves of 21 Australian soldiers who died on 23 August 1918.

Morcourt Communal Cemetery – on the south side of the River Somme about 2km north of here in which three British soldiers were buried by the Germans.

Morcourt Communal Cemetery Extension - containing 41 Australian and eight British men buried in August 1918.

Morcourt German Cemetery - in which the Germans buried two men of the Rifle Brigade in April 1918.

Proyart Communal Cemetery Extension - made by the Germans in April-June 1918 and located about 3km north-east of here. It was used by the British in August and September 1918 for the burial of 64 British and 58 Australian soldiers. It is now a large German Cemetery which is covered elsewhere in this book.

Ridgeway Cemetery, Lihons – found on the road from Lihons to Rosieres about 4km south-east of here, and containing the graves of 23 Australian soldiers who died in August 1918.

Sailly-Laurette Military Cemetery – 800m north of the village which is on the north side of the River Somme about 4km north-west of here. Buried here were 38 British soldiers, mainly of the 58th (London) Division, and two from Australia who died in August 1918.

Vermandovillers German Cemetery – located about 6km south-west of here and in which the grave of one British officer was made by the Germans. A permanent cemetery, with 7544 identified graves, on the east side of the road to Foucaucourt and is covered elsewhere in this book.

UK – 859   Aust – 984   NZ – 6
Can – 9   SAfr – 2   Unnamed – 369

Area - 5,560 sq mts

Special Memorials are erected to 24 Australian and two British soldiers, known or believed to be buried here among the unnamed.

Special Memorials record the names of nineteen British soldiers and two from Australia, buried in other cemeteries, whose graves could not be found upon concentration.

LOCATION

Harbonnieres is situated 1.5km south of the straight main road from Amiens to St. Quentin. Heath Cemetery is on the south side of the main road north of the village. There is not good parking and this is a very busy road.

HEBUTERNE COMMUNAL CEMETERY

HISTORY
The cemetery was used by the French for military burials in October 1914. The British used it from July 1915 to January 1917. Two further graves were made in April 1918.

INFORMATION
The village gave its name to a major action fought by the French on 10-13 June 1915 as part of the Second Battle of Artois. The area was taken over by British troops in the summer of 1915. The village was under shell fire during the Battles of the Somme and served as the area from which the 56th (London) Division made their final move into the trenches before the 'diversionary' attack on Gommecourt on 1 July 1916. It was again the scene of fighting in March 1918, when the New Zealand Division held up the advancing Germans though the village fell for a brief period before its recapture.

Hebuterne Communal Cemetery contains two Plots of British graves. The Plots contain mostly men of the 20th (Light) and 31st Divisions buried in July 1915-January 1917, and two Australian soldiers buried in April 1918. The first burials were men of the Royal Warwickshires. There is also a group grave for men of 'A' Battery, 170th Brigade, Royal Field Artillery killed in a gas attack on 21 October 1916. One man of the Imperial War Graves Commission is buried here. The Plot of 54 French graves are still here. Among them is one man killed on 11 November 1918.

Buried here is Captain Harold Quest, MC, 'A' Company, 14th (2nd Barnsley Pals) York and Lancasters, killed in action on 3 November 1916. He was the youngest son of the Deputy Chief Constable of the West Riding of Yorkshire. He was awarded the Military Cross for his actions in a raid on the night of 3-4 June 1916 when he was still a 2nd Lieutenant. This was followed by two quick promotions. At the time he was killed his elder brother was in hospital suffering from shell-shock.

UK – 56	Aust – 2	French – 54
Other – 1	Unnamed - 6	

LOCATION
Hebuterne is 15km north of Albert. The cemetery is on the southern edge of the village on the east side of the road to Mailly-Mallet. The British graves are near the entrance on either side of the path.

HEBUTERNE MILITARY CEMETERY

HISTORY
The British used this burial ground from August 1915 to January 1917. Further graves were made in 1918.

INFORMATION
The cemetery was begun by the 48th (South Midland) Division in August 1915, particularly by the 56th (London) Division who lost many men nearby on 1 July 1916, until the spring of 1917. The graves of two American soldiers have been removed. There are 61 men in a mass grave forming Row M of Plot 4 who were killed on 1 July 1916.

An inscription for Rifleman Cecil Hugh Rhodes Ravenscroft, 1/1st Londons, killed aged 19 years reads 'One less at home, one more in heaven'. Another for Gunner Albert Brindley Parry, 56th Divisional Ammunition Column, Royal Field Artillery attached 56th Trench Mortar Battery, killed aged 20 years says 'Among the rest, my boy'.

Among those buried here is Captain Richard John Spotswood Seddon, 3rd Battalion, New Zealand Rifle Brigade, killed in action at Bapaume on 21 August 1918 aged 37 years. He had fought in the Boer War and was son of the Right Honourable Richard John Seddon, PC, LLD, Prime Minister of New Zealand from 1893 to 1906.

Also here is Private Milsom Parr, 51st Battalion, Machine Gun Corps, formerly South Lancashires, who died on 12 October 1916. He was one of three brothers killed in the war. One brother, Lance Corporal George Parr, 8th King's Royal Rifle Corps, died on 16 September 1916 aged 30 years and is commemorated on the Thiepval Memorial. Another brother, Sapper Stanley Parr, West Lancashire Division, Royal Engineers, died on 26 February 1915 aged 18 years. He was buried in Eccleston (St. Thomas) Churchyard Extension but the grave cannot be found and he is now commemorated on the screen wall at Manchester Southern Cemetery.

Another to lose two brothers is Lieutenant Henry Paton Nott, MiD, 1/6th Gloucestershires, killed on 27 April 1916 aged 21 years. His brothers Lieutenant Colonel Thomas Walker Nott, DSO, aged 28 years and Captain Louis Nott,

MC, aged 23 years were commanding officer and Adjutant of 1/6th Gloucestershires killed on 18 April 1917 when the Battalion HQ, in a cellar at Villers-Faucon, was destroyed by a German delayed action fuse mine. They were part of a group of officers of the battalion killed by the mine and all buried in Villers-Faucon Communal Cemetery.

There are also at least ten graves of boys who were killed while aged only 17 years.

UK – 699   NZ – 53   Ger – 5
Unnamed - 45

Special Memorials are erected to seventeen British soldiers, known or believed to be buried here.

LOCATION
The cemetery is in a secluded position on the south-west side of the village. It is 100m north of the church near the Fonquevillers road, 50m from the road, and reached by a tree-lined track between the farm and field. It is situated in a former orchard, which may go some way to explain the distribution of graves. It also makes the cemetery interesting as it draws you in to the irregular layout.

HEDAUVILLE COMMUNAL CEMETERY EXTENSION

HISTORY
The Extension was opened in March 1918 when the front-line came to a position east of the village. It remained in use until August 1918. The cemetery was almost doubled in size after the war.

INFORMATION
The Extension was made by the British when they had been forced to retreat to this location by the German spring offensive in 1918. It was used by a Field Ambulance stationed nearby and by front-line units who brought their dead from the trenches for burial here. There are 61 graves of artillerymen.

The cemetery contained 95 graves at the end of the war. A further 83 were concentrated from isolated positions on the surrounding battlefields shortly after the war.

When the British tried to hold the Germans at Albert in May 1940, the village here contained four guns. The Germans captured the village and the artillery on 20 May 1940 when the guns ran out of ammunition. Two of the men were killed and buried here. Sergeant Albert Clement Brown has date of death given as sometime between 11 May and 12 June 1940. He was aged 39 years.

Buried here is Farrier Serjeant Frederick Martin Anderson, MSM, 'B' Battery. 104th Brigade, Royal Field Artillery, killed on 30 March 1918 aged 29 years. He trained as a blacksmith and joined the artillery in March 1908. He went to Belgium with General Rawlinson's 7th Division in October 1914. Farrier Sergeants would make and fit horseshoes, be able to attend to the majority of the veterinary and husbandry needs of the horses and inspect every horse in their charge on a daily basis. The horses with which he worked would be heavy draught horses such as Clydesdales or Suffolk Punches who were used to draw heavy artillery and ammunition wagons. His Meritorious Service Medal was awarded posthumously.

The village also saw the passing of Henry V on his way to Agincourt as well as the Guards Armoured Division in September 1944.

UK – 168   NZ – 9   Aust – 1
Unnamed – 4   WW2 – 2   Area – 797 sq yds

LOCATION
Hedauville is situated about 5km north-west of Albert at the intersection of the Amiens-Arras and Albert-Doullens roads. The cemetery is on the northern edge of the village on the east side of the road to Forceville. The Extension is on the south side of the cemetery about 20m from the road. The two WW2 graves are near the entrance.

HEILLY STATION CEMETERY, MERICOURT-L'ABBE

HISTORY
The cemetery was begun in May 1916 and was used by Casualty Clearing Stations until April 1917. From March to May 1918 it was used by Australian fighting units. It was used again by a Casualty Clearing Station in late 1918.

INFORMATION
The 36th Casualty Clearing Station was at Heilly from 1 April 1916 to April 1917. It was joined in May by the 38th CCS, and in July by the 2/2nd London CCS. The last hospital left Heilly in June 1917, but the 20th CCS was there in August and September 1918.

The CCS was the first level of treatment at which a soldier could find major surgery and nursing treatment. It was still close enough to the front to reach fairly quickly from an advanced Dressing Station, but usually was close to a railway line for the men to be evacuated to a Base Hospital if required. Heilly was one of four major groups of CCS's at Heilly, Corbie, La Neuville and Daours, located in sequence alongside the railway line during the Battle of the Somme. There was significant problems with ambulance trains at the opening of the Battle of the Somme. Rawlinson had requested more trains which caused congestion in which the three CCS's suffered heavily as they took the wounded from the southern sector of the battle covering La Boiselle to where the front line reached the French sector. Ambulances from a large section of the front-line of 1 July 1916 reached the CCS's here while the ambulance trains coming from the south and west reached the other CCS centres first and did not get as far Heilly as they were full so returned to Base Hospitals. There was a mis-match between what was provided and what was needed. Hence, many men died here that could have survived. Approximately 260 men died in the week following 1 July 1916 which is a high mortality rate. The pressure on the four centres eased after the first week as the axis of the battle shifted to the area south-east of the Albert-Bapaume road.

Many of the burials were carried out under shell-fire and extreme pressure, especially in the days on or after 1 July 1916. The cemetery became so congested that men were buried on top of each other and so many headstones contain the names of two or even three men. Hence, 117 national and regimental badges are carved on a cloister wall on the north side of the cemetery which is an extremely attractive feature.

The last British grave was made in May 1919. A small German Plot, near the north-west corner, containing thirteen graves of 1918-19, was removed after the war though there is now a plot of 83 German graves.

Among those here is Brigadier-General Archie Stewart Buckle commanding 17th (Northern) Division's Artillery, who died on 18 August 1916 from meningitis. He was commissioned in the Royal Artillery on 17 February 1888 and served in India. He went to France in 1914 as a Major commanding a Battery, but was soon promoted to Lieutenant Colonel and was then wounded in October 1914 and invalided home. In January 1915 he was appointed GSO1 with 19th (Western) Division, and returned to France. In January 1916 he moved to command XXII Brigade Royal Field Artillery in 7th Division remaining in command until August 1916. On 9 August 1916 he was promoted Brigadier-General and posted to 17th (Northern) Division but within a week he was taken ill and died.

Also here is Brigadier-General Duncan John Glasfurd, GOC 12th Australian Brigade, 4th Australian Division, who died of wounds on 12 November 1916. General Glasford was inspecting the line into which his Brigade was about to move and was in 'Cheese Road', a sunken lane forming the support line in front of Flers, when he was mortally wounded by a shell. A piece of the shell entered his back and is believed to have lodged in his kidneys. It took ten hours to get him here. He was the tenth British General to die in the Battle of the Somme 1916 and the most senior Australian soldier to die in France.

You may notice an interesting memorial in the cemetery which takes the place of the normal CWGC headstone. Lance Corporal John O'Neill, 13th Australian Infantry died accidentally on 6 January 1917 aged 21 years. A court of enquiry established that John O'Neill's fatal head wound, received while training at 1st ANZAC Corps School on 4 January, had been caused by a faulty grenade.

You can find the grave of Sergeant Percy Edward Rowe, 29th Australian Infantry, who died of wounds caused by a shot to the stomach on 5 December 1916 aged 27 years. Percy Rowe was an Australian Rules footballer who played with Collingwood in the Victorian Football League. When he signed for Collingwood in 1911 he had already played with another side during that season so he registered under an assumed name as Paddy Rowan. On 4 September 1915 Rowe had married his pregnant girlfriend Louisa 'Louie' Newby. His best man, Malcolm Sneddon, was also a player at Collingwood and after the war, he returned to Australia and married Newby.

Also buried here is Lieutenant Colonel Owen Howell-Price, 3rd Australian Infantry, DSO, MC, twice MiD, killed in action on 4 November 1916. He was commissioned as a 2nd Lieutenant on 27 August 1914 and arrived in Egypt in December. During this time he was appointed Assistant Adjutant and when the Adjutant was killed on the first day at Gallipoli he succeeded him. He was promoted to Captain on 4 August 1915. During the fighting at Lone Pine he won the Military Cross and was also Mentioned in Despatches. Casualties were heavy and on 5 September he was promoted to temporary Major and assumed command of the battalion. He was wounded on 9 September but remained on duty. The 3rd Battalion arrived in France on 28 March 1916 and Owen was promoted to Lieutenant-Colonel on 12 May. In July and August the battalion fought at Pozières and Mouquet Farm. For his leadership he was awarded the Distinguished Service Order and Mentioned in Despatches again. On 4 November 1916, near Flers, he was shot in the head and died instantly. A brother was 2nd Lieutenant Richmond Gordon Howell-Price, MC, 1st Australian Infantry, killed in action on 4 May 1917 aged 20 years. On 4 May 1917 he was wounded at Bullecourt and died later that day. Three days later it was announced that he had been awarded the Military Cross. He is buried at Vraucourt Copse Cemetery. His elder brother John ran away to sea aged 14 years and served an apprenticeship before obtaining a Master's Certificate. He joined the Royal Naval Reserve as a temporary Sub-Lieutenant on 24 March 1915 and was serving in HMS Alcantara when she met the German raider SMS Greif in the North Sea on 29 February 1916. After a fierce fight both ships were sunk, the survivors nearly freezing to death in open boats before they were rescued. For his part in the engagement John was awarded the Distinguished Service Cross. He later transferred to the submarine service and was promoted to temporary Lieutenant on 24 July 1917. He was second-in-command and navigator of the British submarine C3 which, filled with explosives, was blown up at Zeebrugge, Belgium, on the night of 22-23 April 1918. The commander of the submarine was awarded the Victoria Cross and John the Distinguished Service Order. Another brother, Frederick, was employed as a bank clerk until 17 September 1914 when he enlisted as a driver in the 6th Company, Australian Army Service Corps. On 16 December he was promoted to 2nd Lieutenant and five days later sailed from Sydney with the 2nd Light Horse Divisional Train. He rose through the ranks in the supply service. He served during the Romani, Beersheba, Jericho Valley and Syrian operations, was promoted Major on 1 November 1917, awarded the DSO and twice Mentioned in Despatches. One other brother, Major Philip Llewellyn Howell-Price was a bank clerk before enlisting in the 1st Australian Infantry as a private on 14 September 1914. He was commissioned as a 2nd Lieutenant four days later and embarked for Egypt on 18 October. The battalion landed at Gallipoli on 25 August 1915 and Philip was promoted to Lieutenant. He was Mentioned in Despatches during the Battle of Lone Pine, during which he was severely wounded. Returning after three months in hospital, he was one of the last to evacuate from Gallipoli. He was promoted to Captain on 28 January 1916 and was awarded the DSO for leading a raiding party near Armentieres on 27 June. He fought on the Somme in July, at Flers in November and was wounded at Bullecourt in 1917. Birdwood soon had him appointed to the staff of the 1st ANZAC Division. He was promoted to Major on 7 June 1917 and attached to the staff of the 2nd Brigade. That month he was awarded the Military Cross. On hearing that his old battalion was going into action he begged to be sent back to it and on 4 October was killed in an artillery barrage at Broodseinde and is commemorated on the Menin Gate Memorial in Ieper. His body was never identified. The family accrued one DSC, four DSO's, three MC's and were five times MiD. Three were killed. This is a considerable contribution well worth commemoration.

UK – 2356	Aust – 401	NZ – 118
Can – 7	NF – 8	Ger – 83
BWI – 1	Other – 1	Unnamed - 12

Area – 6211 sq mts

Special Memorials to fifteen British soldiers, four-from New Zealand and two from Australia, who are known or believed to be buried here.

LOCATION
Mericourt-L'Abbe is situated 8km south-west of Albert. Heilly Station Cemetery is 2km south-west of the village, 100m south of the road from Méricourt to Corbie, and 500m south of Heilly Halte on the railway line.

HEM FARM MILITARY CEMETERY, HEM-MONACU

HISTORY
The cemetery was begun by British troops in January 1917 and used until the following March. Further burials were made in September 1918 and many graves were brought in after the war.

INFORMATION
The area was captured from the Germans, who had held it since 1914, by French troops in the Battles of the Somme 1916, and taken over by the British later in the year. The ground in front of the cemetery was the scene of bitter fighting by the French in the first week of July 1916. The line of trenches can still be made out when the fields do not have crops.

The original burials form part of Plot I, Rows E, F and G and were made by a Dressing Station in the farm. The cemetery was greatly enlarged after the war by the concentration of 565 graves from the battlefields on both sides of the River Somme. These include five rows almost completely of South Africans who were overrun on 24 March 1918 by the German advance at Le Foreste.

Two men who won the Victoria Cross are buried here. 2nd Lieutenant George Edward Cates, VC, 2nd Rifle Brigade, killed on 9 March 1917, aged 24 years was making a captured German trench deeper when he uncovered a bomb. He stood on it to protect his men when it exploded killing him. The citation reads 'For most conspicuous bravery and self-sacrifice. When engaged with some other men in deepening a captured trench this officer struck with his spade a buried bomb, which immediately started to burn. 2nd Lt. Gates, in order to save the lives of his comrades, placed his foot on the bomb, which immediately exploded. He showed the most conspicuous gallantry and devotion to duty in performing the act which cost him his life, but saved the lives of others.' His brother, 2nd Lieutenant Geoffrey Cates, 10th attached 2nd Durham Light Infantry was killed in action on 21 March 1918 and is commemorated on the Arras Memorial. Another brother, Private William Frederick Cates, Canadian Army Medical Corps died on 27 June 1918 aged 30 years. He had enlisted in 1915 while working in the Civil Service and spent time in the Salonika Campaign. He was crew on the Hospital Ship Llandovery Castle, bound from Halifax, Nova Scotia, for Liverpool, which was torpedoed 114 miles south-west of the Fastnet Rock by German submarine U-86. Despite showing Red Cross lights, the ship was attacked and most survivors, including fourteen Nursing Sisters were machine gunned. The Llandovery Castle became the rallying cry for the Canadian troops during the Last 100 Days offensive. He is commemorated on the Halifax Memorial, Nova Scotia.

Private Robert MacTier, VC, 23rd Australian Infantry was killed on 1 September 1918 at Peronne on Mont St. Quentin trying to capture a fourth German position having already taken three. The citation reads 'For most conspicuous bravery and devotion to duty on the morning of the 1st September, 1918, during the attack on the village of Mt. St. Quentin. Prior to the advance of the battalion, it was necessary to clear up several enemy strong points close to our line. This the bombing patrols sent forward failed to effect, and the battalion was unable to move. Private Mactier, single handed, and in daylight, thereupon jumped out of the trench, rushed past the block, closed with and killed the machine gun garrison of eight men with his revolver and bombs, and threw the enemy machine gun over the parapet. Then, rushing forward about 20 yards, he jumped into another strong point held by a garrison of six men, who immediately surrendered. Continuing to the next block through the trench, he disposed of an enemy machine gun which had been enfilading our flank advancing troops, and was then killed by another machine gun at close range. It was entirely due to this exceptional valour and determination of Private Mactier that the battalion was able to move on to its "jumping off" trench and carry out the successful operation of capturing the village of Mt. St. Quentin a few hours later.' Originally buried at Clery he was moved here in 1924.

Also here is Major John Douglas Barford Warwick, Huntingdon Cyclist Battalion, attached 1/1st Oxford and Bucks Light Infantry, killed near Peronne on 10 March 1917 aged 23 years. A letter to his parents by his commanding officer said: '… he was killed in action this morning by a gas shell, which burst in the entrance of his dug-out. Although he got out, he died of the effects of the poison five hours later. It will console you in some measure to know that, unlike many cases of gas poisoning, he died without suffering in the least gradually sinking from heart failure. The death of your son will be a very great loss to this Battalion, both as an officer and as a friend. As an officer he was quite one of the most capable and conscientious I have ever had the pleasure to serve with, and after joining us in September last he very rapidly gained the affection and respect of all ranks. Please accept the very sincere sympathy of all ranks of this Battalion your great sorrow, which is shared by us all.'

Concentrated here:

Achille British Cemetery, Flaucourt – this was situated on a trench named Achille Alley which was 1km east of Flaucourt. Although begun by the French, this cemetery was used by the British in February and March 1917, and contained the graves of 55 British soldiers mainly of the 48th (South Midland) Division.

Clery-Sur-Somme German Cemetery - midway between Hem and Clery about 2km east of here. It contained the graves of two British Officers.

Curlu French Military Cemetery – found midway between Curlu and Hem Farm. Curlu was captured by the French on 1 July 1916, and again by the 3rd Australian Division on 28 August 1918. The cemetery contained the graves of 46 Australian and seven British soldiers who died in August and September 1918, with one exception. Thirty-two of these graves were concentrated here and 21 in to Suzanne Military Cemetery No. 3.

Feuilleres British Cemetery – situated in the south part of the village which is directly across the River Somme from here. It contained the graves of 27 Australian soldiers who died in August and September 1918.

Frise French Military Cemetery, Feuilleres – located on the south bank of the canal midway between the two villages about 1km south-west of here. One British soldier was buried in April 1917.

Meudon British Cemetery, Flaucourt – also known as Meudon Quarry Cemetery. It was sited near the north-east corner of Meudon Wood about 4km south of here. This cemetery was made by the 1st Division in February and March 1917 and contained the graves of 22 British soldiers.

Needle Wood Cemetery, Clery-Sur-Somme – also known as Andover Place Cemetery. It was sited between Clery and Rancourt and contained the graves of eighteen British soldiers who died in the winter of 1916-17.

UK – 368	Aust – 138	Can – 4
SAfr – 88	Unnamed - 205	

Area – 2198 sq mts

Special Memorial erected to one British soldier believed to be buried among the unnamed.

Special Memorial records the name of a British soldier, buried in Clery-sur-Somme French Military Cemetery, whose grave was destroyed by shell fire.

LOCATION

Hem-Monacu is a commune including the village of Hem and the hamlet of Monacu. It lies on the north bank of the River Somme about 5km north-west of Peronne. This cemetery is on the west side of a large farm lying south-west of the village, close to the river. It is on a quiet track close to the present Hem Farm. It is not well signed and takes some effort to discover. But it is well worth the effort. The rear of the cemetery gives good views over the River Somme.

HENIN COMMUNAL CEMETERY EXTENSION

HISTORY
The cemetery was in use for a brief period in the middle of 1917. A few burials were made in August 1918 and some graves were added after the war.

INFORMATION
The village was in German hands for much of the war until captured on 2 April 1917. It was lost in March 1918 and retaken on 24 August 1918 by the 52nd (Lowland) Division. The cemetery was made in April-November 1917. Most of the graves were made by 21st and 30th Divisions. Fifteen men were buried here in 1918.

Among those here is Private James William Howard, DCM, 2nd Yorkshires, killed in action on 2 April 1917 aged 25 years. The citation for his Distinguished Conduct Medal gazetted in 1918 reads 'He showed great coolness under heavy barrage, and rendered valuable assistance to his company commander when the trench was being blown in, rallying and organising the men. He also helped to keep the right flank intact after the company on the right had been surrounded.'

Concentrated here:
Henin British Cemetery - was at the south-west end of the village, on the road north of the River Cojeul. It was made in April 1917 for the burial of 68 British men, mostly of the 30th Division.

UK – 192   Can – 1   Unnamed – 18
Area – 906 sq mts

Special Memorials to two British men who were buried in Henin British Cemetery but whose graves have been lost.

LOCATION
Henin-sur-Cojeul is 8km south-east of Arras. The cemetery is on the south side of the village, on the east side of the Communal Cemetery. It is on a ridge 50m west of the road to St. Leger, between the road and the railway. The Extension is nearer the road than the Communal Cemetery.

HENIN CRUCIFIX CEMETERY

HISTORY
The cemetery was made by units of the 30th Division after the capture of the village in 1917.

INFORMATION
The cemetery is named after a shrine standing on the opposite side of the road. It contains the graves of 61 soldiers of the 30th Division in a single row.

The men buried here died mostly in one of two operations. One on 2 April 1917 by 2nd Yorkshires and two Companies of the 19th Manchesters to attack the village of Henin-sur-Cojeul 2km south-west of here. The attack surrounded the village and then cleared it building by building until the Town Hall (Marie) fell at about 3.00pm. The other operation was on 9 April 1917 and includes attacks by several battalions of the Kings (Liverpools) in this area.

Among those here is 2nd Lieutenant Allan Copley, 19th Manchesters, killed in action on 2 April 1917 aged 23 years. The Times of 14 April 1917 said 'For about two years before November, 1915, he was an underwriter on the staff of the Western Australian Insurance Company (Limited), of which company his uncle, Mr. S. W. Copley, is the chairman.' He joined the Reserve Training Battalion of the Honourable Artillery Company in November 1915 and transferred to the 1/28th (Artists Rifles) Londons Officer Training Corps in September 1916. He was commissioned into the Manchesters in October 1916, went to France in February 1917, and was dead within two months.

UK – 61   Unnamed – 2   Area – 375 sq mts

Special Memorials to eight graves destroyed in later fighting.

LOCATION
Hénin Crucifix Cemetery is on the north edge of the village and on the east side of the road to Neuville-Vitasse. It is still opposite a crucifix.

HENINEL COMMUNAL CEMETERY EXTENSION

HISTORY
The cemetery was made in April 1917 by the 56th (London) Division. It remained in use until November.

INFORMATION
The area was behind German lines for much of the war. The village of Heninel was taken by the 56th (London) Division and the 21st Division on 12 April 1917. The 33rd Division was then sent into the attack and captured further ground. The village fell to the Germans in April 1918 and was recaptured in August.

Among those buried here is Captain Hugh Richard Longbourne, DSO, Silver Medal for Bravery (Montenegro), 7th Queens (Royal West Surreys), who died on 3 May 1917 aged 32 years. He raised a Company in the Huntingdon Cyclist Battalion in February 1914 and was transferred to The Queens in 1916. He was awarded the Distinguished Service Order for his actions at the Schwaben Redoubt on 28 September 1916. The citation reads 'He crawled to within 25 yards of an enemy strongpoint and bombed the enemy with good effect. Later, with a sergeant and a private, he rushed the strongpoint, capturing a machine gun and 40 unwounded prisoners.' He was awarded the Montenegrin medal in April 1917. He was killed by a sniper when taking his Company forward to support another battalion. His brother, Brigadier General Francis Cecil Longbourne, CMG, DSO, 172nd Brigade, 57th (West Lancashire) Division, late Queens (Royal West Surreys) was awarded his DSO in 1915 for services in the field, was Mentioned in Despatches on eight occasion and held the Legion d'Honneur (France). He became a member of the Order of St. Michael and St. George in 1919.

UK – 140   Unnamed – 7   Area – 702 sq mts

LOCATION
Heninel is 10km south-east of Arras, 3km south of the straight road from Arras to Cambrai and 1km east of the A1 Autoroute. The cemetery is on the southern edge of the village, and on the south-west side of the Communal Cemetery, to the east of the village. A track leads 50m from the road to the cemetery which overlooks the valley below.

HENINEL-CROISILLES ROAD CEMETERY

HISTORY
The cemetery was opened in April 1917 following the fighting to capture the village from the Germans. The German graves were made when they held this area in 1918. The cemetery was enlarged after the war.

INFORMATION
The cemetery was made by the 33rd Division and most of the graves are men of the 21st or 33rd Divisions. The Germans in Plot I were buried by their comrades. At the end of the war the cemetery contained 225 graves. After the war 93 graves, mostly unidentified, were concentrated here from the battlefields around Heninel.

Among those here is Serjeant Frederick Palmer, DCM, 20th Royal Fusiliers, killed in action on 16 April 1917. The citation for his Distinguished Conduct Medal, awarded while he served as a Private with 2nd Royal Fusiliers, reads 'On 25 April 1915, at Cape Helles, for gallantry and marked ability in collecting men whose section leaders had been killed, and leading them in the attack.'

Also here, and buried almost side by side, are Captain Robert Thomas Patey MC, 1st Kings (Liverpools) and 2nd Lieutenant Arthur Corbridge, MC, 4th Kings (Liverpools), both killed on 20 May 1917 in action at the Hindenburg Line. They had both received their Military Crosses for an attack on Dewdrop Trench, north-east of Lesbœufs, on 28 October 1916.

UK – 297   Aust – 10   Ger – 11
Unnamed – 104   Area – 969 sq mts

LOCATION
Heninel and Croisilles are situated about 5km and 7km south-west of Arras respectively and north of Bapaume. The road between the villages, now little more than a farm track, crosses a ridge between the villages, and runs parallel to the A1 Autoroute about 1km to the east. The cemetery is on the east side of the road about 2km south-east of Heninel and 4km north of Croisilles.

HENU CHURCHYARD

INFORMATION
This is one of four burial grounds located in the southern part of the Pas-de-Calais. They contain 31 British men covering the period 1915-1918. There is a French Military Cemetery next to the British Plot here.
Buried here are Captain Clarence Case Anthony, 13th Royal Fusiliers, died on 15 December 1915 and 2nd Lieutenant W Brunstrom, MC, 'C' Battery, 223rd Brigade Royal Field Artillery died 18 on August 1918. Both have personal memorials erected by their men or family. I also noticed a Captain Christmas buried here, though Captain Bernard Lovell Christmas, 1/3rd Londons died on 19 May 1916.
UK – 17   French - 88

LOCATION
Henu is about 7km east of Doullens and 1km east of Pas-en-Artois. It is south of the Doullens-Arras road. The church is in the centre of the village at a small crossroads. The British graves are at the rear of the cemetery.

HISTORY
The cemetery was used from September 1915 to May 1916. A further two burials, artillerymen of the same battery, were made on 18 August 1918.

HERBECOURT BRITISH CEMETERY

HISTORY
The cemetery was begun in February 1917. It was used by the British until March 1918 and again after the village was re-captured until September 1918.

INFORMATION
The village was in German hands until early 1917. It fell to the Germans again in March 1918 and was recaptured by the 6th Australian Infantry Brigade on the following 29 August.
The first six burials in Row A were made in February and March 1917 by the 48th Division who took the area over from the French. The cemetery was, during the war, situated next to a Communal Cemetery Extension that was being used by the French and Germans at different times. These burials have been removed.
The last burials were made in August and September 1918, mainly men of 55th (NSW) Australian Infantry. Among those here is Captain Frederick James Cotterell, MC, 55th Australian Infantry, killed in action on 2 September 1918 aged 29 years while reconnoitring forward positions near Peronne. He was originally posted to the 6th Light Horse and saw action in Gallipoli. He transferred to the infantry in France winning the Military Cross at Polygon Wood in 1917. His brother was killed in a training accident in 1914 in Australia.
Also here is Lieutenant Stanley Colless, DCM, MC, 55th Australian Infantry, killed in action by machine gun fire in an advance at Peronne on 1 September 1918 aged 25 years. He won the Distinguished Conduct Medal at Fromelles in July 1916 manning two machine guns to cover the retreat of the Australians from no-man's land. He won the Military Cross in March 1918 by leading a raid on German trenches bringing back several prisoners.
UK – 8   Aust – 51   Area – 326 sq mts

LOCATION
Herbecourt is on the Amiens-Peronne road 8km west of Peronne. The British Cemetery is near the western outskirts of the village, 75m north of the main road to Bray. There is a path from the road to the cemetery.

HERISSART COMMUNAL CEMETERY

HISTORY
The cemetery was used for the burial of thirteen British men, all of the 47th (London), 17th and 12th Divisions who were killed from April-July 1918.

INFORMATION
Among those here is Serjeant Charles Robert Hancock, MM, 4th London Field Ambulance, Royal Army Medical Corps, killed 8 on April 1918 aged 37 years. He died leaving a wife in Plumstead.
UK – 13

LOCATION
Herissart is situated 8km north-east of Amiens and 3kms south of Puchevillers. The Communal Cemetery is on the western edge of the village on the north side of the road to Talmas. The graves are on the eastern side of the cemetery.

HERMIES BRITISH CEMETERY

HISTORY
The cemetery was made from April to December 1917.

INFORMATION
The village, having been in German hands since 1914, was seized on the morning of 9 April 1917 in a surprise attack by the 2nd and 3rd Australian Infantry. When the 1st ANZAC Corps was here in 1917, the village green was a large mine crater. Although the village was held by the 17th Division against the advancing Germans on 22 March 1918, they were forced to retreat on the following day. It was finally retaken in September 1918.

Buried here is Brigadier General Roland Boys Bradford, VC, MC, 2nd Durham Light Infantry, commanding 186th Brigade, killed on 30 November 1917 aged 25 years. On 20 November 1917 he was promoted to the rank of Brigadier General, then the youngest General in the British Army. The citation for his Victoria Cross reads 'For most conspicuous bravery and good leadership in attack, whereby he saved the situation on the right flank of his Brigade and of the Division. Lieutenant-Colonel Bradford's Battalion was in support. A leading Battalion having suffered very severe casualties, and the Commander wounded, its flank became dangerously exposed at close quarters to the enemy. Raked by machine-gun fire, the situation of the Battalion was critical. At the request of the wounded Commander, Lieutenant-Colonel Bradford asked permission to command the exposed Battalion in addition to his own. Permission granted, he at once proceeded to the foremost lines. By his fearless energy under fire of all description, and his skilful leadership of the two Battalions, regardless of all danger, he succeeded in rallying the attack, captured and defended the objective, and so secured the flank.' One brother, Lieutenant-Commander George Nicholson Bradford, Royal Navy, also won the Victoria Cross. He was involved the Zeebrugge raid on 23 April 1918, his 31st birthday, in which he was killed and awarded his VC. He is buried in Blankenberge Town Cemetery. George and Roland were the only brothers to win the VC in World War I. Another brother, 2nd Lieutenant James Barker Bradford, MC, 18th Durham Light Infantry, also died on service when he died of wounds on 14 May 1917. He is buried at Duisans British Cemetery.

Also here is Captain, the Reverend, George Harvey Ranking, attached as Chaplain to 18th Heavy Siege Battery, Royal Garrison Artillery, who was killed on 20 November 1917 aged 46 years. On leaving school he devoted his time to the recently formed Rugby Boys' Club in North Kensington and was also a member of the Inns of Court Volunteers. At the age of 34 he was ordained at Winchester Cathedral, becoming curate of Farnham, Surrey. In 1911 he was appointed to a pit village near Doncaster. There his church grew from an iron shed to a permanent building, and he then became the first Vicar of All Saints, Woodlands. In 1915 he was appointed Vicar of Fernhurst, near Haslemere, Sussex but felt he could do more at the Front. On the morning of his death he was walking near Havrincourt Wood to a village near to the front line to help the wounded who might come in, and while in search of wounded men was killed by a shell.

UK – 82   Aust – 27   Unnamed – 3
Area – 731 sq mts
Special Memorial is erected to one British soldier who is believed to be buried here.

LOCATION

Hermies is a large village 3km south of the road from Bapaume to Cambrai. The cemetery is on the south-western outskirts of the village, on the west side of the road to Bertincourt, in the site of an old brick-field.

HERMIES HILL BRITISH CEMETERY

HISTORY

The cemetery was begun in November 1917 and used until March 1918. Further graves were added in the following September. The cemetery was enlarged after the war by the concentration of graves brought in from smaller burial grounds.

INFORMATION

The original burials comprise nearly the whole of Plot I. The remaining three Plots were added after the war by the concentration of 819 graves from a wide area.

Among those buried here is 2nd Lieutenant Frank Edward Young, VC, 1/1st Hertfordshires, killed in action on 18 September 1918 aged 23 years during the action for which he gained his award. He joined the territorial Hertfordshire Regiment as a Boy Bugler in November 1909. His father was the battalion's Regimental Sergeant Major. Following the outbreak of war, Young was declared medically unfit for overseas service and had to undergo an operation. In January 1915 he was passed fit and joined the battalion in France. Both father and son served through 1915, including the Battles of Festubert and Loos and during this period Edward was promoted to Sergeant. In 1916 he was appointed as a bombing instructor at the Rouen Central Bombing School, but was wounded in an accident. After a period of recovery Young was selected for officer training becoming a 2nd Lieutenant on 27 April 1917. Following training with the Royal Flying Corps, Young returned to the infantry and was sent to re-join the 1/1st Hertfordshires in France on 12 September 1918, being appointed commander of No. 4 Company. The Hertfordshires used numbers for Companies as they had served with the Guards, who use numbers rather than letters for their Companies, when they first arrived in France in late 1914. For this, the Hertfordshires were sometimes known as the 'Hertfordshire Guards'. Soon after he re-joined the battalion, it was moved into the front-lines south east of Havrincourt, near a copse named Triangle Wood. In the late afternoon of 18 September 1918, after an intense artillery barrage, German troops launched an assault against this position. Although the Germans gained an initial foothold, ultimately the battalion's line held and the Germans were forced to withdraw. His citation reads 'For most conspicuous bravery, determination and exceptional devotion to duty on 18th September, 1918, south-east of Havrincourt, when during an enemy counter-attack and throughout an extremely intense enemy barrage he visited all posts, warned the garrisons and encouraged the men. In the early stages of the attack he rescued two of his men who had been captured, and bombed and silenced an enemy machine gun. Although surrounded by the enemy, 2nd Lt. Young fought his way back to the main barricade and drove out a party of the enemy who were assembling there. By his further exertions the battalion was able to maintain a line of great tactical value, the loss of which would have meant serious delay to future operations. Throughout four hours of intense hand-to-hand fighting 2nd Lt. Young displayed the utmost valour and devotion to duty, and set an example to which the company gallantly responded. He was last seen fighting hand to hand against a considerable number of the enemy.'

Concentrated here:

Demicourt German Cemetery, Boursies – sited at the north end of Demicourt which is 2km north of here, it contained about 100 German graves and those of fifteen unidentified men of the 7th Argyll and Sutherland Highlanders.

Havrincourt Cottage Garden Cemetery – situated in the southern part of the village which is 2km east of here. It was made by the 47th (London) Division and contained the graves of 30 British soldiers and five Germans who died in the winter of 1917-1918.

Havrincourt Wood British Cemetery – located about 1km south-west of Havrincourt village. It contained the graves of 70 British soldiers who died on 20 November 1917, the first day of the Battle of Cambrai, all but five of whom belonged to the 62nd (West Riding) Division.

Hermies Australian Cemetery - on the north-west side of the village about 2km west of here. It contained the graves of 21 men of the 2nd Australian Infantry who died on 9 April 1917.

| UK – 983 | Aust – 43 | NZ – 7 |
| Can – 3 | Unnamed - 297 | |

Area – 3630 sq mts

Special Memorials are erected to 28 British soldiers and three from Australia known or believed to be buried among the unnamed.

Special Memorials record the names of six British soldiers, buried in two German Cemeteries, whose graves were destroyed by shell fire.

LOCATION

The cemetery is 75m east of the road to Bertincourt, opposite Hermies British Cemetery. It stands on ground rising sharply from the village. The cemetery stands between the brick-fields and houses of the village.

HESBECOURT COMMUNAL CEMETERY

HISTORY
The cemetery was used from September 1918 until the end of the war.

INFORMATION
The first burials were the bodies of two men of the Royal Flying Corps shot down on 16 September 1916 and buried by the Germans. It was subsequently used in April 1917 for two burials, May 1917 for one burial, September 1917 for two men of the Machine Gun Corps killed on 16 September, March 1918 for three burials and finally in September 1918 for two Australians. The bodies of two Americans and five Germans have been removed.

One of the airmen here is Captain Guy Lindsay Cruickshank, DSO, MC, 1st Gordon Highlanders attached Royal Flying Corps. He was known for his long range reconnaissance missions for which he had been decorated. He was killed while flying a Sopwith Camel of No. 70 Squadron while observing German troop movements on the day of the first use of tanks at Flers-Courcelette. He was shot down by Oswald Boelcke, becoming the German fighter ace's 25th success. Cruickshank is buried with his observer.

UK – 12   Aust – 2   Unnamed - 2

LOCATION
Hesbecourt is located just north of the Somme-Aisne boundary, so just within the boundaries of this book, about 2km west of the A26 Autoroute and about 8km east of Peronne. The graves are located in various areas of the cemetery. The Communal Cemetery is 'behind' the church and reached by a path from the road.

HEUDICOURT COMMUNAL CEMETERY EXTENSION

HISTORY
The Extension was opened in March 1917 after this area had been taken by the British as part of the German retreat to the Hindenburg Line. It remained in use until March 1918 and a few further burials were made in September and October 1918.

INFORMATION
The village was behind the German lines for most of the war. It was captured by the British in March 1917 but fell to the Germans at the start of their offensive in March 1918. The British captured it for the final time in September 1918.

The Extension was opened by front-line units who had brought their dead back from the line for burial. When the Germans took over the area in 1918 they made an Extension to the Communal Cemetery between the British graves and the Communal Cemetery so that the British Extension is now a little detached from the Communal Cemetery.

Among those buried here are Lieutenant Colonel Edwin Christian, 18th Lancers, Indian Army and Lieutenant Colonel Malcolm Docherty, DSO, MiD, Lord Strathcona's Horse, aged 40 years, both killed on 1 December 1917 during the Battle of Cambrai in the German counter-offensive when cavalry was in action in Gauche Wood. They are buried side by side in Row C. Docherty was awarded the Distinguished Service Order in the Birthdays Honours List in June 1916.

UK – 81   Can – 2   India – 2

Area – 863 sq mts

LOCATION
Heudicourt is about 10km north-east of Peronne and 15km south-west of Cambrai. The Communal Cemetery is on the eastern edge of the village and the Extension is behind it.

HIBERS TRENCH CEMETERY, WANCOURT

HISTORY
The cemetery was used from April to October 1917. A few graves were added in August and September 1918.

INFORMATION
The village was captured by British troops on 12 April 1917. At the end of March 1918 the village and its neighbourhood were lost but they were recovered by the Canadian Corps on the following 26 August.

The cemetery was begun by the 50th Division. Three Canadian graves were added in August and September 1918 and two further burials in the summer of 1919.

Among those here is Captain Charles Claude Whitley, MC, 7th King's Royal Rifle Corps, killed in action on 11 April 1917 aged 28 years. His father, Edward, was a solicitor, Member of Parliament, Magistrate and Town Councillor in Liverpool as leader of the Conservative Party in the city. His father's London address was 185 Piccadilly. Charles joined the 14th King's Royal Rifle Corps as a Private in 1914, and was given a commission in the 7th Battalion in the following year. He was promoted to Captain in 1916, and was awarded the Military Cross in October 1916. The citation reads 'for conspicuous gallantry in action. Though shot through the arm, he remained in command of his Company, advanced with it, captured and consolidated the enemy's trench, and remained on duty for twelve hours after being wounded until relieved.' He was killed whilst leading his Company into an impossible attack on Germans at Wancourt.

Also of note is Private Harold John Wilkinson, 7th York and Lancasters attached No. 121 Prisoner of War Company, who drowned on 15 June 1919 aged 28 years. He enlisted into the 19th Royal Welsh Fusiliers, serving with the 2nd and 10th battalions, before transfer to the York and Lancasters and served at the Front from 1916 being wounded in July 1917. Buried next to him is Private Albert Percy Swift, 7th York and Lancasters attached No. 121 Prisoner of War Company, who was killed by an explosion on 28 July 1919 aged 36 years.

UK – 133   Can – 3   Unnamed - 6
Area – 636 sq mts

Special Memorials are erected to two British soldiers who are known to be buried here.

LOCATION
Wancourt is situated 8km south-east of Arras. Hibers Trench Cemetery is about 1km north-west of the village on the north side of the road from Wancourt to Arras. The cemetery lies in fields between Tilloy and Wancourt very close to the A1 Autoroute lying between it and the railway.

HILLSIDE CEMETERY, LE QUESNEL

HISTORY
The cemetery was in use in August 1918.

INFORMATION
The village, which had been in British hands since 1915, was captured by the Germans on 27 March 1918, but was retaken on 9 August by the 75th Canadian Infantry.

The cemetery was made by the Canadian Corps in August 1918. Most men are from the 78th (Manitoba) Canadian Infantry. It includes a high proportion of officers – two Majors, two Captains and eight Lieutenants. The seven British graves represent units supporting the Canadians in the August advance. There are four artillerymen, two RAF pilots killed while flying a Bristol Fighter of No. 48 Squadron and a cavalryman of the North Somerset Yeomanry.

Among those buried here is Major Ivan Steele Ralston, MC, 85th Canadian Infantry, killed in action on 10 August 1918 aged 28 years. He was a lawyer before the war and was commissioned as a Captain in September 1915 into the 60th Canadian Infantry. He was awarded the Military Cross in 1916 while with the 60th battalion for staying in the line after twice being buried by shellfire. He briefly served with 87th Canadian Infantry, temporarily as its commander, until he learnt of his brother's promotion to command the 85th battalion to whom he was soon transferred. He was directing fire at Cayeaux Wood when he was killed by machine gun fire. His brother went on to be Minister of National Defence of Canada in 1940.

UK – 7   Can – 101   Unnamed – 3
Area – 586 sq mts

LOCATION
Le Quesnel lies 25km south-east of Amiens on the north side of the road from Amiens to Roye. Hillside Cemetery is near the west side of a small road from Le Quesnel to Caix.

HOURGES ORCHARD CEMETERY, DOMART-SUR-LA-LUCE

HISTORY
The cemetery was made in August 1918 after this area had been won back from the Germans during the Allied advance to victory at the end of the war. Two graves were concentrated here after the war.

INFORMATION
The area was behind Allied lines for most of the war but fell to the Germans for a brief period in 1918. It was the scene of bitter fighting on 1 April 1918 when the 2nd Cavalry Division, including the Canadian Cavalry Brigade, captured the area from the Germans. It fell once more to the Germans and was recaptured, by the 43rd Canadian Infantry on 8 August 1918, as the Canadians, on the extreme right flank of the advance, took Rifle Wood.

The cemetery was made to bury the dead who fell during the August offensive. Hence, 45 of those buried here are from the 43rd (Manitoba) Canadian Infantry, while another 39 were from the 116th Canadian Infantry. The men are buried so close together that many headstones bear more than one name.

Among those here is Company Sergeant Major Cornelius Joseph Enright, DCM, MM, 58th Canadian Infantry, killed in action on 8 August 1918. He enlisted as a Private in January 1916 into the 169th Canadian Infantry. The Battalion War Diary notes that he was recommended for the Military Medal for his diligent work during the raid on Commotion Sap on the night of 13-14 January 1918. The citation for his Distinguished Conduct Medal gazetted in September 1918 reads 'With an officer he rushed an enemy block and machine-gun post, and during a bombing fight he entered an enemy post at great personal risk and captured a machine-gun which his men got away. He did fine work throughout the operations.'

Concentrated here:

Aubercourt Churchyard - the churchyard is behind the church in the centre of the small village which is about 2km north-east of here. It contained the graves of three Canadian artillerymen of the 4th Division Ammunition Column killed in action on 24 August 1918.

Domart-Sur-La-Luce Communal Cemetery - situated on the north side of the village and about 1km north-west of here. 2nd Lieutenant Leslie Caldwell and Private Horace Sutcliffe, both of the 49th Australian Infantry, were killed on 2 August 1918. Privates Henry Hayes and Alfred Moulson, both of the 51st Australian Infantry, were killed on 4 August 1918. They are now buried in Row B.

Thennes Communal Cemetery - the Communal Cemetery is by the River Luce near the church in this village which is about 2km south-west of here. It contained the graves of five British soldiers and three Canadian cavalrymen who were killed in April 1918. Only two could be identified.

Thesy-Glimont Communal Cemetery - situated on the east side of the village that is about 4km west of here. The Communal Cemetery contained the graves of two men of the Royal Field Artillery killed on 4 April 1918 when their truck was hit by a shell.

UK – 13   Can – 127   Aust – 4
Unnamed – 11   Area – 432 sq mts

Special Memorial erected to a Canadian soldier known to be buried among the unnamed graves.

LOCATION
Domart-sur-la-Luce is a small village on the north side of the Amiens-Roye road. Hourges Orchard Cemetery is about 1km south-east of the village and situated at a point where the road splits into two carriageways. The cemetery is between the two carriageways and can be best reached from Domart.

HUMBERCAMPS COMMUNAL CEMETERY EXTENSION

HISTORY
The cemetery was used, mainly by Field Ambulances, from September 1915 to February 1917. A further six burials were made in March 1918.

INFORMATION
This cemetery is part of an old orchard. Two Lieutenants in the Extension are separated from the other burials. One of these is Lieutenant George Dewar, 48th Field Ambulance, Royal Army Medical Corps, killed on 3 February 1916 aged 23 years. He attended Aberdeen University, where he was popular and excelled in rugby and cricket, but at the start of the war he enlisted as a Private in the RAMC. Almost immediately he returned to Aberdeen to complete his medical studies. After his graduation in 1915 he returned

to the RAMC as a Lieutenant and in November 1915 went to France. He was killed soon after by a shell.

UK – 79 Area – 630 sq mts

LOCATION

Humbercamps is situated 20km south-west of Arras. The Communal Cemetery is on the northern edge of the village.

The Extension is on the north-eastern side of the Communal Cemetery. Access to the Extension is by a path at the side of the Communal Cemetery. There is no direct access between the two.

HUNTER'S CEMETERY, BEAUMONT-HAMEL

HISTORY

The cemetery was only used in November 1916.

INFORMATION

Beaumont was in German hands from 1914. It was an objective for 29th Division on 1 July 1916 but it was not captured until 13 November when the 51st (Highland) Division took it with the 63rd (Royal Naval) Division.

Hunters Cemetery is a shell hole in which 46 soldiers of the 51st Division, who died in the capture of the German line here, were buried. It was a normal practice to use available locations such as shell holes for burials. What is unusual is that a relatively small cemetery was not concentrated after the war. This is, in part, due to its location in what is now this preserved section of the battlefield. It stands at the upper end of 'Y' Ravine, within the Newfoundland Memorial Park. It is a small circular cemetery with headstones set into the block upon which stands the Cross of Sacrifice. It is the only cemetery of its type.

Most buried here are of the 1/6th or 1/7th Black Watch. The remainder come from the 1/5th and 1/7th Gordon Highlanders, 9th Royal Scots and one man of the Machine Gun Corps, though his unit, the 153rd Company Machine Gun Corps, was attached to the Brigade which contained the 5th and 7th Gordon Highlanders.

Among them is 2nd Lieutenant John Alexander Wilson, 1/5th Gordon Highlanders, killed in action on 13 November 1916 aged 26 years. Before the war he was a teacher of English though he planned to become a vicar. He enlisted in April 1915 and was commissioned in November. After taking a special course in bayonet and musketry work he went to France. He was the battalion Intelligence Officer when he met his death during the advance on Beaumont. For information about Newfoundland Park, please see Hawthorn Ridge No. 2 Cemetery.

UK – 46 Unnamed - 5

LOCATION

Beaumont-Hamel is a village and commune in the Department of the Somme. But this cemetery is only accessible on foot from the village. In fact it is easier to access from the road between Auchonvillers and Hamel. It is in the north-west corner of Newfoundland Park and access is through the park which is on the north side of the Auchonvillers-Hamel road. There is good parking available outside Newfoundland Park – but the car park closes at 5.00pm promptly. From here you cross the road and follow the paths through the park to the cemetery. It cannot be guaranteed that the paths through the park will be open at all times of the year. They are frequently closed in winter.

JEANCOURT COMMUNAL CEMETERY EXTENSION

HISTORY

The first burials by the British in the Extension were made in April 1917 and it remained in use until February 1918. Further British burials were made in September and October 1918. The Extension was enlarged after the war.

INFORMATION

The Germans made burials here before the British arrived as Jeancourt was behind German lines for much of the war and was used as a German hospital centre. As the Germans withdrew to the Hindenburg Line the area came under British control and they made burials here. The Germans made further burials from March to September 1918 when they had retaken the village. There is still a large plot of German graves in the north-western part of the Extension. Many of the early British burials were made by the 59th and 34th Divisions. There are also graves of men of the

24th and 66th Divisions who were attacked in March 1918. The remainder are mostly Australians who died in late 1918. Plots I and II were made during the war. Plots III to VI are the 369 graves concentrated here after the war, mainly graves of men who died in March and September 1918.

Buried here is Lieutenant Norman James McGuire, MC, MM, 13th Australian Infantry, killed in action on 18 September 1918 aged 25 years. He was a bricklayer before the war and enlisted as a Private in January 1915. The citation for his Military Medal reads 'For conspicuous gallantry and devotion to duty during operations East of MESSINES. On the night of 24th August 1917 when on patrol, he located an enemy listening post and drove it back to its own front line. On this an enemy patrol of about 12 moved out and endeavoured to intercept Sergeant McGUIRE'S party. He withdrew three of his six men to a flank and the remainder made a feint retirement with the object of drawing the enemy on. This manoeuvre took place fully 400 yards in front of our line and only failed through the precipitate retreat of the enemy patrol. Sergeant McGUIRE patrolled No Man's Land throughout every night of the tour, maintaining touch, across a swamp, with the unit on the left flank and holding supremacy in No Man's Land by a vigorous aggressive policy.' That for the Military Cross for action near Morcourt in August 1918 reads 'For conspicuous gallantry and during an advance. When the company on his right was checked by machine gun fire he rushed round to the threatened flank, threw a bomb, and silenced the gun and captured the crew. At the final objective, when he was leading a patrol forward, he assisted in capturing a gun which was hindering consolidation. He set a very fine example of courage, and determination to his men.'

Concentrated here:
Poeuilly British Cemetery - the village is located on the Amiens-St. Quentin road about 5km south-west of here and 10km west of St. Quentin. The British Cemetery was 200m south of the village. It contained the graves of 27 British soldiers and an Australian serviceman who died in September and October 1918.

| UK – 372 | Aust – 114 | Can – 6 |
| Unnamed – 207 | | Ger – 168 |

Area – 2947 sq mts

Special Memorials to one Australian and one British soldier believed to be buried among the unnamed graves.

LOCATION
Jeancourt is situated about 15km north-west of St. Quentin and a similar distance east of Peronne. The Catholic and Protestant Communal Cemeteries are located near each other in a quiet valley on the western edge of the village. The Extension can be found on the east side of the Protestant Cemetery.

KNIGHTSBRIDGE CEMETERY, MESNIL-MARTINSART

This is the larger and newer of the two cemeteries here. The first burials were made by the 29th Division. Their men are in Rows G and H including men of the Division's reserves, the 1st Essex and 1st Royal Newfoundland Regiment. Men in Row I are from the 13th Cheshires who were killed by German shelling at the end of July 1916. Much of the cemetery was made by the 39th Division after an attack on the Schwaben Redoubt on 3 September 1916. Buried here is 2nd Lieutenant Wilfred D Ayre, 1st Newfoundland Regiment, killed on 1 July 1916 aged 21 years. He was one of four from his family, including two sets of brothers, who were killed on that day.

Also of note is Private J Haston, 1st King's Own Scottish Borderers, killed on 1 July 1916 aged 16 years.

Buried here, though not side by side, are brothers Private A E Holman, 1st Essex who died on 5 July 1916 aged 22 years and Private T A A Holman, 1st Essex, died on 12 July 1916 aged 18 years.

HISTORY
The cemetery was begun on 1 July 1916 and used until February 1917. It was later used from March to July 1918. After the war over 100 graves were concentrated here.

INFORMATION
The cemetery gained its name from a communication trench next to which the cemetery was made. It was considered to be a front-line trench throughout the Battles of the Somme and the winter of 1916-1917. After the Germans withdrew to the Hindenburg Line the cemetery fell out of use. When the German advance of 1918 brought the front-line back to the River Ancre the cemetery was again used as a front-line burial ground. Rows G, H and J were made after the war when 112 graves were concentrated from isolated positions on the battlefields.

| UK – 490 | Newf – 39 | NZ – 18 |
| Aust – 1 | KUG – 65 | Unnamed – 141 |

Area – 2437 sq mts

LOCATION
The cemetery lies in fields south of Newfoundland Park about 1km north of Mesnil. It is difficult to approach, especially in winter, being reached from Mesnil by a road that becomes a farm track for the last 300m. At the head of the valley, in sight of Newfoundland Park car park, but not accessible from the car park, are two cemeteries, Knightsbridge and Mesnil Ridge. This is the nearer to the front line of 1 July 1916. It is very peaceful and has very few visitors.

LA CAUCHIE COMMUNAL CEMETERY

HISTORY
There are a group of thirteen soldiers buried at the end of March with one buried in April 1918.

INFORMATION
The men were buried by the 62nd Division. There are fourteen CWGC records for this cemetery as one man, Edward Ellis Smith, 13th Australian Infantry, served as Edgar Ellis Hudson. Both names are recorded by the CWGC register. A labourer from New South Wales, he had enlisted on 1 October 1914 and survived until dying of wounds on 23 March 1918.

UK – 8 Aust - 5

LOCATION
La Cauchie is situated just south of the N25, half way between Doullens and Arras. The cemetery is on the south-western edge of the village 200m south-west of the church. The row of graves are at the rear of the cemetery.

LA CHAPELETTE BRITISH AND INDIAN CEMETERIES, PERONNE

HISTORY
The cemetery was begun in late April 1917. It remained in use until March 1918 and was used again in late 1918. There are burials of men killed at other times and brought in from the surrounding battlefields or men that were buried by the Germans when they occupied the area.

INFORMATION
Peronne and La Chapelette were in German hands until taken from them on 18 March 1917. They were lost on 23 March 1918 and regained on 1 September 1918.

Several Casualty Clearing Stations were here at times during the war. The 34th CCS was at La Chapelette from April to July 1917, the 55th for a short time in April, the 48th in May, the Lucknow from May 1917 to March 1918, the 53rd and the 12th for short periods in September 1918. In the spring of 1918 the Germans made eleven burials in the two cemeteries.

The burials in the British section are unusual in that every man is identified as most of those buried here died of wounds in the hospitals. The only unidentified burials are in the Indian section. The British section includes a small number of 'Christian Indians' who were not buried with the other Indians. The Indians are almost entirely Labour Corps who worked in the town when it was behind the lines. Three Italian graves have been removed. Three men of the Egyptian Labour Corps are here.

Among those here is Risaldar (Major) Hardit Singh Dhillon, IDSM (Indian Distinguished Service Medal), 9th Hodson's Horse, died of wounds received on 2 December when in surgery on 5 December 1917 aged 25 years. Hardit Singh Dhillon was the eldest son of Risaldar Major Honorary Captain Sardar Bahadur Ram Singh. He joined the 9th Hodson's Horse on 1 March 1908 as a Sowar, was promoted Jemanar in 1909 and Risaldar on 14 November 1916 shortly before his death.

UK – 207	Aust – 49	NZ – 1
India – 320	Egypt – 3	
Unnamed – 6		Area – 2937 sq mts

LOCATION
Peronne is about 25km east of Amiens and 15km north-west of St. Quentin on the River Somme. La Chapelette is a hamlet on the southern edge of Peronne on the main road to Roye and Paris. The two cemeteries are together on the east side of the road, on the edge of an industrial estate, below the level of the road.

LA NEUVILLE BRITISH CEMETERY, CORBIE

HISTORY
The cemetery was opened early in July 1916 for the burial of men who were wounded in the attack on 1 July. It remained in use until the German withdrawal to the Hindenburg Line in early 1917. A few burials were made in 1918.

INFORMATION
Burials in the village were begun by 21st Casualty Clearing Station when it was posted here in April 1916. Hence, this is a typical cemetery associated with a CCS. The earliest burials, from 1 July 1916, are now Plot 1. They are mostly men of 18th and 30th Divisions from Mametz and Montauban. The CCS remained through the Battle of the Somme in 1916 and departed with the German withdrawal in 1917. The majority of British burials in this cemetery are from this CCS. There are 27 Germans buried here who died as Prisoners of War.

Among those buried here is Captain Robert Colgate, 114th Company, Machine Gun Corps who died on 13 July 1916 aged 35 years. A former pupil of Winchester School and Trinity College, he was the son of Lieutenant Colonel Henry Colgate MD, Royal Army Medical Corps. In the first days of the war he enlisted in a Public Schools Battalion and was then commissioned in the Armoured Car Division of the Royal Naval Volunteer Reserve. He went to Gallipoli and was wounded at Suvla Bay. On his recovery he was posted as Captain to the newly-formed 114th Company, Machine Gun Corps. He was mortally wounded in Mametz Wood, while on his way to help an isolated party of his machine-gunners.

UK - 821   Aust - 21   SAfr – 24
Ger – 27   Unnamed – 5
Area – 2215 sq mts

LOCATION
Corbie is a town about 10km east of Amiens on the River Somme. La Neuville is a suburb of Corbie on the western edge of the town towards Amiens. The British Cemetery is to the north of the village on the east side of the road to Pont-Noyelles in a valley. The cemetery is reached by a track that becomes rough for the last 200m, so is best approached on foot. The CWGC site says 'The track is regularly used by large agricultural machinery and lorries. Please accept our apologies for any inconvenience caused.'

LA NEUVILLE COMMUNAL CEMETERY, CORBIE

INFORMATION
See La Neuville British Cemetery.

Most buried here were medical cases rather than battle wounds.

Among those buried here is 2nd Lieutenant Ian Forbes Clark Badenoch, AM, 20th Royal Fusiliers, died of wounds on 19 March 1917 aged 19 years. He was leading men training in throwing grenades (bombs) when an accident happened during which he was killed trying to save the life of his men. He is one of only two men to receive the Albert Medal to be buried on the Somme.

UK - 173   Aust - 13

LOCATION
The Communal Cemetery is to the north of the village on the east side of the road to Pont-Noyelles. The cemetery is between two roads with access from either end. The graves form one long row on the northern side of the cemetery.

HISTORY
The Cemetery was opened early in April 1916. It remained in use until the German withdrawal to the Hindenburg Line in early 1917. A few burials were made in 1918.

LAGNICOURT HEDGE CEMETERY

HISTORY
The cemetery was begun in June 1917 and remained in use until November 1917. The Germans made burials here in March 1918. The final burials by the British were in September 1918.

INFORMATION
Lagnicourt was behind the German lines for much of the war. It was captured in the actions following the German retreat to the Hindenburg Line in April 1917 despite a counter-attack by the Prussian Guards on 15 April. The Germans recaptured the village on 21 March 1918 and it fell for the final time, to the 2nd Guards Brigade, on 3 September 1918.

The first burials were men killed when the Somerset Light Infantry were relieving the 12th Kings (Liverpools) on 5 June 1917, some killed by shellfire and some by snipers. Plot II was made by the Germans when they occupied the village in 1918. They called it Lagnicourt Cemetery No. 2, one of four in the area. The cemetery was completed by the Guards Division.

Among those buried here is Private Francis Maurice Prentice, 1/14th (London Scottish) Londons, died on 25 September 1917 aged 24 years. His brother, Private Howard Prentice, 11th Middlesex, died on 30 November 1917 and is commemorated on the Cambrai Memorial at Louverval. Another brother, Private Jack Alan Prentice, 1st Bedfordshires died while on active service on 25 March 1920 aged 21 years and is buried in Bedford Cemetery, Bedfordshire.

Also here is 2nd Lieutenant Eric Francis Seaforth Hayter, 87th Battery, Royal Field Artillery, killed in action on 21 March 1918, aged 25 years. In 1916 he was commissioned with the Royal Field Artillery, but in early in 1917 he was invalided home, with fever and the effects of gas, where he spent some time in hospital. In January 1918 he returned to his unit. His obituary contains a quote from his Commanding Officer: 'He was with the forward section of the guns, and the attack developed so quickly that none of them came back. It was only known that they fought their guns up till the last minute.' He was originally buried in an isolated grave about 1km west of the cemetery.

UK – 62   Aust – 1   Ger – 15
Unnamed – 1
Area – 654 sq mts

LOCATION
Lagnicourt is situated about 10km north-east of Bapaume. This cemetery is on the south-western edge of the village near the north side of the road to Morchies. It is reached as the road climbs about 400m from the church.

LE FERMONT MILITARY CEMETERY, RIVIERE

HISTORY
The cemetery was opened in early 1916 and closed in March 1917, though there were three burials made in 1918.

INFORMATION
The cemetery was opened and used by the 55th (West Lancashire) Division as a front-line cemetery. Among those buried here is Pioneer George Harvey, 4th Battalion, Special Brigade, Royal Engineers, who died on 26 June 1916 aged 18 years. His real name is Henry George Denne and he was from Camberwell in London. The Special Companies and Brigades of the Royal Engineers were those who specialised in chemical gas warfare. He had previously been with the King's Royal Rifle Corps and seems to be an example of the young men who joined up under assumed names so they could be in the army, but was at the front for a short time.

UK – 78   Chinese Labour Corps – 2
Area – 660 sq mts

LOCATION
Riviere lies about 8km south-west of Arras in the valley of the River Crinchon. Le Fermont is a hamlet north-east of Riviere on the valley road to Wailly and Arras. It is easy to get lost in the small roads in this valley so it may take some time to find the cemetery which is just to the east of the hamlet. If you are on the north bank of the river on the road east from Riviere you will find it.

LE QUESNEL COMMUNAL CEMETERY

HISTORY
The cemetery contains three British soldiers who died in February and March 1917, and three from Canada who died in August 1918. It contained over 400 French and German graves, many of which have been removed.

INFORMATION
The village, which had been in British hands since 1915, was captured by the Germans on 27 March 1918, but was retaken on the following 9 August, by the 75th Canadian Infantry Battalion.

Among those buried here is The Honourable Captain Reverend William Henry Davis, MC, one of fourteen serving clergymen in the 4th Canadian Mounted Rifles. He was killed on 9 August 1918 aged 34 years. Having gone to Le Quesnel Hospital to secure a stretcher party, he was returning with that party 'when a German shell exploded at his feet instantly killing him'.

To the west of the village is a Canadian Memorial. It is on the Amiens-Roye road and marks the boundary between the Canadians and French in August 1918 and lies just behind the line reached by the Canadians on 8 August 1918. This memorial is in a park on the Canadian side of the boundary.

UK – 3   Can – 3   Fr - 147

LOCATION
Le Quesnel lies 25kms south-east of Amiens on the north side of the road from Amiens to Roye. The cemetery is on the north-east outskirts of the village. Five of these graves are on the west side of the centre path and one is near the south-east corner.

LE QUESNEL COMMUNAL CEMETERY EXTENSION

HISTORY
The cemetery was used for three burials in February 1918 and then exclusively in August 1918. Further burials were made in WW2.

INFORMATION
The cemetery was made by the Canadian Corps in August 1918. It is a simple walled plot. Most of the burials are in a mass grave and most of the men here were killed on 9 August 1918.

The first grave as you enter is of Lieutenant D Gibson, MC, MM & Bar of the 5th Canadian Infantry, killed on 9 August 1918. Also here are three British men of the Tank Corps, and three men from Lancashire killed in an accident in February 1918 in a local Trench Mortar School.

There are seven men from the Royal Air Force, No. 18 and No. 57 Squadrons, killed in accidents or on missions in late 1939 and 1940 when based nearby. Among them is Sergeant (Observer) Victor Harvey, No. 18 Squadron, Royal Air Force, killed in action on 27 December 1939 aged 19 years. He was the first man from Loughborough to be killed in action in WW2 and was one of the youngest Sergeants in the RAF at the time, having joined during the Munich Crisis in 1938. All four crew of the Blenheim bomber, who were on a leaflet dropping mission, were killed when their plane was shot down. They are all buried here - Aircraftman 1st Class (Wireless Operator) William Martin aged 21 years, Sergeant (Pilot) Leonard James Sabin, aged 23 years and Leading Aircraftman Jasen Job aged 21 years.

UK – 11   Can – 54   Unnamed – 6
WW2 – 7   Area – 486 sq mts

LOCATION
The Extension is on the east side of the Communal Cemetery.

LEBUQUIERE COMMUNAL CEMETERY EXTENSION

HISTORY
The Extension was begun on 24 March 1917 and remained in use until the German advance in March 1918. It was used again for two weeks in September 1918 and was greatly enlarged after the war.

INFORMATION
Lebuquiere was first occupied by the British on 19 March 1917. The Germans recaptured the village, from the 19th Division, on 23 March 1918 and it changed hands for the

final time on 3 September 1918 when it was taken by the 5th Division.

The 1st Australian Division opened the Extension and, by the end of the war, it contained 150 graves. After the war it was used for the concentration of graves from the surrounding battlefields.

Among those buried here is Lieutenant Colonel Francis Holden Shuttleworth Rendall, DSO, Duke of Cornwall's Light Infantry attached 1/5th York and Lancasters who died on Sunday 9 July 1916, aged 37 years. On 7 July, the 1/5th York & Lancasters were defending an attack by the Germans on a salient north of Thiepval which was itself the base for a planned attack by the British on Ovillers. The German attack was at 2.30am, following a two hour bombardment, and was launched by 'storm troops' using the new 'egg' grenade. By 6.00am, the salient had been lost. Rendall was buried by the Germans and concentrated into this cemetery after the war.

Also here is Private Colin Burchett, 17th (1st Football) Middlesex, died on 11 December 1917 aged 24 years. A brother, Serjeant Arthur Burchett, 1st Coldstream Guards, died on 14 September 1914 aged 24 years and is buried in Vailly British Cemetery which is east of Soissons, though he was originally buried by the Germans in one of their cemeteries. Another brother, Private Edwin Burchett, 1/4th Wiltshires, died of Malaria on 1 November 1918 and is buried in Haifa War Cemetery.

Another burial of note is 2nd Lieutenant Roderick Kyrle Matheson, 3rd Queen's Own (Royal West Kents) attached 20th (5th Manchester Pals) Manchesters, who died of wounds on 8 September 1916 aged 20 years. He enlisted in 1914 at the age of 17 years into the Royal Fusiliers, was soon commissioned, in January 1916, into the Royal West Kents, and then attached to the Manchesters. He went to France in June 1916 and was reported wounded and missing on 3 September. He was buried by the Germans having died of his wounds in captivity. One brother Lieutenant Alexander Perceval Matheson, No. 55 Squadron, Royal Flying Corps and General List died on 13 July 1917 aged 23 years and is buried in Oudenaarde Communal Cemetery. Another brother, Lieutenant Ian Kenneth Matheson, 2nd Seaforth Highlanders, died of wounds on 13 May 1917 aged 23 years and is buried in Etaples Military Cemetery. There were no other brothers in the family all boys dying within a ten month period.

UK – 685	Aust – 66	NZ – 21
Can – 1	SAfr – 1	Ger – 5
Unnamed – 266		Area – 2950 sq mts

Special Memorials to 20 British soldiers and a South African who are known, or believed, to be buried here.

Special Memorial to a British soldier, who was buried in Bertincourt German Military Cemetery, whose grave could not be found on concentration.

LOCATION
Lebuquiere lies 1km south of the Bapaume-Cambrai road about 6km east of Bapaume. The Communal Cemetery is on the south-east side of the village and the Extension is on its north-east side. Access is behind the church into what seems to be a farmyard. The Extension is at the end of the farm track on the south side of the Communal Cemetery.

LEMPIRE COMMUNAL CEMETERY

INFORMATION
The village was in German hands from 1914 until it was captured in April 1917 by the British, lost in March 1918 and retaken in September 1918 by the 18th Division. The village at one time contained a German Prison Camp.

There were seven graves of men of the Royal Field Artillery buried outside the walls of the Communal Cemetery. They had now been concentrated into Unicorn Cemetery.

Among those here is Lance Corporal Ernest John Ryder, MM, 'A' Company, 1/5th Gloucestershires, killed in action in the attacks on Tombois and Petit Priel Farms about 1km north-east of Lempire on 17 April 1917 aged 21 years.

UK – 12   Unnamed - 1

LOCATION
Lempire is 17km north-west of St. Quentin and 3km north of Hargicourt. The graves are at the rear of the Communal Cemetery which is behind a small chapel. The graves are together in the south-east corner of the cemetery.

HISTORY
The cemetery was used for the burial of eight men of the 19th Durham Light Infantry on 20 July 1917. There are also one burial from January 1917, one from 5 April 1917 and one from 17 April 1917. Another is of an unidentified man.

L'HOMME MORT BRITISH CEMETERY, ECOUST-ST. MEIN

HISTORY
The cemetery was used in August 1918 and again after the war.

INFORMATION
L'Homme Mort saw fighting in March and August 1918. It had been in German hands from 1914 until their withdrawal in 1917.

Plot I, Row A, was made in August 1918 by the Grenadier Guards. The rest of the cemetery was made after the war for the concentration of graves from the neighbouring battlefields.

Next to the cemetery is a memorial to Captain Pulteney Malcolm. He is buried in the cemetery in a row of Guardsmen, some of whom died with him. He was commanding Kings Company, 1st Grenadier Guards when he was killed on 25 August 1918 at the Sunken Road, L'Homme Mort aged 24 years. Educated at Eton College and Oxford, he joined the King's Own Scottish Borderers in August 1914 and transferred to the Grenadier Guards in 1915. He was wounded at Loos in September 1915 and at Arras in April 1917 before his death. He was called back to his battalion from the rear for this attack. The weather was misty and the tanks that were to support the attack got lost or broke down. He was buried by the Germans with several of his men were they died. He was the only child of Lieutenant Colonel Pulteney Malcolm, AM, MVO, DSO, MiD, grandson of General Sir George Malcolm, GCB and descendent of a cast of men who had senior military or naval service.

UK – 126	NZ – 37	Can – 3
Unnamed – 104		Area - 926 sq mts

Special Memorial is erected to one British soldier buried here.

LOCATION
Ecoust-St. Mein is 10km north-east of Bapaume, and L'Homme Mort is a hamlet nearly 3km to the south-west. The cemetery is near the east side of the Vraucourt-St. Leger road. It now finds itself squeezed between the motorway and the railway. There is a large area to park and turn.

LONDON CEMETERY AND EXTENSION, HIGH WOOD, LONGUEVAL

HISTORY
London Cemetery was opened on 18 September 1916 and enlarged on 21 September. A few further burials were made later in the war. It was greatly enlarged after the war.

INFORMATION
High Wood was the name given to a privately owned wood standing on one of the highest parts of the Somme battlefield. It is known locally as Bois de Fourreaux (Ravens Wood).

High Wood was taken by the 7th Division and the Cavalry Corps, in one of the last actions involving mounted troops, on 14 July 1916, but the British advantage was not pressed forward and the wood was lost within the day. On the morning of 14 July the Brigade commander walked to the wood and returned without being fired upon. No further advance was attempted until the cavalry had been brought up. Then 2nd Queens, 1st South Staffordshires, 7th Dragoon Guards and the Deccan Horse moved forward in the afternoon, but they were not able to fully occupy the wood by sunset. The cavalry advance to the east of the wood was the only real cavalry action on the Somme in 1916, though they were soon stopped by machine gun fire. The Germans sent reinforcements and quickly recaptured the wood. It took two months to fully capture the wood.

A number of Divisions were used to capture the wood between 20 July (33rd Division), 7 August (51st Division) and 15 September (47th Division). The Germans re-occupied the wood from April to August 1918.

The cemetery is in Longueval Commune although High Wood is in the Commune of Flers. The original cemetery, now making up Plot 1A, was begun when 47 men of the 47th (London) Division were buried in a shell-hole in September 1916. It is from this original set of burials that the cemetery gained its name. Further graves were added at various times during the war so that at the end of the war it comprised a group of 101 British soldiers, 94 of the

47th Division, most of whom fell on 15 September 1916. All but three were identified though the exact location of the graves could not be ascertained so most of the headstones bear the words 'Believed to be ...'. A memorial at the entrance indicates that there are men buried here but the exact position is unknown.

The Extension was created after the war as many graves were found in smaller cemeteries and isolated positions on the surrounding battlefields and needed to be concentrated. It was felt that one burial ground would serve the needs of the British Army to take graves from a wide area. The enlarged cemetery was designed to incorporate the original cemetery yet retain its distinct character. The resulting Cemetery and Extension is the third largest on the Somme.

London Cemetery and Extension was used again in 1946 by the Army Graves Service for the reburial of Second World War casualties recovered from various temporary burial grounds, French military cemeteries, small communal cemeteries, churchyards and isolated graves, where permanent maintenance was not possible. These graves are in one central plot at the extreme end of the cemetery, behind the Cross of Sacrifice.

So, we can see a cemetery of four stages:
1. A small cemetery made at the side of the road soon after the capture of the wood.
2. When Serre Road No. 2 Cemetery was completed in 1934, there were still many bodies to be buried so an extension to this small wartime cemetery was commenced. Nearly 3000 bodies were buried from 1934-39. The work was stopped by WW2. Bodies came from all over the 1916 battlefield and are buried in Plots 1-10 except the last two rows of each Plot.
3. After 1945 the bodies of WW1 were still being found and were buried in Plots 11 and 12. Plot 13 was made for the WW2 burials.
4. The last two rows of Plots 1-10 contain the last burials. These are bodies found after 1945 from all over the Western Front. Approximately 900 bodies of men who fell in WW1 have been buried since 1945. This is now the third largest cemetery on the Somme. Nearly 83% of the graves are unidentified, the highest of any major cemetery on the Somme. This reflects the way in which a large number of bodies were found so long after the war. The post-1945 burials are nearly 95% unidentified. The cemetery was officially closed in 1961.

There are a number of memorials nearby. At the south-east corner of the wood are memorials to the Cameron Highlanders and Black Watch. The 1st battalion of each regiment attacked the wood on 3 September 1916.

The first memorial erected was to the 47th (London) Division. They captured the wood on 15 September 1916 as part of the Battle of Flers-Courcelette. They had been told they would attack with tanks rather than a preliminary artillery bombardment. The tanks did not arrive, but the Division attacked anyway, losing many casualties. Later in the day a tank almost destroyed the Battalion HQ and ended up in a communication trench disrupting activities.

There is also a memorial to the 1/9th (Glasgow Highlanders) Highland Light Infantry of the 33rd Division. It is a cairn reflecting the Scottish tradition that on the eve of a battle each man coming to battle would leave a stone at a cairn. Each man who survived the battle took a stone. The cairn that remains represents the men who died in battle. A cairn of 192 stones was created in the 1970's using stones from High Wood near Culloden in Scotland to commemorate the men of the Glasgow Highlanders who fell here in 1916. It is 5 feet 7 inches (1.70m) high as this was the minimum height for recruitment to the battalion.

There is a mine crater in the wood which is unusual in that it is filled with water. It is the result of mines blown under the German line in early September 1916.

Among those buried here is Captain David Henderson, 8th attached 19th (2nd Public Works Pioneers) Middlesex, died on 15 September 1916 aged 27 years. He was son of Right Honourable Arthur Henderson, MP, leader of the British Labour Party in 1916 and the first Labour member of a British Government Cabinet when Prime Minister Herbert Asquith invited him to join his coalition government. He was later award the Nobel Peace Prize.

Also here is Captain Edward David Murray Fincastle, 4th Queen's Own Cameron Highlanders who died in the Battle of Abbeville on 6 June 1940. He was Viscount Fincastle and son of Alexander Edward Murray, 8th Earl of Dunmore VC, DSO, MVO, DL. His son became the 9th Earl of Dunmore.

Another here is Lance Corporal Harry Woodfield, 1/2nd Londons (Royal Fusiliers), killed in action on 17 September 1916 near Leuze Wood. His body was not originally identified so his name was added to the Thiepval Memorial until, in 1938, a local farmer found his body which was then buried here.

Concentrated here:

Ytres Communal Cemetery – on the western outskirts of the village which is about 10km north-east of here. It contained three British men who died in March and April 1917.

Ytres Churchyard – in the centre of the village. It contained the graves of fourteen British soldiers who died in September 1918. There was an Italian grave which has also been removed.

UK – 3339	Aust – 300	Can – 162
NZ – 35	SAfr – 33	India - 2
Fr – 2	Ger – 2	Unnamed – 3114
WW2 - 165		

Special Memorial erected to a British soldier, buried in Qusnoy-sur-Deule Communal Cemetery, whose grave could not be identified after the war.

LOCATION

The cemetery is situated about 8km north-east of Albert, 2km south-east of Martinpuich and 3km north-west of Longueval. It is on the south side of the Longueval-Martinpuich road opposite High Wood. This is an impressive cemetery with attractive features but it is indeed notable how few headstones have names.

LONDON CEMETERY, NEUVILLE-VITASSE

HISTORY
The cemetery was begun in April 1917. It was enlarged after the war by the concentration of graves from other burial grounds and from the battlefields between Arras, Vis-en-Artois and Croisilles.

INFORMATION
The village was behind German lines for much of the war until attacked and captured by the 56th (London) Division on 7-9 April 1917. The Germans took it back in March 1918. It changed hands again and was finally captured at the end of August 1918.

The London Cemetery was made by the 56th Division and it is from this Division that the cemetery gained its name. There are eight men buried in grave reference number I. C. I. This seems to be a mass grave for bodies that may have been found buried together and indistinguishable from each other but it includes Cunnington below so the story is not fully explained.

Among those buried here is Private Samuel H. Cunnington, 2nd Royal Warwickshires, executed for desertion on 19 May 1917 aged 20 years. He was a regular from 1914 and absconded as his battalion went to fight on the Somme. He was captured at the end of 1916. He probably escaped once as he was charged with two cases of desertion. His brother, Private David John Cunnington, 2nd Royal Warwickshires, was killed on 25 September 1915 during the Battle of Loos and is commemorated on the Loos Memorial.

Another here is Lieutenant Colonel Valerio Magawly de Calry, DSO, Legion of Honour, 6th (Inniskilling) Dragoons, commanding 7th Rifle Brigade when he died on 10 May 1917 aged 34 years. He was son of the 6th Count Magawly Cerati de Calry. He received his Distinguished Service Order in the New Years Honours List in January 1917.

Also here is Lieutenant Colonel Maurice Edwin McConaghey, DSO, MiD, 2nd Royal Scots Fusiliers, though showing on CWGC website as 1st battalion. He was killed in action on 23 April 1917 leading his men into battle in an attack on the high ground overlooking Cherisy. The battalion advanced at 4.45am on a two-Company front, and immediately came under intense machine-gun fire. At 6.00am, the Germans counter-attacked, though this was repelled. At 6.00pm the 21st Brigade attempted to repeat the morning's attack, but it too suffered heavily. At 9.00pm the survivors of the Scots Fusiliers were withdrawn to the rear having lost half of their number. The dead included the commanding officer, Lieutenant-Colonel McConaghey, five other officers and 55 other ranks, four officers and 195 men were wounded, four officers and 209 men missing. McConaghey received his Distinguished Service Order in the Birthday Honours List in June 1916.

Another of note is Regimental Serjeant Major Henry James Bartholomew, DCM, MiD, 6th Royal Berkshires, killed on 8 May 1917 aged 37 years. He had served with the police and the army including time in West Africa but had retired in early 1914. As soon as the war began he returned to the colours. He was awarded the Distinguished Conduct Medal for his actions while still a Company Sergeant Major near Montauban on 1 July 1916. He was killed by a shell with two other men while standing in the trenches distributing rations.

Also here is Captain Paul Raymond Meautys, MC, MiD, 2nd North Staffordshires, Brigade Major 53rd Division, died on 16 June 1917 aged 26 years. His Military Cross was awarded the in 1917 New Years Honours List. His brother Lieutenant Thomas Gilliat Meautys, 1st West Yorkshires was killed on 22 September 1914 aged 25 years and is buried in Vendresse British Cemetery. Thomas had served in India before the war and was killed while reconnoitering the positions. Thomas's son, also Thomas Gilliat Meautys, died on active service in 1947. Another brother, Lieutenant Denzil Hatfeild Meautys, 1st attached 12th West Yorkshires died of wounds on 7 May 1917 aged 19 years and is buried in Etaples Military Cemetery.

Concentrated here:
- Wancourt Road Cemetery No. 2 - just east of Neuville-Vitasse.
- Neuville-Vitasse Mill Cemetery - close to a German strong point on the road to Mercatel.
- Beaurains Road Cemetery No. 2 - just north-west of Neuville-Vitasse.
- Beaurains German Cemetery.
- Erchin German Cemetery (Nord).

UK – 713　　Aust – 11　　Can – 19
NF – 4　　Unnamed – 318　　Area – 2028 sq mts

Special Memorials to 138 British soldiers, buried in four cemeteries whose graves were destroyed by shell fire. These are represented on a series of panels on a wall at the rear of the cemetery.

LOCATION
Neuville-Vitasse is situated 5km south-east of Arras. London Cemetery stands on the south-west side of the road to Arras in a shallow valley. The cemetery is 1.5km north-west of the village.

LONGUEAU BRITISH CEMETERY

HISTORY
This cemetery was begun in April 1918 when the British established a new line to the east of Amiens. It remained in use until August when the Germans were pushed back. After the war the cemetery was enlarged by the concentration of graves from the surrounding battlefields.

INFORMATION
Longueau was in Allied hands throughout the war. Its railway yards were a major link in the British support organisation. In spring 1918, when the Germans threatened Amiens, trains bringing reinforcements stopped here before men marched 10km to the Front. Hence, the Germans bombed the railway yards in 1918. Ironically, the RAF bombed the yards in 1944 to prevent the Germans sending reinforcements to Normandy.

The cemetery was in the countryside when made in 1918 but it is now surrounded by the town. Most of the graves were made late in the war when the British were trying to halt the German advance in 1918. Plot IV was made after the war by the concentration of 36 graves from smaller cemeteries and isolated positions on the battlefields east of Longueau. Three American, one French and 39 German graves have been removed.

Among those buried here is Lieutenant Colonel Elmer Watson Jones, DSO & Bar, three times MiD, commanding 21st Canadian Infantry when killed on 8 August 1918. When war broke out he was practising law in Vancouver. He became the first Officer Commanding 'A' Company of the battalion and was promoted to Major in February 1915. He had a period of convalescence in England from wounds received in the attack at Vimy Ridge on 9 April 1917 and returned to France to command the battalion on 6 July 1917 when he was also temporarily in charge of 4th Canadian Brigade. He had several further encounters with medical units and training for senior command before taking command of his battalion again in July 1918. On 8 August 1918, he was mortally wounded when advancing with his men. He was awarded the Distinguished Service Order in the New Year's Honours List of January 1917 for his leadership in 1916 rather than for one act. He received the Bar to his DSO in May 1918. The citation reads 'For marked devotion to duty and exceptional gallantry, in connection with a strong hostile operation followed by a successful raid made upon the enemy. Hostile forces, strength about 280, having entered our trenches under an intense barrage and liquid fire, he promptly, and under very heavy fire, went forward, to direct the Counter Attack which was entirely successful. His well prepared plans and promptness in action, turned the operation entirely in our favour with few casualties, and restored our line without the enemy having gained identification. Under his direction, this success was followed by a raiding party, entering the German lines, and with few casualties, bringing back prisoners, and inflicting on the enemy, severe losses, in killed, and destruction of dug-outs. This officer had displayed marked resourcefulness in action, on numerous occasions.'

Concentrated here:

Blangy-Tronville French Military Cemetery and Communal Cemetery Extension - these were in effect one cemetery on the north side of Blangy-Tronville Communal Cemetery. This is found on the south bank of the Somme about 5km east of here. The French Cemetery contained 84 French graves which have been removed to Montdidier French National Cemetery. The Extension contained nine Australian and five British graves of men who died mainly in July 1918.

Cottenchy Churchyard Extension - Cottenchy is a village on the west bank of the River Noye about 10km south of here. The Extension contained 555 French soldiers, three Germans who died as prisoners, three British men and an airman from Canada.

Cagny Communal Cemetery - this was situated about 1km south of here. It contained the graves of two British soldiers killed in April 1918 who were concentrated here in 1934.

| UK – 72 | Can – 65 | Aust – 65 |
| BWI – 2 | Unnamed – 14 | WW2 – 2 |

Area – 1143 sq mts

LOCATION
Longueau is a suburb of Amiens to the south-east of the city centre. The British Cemetery is now in a built-up area on the west side of the main road to Roye about 1km from the bypass junction.

LONGUEVAL ROAD CEMETERY

HISTORY
The cemetery was opened in September 1916. It remained in use until February 1917 when the Germans withdrew to the Hindenburg Line and the fighting moved away from this area. Further burials were made in August and September 1918 as this area was recaptured during the final advance to victory. In 1923-24 graves were concentrated here from isolated positions on the battlefields surrounding Longueval.

INFORMATION

Longueval was in German hands from 19814. It was the site of heavy fighting from 14 to 29 July 1916 when this area fell to the British 5th Division. On 14 July the 8th Black Watch waited here in no-man's land before the dawn assault on Longueval. The Germans recaptured it in March 1918 but the 38th Division took it for the last time on 28 August 1918.

The cemetery served a Dressing Station situated here from September 1916 known as 'Longueval Alley' or 'Longueval Water Point'. The cemetery contained 171 graves at the end of the war, mostly men who died in the September fighting for Leuze (Louzy) Wood. A number of, mostly unidentified, graves were concentrated here after the war in 1923-4.

Among those here is Private Stanley Callaghan, 18th Australian Infantry, killed in action on 15 November 1916 aged 22 years. He enlisted in October 1915, left Australia in April 1916 and arrived in France a few weeks later. He was killed near Flers. His brothers both died in the war. They are Private Horace William James Callaghan, 9th Australian Infantry, killed in action at Pozieres on 23 July 1916 aged 19 years and commemorated on the Villers-Bretonneux Memorial and Private Walter Leslie James Callaghan, 54th Australian Infantry, died of wounds on 4 September 1918 aged 31 years and buried at St. Sever Cemetery Extension, Rouen.

Similarly here is Driver Alexander Lawrence Carraill, 14th Brigade, Australian Field Artillery, who died on 8 August 1918. His brother, Private Stanley James Carraill, 19th Australian Infantry, died on 14 November 1916 aged 25 years and is commemorated on the Villers-Bretonneux Memorial. Another brother, Private Leslie McNiel Carraill, 32nd Australian Infantry, died on 3 September 1918 aged 22 years, is buried in Peronne Communal Cemetery Extension.

There is a shrine outside the cemetery which marks the spot where Julius Caesar is reputed to have addressed his legions.

UK – 185	Aust – 22	Can – 7
NZ – 7	Newf – 1	Ger – 1
Unnamed – 49		Area – 1015 sq mts

Special Memorials erected to three British soldiers known, or believed, to be buried among the unnamed graves.

LOCATION

Longeval is situated about 10km east of Albert. The cemetery is 1km south of the village on the east side of the road to Guillemont.

LONSDALE CEMETERY, AVELUY AND AUTHUILLE

HISTORY

The cemetery was made in the spring of 1917 when the surrounding battlefields were cleared, by V Corps, of the bodies of men who had died during the battles of 1916. It was greatly enlarged after the war.

INFORMATION

During the war the valley here was known by the British Army as Nab Valley which further up the valley becomes known as Blighty Valley.

The area was in German hands from 1914. The German line at this point was one of their strongholds, this one being known as the Leipzig Salient. It was attacked 30 minutes after zero hour on 1 July 1916 by the 11th (Lonsdale) Borders but they failed to capture the position suffering heavy casualties. It was taken later in the day by 17th (3rd Glasgow Pals) Highland Light Infantry, the only Divisional success of the day. Even though the rest of the salient was captured on 24 August 1916 by 3rd Worcestershires and 1st Wiltshires of 25th Division, the area did not become safe until the Germans withdrew to the Hindenburg Line in March 1917.

At that time V Corps made two cemeteries in this area known as Lonsdale Cemeteries No.'s 1 and 2. Lonsdale Cemetery No. 1 contained 96 graves at the end of the war, mostly men of the 1st Dorsets and 11th Borders in Plot 1. After the war many graves were concentrated here from smaller cemeteries and isolated positions on the surrounding battlefields. Most of the concentrated graves were men who died in 1916 and many of them had lain in no-man's land through the winter of 1916-1917. Consequently, over 50% of the graves are unnamed.

Buried here is Serjeant James Yuill Turnbull, VC, 17th Highland Light Infantry, killed in action on 1 July 1916, aged 32 years. His citation reads 'For most conspicuous bravery and devotion to duty, when, having with his party captured a post apparently of great importance to the enemy, he was subjected to severe counter-attacks, which were continuous throughout the whole day. Although his party was wiped out and replaced several times during the day, Serjeant Turnbull never wavered in his determination to hold the post, the loss of which would have been very serious. Almost, single-handed, he maintained his position, and displayed the highest degree of valour and skill in the performance of his duties. Later in the day this very gallant soldier was killed whilst bombing a counter-attack from the parados of our trench.'

Also here is Captain Colin Selwyn Brown, 11th Borders, killed on 1 July 1916. He was one of 63 soldiers in the battalion who were killed, including the Commanding Officer, Lieutenant Colonel Percy Wifrid Machel, CMG, DSO, husband of Valda, Countess of Gleichen. Lieutenant Colonel Machell went 'over the top' to lead his men against the German trenches despite orders that Commanding Officers were not to take part in the attack.

Concentrated here:

Lonsdale Cemetery No. 2 - situated about 450m to the east. It was made at the same time as Lonsdale No. 1 Cemetery and contained 38 British burials, 31 of the 11th Borders, and 2 German men.

Nab Road Cemetery, Ovillers-La Boiselle - situated about 1km east of here on the road running up Nab Valley. It contained the graves of 27 British soldiers who died from July to October 1916.

Paisley Avenue and Paisley Hillside Cemeteries, Authuille - situated on the south side of Thiepval Wood about 1km north of here. They contained the graves of 284 British soldiers, mainly of the 49th (West Riding) Division, who died from July 1916 to February 1917. There were also two German graves.

UK – 1538   Aust – 4   Fr – 1
Unnamed – 816   Area – 3869 sq mts

Special Memorials to 22 British soldiers known, or believed, to be buried among the unnamed graves.

LOCATION

Authuille is about 4km north of Albert on the east bank of the River Ancre. This cemetery is east of the village at the head of Nab Valley on the west side of the road to Ovillers. The cemetery is in a field reached by a long path. The CWGC website indicates there may sometimes be problems of access.

LOUVENCOURT MILITARY CEMETERY

HISTORY

The cemetery was begun by the French in June 1915. The British began their burials here on 30 July 1915 and continued until 22 July 1918.

INFORMATION

The French had a medical centre here in 1915 which they handed over to the British. Rows A and B contain the French Graves. The early British graves were buried by the Field Ambulances that were stationed here from July 1915 to August 1916 at which time the village was 10km behind the front-line.

The number of burials declined in 1917 as the German retreat took the front-line to the east. The final burials were made here during the German offensive of 1918. They are in rows D and E. The cemetery is one of the first three CWGC cemeteries to be built after the war. It was a test site. The French were also testing possible headstones, which is why the French memorials are unusual.

The first burial here is of Captain Arthur Gilbert Rollason, 1/7th Worcestershires who died of pneumonia on 30 July 1915, aged 23 years. He was the first British officer to die on the Somme. He is buried among five officers. One is 2nd Lieutenant Roland Aubrey Leighton, 1/7th Worcestershires, killed in action at Hebuterne on 23 December 1915 aged 19 years. He had been hit on the previous night while leading a party mending wire in front of the trenches. He was the fiancée of Vera Brittain whose brother was killed in Italy in 1918. She wrote 'Testament of Youth' about her experiences and was mother of Shirley Williams the renowned politician.

Also here is Brigadier General Charles Bertie Prowse, DSO, 1st Somerset Light Infantry commanding 11th Brigade who was killed on 1 July 1916 aged 47 years. He was the most senior officer to die on 1 July, wounded when he went forward to find out what was happening to his Brigade. They were, in fact, taking heavy casualties across the Serre Road near the Heidenkopf. Many men were already dead while many others lay in no-man's land. Most of those who died in no-man's land were not buried until February 1917. Prowse is one of the bodies concentrated from Vauchelles. Prowse has a farm named after him near Ieper and is believed to be the only person to have a cemetery named after him, also near Ieper, where he fought a famous action in 1914. His brother was Captain of the battle-cruiser HMS Queen Mary which blew up at the Battle of Jutland on 31 May 1916 for the loss of all hands except nine.

You can find the graves of two men 'shot at dawn'. Private Harry MacDonald, 12th West Yorkshires, a father of three had fought and was wounded at Gallipoli while with the Duke of Wellington's Regiment. He was on leave when his wife became pregnant with their third child so MacDonald asked for an extension of his sick leave which was refused and he went absent. He was arrested and posted to the 12th West Yorkshires with whom he was subsequently buried by an explosion which may have caused shell-shock. On 12 September, and having already reported sick again, MacDonald absented himself from the trenches at Hulluch. He remained free for a month before being picked up at Boulogne. The fact that he was carrying a false ID was enough evidence at his trial that he had no intention of returning to duty. He was medically examined after the trial but the doctors declared that there was nothing wrong with him. His Divisional Commander promptly declared him 'worthless' and MacDonald's fate was sealed. MacDonald's circumstances were raised in Parliament but a pardon was refused due to the lack of medical evidence. He was executed on 4 November 1916 aged 32 years.

Rifleman Frederick Martin Barratt, 7th Kings Royal Rifle Corps, was executed on 10 July 1917 aged 23 years. Barratt was a regular soldier who had been fighting on the Western Front for a number of years. He had been sentenced to three years in March 1916 for falling asleep at his post. Sentences of imprisonment were usually suspended to ensure that the offender was sent back to his unit rather than spending the rest of the war in comparative safety. Following this, and whilst his battalion were at Arras, Barratt deserted. He was soon retrieved and sent before a Court Martial on 21 June 1916 but with a previous offence against him, a death sentence was almost a certainty.

There are three Royal Engineers killed in May 1940 buried here.

Concentrated here:

Vauchelles-Les-Authie Communal Cemetery Extension - situated about 1.5km to the north-west on the road to Doullens. It was opened in July 1916 by the Field Ambulances in the village but was only used for eight burials.

UK – 133   Canada – 1   NZ – 17
Fr – 76   WW2 - 3

LOCATION

The village is 13km south-east of Doullens on the road to Albert. The Cemetery is on the south-eastern side of the village.

LOUVERVAL MILITARY CEMETERY, DOIGNIES

HISTORY

The first burials were made in April 1917. It remained in use until December. The remaining graves were concentrated here after the war.

INFORMATION

The village was in German hands for most of the war. The Chateau was taken by the 56th Australian Infantry at dawn on 2 April 1917. The Germans re-took it on 21 March 1918, pushing the 51st (Highland) Division out. The position was retaken in the-following September.

Parts of Rows B and C were made in April-December 1917. In 1927 the remaining graves were brought in from Louverval Chateau Cemetery, and seven German graves were removed.

Among those buried here is Surgeon Lieutenant Frank Pearce Pocock, DSO, MC & Bar, Drake Battalion, Royal Naval Division, Royal Navy, killed in action on 29 September 1918 aged 27 years. He was the Medical Officer on board HMS Iris II for the Zeebrugge Raid in April 1918 for which he was awarded his Distinguished Service Order. He enlisted in September 1915 and was sent to join the 1st (RN) Field Ambulance at Mudros in the Mediterranean in January 1916. He joined Drake Battalion in March 1916 and stayed with them, though he had a few periods of illness, until January 1918. He was then transferred for the Zeebrugge Raid but returned to Drake Battalion in August 1918. He was awarded the Military Cross for gallantry and devotion to duty in operations north of the Ancre in November 1916. He was posthumously awarded a Bar to his Military Cross in January 1919, though this is not recorded by the CWGC. The citation reads 'He attended to the wounded under very heavy fire and most adverse circumstances during operations lasting several days. His courage & self-sacrificing devotion to duty were a splendid example to his stretcher-bearers and his skill was instrumental in saving the lives of many wounded men'.

Concentrated here:

Louverval Chateau Cemetery – it was in a meadow near the southern edge of the Chateau grounds. It was begun by the Germans in March 1918 and was used by the British in September and October 1918. It contained the graves of 78 British men, one Australian soldier, one New Zealand man, and 23 German soldiers.

Louverval German Cemetery – it was at the eastern edge of the Chateau grounds. It contained the graves of 138 German soldiers and seven unidentified Highlanders.

UK – 118   Aust – 4   NZ - 2
Unnamed – 6   Area – 682 sq mts

CAMBRAI MEMORIAL

Located on the east side of the cemetery, the Memorial was unveiled by Lieutenant-General Sir Louis Vaughan on 4 August 1930. The Memorial commemorates 7058 servicemen, mostly British but also South Africans and the Channel Islands Militia, who died in the Battle of Cambrai in November and December 1917 and whose graves are not known.

Sir Douglas Haig described the object of the Cambrai operations as the gaining of a 'local success by a sudden attack at a point where the enemy did not expect it' and to some extent they succeeded. The proposed method of assault was new, with no preliminary artillery bombardment. Instead, tanks would be used to break through the German wire, with the infantry following under the cover of smoke barrages.

Most battles of WW1 are historically arranged in groups, but Cambrai stands alone. It followed Third Ieper but was fought by a different army, in a different area, and it preceded several more months of trench warfare before the nature of the war changed with the German offensive of March 1918.

The attack began early on the morning of 20 November 1917 and initial advances were excellent. However, by 22 November, a halt was called for rest and reorganisation, which allowed the Germans to reinforce. From 23-28 November, the fighting was concentrated almost entirely around Bourlon Wood and by 29 November, it was clear that the Germans were ready for a major counter attack. During the fierce fighting of the next five days, much of the ground gained in the initial days of the attack was lost. The Third Army lost about 20,000 dead in the battle.

For the Allies, the results of the battle were disappointing but, importantly, valuable lessons were learnt.

There are seven men who won the Victoria Cross honoured on the Memorial.

Private George William Burdett Clare, VC, 5th (Royal Irish) Lancers, died on 28 November 1917, aged 28 years. His citation reads 'For most conspicuous bravery and devotion to duty when, acting as a stretcher-bearer during a most intense and continuous enemy bombardment, Pte. Clare dressed and conducted wounded over the open to the dressing-station about 500 yards away. At one period when all the garrison of a detached post, which was lying out in the open about 150 yards to the left of the line occupied, had become casualties, he crossed the intervening space, which was continually swept by heavy rifle and machine-gun fire, and, having dressed all the cases, manned the post single-handed till a relief could be sent. Pte. Clare then carried a seriously wounded man through intense fire to cover, and later succeeded in getting him to the dressing station. At the dressing-station he was told that the enemy was using gas shells to a large extent in the valley below, and as the wind was blowing the gas towards the line of trenches and shell-holes occupied, he started on the right of the line and personally warned every company post of the danger, the whole time under shell and rifle fire. This very gallant soldier was subsequently killed by a shell.'

Private Frederick George Dancox, VC, 4th Worcestershires, died on 30 November 1917 aged 38 years. Citation – 'For most conspicuous bravery and devotion to duty in attack. After the first objective had been captured and consolidation had been started, work was considerably hampered, and numerous casualties were caused, by an enemy machine gun firing from a concrete emplacement situated on the edge of our protective barrage. Pte. Dancox was one of a party of about ten men detailed as moppers-up. Owing to the position of the machine gun emplacement, it was extremely difficult to work round a flank. However, this man with great gallantry worked his way round through the barrage and entered the Pillbox from the rear, threatening the garrison with a Mills bomb. Shortly afterwards he reappeared with a machine gun under his arm, followed by about 40 enemy. The machine gun was brought back to our position by Pte. Dancox, and he kept it in action all day. By his resolution, absolute disregard of danger and cheerful disposition, the morale of his comrades was maintained at a very high standard under extremely trying circumstances.'

2nd Lieutenant James Samuel Emerson, VC, 9th Royal Inniskilling Fusiliers, died on 6 December 1917 aged 22 years. Citation – 'For repeated acts of most conspicuous bravery. He led his company in an attack and cleared 400 yards of trench. Though wounded, when the enemy attacked in superior numbers, he sprang out of the trench with eight men and met the attack in the open, killing many and taking six prisoners. For three hours after this, all other Officers having become casualties, he remained with his company, refusing to go to the dressing station, and repeatedly repelled bombing attacks. Later, when the enemy again attacked in superior numbers, he led his men to repel the attack and was mortally wounded. His heroism, when worn out and exhausted from loss of blood, inspired his men to hold out, though almost surrounded, till reinforcements arrived and dislodged the enemy.'

Major Frederick Henry Johnson, VC, 73rd Field Company, Royal Engineers, died on 26 November 1917 aged 27 years. Citation – 'For most conspicuous bravery and devotion to duty in the attack on Hill 70 on 25th Sept., 1915. Second Lieutenant Johnson was with a section of his company of the Royal Engineers. Although wounded in the leg, he stuck to his duty throughout the attack, led several charges on the German redoubt, and at a very critical time, under very heavy fire, repeatedly rallied the men who were near him. By his splendid example and cool courage he was mainly instrumental in saving the situation and in establishing firmly his part of the position which had been taken. He remained at his post until relieved in the evening.'

Captain Allastair Malcolm Cluny Mcready-Diarmid, VC, 4th attached 17th Middlesex, died on 1 December 1917 aged 29 years. Citation – 'For most conspicuous bravery and brilliant leadership. When the enemy penetrated some distance into our position and the situation was extremely critical, Capt. McReady-Diarmid at once led his company forward through a heavy barrage. He immediately engaged the enemy, with such success that he drove them back at least 300 yards, causing numerous casualties and capturing 27 prisoners. The following day the enemy again attacked and drove back another company which had lost all it's officers. This gallant officer at once called for volunteers and attacked. He drove them back again for 300 yards, with heavy casualties. Throughout this attack Capt. McReady-Diarmid led the way himself, and it was absolutely and entirely due to his marvellous throwing of bombs that the ground was regained. His absolute disregard for danger, his cheerfulness and coolness at a most trying time, inspired all who saw him. This most gallant officer was eventually killed by a bomb when the enemy had been driven right back to their original starting point.'

Captain Walter Napleton Stone, VC, 3rd attached 17th Royal Fusiliers, died on 30 November 1917. Citation – 'For most conspicuous bravery when in command of a company in an isolated position 1,000 yards in front of the main line, and overlooking the enemy's position. He observed the enemy massing for an attack, and afforded invaluable information to battalion headquarters. He was ordered to withdraw his company, leaving a rearguard to cover the withdrawal. The attack developing with unexpected speed, Capt. Stone sent three platoons back and remained with the rearguard himself. He stood on the parapet with the telephone under a tremendous bombardment, observing the enemy and continued to send back valuable information until the wire was cut by his orders. The rearguard was eventually surrounded and cut to pieces, and Capt. Stone was seen fighting to the last till he was shot through the head. The extraordinary coolness of this heroic officer and the accuracy of his information enabled dispositions to be made just in time to save the line and avert disaster.' His brother Lieutenant Colonel Arthur Stone, DSO, 16th Lancashire Fusiliers killed in action on 2 October 1918 aged 41 years is buried in Hancourt British Cemetery.

Captain Richard William Leslie Wain, VC, 25th Manchesters attached 'A' Battalion, Tank Corps, died on 20 November 1917 aged 20 years. Citation – 'For most conspicuous bravery in command of a section of Tanks. During an attack the Tank in which he was, was disabled by a direct hit near an enemy strong point which was holding up the attack. Capt. Wain and one man, both seriously wounded, were the only survivors. Though bleeding profusely from his wounds, he refused the attention of stretcher-bearers, rushed from behind the Tank with a Lewis gun, and captured the strong point, taking about half the garrison prisoners. Although his wounds were very serious he picked up a rifle and continued to fire at the retiring enemy until he received a fatal wound in the head. It was due to the valour displayed by Captain Wain that the infantry were able to advance.'

Among those commemorated here is Private Howard Prentice, 11th Middlesex who died on 30 November 1917. His brother, Private Francis Maurice Prentice, 1/14th (London Scottish) Londons, died on 25 September 1917 aged 24 years is buried at Lagnicourt Hedge Cemetery. Another brother, Private Jack Alan Prentice, 1st Bedfordshires died while on active service on 25 March 1920 aged 21 years and is buried in Bedford Cemetery, Bedfordshire.

Similarly commemorated here is Lieutenant Randle William Gascoyne-Cecil, Royal Horse Artillery and Royal Field Artillery, killed on 1 December 1917 aged 28 years. It is interesting to note that Randle had been sent down from Oxford in 1908 for 'a breach of discipline' after throwing rocks through the windows of Balliol College. He had appeared as an actor in Gaiety plays and had travelled with actor George Grossmith to America. Additionally, he married Dorothy Janaway in June of 1914 and divorced her in July of 1915. His brother, Captain John Arthur Gascoyne-Cecil, MC, 75th Brigade, Royal Field Artillery, who died on 27 August 1918 aged 25 years is buried in Bucquoy Road Cemetery. Another brother, Lieutenant Rupert Edward Gascoyne-Cecil, 1st Bedfordshires, died on 11 July 1915 and is buried in Railway Dugouts Burial Ground (Transport Farm) near Ieper. Their father was later the Bishop of Exeter and of Salisbury. Their grandfather was Lord Salisbury, three time Prime Minister of the United Kingdom.

Another to lose two brothers, though there are some I have not included here, is Private Thomas John Gallienne, 1st Royal Guernsey Light Infantry, killed on 30 November 1917 aged 35 years. His brothers, twins, Private Adolphus Gallienne, and Private Archibald Gallienne, both 1st Royal Guernsey Light Infantry, died on 23 and 21 March 1918 respectively. They were aged 24 years and are both commemorated on the Tyne Cot Memorial near Ieper.

You may be interested in Lieutenant Gavin Patrick Bowes-Lyon, 3rd Grenadier Guards, killed in action on 27 November 1917 aged 20 years while leading his Company at Fontaine-Notre-Dame, near Cambrai. He was a cousin to the mother of Queen Elizabeth II. His father was Wimbledon Doubles Tennis Champion in 1887 and 1888.

You will also want to think about two young men. Private Albert Arthur Fryer, 14th Durham Light Infantry, killed on 3 December 1917 aged 16 years and Private Thomas Henry Anderson, 4th South African Infantry, died on 7 December 1917 aged 16 years.

LOCATION

Louverval is a hamlet in the commune of Doignies. It is 13km north-east of Bapaume and 16km south-west of Cambrai. Louverval Military Cemetery is on the north side of the Bapaume-Cambrai road. The cemetery is in a ravine below and next to the road out of view, however the Memorial is clearly visible on this often very busy road. This is a very effective tribute to the men buried and commemorated here.

LOWRIE CEMETERY, HAVRINCOURT

HISTORY
The cemetery was opened and closed in October 1918. It was used after the war for the concentration of graves from the surrounding battlefields.

INFORMATION
Havrincourt was well behind German lines for most of the war. It was attacked by the 62nd Division in November 1917 as part of the Battle of Cambrai and then remained in British hands through the winter. On 23 March 1918 the Germans captured the village at the start of their offensive and it remained in German hands until the final advance to victory when, on 12 September 1918, the 62nd Division again captured the village and held it during a counter-attack on the following day.

This cemetery was made by the Burial Officer of the 3rd Division, and named after him, for the burial of men who fell in the final capture of Havrincourt in September 1918. The cemetery was enlarged after the war when 40 graves were concentrated here from isolated positions in the surrounding area.

Buried here is Company Serjeant Major James K Rollo, DCM, MM, 1st Gordon Highlanders, killed in action on 28 September 1918 aged 26 years. His Distinguished Conduct Medal was gazetted in early September 1918. The citation reads 'He located the enemy by a daring reconnaissance at a critical period. Later, led a bombing party against the enemy and put them to flight. Although wounded in the head he refused to leave them for twelve hours.'

UK – 251   Unnamed – 47   Area – 774 sq mts

LOCATION
Havrincourt is a village about 15km south-west of Cambrai and 25km directly east of Bapaume. It lies next to, and just south of, the A2/E19 Autoroute. Lowrie Cemetery is about 1km north of the village on the east side of the road to Moeuvres at the bottom of the bank that carries the road over the autoroute.

LUKE COPSE BRITISH CEMETERY, PUISIEUX

HISTORY
The cemetery was created as part of the battlefield clearance that took place in February 1917.

INFORMATION
Luke Copse British Cemetery is in the no-man's land in front of the British front line of 1 July 1916. It lies on the position of the attack by 12th (Sheffield City Battalion) York and Lancasters followed by the 14th (2nd Barnsley Pals) York & Lancasters. On 13 November 1916 the attack was repeated by 2nd Suffolks and 8th Kings Own (Royal Lancasters), many of whom can now be found in cemeteries nearby.

The name came from the small copses, Matthew, Mark, Luke and John, situated behind this cemetery along the edge of which ran the British front line. This is the most northerly cemetery, with the exception of the diversion at Gommecourt, on the battlefields of 1 July 1916.

The cemetery was made by the V Corps in 1917, as V Corps Cemetery No. 19, when the battlefields were cleared. The men buried here belong to the 31st and 3rd Divisions who attacked the German line on 1 July and on 13 November 1916. It is a mass grave.

Among those buried here are two brothers from Sheffield who joined up together into the 12th (Sheffield City Battalion) York and Lancasters and were both killed in the attack here on 1 July 1916. They are Lance Corporal Frank Gunstone, 660 and Private William Walter Gunstone, 661. Note the consecutive service numbers showing they joined up together.

UK – 72   Unnamed – 28   Area – 314 sq mts

LOCATION
Serre is situated about 20km south of Arras on the road to Amiens. The cemetery is reached by a farm track from the road. The farm track leads 200m to Serre Road No. 3 Cemetery and another 200m past Sheffield Memorial Park to Luke Copse Cemetery. The last part is the most difficult section of track. There is no easy turning at the cemetery. The cemetery is a further 20m from the track in the middle of no-man's land. It is best to park at the road and take a stroll to this cemetery as well as the other local burial grounds and the Memorial Park.

MAILLY WOOD CEMETERY

HISTORY
The cemetery was begun in June 1916. It was used again after the attack by the 51st Division on Beaumont-Hamel in November 1916. The main period of use was during the German offensive in 1918.

INFORMATION
Mailly-Maillet was behind the French and British front-lines for most of the war, coming under British control when the Third Army took it over from the French in 1915, but it was damaged by shelling from the German guns. The village, one of the largest in the area, and the surrounding district were used as a base for Field Ambulances and Dressing Stations from August 1915 to the German advance in March 1918. In the German offensive in March 1918 the front- came to a line just east of this cemetery. The area was defended in March by the 12th Division and in August by the 21st Division, both of whom buried their dead here. The Germans also used it for billets in WW2.

The cemetery was opened with the burial of thirteen men of the 2nd Seaforth Highlanders on 25 June 1916. These were men killed by German shelling answering the British bombardment before the Battle of the Somme on 1 July 1916. Many of the men buried here are of the 51st (Highland) Division and died during November 1916.

The cemetery was extended after the war when 101 graves were concentrated here from the surrounding battlefields. Buried here is Sergeant Harold John Colley, VC, MM, 10th Lancashire Fusiliers, who died of wounds, suffered in the action for which he was awarded the Victoria Cross, in one of the Field Ambulances in the village on 25 August 1918, aged 23 years. His citation reads 'For most conspicuous bravery and initiative when in command of a platoon in support of forward platoons which had been ordered to hold on at all costs. When the enemy counter-attacked in force, he rushed forward on his own initiative to help the forward line, rallying and controlling the men holding it. The enemy by this time were advancing quickly, and had already obtained a footing in the trench. Sergeant Colley then formed a defensive flank and held it. Out of the two platoons only three men remained unwounded, and he himself was dangerously wounded. It was entirely due to Sergeant Colley's action that the enemy were prevented from breaking through, and were eventually driven off. His courage and tenacity saved a very critical situation.' He enlisted on 1 September 1914, with the Duke of Cornwall's Light Infantry, initially serving in the Army Cycling Corps and then as a despatch rider. He received a Certificate for Meritorious Conduct for his actions on 30 March 1917, when he was wounded while digging out two men, who had been buried by a mortar bomb, while under heavy fire. After time in England to recover from his injuries, Harold was then posted to the 10th Lancashire Fusiliers. He was awarded the Military Medal for his actions at Beaumont Hamel on 4 June 1918. With two others he beat off a German advance and saved the Fusiliers positions. As well as his MM he was promoted to acting Sergeant.

Also here is Captain Herbert Geoffrey Lush-Wilson, Royal Horse Artillery, killed in action on 21 July 1916. Serving in 'Y' Battery he fought at Gallipoli with the 29th Division and he and his Battery came to France in April 1916. He was awarded the Chevalier of the Legion of Honour and was killed near Mailly by counter-battery fire.

Concentrated here:
Mailly-Mailly Military Cemetery - located within the village. Thirty soldiers had been buried in June 1916 and July-August 1918. Six of the graves had been destroyed by shell-fire and they are now represented by Special Memorials.

UK – 631   NZ – 28   SAfr – 3
KUG – 40   Unnamed - 60

Area – 2100 sq mts

Special Memorials to six soldiers buried in Maiily-Maillet Military Cemetery whose graves had been destroyed by shellfire.

Special Memorials to two British soldiers whose graves cannot now be identified.

LOCATION
Mailly-Maillet lies about 8km north-west of Albert on the Amiens-Arras road. The cemetery is 400m south of the centre of the village on the edge of the wood in the direction of Hedauville. A track leads from the road to the cemetery. The CWGC website says 'Access can be difficult during winter due to the condition of the mud track and a four-wheel drive vehicle would be required. It should however be emphasised that even with this type of vehicle there is a danger of the vehicle slipping as the track is narrow, becomes very muddy and the fields are below the level of the track.'

MAILLY-MAILLET COMMUNAL CEMETERY EXTENSION

HISTORY
The Extension was begun by the French Army in June 1915 when they still occupied this sector of the front. The British began to make burials here in August 1915 and continued until December 1916. It was used again during the German offensive from March to July 1918.

INFORMATION
The Extension was first used by medical units. The first burial was 2nd Lieutenant George Hanson Wheatcroft, 16th Heavy Battery, Royal Garrison Artillery killed on 11 August 1915 aged 26 years.

Burials were made by fighting units in 1918. The 51 French graves and the graves of two German Prisoners of War have been removed.

Buried here are Rifleman James F McCracken and Rifleman James Templeton, both 15th Royal Irish Rifles, court-martialled on 27 February and executed for desertion on 19 March 1916. Sadly, both also had poor disciplinary records, but both returned to their comrades before being arrested. McCracken was aged 19 and had gone absent on 21 February 1916 after being informed he would be sent for duty in the trenches. Templeton was 20 years old and had gone absent on 20 February after being told to prepare for sentry duty. They were executed side by side and are buried together.

UK – 122   NZ – 3   Newf – 1
Area – 868 sq mts

LOCATION
The Communal Cemetery is situated about 1km north of the village, a little to the west of the road to Courcelles-au-Bois. The Extension is on the east side of the Communal Cemetery.

MANCHESTER CEMETERY, RIENCOURT-LES-BAPAUME

HISTORY
The cemetery was opened and closed in September 1918 when this area had been captured from the Germans during the final advance to victory.

INFORMATION
Riencourt was behind German lines until they withdrew to the Hindenburg Line in March 1917. The British held the village for a year until the German spring offensive in 1918. It was recaptured by the 42nd Division on 30 August 1918. Who then opened the cemetery. The graves of 21 German soldiers have been removed elsewhere.

Of those buried here 62 were from territorial battalions, 1/5th to 1/8th, of the Manchester Regiment. One of these is Captain Clarence James Thody, 'B' Company, 1/8th Manchesters, killed in action on 30 August 1918 aged 33 years. Before the war he was a teacher at Ardwick Green Industrial School in Manchester. He arrived in France in March 1917.

UK – 67   NZ – 1   KUG – 3
Unnamed – 8   Area – 307 sq mts

Special Memorial to a British soldier, of the 1/5th Manchesters, known to be buried among the unnamed graves.

LOCATION
Riencourt-les-Bapaume is situated 3km south-east of Bapaume just to the east of the road to Peronne. The cemetery is south-east of the village on the north-east side of the road to Villers-au-Flos.

MANITOBA CEMETERY, CAIX

HISTORY
The cemetery was opened by the 1st Canadian Division who captured the village in 1918. It was used for burials over a ten day period in 1918 from 8 to 18 August.

INFORMATION
The village was in German hands until taken by British troops in March 1917 during the German retreat to the Hindenburg Line. The Germans re-captured the village in March 1918 and the Canadian Corps re-took the village on 8 August 1918.

Almost all of the men buried here are Canadian, most from the 8th (Manitoba) Canadian Infantry, which fought here on 9 August 1918 and gave the cemetery its name. The 1st Canadian Division's Burial Officer was also Chaplain of 8th Canadian Infantry.

Among those buried here is Lieutenant Colonel Thomas Head Raddall, DSO, commanding 8th Canadian Infantry, also known as the 90th Winnipeg Rifles, who died with his men when killed by machine gun fire on 9 August 1918 aged 40 years. He was born in Farnborough, England but lived in Nova Scotia. He had served 21 years in the British Army before joining the Canadian Permanent Force as a musketry instructor with the Royal Canadian Regiment when he emigrated to Canada in 1913. He represented Great Britain in shooting at the 1908 Olympics. His son of the same name became a noted author and historian and an Officer of the Order of Canada.

South of the cemetery, on the same road, is a memorial at the spot where, on 7 June 1940, 31 disarmed French soldiers of the 41st Infantry Regiment and 10th Artillery Regiments were massacred by the Germans.

UK – 2	Can – 118	KUG – 8
Unnamed – 3		Area – 507 sq mts

Special Memorial to one Canadian soldier believed to be buried here among the unnamed.

LOCATION
Caix is a village 24km east of Amiens, between the roads to St. Quentin and Roye. Manitoba Cemetery is situated 2km south of Caix between the village of Caix and Beaufort on the road from the Caix Communal Cemetery. The small, peaceful and isolated cemetery is on the east side of the road.

MARTEVILLE COMMUNAL CEMETERY, ATTILLY

HISTORY
The cemetery was used for the burial of men killed in battle during April and May 1917. It was later used in January, March, September and October 1918. The Germans made some burials here in March 1918.

INFORMATION
The village was the scene of fighting in April 1917, March 1918 and September-October 1918.

Among those buried here is Serjeant Thomas George Earl, DCM & Bar, 2nd Welsh, killed in action on 24 September 1918. The citation for his Distinguished Conduct Medal reads 'For conspicuous gallantry on the 9th May 1915, at Richebourg L'Avoue in going out on five separate occasions under heavy fire, and successfully bringing in five wounded men, ultimately being wounded himself. Also on 2nd August at Vermelles, Corporal Earl, accompanied by another man, left our parapet and crawled through the grass to within 30 yards of a sap occupied by the enemy. while taking observations, a party of the enemy approached to within 10 yards, and when one raised himself above the grass Corporal Earl shot him, the remainder of the enemy lying flat in the grass; after waiting a short time, both men cralwed back and regained our parapet. The reconnaissance was carried out with great judgment and bravery, and valuable information was gained.' The citation for the Bar to his DCM, won in 1918, reads 'For conspicuous gallantry and devotion to duty as a Bn. Scout Serjeant and observer during three days' operations. He obtained connection with the right and centre companies both by day and night, and when all other guides failed. During an attack he led a ration party to the rear company through heavy shelling, and, though suffering several casualties, arrived at his destination with the rations.' He had served before the First World War joining the Regiment in 1894, seeing action in India and the

South African Wars. On leaving the Welsh Regiment he joined the Natal Carbineers, and took part in putting down the Zulu Bambatha Rebellion in 1906. He was killed in an attack on Fresnoy-le-Petit.

UK – 76　　　　Fr – 2　　　　Ger – 1
Unnamed – 9　　　　　　　　Area – 507 sq mts
Special Memorial to one soldier whose grave was destroyed by shellfire.

LOCATION
The village is found about 5km west of St. Quentin and 1km south of the Amiens-St. Quentin road. The cemetery is on the south side of the village on the Vermand-Attilly road. It is on the north side of the road with a large car park. The British burials are on the north edge of the Communal Cemetery at the rear near the wall.

MARTINPUICH BRITISH CEMETERY

HISTORY
The cemetery was opened in November 1916 and remained in use until June 1917. It was used again at the end of August 1918 when this area had again been captured from the Germans. A few graves were concentrated here after the war.

INFORMATION
Martinpuich was in German hands from 1915. It was a first-day objective on 1 July 1916 but was not captured until the morning of 15 September 1916 when it fell to the 15th Division with a tank in support. The Germans re-occupied the village from April to August 1918.

In 1931 the graves of ten British soldiers who were buried by the Germans in the Communal Cemetery, and whose graves were lost in subsequent fighting, were rediscovered and concentrated here. Among them were 2nd Lieutenant Noel Carleton Blakeway and three men, Lance Corporal Alfred James Way, Privates Francis Henry Fielding and James Gallivan, all of 1st Dorsets, killed on 27 March 1916 in a night raid on Y Sap near La Boiselle.

Also here is 2nd Lieutenant William Ritchie Sellar, No. 98 Squadron, RAF, a Scottish pilot shot down aged 18 years while flying a DH9 on 29 August 1918.

There are still some British soldiers in the Communal Cemetery. A German Military Cemetery has been removed from the village. The grave of an American Medical Officer was removed after the war.

The original village school playground was paid for by the 47th (London) Division as a memorial to their men who died fighting in France, particularly those who were killed at High Wood on 15 September 1916.

UK – 80　　　　Aust – 34　　　　Can – 1
Area – 638 sq mts

Special Memorials erected to four British soldiers of the Royal Warwickshires, killed in November 1916, who are known to be buried within the cemetery boundary but whose graves cannot now be identified.

LOCATION
Martinpuich is situated 1km south of the Albert-Bapaume road about 10km from each town. The British Cemetery is on the southern edge of the village on the road to Longueval near the Communal Cemetery. A farm road and a path lead to the cemetery on the south side of the valley.

MARTINSART BRITISH CEMETERY

HISTORY
This cemetery was begun in June 1916 and used as a front-line cemetery until October 1916. It was used again in September 1918. After the war the cemetery was greatly enlarged when most of the burials were made.

INFORMATION
The village was close to the British front-line until September 1916 by which time the Germans had been pushed back in this area. It came close to the front-line again from March to August 1918.

The first burials here were of seventeen men, including the Regimental Sergeant Major and a Company Sergeant Major of the 13th Royal Irish Rifles, who were killed by a shell on 28 June 1916 as they prepared for 1 July 1916 and who are buried in Plot I, Row A. The battalion was marching out of Martinsart to relieve the 11th Royal Irish Rifles in

Thiepval Wood. As No. 11 Platoon and the battalion headquarters were about to march out together a shell fell in the midst of the group. Fourteen were killed immediately and ten more died later. Most of the other men were wounded, including the second-in-command Major R. P. Maxwell, and the adjutant, Captain Wright.

The V Corps Burial Officer used the cemetery in September 1918 for the burial of several officers and men found on the surrounding battlefield.

After the war 346 graves were concentrated here from the battlefields north, east and south of the village. This is when most of the cemetery was made. There were sixteen German Prisoners of War buried here but they have been removed.

Among those buried here is Lieutenant Commander Frederick Septimus Kelly, DSC, Hood Battalion, Royal Naval Division, RNVR who died on 13 November 1916 aged 35 years. He was one of the pall bearers at Rupert Brookes' funeral in 1915. He was an Old Etonian who had been a concert pianist, won a rowing Gold at the Olympics in 1908 and had aspirations to be a composer. He won the Distinguished Service Cross during the withdrawal from Gallipoli and was killed in one of the final acts of the Battles of the Somme in 1916 while leading an attack on a German machine-gun position.

Also here is Colonel Herbert Clifford Bernard, commanding 10th Royal Irish Rifles, killed in action at Thiepval Wood encouraging his men forward at a point known as Gordon's Castle, on 1 July 1916, aged 50 years. He had served in the sub-continent for most of his career, including involvement in the Burmese War from 1885 to 1891, and commanding the 45th (Rattray's) Sikhs from 1909 to 1914, after which he retired from the Indian Army.

Two men who had emigrated to Canada but returned to fight with the same battalion of the Lancashire Fusiliers are here. Private Ronald Everest Simpson, 18th Lancashire Fusiliers was killed in action on 16 April 1918, aged 32 years. Private Thomas John Brightwell, 18th Lancashire Fusiliers, formerly Northants Yeomanry, was killed in action on 1 June 1918, aged 34 years.

UK – 383   NZ – 8   Aust – 1
KUG – 96   Unnamed – 156   Area – 2003 sq mts

Special Memorials to six British soldiers believed to be buried among the unidentified graves.

LOCATION

Martinsart lies about 5km north of Albert on the west side of Aveluy Wood on the ridge above the River Ancre. The cemetery is on the south side of the village, 100m south of the Communal Cemetery, beside the road to Aveluy.

MEATH CEMETERY, VILLERS-GUISLAIN

HISTORY

The cemetery was opened in October 1918 and remained in use only for a few weeks.

INFORMATION

Villers-Guislain was behind the German lines for much of the war. The village was attacked and captured by the British in April 1917. The Germans recaptured the village on 30 November during the Battle of Cambrai and held it against an attack by the Tank Corps and Guards Division on the following day. The British did not regain the village until 30 September 1918.

The cemetery was begun by the 33rd Division. Most of the men buried here were from the Cameronians, the Queen's or the Londons.

Among those buried here is Sergeant Herbert E. Randall, DCM, 1st Queen's (Royal West Surreys), killed on 21 September 1918, aged 20 years. He was awarded the Distinguished Conduct Medal in March 1918 for 'On hearing cries for help coming from a detached post, he, heedless of the very hostile shelling, went to the spot and found a N.C.O. and two men buried under some debris. Returning for assistance, he, with two men, who volunteered to aid him succeeded in extricating the buried men under the most dangerous and difficult circumstances. This gallant act occupied an hour under heavy fire in the open, undoubtedly saved the lives of the three men.'

UK – 125   Unnamed – 21   Area – 418 sq mts

Special Memorials erected to three British soldiers of the 1st Cameronians known, or believed, to be buried among the unnamed graves.

LOCATION

Villers-Guislain is located about 15km south of Cambrai, a similar distance north-east of Peronne and 2km west of the A26 motorway. The cemetery is about 1km south-east of the village on the ridge separating 'Targelle Ravine' and 'Pigeon Ravine'. Meath Cemetery is located in the middle of fields and is approached from the village by a rough track which takes you first past Villers Hill Cemetery on your right and then Targelle Ravine Cemetery on the left though you turn right just before the cemetery. It is possible to continue further in your vehicle and you can get to Meath Cemetery in a 4x4 in winter as I have achieved this. However, you may wish to stop at Targelle Ravine Cemetery and walk the remaining distance which should take 10-15 minutes.

MEAULTE MILITARY CEMETERY

HISTORY
The cemetery was opened in December 1915 and remained in use until the front-line moved away from here in February 1917. A few burials were made in September 1918. The cemetery was enlarged after the war.

INFORMATION
Meaulte was held by the French until the British arrived in early 1915. The village saw little effect from the fighting for much of the war as 75% of its civilian population remained until March 1918. However, the village fell to the Germans, taking it from the 9th Division, on 26 March 1918. The 12th Division, aided by the Tank Corps, recaptured the village on 22 August 1918.

Of the burials here 154 were concentrated after the war. One man buried here was moved after the war from Meaulte Churchyard but he remains unidentified.

Among those buried here is 2nd Lieutenant Henry 'Harry' Augustus Butters. The son of a prominent San Francisco industrialist, Butters was raised partially in England before inheriting his father's fortune in 1906 when he moved to California where he worked briefly for Standard Oil and purchased his own ranch. When the war began in 1914, Butters decided to join the British army and received a commission in the Royal Artillery, 107th Brigade, 24th Division in April 1915. In September 1915 Butters travelled to France where he took part in the Battle of Loos. At Ploegsteert in April 1916 he met Winston Churchill. After suffering from shell shock Butters was sent on leave in June, but returned to the Front on 2 July. On 31 August 1916, Butters and his unit were firing on Trones Woods, outside Guillemont, when his gun received a direct German hit by which he and all the members of his battery were killed. His book, 'An American Citizen' was published in 1918.

Concentrated here:

Sandpit Cemetery, Meaulte - situated on the eastern edge of the village on the Albert-Bray road. The Sandpit was a military camp in January 1917. The cemetery was made by the 12th Division and contained the graves of 93 British soldiers with a Canadian airman killed between 22 and 29 August 1918.

Meaulte Triangle Cemetery - situated on the southern edge of the village at the site of the former light railway crossing of the Morlancourt road. It was created by the III Corps Heavy Artillery and the 12th Division. It contained the graves of 36 British soldiers who were killed from 23 to 25 August 1918.

UK – 296	India – 6	Can – 2
Aust – 1	KUG – 7	Unnamed – 21

Area - 1522 sq mts

Special Memorials are erected to eleven British soldiers believed to be buried among the unnamed graves.

LOCATION
Meaulte is a village 1km south-east of Albert and is now almost a suburb of the larger town. The Military Cemetery is south of the village on the west side of the road to Etinehem as the road begins to climb out of the village.

MEHARICOURT COMMUNAL CEMETERY

HISTORY
The cemetery was used by the Germans for the burial of WW2 flying crew who had been shot down and killed.

INFORMATION
Most of the crew were shot down during 1944 in attacks on French railways during the build up to D-Day.

Among those buried here is Pilot Officer Andrew Charles Mynarski, VC, No. 419 Squadron, Royal Canadian Air Force, who was killed when attacked over Cambrai on 13 June 1944 aged 27 years while flying a Lancaster bomber. He is the only WW2 Victoria Cross holder buried on the Somme and his award was the last to a Canadian airman in WW2. His citation reads 'Pilot Officer Mynarski was the mid-upper gunner of a Lancaster aircraft, detailed to attack a target at Cambrai in France, on the night of 12th June, 1944. The aircraft was attacked from below and astern by an enemy fighter and ultimately came down in flames. As an immediate result of the attack, both port engines failed. Fire broke out between the mid-upper turret and the rear turret, as well as in the port wing. The flames soon became fierce and the captain ordered the crew to abandon the aircraft. Pilot Officer Mynarski left his turret and went towards the escape hatch. He then saw that the rear gunner was still in his turret and apparently unable to leave it. The turret was, in fact, immovable, since the hydraulic gear had been put out of action when the port engines failed, and the manual gear had been broken by the gunner in his attempts to escape. Without hesitation, Pilot Officer Mynarski made his way through the flames in an endeavour to reach the rear turret and release the gunner. Whilst so doing, his parachute and his clothing, up to the waist, were set on fire. All his efforts to move the turret and free the gunner were in vain. Eventually the rear gunner clearly indicated to him that there was nothing more he could do and that he should try to save his own life. Pilot Officer Mynarski reluctantly went back through the flames to the escape hatch. There, as a last gesture to the trapper gunner, he turned towards him, stood to attention in his flaming clothing and saluted, before he jumped out of the aircraft. Pilot Officer Mynarski's descent was seen by French people on the ground. Both his parachute and clothing were on fire. He was found eventually by the French, but was so severely burnt that he died from his injuries. The rear gunner had a miraculous escape when the aircraft crashed. He subsequently testified that, had Pilot Officer Mynarski not attempted to save his comrade's life, he could have left the aircraft in safety and would, doubtless, have escaped death. Pilot Officer Mynarski must have been fully aware that in trying to free the rear gunner he was almost certain to lose his own life. Despite this, with outstanding courage and complete disregard for his own safety, he went to the rescue. Willingly accepting the danger, Pilot Officer Mynarski lost his life by a most conspicuous act of heroism which called for valour of the highest order.'

Also here are six of Pilot Officer Gordon Herbert Weeden's crew, No. 617 Squadron, shot down in December 1943 as they were dropping equipment for the French Resistance. Pilot Officer Claude Weaver, a Spitfire Pilot of No. 403 (Canadian) Squadron was shot down in a dog fight in January 1944. He tried to escape his from Spitfire but his parachute was entangled with the tailplane as it crashed. He survived for three hours before he died in hospital. He was an American, though recorded below as Canadian, from Tulsa, Oklahoma who had already received the DFC, DFM and MiD when he was killed aged 19 years. He had enlisted in February 1941 aged 17 years. After training he joined No. 412 Squadron and then No. 185 Squadron in the Middle East and Malta. He was shot down and captured by the Italians but escaped in May 1943 and was with No. 403 Squadron in October 1943. He received his Distinguished Flying Medal in November 1943 for his part in a series of successes in July 1942. He received the Distinguished Flying Cross posthumously for his actions in 1944. He was Mentioned in Despatches in June 1944. His brother, David Overton Weaver, was killed at Iwo Jima with the US Marines.

WW2 – 41 (Aust – 6, Can – 12, NZ – 2, UK – 21)

LOCATION
Méharicourt is located 38km south-east of Amiens and 24km south-west of Peronne. The Communal Cemetery is on the Rue de Rosieres on the north-western side of the village. There is a large obelisk to draw your attention. The British graves are at the rear right of the cemetery behind a low hedge with a cross of sacrifice.

MERCATEL COMMUNAL CEMETERY

HISTORY
The cemetery was used for the burial of seven men killed on 20 May 1940. There are also another 13 unidentified burials. So there are a total of 20 WW2 burials.

INFORMATION
All of the men buried here are Privates of the 1st Tyneside Scottish, Black Watch (Royal Highlanders). The battalion was a territorial force raised in January 1940. It was overrun at Fichuex in May 1940 in its only battle while covering the retreat of the British Expeditionary Force to Dunkirk. The lightly armed men faced tanks so the battalion ceased to exist but held up the Germans for a valuable five hours. Of note are Private Albert Edward McLuckie and Private Ernest Nixon who have consecutive service numbers.

WW2 UK – 20 (Unnamed – 13)

LOCATION
Mercatel is situated 7km south of Arras on the road to Bapaume. The Communal Cemetery is south of the village, about 460m south of the church on the road to Boisleux-St.-Marc. East of the entrance, on the south side of the main path are the 1939-1945 graves. It is better to use the side entrance rather than the usually locked main gate.

MERICOURT-L'ABBE COMMUNAL CEMETERY EXTENSION

HISTORY
The Extension was begun in August 1915 and remained in use until July 1916 when it was closed. It was opened again in March 1918 and used until August 1918. After the war it was enlarged by the concentration of graves from the battlefields north-east of Mericourt.

INFORMATION
The British took over this sector in the summer of 1915 and the railway station became a major railhead for the British Army. As such medical units were stationed in the area.
Field Ambulances opened the Extension and used it until the start of the Battles of the Somme in 1916. Plot II was the result of the July 1916 fighting including many who died with the 34th Division at La Boiselle.
From March to August 1918 the cemetery was used again, this time by units defending Amiens during the German offensive. After the war Rows G to K of Plot III were created when 74 graves, only one of which could be identified, were brought in from the surrounding battlefields.

Two soldiers, one killed in March 1916 and one in April 1918, buried in Heilly Churchyard were concentrated here in 1934. A French soldier buried here has been removed. Among those here is 2nd Lieutenant Tobias Mortimer Moll, 9th Leicestershires, died of wounds on 15 July 1916 aged 26 years. A South African, he played for Leicester Tigers as a Rugby Union prop forward. He also represented Cape Colony, Transvaal and on one occasion his country, South Africa, in a defeat against the 1910 touring British Isles. He was mortally wounded by shrapnel at Bazentin-le-Petit.

South of the village on the D1 Corbie-Bray road is the 3rd Australian Division Memorial. The Division did not arrive in France until November 1916 and went into its first battle at Messines in June 1917. The Memorial is at the centre of a triangle formed by the villages of Morlancourt, Treux and Hamel, which make up the Divisions' battle honours as they defended the German attack in the spring of 1918 and pushed the Germans back in August 1918.

UK – 234   Aust – 122   Can – 5
KUG – 51   Ger – 11
Unnamed – 73   Area – 1777 sq mts

Special Memorials to two British soldiers who were buried in Clery-sur-Somme German Cemetery but whose graves could not be found after the war. They are Sergeant Frank Kerman, MM, 7th The Buffs (East Kents), died of wounds on 7 August 1918 and Lance Corporal Frederick Smith, 10th Essex, died of wounds on 9 August 1918.

LOCATION
Mericourt-L'Abbe lies in the valley of the River Ancre about 8km south-west of Albert and 2km south of the Albert-Amiens road. The Communal Cemetery is on the eastern edge of the village and the Extension is on the southern side of the cemetery towards the road to Treux.

MESNIL COMMUNAL CEMETERY EXTENSION

HISTORY
The Extension was begun in July 1916. It was used again in 1918. After the war the cemetery was greatly enlarged when most of the burials were made here.

INFORMATION
The village was close to the British front-line until September 1916 by which time the Germans had been pushed back in this area. It came close to the front-line again from March to August 1918.

The road from Mesnil to Martinsart was a main artery for the British from 1915 to 1916 as it was concealed from the enemy. At the end of the war there were 79 graves here mostly men killed in July 1916 and August 1918. After the war 244 graves were concentrated here from the battlefields north-east of the village.

Among those buried here is Captain Charles Moore Johnston, 'C' Company, 9th Royal Irish Fusiliers, killed in action on 1 July 1916. Before enlisting in the Royal Irish Fusiliers he was a Company commander in the Ulster Volunteer Force. His son, born in 1915, fought with the Royal Artillery in WW2, became Treasurer of the Conservative Party and was made Baron Johnston of Rockport, of Caversham in 1987.

Concentrated here:
Mesnil Dressing Station Cemetery - situated to the west of the village, it was used from June 1916 to February 1917 and from March to July 1918. It contained 141 British men, mostly of the 63rd (Royal Navy) Division, and five Canadian

soldiers with two German prisoners who have been removed elsewhere.

UK – 262   NZ – 7   Can – 5
KUG – 59   Unnamed – 94   Area – 1172 sq mts

Special Memorials to ten British soldiers, buried in Mesnil Dressing Station Cemetery, whose graves could not be found at the time of concentration.

LOCATION
Martinsart lies about 5km north-west of Albert on the north side of Aveluy Wood on a ridge above the River Ancre. The cemetery is on the south side of the village on the east side of the road to Martinsart near the north-west corner of Aveluy Wood. The Extension is on the south side of the Communal Cemetery.

MESNIL RIDGE CEMETERY, MESNIL-MARTINSART

HISTORY
The cemetery was used between August 1915 and August 1916.

INFORMATION
Most of the cemetery was made by the 29th and 36th (Ulster) Divisions who were fighting nearby in 1916. The first burials were made by 1st Rifle Brigade in August 1915.

There is a row of Irish graves made by 36th Division at the back of the cemetery when they held the line here. There are also 25 graves of 2nd South Wales Borderers killed in a German raid on 6 April 1916. No officers are buried here. Among those here is Private James Oliver Bridgewater, 1st Royal Munster Fusiliers, killed when accidentally shot on 18 April 1916 aged 30 years. He was from Sparkhill, Birmingham and had a wife and family. He served as Sutton rather than under his own name.

UK – 94   NF – 1   Unnamed – 1
Area – 747 sq mts

LOCATION
The cemetery lies in fields in a valley to the south of Newfoundland Park about 1km north of Mesnil. The valley runs north from the village towards Newfoundland Park. It is difficult to approach, especially in winter, being reached from Mesnil by a road that becomes a farm track for the last 300m. It is possible in a car, but better in a 4x4. At the head of the valley, in sight of Newfoundland Park car park, but not accessible from the car park, are two cemeteries. This is the nearer to the front line of 1 July 1916. It is very peaceful and has very few visitors.

METZ-EN-COUTURE COMMUNAL CEMETERY BRITISH EXTENSION

HISTORY
The British Extension was begun in April 1917, used until March 1918, and used again for two burials in September 1918. It was enlarged after the war.

INFORMATION
The village was in German hands until captured by the 10th and 11th King's Royal Rifle Corps on 4 and 5 April 1917. It was lost on 23 March 1918, and retaken by the 1st Otago Regiment, NZEF on 6 September. It was noted for its extensive system of underground cellars.

The Communal Cemetery was used by the Germans for the burial of their dead while they held the village. Three Royal Flying Corps Officers buried by the Germans in the Communal Cemetery have been moved to the British Extension.

The Germans also made an Extension next to the Communal Cemetery for 252 German dead. With them they buried one man of the Chinese Labour Corps who has since been moved to the British Extension while the German graves have been removed.

The original burials are in Plots I and II. Plots III and IV were added after the war by the concentration of 204 graves.

Buried here is Acting Captain George Henry Tatham Paton, VC, MC, 4th Grenadier Guards, who died on 1 December 1917, aged 22 years. The citation for his Victoria Cross reads 'For most conspicuous bravery and self-sacrifice. When a unit on his left was driven back, thus leaving, his flank in the air and his company practically surrounded, he fearlessly exposed himself to re-adjust the line, walking up and down within fifty yards of the enemy under a withering fire. He personally removed several wounded men, and was the last to leave the village [Gonnelieu]. Later, he again re-adjusted the line, exposing himself regardless of all danger the whole time, and when the enemy four times counter-attacked he sprang each time upon the parapet, deliberately risking his life, and being eventually mortally wounded, in order to stimulate his command. After the enemy had broken through on his left, he again mounted the parapet, and with a few men, who were inspired by his great example, forced them once more to withdraw, thereby undoubtedly saving the left flank.' Paton was the first officer of the Grenadier Guards to win the VC since the Crimean War. He was awarded the Military Cross for his leadership and bravery on the Pilkem Ridge near Ieper on 31 July 1917, the first day of the Third Battles of Ieper. His father was Managing Director and Deputy Chairman of Bryant and May, the match manufacturer. He was commissioned into the 1/17th (Poplar and Stepney Rifles) Londons and joined the Guards at the start of 1916.

Also buried here is Major Robert Oscar Cyril Ward, 'D' Battalion, Tank Corps, twice MiD, killed in action on 20 November 1917 aged 36 years. He left two sons - Major Patrick Vernon Ward, Royal Tank Regiment, who was killed in Normandy in July 1944; and 2nd Lieutenant Robert Adrian Horace Ward, 18th Royal Garhwal Rifles, Indian Army who was killed at the fall of Singapore on 15 February 1942 and is commemorated on the Singapore Memorial.

Another here is Lieutenant Ivan Laing, MC, 2nd Coldstream Guards, killed in action on 30 November 1917 aged 32 years. He had won the Bronze medal in Hockey at the 1908 London summer Olympics. Great Britain were represented by a team from each Home Country who shared the medals. The only other participants were Germany and France.

Another here is Lance Serjeant Ernest Henry Dodd, 2nd Battalion, 3rd New Zealand Rifle Brigade, died 11 September 1918 aged 38 years. He had played three times for the New Zealand All Blacks rugby union team including one international victory against Australia.

Concentrated here:

Metz-en-Couture British Cemetery No. 2 – situated on the west side of the village, a little south of the road to Ruyaulcourt. It contained the graves of 35 British soldiers, mainly of the 58th (London) and 47th (London) Divisions, who died in 1917 and 1918.

UK – 415	NZ – 43	SAfr – 7
Can – 1	Aust – 5	Chinese – 1
Ger – 12	Unnamed – 44	KUG – 2

Area – 2212 sq mts

Special Memorials are erected to four British soldiers, buried in Metz-en-Couture British Cemetery No. 2, whose graves could not be found at the time of concentration.

LOCATION

Metz-En-Couture is found midway between Cambrai and Peronne. The Communal Cemetery British Extension is about 500m south-east of the village, on the south side of the road to Gouzeaucourt. It is next to the civilian cemetery.

MEZIERES COMMUNAL CEMETERY EXTENSION

HISTORY

The Extension was begun in August 1918, and was increased after the war by the concentration of 107 graves from a wide area south-east of Amiens.

INFORMATION

The area was the scene of rear-guard actions during the withdrawal by French and British troops in March 1918. The village was on the right flank of the Canadian advance in August 1918 when it was recaptured. Most of the Canadian graves were made during that advance.

It was called at times White House Cemetery from the name of a house on the road to the north.

Buried here is Captain Horatio Alfred Fane, MC, Queen's Own Oxfordshire Hussars, killed on 11 August 1918. Grandson of the 6th Duke of Marlborough, he was one of three brothers killed in the war. Commander Robert Gerald Fane, Silver Medal for Military Valour (Italy), HMS Dartmouth, Royal Navy, died on 15 May 1917 aged 35 years and is buried in Bari War Cemetery. Originally, buried in Brindisi Communal Cemetery, he and several others were moved to Bari in 1981. Major Octavius Edward Fane, DSO, MC, 128th Heavy Battery, Royal Garrison Artillery died of wounds on 18 September 1918 aged 31 years and is buried in Hancourt British Cemetery about 25km south-west of here.

Also here is Major Charles Frederic Somes Stewart, MC, Royal Munster Fusiliers attached 6th Northamptonshires, killed in action on 5 April 1918, aged 34 years. In 1906 he became amateur middleweight champion of South Africa. He and was awarded the Military Cross on 19 August 1916.

| UK – 95 | Can – 37 | Aust – 1 |
| Unnamed – 63 | | Area – 581 sq mts |

Special Memorial erected to one soldier from Canada, known to be buried in an unnamed grave.

LOCATION

Mezieres-en-Santerre is located on the south-west side of the main from Amiens to Roye, 20km south-east of Amiens. It is on the northern edge of the village on the south-west side of the Communal Cemetery. It feels peaceful and isolated.

MILL ROAD CEMETERY, THIEPVAL

HISTORY
The cemetery was made in the spring of 1917 when the battlefield was cleared by V Corps as the Germans withdrew to the Hindenburg Line. It was greatly enlarged after the war by further clearance of the battlefields.

INFORMATION
The village of Thiepval was in German hands from 1914. It was a first day objective on 1 July 1916. The 36th (Ulster) Division attacked the 180th Wurttemburgers in the Schwaben Redoubt at the crest of the ridge upon which the cemetery rests. The main part of the redoubt is about 200m north of the cemetery. The 36th Division made early gains but the attack failed, as the attacks by the Divisions to the left and right had not made any gains so the Germans could enfilade them with fire from both sides. Hence the Ulstermen had to withdraw on 1 and 2 July from the positions they had captured at great cost. The Ulster Division suffered casualties of approximately 5000 men. They won four Victoria Crosses.

The 39th Division completed the capture of the Schwaben Redoubt in mid-October, fifteen weeks after the men of Ulster had first occupied the trenches on 1 July 1916.

Thiepval, by then destroyed, was captured in September by the 18th Division. The village remained in British hands until 25 March 1918 but was retaken on 24 August by the 38th and 17th Divisions.

The Ulster Tower, a copy of Helen's Tower in the training area of the Ulster Division at Clandeboyne in Ireland, was erected in memory of the men who died during the attack in 1916. The 18th Division have erected a memorial on the edge of Thiepval village.

The cemetery was first called Mill Road Cemetery No. 2 which at the end of the war contained 260 graves. The original cemetery is easy to identify because the area in which the bodies are buried was on the old German trenches, so the ground is unstable and the headstones are laid flat. After the war 1038 graves were concentrated from smaller cemeteries and isolated positions on the surrounding battlefields. The concentrated graves are on firmer, safer ground.

More than 60% of the burials are of unidentified bodies. They are almost all men who died in this area from the 32nd and 36th Division killed on 1 July attacking from Thiepval Wood, and the 49th, 18th and 39th Divisions killed in July-September 1916.

Buried here is Major William Tait Sewell, 11th Royal Inniskilling Fusiliers, killed in action on 1 July 1916 aged 34 years. He lectured in pathology at Durham University and was posted missing on 1 July 1916. Two months later his identity disk was returned to his father who then interviewed a Private in his Company who confirmed that Major Sewell died from bullet wounds to head and chest.

Also here is Lieutenant Holt Montgomery Hewitt, 109th Machine Gun Company, Machine Gun Corps (Infantry), killed in action on 1 July 1916 aged 29 years. His brother, 2nd Lieutenant William Arthur Hewitt, 9th (County Tyrone) Royal Inniskilling Fusiliers also died in action on 1 July 1916, aged 23 years and is commemorated on the Thiepval Memorial. 109th Machine Gun Company was attached to 109th Brigade of which 9th Royal Inniskilling Fusiliers formed a part. So, these two brothers died close to each other on the same day. Another brother, Lieutenant Ernest Henry Hewitt, MiD, 4th King's Own died sometime between 15 and 16 June 1915 aged 29 years and is commemorated on the Thiepval Memorial.

Concentrated here:

Divion Road Cemetery No. 1 - situated about 500m west of here and 400m south of St. Pierre Divion. It contained the graves of 29 British soldiers who died in the attacks of July and September 1916.

Divion Road Cemetery No. 3 - situated close to No. 1 and No. 2 Cemeteries. It contained the graves of 44 British soldiers who died in September and October 1916. Divion Road Cemetery No. 2 was concentrated into Connaught Cemetery.

Mill Road Cemetery No. 1 - situated just to the west of this cemetery. It contained the graves of 39 British soldiers who died in September 1916.

St. Pierre Divion Cemetery No. 2 - situated about 400m north of here, next to St. Pierre Divion Cemetery No. 1 cemetery which was concentrated into Connaught Cemetery, on the old road from St. Pierre Divion to Thiepval. It contained the graves of 28 British soldiers who died from September to November 1916.

UK – 1304   Unnamed – 815   Area - 3440 sq mts

Special Memorials erected to three British soldiers believed to be buried among the unnamed graves.

Special Memorials erected to three British soldiers, buried in Divion Road Cemetery No. 1, whose graves were destroyed by shell-fire.

LOCATION
Thiepval is located on the ridge to the east of the River Ancre about 5km north of Albert. This cemetery is in the fields on the ridge between the village and the river. It is about 100m north of the Thiepval-Hamel road. It is safest to park at Connaught Cemetery, or the Ulster Tower, and walk to the cemetery. The view into Newfoundland Park across the valley of the Ancre is outstanding. At the right time of the year you can still make out the lines of the trenches by the chalk showing in the fields.

MILLENCOURT COMMUNAL CEMETERY EXTENSION

HISTORY
The cemetery was used for a few burials in 1916, again in March and April 1918, and a few graves were concentrated here after the war.

INFORMATION
The valley, known as 'Long Valley', between the village and Albert was used for training troops of the 8th Division before their attack at Ovillers on 1 July 1916 because it was similar to 'Mash Valley'.

The Communal Cemetery was used from August 1915 to May 1916 and again in April 1918 by which time 61 British and three Australian soldiers had been buried. These were all moved into the Extension after the war.

The Extension was opened by Field Ambulances and the III Corps Main Dressing Station who were stationed in the village in 1916. It was used by the 4th Australian Division in 1918. Many of those who died here were killed in the fighting at La Boiselle and Ovillers in 1916. There is also a row of Australians, mostly of the 46th Australian Infantry, who were killed in early April 1918.

Among those buried here is Captain Maurice Fletcher, MC, killed in action on Saturday 9 September 1916 aged 31 years. He was educated at St. Edmund's School, Canterbury, subsequently gaining a Scholarship at Selwyn College, Cambridge, where he read Classics. He taught in a French school and then Merchant Taylors, Crosby. On the outbreak of the war he was assistant master in Wakefield Grammar School, but enlisted in the 18th (1st Public Schools) Royal Fusiliers, and in December 1914 was given his commission in the Munster Fusiliers, being promoted to Captain in the following October having been in France since December 1915. He was awarded his Military Cross for leading a working party under fire close to the German line about a month before he was killed. He is recorded by the CWGC as being in 'C' Company, 9th Royal Munster Fusiliers. However, the 9th battalion had been disbanded in May 1916. He is recorded in the Battalion War Diary of the 2nd Royal Munster Fusiliers as having been wounded with them on 8 September 1916 and died of wounds the next day. He was commanding 'C' Company which had been with the 1st South Wales Borderers during an attack on High Wood while the rest of the Fusiliers had been withdrawn for the day.

UK – 273   Aust – 50   Can – 7
NZ – 7   SAfr – 1   Ger – 5
KUG – 2   Unnamed - 4
Area – 1151 sq mts

LOCATION
Millencourt is located about 4km west of Albert and is easily reached from the main road to Amiens. The Communal Cemetery is west of the village on the north side of the road to Henencourt and the Extension is on the north side of the Communal Cemetery. It is reached through the Communal Cemetery.

MIRAUMONT COMMUNAL CEMETERY

HISTORY
The Communal Cemetery was largely used by German troops. Twenty-seven British soldiers, of whom six are unidentified, were buried by the Germans.

INFORMATION
The village was in German hands for much of the war until occupied by British troops at the end of February 1917. It was lost on 25 March 1918 and retaken by the 42nd (East Lancashire) Division on 24 August. The village was destroyed by British artillery in August 1916 when it was being used as a German supply base.

Four French graves have been removed. A worker of the IWGC is also buried here, as are two airmen killed on 23 May 1940. They were killed when their Blenheim was shot down nearby during an operation on Arras. The third member of the crew was taken prisoner.

Among those here is Major Victor Annesley Barrington-Kennett, MiD, No. 4 Squadron, Royal Flying Corps formerly Grenadier Guards, killed in action on 13 March 1916. He graduated from Oxford University in 1910 and was briefly working in the City of London as a banker. In 1911 he joined the London Balloon Company, Royal Engineers, (TF) as a 2nd Lieutenant. This introduced him to flying and he gained his Aviator's Certificate, No. 190, in March 1912. In August 1913 he joined the Royal Flying Corps and by August 1914 he had been promoted to Flying Officer. In March 1915 he went to France and in June 1915 he became Flight Commander and Captain, followed by promotion to Squadron Commander of No. 4 Squadron and Major in January 1916. He was shot down in his Bristol Scout by the German Ace, Max Immelmann. The Germans buried him and got a note to the British saying where his body lay. His father was a member of the King's bodyguard. Two brothers were also killed in the war. They are Major Basil Herbert Barrington-Kennett, 2nd Grenadier Guards, killed in action on 18 May 1915 aged 30 years and buried in Le Touret Military Cemetery, and youngest brother 2nd Lieutenant Aubrey Hampden Barrington-Kennett, 2nd Oxford and Bucks Light Infantry, killed in action on 20 September 1914 aged 24 years and buried at Vailly British Cemetery.

UK – 27   IWGC – 1   WW2 – 2
Unnamed - 4

LOCATION
Miraumont is located 5km west of Bapaume. The cemetery is on the west edge of the village. Access is by the Rue du Cimetiere from the village centre. The British plot is at the east end of the cemetery through an avenue of trees. Two British men are near the north boundary.

MOEUVRES BRITISH CEMETERY

HISTORY
The cemetery was opened on 6 October 1918 for the burial of men who had been killed during the battles to capture the villages nearby in the final advance to victory. A few later burials were made.

INFORMATION
Moeuvres was behind the German lines for almost all of the war. It was close to the front-line during the Battle of Cambrai in 1917 but, despite three days of constant pressure by the 36th Division, it remained in German hands. It did not fall to the British until the 57th Division captured part of the village on 11 September 1918. The task was continued by the 63rd Division on 19 September and completed by the 52nd Division after five days fighting. The first burials were, therefore, men who died on 12 September 1918. The last was made on 1 October 1918. Only eighteen burials are of men who did not die on 27 September. Three of the four Germans buried here died after the end of the war while Prisoners of War.

Buried here is Lieutenant Aubrey Meldum Wood Hawks, 1/4th Royal Scots, killed in action on 27 September 1918 aged 22 years. He was a student at Edinburgh University when he left to take a commission in the 1/6th Gloucestershires in October 1915. He saw action in France and Egypt with 7th Field Company, Royal Engineers and the Royal Scots before his death at the Canal du Nord.

UK – 102   Can – 1   Ger – 4
Unnamed – 13   Area – 554 sq mts

Special Memorials to four British soldiers known, or believed, to be buried here.

LOCATION
Moeuvres is about 1.5km north of the road from Bapaume to Cambrai. It is about 2km west of the A26 Autoroute about 2km north of its junction with the A2 Autoroute. The cemetery is south of the village between the road to Havrincourt and the canal. It is located about 100m east of the road in fields. There is a CWGC path from the road.

MOEUVRES COMMUNAL CEMETERY EXTENSION

HISTORY
The civil cemetery was used by the Germans from November 1917 to March 1918. The British Extension was made in September and October 1918 for the burial of men killed nearby in the fighting. It was enlarged after the war.

INFORMATION
Among those buried here is Lieutenant Charles Pope, VC, 11th Australian Infantry, killed in action at Louverval on 15 April 1917 aged 34 years. The citation for his Victoria Cross reads 'For most conspicuous bravery and devotion to duty when in command of a very important picquet post in the sector held by his battalion, his orders being to hold this post at all costs. After the picquet post had been heavily attacked, the enemy, in greatly superior numbers, surrounded the post. Lt. Pope, finding that he was running

short of ammunition, sent back for further supplies. But the situation culminated before it could arrive, and in the hope of saving the position, this very gallant officer was seen to charge with his picquet into a superior force, by which it was overpowered. By his sacrifice Lt. Pope not only inflicted heavy loss on the enemy, but obeyed his order to hold the position to the last. His body, together with those of most of his men, was found in close proximity to eighty enemy dead, a sure proof of the gallant resistance which had been made.'

Also here is Lieutenant Colonel Clinton Wynard Battye, DSO, King's Shropshire Light Infantry attached 14th Highland Light Infantry, died on 24 November 1917 aged 43 years. He was awarded the Distinguished Service Order during the South African Wars.

UK – 500   Aust – 8   Can – 22
Ger – 90 (46 unnamed)   Russ – 4
Unnamed – 262   Area – 2182 sq mts

Special Memorials to 31 British soldiers known or believed to be buried among the unnamed.

Special Memorials to three British soldiers buried in Boursies Communal Cemetery German Extension, whose graves could not be found at the time of concentration.

LOCATION
The Communal Cemetery is at the north-west corner of the village, 500m from the village centre, on the road to Inchy. The British Extension is on the north side of the Communal Cemetery.

MONDICOURT COMMUNAL CEMETERY

INFORMATION
The cemetery was used first for the burial six men of the 8th Leicestershires who were killed in an accident on 31 August 1915 whilst they were practicing bomb (grenade) throwing. A man of the Chinese Labour Corps, killed on 22 March 1918, is buried in the south-west corner. The burials include several who died of illness, accident or injury.

The WW2 men are almost entirely men of the Buffs or Royal Army Service Corps killed in May 1940 though there is one artilleryman who died in 1939.

UK – 12   Chinese – 1   WW2 (UK) - 13

LOCATION
Mondicourt is about 25km south-west of Arras on the road to Doullens. The cemetery is on the southern side of Mondicourt about 1km south-east of the road on a by-road off the road to Pas-en-Artois. It is on a rise about 50m east of the road to Pas-en-Artois. This is not easy to find. Two of the WW1 dead are on the western edge of the cemetery. The other CWGC burials are along the northern edge

HISTORY
The cemetery was begun in August 1915. Other burials were made at various times during the war. It was used again in WW2 before the 'Fall of France'.

MONTIGNY COMMUNAL CEMETERY (SOMME)

INFORMATION
Among those buried here is Pioneer W T Greenslade, 312th Road Construction Company, Royal Engineers who died on 1 June 1918. His parents had this inscription added to a private memorial cross that is found near his grave 'The last words of my dear boy. 19.3.1918 "Mother, it is hard for me, but promise you will not grieve for me. It won't be long"'. Eight other men from his unit were killed in June 1918.

UK – 56   Unnamed - 3

LOCATION
Montigy-sur-L'Hallue is about 10km north-east of Amiens and 15km south-west of Albert. It is about 2.5km north of the D929. The cemetery is on the southern edge of the village in the valley of the River L'Hallue 50m west of the road to Frechencourt. The men are found together at the east end of the cemetery.

HISTORY
The Communal Cemetery was used from May to August 1918 by the 47th (London) and 58th (London) Divisions.

MONTIGNY COMMUNAL CEMETERY EXTENSION (SOMME)

HISTORY
The Extension was used in August 1918.

INFORMATION
The Germans were buried here in June 1918. Four American bodies have been removed. Among those buried here is Private John Swain, 5th Royal Berkshires who was executed for desertion on 11 August 1918. He was already under two suspended sentences of death and was found hiding in a cornfield after his third attempt at desertion. His grave is set apart from the others at the north end of the Extension.

UK – 19   Ger - 3

LOCATION
The Extension is at the west end of the Communal Cemetery.

MORCHIES AUSTRALIAN CEMETERY

HISTORY
The cemetery was begun at the end of March 1917. It remained in use until the end of April. Further burials were made in September 1918.

INFORMATION
The village was behind the German lines for most of the war until it was occupied by the British on 20 March 1917. The Germans retook the village on 21 March 1918 and Morchies fell for the final time in September 1918.
The cemetery was begun by Australian troops soon after the capture of the village in 1917. The Germans buried four men here in March 1918.

Among those buried here is Major Thomas Francis Pennefather Breen, 142nd Field Ambulance, Royal Army Medical Corps, killed on 10 September 1918 aged 28 years. Breen studied medicine at Trinity College, Dublin where he graduated in 1912. He gained a commission as a Lieutenant in the Army Medical Services on 30 January 1914 and on 24 August 1914 was at the Front with the 11th Field Ambulance being involved in the retreat from Mons. He was promoted to Captain on 30 March 1915, and Major from 4 January to 4 April 1918. He was then attached to the 1st Rifle Brigade as Medical Officer, and later twice appointed Deputy Assistant Director of Medical Services. In 1918 he was attached to the 142nd Field Ambulance, and during the advance in autumn 1918, when the Colonel was wounded, commanded the Field Ambulance. He was killed whilst rescuing wounded under heavy shell fire.

UK – 41   Aust – 20   Ger – 2
Unnamed – 3   KUG - 1   Area – 404 sq mts

LOCATION
Morchies is situated between Bapaume and Cambrai about 2km north of the road between the two towns. The Australian Cemetery is south-west of the village on the south-east side of the road to Beugny. It lies on a bank above the level of the road.

MORCHIES MILITARY CEMETERY

HISTORY
The cemetery was begun in April 1917 and remained in use until January 1918. The Germans buried a few British dead in March 1918. Further burials were made by the British later in 1918.

INFORMATION
Following the period of British use in 1917, 76 British and 15 German burials were made in Rows B, C and D by the Germans in March 1918.

Among those buried here is Lieutenant Arthur William MacNamara, DFC, No. 12 Squadron, Royal Air Force, died on 3 September 1918 aged 19 years. In August and September 1918 No. 12 Squadron was undertaking Corps Reconnaissance duties and some night bombing using RE8s. His Distinguished Flying Cross was awarded for several photographic reconnaissance missions in the face of enemy fighter attacks in August 1918. His observer Lieutenant Hallgrimur Jonsson, MC, originally in the

Canadian Expeditionary Force, was also killed but is commemorated on the Arras Flying Services Memorial.

UK – 133 Aust – 17 Ger – 15
Unnamed – 74 Area – 657 sq mts

Special Memorials erected to eight British soldiers known to be buried among the unnamed graves.

Special Memorials erected to ten British soldiers, buried in the village by the Germans, whose graves were destroyed by later shell-fire.

LOCATION
The Military Cemetery is on the north edge of the village on the west side of the road to Lagnicourt. It is just south of the Communal Cemetery lying in fields and reached from the road by a CWGC path. There is no access from the Communal Cemetery.

MOREUIL COMMUNAL CEMETERY ALLIED EXTENSION.

HISTORY
This is a concentration cemetery made after the war.

INFORMATION
The village was part of the boundary between the British and French forces in March 1918.

The village and nearby Moreuil Wood were the scene of bitter fighting in March and April 1918. The forces here at that time included British, Australian and French Infantry with Canadian Cavalry. In late March, as the Germans approached Moreuil and threatened to cross the River L'Avre, the last natural barrier before Amiens, the Canadian Cavalry Corps was assigned the task of stopping them. The charge by a squadron of Lord Strathcona's Horse so unnerved the Germans that they failed to capture Moreuil Wood. The village was lost to the Germans but was retaken on 8 August by the French XXXI Corps. Their Memorial is at the road junction 1.5km east of the Communal Cemetery. It was destroyed in 1940 and rebuilt in 1955.

Most burials here date from April 1918 though there are some of March 1918 and a few of August 1918. The burials represent the desperate the defence here in 1918 and include a range of cavalry regiments not often seen. Over 50% of the burials are unidentified having been brought in from isolated burial grounds on the battlefields.

In the space between the Communal Cemetery and this Extension were 1204 French war graves, now removed to Montdidier French National Cemetery. Hence, this is separated from the Communal Cemetery.

Among those buried here is Lieutenant Albert Victor Seymour Nordheimer, Royal Canadian Dragoons, killed in action on 30 March 1918 aged 33 years. He was a Major in the Canadian Rearmament Forces but reverted to Lieutenant to get to the front.

Also here is Captain Charles Thomas Anderdon Pollock, Inns of Court OTC attached 1/4th East Yorkshires, died of wounds on 31 March 1918 aged 38 years. He was mortally wounded while carrying his batman to safety.

Another buried here is Lieutenant Colonel John Evelyn Carmichael Darley, MiD, 4th (Queen's Own) Hussars, killed in action on 31 March 1918 (Easter Sunday) aged 38 years. It was his birthday. He was obtained a commission in the 5th Lancers in November 1899 and served throughout the South African Wars. In December 1901, he was promoted to Captain in the Hussars, but in January 1902 he was severely wounded. He was ADC to General Sir Archibald Hunter, Governor of Gibraltar, from 1910 to 1913, when he was promoted to Major. He went to France on 15 August 1914 being involved in the retreat from Mons and in the First and Second Battles of Ypres. In April 1916 he became Lieutenant Colonel of his regiment. His brother Commander Arthur Tudor Darley, RN was killed in one of the earliest naval actions of the war, the Battle of Coronel off the Chilean coast, on 1 November 1914 when his ship, HMS Good Hope, was sunk.

You will find a memorial to Captain Aubry east of the town on the road to Plessiers. He was a French Chausseur officer who became a pilot and died in May 1915.

UK – 177 Can – 9 Aust - 3
Unnamed - 96 Area – 1344 sq mts

Special Memorial to one man believed to be buried among the unnamed.

LOCATION
Moreuil is located in the valley of the River L'Avre about 15km south-east of Amiens and 5km south of Villers-Bretonneux on the Montdidier road. The Extension is 100m east of the Communal Cemetery. The cemetery is small and peaceful set in the suburbs of the town.

MORLANCOURT BRITISH CEMETERY No. 1

HISTORY
Morlancourt British Cemetery No. 1 was made in June and July 1916. Most burials date from the early part of the Battle of the Somme and are men who died in Casualty Clearing Stations. One grave of September 1915 was brought from Morlancourt Communal Cemetery in 1926.

INFORMATION
For most of the war Morlancourt was used as a location for Divisional Camps and medical units, though it was less busy than some of the others. At the end of March 1918 the village was captured by the Germans. Actions in May and June brought the Allies close to the village but it remained in German hands until 9 August 1918. Then it was taken by the 1/1st Cambridgeshires and tanks.

For some time this was known as Morlancourt Military Cemetery. Five German graves have been removed. Many of the burials are men of the 38th (Welsh) Division wounded in the Battle of Mametz Wood in July 1916. Among them is Lieutenant Colonel Oswald Swift Flower, 13th Royal Welsh Fusiliers, died on 12 July 1916 aged 45 years. He joined the Royal Welsh Fusiliers as a 2nd Lieutenant and served in Crete, Malta, Burma, India and China. During the Boxer Rising of 1900 Lieutenant Flower was twice Mentioned in Despatches. In India he was an excellent polo player, winning the Regimental Cup while serving at Quetta. However, the climate affected his health so he was forced to retire in 1913. At the outbreak of the war, he re-joined his old regiment. While a Brigade Major he raised a number of service battalions and in May 1915 was asked to command the 13th Royal Welsh Fusiliers, the 'North Wales Pals', one of the battalions he had raised. When he returned home on leave in June 1916 it was apparent that his health was poor, but he insisted on returning to the Front. His adjutant described how, despite fainting from exhaustion, Flower was always up with the front line, saying 'the boys are going on and I must go with them'. On 10 July the Battalion attacked Mametz Wood where Flower spent the night sleeping in a shell-hole. On 11 July Colonel Flower was at Battalion HQ when a British shell, landing short, badly wounded Colonel Flower, his Adjutant and Major Lawrence, the Medical Officer. Flower was brought here where he died of his wounds. One brother was the Mayor of Stratford upon Avon. Another brother, Lieutenant Fordham Flower, had been killed during the South African Wars.

UK – 74   Indian – 1   Unnamed – 4
Area – 530 sq mts

LOCATION
Morlancourt is situated about 5km south of Albert. The cemetery is in fields to the west of the village. Both this and No. 2 are in a valley running south from the River Ancre. A track leads to No. 2 cemetery and a path leads from that track to No. 1 cemetery on the other side of the valley 400m to the west.

MORLANCOURT BRITISH CEMETERY No. 2

HISTORY
The cemetery was made in August 1918 for the burial of men who died in capturing the village.

INFORMATION
The cemetery was made by the 12th Division. For some time this was known as Morlancourt British Cemetery. Five German graves have been removed.

Among those here is Lieutenant Reginald Francis Clements, MC, 7th Royal Sussex, died on 14 August 1918 aged 26 years. The citation for his Military Cross, gazetted in May 1918, reads 'For conspicuous gallantry and devotion to duty. In preparation for a raid on the enemy's lines he carried out several patrols, and the accurate information which he obtained contributed very largely to the success of the operation. He led his men in the raid with great skill and determination, and rushed an enemy post which offered strong opposition, with the result that six of the enemy were killed and two prisoners were captured. He showed splendid initiative and coolness.' He was killed by a shell.

UK – 55   Aust – 2   Unnamed – 2
Area – 530 sq mts

LOCATION
See Morlancourt No. 1 Cemetery.

MORVAL BRITISH CEMETERY

HISTORY
This cemetery was opened in early September 1918 and was closed by the middle of the month.

INFORMATION
Morval, having been in German hands since 1914, was the objective of the successful attack by the 5th and 6th Divisions on 25 September 1916. It fell on 24 March 1918 during the first stages of the German advance in 1918 and was not recaptured until 1 September 1918 when it was taken by the 38th (Welsh) Division.

The cemetery was made by the V Corps. The men buried here fell between 26 August and 6 September 1918 and almost all of them were men of the 38th Division. There is also a German prisoner buried here. This is the only cemetery in the area of the 1916 battles which does not contain a grave dating from those battles. You can find a Captain and six subalterns buried together.

Buried here is Captain Tom Cecil Haydn Berry, 5th Welsh, died of illness on 30 August 1918 aged 26 years. He studied at Exeter College, Oxford and had served mostly in the Middle East during the war.

UK – 54   Ger – 1   Area – 234 sq mts

LOCATION
Morval is situated about 10km south of Bapaume just west of the Autoroute. The British Cemetery is on the eastern edge of the village on the north side of the road to Ginchy. The access track from the centre of the village to the cemetery, which runs behind a farm and is not marked with a CWGC sign, may be difficult under bad weather conditions.

MORY ABBEY MILITARY CEMETERY, MORY

HISTORY
The cemetery was opened in March 1917 and used mainly when fighting was taking place in the local area up to September 1918. It was used again for the concentration of graves after the war.

INFORMATION
Mory was in German hands for much of the war but was occupied by British troops in the middle of March 1917 as the Germans retreated to the Hindenburg Line. It was retaken by the Germans during their advance in March 1918. It fell for the final time in late August 1918, being captured by 62nd (West Riding) and Guards Divisions.

The 189 German burials in a Plot on the west side of the cemetery were made by German troops in March to August 1918. Thirteen Germans were buried by the British in September 1918.

Plots I–III were made during the war. The 287 graves, including many of the Guards Division, and chiefly of 1918, in Plots IV and V were added after the war by the concentration of graves from the battlefields between St. Leger and Bapaume. The grave of one American airman has been removed.

Buried here is Lieutenant Colonel Richard Annesley West, VC, DSO and Bar, MC, North Irish Horse, attached 6th Battalion, Tank Corps, killed in action on 2 September 1918 aged 40 years. He served in the Boer War. He won his Victoria Cross for actions at Courcelles & Vaulx Vraucourt on 21 August & 2 September 1918. His citation reads 'For most conspicuous bravery, leadership and self-sacrifice. During an attack, the infantry having lost their bearings in the dense fog, this officer at once collected and re-organised any men he could find and led them to their objective in face of heavy machine-gun fire. Throughout the whole action he displayed the most utter disregard of danger, and the capture of the objective was in a great part due to his initiative and gallantry.' He was awarded the Distinguished Service Order in the New Years Honours List in January 1918, the Bar to his DSO and a Military Cross posthumously in November 1918.

Also buried here is Captain Eldred Wolfrestan Bowyer-Bower, No. 59 Squadron, Royal Flying Corps, formerly East Surreys killed in action on 19 March 1917 with his Observer, 2nd Lieutenant Eric Elgey. They were buried by the Germans and a few weeks later, following the capture of Croisilles, Bowyer-Bowers father, Captain Thomas Bowyer-Bower, Royal Engineers discovered a grave with a marker made of pieces of a wrecked plane which had written on it 'Two Unknown Captains of the Flying Corps'.

He gained permission to exhume the bodies and discovered that one was his son. He brought the two men here for burial.

Another here is Lieutenant Colonel James Houghton Henry Chadwick, DSO, MiD, 24th (Oldham Pals) Manchesters, killed in action on 4 May 1917 aged 36 years. He was posthumously Mentioned in Despatches on 25 May 1917 and awarded the Distinguished Service Order in the Birthday Honours List in June 1917. He was killed with his batman, Lance Corporal Robert Archer, MM by a German shell as they went forward to confirm where a new trench was to be made as his battalion were a Pioneer battalion and there had been some confusion about the location of the new trench.

Concentrated here:

Grenadier Guards Cemetery, St. Leger - on the road to Vraucourt, which contained the graves of 24 men of the 2nd Grenadier Guards and two other British soldiers who died on 27 August 1918.

Hally Copse East Cemetery, St. Leger - between 'Hally Copse' and the road to Vraucourt, which contained the graves of 49 British soldiers, all of the Guards Division except one, who died in August 1918.

Mory French Cemetery - nearly 1km south—west of the village, in which three British soldiers were buried in February and March 1917.

UK – 616   Aust – 1   NZ – 1
Ger – 230   Unnamed – 101   Area – 2794 sq mts

Special Memorial to one soldier known to be buried among the unnamed.

LOCATION
Mory is located between Arras and Bapaume about 5km north of Bapaume. This cemetery is 500m north-east of the village, on the north side of the road to Ecoust-St. Mein near a fork with the road to St. Leger. The cemetery is above the level of the road. At the east end of the cemetery is the civilian cemetery.

MORY STREET MILITARY CEMETERY, ST. LEGER

HISTORY
The first six burials were made in March and April 1917. They are now marked by Special Memorials. The other graves are for men who fell in the fighting for the village in August and September 1918.

INFORMATION
See Mory Abbey Military Cemetery for details of history of St. Leger village in WW1.

Most of the men buried here are from the Guards Division, many from the 2nd Coldstream Guards. The cemetery was once considerably larger, but 48 German and some French graves have been removed.

Buried here is Lieutenant Guy Frederick Beckham Handley, MC & Bar, twice MiD, No. 3 Company, 2nd Coldstream Guards, formerly 4th Nigeria Regiment, died on 27 August 1918 aged 35 years. He had worked with the Nigeria Political Service, and served with the Nigeria Regiment from November 1914 to April 1916. He then served with the York and Lancasters and had been with 2nd Coldstream Guards since December 1917. He was awarded the Military Cross in November 1916 and the Bar in August 1917. His name is on the cenotaph near the bridge at Victoria Falls between Zimbabwe and Zambia.

UK – 66   Unnamed – 5   Area – 2794 sq mts

Special Memorials to six graves destroyed by shell-fire.

LOCATION
St. Leger is located between Arras and Bapaume about 7km north of Bapaume. This cemetery is on the west side of the Mory-St. Leger road as the road climbs onto a ridge.

MOYENNEVILLE (TWO TREE) CEMETERY

HISTORY
The cemetery was made in August 1918.

INFORMATION
Moyenneville was in German hands from 1914 until the German withdrawal to the Hindenburg Line when the 7th Division took the village on 17 March 1917. The Germans recaptured the village in March 1918. The Guards Division took the village for the final time on 21 August 1918.

The cemetery was named after two large trees situated here during the war. Those buried here are almost all men of the 15th West Yorkshires who defended the village in March 1918 or men of the Guards Division who captured the village in August 1918.

Buried here is Lance Corporal John William Langley, MM, 1st King's (Liverpools), killed in action on 11 August 1918. Before the war he was an apprentice plumber, a member of the Boy Scouts and a keen footballer winning many trophies and medals. After his death his Company commander wrote to his parents saying 'I was ordered to take out a patrol at 2.30 in the afternoon (August 14) to locate the Boches, so I asked for volunteers. Your son asked me to let him come along, which I did, so with your son and two others I proceeded out. The Boches were over one and three-quarter miles away, so we all strolled along joking and looking for pieces of Boches equipment etc. At about 4 p.m. we got to the Boches position without being seen, but as soon as we got in their trench they started coming along in large numbers so we decided to withdraw. I told your son to crawl along the side of the road and get back towards our line whilst I would cover his withdrawal. As soon as I started crawling a concealed sniper shot your son through the side in line with his heart. He died instantaneously. I might say that the others of the patrol were wounded. Your boy was the bravest of the brave. Four times previously he volunteered to come out on night patrol with me. He was the best N.C.O. in my patrol, and I had just previously recommended him for promotion. He was beloved by all the men in his section, and was most popular with all who knew him. I miss him tremendously. He was my right-hand man. It must be a most extremely heavy blow to you all, but I am sure you will find a little consolation in the knowledge of his great bravery and the gloriously brave manner in which he met his death. In conclusion I implore you to accept my sincere sympathy and also the sympathy of all his pals.' He won his Military Medal at Ieper in 1917.

UK – 49   Unnamed – 17   Area – 208 sq mts

LOCATION
Moyenneville, not to be confused with the village near Abbeville, is about 15km south of Arras and 8km north-west of Bapaume. It is 2km west of the Arras-Bapaume road. The small cemetery lies in open fields 500m south-west of the village. A rough track leads 300m to the cemetery from its junction with the road leading south-west from the village.

MUNICH TRENCH BRITISH CEMETERY, BEAUMONT-HAMEL

HISTORY
The cemetery was created in early 1917 and only used at that time.

INFORMATION
Beaumont-Hamel was behind lines from 1914. It was an objective on 1 July 1916 but was not captured until November 1916, in the Battle of the Ancre, and the graves in this cemetery are largely those of men who died at that time. When the Germans withdrew to the Hindenburg Line in early 1917 the British had the opportunity to bury the dead who had been killed during the Battle of the Ancre in November 1916. The V Corps created a number of cemeteries in this area at that time. This cemetery was originally known as V Corps Cemetery No. 8. It gained its present name after the war and was named after the German trench captured by the 7th Division on 11 January 1917.

Buried here is Lieutenant (Acting Captain) Vivian Edward Fanning, 2nd Oxford & Bucks Light Infantry, killed in action on 14 November 1916 aged 19 years. His headstone bears the inscription 'After 3 months fighting he was killed leading his Company.' The 2nd Oxford & Bucks Light Infantry arrived on the Somme on 20 July 1916 and was engaged in the unsuccessful attack on Waterlot Farm on 30 July. They were involved in battle frequently until they moved from Mailly-Maillet to assembly positions after dark on 12 November 1916 in support of 24th Royal Fusiliers during operations along the Redan Ridge and towards Beaumont Trench. A small party reached Frankfurt Trench before they were driven back.

In the fields just west of the cemetery the author 'Saki', Lance-Sergeant H H Munro, of the 22nd (Kensington) Royal Fusiliers was killed in action on 14 November 1916. He has no known grave and is commemorated on the Thiepval Memorial. We also know that Wilfred Owen was in the front-line here in January 1917 when he joined the 2nd Manchesters. He may have written 'The Sentry' while here. As Munich Trench was one of the last actions of the 1916 Battles of the Somme in this area, it is possible to see how little was gained here for such great cost.

UK – 126   Unnamed – 28   Area - 408 sq mts

LOCATION
Beaumont lies on the high ground above the River Ancre about 8km north of Albert. The cemetery can be found on the ridge in the area north of the village between it and Serre. This is on the same farm track as Waggon Road Cemetery, though this is further from the village and the road. This is not an easy cemetery to reach but there are excellent views of the battlefield.

NESLE COMMUNAL CEMETERY

UK – 135   Unnamed – 1

HISTORY
The cemetery was used from April to June 1917. A further five British burials were made in May 1918.

INFORMATION
The village was captured by the Germans in 1914 and held until it fell to British and French cavalry on 18 March 1917. The Germans re-took the town as part of their advance in 1918 reaching it on 25 March causing the Fifth Army Headquarters to withdraw, though it was only captured after fierce fighting. The town fell for the final time on 28 August 1918 when the French re-took it.

The British burials here were made between two German Plots when 21st Casualty Clearing Station were stationed in Nesle. The German burials have been removed. Most British burials date from April 1917 during the actions when the Germans withdrew. Over half of the graves are men of the 32nd Division. The five British graves of 1918 were Prisoners of War buried by the Germans.

Among those here is 2nd Lieutenant Morris Villiers Godwin Tanner, 3rd attached 2/8th Sherwood Foresters (Notts and Derby Regiment), who died of wounds on 7 April 1917 aged 21 years. During an attack on Le Verguier on the night of 6 April 1917, he was struck by shrapnel and taken to 107th Field Ambulance where he died.

LOCATION
Nesle is located about 25km south-east of Amiens and 20km south-west of St. Quentin. The cemetery is on the eastern edge of town in what is now a built up area. The easiest way to find it is from the northern bypass which is the Ham-Roye road. Use the side entrance to the cemetery to get to the CWGC graves which are a quiet oasis of green in a typical French civil cemetery.

NEUVILLE-BOURJONVAL BRITISH CEMETERY

HISTORY
The cemetery was opened by the 11th Rifle Brigade in April 1917 and remained in use until March 1918. It was used again in September 1918 and a few burials were added after the war.

INFORMATION
The village was in German hands for most of the war. It was captured by 12th Kings (Liverpools) on 28-29 March 1917. It was lost to the Germans again on 22 March 1918 and captured for the final time on 4-5 September 1918 when it fell to men of the 42nd (East Lancashire) Division.

The cemetery stands on what was known as 'Green Jacket Ridge' during the war. The Communal Cemetery in the village contained the graves of twelve British men and one from New Zealand. Seven died in the fighting in March-May 1917 and six in September 1918. They were moved into what is now Row D in the British Cemetery in 1930. A set of German graves have been removed from the Communal Cemetery.

Among those buried here is Private George Hanna, 1st Royal Irish Fusiliers, executed for desertion on 6 November 1917, aged 26 years. He had served in Gallipoli and Salonika with the 2nd Royal Irish Fusiliers and was already under a sentence of death when he absconded again. Hanna had a poor disciplinary record, notable for several disappearances during times of action. He had been sentenced to death after a brief period of desertion in 1915 when he fled from action at Hill 70 at Gallipoli but this was commuted to a ten year prison sentence and then suspended. After a brief period of good conduct he fled again in late 1916 while his battalion were serving in the Salonika Campaign. Hence, by 1917 he found himself in prison on his second commuted death sentence serving seven years in prison for desertion. He was informed of the suspension of his sentence and a return to the Front. He was sent back to the unit from whom he had deserted twice before. Once in France with his battalion he went absent on 29 August and again on 28 September 1917 but gave himself up a few days later while in Amiens. He faced his final Court Martial on 19 October and was executed at Barrosa Hall at Metz-en-Couture. His brother, Private David Loftus Hanna, 1st Royal Inniskilling Fusiliers, died of wounds on 9 August 1916 aged 32 years and is buried in Lijssenthoek Military Cemetery near Ieper. Hann claimed another brother died at sea but I can find no record of him. Also here is Captain Alfred Percy Brewis, 1st Northumberland Fusiliers attached 1/5th East Lancashires,

MiD, killed in action at Havrincourt Wood just north-east of this village on 1 June 1917 aged 22 years. His father is recorded as a ship-owner and Alfred was educated at Uppingham School and Oxford. He was commissioned in October 1914, promoted to Lieutenant in December and Captain in September 1915 while attached to the 1/5th East Lancashires and serving in Gallipoli.

Lieutenant Colonel George Herbert St. Hill, Royal North Devon Hussars attached and commanding 2/5th Sherwood Forresters, MiD, killed in action on 8 July 1917 aged 52 years is buried here. He served in the Royal North Devon Hussars for eighteen years and fought in the Matabele, Angoni, and South African Campaigns. He also served at Gallipoli, where he commanded the 6th Lincolnshires at the evacuation of Suvla Bay. He was killed by a sniper while his battalion, which he had led since June 1916, were occupying and improving trenches east of Villers-Plouich. His men carried his body back from the trenches when relieved and buried him here in a brief ceremony on route to the rear. He was the son of the Reverend Canon Woodford St. Hill who at one time had been Canon of Hawkes Bay, New Zealand.

Another here is Private Percy Courtman, 'D' Coy. 1/6th Manchesters, killed in action on 2 June 1917. He won Bronze in swimming the 400m Breaststroke for Great Britain at the 1912 Olympics.

UK – 209   NZ – 5   Unnamed – 9
Area – 829 sq mts

Special Memorials to three men whose graves were destroyed by shellfire.

LOCATION
The village is located about 6km south-east of Bapaume and 10km south-west of Cambrai. It is on the south side of the A2 Autoroute. The cemetery is north-east of the village on the road to Metz-en-Couture. It is 50m from the road in fields next to a farm track.

NEUVILLE-VITASSE ROAD CEMETERY

HISTORY
The cemetery was made by the 33rd Division in April 1917 with further burials in June.

INFORMATION
Neuville-Vitasse was in German hands until taken by the 56th (London) Division on Easter Monday 9 April 1917. The Germans attacked and almost captured the village in March 1918 though some parts remained in Allied hands. The advance of August 1918 saw it fall for the last time.

Among those buried here is Company Serjeant Major Thomas Chrisp, MM, 1/8th Durham Light Infantry, killed in action on 23 June 1917 aged 24 years. When the war began he had just completed his teacher training course. His Territorial Force battalion all volunteered for overseas service, arrived in France on 20 April 1915 and travelled in horse trucks to Vlamertinge just west of Ieper. They entered the trenches during the Second Battles of Ypres, the first time gas was used during the war. From 24-26 April they lost 90 dead, 162 wounded and 342 missing, most of whom had been killed. Chrisp had been shot in his right arm and left leg so returned to 'Blighty'. On recovery he trained new recruits and was promoted to Sergeant Major. He married at Hexham Abbey in June 1916 and returned to France in July arriving on the Somme, via the Ypres Salient, in September to see the first tanks. The battalion was in action between Flers and Le Sars from 28 September–3 October. For leading his platoon during this period Chrisp was awarded the Military Medal. He then survived the disaster at the Butte de Warlencourt in November 1916 when his battalion was almost wiped out. He was involved in the battles on the Hindenburg Line in April 1917 and by June was in trenches near Cherisy. At 8.00am on Saturday 23 June 1917 Chrisp was entering his dug out when he was hit by a fishtail bomb (whizz-bang) and killed. His father had been Inspector of Police in Wooler, Cumberland.

Also here is 2nd Lieutenant Frederick Ashcroft, 18th (2nd Liverpool Pals) King's (Liverpools), killed in action on 9 April 1917. He had been in France since January 1917. His brother Lieutenant William Ashcroft, 19th (3rd Liverpool Pals) King's (Liverpools) was killed in action on 22 March 1918 and is commemorated by a Special Memorial in Savy British Cemetery. Another brother, Lieutenant Edwin Stanley Ashcroft, 17th (1st Livepool Pals) King's (Liverpools), died of wounds in German hands and is buried in Harlebeke New British Cemetery.

UK – 86   Unnamed – 11   Area – 389 sq mts

LOCATION
The village is on the south-eastern edge of Arras about 1km from the suburbs of the town. The cemetery is on the western side of the D5 road that runs south-east from Arras along the line of the old Hindenburg Line – if you give a little poetic licence. It is reached by a farm track from the D5 road. If you continue on down the track you will come out in St. Martin sur Cojeul. The cemetery is on top of the ridge between St. Martin sur Cojeul and Neuville-Vitasse.

NEW MUNICH TRENCH CEMETERY

HISTORY
The cemetery was made by V Corps in the spring of 1917, when their units cleared the battlefield. It was only used at that time.

INFORMATION
Beaumont-Hamel was in German hands from 1914. It was an early objective for 1 July 1916 but was not reached or even approached as the men cut down in what is now Newfoundland Park failed to get far from their own lines. Beaumont was attacked again, and taken on 13 November 1916, by the 51st (Highland) and 63rd (Royal Naval) Divisions.

After the capture of Beaumont on 13-14 November some objectives remained untaken. These included the German positions overlooking Beaumont known as Munich Trench and Frankfurt Trench. Munich Trench was entered by the 51st (Highland) Division on 15 November but they were forced back to New Munich Trench which was dug on the previous night by the 2/2nd Highland Field Company and a company of the 8th Royal Scots. The trench was lengthened by the 8th Devonshires in December. On 18 November units of the 32nd Division, including 16th (Glasgow Boys' Brigade) Highland Light Infantry, advanced at 6.10am through a snowstorm which later turned to sleet and then freezing rain. The attack failed and was called off, leaving 1387 men killed or wounded in front of Munich Trench. However, a small force of around 60 men of 'D' Company from the 16th Highland Light Infantry, plus some men of the 11th Borders, had managed to cross Munich Trench and had become cut off, surrounded and behind enemy lines, in the next German position, Frankfurt Trench. No-one knew that this small force was there, until some men managed to cross back to the British lines. Several rescue attempts were mounted, for example that by the 16th (2nd Salford Pals) Lancashire Fusiliers on 23 November, but they all failed with even further losses. The men in Frankfurt Trench managed to hold on until a week after they originally reached their objective. The Germans stormed the trench on 25 November and found only 15 wounded men alive, three of whom died soon afterwards. General Sir Hubert Gough praised their stand under Army Order 193.

When the Germans withdrew to the Hindenburg Line in early 1917 the British had the opportunity to bury the dead who had been killed during the Battle of the Ancre in November 1916, one of the last offensives of the Battle of the Somme. The V Corps created a number of cemeteries in this area at that time. This cemetery was originally known as V Corps Cemetery No. 25 and gained its present name after the war.

The graves in this cemetery are largely those of men who died at that time, the majority belonged to the 16th or 17th (Glasgow Commercials) Highland Light Infantry.

One of those involved in the attempted rescue of those in Frankfurt Trench is Private W Taylor, 16th Lancashire Fusiliers, killed in action on 23 November 1916 aged 23 years. One of those killed in the attack on 18 November is Private Alexander Park Knight Scott, 'B' Company, 16th Highland Light Infantry, aged 19 years. He had started his war in the Highland Cyclist Battalion in Kirkcaldy where he lived, was then attached to the 21st Infantry Base Depot at Etaples before being posted to the Highland Light Infantry in July 1916 with several others.

Also buried here is Private Thomas Clarke, 1st Royal Berkshires, killed in action on 14 November 1918 nearby. He was sent to borstal for theft but was later allowed to join the army. He was sent to France aged 18 years, deserted, was court-martialled and sentenced to death before the action in which he was killed.

UK – 146   Unnamed – 18   Area – 404 sq mts

LOCATION
Beaumont lies on the high ground above the River Ancre about 8km north of Albert. The cemetery can be found on the ridge north of the village between Beaumont and Serre. Signs lead from the village centre to the cemetery which is on the road to Miraumont. At the top of the ridge a sign leads from the road along a farm track to the cemetery which is about 100m from the road. Only the brave should attempt this by vehicle in winter, unless you have a good 4x4, but there is no turning place at the cemetery. The cemetery commands wide views in all directions over the battlefields of 1916-18, including the town of Albert, Newfoundland Park, and the 36th (Ulster) Division Memorial Tower.

NOREUIL AUSTRALIAN CEMETERY

HISTORY
The cemetery was begun to bury the dead of the battle here in April 1917 and remained in use until December 1917. A further set of burials were made in September 1918 during the fighting nearby.

INFORMATION
The village was in German hands since 1914 but it was one of the villages the Germans chose to temporarily defend in the retreat to the Hindenburg Line in 1917. It was attacked by 13th Australian Infantry Brigade, notably 50th and 51st

Australian Infantry, on 2 April and captured by the end of 3 April, but at heavy cost. The 50th battalion suffered 360 casualties many of whom are buried here. The 82 unidentified graves here almost certainly belong to men of the 50th Australian Infantry.

Among those buried here is Major George Tostevin, 1st Company, Australian Machine Gun Corps, who died of wounds on 5 May 1917 aged 25 years. Originally from the Channel Islands he had enlisted in Australia in October 1914 as a Private in the 12th Australian Infantry. He was commissioned soon after and was killed while reconnoitring the area.

Two brothers are buried here. Privates Edward Charles Clayton and William Alfred Clayton, 52nd Australian Infantry, killed on 12 April 1917. Edward was 29 while William was 42 years. They are buried together.

Another pair of brothers buried here are Private Angus Boston aged 28 years, and Corporal Thomas Boston aged 25 years, both 50th Australian Infantry with consecutive service numbers, both killed in action on 2 April 1917. Angus is commemorated by a Special Memorial as his grave could not be identified but he is known to be buried here among the unnamed.

Also of note is Lieutenant William Paton Hoggarth, 50th Australian Infantry, killed in action on 2 April 1917. He was the first Australian to enter Mouquet Farm in August 1916 though he was wounded in the action.

UK – 62 Aust – 182 Unnamed – 28
Area – 1069 sq mts

Special Memorials to 82 men whose graves in this cemetery cannot be identified as they were destroyed by shellfire.

LOCATION
Noreuil is located about 5km north-east of Bapaume on the area of the German Hindenburg Line. The Australian Cemetery is near the southern edge of the village, on the east side of the road to Morchies.

NORFOLK CEMETERY, BECOURT-BECORDEL

HISTORY
The cemetery was opened in August 1915 soon after the British took over this sector. It remained in use until August 1916. After the war it was greatly enlarged.

INFORMATION
The cemetery was begun by the 1st Norfolks from whom it got its name though the 8th Norfolks were later to make burials here. The first burial was Private Isaac Albert Laud, 'A' Company, 1st Norfolks killed on 9 August 1915. He was aged 16 years old. The cemetery is in a long valley where artillery batteries were located during the prelude to 1 July 1916.

Most of Plot I was completed by the end of the war when there were 281 graves in the cemetery. After the war a further 268 graves were concentrated in Plot I, Row D and Plot II. Almost all of the unnamed graves were among those concentrated here.

One of the last burials here in 1916 was that of Temporary Major Stewart Walter Loudoun-Shand, VC, 10th Yorkshires (Green Howards), killed in action on 1 July 1916 aged 36 years. The citation for his Victoria Cross reads 'For most conspicuous bravery. When his company attempted to climb over the parapet to attack the enemy's trenches, they were met by very fierce machine gun fire, which temporarily stopped their progress. Maj. Loudoun-Shand leapt on the parapet, helped the men over it, and encouraged them in every way until fell mortally wounded. Even then he insisted on being propped up in the trench, and went on encouraging the non-commissioned officers and men until he died'. His was the first Victoria Cross awarded to a man in the New Army battalions raised in Yorkshire for an act in the battles of 1916 on the Somme.

Another battalion commander buried here is Lieutenant-Colonel Colmer William Donald Lynch, DSO, 9th King's Own Yorkshire Light Infantry who was killed in action on 1 July 1916 aged 35 years when leading his battalion in attack north of Fricourt. The battalion lost fifteen officers killed on that day with over 400 men as they were ordered to walk across no-man's land allowing the German defenders time to get machine guns into place. Even so, the attack in that area took and held the German lines so that Fricourt was given up by the Germans in the next few days. He received his Distinguished Service Order in the New Years Honours List in January 1916. His father was Major General William

Wiltshire Lynch who served during the Indian Mutiny and died of cholera in India.

Also buried here are Privates John Jennings and Griffith Lewis, both 2nd South Lancashires, and both executed for desertion on 26 June 1916. There were both pre-war reservists who had been on the Western Front since 15 September 1914. They deserted in London in October 1915 while returning from leave but were caught in May 1916. Their trial was on 20 June 1916 and they may have been executed at that time 'to encourage others' just before the 'Big Push'. They are buried side by side.

Buried here is Private Charles Wadey, 7th Queen's (Royal West Surreys) who died on 4 January 1916 aged 28 years. His brother, Private Edmund Wadey, 1st Queen's (Royal West Surreys) was killed on 25 September 1915 during the Battle of Loos and is commemorated on the Loos Memorial. Another brother, Private Frederick Wadey, 2nd Queen's (Royal West Surreys) was killed on 9 May 1915 during the Battle of Aubers Ridge and is commemorated on the Le Touret Memorial.

Also here is Private William Arthur Cook, 8th Norfolks killed in action on 23 November 1915 aged 30 years. He was the eldest of five brothers who served. Private John Robert Cook, 1/8th Worcestershires, died on 4 November 1916 aged 23 years and is buried in the A.I.F. Burial Ground, Flers. The other brothers are Albert, George and Charles.

Two brothers are buried here though not side by side. Sapper Richard Farnell, 178th Company, Royal Engineers who died on 2 July 1916 and Sapper Samson Farnell, 179th Company, Royal Engineers who died of natural causes on 23 December 1915 aged 38 years. Another brother, Private George Farnell, 8th South Staffordshires Regiment, died of wounds on 4 March 1916 and is buried in Etaples Military Cemetery.

Also of note is Lieutenant Wolfred Reeve Cloutman, twice MiD, 178th Tunnelling Company, Royal Engineers, died on 21 August 1915 aged 25 years. He died while rescuing a Serjeant whom he carried on his shoulder 15m up a ladder from the bottom of a mine. As soon as the Serjeant was lifted off, this officer, overcome with gas, fell to the bottom of the shaft. Cloutman studied Mining Engineering at Imperial College, London, before undertaking post-graduate research in Australia and Malaya. His brother, Lieutenant-Colonel Brett Cloutman, was commanding 59th Field Company, Royal Engineers, when he was awarded the Victoria Cross on 6 November 1918, at Pont-sur-Sambre, France, for 'after reconnoitring the river crossings, found the Quartes Bridge almost intact but prepared for demolition. Leaving his party under cover he went forward alone, swam across the river and having cut the 'leads' from the charges returned the same way, despite the fact that the bridge and all the approaches were swept by enemy shells and machine-gun fire. Although the bridge was blown up later in the day by other means, the abutments remained intact.' His was the last action in WW1 to receive the VC. He was knighted for serving in senior judicial positions. On his death, his ashes were brought here to be buried with his brother.

As well as Laud mentioned above, Private John Edward Hart, 'C' Company, 1st East Yorkshires, died on 4 June 1916 aged 16 years.

UK – 407	Aust – 9	SAfr – 3
Can – 2	NZ – 1	India – 1
KUG – 126	Unnamed – 226	Area – 2539 sq mts

LOCATION
Norfolk Cemetery lies on the east side of the road from Becourt to Becordel. This is in a valley that runs north-south between the two villages. It is east of Albert and about 1km north of the road to Peronne.

ONTARIO CEMETERY, SAINS-LES-MARQUION

HISTORY
The cemetery was opened in the last weeks of September 1918 and was used for a few weeks until the middle of October. It was substantially enlarged after the war.

INFORMATION
The area was behind German lines for almost all of the war but fell to the 1st Canadian Division on 27 September 1918 who then opened the cemetery.

At the end of the war the cemetery contained 144 graves, mostly men of the 1st, 2nd, 3rd and 4th Canadian Infantry. After the war 182 graves were concentrated here, a few from isolated positions on the surrounding battlefields, but mostly men brought from German cemeteries that were being removed. The Maple Leaf at the gate marks this as a Canadian cemetery.

Among those buried here is Lieutenant Colonel Charles James Townshend Stewart, DSO and Bar, Croix de Guerre (France), twice MiD, commanding Princess Patricia's Canadian Light Infantry, killed in action on 28 September 1918 aged 44 years. Charlie Stewart, as he was called, belonged to a prominent and wealthy Nova Scotia family. A superb athlete, he was good at cricket, hockey, football, tennis, and golf, but while attending the Royal Military College of Canada he was expelled for gambling. He joined the North-West Mounted Police Stewart and was promoted to Corporal but reverted to Constable for having struck a bullying non-commissioned officer. He was appointed Lieutenant in Princess Patricia's Canadian Light Infantry on 12 August 1914 and arrived in England in October. He accidentally set fire to his tent so could not travel with his unit to France but joined them later. On 15 March 1915, while commanding a Platoon, he was shot in the chest and was invalided to England but it was clearly not too serious as he re-joined his unit on 17 July 1915 and was promoted to Captain. Stewart was on leave so missed the Battle of Mount Sorrel in 1916 in which the unit suffered 400 casualties, including nineteen of 23 officers. When Stewart returned on 5 June he was a Major. At the Battle of Flers-Courcelette, on 15 September, Stewart 'led an attack which captured two enemy trenches, and showed great determination, both in the attack and in the consolidation of the position won.' For this he was awarded the Distinguished Service Order, and was later Mentioned in Despatches. He missed the Battles of Vimy Ridge and Passendale due to his recovery from other wounds. On 30 March 1918, following the previous commanding officers' resignation, Stewart was promoted to Lieutenant-Colonel. Under Stewart's leadership the PPCLI took part in the Battles of Amiens and The Scarpe. In the latter battle it lost 60% of its officers and 30 per cent of its men but, on 27 September, tired and under strength, the PPCLI entered the Battle of Cambrai (1918). The following day, while advancing with his battalion across open ground near Raillencourt, west of Cambrai, Stewart was killed by a German shell. The citation for a Bar to the DSO, awarded posthumously, praised 'his extraordinary energy and resourcefulness, his sound tactical knowledge and ability' and added that 'his consistent cheerfulness, his complete disregard of danger and his personal example were undoubtedly instrumental in the success of his Battalion.' He was also awarded the French Croix de Guerre and received a second MiD.

Concentrated here:

Aubencheul-au-Bac German Cemetery - situated about 8km north-east of here in the chateau wood near the Canal du Nord. The cemetery contained 494 Germans and a Russian soldier. It also contained the graves of twelve British and two Australian soldiers who died as prisoners of the Germans in 1917 and 1918.

Bantigny Communal Cemetery and German Extension - situated in the village about 10km north-east of here and 5km north of Cambrai. Among the 563 Germans were the graves of eight British and four Australian soldiers who had died as prisoners of the Germans.

Epinoy German Cemetery - situated about 6km north-east of here next to the Cambrai-Douai road. It contained the graves of five British soldiers who died as prisoners in April 1918, six Italian soldiers who died as prisoners between December 1917 and January 1918 and over 200 Germans.

Flesquieres Communal Cemetery German Extension - situated on the western edge of the village which is about 8km south of here. It contained the graves of three unidentified British soldiers among the 350 German graves.

Flesquieres German Cemetery No. 2 - this was made next to Flesquieres Hill British Cemetery which is on the eastern edge of the village. Among the Germans were the graves of three British soldiers who died as prisoners in October and November 1916.

Graincourt-Les-Havrincourt Communal Cemetery German Extension - situated on the eastern edge of the village which is about 5km south of here. Among the 487 German graves were five unidentified British soldiers with one Australian and one Russian who died as prisoners.

Inchy-En-Artois Churchyard - in the village about 2km west of here. Among 50 Germans it contained the grave of a British soldier who died as a prisoner.

Longavesnes German Cemetery - situated south of the village, which is 25km south of here and 7km east of Peronne, on the road to Tincourt. It contained the graves of 726 Germans and 29 British soldiers who died as prisoners. Of the British graves twenty were concentrated into Tincourt New British Cemetery with the graves from Longavesnes British Cemetery.

Oisy-Le-Verger German Cemetery - situated at the east end of the village that is about 10km north of here. Among the 247 Germans were the graves of 24 British, six Italian and three Russian soldiers who died as prisoners.

Palleul Communal Cemetery German Extension - situated in the village on the Canal du Nord about 10km north of here. It contained the graves of 91 Germans and, among them, nine British soldiers who died as prisoners in 1918.

Sauchy-Lestree Communal Cemetery German Extension - situated in the village which is about 7km north of here. It contained the graves of 23 British soldiers who died as prisoners buried among the 303 German soldiers.

UK – 182	Can – 144	Aust – 9
NZ – 1	Unnamed – 84	Area – 949 sq mts

Special Memorials erected to four British servicemen and a Canadian soldier, buried in other cemeteries, whose graves could not be located at the time of concentration.

LOCATION

Sains-les-Marquion is at the extreme north-east corner of the area covered in this book. It is about 2km south-west of the point where the A26/E17 Autoroute has a junction with the Cambrai-Arras road. The cemetery is about 1km south of the village on the road to Trescault at a point where a small track to Moeuvres leaves the road.

ORIVAL WOOD CEMETERY

HISTORY

The cemetery was begun in November 1917 during the Battle of Cambrai. It was used again in September and October 1918. It was enlarged after the war by the concentration of graves from two cemeteries.

INFORMATION

The village was in German hands from 1914 until attacked by the 51st (Highland) Division supported by tanks on 20 November 1917 in the Battle of Cambrai. A German officer with a few men held out for some time but the village was captured on the next day. It was lost again to the Germans in the late stages of the battle who remained there until 27 September 1918 when it was captured by the 3rd Division. The German burials here include men of the German Naval Division.

Among those buried here is Lieutenant Ewart Alan Mackintosh, MC, 1/5th (The Sutherland and Caithness Highland) Seaforth Highlanders, killed in action on 21 November 1917. A war poet he had been an officer in the Seaforth Highlanders from December 1914. Having tried to join the army immediately war broke out and while still in his university course, he was rejected on the grounds of his poor eyesight. He reapplied, was accepted by the Seaforth Highlanders, and was commissioned as a 2nd Lieutenant on 31 December 1914 with the 1/5th Seaforth Highlanders. On 16 May 1915 he led a raid near Arras where several of his men were killed. Mackintosh had tried to bring Private David Sutherland, who had severe wounds, back to the trenches. Sutherland died of his wounds and had to be left behind, so he has no known burial place and is commemorated on the Arras Memorial. This event inspired a poem 'In Memoriam' and Mackintosh, by now a Lieutenant, was awarded the Military Cross. At the age of 23, Mackintosh regarded himself as a father to his men, and they affectionately called him "Tosh". One of Mackintosh's final poems, Cha Till Maccrimmein, appears to foretell his own death. He returned to England in August 1916 after being wounded in High Wood on the Somme to be stationed near Cambridge for eight months during which time he was training cadets. Mackintosh was killed while observing action near the village of Cantaing.

Concentrated here:

The 51st Division Cemetery, Flesquiéres –about 1km south of Flesquiéres on a sunken track running towards Havrincourt. It contained 74 officers and men of the 51st (Highland) Division and the Tank Corps who died in the last eleven days of November 1917.

Flesquiéres Chateau Cemetery – near the Havrincourt road and just outside the chateau grounds. It was used from November 1917 to March 1918 and for one burial in September 1918. It was also used for the burial of a Chinese labourer in February 1919. It contained 135 graves.

UK – 281   Chinese – 1   Ger – 20
Unnamed – 10   Area – 794 sq mts

Special Memorials to five men who are known to be buried here but it is not known where.

Special Memorials to two British soldiers buried in Flesquiéres Chateau Cemetery whose graves could not be identified at the time of concentration.

LOCATION

Flesquiéres is located about 10km east of Bapaume and 10km south-west of Cambrai. It is just south-west of the junctions of the A2 and A25 Autoroutes. The cemetery is 50m south of Orival Wood. It is on the east edge of the village on the road that runs north from Flesquieres Hill Cemetery.

OVILLERS MILITARY CEMETERY

HISTORY

The cemetery was opened in July 1916 after the village had been captured. It remained in use by Dressing Stations until March 1917 and was greatly enlarged after the war.

INFORMATION

The village is situated on one of two spurs of ridges with Nab Valley to the north and Mash Valley to the south. It was in German hands from 1914. While 70th Brigade attacked Nab Valley on 1 July 1916 (see Blighty Valley Cemetery) the rest of 8th Division attacked this spur and part of Mash Valley with 34th Division to their south in the valley, at La Boiselle, and in Sausage Valley. They suffered terrible casualties as the German line ran along the southern edge of the valley so that all of Mash Valley, across which 8th and 34th Divisions had to pass to reach the German line at Ovillers, was within no-man's land. Mash Valley became a killing ground in the crossfire of German machine guns from several directions. The village was held by the Germans on 1 July 1916 and was attacked again on 2 July, this time by 12th Division, which also failed. The German Guard Fusilier Regiment held out until 15 July when Ovillers fell to units of the 25th and 48th Divisions who attacked from the Bapaume Road. The village was lost in March 1918 during the German offensive but was taken for the last time on 24 August by the 38th Division.

Begun by a Dressing Station in the village, the earliest burials date from August 1916. It stands in what was no man's land and is the largest local cemetery.

It is easy to stand at the front of the cemetery looking along Mash Valley, over the area across which 2nd Middlesex attacked, and back towards Albert to the jumping off point at the Tara-Usna Line, to understand why casualties here were so high. Of the 2nd Middlesex, only 28 men answered roll call that evening. The battalion commander Lieutenant-Colonel Edwin Thomas Falkner Sandys, DSO, had complained before the attack that the German defences had not been destroyed but was ignored. He was wounded on the day and was so distressed by his experiences and the horrors his men faced that he took his own life, shooting himself with his service revolver on 6 September 1916 in his room in the Cavendish Hotel, London. He died a week later and is buried in Brompton Cemetery, London. He was reported in the Daily Mirror as a five times wounded hero dying of a gunshot wound, found in his bed with his revolver by his side, and having said that he wished he had died with his men.

At the end of the war the cemetery contained 143 graves now in Plot I. The cemetery was enlarged by the concentration of 3329 graves from the battlefields of Pozieres, Ovillers, La Boisselle and Contalmaison. Most of the concentrated graves were men who died in July 1916 but there were also 121 graves of French troops who were killed when they held the line here from 1914 to 1915. Over 70% of the graves are unidentified.

Buried here is Captain John Lauder, 1/8th Argyll and Sutherland Highlanders, killed on 28 December 1916 aged 25 Years. He was the son of the Variety and Music Hall artist, Harry Lauder, at that time the highest-paid performer in the world. There are many stories about the origin of the well known song 'Keep Right on to the End of the Road' but one that I credit is that he wrote the song after visiting his son's grave in 1924.

Also here are three battalion commanders involved in attacks nearby in early July 1916. Lieutenant Colonel Frederick Christian Heneker, was commanding 21st (2nd Tyneside Scots) Northumberland Fusiliers on 1 July 1916 having been transferred from the 20th Northumberland Fusiliers on the afternoon of 30 June 1916. Graduating from the Royal Military College, Canada, and carrying off the Sword of Honour as the best cadet of his year, he was given a commission in the Prince of Wales' Leinster (Royal Canadians) Regiment in 1894. He became a Captain in 1900 and Major in September 1915. He served in the Egyptian Army for four years and was an instructor at Sandhurst from 1909-1913. He went to France in September 1914, and was wounded in January 1915 near Armentieres. He went to France again in January 1916 and was killed in front of La Boiselle with 'his' men.

Lieutenant Colonel Louis Meredith Howard, 24th (1st Tyneside Irish) Northumberland Fusiliers, died of wounds on 2 July 1916 aged 37 years. He served in the South African Wars as a Corporal and was then commissioned. In 1914 he was a Captain in the Queen's (Royal West Surreys), but soon transferred to the Leeds 'Pals', the 15th West Yorkshires. He left them to take command of the Fusiliers in August 1915 and was mortally wounded south-east of La Boiselle on 1 July.

Lieutenant Colonel George Arthur Royston-Piggott, DSO, MiD, Northamptonshire Regiment attached and commanding 10th Worcestershires, was killed in action on the night of 2-3 July 1917 shot through the heart at his battalion HQ on the lip of Lochnagar Crater while his men were involved in hand to hand fighting in the village of La Boiselle. He had been commissioned into the 2nd Northamptonshires in 1895, and served in the South African Wars. He was in command of this battalion at the Battle of Loos in 1915, when he was Mentioned in Despatches and obtained the Distinguished Service Order. He joined the 10th Worcestershires in February 1916.

Also remembered here is Private James Walters, 9th Royal Fusiliers, killed in action on 7 July 1916, aged 16 years.

In the area between the cemetery and the village 49 British and two German remains were discovered in November 1982. The British have been buried at Terlincthun British Cemetery near Boulogne. They were men of the Royal Fusiliers, West Yorkshires, Royal Sussex, Essex and Royal Berkshires killed in attacks on 1 and 2 July 1916.

Concentrated here:

Mash Valley Cemetery, Ovillers-La-Boisselle - situated 200m north of here. The cemetery contained the graves of 76 British men who died from July to September 1916.

Red Dragon Cemetery, Ovillers-La-Boisselle - situated in Mash Valley midway between Ovillers and La Boiselle. It was created by the 16th and 17th (2nd North wales Pals) Royal Welsh Fusiliers and was named after their badge. It contained the graves of 25 British men, all from the 38th (Welsh) Division, including 22 of the Royal Welsh Fusiliers, who died in August 1918.

UK – 3208	Can – 95	Aust – 57
SAfr – 13	NZ - 6	Fr – 121
Unnamed – 2480		Area – 9476 sq mts

Special Memorials erected to 23 British soldiers and one Australian believed to be buried among the unnamed.

Special Memorials erected to 36 British soldiers, buried in Mash Valley Cemetery, whose graves were destroyed.

LOCATION

Ovillers is situated 1km north of the Albert-Bapaume road and about 5km north-east of Albert. The cemetery is on the south-western edge of the village on the north side of the road to Aveluy and the north side of Mash Valley. The cemetery gives excellent views of the battlefields.

OWL TRENCH CEMETERY, HEBUTERNE

HISTORY
The cemetery was only used in February 1917.

INFORMATION
Hebuterne was held by the French from the start of the war and taken over by the British in the summer of 1915. It was close to the front-line at the point at which the German advance in 1914 was held in this area. The Germans only occupied the village for a brief period during the summer of 1918.

Owl Trench was a German trench in front of Rossignol Wood. The 31st Division attacked the Germans as they withdrew in 1917 though the attack was considered a failure. The Germans re-occupied the area in early 1918. It was attacked by the 4th New Zealand Rifle Brigade on 15

July 1918, and cleared by the 1st Auckland Regiment five days later.

The cemetery was made for the burial of men killed on 27 February 1917, with one exception.

Row A is a mass grave in which are buried 46 British soldiers, of whom 43 belonged to the 16th (1st Bradford Pals) West Yorkshires. The battalion's most senior officer killed in the attack and buried here is Captain Geoffrey Armitage aged 30 years on 27 February 1917. He was a mohair merchant's manager and had been a member of Bradford Rowing Club. He was married and living in London at the start of the war and had survived the disaster at Serre on 1 July 1916.

UK – 53   Unnamed – 10   Area 184 sq mts

LOCATION

Hebuterne is about 7km west of Bapaume and a similar distance north of Albert. The cemetery is on the south side of the Puisieux-Gommecourt road between the two villages in open fields. It is very close to Rossignol Wood Cemetery opposite it on the other side of the valley.

PARGNY BRITISH CEMETERY

HISTORY

This is a concentration cemetery made after the war.

INFORMATION

The village was in German hands for much of the war. It fell to the British in 1917 and was retaken by the Germans for a few months in 1918.

The village was just behind the line at the crossings of the Somme at which the 8th Division tried to hold the Germans on 24 March 1918. The 1st Worcestershires took up positions at 2.30am on 23 March with orders to hold the west bank of the River Somme and cover the withdrawal of the Fifth Army. The bridge was congested with refugees and army units just in front of the advancing Germans. At 8.00pm the Germans began to try to cross the bridge. The commanding officer, Major, Acting Lieutenant Colonel (later Major General) Frank Crowther Roberts, VC, DSO, OBE, MC, took 45 men to push the Germans back. He was awarded the Victoria Cross for his actions on that and subsequent days including leading a bayonet charge through Pargny. He captured six machine guns, twenty prisoners and killed 80 other Germans though the battalion suffered heavy losses. The Germans had made footbridges during the night and crossed the river in strength so the battalions at the bridge and river were driven back while those in the village were pushed out.

Many of those here were killed in fighting on 24 March 1918. A large number of men are from 8th and 61st (South Midland) Divisions. While most of the burials here date from the fighting of March 1918, some later concentrations were from the battlefields at Serre and date from 1 July 1916. This includes men from the territorial battalions that suffered on the Serre Road. The Canadians are men of the Canadian Motor Machine Gun Service.

Among those buried here is Private Ephrahim Moore, 1/6th Royal Warwickshires, killed in action on 1 July 1916. We know the battalion were on the Serre road when he was killed and was originally buried just next to what is now Serre Road No. 2 Cemetery and that he was moved here in 1924. The CWGC website shows him to have been awarded the Military Cross but the hard copy register does not. Neither do any of his other records and I think the error is a confusion with 2nd Lieutenant Ernest Moore also concentrated into the cemetery who was awarded the MC. There is a nearby memorial to French Naval Pilot, Lieutenant Georges Faltz, and his radio operator, shot down on 20 May 1940.

Concentrated here:

Pargny German Cemetery – located north-east of Pargny Church. It contained the graves of 32 British soldiers.

UK – 613   Can – 6   Unnamed – 489

Area 2510 sq mts

Special Memorials to sixteen British men known to be among the unnamed.

Special Memorials to two RAF officers buried in Pertain Military Cemetery whose graves were destroyed.

LOCATION

Pargny is situated about 15km west of St. Quentin and 25km east of Amiens. It is about 5km south of the old road between the two cities. The cemetery is south of the village on the road to Nesle. The cemetery is on the east side of the road by a copse on the edge of a ridge. There is now excellent parking and a safe 100m path from the car park to the cemetery.

PEAKE WOOD CEMETERY, FRICOURT

HISTORY
The cemetery was begun at the end of July 1916 when it was used as a front-line cemetery. It remained in use until February 1917 when the Germans withdrew to the Hindenburg Line.

INFORMATION
Peake Wood was the name given by the British Army to a small copse on the south-east side of the Fricourt-Contalmaison road at the crest of the rise leading out of Fricourt. Having been in German hands since 1914, the copse fell to the British on 5 July 1916 following the fall of Fricourt and before the attack on Contalmaison. The copse has since gone.

The cemetery was in German hands during March to August 1918. This was one of the first war cemeteries to be constructed and completed after the war.

Among those buried here is 2nd Lieutenant Henry Alfred Stanley Carpenter, 103rd Company, Machine Gun Corps (Infantry), killed in action on 2 September 1916 aged 22 years. Carpenter served first with 9th East Yorkshires as a drill instructor, taking his officers course in Glasgow and then being gazetted into the 14th Royal Scots, later transferring to the Machine Gun Corps. He was killed by a shell just outside Contalmaison, where he was commanding four machine guns.

UK – 89   Aust – 7   Can - 1
Area - 792 sq mts
Special Memorials to five British and one Australian soldiers who are believed to be buried here.

LOCATION
Peake Wood Cemetery lies on the north-west side of the Fricourt-Contalmaison road about 1km south-west of Contalmaison and 3km north of Fricourt.

PERONNE COMMUNAL CEMETERY

HISTORY
The cemetery was used by the British for the burial of one member of the Royal Flying Corps who was killed when his plane crashed while returning from reconnaissance in August 1914. The French made burials at various times during the war.

INFORMATION
Corporal Frederick John Parsons Geard joined the Royal Engineers in 1910, transferred to the Air Battalion of the Royal Engineers in 1911 before transferring to the Royal Flying Corps in 1912 when it formed. He was killed while serving in No. 5 Squadron when he was the observer in BE8 391, piloted by Lieutenant Robert Raymond Smith-Barry, when it crashed at Peronne on 18 August 1914. Lieutenant Smith-Barry broke both legs in the crash, but went on to become the founder of modern flying training. Geard was the fifth member of the Royal Flying Corps to be killed in the war and one of the earliest British casualties of the war. There are also 66 French military burials in this cemetery.

UK – 1   FR - 66

LOCATION
Peronne is situated 12km south of Bapaume in the valley of the River Somme on one of the important river crossings. The Communal Cemetery is between Peronne and Mont-St. Quentin, and the Extension is on the south-west side of it. The Communal Cemetery is in the commune of Peronne, and the Extension in that of Ste. Radegonde. The Communal Cemetery and Extension are on the north side of the road. The main gates are often locked so use a gate at the south-west corner of the cemetery. The grave is on the left-hand side of the centre path, opposite the 1870 Memorial, about 50m from the main entrance.

PERONNE COMMUNAL CEMETERY EXTENSION, STE. RADEGONDE

HISTORY

The Extension was begun by the 48th (South Midland) Division in March 1917, used by the Germans in 1918, and by Australian units in September 1918. It was enlarged after the war by the concentration of graves from the battlefields north and east of Peronne.

INFORMATION

Peronne has withstood many sieges in French history. It was fortified by Vauban in the 1700's. It was captured by the Germans on 9 January 1871, after a twelve days siege and bombardment, during the Franco-Prussian War. The Germans swept through the town in May 1940 and remained until the town's liberation by American troops in September 1944.

In WW1 the town fell into German hands on 24 September 1914 and remained behind their lines, used as a base, until 18 March 1917 by which time it was almost demolished by Allied shelling. During the German withdrawal to the Hindenburg Line the 40th and 48th Divisions entered the town which had been set on fire by the Germans. In the German advance on 23 March 1918 the Germans recaptured the town when the remnants of the 66th Division retreated through the town. On 30 August to 1 September 1918, the 2nd Australian Division took Mont-St. Quentin, a feat commemorated by the Memorial, and on 1 September they entered Peronne. During the battle for Mont St. Quentin and Peronne five Victoria Crosses were awarded, all to men who survived the war.

The cemetery consisted of Plots I and II at the end of the war. The bodies of one French and one American soldier have been removed to other cemeteries.

Among those buried here is Corporal Alexander Henry Buckley, VC, 54th Australian Infantry, killed in action on 1 September 1918. The citation for his Victoria Cross says 'For most conspicuous bravery and self-sacrifice at Peronne during the operations on the 1st/2nd Sept., 1918. After passing the first objective his half company and part of the company on the flank were held up by a machine gun nest. With one man he rushed the post shooting four of the occupants and taking 22 prisoners. Later on reaching a moat, it was found that another machine gun nest commanded the only available footbridge. Whilst this was being engaged from a flank Corporal Buckley endeavoured to cross the bridge and rush the post, but was killed in the attempt. Throughout the advance he had displayed great initiative, resource and courage, and by his efforts to save his comrades from casualties, he set a fine example of self-sacrificing devotion to duty.' He is buried in the British/German Plot near the entrance.

Also here is Brigadier General George Augustus Stewart Cape, CMG, Royal Artillery, commanding 39th Division, killed on 18 March 1918 aged 51 years. He was commissioned into the Royal Artillery as a 2nd Lieutenant in November 1889, promoted to Lieutenant in November 1892, Captain in January 1900, and by October 1917 he was a Brigadier General commanding the 39th Division artillery. He had served in Uganda in 1898, the South African Wars and the Gambia Expedition in 1901. He was killed, while commanding the Division when Major General Feetham was home on leave, by a shell from the British artillery during an exercise.

Buried here is Corporal Frederick Arthur Thurston, MM and two Bars, 33rd Australian Infantry, killed by a shell near Hem on 30 August 1918 aged 24 years. He won the Military Medal at Messines near Ieper in June 1917 when he was a Company runner under heavy fire for 96 hours. A Bar was awarded in early March 1918 after he led a group to attack a German trench. A second Bar was awarded for leading a counter attack at Marcelcave on 30 March 1918.

Buried here is Corporal John William E Saunders, MM, 110th Brigade, Royal Field Artillery, died on 18 September 1918 aged 23 years. His brother, Rifleman William E Saunders, 16th (St. Pancras) Rifle Brigade, died on 23 December 1916 aged 20 years and is buried in Essex Farm Cemetery near Ieper. Another brother, Private Edward Robert Saunders, 21st (Islington) Middlesex, died on 9 April 1918 aged 18 years and is commemorated on the Ploegsteert Memorial.

Similarly here is Private Leslie McNiel Carraill, 32nd Australian Infantry, died on 3 September 1918 aged 22 years. His brother, Private Stanley James Carraill, 19th Australian Infantry, died on 14 November 1916 aged 25 years and is commemorated on the Villers-Bretonneux Memorial. Another brother, Driver Alexander Lawrence Carraill, 14th Brigade, Australian Field Artillery, died on 8 August 1918 and is buried in Longueau British Cemetery.

Two brothers are buried here though not side by side although both were killed in action on 31 August 1918. They are Private Frankland Bailey, 34th Australian Infantry, aged 20 years and Private Robert Bailey, 19th Australian Infantry aged 21 years.

The WW2 burials include the pilot and observer of a Lysander reconnaissance aircraft of No. 13 Squadron, RAF who crashed in December 1939. They are some of the earliest casualties of WW2 and reflect the accident in which Corporal Beard, buried in the Communal Cemetery, was killed in WW1.

Concentrated here:

Aizecourt-Le-Haut Churchyard Extension – 2km north-east of Peronne. It contained the graves of eighteen British soldiers and two from South Africa who died in March 1918.

Cartigny Communal Cemetery and German Extension – 2km south-east of Peronne. It contained the graves of 5250 Germans, now removed, two British and one Australian soldiers.

Copse Trench Cemetery, Allaines – situated between Allaines and Moislains about 3km north of Peronne. Buried here were 64 British soldiers, mainly 14th Black Watch and 12th Somerset Light Infantry, who died in September 1918.

Driencourt British Cemetery – found on the south side of the village about 3km east of Peronne. It was made by the 74th (Yeomanry) Division in September 1918, and contained the graves of 20 British soldiers.

Lieramont Communal Cemetery German Extension – situated about 7km north-east of Peronne. It contained 63 British soldiers who were buried by the Germans in 1916-1918 and by the 58th (London) Division in September 1918.

Moislains British Cemetery – found a little south-west of the village about 4km north of Peronne. Buried here were 54 soldiers of the 47th (London) Division who died in September 1918.

Moislains Churchyard - about 4km north of Peronne. It contained the graves of three British soldiers and one from Canada.

Moislains German Hospital Cemetery - at the north-east end of the village which is about 4km north of Peronne. Buried here, with 281 Germans, were 38 Allied soldiers who died in 1917 and 1918.

Templeux-La-Fosse German Cemetery – the village is about 6km north-east of Peronne. The cemetery was on the east side of the village. It contained 34 British soldiers, of whom 33 were buried in September 1918.

Vaux Wood British Cemetery, Vaux-Sur-Somme – the village is about 20km west of Peronne and 10km east of Amiens and lies in the valley of the River Somme. The wood is about 2km east of the village and the cemetery was within the eastern edge of the wood. Here were buried, in September 1918, 25 British soldiers, mainly of the London Regiment.

UK – 1065	Aust – 512	SAfr – 6
Can – 1	Ger – 97	Unnamed – 220
WW2 - 5		

Special Memorials to four Australian, two South African and one British soldiers, known or believed to be buried among the unnamed.

Special Memorials to nine British soldiers and one from South Africa, buried in German Cemeteries, whose graves could not be found.

Area - 5536 sq mts

LOCATION

The Extension is at the south-west corner of the Communal Cemetery.

PERONNE ROAD CEMETERY, MARICOURT

HISTORY

The cemetery was opened during the Battles of the Somme by local Field Ambulances and remained in use until August 1917. It was greatly enlarged after the war when remains were brought in from surrounding battlefields and burial grounds. Hence, there are now burials here of men who were killed in 1915 before the cemetery was begun.

INFORMATION

The village was, at the beginning of the 1916 Battles of the Somme, the point at which the boundary existed between the British and French armies. This was the extreme right flank of the British army in 1916 and was held by the British Fourth Army with the French Sixth Army on its right.

Two roads lead north from Maricourt to the front-lines. One is to Bernafay Wood and Longueval. The other leads to Montauban. It reaches the frontline of 1 July 1916 about 350m north of the village where the 30th Division attacked. The Division had four regular battalions with a Brigade of Manchester Pals and a Brigade of Liverpool Pals. They were helped by French artillery causing great damage to the German defences. The attack by 30th Division captured 500 Germans and several guns taking all their objectives, one of the few successes of the day. The village fell during the German advance in 1918 and was retaken in August 1918.

The wartime cemetery, originally called Maricourt Military Cemetery No. 3, is now Plot I.

Among those buried here is Lieutenant Colonel William Anderson, VC, commanding 12th Highland Light Infantry, killed in action on 25 March 1918 aged 36 years. The citation for his Victoria Cross reads 'For most conspicuous bravery, determination, and gallant leading of his command. The enemy attacked on the right of the battalion frontage and succeeded in penetrating the wood held by our men. Owing to successive lines of the enemy following on closely there was the greatest danger that the flank of the whole position would be turned. Grasping the seriousness of the situation, Colonel Anderson made his way across the open in full view of the enemy now holding the wood on the right, and after much effort succeeded in gathering the remainder of the two right companies. He personally led the counter-attack and drove the enemy from the wood, capturing twelve machine guns and seventy prisoners, and restoring the original line. His conduct in leading the charge was quite fearless and his most splendid example was the means of rallying and inspiring the men during the most critical hour. Later on the same day, in another position, the enemy had penetrated to within three hundred yards of the village and were holding a timber yard in force. Colonel Anderson reorganised his men after they had been driven in and brought them forward to a position of readiness for a counter attack. He led the attack in person and throughout showed the utmost disregard for his own safety. The counter-attack drove the enemy from his position, but resulted in this very gallant officer losing his life. He died fighting within the enemy's lines, setting a magnificent example to all who were privileged to serve under him.'

Also believed to be here is Private John Mayhew, 2nd Queen's (Royal West Surreys) who died on 1 July 1916 aged 16 years. He was from London.

Buried here is Lieutenant Colonel Edward Henry Trotter, DSO, 1st Grenadier Guards attached and commanding 18th (2nd Liverpool Pals) King's (Liverpools), killed in action on 8 July 1916 aged 44 years. Trotter had previously served in the Sudan under Lord Kitchener and had won his Distinguished Service Order during the Boer War whilst attached to the City of London Imperial Yeomanry. In August 1914 he took command of the 18th Kings (Liverpools). He was very keen on Physical Education and his men became known as 'Trotters Greyhounds'. The battalion suffered over 500 casualties attacking Montauban on 1 July 1916 but took its objectives. On 8 July the battalion was moving back into the front line and Trotter went ahead in preparation for the move. He was in the new Brigade HQ when the enemy noticed the troop movements and shelled the area. One of these shells killed him as well as the commander of the 18th (3rd Manchester Pals) Manchesters. His brother, Captain Reginald Baird Trotter, MiD, 2nd Cameron Highlanders, was killed in action on 9 May 1915 in the Battle of Aubers Ridge aged 41 years and is commemorated on the Le Touret Memorial.

Also here is Lieutenant Colonel Frank Aubrey Jones, CMG, DSO, MiD, 4th South African Infantry formerly Welsh Regiment, killed in action on 11 July 1916. He joined the Welsh Regiment in 1895, became Lieutenant in 1898, and served in Sierra Leone from 1898-99 on the Protectorate Expedition where he was wounded. He also served in South Africa 1899-1902 when he was severely wounded, Mentioned in Despatches and received a Distinguished Service Order. He retired as a Captain from the Welsh Regiment but re-joined in 1914. He was posted to the South African Infantry and was killed by a piece of shrapnel on 11 July 1916 just before the rest of the Battalion were decimated at Delville Wood.

East of the village on the Peronne road is a large granite memorial to Lieutenant Robert Brodu, company commander with the French 224th Infantry Regiment and to his men who died here in December 1914. It is in the middle of the no man's land over which the French 11th Division attacked on 1 July 1916.

Concentrated here:

Authuile Communal Cemetery Extension – located about 10km north-west of here. It was on the south side of the Communal Cemetery. It contained the graves of 108 French and 23 British soldiers who died in 1915 and early 1916.

Briqueterie East Cemetery, Montauban - about 3km north of here and on the east side of the brickworks between Maricourt and Montauban. It contained the graves of 46 British soldiers who died in the later battles of the Somme in 1916.

Carnoy Communal Cemetery Extension – located about 1km west of here. Here were 36 French soldiers and one British man buried in March 1918.

Casement Trench Cemetery, Maricourt - on the west side of the road to Montauban. Here were 163 British soldiers and one from South Africa buried from 1916 to 1918.

Fargny Mill French Military Cemetery, Curlu – about 2km south-east of here on the north bank of the Somme. It contained, among the French graves, six British soldiers and two from Australia who were buried from 1916 to 1918.

La Cote Military Cemetery, Maricourt – situated a short distance west of Péronne Road Cemetery. It contained the graves of 38 British soldiers and one from Australia who died from 1916 to 1917.

Maricourt French Military Cemetery – found on the south side of the village near this cemetery. Buried here were two British soldiers who died in December 1916.

Montauban Road French Military Cemetery, Maricourt – north of this cemetery. It contained among the French burials six men of the 1/8th King's (Liverpools) who were buried in August 1916.

Talus Boise British Cemetery, Carnoy - located less than 1km west of here, between Carnoy and Maricourt, at the south end of a copse. It was used mainly by the 1/5th Royal Berkshires in August 1918 and contained the graves of 175 British soldiers and five from South Africa.

UK – 1299 SAfr – 34 Aust – 14
Can – 1 Unnamed – 366 Area – 3788 sq mts

Special Memorials to 22 British soldiers known or believed to be among the unnamed graves.

Special Memorials to three British soldiers, buried in other cemeteries, one in Authuille Communal Cemetery Extension and two in Fargny French Military Cemetery, whose graves could not be identified at the time of concentration.

LOCATION

Maricourt is located about 6km east of Albert on the north side of the River Somme and north of the road from Albert to Peronne. The cemetery is on the north side of the Albert-Peronne road on the western edge of the village.

PIGEON RAVINE CEMETERY, EPEHY

HISTORY
The cemetery was made by the 33rd Division at the beginning of October 1918.

INFORMATION
Epehy was captured at the beginning of April 1917 during the attacks on the Hindenburg Line. The Germans re-took it on 22 March 1918. The British front-line, held by the 8th Leicestershires, ran across a valley about 1km north of the village. They fell back to the village where they, with 6th and 7th Leicestershires, inflicted heavy casualties on the Germans caught in the open ground in front of the village. It fell for the final time, in the Battle of Epéhy, on 18 September 1918 when it was captured by the 12th (Eastern) Division.

The cemetery is situated at the site of a charge led by the Indian Army 2nd Lancers on 1 December 1917. This was to halt the German advance from Cambrai. The commanding officer, Lieutenant Colonel H H F Turner, led his Dragoons in an attack along this shallow valley, under intense fire from German machine guns, supported by the 6th Inniskilling Dragoons and a mounted machine gun section. The 2nd Lancers lost two British officers, including Turner, one Indian officer and six Indian other ranks killed. One Victoria Cross, one Distinguished Service Oreder and one Bar, three Military Crosses, two Indian Order of Merits (2nd Class), seven Indian Distinguished Service Medals and one Bar were awarded. Turner was the third cavalry commanding officer to die on that day. He is buried in Tincourt New British Cemetery.

Most burials here are men of 2nd Worcestershires. This is the most easterly military cemetery in the Department of the Somme. The most easterly burial is that of an unidentified soldier. One of the 2nd Worcestershires buried here is 2nd Lieutenant George Ernest Woodward, killed in action on 29 September 1918 aged 28 years while taking part in a diversionary attack near Epehy. His relative, Private James Thomas Thompson, 8th Battalion, Tank Corps was killed on the same day whilst serving as a gunner in the assault on the Hindenburg Line at Bellicourt. He is commemorated on the Vis-en-Artois Memorial.

UK – 135   Unnamed – 16   Area – 514 sq mts
Special Memorials to two British soldiers believed to be buried here among the unnamed.

LOCATION
Epehy is located about midway between Bapaume and St. Quentin and 15km south-west of Cambrai. The village is about 1km west of the A26 Autoroute. The cemetery is 3km north-east of the village on the south side of a small valley running east-west.

POINT 110 NEW MILITARY CEMETERY

HISTORY
This cemetery was begun by the French 403rd Infantry Regiment who used it from May-July 1915. It was used by the British from February-July 1916.

INFORMATION
The cemeteries here are named after the 100m contour on military maps, though in 1916 this area was called 'King George's Hill'. This cemetery was used by the British after space in the 'Old' Cemetery (see below) was almost filled. Almost 50% of the burials are men of the Manchester Pals including eleven of the 24th Manchesters killed in February 1916 when a German shell hit their dugout. The 26 French and two German graves have been removed.

Among those buried here are three friends of the poet Robert Graves killed over two days in March 1916 and buried side by side. 2nd Lieutenant David Cuthbert Thomas, 3rd Royal Welsh Fusiliers, died of wounds on 18 March 1916 aged 20 years. Graves describes in his autobiography 'Goodbye to All That' what happened to Thomas. 'A' Company (Graves') and 'C' Company (Thomas') were working putting sandbags in position when rifle fire broke out and sentries passed the news "Officer hit." Captain Richardson went to investigate and came back and said "It's young Thomas, a bullet through the neck but I think he's all right, it can't have hit his spine or an artery because he's walking to the dressing station." Later came news that Thomas was dead. The regimental doctor, a throat specialist, had told Thomas at the dressing-station "You'll be alright, only don't raise your head for a bit". David then took a letter from his pocket and gave it to an orderly and said "Post this." It had been written to a girl in

Glamorgan for delivery if he got killed. The doctor saw that he was choking and tried a tracheotomy but was too late. Captain Mervyn Stronge Richardson, 1st Royal Welsh Fusiliers, died of wounds on 19 March 1916 aged 21 years. Graves in 'Goodbye to All That' describes that following completion by the working party, Captain Richardson invited Graves to take his Company down for their rum and tea and said he was going with Corporal Chamberlain to see what the wiring-party had done. As he was doing this Graves heard a couple of shells fall. There was a call for stretcher bearers and a man ran up and said "Captain Richardson is hit!" Graves sent a stretcher party to investigate and found that Richardson and Chamberlain had been caught by shells among the wire. Chamberlain lost his leg and died of wounds. Richardson, blown into a shell-hole full of water, lay there stunned for some minutes before the sentries heard his cries and realized what had happened. The stretcher bearers brought Richardson down semi-conscious but he recognised Graves and said he wouldn't be long away from the Company and gave Graves instructions. The doctor found no wound in any vital spot though the skin of his left side had been riddled with chalky soil blown against it. A little later Graves was told that Richardson was dead, the explosion and the cold water had over strained his heart, weakened by rowing in the Eight at Radley College.

2nd Lieutenant David Pritchard, 1st Royal Welsh Fusiliers, was killed in action on 19 March 1916 aged 19 years. He was the battalion trench mortar officer. Graves describes that Pritchard had just been given two Stokes mortar-guns which he had been testing and told Graves he could get his own back on the Germans as he could put four or five shells in the air at once. Shortly after hearing about the death of Captain Richardson shells burst nearby and again the cry went up "Stretcher-bearers". David Pritchard had fought his duel with the Germans all night, had finally silenced them, and was coming off duty when a shell hit him at a point where the communication trench reached Maple Redoubt.

UK – 64   Area – 729 sq mts

LOCATION
Fricourt is about 3km east of Albert. The cemetery is located on the south side of a ridge south of Fricourt. There is a small, easy to miss, crossroads about 100m east of the crossroads of the Fricourt-Bray and Albert-Peronne roads. The road north leads back into Fricourt. The road south leads up onto a ridge where the road becomes a farm track. The New Cemetery is 100m further south than the Old Cemetery. It can also be reached by farm tracks from the Bray-Fricourt road. The cemetery is 50m from the track.

POINT 110 OLD MILITARY CEMETERY

INFORMATION
Forty-nine French graves have been removed to the National Cemetery in Albert. This cemetery is closer to the front-line and is at the point where the communication trenches began.

The first British soldier to die in this area is buried here. He is Private Frank Footman, 1st Duke of Cornwall's Light Infantry who drowned on 2 August 1915 having been in France since 10 December 1914. He was moved here with several other sets of remains in 1935 from Etinehem Communal Cemetery.

In the nearby Bois Francais is the grave of French soldier H Thomasin of the 26th Infantry Regiment. He was killed in 1915 and his family made the grave permanent after the war. It lies a few yards from the former French front-line.

UK – 100   Unnamed – 3   Area – 879 sq mts

HISTORY
This was begun by the French in February 1915. It was used by the British from August 1915 to September 1916. A few burials were concentrated here after the war.

LOCATION
See Point 110 New Military Cemetery.

POMMIER COMMUNAL CEMETERY

HISTORY
The cemetery was used for the burial of 26 British soldiers who fell at various dates during the war when the British army was in this area.

INFORMATION
Buried here are mostly men of the Royal Field Artillery and 62nd (West Riding) Division. The French military graves have been removed.

One burial was made in 1915, eleven in 1916 including eight gunners killed on 3-4 February, three men of the 2/3rd Londons killed in 1917 and eleven men of the Duke of Wellingtons killed from 26-28 March 1918.

The first to be buried is Gunner Patrick Donohoe (Donohue), 20th Heavy Battery, Royal Garrison Artillery who died on 20 September 1915. The Battery had been in France since 7 August 1915.

UK - 26

LOCATION

Pommier is about 10km east of Doullens and about 2km south of the N25 Doullens to Arras road. The Communal Cemetery is on the south-east side of the village at a junction of the roads to Humbercamps, Berles and Bienvillers. The graves are on the east side of the cemetery in a small valley.

POZIERES BRITISH CEMETERY

HISTORY

The cemetery was started as a battlefield cemetery in July 1916. This now makes up Plot II. Further burials were made throughout the war. The cemetery was greatly enlarged after the war by the concentration of burials from the surrounding battlefields.

INFORMATION

The village was in German hands from 1914. It was important for two reasons. First, it is astride the road that was the main axis of the attack on 1 July 1916. Second, it is on a crest known as the Pozieres Ridge, one of the highest points on, and with commanding views across, the battlefield. It was an objective for 8th Division on 1 July 1916 but the attack foundered in Mash Valley at the German wire in front of Ovillers over 1km away.

Pozieres was attacked by the Australians with the 48th Division in late July 1916. It was captured in a few days but had to be held against German counter-attacks and shelling until the end of August. The Australian attack was made from the south as the axis of the attacks had changed due to the failures of 1 July 1916. At the start of September the Australians, having suffered huge casualties across four Divisions of 701 officers and 22592 men, or 60% of the infantry in action, with nearly 8000 killed, were replaced by Canadians as the focus moved on to Mouquet Farm and Courcelette. The village of Pozieres had disappeared by the end of the battle. There were five Victoria Crosses won by the Australians here and a container of soil was taken from Pozieres to the Australian National War Memorial in Canberra.

The village was lost in March 1918 and retaken by the 17th Division on 24 August 1918.

The location of the cemetery was known in 1916 as 'Tramway Crossing' or 'Red Cross Corner'. Around 50% of the burials here are unnamed which reflects the nature of the cemetery being mainly a concentration burial ground. There are 690 Australian and 218 Canadians known to be among the unidentified graves. The Germans buried 57 of their men in 1918 but they have been removed.

Among those buried here are brothers Privates John W Christy, aged 21 years, and Robert Christy, aged 25 years, 1st Kings (Liverpools), both killed on 17 January 1917. They came from Manchester, had both formerly been in the Manchester Regiment, and have consecutive service numbers so joined up together. They are buried side by side.

Also buried here is Sergeant Claude Castleton, VC, 5th Battalion, Australian Machine Gun Corps, killed in action on 29 July 1916 aged 23 years. The citation for his Victoria Cross reads 'For most conspicuous bravery. During an attack on the enemy's trenches the infantry was temporarily driven back by the intense machine gun fire opened by the enemy. Many wounded were left in no mans land lying in shell holes. Serjeant Castleton went out twice in face of this intense fire and each time brought in a wounded man on his back. He went out a third time and was bringing in another wounded man when he was himself hit in the back and killed instantly. He set a splendid example of courage and self-sacrifice.'

And buried here is Private William McHardy, 5th Australian Infantry, who was killed in action on 25 July 1916 aged 20 years. His 27 year old brother Private Frank McHardy, of the same Battalion, was killed on the same day but has no known grave. He is commemorated on the Australian Memorial at Villers-Bretonneux.

Also here is Private Charles Frank Church, 8th Australian Infantry, who was born in North Adelaide, South Australia on 15 September 1900. He was killed in action near Pozieres on 18 August 1916 so was 15 years 11 months old when he died.

Another buried here is Major Duncan Chapman, 45th Australian Infantry, killed by shellfire at Pozieres on the night of 6 August 1916. He was the first Australian ashore at Gallipoli on 25 April 1915.

You will find on the south side of the village two memorials. One is to the 1st Australian Division. This is opposite Fort Gibraltar, a large German bunker destroyed, and captured on 24 July 1916 by 1st Australian Division, in 1916. Nearby is the Memorial to the Kings Royal Rifle Corps who fought on the Somme, though interestingly not at Pozieres.

North of the village is the site of the Pozieres Windmill. It was destroyed in the fighting and its position has been made into a Memorial. It commemorates the three 'battles' the Australians had over 45 days in taking the village by late August 1916.

On the other side of the road is the Tank Memorial as tanks were first used in battle nearby. Three tanks of 'C' Company, Heavy Branch, Machine Gun Corps (as the tanks units were known before the formation of the Tank Corps) passed through this location on 15 September 1916 headed to the front line. This unit later became the 3rd Tank Battalion. They supported the 2nd Canadian Division and helped in the capture of the old sugar factory and the nearby trenches. You can see bullet marks made during WW2.

Concentrated here:

Casualty Corner Cemetery, Contalmaison - on the road from Pozieres to Fricourt. It was used in the summer and autumn of 1916, and contained the graves of 21 Canadian, 21 Australian and thirteen British soldiers

Danube Post Cemetery, Thiepval – located between Thiepval and Mouquet Farm. It was named after a trench and a Dressing Station and contained 34 British soldiers, mainly of the Royal Field Artillery, who were buried in the winter of 1916-17

Nab Junction Cemetery, Ovillers-La Boisselle – found at the crossing of the Thiepval-Pozieres Road and 'Nab Valley'. It contained the graves of 60 British soldiers and one German prisoner who were buried in the winter of 1916-17.

| UK – 1809 | Aust – 700 | Can – 214 |
| Ger – 1 | Unnamed – 1382 | KUG - 11 |

Area – 7194 sq mts

Special Memorials to 23 casualties known or believed to be buried among the unnamed.

POZIERES MEMORIAL

The cemetery is enclosed by the Memorial to the Missing of 1918 on the Somme. This was made by adding panels of names to the walls of the cemetery. It is a Memorial to the missing of the Fifth Army killed in the German offensive in 1918 which pushed the Fifth and Third Armies back 50km in sixteen days. It was originally intended that each Army would have a Memorial to its missing of that campaign but the French protested at the amount of land required. Hence, the idea was dropped. Third Army's missing are on the walls of a Memorial in Arras while Fifth Army are here. This is ironic as it was Third Army that fought here while the Fifth Army was in the valley of the River Somme. There are 14644 names including 3205 South Africans – this includes all those who died in the retreat and the period up to 7 August 1918.

It should be noted that, although the memorial stands upon a battlefield of importance to Australians and contains 700 Australian graves, there are no Australians on the Memorial. All Australian soldiers who fell in France and whose graves are not identified are commemorated on the Villers-Bretonneux Memorial.

Listed on the memorial is Brigadier General George Norman Bowes Forster, CMG, DSO, General Staff commanding 42nd Infantry Brigade, and Royal Warwickshire Regiment, who died on 4 April 1918 aged 45 years. He served in the Nile Expedition of 1898 and in the South African Wars. In 1914, he went to France with the 7th Royal Warwickshires, eventually commanding it. He was wounded twice, and was awarded the Distinguished Service Order in the New Year's Honours List of January 1917. In August 1917 he was appointed to command the 42nd Infantry Brigade, 14th (Light) Division. On 4 April 1918 his brigade HQ was overrun near Villers Bretonneux, he was killed and his body was never identified. The Brigade war diary says '11.00am. The enemy at this hour were heavily attacking and by 12 noon had captured the whole of the trench line and entered the village. Brigade HQs (only 500 yards behind the front line) was surrounded before any message was received and the Brigadier-General and the Staff-Captain and Signalling Officer are missing together with 15 other ranks. The Brigade-Major hid in a ditch about 200 yards from the late HQ and escaped through the enemy's outposts at night.'

There are also twelve men of the rank of Lieutenant Colonel commemorated on the Memorial.

Commemorated upon the Memorial are the following winners of the Victoria Cross.

Private Herbert George Columbine, VC, 9th Squadron Machine Gun Corps (Cavalry) killed in action on 22 March 1918 aged 24 years. His citation reads 'For most conspicuous bravery and self-sacrifice displayed, when, owing to casualties, Pte. Columbine took over command of a gun and kept it firing from 9 a.m. till 1 p.m. in an isolated position with no wire in front. During this time wave after wave of the enemy failed to get up to him. Owing to his being attacked by a low-flying aeroplane the enemy at last gained a strong footing in the trench on either side. The position being untenable he ordered the two remaining men to get away, and, though being bombed from either side, kept his gun firing and inflicting tremendous losses. He was eventually killed by a bomb which blew up him and his gun. He showed throughout the highest valour, determination and self-sacrifice.'

2nd Lieutenant Edmund de Wind, VC, 15th Royal Irish Rifles, killed in action on 21 March 1918 aged 34 years. His citation reads 'For most conspicuous bravery and self-sacrifice on the 21st March, 1918, at the Race Course Redoubt, near Grugies. For seven hours he held this most important post, and though twice wounded and practically single-handed, he maintained his position until another section could be got to his help. On two occasions, with two NCO's only, he got out on top under heavy machine gun and rifle fire, and cleared the enemy out of the trench, killing many. He continued to repel attack after attack until he was mortally wounded and collapsed. His valour, self-sacrifice and example were of the highest order.'

Lieutenant Colonel Wilfrith Elstob, VC, DSO, MC, 16th Manchester Regiment, killed in action on 21 March 1918 aged 29 years. His citation reads 'For most conspicuous bravery, devotion to duty and self-sacrifice during operations at Manchester Redoubt, near St. Quentin, on the 21st March, 1918. During the preliminary bombardment he encouraged his men in the posts in the Redoubt by frequent visits, and when repeated attacks developed controlled the defence at the points threatened, giving personal support with revolver, rifle and bombs. Single-handed he repulsed one bombing assault driving back the enemy and inflicting severe casualties. Later, when ammunition was required, he made several journeys under severe fire in order to replenish the supply. Throughout the day Lieutenant-Colonel Elstob, although twice wounded, showed the most fearless disregard of his own safety, and by his encouragement and noble example inspired his command to the fullest degree. The Manchester Redoubt was surrounded in the first wave of the enemy attack, but by means of the buried cable Lieutenant-Colonel Elstob was able to assure his Brigade Commander that "The Manchester Regiment will defend Manchester Hill to the last." Sometime after this post was overcome by vastly superior forces, and this very gallant officer was killed in the final assault, having maintained to the end the duty which he had impressed on his men - namely, "Here we fight, and here we die." He set throughout the highest example of valour, determination, endurance and fine soldierly bearing.' He received the Military Cross for his leadership during the Battle of the Somme and the Distinguished Service Order for his leadership during Third Ieper.

Also commemorated here is Lance Corporal William Richard Deal, 490th Field Company, Royal Engineers, killed on 25 March 1918. He was a pre-war amateur international footballer. Another footballer commemorated is Private Harry Hanger, who played for Northampton Town, Bradford City and Crystal Palace. He joined up with the 5th (Royal Irish) Lancers in 1914 and was killed on 23 March 1918.

LOCATION
Pozieres is situated astride the Albert-Bapaume road about 3km north-east of Albert. The cemetery is about 200m south-west of the village on the north side of the road. There is good parking in front of the cemetery.

PUCHEVILLERS BRITISH CEMETERY

HISTORY
The cemetery was opened in preparation for the Battles of 1916 and the largest number of men buried here date from 1916 and early 1917. The next large group of burials date from the German advance of 1918.

INFORMATION
The village was behind Allied lines during the war. The 3rd and 44th Casualty Clearing Stations were posted to the village in June 1916 in preparation for the Battles of the Somme in 1916. They made the burials in Plot I to VI in the period to March 1917. The 2/1st South Midland CCS used the cemetery until May 1917. The 49th CCS made the burials in Plot VII, found at the rear of the cemetery, during the German offensive in 1918 though some additions were made by the 48th Labour Group in August.

When the cemetery was opened men were dying at the rate of about twenty per day. The local CCS's served 36th, 32nd and 34th Divisions who fought on 1 July 1916 from Thiepval to La Boiselle. The burials from that time are close together. Later battles at Pozieres and Courcelette are represented by the Australian and Canadian dead buried here. A group of 74 Germans who died as Prisoners of War have been removed as have some French graves.

Among those buried here is Captain Marcus Herbert Goodall, 1/5th York and Lancasters who died of wounds on 14 July 1916 aged 21 years. He was a friend of Siegfried Sassoon who had been at Marlborough College, though not at the same time, and at the Fourth Army School for Junior Officers. Goodall was a Company commander who, two nights after the disastrous Ulster Division attack at Thiepval, took out a patrol of 20 volunteers to 'assess the strength of the Bosch line'. However, the patrol was fired on as it tried to cut through the German wire. Goodall and one other man were hit. When the news of his death reached Sassoon, he was in hospital where he wrote 'Elegy for Marcus Goodall'. Goodall is buried among a group of officers and his headstone reads 'Tell England that we who died serving here rest here content.'

Also here is 2nd Lieutenant Herbert Walter Crowle, 10th Australian Infantry, who died of wounds on 25 August 1916 aged 32 years. In October 1919 his wife and brother visited his grave and had a private cross erected which remains today. It shows he was at Gallipoli and mortally wounded at Mouquet Farm five days before he died.

There are several young soldiers buried here. They include 16 year olds Private Victor Apps, 6th Borders who died on 29 September 1916; Private Albert Henry Thomas Bowl, 10th Royal Fusiliers, who died on 10 July 1916. With them are 17 year olds Lance Corporal James Skinn, 1/5th King's Own Yorkshire Light Infantry, who died on 3 July 1916; Private Charles John Foakes, 7th Royal Fusiliers, who died on 12 July 1916; Private Alfred Wilsdon, 10th Gloucestershires, who on died 23 July 1916; Private Walter Shepherd, 10th Gloucestershires, who died on 23 July

1916; Lance Corporal H Howard, 8th Duke of Wellington's (West Riding Regiment), who died on 17 September 1916; Private Wilfred Bentley, 1/5th West Yorkshires, who died on 29 September 1916; Private Stephen Cuthbert, 15th Northumberland Fusiliers, who died on 30 September 1916; and Gunner Arthur Smith, 106th Siege Battery, Royal Garrison Artillery, who died on 25 October 1916.

| UK – 1132 | Aust – 417 | Can – 213 |
| NZ - 1 | Unnamed – 7 | Area - 4753 sq mts |

LOCATION
Puchevillers is 19km north-east of Amiens and a similar distance west of Albert. The British Cemetery can be found about 400m west of the village in open countryside at the end of a small dead-end road.

QUARRY CEMETERY, MARQUION

HISTORY
The cemetery was only used in October 1918.

INFORMATION
Marquion had been in German hands from 1914 until it was captured by the 11th Division and 1st Canadian Division on 27 September 1918.

The cemetery was also known as Chalk Pit Cemetery. The graves of seventeen Germans have been removed to Baralle German Cemetery. A Canadian grave was moved here from Marquion German Cemetery, which has since been removed, after the war.

Among those buried here is Captain Gordon Stevenson Winnifrith, MC, 15th Canadian Infantry (48th Highlanders of Canada), killed in action on 27 September 1918 aged 27 years. The Toronto Star of 12 October 1918 records that he enlisted as a Private on 8 June 1915 and was commissioned in the field. He had three months prior service with the Canadian Field Artillery and before enlisting he had been an accountant. He was the only surviving officer in the battalion after one encounter with the Germans. He was killed leading his Company during the assault on the Canal du Nord.

| UK – 23 | Can – 45 | Area – 544 sq mts |

LOCATION
Marquion is situated at the extreme north-east corner of the area covered by this book. It is about 10km north-west of Cambrai on the south side of the Cambrai-Arras road. The cemetery is about 1km south-east of the village on a small road signed from the centre of the village. The cemetery lies below the level of the road and is a beautiful and tranquil place to be buried.

QUARRY CEMETERY, MONTAUBAN

HISTORY
The cemetery was first used on 16 July 1916 and remained in use until February 1917. It was greatly enlarged after the war.

INFORMATION
Montauban was in German hands from 1914. It was captured by the 30th and 18th Divisions by 10.30am on 1 July 1916 in one of the few successes of the day. However, the British failed to press home their advantage as they expected a counter-attack from the Germans. There is a position just north of the village called 'Triangle Point' where the German Trench 'Montauban Alley' crosses the road heading north. The 17th (2nd Manchester Pals) Manchesters reached this location by midday on 1 July 1916 to find the German infantry and artillery in chaos as they withdrew. Hence, this point was the location of the furthest advance on 1 July 1916. Rawlinson had not expected such success by the 30th Division which partly explains why it was not exploited by the cavalry.

The Germans retook the village during their spring offensive in March 1918. The village fell to the 7th Buffs and 11th Royal Fusiliers of the 18th Division on 25 August 1918.

The cemetery is found in a valley in which the German artillery was positioned on 1 July 1916 before the Manchesters took the village.

The quarry became a busy place after it had been captured and as the advance pressed on in 1916. Medical units arrived nearby in August and the cemetery served an advanced Dressing Station that was in the quarry for much of the Battles of the Somme in 1916. Many of the burials, including those concentrated here, are men from the 3rd and 9th Divisions who were killed in the attacks from this village on 14 July 1916 that took the Longueval Ridge. There are also artillerymen buried here as the British used the valley for artillery positions as the Germans had done before them.

The Germans made some burials in April and May 1918, now in Plot V. At the end of the war the cemetery contained 152 graves, now in Plots V and VI. After the war 580 graves were concentrated here, mostly of men who were killed from July to December 1916, from the surrounding battlefields. However, it is notable that of the 800 men of the Manchesters and Kings (Liverpools) who died in the capture of the village on 1 July 1916 none is buried here.

Among those here is Captain Walter Joel Ralphs, 12th Battery, Royal Field Artillery, killed on 15 July 1916. He is shown as being late officer commanding Shanghai Light Horse who joined the RFA as a 2nd Lieutenant in December 1914.

Also buried here is Air Mechanic Reginald Hobbs, No. 3 Squadron, Royal Flying Corps who died on 29 August 1916 aged 16 years. He is one of the youngest men killed while with the RFC. He lied about his age to join up in 1915, trained as a wireless operator and signaller, and went to France in May 1916. However, the artillery had a desperate need for signallers so he was posted to 14th Brigade, Royal Horse Artillery and was killed soon after by shellfire having been at the Front for three months.

There is now a Memorial in the village centre to the men of the Manchester and Liverpool Pals who took this village in 1916.

Concentrated here:

Briqueterie Cemetery No. 3, Montauban - situated about 500m east of here on the east side of the Longueval-Maricourt road next to the old brickworks. It contained the graves of 23 British soldiers, mainly 1/5th King's Own, who died in July and August 1916.

Caterpillar Wood Cemetery No. 2, Montauban - situated about 500m west of here on the eastern edge of a wood that is now removed. It was begun by the 2nd Suffolks in July 1916 and remained in use until January 1917 for the burial of 50 British soldiers.

Green Dump Cemetery, Longeuval - situated in the fields 1km north-east of here. It contained the graves of 42 British and eleven New Zealand soldiers, with one who is only 'Known Unto God', who were killed from August to October 1916.

Quarry Scottish Cemetery, Montauban - about 200m east of here between the quarry and Bernafay Wood. It contained the graves of 55 British soldiers, mainly of the 11th and 12th Royal Scots, who were killed in July 1916.

UK – 674	NZ – 36	Aust – 25
SAfr – 5	Fr – 1	Ger - 15
Unnamed – 157		Area – 3459 sq mts

Special Memorials erected to seven soldiers known, or believed, to be buried among the unnamed graves.

Special Memorials erected to seventeen British and two New Zealand soldiers, buried in Quarry Scottish Cemetery, Green Dump Cemetery and Caterpillar Wood Cemetery No. 2 whose graves could not be identified at the time of concentration.

LOCATION
Montauban is situated about 10km east of Albert. The cemetery is 1km north of the village on the north-west side of an old quarry which is on the east side of the road to Bazentin.

QUARRY WOOD CEMETERY

HISTORY
The cemetery was made by the 102nd Canadian Infantry in October 1918.

INFORMATION
The village of Sains-lès-Marquion had been in German hands until it was captured by the 1st Canadian Division on 27 September 1918.

All of those who are buried here, most of whom are Canadian, died in September 1918 except for two men buried on 1 and 2 October 1918.

Among those here is Major David Fraser, 50th Canadian Infantry, killed in action on 27 September 1918 aged 34 years. Born in Scotland, he had served seven years with the 3rd Volunteer Battalion, Seaforth Highlanders before emigrating to Canada. He enlisted on 6 February 1915 as a Private in the 13th Canadian Mounted Rifles and was commissioned as Lieutenant to 192nd Battalion on 17 February 1916 at Blairmore, Alberta before transfer to the 50th Canadian Infantry.

UK – 14	Can – 263	Unnamed – 5
Area – 1249 sq mts		

Special Memorial to one Canadian Officer believed to be buried among the unnamed.

LOCATION
Sains-les-Marquion is about 5km west of Cambrai at the north-east corner of the area covered by this book. The cemetery is about 1.5km south of the village close to Ontario Cemetery but further from the village. It is situated on a ridge near a wood containing disused quarries. A farm track leads 150m from the road to the cemetery.

QUEANT COMMUNAL CEMETERY BRITISH EXTENSION

HISTORY
The cemetery was made in September and October 1918.

INFORMATION
The village was in German hands for most of the war. It was behind the Hindenburg Line and formed part of the Drocourt-Quéant Line defence system lying at its southern end. It did not fall into Allied hands until 2 September 1918 when it fell to the Canadian Corps.

A German cemetery was made during the war on the north side of the Communal Cemetery with nearly 600 burials. This British Extension was made on the east side of the German extension. Many of the Canadians buried here died as a consequence of fighting at the Canal du Nord in late September and October 1918. At that time the 4th Canadian Divisional Advanced Dressing Station was here and buried many of those in this cemetery.

Among those buried here is Lieutenant Samuel Lewis Honey, VC, DCM, MM, 78th (Manitoba Regiment) Canadian Infantry, who died of wounds on 30 September 1918 aged 24 years. The citation for his Victoria Cross reads 'For most conspicuous bravery during the Bourlon Wood operations, 27th September to 2nd October, 1918. On 27th September, when his company commander and all other officers of his company had become casualties, Lt. Honey took command and skilfully reorganised under very severe fire. He continued the advance with great dash and gained the objective. Then finding that his company was suffering casualties from enfilade machine-gun fire he located the machine-gun nest and rushed it single-handed, capturing the guns and ten prisoners. Subsequently he repelled four enemy counter-attacks and after dark again went out alone, and having located an enemy post, led a party which captured the post and three guns. On the 29th September he led his company against a strong enemy position with great skill and daring and continued in the succeeding days of the battle to display the same high example of valour and self-sacrifice. He died of wounds received during the last day of the attack by his battalion.' He enlisted in January 1915 and earned the Military Medal raiding German trenches on 22 February 1917. He was awarded the Distinguished Conduct Medal for leadership and maintaining morale in the face of extremely heavy fire at Vimy Ridge in April 1917. He was commissioned in early 1918.

Also here is Major General Louis James Lipsett, CB, CMG, twice MiD, Croix de Guerre (France), Officier de la Legion d'Honneur, General Staff, commanding 4th Division late Royal Irish Regiment, killed in action on 14 October 1918 aged 44 years. He was commissioned into the Royal Irish in 1894, then serving in India including the Tirah Campaign, following which he was promoted to Lieutenant. He fought in the South African Wars when he was promoted to Captain. He was in charge of training Canadian officers from 1913 and brought the 8th Canadian Infantry to France in 1915 who were then heavily involved in the Second Battle of Ypres. He is credited with issuing the first order to counteract the effects of poison gas, when he ordered his men to urinate on strips of cloth and tie them to their faces to neutralise the chlorine. However, the idea was probably that of a more junior officer. He was subsequently promoted to Brigadier-General commanding the 2nd Canadian Infantry Brigade and was made a member of the Order of Companion of St. Michael and St. George. He commanded the 3rd Canadian Division during some of the bitterest battles of the war, taking over after his predecessor, Major-General Malcolm Smith Mercer was killed during the Battle of Mount Sorrel. He led them through all the battles in 1916, 1917 and early 1918. He prepared the Division for the 1918 '100 Days Campaign' and led them in the initial attacks in August, for which he was made a Companion of the Order of the Bath. He was transferred, against his wishes, to the British 4th Division at the start of September 1918 as it had been agreed that Canadian Divisions were to be led by Canadians. He was killed in action less than a month before the end of the war during a reconnaissance mission observing German positions along the River Selle. At about 3.15pm the party was spotted and a German machine gun opened fire from across the river. The party went to ground but a single bullet struck Lipsett in the face. He was able to stagger back to his own lines but collapsed from massive blood loss and never regained consciousness. He was the last British General to be killed during the war.

You will also find Lieutenant Colonel Edward Stephen Gibbons, DSO, three times MiD, Middlesex Regiment, attached and commanding 7th Highland Light Infantry, killed in action on 19 September 1918 aged 35 years. He had fought on the North-West Frontier before the war, was seriously wounded during the war and led his battalion for nearly a year. He was awarded the Distinguished Service Order for his leadership at Le Maisnil on 21 October 1914 while a Captain with 1st Middlesex.

Another buried here is Private Alexander Bulloch, 7th Cameronians (Scottish Rifles) who died on 19 September 1918 aged 20 years. His brother, Corporal Walter Bulloch, 5th/6th Cameronians (Scottish Rifles), was killed on 21 May 1917 aged 24 years and is commemorated on the Arras Memorial. Another brother, Sapper William Bulloch, 2nd Field Company, Australian Engineers, died of wounds on 31 December 1917 aged 33 years and is buried in Trois Arbres Cemetery, Steenwerck.

Also of note is Sergeant Tom Hobart Scott, Canadian Corps Gas Services, who died on 22 September 1918 aged 37 years. He is one of only two men from his unit to die in the war. The CCGS was created in response to the German gas attack in April 1915 with the aim of training men to survive the use of poison gas on the battlefield.

UK – 159   Can – 112   NZ – 3
Chinese – 1   KUG – 1   Unnamed – 6
Area – 1011 sq mts

LOCATION
Queant is about 10km west of Cambrai and a similar distance north-east of Bapaume. The Communal Cemetery is near the north-west outskirts of the village on the west side of the road to Riencourt-les-Cagnicourt. The British cemetery is at the north-west corner of the Communal Cemetery and is now 50m from the road. There is access from the Communal Cemetery but also from the road at the north end of the old German extension.

QUEANT ROAD CEMETERY

HISTORY
The cemetery was made by the 2nd and 57th Casualty Clearing Stations in October and November 1918. Many graves were concentrated here after the war from the surrounding battlefields of 1917 and 1918 and smaller burial grounds.

INFORMATION
The village was in German hands from 1914 until it was reached by the Third Army on 2 September 1918, after the storming of the Drocourt-Quéant line. It was taken from the Germans on 3 September.

The original cemetery of 71 burials is now Plot I, Rows A and B. Many of the burials concentrated here after the war were men who had died in German hands as Prisoners of War. Approximately 65% of the burials here are unidentified. The graves of three Americans have been removed.

Buried here is Captain Percy Cherry, VC, MC, 26th Australian Infantry, killed in action on 26 March 1917 aged 21 years. The citation for his Victoria Cross reads 'For most conspicuous bravery, determination and leadership when in command of a company detailed to storm and clear a village. After all the officers of his company had become casualties he carried on with care and determination in the face of fierce opposition, and cleared the village of the enemy. He sent frequent reports of progress made, and when held up for some time by an enemy strong point, he organised machine gun and bomb parties and captured the position. His leadership, coolness and bravery set a wonderful example to his men. Having cleared the village, he took charge of the situation and beat off the most resolute and heavy counter-attacks made by the enemy. Wounded about 6.30 a.m., he refused to leave his post, and there remained, encouraging all to hold out at all costs, until, about 4.30 p.m. this very gallant officer was killed by an enemy shell.' He had been with the Citizen's Militia Force as a 2nd Lieutenant in 1913 and was soon in the Army, serving in Gallipoli as a Quarter Master Sergeant, being wounded, before being commissioned and transferring to the 7th Machine Gun Company. On 5 August 1916, he and a German officer, who was leading an attack against Cherry's position, were exchanging shots from neighbouring shell-holes until they both rose, firing simultaneously. The German officer hit Cherry in the neck but was mortally wounded by Cherry who approached the man. The German pulled letters from his pocket and asked Cherry to have them posted. Cherry promised to do so and took the letters as the German said 'And so it ends' before dying. Cherry was awarded the Military Cross for his part in an attack on Malt Trench at the Butte de Warlencourt on 2 March 1917. In the afternoon of 26 March 1917, a shell burst in a sunken road to the east of Lagnicourt, killing Cherry and several other men.

Also here is Major Benjamin Bennett Leane, 48th Australian Infantry, Order of the White Eagle (Serbia), killed in action at Bullecourt on 10 April 1917 aged 27 years. His unit was withdrawing as the attack had been postponed when the Germans shelled their position in no-man's land. He was the brother of the Battalion's commander, Lieutenant Colonel Raymond Lionel Leane, later Brigadier General and holder of the CB, CMG, DSO & Bar, MC. His cousin, Lieutenant Colonel Allan William Leane, 28th Australian Infantry, died of wounds received at Delville Wood on 4 January 1917 and is buried in Dernancourt Communal Cemetery.

Another here is Sergeant John James White, 22nd Australian Infantry, killed in action on 3 May 1917 aged 29 years. Initially registered as missing in action during the Second Battle of Bullecourt his body was not recovered and his name is on the Australian Memorial at Villers-Bretonneux. In November 1994, while ploughing his field near to the Digger Memorial at Bullecourt, a local farmer found John's remains. His identity disc was still intact as was his wallet containing a letter and a lock of hair which is thought to be from his wife, Lilian. In November 1995 Sergeant White was carried by six Australian soldiers to this grave and buried, with the lock of hair he had brought from Australia, with full military honours in the presence of his 80 year old daughter.

Also here is Reverend The Honourable Maurice Berkeley Peel, MC and Bar, Chaplain 4th Class, Army Chaplains' Department, killed in action on 14 May 1917 aged 44 years.

He was son of Arthur Wellesley Peel, 1st Viscount Peel, former Speaker of the House of Commons and grandson of Conservative Prime Minister Sir Robert Peel. He was educated at Winchester and Oxford becoming ordained in 1899. When the war began he volunteered his services as a chaplain and went to France in October 1914 with the 7th Division, being awarded the Military Cross early in 1915. At the Battle of Festubert he led one of the battalions of his Brigade into attack, carrying only a walking stick. He was severely wounded but refused attention until all the men had been cared for. He was sent home to England to be Vicar of Tamworth. In 1917 he again volunteered, and was sent to his old battalion. He would go into attacks with the third wave so that he might tend to all those who had been wounded or were dying. After the capture of Puisieux in early 1917 he received a Bar to his MC. He was killed by a sniper at Bullecourt, while going out to rescue a wounded man. His son, Major David Arthur George Peel, 2nd Irish Guards, MC, was killed in action on the 12 September 1944 aged 33 years during the advance to the Escaut Canal and is buried in Leopoldsburg War Cemetery in northern Belgium.

Another of note is Private George M Gray, 7th Cameronians (Scottish Rifles), died on 2 September 1918. His brother, Engine Room Artificer 4th Class Frederick Balfour Gray, HMS Laurentic, Royal Naval Volunteer Reserve, died on 25 January 1917 and is buried in Upper Fahan (St. Mura's) Church Of Ireland Churchyard. The SS Laurentic was a liner of the White Star Line. She was commissioned as a troop transport for the Canadian Expeditionary Force. After conversion to armed merchant cruiser service in 1915, she struck two mines off Lough Swilly to the north of Ireland on 25 January 1917 and sank within an hour. Only 121 of the 475 aboard survived. Another brother, Lance Corporal John Gray, 5th Royal Scots, died on 15 April 1918 aged 32 years and is commemorated on the Ploegsteert Memorial.

Concentrated here:

Cagnicourt Communal Cemetery – about 2km north-west of here. It contained the grave of one British soldier who died in September 1918.

Lagnicourt (6th Jaeger Regiment) German Cemetery – situated 1.5km east of the village and about 5km south of here. Among the 137 German graves was one British soldier.

Noreuil British Cemeteries No. 1 and No. 2 - these were close together, about 400m north of the village about 5km south-west of here. The cemeteries were made in April-August 1917 and contained the graves of 50 Australian and sixteen British soldiers. Some were re-buried in H.A.C. Cemetery, Ecoust-St. Mein.

Noreuil German Cemetery No. 1 – this was next to Noreuil Australian Cemetery which is on the southern edge of the village about 5km south-west of here. It contained 78 German graves and ten British burials.

Pronville German Cemetery – located on the western outskirts of Pronville about 2km south of here. There were seventeen British graves among the German burials.

Pronville German Cemetery No. 4 – 1.5km south of Pronville about 2km south of here on the road to Beaumetz-les-Cambrai. It contained 83 German and 83 British graves, 52 of which were soldiers of the Black Watch.

Proville Churchyard – in the southern suburbs of Cambrai. Two British men were buried here.

UK – 1289   Aust – 995   Can – 87
BWI – 2   NZ – 1   Ger – 3
KUG - 5   Unnamed – 1443

Area – 7278 sq mts

Special Memorials to 43 soldiers from Australia, and thirteen British servicemen, known or believed to be buried among the unnamed.

Special Memorials to 26 British soldiers, buried in German cemeteries in the neighbourhood, whose graves could not be found on concentration.

LOCATION

Buissy is about 8km west of Cambrai. The village is situated 1km south of the Arras-Cambrai road. The cemetery is about 2km south-west of the village and 2km north-east of Queant. It lies on the north-west side of the road between the two villages.

QUEBEC CEMETERY, CHERISY

HISTORY

The cemetery was opened after the village fell to the British advance in September 1918. It remained in use during the following month.

INFORMATION

The village was behind the German lines for most of the war. It was entered by the 18th Division on 3 May 1917 but retaken by the Germans at the end of the day. It finally fell to the Allies on the 27 August 1918 when it was captured by the Canadian Corps.

The cemetery was made for the burial of men who died in local fighting from 27 August to 11 September 1918. Most of the Canadians fought in the 22nd and 24th Canadian Infantry, both from Quebec, hence the name of the cemetery.

Among those buried here is Corporal Lucien Savarie, 22nd Canadian Infantry, killed in action on 28 August 1918. Interestingly, the CWGC has his age recorded as 58 years yet the only record of birth I can find is 12 March 1894 which makes him 24 years old when he died.

UK – 6   Can – 189   Unnamed - 12
Area – 703 sq mts

LOCATION
Cherisy is situated about 30km west of Cambrai and 10km south-east of Arras. It is about 2km south of the Arras-Cambrai road. The cemetery is east of the village on a side road on the plateau towards Cambrai. It is in open fields between Cherisy and Vis-en-Artois and best reached by the farm track, and on foot at some times of the year, from Sun Quarry Cemetery on the D38 south-east of the village. This is a very peaceful cemetery with excellent views.

QUEENS CEMETERY, BUCQUOY

HISTORY
The cemetery was begun in March 1917, used until March 1918 and again in April-August 1918. The cemetery was enlarged after the war by the concentration of 690 graves from small cemeteries in the neighbourhood and from the battlefields of the Ancre.

INFORMATION
The village was in German hands from 1914 until March 1917, when it was taken by the 7th Division during the German withdrawal to the Hindenburg Line. It was attacked by the Germans in April 1918, but was partially held by the 62nd (West Riding), 37th and 42nd (East Lancashire) Divisions. It was cleared on the following 21 August.

The cemetery began when 23 men of the 2nd Queen's (Royal West Surreys) were buried in what is now Plot II, Row A. Thirteen graves of April-August 1918 were added in Plot II, Row B in September 1918 by the 5th Division. Approximately 100 burials are men from the Royal Naval Division. When the cemetery was enlarged after the war, fifteen French graves and one American grave were brought here. Ten French graves and the American have since been removed.

Among those here are 2nd Lieutenants Geoffrey Richard Bolitho, and Stanley Norman Williams, both No. 4 Squadron, Royal Flying Corps, killed in action on 25 October 1916. Bolitho, the observer, is recorded as formerly Devonshire Regiment, joining the RFC in May 1916, and aged 23 years when he died. Williams, the pilot, is shown as on the General List. They were flying a BE2c on a bombing mission, took off at 8.45am and were in combat at 10.50am in which Lieutenant O Hohne of Ja2 claims to have shot them down. They were originally buried about 2.5km east of Puisieux and south-east of here.

Concentrated here:

Baillescourt Farm Cemetery, Beaucourt-Sur-Ancre – about 6km south of here in marshy ground between the Farm and the River Ancre. It was made by the V Corps in early 1917. It contained the graves of 64 British men who died in the winter of 1916-17, and in August and September 1918. The Farm was taken by the Honourable Artillery Company in February 1917.

Miraumont Churchyard – about 4km south of here. It contained the graves of ten British men, mostly artillerymen who were buried in February and March 1917.

Miraumont German Cemetery - about 4km south of here. Among the Germans were six British soldiers buried by the Germans in 1915-16.

River Trench Cemetery, Puisieux – the village is 2km south of here and the cemetery a further 1km south in the open country between Grandcourt and Puisieux. It was made by V Corps in 1917. It contained the graves of 117 British soldiers, almost all of the Royal Naval Division, who died in February 1917.

Swan Trench Cemetery, Puisieux - the village is 2km south of here and the cemetery was near the Grandcourt-Puisieux road south of the village. This was made by V Corps when clearing the battlefields in 1917. Buried here were 27 officers and men of the Royal Naval Division, who died in February 1917.

Triangle Cemetery, Miraumont – the village is about 4km south of here and the cemetery was 500m east of the village on the road to Pys. This was a German cemetery containing the graves of 181 German soldiers among which were eight British men.

UK – 698   NZ – 28   Fr – 5
Unnamed – 214   Area – 2631 sq mts

Special Memorials are erected to four British servicemen, known or believed to be buried among the unnamed graves.

Special Memorials record the names of six British soldiers, buried in Miraumont German Cemetery, whose graves were destroyed by shell fire.

LOCATION
Bucquoy is situated about 5km north-west of Bapaume and midway between Albert and Arras. Queens Cemetery is at the south end of the village, on the north-west side of the road to Puisieux and Amiens as the road climbs out of the village.

QUEENS CEMETERY, PUISIEUX

HISTORY
The cemetery was created as part of the battlefield clearance that took place in February 1917.

INFORMATION
The French held the German advance here in 1914 and remained until 1915 when the area was handed over to the British. The village was an objective to be taken early on 1 July 1916 but remained in German hands. It was attacked again in November 1916 but did not fall. The villages of Puisieux and Serre were taken from the Germans on 28 February 1917, lost to them on 26 March 1918 and taken for the final time on 21 August 1918.

Queen Cemetery is on the old British front line, south of Mark Copse. The approximate position of the German line is 50m north of the cemetery. The cemetery was made by the V Corps, as 'The Queens's V Corps Cemetery No. 4', in early 1917, one of a number of cemeteries made during the battlefield clearance. You can see a string of small cemeteries across the ridges following the line of no-man's land of 1 July 1916. The burials here are men of the 31st, 3rd and 19th Divisions who died in July and November 1916 and February 1917.

Many of the unnamed will be men of the 11th (Accrington Pals) East Lancashires who attacked over this ground on 1 July 1916. Accrington was the smallest town in the country to raise a 'Pals' battalion and it was one that paid a heavy price. An identified Accrington Pal buried here is Lance Corporal Alfred Boon Dix who was killed in action on 1 July 1916 aged 39 years. He had enlisted in January 1916 and spent three months in Egypt before arriving in France.

Also here is Captain Arnold Banatyne Tough, 11th (Accrington Pals) East Lancashires, killed in action on 1 July 1916 aged 26 years. He was one of the first to leave Mark Copse at 7.20am, now the edge of Sheffield Memorial Park. He was soon wounded but carried on to lie down in a shell hole just about where he is now buried. At 7.30am, as the rest of his battalion reached him, he stood up to encourage his men in the attack, but was shot and killed.

UK – 311   Unnamed – 131   Area 681 sq mts

LOCATION
Serre-les-Puisieux, commonly called Serre, is situated about 20km south of Arras and 5km west of Bapaume. The cemetery is situated on the Serre battlefield 750m south-west of Puisieux and south of the hamlet of Serre-les-Puisieux. The cemetery is only accessible on foot and is reached by a farm track from the D929 road. The farm track leads 200m to Serre Road No. 3 Cemetery and another 100m to Sheffield Memorial Park from which a path leads back into no-man's land and Queens Cemetery. It is best to park at the road and take a stroll to this cemetery, the other local burial grounds and the Memorial Park. This is not easy to reach if you are not very mobile.

QUERRIEU BRITISH CEMETERY

HISTORY
The cemetery was used from March to August 1918 by Divisions involved in the defence of Amiens.

INFORMATION
The town was the scene of fighting during the Franco-Prussian War of 1870 and there are now Monuments in the village commemorating the action and the dead.

Rawlinson used the chateau at Querrieu as his HQ during the Battle of the Somme in 1916. The Germans used the chateau from 1940-44. Two members of the family who own the chateau died in WW2, one with the Belgian Air Force in 1940 and one in a concentration camp after being caught by the Germans while working with the French Resistance. Another son survived the concentration camp. Buried here is Lieutenant Colonel Christopher Bushell, VC, DSO, 7th Queen's (Royal West Surreys), killed in action on 8 August 1918, aged 30 years. He had served since 1914, being wounded. His Distinguished Service Order was awarded in the New Years Honours List in January 1918 for service during the winter of 1917-18. He won his Victoria Cross on 22 March 1918 and was later killed at Morlancourt. His citation reads 'For most conspicuous bravery and devotion to duty when in command of his battalion. Lt. Col. Bushell personally led "C" Company of his battalion, who were co-operating with an Allied regiment in a counter-attack, in face of very heavy machine gun fire. In the course of this attack he was severely wounded in the head, but he continued to carry on, walking about in front of both English and Allied troops encouraging and re-organising them. He refused even to have his wound attended to until he had placed the whole line in a sound position, and formed a defensive flank to meet a turning movement by the enemy. He then went to brigade headquarters and reported the situation, had his wound dressed, and returned to the firing line, which had come back a short distance. He visited every portion of the line, both English and Allied, in the face of terrific machine-gun and rifle fire, exhorting the troops to remain where they were, and to kill the enemy. In spite of his wounds this gallant officer refused to go to the rear, and had eventually to be removed to the dressing station in a fainting condition. To the magnificent example of energy, devotion and courage shown by their Commanding officer is attributed the fine spirit displayed and the keen fight put up by his battalion not only on the day in question but on each succeeding day of the withdrawal.'

Also buried here is Captain Thomas George Peyton Winmill, 'U' Battery, 16th Brigade, Royal Horse Artillery killed in action on 11 June 1918. He was born in Lucknow in India while he father was serving there. His brother Lieutenant Westropp Orbell Peyton Winmill, 1st Bedfordshires, was killed in action on 23 March 1918 aged 23 years. He had served with the Royal Flying Corps and has no known grave. He is commemorated on the Pozieres Memorial.

The WW2 burial is of Pilot Officer Roger William Burton, No. 85 Squadron, Royal Air Force Volunteer Reserve, killed in action on 20 May 1940. He was shot down in his Mark I Hurricane by Bf109s while ground strafing enemy columns east of Arras. He crashed near Querrieu at 3.30pm.

There is a group of Germans buried here who died as Prisoners of War.

| UK - 102 | Aust – 84 | Chinese – 1 |
| Ger - 12 | WW2 – 1 | Area – 934 sq mts |

LOCATION
Querrieu lies on the road from Albert to Amiens, where it crosses the River Hallue, about 9km north-east of Amiens. The cemetery lies on the eastern side of the road to Bussy-les-Daours beyond an orchard and about 300m from the edge of the village.

QUESNOY FARM MILITARY CEMETERY

HISTORY
The cemetery was only used in April 1918.

INFORMATION
Bucquoy was in German hands until 1917, though it was an objective on 1 July 1916. It was taken by the 7th Division in March 1917 during the German withdrawal to the Hindenburg Line. It was attacked by the Germans in April 1918, but was partially held by the 62nd (West Riding), 37th and 42nd (East Lancashire) Divisions. It was cleared on the following 21 August.

Most of those buried here are 15th or 16th Lancashire Fusiliers though there are also some Manchesters. One of these is 2nd Lieutenant John Baron Rittson Thomas, 4th attached 2nd Manchesters, killed in action on 18 April 1918 aged 20 years. He had started his war as a Lance Corporal in the Buffs (East Kents). Another is 2nd Lieutenant Thomas Lines, MC, DCM, 16th Lancashire Fusiliers, died of wounds on 5 April 1918 aged 33 years. He was a felt hat finisher from Stockport who enlisted into the 10th Cheshires in September 1914. He was promoted to Company Sergeant Major in March 1916 and was awarded the Distinguished Conduct Medal for actions in late 1916 when he held a trench for four hours against a German attack. Despite several disciplinary infringements and a transfer to the 13th Cheshires, he was commissioned in September 1917 and attached to the Lancashire Fusiliers. He was awarded the Military Cross in February 1918 for an action when he commanded a party of 32 men undertaking a night raid near Houthulst Forest north of Ieper. He attacked a position of about nine Germans and shot three men taking another man prisoner. He was mortally wounded in another raid, this time at Ayette, on the nights of 1-3 April 1918.

After the war further burials were made of French bodies concentrated from the surrounding battlefields of 1914-15. They and four German graves were removed in 1923.

| UK – 60 | Unnamed – 1 | Area – 334 sq mts |

LOCATION
Bucquoy is situated about 5km north-west of Bapaume and midway between Albert and Arras. Quesnoy Farm is a large farm in the open country between Bucquoy, Douchy-les-Ayette and Monchy-au-Bois, and the cemetery is 270m north-west of the farm house. There is a rough but passable farm track from Monchy-au-Bois, but it is better to follow the CWGC sign from the D919 in Bucquoy along the farm track for 3km to the farm and the cemetery. It is very isolated and peaceful with great views.

RAILWAY CUTTING CEMETERY, COURCELLES-LE-COMTE

HISTORY

The cemetery was made in August 1918 after the capture of the village.

INFORMATION

The village was in German hands from 1914 until 1917 when they withdrew to the Hindenburg Line. It fell to them again in March 1918. The village was taken, for the final time, by the 3rd Division on the 21 August 1918.

The cemetery contains the graves of soldiers who belonged to the 2nd, 3rd, 37th and 63rd Divisions and most died between 21 and 28 August 1918.

Among those buried here is Captain Barrie Dow Robertson, 4th Royal Fusiliers, killed in action during a British advance near Achiet-le-Grand on 22 August 1918 aged 27 years. He joined the 17th (Empire) Royal Fusiliers as a Private in September 1914 and arrived in France in October 1915. He fought on the Somme in 1916, notably at Beaumont-Hamel. He was then recommended for a commission so went to train in England and returned to France as a 2nd Lieutenant in the 4th Royal Fusiliers. In March 1918, as a consequence of holding an important position against the German advance with only twenty men, he was promoted to Captain.

UK – 107   Unnamed – 16
Area – 650 sq mts

Special Memorial erected to one British soldier believed to be buried among the unnamed.

LOCATION

Courcelles-Le-Comte is about 4km north-west of Bapaume and 20km south of Arras. The cemetery is about 2km south of the village and lies in open countryside on the west side of the Albert-Arras railway. From Gomiecourt, follow the CWGC sign down a track. Park your vehicle after crossing the railway line, then follow the grass path beside the railway to the cemetery.

RAILWAY HOLLOW CEMETERY

HISTORY

The cemetery was used in early 1917.

INFORMATION

The cemetery was made as V Corps Cemetery No. 3 in early 1917 when the battlefields of the Somme and Ancre were cleared by V Corps. You can see a string of small cemeteries across the ridges following the line of the no-man's land of 1 July 1916. The burials here are men of the 31st, 3rd and 19th Divisions who died in July and November 1916 and February 1917.

Among those buried here is Serjeant Maurice Charles Pilford Headeach, MM, 12th (Sheffield City Battalion) York and Lancasters, killed in action on 1 July 1916 aged 42 years. He had enlisted in the battalion as a Private at the start of the war. He had been a scout master before the war and had founded the 2nd Harrow Seas Scouts in 1910.

Sheffield Memorial Park

Sheffield Memorial Park is a wooded area where the frontline trenches and shell-holes have been preserved. It was opened in 1936 to remember the Pals Battalions of the 31st Division. There is an information tablet placed by Sheffield City Council which shows the positions of the battalions on 1 July 1916, along with the German trenches and machine-gun positions. The wood that contains Sheffield Memorial Park was known as Mark Copse, one of four here on the front-line named after the books of the New Testament.

There are several memorials within the park. The largest is a brick built structure commemorating the Accrington Pals (11th East Lancashires) who attacked from the trenches in the Park. The bricks used to construct this memorial are known as 'Accrington NORI' bricks which are still made in Accrington. They are very red in colour from the iron oxides in the clay, and the name 'NORI' apparently comes from the accidental printing in reverse of the word 'IRON'. Next to the Accrington Pals memorial are two smaller memorials with bronze plaques set on their fronts. These commemorate the 'Y' (Chorley) and 'Z' (Burnley and district) Companies of the Accrington Pals.

The shelter is in memory of the Sheffield City Battalion who did not attack from here but from a line approximately 200m north of here. This battalion suffered tremendous losses, with just under 500 casualties, which included 246 killed. Only four officers survived.

The memorial to the Barnsley Pals is made of black granite. It was unveiled in 1998, seven years after the last Barnsley Pal died.

Another memorial is a stone cross to Private Albert Edward Bull. Bull was from Apperknowle in Derbyshire, and was with the Sheffield City Battalion when he was killed on 1 July 1916 aged 22 years. He is buried in the Serre Road No. 2 Cemetery.

At the front of the memorial park, the shallow frontline trench of 1 July can still be made out. The memorial park slopes downhill, and the land still bears the scars of battle. A path leads through the park to Railway Hollow Cemetery in the valley. A trench called Railway Avenue ran 3km to Colincamps.

A memorial to the 12th York and Lancasters (Sheffield City Battalion) can be found in the village of Serre.

UK – 107   Fr – 2   Unnamed – 44
Area – 370 sq mts

LOCATION
Serre-les-Puisieux, commonly called Serre, is situated about 20km south of Arras and 5km west of Bapaume. The cemetery is situated on the Serre battlefield 750m south-west of Puisieux and south of the hamlet of Serre-les-Puisieux. The cemetery is only accessible on foot and is reached by a farm track from the D929 road. The farm track leads 200m to Serre Road No. 3 Cemetery and another 100m to Sheffield Memorial Park through which you pass to reach this cemetery at the foot of a valley. It is best to park at the road and take a stroll to this cemetery, the other local burial grounds and the Memorial Park. This is not easy to reach if you are not very mobile.

RANCOURT MILITARY CEMETERY

HISTORY
This cemetery was begun in late 1916 following the Battles of the Somme. It remained in use until the German withdrawal to the Hindenburg Line in early 1917. It was used again during September 1918 and for the burial of six men after the war.

INFORMATION
Rancourt was captured by the French on 26 September 1916 and handed over to the British soon after. It came to be behind the front-lines following the German withdrawal in 1917. However, the village fell to the Germans in the early stages of their advance in 1918 and was not recaptured until 1 September 1918 when the 47th (London) Division attacked this area.

This cemetery was begun by the Guards Division but the majority of the burials here were made by the 12th and 18th Divisions in September 1918. The six men concentrated here after the war were brought in from isolated positions in the surrounding battlefields.

Also to be found nearby are the French National Cemetery, opposite this Cemetery, containing nearly 4300 graves and the German Cemetery with nearly 4000 burials.

The WW2 burials are of three airmen who died in May 1940. The CWGC records for 1957 show they were unidentified but, following a prolonged effort by local amateur historians and a Canadian researcher, the CWGC recognised the graves of these three airmen in June 2015. We now know they were Pilot Officer Cyril Light, aged 22 years, and two Sergeants, Arthur Ernest Craig aged 33 years and George Hawkins, DFM, aged 30 years, of No. 18 Squadron, killed while flying a Blenheim IV which was shot down by German flak while trying to prevent the German advance on the Channel. They took off from RAF Watton in Norfolk at about midday and were shot down at 3.00pm. Hawkins was awarded his Distinguished Flying Medal in March 1940. He and Craig had been involved in a crash on take-off only two days before their deaths.

UK – 93   Unnamed – 17   WW2 – 3
Area – 334 sq mts
Special Memorial to a British soldier who is known to be buried in one of the unnamed graves.

LOCATION
Rancourt lies astride the Arras-Peronne road about 10km south-east of Bapaume and a similar distance north of Peronne. This cemetery lies on the west side of the road about 1km south of the village. It is opposite the much larger French National Cemetery and set back from the road so access is by a track.

RED CROSS CORNER CEMETERY, BEUGNY

HISTORY
The cemetery was begun by the British in April 1917. It remained in use until March 1918 when the Germans began their offensive. The Germans used the cemetery during their occupation of the village in 1918. Further burials were made by the British in September 1918.

INFORMATION
The village of Beugny was behind the German lines until it fell to the British in March 1917 during the actions following the German withdrawal to the Hindenburg Line. At the time of the British occupation they named the point where the light railway crossed the road at the west end of

the village as 'Red Cross Corner'. Field Ambulances and front-line units made Plot I of the cemetery before the village fell to the Germans in 1918.

While the Germans occupied the village, from March to August 1918, they incorporated the cemetery into Beugny Military Cemetery No. 3. They buried 350 Germans and 35 British soldiers, 25 of whom died on 21 March 1918, on the north and west sides of the British burials. In September 1918 Plot II was made by the British. After the war the German graves were removed and the British graves in the German section were concentrated in Delsaux Farm or Favreuil British Cemeteries.

Among those buried here are Canadian 2nd Lieutenant Wilfred Ferguson MacDonald and British Lieutenant Frank Charles Shackell, pilot and observer of a FE2b of No 18. Squadron, Royal Flying Corps shot down and killed at about 1.30pm on 23 May 1917. Observer-Gunner Shackell had been commissioned as a 2nd Lieutenant in March 1916 having been a Company Quartermaster Sergeant. Pilot MacDonald was born in Ottawa in 1894 was awarded Aviators' Certificate No. AM437 in March 1916 and claimed one enemy aircraft shot down.

Also here is Lieutenant Philip Dudley Waller, 71st Siege Battery, South African Heavy Artillery, died on 14 December 1917 aged 28 years. He played Rugby Union for Wales in five Tests and the British 'Lions' who toured South Africa in 1910, winning two of three matches in which Waller featured in all matches. Waller stayed in South Africa after the tour. He was killed by shellfire.

UK – 205   Aust – 10   SAfr – 4
Ger - 1   Unnamed - 12   Area – 958 sq mts

Special Memorial erected to one British soldier whose grave was destroyed by shell-fire.

LOCATION
Beugny is a village on the Bapaume-Cambrai road about 5km from Bapaume. The cemetery is 50m south of the main road at the west end of the village. There is a path which leads to the cemetery from the road.

REDAN RIDGE CEMETERY No. 1, BEAUMONT-HAMEL

HISTORY
The cemetery was created in February 1917.

INFORMATION
The cemetery was made by the V Corps in early 1917 when the battlefields of the Somme and Ancre were cleared by V Corps. You can see a string of small cemeteries across the ridges following the line of no-man's land of 1 July 1916. The burials here are men of the 4th and 2nd Divisions who died in July and November 1916. The 2nd Division captured this location in November 1916. Most burials here are from that attack.

Among those here is Captain Ronald John Ranulph Leacroft, MC, 1st Somerset Light Infantry, killed in action on 1 July 1916 aged 22 years. He and his brother joined the Somerset Light Infantry in which Ronald was commissioned in March 1913. He was wounded at Mons in 1914. In February 1915 he was made Captain after being awarded the Military Cross. The citation for his Military Cross reads 'For conspicuous gallantry when leading a raid on the enemy's trenches. When the enemy exploded a mine he directed his parties for over two hours under heavy fire. It was mainly, owing to his coolness and personal example that his men succeeded in covering the working parties during the consolidation.' Unfortunately for Ronald, he did not get credit for the award properly as it was initially gazetted to Captain Geoffrey Charles Ranulph Leacroft and later corrected.

UK – 154   Unnamed – 74   Area – 600 sq mts

LOCATION
Beaumont is about 24km south of Arras and 6km north of Albert. The Redan Ridge Cemeteries (Nos. 1, 2 and 3) are situated to the north of the village. The three are accessed by a road that runs between Beaumont-Hamel and the D919 at Serre Road No. 1 Cemetery. No. 1 and No. 3 are close together with this being about 150m further north from the road. It is close to the rear of Serre Road No. 2 Cemetery. This cemetery has excellent views of the battlefield from its position on top of the ridge. It is best to park and walk the last 300m on the farm track.

REDAN RIDGE CEMETERY No. 2, BEAUMONT-HAMEL

HISTORY
The cemetery was created in February 1917.

INFORMATION
See Redan Ridge No. 1 Cemetery.

Redan Ridge Cemetery No. 2 is about 90m west of the old German front line. Most headstones bear two names and most date from 1 July 1916.

Buried here is Serjeant Frederick Joseph Allsworth, MM, 'A' Company, 1st Hampshires, killed in action on 1 July 1916 aged 42 years. He enlisted in the 3rd Royal Berkshires militia at the age of 17 years in November 1890 and joined the army, following in his elder brother's footsteps, in 1891 leaving his job as a plumber's labourer. He served in England until December 1893, and then Bermuda, Canada, and the West Indies again until he returned to England in 1898. From December 1899 to September 1902 he was involved in the South African Wars during which he was promoted to Lance-Corporal and then Corporal. His younger brother Walter had joined the Royal Berkshires in 1897 and also served in South Africa. He left the army in 1903 and re-joined the militia. For a time he worked for the Great Western Railway as a Mechanic's Labourer in the Locomotive and Carriage Department in Oxford. He returned to the army in 1914 and was awarded his Military Medal posthumously for bravery in the actions in which he was killed. He and another member of his regiment awarded the Military Medal, Corporal G. Mills, share a gravestone.

UK – 279   Unnamed – 124   Area – 364 sq mts

LOCATION
Of the three Redan Ridge cemeteries this is the closest to the village being about 200m north of the village centre. It is accessed by a track from the road. It is at the head of the valley which leads to Beaumont-Hamel Cemetery. This position gives excellent views of the German lines.

REDAN RIDGE CEMETERY No. 3, BEAUMONT-HAMEL

This cemetery lies within the old German front line trenches. Most burials here are men of the 2nd Division who died in November 1916. There are no identified officers buried here.

Among those here is Serjeant William George Saunders, MM, 2nd Oxford and Bucks Light Infantry, killed in action on 13 November 1916. He was from London and was a policeman before the war earning the Police Service, Police Long Service and Good Conduct Medals. He entered the Western Front as a Private in September 1914.

UK – 67   Unnamed – 34   Area – 283 sq mts

Special Memorials to thirteen men whose graves were destroyed by shell fire.

LOCATION
No. 1 and No. 3 Redan Ridge cemeteries are close together with this being closer to the road. This cemetery has excellent views of the battlefield from its position on top of the ridge.

HISTORY
The cemetery was created in February 1917.

INFORMATION
See Redan Ridge No. 1 Cemetery.

REGINA TRENCH CEMETERY, GRANDCOURT

HISTORY
The cemetery was opened in November 1916 when this area had been captured during the Battles of the Somme. It remained in use until March 1917 when the Germans withdrew to the Hindenburg Line. The cemetery was greatly enlarged after the war by the concentration of graves from the surrounding battlefields.

INFORMATION
Grandcourt, to the north-west, was entered by units of the 36th (Ulster) Division on 1 July 1916 but was not held. It was occupied by the Howe Battalion of the 63rd (Royal Naval) Division in February 1917. Courcelette, to the south-east, was taken by the 2nd Canadian Division on 15 September 1916 after heavy fighting. Both villages fell to

the Germans during the spring advance in 1918 and were retaken by the Allies late in 1918.

Regina Trench was a major German communication trench, and later a defensive position, between Grandcourt and Courcelette. It was the longest trench built by the Germans in WW1. It was captured briefly by the 5th Canadian Brigade on 1 October 1916 but soon lost. Another attempt was made on 8 October by the 1st and 3rd Canadian Divisions but it was not until 21 October that the British 18th and 4th Canadian Divisions managed to capture and hold part of the trench. The rest of the position was taken on 11 November by the 4th Canadian Division.

The cemetery that now makes up Rows A to D of Plot II containing 179 graves was begun in the trench. The rest of the cemetery was made after the war when 2086 graves were concentrated from isolated positions and smaller cemeteries around Courcelette, Grandcourt and Miraumont. The majority of the concentrated graves were men who died from October 1916 to February 1917. Many of the graves in this cemetery contain more than one burial and the cemetery is designated a Canadian cemetery.

Among those buried here are four airmen near the War Stone, two of whom are unidentified. The others are First Lieutenant Ervin Shaw, Signal Reserve Corps, USA, who was attached to the Royal Air Force, and his observer Sergeant Thomas Walter Smith. They were killed when their Bristol Fighter of No. 48 Squadron, RAF was shot down nearby on the evening of 9 July 1918. No. 48 Squadron had been the first to be equipped with the new Bristol aircraft which proved highly successful throughout the remainder of the war. Ervin Shaw was a native of South Carolina, USA and the Shaw Air Force Base there, named in his honour, ranks as one of the oldest installations in the United States Air Force. Today, Shaw Air Force Base is the home of 9th Air Force Headquarters and the 20th Fighter Wing and is the largest combat F-16 fighting wing.

Concentrated here:

Courcelette Road Cemetery, Miraumont - situated about 1km north of here on the west side of the road between Courcelette and Miraumont. It was used for the burial of 45 Canadian and 33 British soldiers who died from September to November 1916.

Miraumont British Cemetery - situated close to Courcelette Road Cemetery on the east side of the road. It contained 47 Canadian and 32 British soldiers who died from September to December 1916.

UK – 1667   Can – 563   Aust – 35
Others – 1   Unnamed - 1077
Area – 6847 sq mts

Special Memorials to thirteen British soldiers and one Canadian who are believed to be buried among the unidentified graves.

LOCATION

Grandcourt is situated in the valley of the River Ancre about 10km north of Albert. Courcelette lies just to the north of the Albert-Bapaume road about 10km north-east of Albert. The cemetery is found on the plateau, known as the 'Plaine de Courcelette', between the two villages. It is CWGC signed from both villages but is reached by means of a farm track that can be treacherous for vehicles in winter. This track, known to the Army as 'Twenty-Three Road', undulates over the farmland between the villages and has a small turning crossroads of farm tracks on the Courcelette side of the cemetery.

RIBECOURT BRITISH CEMETERY

HISTORY

The cemetery was begun in November 1917 and used until March 1918. It was used again in September and October 1918.

INFORMATION

Ribecourt was behind the German lines for most of the war. The village was captured by the 9th Norfolks on 20 November 1917 as part of the Battle of Cambrai and remained as a front-line village in British hands through the winter. The Germans recaptured the village at the start of their offensive in March 1918 but the village was taken for the last time by the British 3rd and 42nd Divisions on 27 September 1918. The cemetery was made by the 3rd Division in October 1918 for the burial of their men who died in taking the village.

There are several officers and men of 'E' Battalion, Tank Corps buried here who were killed in the Battle of Cambrai.

Some of the battalion were tasked to attack Flesquieres just north of here on 20 November 1917 in which attack 'E' Battalion deployed 35 tanks. By the afternoon, eighteen had been destroyed or disabled by enemy action, one was ditched and further nine were unserviceable due to technical difficulties. Of the men, 29 were dead, 31 were missing and 64 were wounded. The officers include 2nd Lieutenant John Howells commanding Female tank No. 16 'Empress II', 2nd Lieutenant G Testi commanding Male tank No. 11 'Egypt II', 2nd Lieutenant Thomas Wilson commanding Wire Crusher 'Exquisite' and 2nd Lieutenant M Atkinson commanding Male tank No. 17 'Edinburgh', all from No. 15 Company.

A mystery surrounds Captain Samuel Blackwell, DSO, killed on 20 November 1917. He is recorded by the CWGC as serving with 'D' Company, 9th Norfolks. He is also shown in several sources, including his headstone, as being in the Tank Corps. However, a 2nd Lieutenant Blackwell is shown as commanding Male tank No. 23 'Egbert II' of No. 14 Company, 'E' Battalion at the Battle of Cambrai. He originally enlisted in the Motor Cyclist Section, Royal Engineers and received a Distinguished Service Order whilst serving as a 2nd Lieutenant with the 9th Norfolks in 1916. The citation reads 'He led a reinforcement party over the open under very heavy fire, bombing back the enemy and maintaining his position against three enemy counter-attacks for 36 hours. Later, he led a daring patrol, and proceeded over 100 yards along the enemy line and obtained valuable information'.

UK – 266   NZ – 22   RGLI – 1
Ger – 6   Unnamed – 18
Area – 1002 sq mts

Special Memorials to 81 British soldiers whose graves were destroyed by shell fire.

LOCATION
Ribecourt-la-Tour is situated about 10km south-west of Cambrai and about 30km directly east of Bapaume. It is just to the west of the A26-E17 Autoroute. The cemetery is on the south side of the village on the road to Villers-Plouich.

RIBECOURT RAILWAY CEMETERY, RIBECOURT-LA-TOUR

HISTORY
The cemetery was opened and closed in October 1918 for the burial of men who were killed in the final capture of the village.

INFORMATION
The cemetery was made by the 3rd Division in October 1918 for the burial of their men who died taking the village. Among those here is Serjeant Percy Dolman, MM & Bar, 1st Gordon Highlanders, killed in action on 1 October 1918 aged 21 years. He enlisted in the Highlanders in May 1915 arriving in France in December. He was wounded and sent home in June 1917, returned to France in August and was gassed in June 1918. At some point he had been serving with the Royal Engineers. He was killed leading a successful attack on a German position which had resisted previous attacks during the day. While the CWGC website shows Military Medal and Bar, other records show only the award of a Military Medal but no Bar.

UK – 52   NZ – 1   Unnamed – 1
Area – 329 sq mts

LOCATION
The Railway Cemetery is at the north-east edge of the village on a side road about 30m south of the road to Marcoing. The railway is now gone but the cemetery lies on the edge of the valley where the route of the former railway can still be made out.

RIBECOURT ROAD CEMETERY

HISTORY
The cemetery was opened in November 1917 and remained in use until February 1918. It was used again in October 1918.

INFORMATION
The first burials are now in Plot I Rows B, C and D. They are mostly men from the 51st (Highland) and 59th (North Midland) Divisions. The other burials are almost all men of the 42nd Division killed in capturing Ribecourt. The cemetery was at that time known as the Divisional Cemetery, Trescault.

Among those here is Private George Heard, DCM, MM, 1/7th Lancashire Fusiliers, killed in action on 27 September 1918 aged 33 years. He was awarded the Military Medal for acts in the field in March 1918. The Distinguished Conduct Medal followed for the following on 29 July 1918: 'During an attack by our troops when the leader of his section was severely wounded, he carried him under point-blank machine-gun fire to a place of cover, and then returned and took command of his section and fought the enemy under heavy machine-gun fire and bombing. Two days later he commanded a section in a daylight raid, and though wounded before leaving our lines, he carried on with admirable courage and endurance, attacking a party of 40 of the enemy in their trenches and killing several. His gallant conduct and devotion to duty and endurance were admirable.' It is of note that he served, and was awarded his medals, under the name of Heardley.

UK – 255   NZ – 6   Unnamed – 8
Area – 1015 sq mts

LOCATION
Trescault is a small village about 10km south-west of Cambrai. The cemetery is on the north-eastern edge of the village on the south side of the road to Ribecourt. It stands in fields about 20m from the road.

RIBEMONT COMMUNAL CEMETERY EXTENSION

HISTORY
The Extension was used from May to August 1918 when burials were made by units engaged in the defence of Amiens. The Extension was greatly enlarged after the war by the concentration of graves from east of Ribemont.

INFORMATION
The British took over this sector in 1915 and the railway station became a major railhead. Burials began in the Communal Cemetery in March 1918 and over the next four months fourteen Australians were buried there.

The Communal Cemetery Extension was opened in May 1918 and by the end of the war 68 burials had been made. After the war over 400 graves were concentrated in the Extension. In 1929 the graves from the Communal Cemetery were moved into the Extension and buried near the Cross of Sacrifice.

Buried here is Lieutenant John Algernon Wynyard Peyton, 7th Norfolks, killed in action on 22 August 1918. He left Oxford University with a degree in History and joined the army as a 2nd Lieutenant in the Norfolks in March 1915. He went to France in April 1916 and was wounded a month later. After recovery he returned to the Front in January 1917 and was again severely wounded a few weeks later. His final move to the Front was in April 1918 by which time he had been made a Lieutenant. His only brother, 2nd Lieutenant Montagu Frank Peyton, 16th Northumberland Fusiliers, was killed in action on 12 July 1917 in the Battle of the Dunes at Nieuwpoort aged 19 years. He is buried in Ramscappelle Road Military Cemetery in Niewport.

Several men buried here were executed. Trooper Alexander Butler, Royal Canadian Dragoons, was executed on 2 July 1916 for murder. He was British and had served with the 7th Hussars before re-enlisting in Canada. He shot Trooper E Mickleburgh on 8 June 1916 firing five shots at him. Butler's good character had been affected following at least two serious falls from a horse.

Driver Thomas Grant Hamilton, 72nd Battery, 38th Brigade, Royal Field Artillery, executed on 3 October 1916 for striking a senior officer, 2nd Lieutenant Oates, who disciplined him for smoking on parade. It was agreed by General Rawlinson that 2nd Lieutenant Oates had not handled the incident well so Rawlinson suggested a prison sentence. Haig disagreed which led to his execution.

Driver James Mullany, 72nd Battery, 38th Brigade, Royal Field Artillery, executed on 3 October 1916 for striking a senior officer. He struck the Battery Sergeant Major when instructed to prepare the transport as it meant he would miss his tea. He and Hamilton had been tried on 20 September. One other man from the unit was executed for the same offence, three of only six men executed for striking an officer.

Private John Cameron, 1/5th Northumberland Fusiliers, executed on 4 December 1916, the only man here executed for desertion. He had been on the Western Front for a year.

Concentrated here:

Heilly British Cemetery No. 2 - situated in the grounds of Heilly Chateau about 3km south-west of this Extension. It was made from April to August 1918 and contained the graves of 79 Australian and 24 British soldiers. Heilly No. 1 Cemetery is now called Heilly Station Cemetery.

Henencourt Wood Cemetery - situated about 5km north of this Extension. It was located in the wood about 1km west of Henencourt on the north side of the Henencourt-Warloy road. It was made from June 1916 to August 1918 and contained the graves of 71 British and 34 Australian soldiers, one Canadian, one South African and a soldier who remains unidentified.

Henencourt Communal Cemetery And Extension - situated on the eastern edge of the village that is about 5km north of here. The Communal Cemetery contained one British and one Australian soldier while the Extension contained 26 British and nine Australian soldiers buried in 1918.

Point 106 British Cemetery, Bresle - situated about 2km north-west of Bresle which is about 3km north of here. It was used from March to May 1918 for the burial of a British soldier and 24 Australians.

UK – 269	Aust – 190	Can – 4
SAfr – 2	India - 1	
KUG - 15	Unnamed – 33	

Special Memorials to two Australians buried in Ribemont Communal Cemetery whose graves were destroyed.

Special Memorial to one Australian soldier buried in Heilly British Cemetery No. 2 whose grave was destroyed.

Special Memorials to five British and three Australian soldiers buried in Henencourt Wood Cemetery whose graves were destroyed in later fighting.

Special Memorials to seven Australian soldiers buried in Point 106 British Cemetery whose graves were destroyed.

LOCATION
Ribemont lies in the valley of the River Ancre about 8km south-west of Albert. The Communal Cemetery is on the northern edge of the village on the west side of the road to Baizieux. The Extension is on the south-west side of the Communal Cemetery.

ROCQUIGNY-EQUANCOURT ROAD BRITISH CEMETERY, MANANCOURT

HISTORY
The cemetery was opened in May 1917 and it remained in use until March 1918. The British made further burials in September 1918.

INFORMATION
This area was under German control for much of the war until it fell to the British in April 1917. The Germans retook the area on 23 March 1918 but the British re-occupied it at the start of September.

The cemetery was mainly used by the 21st and 48th Casualty Clearing Stations that were stationed here and in the nearby village of Ytres until March 1918. The later burials were made by the 3rd Canadian and 18th CCS. The Germans made burials of British troops when they held the area in 1918. They called it Etricourt Old English Cemetery. The bodies of two French soldiers and an American Medical Officer have been removed.

Among those buried here is Sergeant John Harold Rhodes, VC, DCM and Bar, 3rd Grenadier Guards, died on 27 November 1917 aged 26 years. A former miner who had served three years in the 3rd Grenadier Guards before the war he was called back to the colours in 1914 serving through the Retreat from Mons, the Battle of the Aisne and First Ypres. He won the Distinguished Conduct Medal as a Lance Corporal in the 2nd Grenadier Guards in May 1915 for gathering intelligence and rescuing men from no-man's land on more than one occasion. In August, as a Corporal, he dug men out of a collapsed trench for which he was awarded a Bar to his DCM. In January 1917 he returned to the 3rd Grenadier Guards. He won his Victoria Cross in October 1917 during the Battle of Poelkapelle at Ieper. The citation reads 'For most conspicuous bravery when in charge of a Lewis gun section covering the consolidation of the right front company. He accounted for several enemy with his rifle as well as by Lewis gun fire, and, upon seeing three enemy leave a "pill-box," he went out single handed through our own barrage and hostile machine-gun fire, and effected an entry into the "pill-box." He there captured nine enemy including a forward observation officer connected by telephone with his battery. These prisoners he brought back with him, together with valuable information.' He was killed a few weeks later at the start of the Battle of Cambrai dying in 48th CCS of wounds received while attacking Fontaine Notre Dame.

Also here is Private Joseph Bateman, 2nd South Staffordshires, executed for desertion on 3 December 1917. He went absent in late September 1917 when his unit were told they were being sent to the trenches. He surrendered a few days later at a Prisoner of War Camp dressed as a Sergeant. He escaped from prison on 18 October and was captured again six days later at Boulogne.

Nearby is an isolated grave, that of Captain Cecil Robert Tidswell, No. 19 Squadron, Royal Flying Corps and 1st (Royal) Dragoons who was shot down on 16 October 1916 aged 36 years. He was flying one of seven BE12's from his Squadron who had attacked Hermies station and aerodrome in the afternoon. It is about 1km south of here.

UK – 1764	Newf – 22	NZ – 21
Can – 12	SAfr – 12	Aust – 5
RGLI – 2	Fr Civ – 10	Ger – 198
Unnamed – 21		Area – 6808 sq mts

Special Memorials erected to nine British soldiers, buried here by the Germans, but whose graves are lost.

LOCATION
Manancourt is situated 10km north of Peronne and a similar distance south-east of Bapaume. It lies on the west bank of the Canal du Nord. The Rocquigny-Equancourt road is 2km north of Manancourt on the northern edge of Etricourt. It used to be a straight road but has been diverted by the Autoroute. The cemetery is on the north side of the road 100m west of the crossroads with the Manancourt-Ytres road.

ROISEL COMMUNAL CEMETERY EXTENSION

HISTORY

This cemetery was begun by the Germans, who made a burial ground to the north of the Communal Cemetery. It was used by the 41st, 48th, 53rd and 58th Casualty Clearing Stations who made burials north of the German cemetery in October and November 1918. The cemetery was enlarged after the war by the concentration of graves from isolated positions and small burial grounds around Roisel.

INFORMATION

Roisel was in German hands for most of the war. It was occupied by British troops in April 1917, and lost on the evening of the 22 March 1918 despite a strong defence by the 66th (East Lancashire) Division. It was retaken in the following September and then became an important centre for medical units.

Burials were first made in the Communal Cemetery. At the end of the war, besides German graves, 94 British men, 24 Australian soldiers, and one man of the United States Army had been buried here. All of the graves, except that of 2nd Lieutenant Eric Allan Gifford Coules (See Roisel Communal Cemetery), have been removed into the Extension. The graves of 88 soldiers from the USA have been removed.

Buried here is 2nd Lieutenant John Crawford Buchan, VC, 7th attached 8th Argyll and Sutherland Highlanders, killed in action on 22 March 1918 aged 25 years. The citation for his Victoria Cross says 'For most conspicuous bravery and devotion to duty. When fighting with his platoon in the forward position of the battle zone, 2nd Lt. Buchan, although wounded early in the day, insisted on remaining with his men, and continually visited all his posts, encouraging and cheering his men in spite of most severe shell fire, from which his platoon was suffering heavy casualties. Later, when the enemy were creeping closer, and heavy machine-gun fire was raking his position, 2nd Lt. Buchan, with utter disregard of his personal safety, continued to visit his posts, and though still further injured accidentally, he continued to encourage his men and visit his posts. Eventually, when he saw the enemy had practically surrounded his command, he collected his platoon and prepared to fight his way back to the supporting line. At this point the enemy, who had crept round his right flank, rushed towards him, shouting out "Surrender." "To hell with surrender," he replied, and shooting the foremost of the enemy, he finally repelled this advance with his platoon. He then fought his way back to the supporting line of the forward position, where he held out till dusk. At dusk he fell back as ordered, but in spite of his injuries again refused to go to the aid post, saying his place was beside his men. Owing to the unexpected withdrawal of troops on the left flank it was impossible to send orders to 2nd Lt. Buchan to withdraw, as he was already cut off, and he was last seen holding out against overwhelming odds. The gallantry, self-sacrifice, and utter disregard of personal safety displayed by this officer during these two days of most severe fighting is in keeping with the highest traditions of the British Army.'

Also here is Captain Thomas Pilling Gibbons, MC, MiD, 1/1st Hertfordshires, killed in action on 22 March 1918. Thomas joined up and received his commission as Lieutenant in October 1914 and went to France in January 1915. When the German spring offensive of 1918 began the Hertfordshires were in reserve, but were soon moved into the line, between Epehy and St. Emilie, on 21 March. As the 16th Division withdrew the following day, the Hertfordshires, serving as the rearguard, were heavily involved all day, suffering 21 killed in action over two days. Gibbons was posthumously awarded the Military Cross in May 1918. Three other officers were killed with Thomas that day covering the retreat - Major John Bolle Tyndale Gough, Lieutenant Donovan Perry and 2nd Lieutenant Charles Leonard King who is also buried here. Gough is at Ste. Emilie Valley Cemetery, Villers-Faucon while Perry's body was lost and he is commemorated on the Pozieres Memorial.

A burial of note is The Reverend William Edgar Jones (or Evans or Evans-Jones). He was Chaplain 4th Class attached to the 9th Yorkshires and died at a casualty clearing station on 24 October 1918 from the wounds he had previously received during the Battle of the Selle. He was 30 years of age.

A battalion commander here is Lieutenant Colonel Alfred Durham Murphy, DSO, MC, three times MiD, 2nd Leinsters, killed in action on 6 November 1917 aged 27 years. He went to France as Transport Officer and Lieutenant in 1914, was promoted to Captain and Adjutant in early 1915, Major in May 1916 and took command of the battalion in August 1916. He was awarded his Distinguished Service Order for for gallantry at Wytschaete on 7 June 1917 during the Battle of Messines. He was killed while inspecting a group of his men in the trenches when a large German shell exploded in the middle of them, instantly killing him and seven soldiers. They are buried together.

Another battalion commander here is Lieutenant Colonel Bernard Hedley Charlton, MC, twice MiD, 4th Yorkshires, killed in action on 22 March 1918 aged 32 years. He had joined this unit before 1908 serving as a 2nd Lieutenant. As a Captain, Charlton was with the battalion when they first went to France in April 1915 and were almost immediately involved in the Second Battle of Ypres. On 25 May 1915 in a German attack outside Bellewaarde, he was badly gassed and spent some time in hospital. On 28 October he was appointed Adjutant of the Battalion, on 10 November

Mentioned in Despatches and in the New Year's Honours List for 1916 he was awarded the Military Cross. At Kemmel on 16 June 1916 he was wounded when the 4th Yorkshires suffered a heavy German bombardment of their trenches. By September 1916 the 4th Yorkshires were involved in the latter stages of the Battle of the Somme. Charlton had by this time been promoted to Major and was signing the War Diary as the Officer Commanding. During 1917 Major Charlton was again Mentioned in Despatches. In the German advance in March 1918 the 4th Yorkshires were placed in the centre of the line defending against the offensive during which he was killed.

Concentrated here:

Bernes Churchyard – about 6km south of here. It contained the graves of 49 British soldiers of the 46th (North Midland) Division and the Royal Field Artillery buried in September 1918.

Bernes Churchyard German Extension - among the Germans was one British soldier buried in September 1917.

Hesbecourt Communal Cemetery Extension – located 2km east of here. It contained 35 Australian and 28 British soldiers buried by the 59th (North Midland) Division in April 1917, and by Australian units in September and October 1918.

L'abbaye German Cemetery, Vermand – Villecholles is on the north-eastern edge of Vermand which is situated 6km south of here. The cemetery lay between the village of Vermand and the hamlet of Villecholles. Among the graves of 300 German soldiers were ten British men and one Canadian who died in April and May 1917.

Roisel Churchyard – in the centre of the village. One officer of the Royal Flying Corps was buried here in August 1916.

Vermand Communal Cemetery German Extension - situated 6km south of here. Among the Germans were seven British soldiers buried by the Germans in March and April 1918.

UK – 721   Aust – 106   S Afr – 29
Can – 6   Ger – 514   Unnamed - 120
Area – 6010 sq mts

Special Memorials are erected to twelve British soldiers and one from Australia who are known or believed to be buried among the unnamed.

Special Memorials record the names of two British soldiers, buried in other cemeteries, whose graves could not be found on concentration.

LOCATION

Roisel is a small village about 8km east of Peronne and 15km north-west of St. Quentin. The Communal Cemetery Extension is on the north-west edge of town on the east side of the road to Villers-Faucon and Nurlu.

RONSSOY COMMUNAL CEMETERY

HISTORY

The Communal Cemetery was used for burials by the Germans throughout the war until the village fell. During this time they buried eight British soldiers. The other British burials were made in September-October 1918.

INFORMATION

One group of six graves can be found near the entrance. They are men of the 6th Connaught Rangers, including the Medical Officer, killed in December 1917. With them is an unidentified soldier from the Royal Inniskilling Fusiliers. One soldier from the 7th Queens (Royal West Surreys), killed in January 1917, is buried alone among the graves of French soldiers. These make up the eight men buried by the Germans.

The main plot contains the graves of 38 British and Australian men and a German soldier killed in September 1918. Three American graves have been removed.

The Medical Officer mentioned above was Captain James McKee Ferguson, MiD, 6th Connaught Rangers, killed in action on 27 December 1917 aged 31 years. He graduated in March 1914 and was appointed Medical Officer in the Union Infirmary, Belfast. He took a temporary commission as a Lieutenant in the Royal Army Medical Corps in December 1914. He went to France in October 1915 as Medical Officer with the 9th Royal Dublin Fusiliers and was promoted to Captain in December 1915. He was then transferred to the 6th Connaught Rangers, and was serving with them when he was killed.

UK – 38   Aust – 7   Ger – 1
Unnamed – 7   Area – 174 sq mts

LOCATION

Ronssoy is a village situated about 20km south of Cambrai and 10km east of Peronne. It is 1km west of the A26 Autoroute so is on the edge of the area covered by this book. The cemetery is in the village just north-west of the centre on Rue Marie-Louise Frison near a large factory entrance tucked behind the houses on the main road through the town. The main group of graves are on the southern edge of the cemetery surrounded by a hedge.

ROOKERY BRITISH CEMETERY, HENINEL

HISTORY
The cemetery was used from April to November 1917, though a further two burials were made in August 1918.

INFORMATION
The village of Heninel was captured in a snowstorm on 12 April 1917 by the 56th (London) and 21st Divisions. The 50th (Northumbrian) Division, advancing from Heninel on the two following days, captured Wancourt.

The cemetery, begun by the 18th and 50th Division Burial Officers, was named after a trench system here.

Interestingly, this cemetery has neither a Remembrance Stone or a Cross of Sacrifice.

Among those here is Lieutenant Charles David Calcott, 18th (2nd Liverpool Pals) King's (Liverpools), killed on 23 April 1917 aged 23 years. He was a former pupil of Shrewsbury School. He was commissioned as a 2nd Lieutenant in July 1915 having served with the Shropshire Yeomanry and then been in Officer Training. He arrived in France in February 1916. He is shown in the CWGC records as being with the 15th King's (Liverpools) but this was a 'Reserve' battalion and the one from which he was transferred to the 18th King's (Liverpools).

UK – 55   Unnamed – 1   Area – 334 sq mts

LOCATION
Heninel is situated about 5km south-east of Arras in the valley of the River Cojeul. The cemetery is about 1km south-east of the village. It is reached by taking a small road or farm track south from the Heninel-Cherisy road. This small road takes you past Cherisy Road East Cemetery. About 400m south of Cherisy Road East Cemetery is a path leading north-east from the road which leads about 100m to this cemetery. It stands in farmland and is very peaceful in an attractive location but it can be difficult to reach.

ROSIERES BRITISH CEMETERY

HISTORY
The cemetery was used for the burial of men who died from 23 to 25 March 1918.

INFORMATION
Rosieres was the scene of heavy fighting between the French Sixth Army and the German First Army at the end of August 1914. It was then in German hands until it fell to the British in February 1917. In the German offensive of March 1918, the town was defended by the 8th Division and the 16th Brigade, Royal Horse Artillery in what is called the Battle of Rosieres, but they withdrew on the evening of 27 March. On the 9 August 1918 the town was retaken by the 2nd Canadian Division supported by tanks.

The cemetery consists of one row of graves. An American grave has been removed. One man buried here did not die in 1918. He is Private George Frankis, 1st Leinsters, who died on 3 October 1915. He was originally buried in Proyart Communal Cemetery about 5km north of here and was moved here in 1935. He was the only burial in the Communal Cemetery, while an extension had several British graves. That is now a German Cemetery.

Also here is Corporal Vernon H Andrews, MM & Bar, twice MiD, 3rd Cavalry Field Ambulance, Royal Army Medical Corps, died on 24 March 1918 aged 21 years. He was an Assistant Scout Master in 1st Jersey (St. Simon's) Troop of Boy Scouts and had been at the Front throughout the war going to France with the 1st Cavalry Division. He had been Mentioned in Despatches by French and Haig and had been awarded the Military Medal for gallantry in action on several occasions in 1914 and 1915 in March 1915, though he himself had been wounded and had been recommended for the Distinguished Conduct Medal. He received a Bar or Silver Rose to his MM in the Birthday Honours List in June 1916. He was the only man from Jersey to receive a MM & Bar. He died at a Casualty Clearing Station on Palm Sunday having been struck in the face by a bomb.

UK – 60   Unnamed – 6   Area – 436 sq mts

LOCATION
Rosieres-en-Santerre is a small village in the southern area covered by this book. It lies about 15km south-west of Peronne and 20km east of Amiens. It is about 2km south of the A29 Autoroute. The cemetery lies in open country about 1km north of Rosieres between the village and Vauvillers. It is about 100m from the D337 road and is accessed by a CWGC path.

ROSIERES COMMUNAL CEMETERY

Buried here is 2nd Lieutenant Cyril Rayner, 18th (2nd South East Lancashire Pals) Lancashire Fusiliers, killed in action on 24 February 1917 aged 24 years. A former pupil of Reigate Grammar School he had joined the 1/5th Queen's (Royal West Surreys) territorials on leaving school while also working with an insurance company. He won prizes for shooting. At the start of the war, the 1/5th Queen's went to India while 'Regulars' were called to the Western Front. However, like many others Rayner wished to be fighting the Germans so he applied for a commission, which he obtained bringing him to the Lancashire Fusiliers as the Lewis Gun Officer. He went to France in June 1916 where he served for several months before his death.

UK – 10   Fr - 140

LOCATION
The Communal Cemetery is on the north side of the village and is best accessed from the D28. It is south of the railway and the new industrial developments. The graves are in one Plot in the south-west corner next to a Plot of French graves.

HISTORY
The Communal Cemetery was used for the burial of British soldiers in February and March 1917.

INFORMATION
See Rosieres British Cemetery.

ROSIERES COMMUNAL CEMETERY EXTENSION

Regimental Quartermaster Sergeant. He was awarded his Distinguished Conduct Medal for 'conspicuous gallantry and devotion to duty. As a non-commissioned officer he set a fine example throughout the campaign. His cheerfulness and courage, many times under the most trying circumstances, had proved invaluable.'

Concentrated here:

Camouflage Cemetery, Rouvroy-en-Santerre – about 3km south of here, near the south-west side of the road from Rouvroy to Warvillers. It was made by the 32nd Division in March 1917 and contained sixteen graves of British soldiers, thirteen of whom belonged to the 2nd King's Own Yorkshire Light Infantry.

Poplar Trench Cemetery, Meharicourt - 2km south-east of here. It contained nineteen British graves.

UK –123   Can – 156   Aust – 66
Chinese – 1   KUG – 82   Unnamed - 157
Area – 1699 sq mts

Special Memorials to three British soldiers, two from Australia and one from Canada, known or believed to be buried among the unknown graves.

Special Memorials to five soldiers buried in Camouflage Cemetery, Rouvroy, and one buried in Rosieres German Cemetery, whose graves were not found on concentration.

LOCATION
The Extension is at the west end of the Communal Cemetery.

HISTORY
The Extension was made after August 1918 and enlarged after the war.

INFORMATION
The Extension was begun as a Canadian burial ground which is now Plot I, Rows A-E. It was enlarged after the war by the concentration of 329 graves from the small cemeteries and battlefields surrounding Rosieres.

Among those buried here is Serjeant Mark Abraham Mayson, DCM, MM, 5th (Royal Irish) Lancers, killed in action on 9 August 1918 aged 30 years. He had served with 'A' Squadron, 5th Lancers for ten years, and also acted as

ROSSIGNOL WOOD CEMETERY

HISTORY
The cemetery was begun in March 1917 by the 4th Division. A German plot was added after the war by concentration from the battlefields immediately to the south and south-west.

INFORMATION
Hebuterne was held by the French from the start of the war and taken over by the British in the summer of 1915. It was close to the front-line when the German advance in this area in 1914 was held. The Germans only occupied the village and wood for a brief period from March to July during the summer of 1918. The wood dominates the area and was a strong-point in German defences in 1916 and 1918.

The burials here reflect distinct periods and actions. First, the majority are men killed on 14 March 1917 when an attack by 1/5th and 1/6th North Staffordshires, who had been involved in the disastrous action at Gommecourt on 1 July 1916, was ordered during the German withdrawal to encourage them to speed up their retreat. It was a poorly prepared night attack against the German position on the edge of Rossignol Wood. The attack suffered 133 killed of which 32 are buried here. This includes two Company commanders, Captain Samuel Brammer Wilton, MC, and Captain Arthur Felix Wedgwood, as well as a senior Non-Commissioned Officer, Company Sergeant Major Wingate all of the 1/5th battalion. The second group are the German dead killed during the advance of 1918. The third are the New Zealanders killed in August 1918.

Captain Samuel Brammer Wilton, MC, 'C' Company, 1/5th North Staffordshire Regiment, killed in action on 14 March 1917 aged 25 years, was a student at Cambridge when war broke out. He joined the battalion as a Private in August 1914 and was commissioned in December. He was wounded by shrapnel in August 1915 returning to France in June 1916. He was awarded the Military Cross posthumously for his service as a whole rather than a specific act.

UK – 34   NZ – 7   Ger – 70
Unnamed - 2

LOCATION
Hebuterne lies about 20km south-west of Arras and about 7km west of Bapaume. Rossignol Wood Cemetery lies approximately 1km north-east of the village, on the south side of the road between Gommecourt and Puisieux midway between the two villages. It is about 400m west of Rossignol Wood and very close to Owl Trench Cemetery opposite it on the other side of the valley.

ROUPY COMMUNAL CEMETERY

HISTORY
The cemetery was only used to bury men killed on 1 April 1917.

INFORMATION
Ten of the men buried here belonged to the 2nd Royal Inniskilling Fusiliers. Among them is 2nd Lieutenant Henry Howard Cockburn who was killed in action on Sunday 1 April 1917 at Savy Wood. He enlisted on 1 December 1915 and joined the Inns of Court Officer Training Corps. At the time of his enlistment he was 31 years old and a commercial traveller. He was posted to No. 7 Officer Cadet Battalion at Fermoy on 11 August 1916 where he underwent officer training, finishing on 18 December 1916. He was commissioned into the 4th Royal Irish (Special Reserve) as a 2nd Lieutenant on 8 January 1917, a battalion on home service, handling drafts to and from France. After three months, Cockburn received orders to proceed to France, to join the 2nd Royal Inniskilling Fusiliers embarking on 15 March 1917. He survived less than two weeks at the front.

UK – 12   Unnamed - 1

LOCATION
Roupy is about 5km south-west of St. Quentin. The cemetery is about 500m north of the village on the road to Savy. The British graves are together at the rear on the right of the main path.

ROYE NEW BRITISH CEMETERY

HISTORY

The cemetery is a concentration cemetery made entirely after the war by the concentration of graves, almost all of 1918, from the battlefields and from other burial grounds.

INFORMATION

Roye fell to the Germans on 30 August 1914 and remained in their hands until the French captured the town on 17 March 1917. It fell again to the Germans on 28 March 1918 before the French took it for the final time on 27 August 1918.

Most of the men buried here were Prisoners of War or casualties of the 1918 fighting when the Army boundary between the French and British was just north of the town. Among those here is Captain Harold Augustus Hodges, twice MiD, 3rd Monmouthshires attached 11th (St. Helens Pioneers) South Lancashires, killed in action near Ham on 24 March 1918. Hodges, a Rugby Union prop-forward, was capped twice for England in the 1906 Home Nations Championship. In 1911 he made his first-class cricket debut for Nottinghamshire against Derbyshire. He was Mentioned in Despatches in April and November 1917. On the night of 24 March 1918, he entered a small factory on a road between Ham and Eppeville, hoping to make contact with a British battalion, but he encountered enemy troops and was killed.

The cemetery also contains the graves of 43 Second World War airmen. Most were men of Bomber Command and nearly all date from the spring of 1944 when raids on the French railways were made in preparation for D-Day. One crew, flying a Stirling of No. 90 Squadron, was shot down flying supplies to the French Resistance.

One of the airmen buried here is Wing Commander Alan George Seymour Cousens, DSO, DFC, Military Cross (Czechoslovakia), No. 635 Squadron, Royal Air Force, killed in action on 22 April 1944 aged 30 years. His Lancaster was shot down in a raid in the railway yards at Laon. His crew, with one exception, are all buried here, the exception survived and was taken prisoner. Cousens received his Distinguished Flying Cross in January 1942 with the following citation after 39 sorties 'Three of Squadron Leader Cousens' flights were to Berlin, and when returning from one of these operations, one night in February 1940, fog compelled him to abandon the aircraft by parachute. In so doing he broke his ankle. Since he was selected in June 1941 as Group Navigation Officer, he has set an admirable example by taking every opportunity to engage in night operations. His skill as a navigator and total disregard for his own safety have been quite outstanding. His flights have been mostly against heavily defended targets in Germany.' His Distinguished Service Order was awarded in November 1942 with the following citation 'By his untiring efforts as navigator and his terrific keenness to press home the attack, this officer has contributed in a large measure to the success achieved by his squadron. He is a fine squadron commander, who has raided many of the highly important industrial targets in enemy territory.'

Concentrated here:

Cressy Churchyard French Extension – the village of Cressy-Omencourt is about 10km north-west of here and the churchyard is in the village centre. It contained 36 British soldiers who were reburied by the French authorities after the war and later moved here.

Dancourt German Cemetery No. 1 – the village of Dancourt-Popincourt is about 2km south-west of Roye and the cemetery was west of the village. It contained the graves of two Royal Air Force officers killed in June 1918.

Dreslincourt German Cemetery – situated about 10km north-east of here on the road to Potte. Among the Germans were buried four British soldiers.

Ferme D'ereuse French Military Cemetery, Berny-sur-Noye – about 20km west of here and on the west side of the farm. Two men of the Tank Corps were buried in July 1918, and one Royal Air Force Officer was added in August 1918.

Goyencourt German Cemetery – the village is about 2km north-west of Roye and the cemetery was on the road to Roye. Here were buried six British men in March-June 1918.

Hattencourt French and German Cemeteries – the village is 5km north of Roye and the cemeteries were on the road to Fresnoy-les-Roye which is between Roye and Hattencourt. Among the French and German graves were fifteen British men.

La Faloise French Military Cemetery – located about 20km west of Roye. The cemetery was near the road to Esclainvillers which is 2km east of La Faloise. Here were nine men of the Tank Corps buried in July 1918 and one Royal Air Force Officer buried in August 1918.

Marchelepot British Cemetery – the village is about 10km north of Roye and the cemetery was on the north-east side of the village. It was used by the British in the early months of 1918 and by the Germans in March—August 1918. It contained 115 British graves.

Roye Communal Cemetery – on the road to Nesle on the east side of town. It contained the grave of one unidentified British soldier buried in 1918.

Roye German Cemetery – among the Germans were 85 British soldiers buried by the Germans in March and April 1918.

Roye Old British Cemetery – this was 1.5km south of the town, between the roads to Lassigny and Montdidier. It was made in March 1918 by the 53rd Casualty Clearing Station just before the German advance and capture of

Roye. The Germans then used the burial ground. The British graves were moved here in 1920.

Solente Communal Cemetery (Oise) – about 4km east of Roye. It contained the grave of one British officer buried in March 1918.

UK – 350	Can – 65	SAfr – 6
Aust – 1	Ger – 2	WW2 – 43
Unnamed – 153		Area – 1579 sq mts

Special Memorials are erected to twelve British soldiers and one from South Africa known or believed to be buried among the unnamed.

Special Memorials record the names of 109 British soldiers, seven South Africans and one Canadian, buried in Marchélepot British Cemetery and in three German cemeteries, whose graves could not be found upon concentration.

LOCATION
Roye is at the southern edge of the area covered by this book. It is about 25km south-east of Amiens and a similar distance south-west of St. Quentin. This cemetery is south-east of Roye near the N17 or D1017 bypass. From the N17 take the D934 towards Noyon. Roye New British Cemetery will be found on the right about 250m along this road.

RUYAULCOURT MILITARY CEMETERY

HISTORY
This cemetery was begun in April 1917 and remained in use, mainly by the 42nd (East Lancashire) Division, until March 1918. It was used again briefly in September 1918.

INFORMATION
Ruyaulcourt village was in German hands from 1914. It was attacked by the 7th Duke of Cornwall's Light Infantry on the night of 28-29 March 1917. Although the Germans withheld the attack the village was found unoccupied the next night by the 7th Somerset Light Infantry. The Germans re-captured the village again on 23 March 1918. It changed hands for the final time when it was captured by the New Zealand Division on 4 September 1918.

Ruyaulcourt German Cemetery was used by the Germans from July 1916 to March 1917 and in August 1918. At the end of the war it contained 405 German graves. With them were the graves of two Royal Air Force officers, two British soldiers and one New Zealand soldier. The cemetery was removed in 1924. At that time the British graves were brought into the Military Cemetery.

Among those buried here is Lieutenant Colonel Thomas Andrew Dunlop Best, DSO and Bar, Royal Inniskilling Fusiliers commanding 2/5th Duke of Wellingtons, killed in action on 20 November 1917 the first day of the Battle of Cambrai, aged 38 years. He served in the South African War, being severely wounded at the Battle of Colenso. In 1914 he joined a battalion of the Inniskillings and accompanied it to Gallipoli. He was severely wounded at the landing at Suvla Bay, where he displayed the greatest courage, and was decorated with the Distinguished Service Order. He was not fully recovered from his wounds when he insisted on going to France in command of the Duke of Wellingtons, and was killed leading his men in the advance on Cambrai.

Also here is Lieutenant The Honourable Arthur Middleton Kinnaird, MC, 1st Scots Guards killed in action on 27 November 1917 aged 32 years. He was son of the 11th Baron Kinnaird. His brother Captain The Honourable Douglas Arthur Master of Kinnaird, 1st Scots Guards, was killed on 24 October 1914 aged 35 years and is buried in Godezonne Farm Cemetery near Ieper.

Another grave of note is that of Lieutenant Colonel Adrian Charles Gordon, DSO, MiD, 235th Brigade, Royal Field Artillery, killed on 12 December 1917. He followed in his father's footsteps and pursued an early career in shipping but also joined the Territorial Force. When war broke out he immediately put his name down to join up and eventually went to France on 6 March 1915 as a Major with the 16th (County of London) Battery, 6th London Brigade, Royal Field Artillery. He saw action at the Battle of Loos where he won the Distinguished Service Order. The citation reads 'For conspicuous gallantry, ability and resource at Maroc 25 Sept. 1915, when he got close although under heavy fire, captured 12 Germans, after shooting one man with a revolver. On the afternoon of the same day he again went up to reconnoitre the enemy's second line under very heavy fire. On the following day Major Gordon rendered valuable service at Loos by reorganising men who had become detached and taking them to the firing line.' He continued to lead his men, achieving a promotion to the rank of Lieutenant-Colonel in 1916, until he was killed.

| UK – 324 | NZ – 20 | Can – 2 |
| Aust – 2 | Unnamed – 10 | Area – 1608 sq mts |

Special Memorials to two airmen, buried in Ruyaulcourt German Cemetery, whose graves could not be found in 1924.

LOCATION
Ruyaulcourt is situated 10km east of Bapaume, 20km south-west of Cambrai and just on the north side of the A2 Autoroute. The cemetery is about 1km north of the village on the west side of a narrow sunken road leading to Hermies.

SAILLY-AU-BOIS MILITARY CEMETERY

HISTORY
The cemetery was opened in May 1916 in preparation for the coming Battles of the Somme in 1916. It remained in use until March 1917 when the Germans withdrew to the Hindenburg Line. It was used again during the summer of 1918.

INFORMATION
The cemetery was begun opposite the Town Major's dugout. It was used by Field Ambulances in 1916. It was used as a front-line cemetery from April to August 1918.

Among those here is Captain Douglas Stuart Phorson, 18th (1st Durham Pals) Durham Light Infantry, killed on 16 December 1916 aged 27 years. He had studied at Edinburgh University to be a vet and was also in the Territorial Force 3rd Durham Light Infantry. Hence, he was commissioned in May 1915 into the 16th Durham Light Infantry before transferring to 18th Durham Light Infantry where he was promoted to Captain. He was wounded in the attack at Serre on 1 July 1916 but not severely. He was killed when a shell hit his dugout near Hebuterne.

Also here is Captain Geoffroy De Carteret Millais, 1st Bedfordshires, died of wounds, received in an attack on the German line earlier in the day, on 21 August 1918 aged 21 years. His father, John Guille 'Johnny' Millais, was a British artist, naturalist, gardener and travel writer who specialised in painting wildlife and flowers.

Another here is Captain George Clifford Whitaker, 15th (1st Leeds Pals) West Yorkshires, killed in action on 1 July 1916 aged 28 years. A Rugby Union forward for the Headingley (Leeds) club, he had served for two years with the Territorials in the 1/5th Kings Own Yorkshire Light Infantry but joined the Pals as a Private when the war began. He was soon commissioned and promoted to Captain in May 1915. He was part of the recruiting party for the Pals which also included former England and Yorkshire cricketer Major William Booth who was also killed at Serre on 1 July 1916 and who is buried in Serre Road No. 1 Cemetery. Whitaker's body, and that of Booth, were found in the battlefield clearances of 1917 by V Corps.

Another buried here is 2nd Lieutenant Hugh Joseph Fleming, 7th attached 6th Dorsetshires, killed in action on 24 August 1916 aged 20 years. His father, Sir Francis Fleming, KCMG, was a British colonial administrator who had served in the West Indies, Sri Lanka and Mauritius before becoming Colonial Secretary of Hong Kong, Governor of Sierra Leone later of the Leeward Islands.

UK – 212 NZ – 24 SAfr – 2
Aust – 1 Ger – 1 Unnamed – 1
Area – 1789 sq mts

LOCATION
Sailly-au-Bois is situated in the open downland between Arras and Amiens. It is about 15km north of Albert and 20km east of Doullens. The Military Cemetery can be found on the western edge of the village on the south side of the road to Couin.

SAILLY-SAILLISEL BRITISH CEMETERY

HISTORY
This is a concentration cemetery made entirely after the war by the concentration of graves from smaller cemeteries and isolated positions in the surrounding battlefields mainly to the south and east of the village.

INFORMATION
Sailly-Saillisel was in German hands from 1914 and attacked by units of the French Army in September and October 1916 falling on 18 October. It was captured by the Germans again on 24 March 1918 and recaptured, by the British 18th and 38th Divisions, on 1 September 1918.

The deaths of most of those here date from September 1916, March 1917, August and September 1918.

Among those buried here is Private David Condon, 1st Irish Guards, killed in action on 15 March 1917. He was from Tipperary, Ireland and aged 22 years when he was killed. He arrived in France in September 1916 after a year of 'home' duty. His first experience of the trenches will have been on 13 November 1916 north of Lesboeufs where he had three days and nights in the line. In January 1917 the Guards Division took over the trenches in this area from the French. The Germans began to withdraw to the Hindenburg Line in early 1917 mainly on 16-19 March in this area. On 15 March the Guards Division found the German trenches opposite the British line to be

unoccupied so the 1st Irish Guards advanced. They came under long-range machine-gun and artillery fire while they were consolidating captured German trenches named 'Bayreuth' and 'Gotha'. They remained under fire taking casualties including the battalion second in command who died of his wounds. Condon was one of thirteen killed.
Concentrated here:
Aldershot Cemetery, Bouchavesnes - situated about 1km north of the village which is about 4km south of here. It contained 34 British graves, mostly men of the 58th Division that captured the village on 1 September 1918, though the cemetery had been opened in February 1917.
Charing Cross Cemetery, Sailly-Saillisel - situated in the fields about 1km south-west of the village. It contained 46 British graves, 34 from Guards units, and was made from December 1916 to March 1917.
Hebule Military Cemetery, Sailly-Saillisel - situated west of the village on the south side of the road to Morval. It gained its name from a nearby quarry. It contained 30 British soldiers, 28 from Guards units, and was made between December 1916 and March 1917.
Morval New Cemetery - situated on the north side of the Sailly-Morval road at the site of the present Autoroute. It contained 39 men of the 38th Division who died from 31 August to 4 September 1918.

UK – 559   Aust – 12   Newf – 7
KUG - 185   Unnamed – 301
Area – 2313 sq mts

Special Memorials to eight British soldiers known, or believed, to be among the unidentified graves.

LOCATION
Sailly and Saillisel are two villages that seem to be one on the east side of the Arras-Peronne road. They are about 10km south of Bapaume and a similar distance north of Peronne. The cemetery lies on the west side of the Arras-Peronne road about 1km south of the village.

SAINS-EN-AMIENOIS COMMUNAL CEMETERY

HISTORY
This cemetery contains four British and two Canadian burials who died from 29 to 31 March 1918. The French burials are almost all of April and May 1918 with one who died on 16 July 1916.

INFORMATION
This is one of seven burial grounds north of the River Somme and behind the line for most of the war that contain a very few Allied military burials.
Among those here is Lieutenant John Harry Knox, 2nd Canadian Railway Troops, killed in action on 30 March 1918 aged 23 years. He enlisted in September 1915 becoming the recruiting officer for the 127th Canadian Infantry. He went to France in January 1917 and was killed by shrapnel when returning to his trench from a machine-gun position.

UK – 4   Can - 2   Fr - 52

LOCATION
Sains-en-Amienois is situated about 5km south of Amiens. The cemetery lies on the western edge of the village on the north side of Rue de Cauriers. The graves are at the rear of a plot of French military burials and hidden from the road by a high hedge.

SAINS-LES-MARQUION BRITISH CEMETERY

HISTORY
The cemetery was begun on 28 September 1918 and remained in use until the middle of October. It was enlarged after the war by the concentration of graves from the surrounding battlefields.

INFORMATION
The village was behind German lines for much of the war until captured by the 1st Canadian Division on 27 September 1918. The 3rd Canadian Infantry Brigade began the cemetery on the following day. At the end of the war it contained 222 graves and another 61 were concentrated here from the local area and Marquion Churchyard.
Marquion Churchyard was destroyed in the war and the burial ground is now closed. Eight German graves were removed to Maison-Blanche German Cemetery, Neuville-St. Vaast while the British graves were brought here.

Among those buried here is Private James Young, 7th Canadian Infantry, killed in action on 27 September 1918.

Young owned a grocery store in Vancouver so did not volunteer. Once the Canadian government had introduced conscription Young was called up in January 1918. He arrived in France in June 1918. Young was killed by German machine-gun fire during the crossing of the Canal du Nord. Jim Vallance, a Canadian songwriter who collaborates with Canadian singer Bryan Adams is James Young's relative. In 1986 Vallance and Adams wrote a song entitled Remembrance Day which commemorates both James Young and Bryan Adams' own grandfather.

Also here is Captain Walter De Mayhew King, MC, Adjutant of the Canadian Light Horse, killed in action on 30 September 1918. He joined up with the 1st Canadian Divisional Cavalry Squadron as a Squadron Sergeant Major on 21 September 1914. He had prior military service of six years with Lord Strathcona's Horse (Royal Canadians) and 19th Alberta Dragoons (militia). He was single and a 'prospector'. He was awarded the Military Cross in January 1918.

| UK – 69 | Can – 185 | Aust – 1 |
| Unnamed - 28 | | Area – 722 sq mts |

LOCATION
Sains-les-Marquion can be found 10km west of Cambrai and about 3km south of the Arras-Cambrai road. It is in the north-eastern sector of the Somme battlefields. The cemetery is at the crossroads on the eastern edge of the village.

SANDERS KEEP MILITARY CEMETERY

HISTORY
The cemetery was created by the Guards Division in the days after the Scots Guards captured the village of Graincourt-les-Havrincourt in 1918.

INFORMATION
The village and this area was in German control for much of the war. It was taken briefly during the Battle of Cambrai but ended the battle in German hands, though it was on the front-line until the German advance of March 1918. Sanders Keep was a German redoubt or defensive position close by which was taken by the Scots Guards on 27 September 1918.

There had been a Plot of German graves on the north side outside the walls of the cemetery. They have been removed.

Buried here is Lance Corporal Thomas Norman Jackson, VC, 1st Coldstream Guards, killed in action on 27 September 1918 aged 21 years. The citation for his Victoria Cross reads 'For most conspicuous bravery and self-sacrifice in the attack across the Canal Du Nord, near Graincourt. On the morning of the 27th September, 1918, Lce. Cpl. Jackson was the first to volunteer to follow Capt. C. H. Frisby, Coldstream Guards, across the Canal du Nord in his rush against an enemy machine-gun post, with two comrades he followed his officer across the Canal, rushed the post, captured the two machine-guns, and so enabled the companies to advance. Later in the morning, Lce. Cpl. Jackson was the first to jump into a German trench which his platoon had to clear, and after doing further excellent work he was unfortunately killed. Throughout the whole day until he was killed this young NCO showed the greatest valour and devotion to duty and set an inspiring example to all.' Frisby was also awarded the Victoria Cross. He survived the war.

Also here is Captain William Herbert Gladstone, MC, 1st Coldstream Guards, killed in action on 27 September 1918 aged 20 years. He was commissioned in January 1917 joining the army straight from school and was awarded the Military Cross in April 1918, the citation reads 'For conspicuous gallantry and devotion to duty. When in command of the main attacking party during a raid, he led his party with splendid dash, and on the barrage lifting gauged the right moment to rush the enemy front line. By his prompt action he forestalled the enemy taking the offensive, and rendered possible the unmolested approach of the whole raiding party to hostile lines'. He was commanding 'A' Company when killed. He was grandson of the British Prime Minister, William Ewart Gladstone. His brother, Lieutenant Charles Andrew Gladstone, Intelligence Department, attached to Royal Flying Corps from April 1915, became a Prisoner of War in Germany when shot down over Ieper on 30 April 1915. Another brother, Sir Albert Charles Gladstone, served throughout the war and had won a gold medal in rowing at the 1908 Olympics A cousin, Lieutenant William Glynne Charles Gladstone, MP, 1st Royal Welsh Fusiliers, was killed in action, shot by a sniper, on 13 April 1915 aged 29 years. He had been an MP since 1911 and his body was the last to be officially repatriated during the war so he lies in Hawarden (St. Deiniol) Churchyard near Chester.

| UK – 142 | Unnamed – 7 | Ger - 49 |

Area – 755 sq mts

LOCATION
Graincourt-les-Havrincourt is about 10km south-west of Cambrai and 1km west of the junction of the A2 and A26 Autoroutes. It is at the eastern border of the area covered by this book. The cemetery is on a ridge between Graincourt and Havrincourt 100m east of the D15 road between the two villages and about 2km south-west of Graincourt. There is a mainly tarmac track from the road.

SAULCOURT CHURCHYARD EXTENSION

HISTORY
Burials began in April 1917 and continued until September 1918 though some burials of British men were made by the Germans.

INFORMATION
The villages of Saulcourt and Guyencourt were in German hands for most of the war until they were captured by the British 5th Cavalry Brigade and armoured cars on 27 March 1917. Supplies of armour-piercing bullets had been sent forward by the Germans after Roisel was captured on the previous day, resulting in the armoured cars being peppered with bullet-holes. However, the armoured cars decoyed the German defenders, while cavalry got round the flanks and captured the villages. The villages were lost during the German spring offensive in March 1918 and retaken in September 1918.

The graves in Rows C and D were made by the Germans, when they held this area, for the burial of men who fell in the March 1918 German offensive. The grave of an American soldier has been removed. There was a German Extension on the south-west side of this cemetery which has been removed, though there remain a few Germans within this cemetery.

Among those buried here is 2nd Lieutenant Robert Oakley Vavasour Thorp, MC, 1st Northumberland Fusiliers attached 64th Trench Mortar Battery, killed in action on 22 March 1918 aged 39 years. He was a teacher before the war having graduated and taken a Masters at Cambridge University. He enlisted with the 21st (4th Public Schools and Universities) Royal Fusiliers in October 1914, and was a Sergeant before being posted for officer training in 1916. He joined the 1st Northumberland Fusiliers as a 2nd Lieutenant in July 1916. He was awarded the Military Cross for conspicuous gallantry in action when he led a successful raid with great courage and determination, killing two Germans and capturing a prisoner. He was later invalided home with Trench Fever but returned to his regiment in 1917 to be attached to a trench-mortar battery. His nephew, 2nd Lieutenant Thomas Tudor Thorp, 'D' Battery, 83rd Brigade, Royal Field Artillery, was killed in action on 16 August 1917 aged 20 years and is buried in Tyne Cot Cemetery near Ieper.

UK – 95   Ger – 7   Unnamed – 33
Area – 630 sq mts
Special Memorials to eight British soldiers who are known or believed to be among the unnamed.

LOCATION
Guyencourt-Saulcourt is a small village located about 10km north-east of Peronne and about 20km south-west of Cambrai. The British cemetery is at the rear of the church which is on the east of the main road through the village. Access is from the churchyard.

SAVY BRITISH CEMETERY

HISTORY
The cemetery is a concentration cemetery made entirely after the war.

INFORMATION
The village was in German hands for much of the war. Savy was taken by the 32nd Division on 1 April 1917, after hard fighting, and Savy Wood, about 1km north-east of the village, on 2 April. On 21 March 1918 Savy was successfully defended by the 30th Division, but they withdrew overnight falling back in the face of the weight of German numbers. The village and the wood were retaken on 17 September 1918 by the French 34th Division, fighting on the flank of the British IX Corps.

Burials were concentrated here in 1919. The burials are mainly men of the 6th, 30th, 32nd, 36th (Ulster) and 61st Divisions.

Among those buried here is Lieutenant Colonel Alexander Fraser Campbell MacLachlan, CMG, DSO and Bar, twice MiD, King's Royal Rifle Corps attached and commanding 12th Rifle Brigade, killed in action on 22 March 1918. He was born in 1875, son of the Reverend A. N. Campbell MacLachlan, vicar of Newton Valence, Hampshire. He was educated at Cheam School, Eton and Magdalen College, Oxford gaining his degree in 1897. He entered the army in 1899 as a 2nd Lieutenant in the King's Royal Rifle Corps, in which he was promoted to Lieutenant in 1900. He served in the South African War where he was wounded,

Mentioned in Despatches and received the Distinguished Service Order for gallantry. He was promoted to Captain in 1906, and was Adjutant of the King's Royal Rifle Corps from 1907-1910. He was at the Retreat from Mons, being severely wounded in September 1914. He was promoted to Major in September 1915, became Lieutenant-Colonel commanding the 13th Manchesters from November 1916 to December 1917 and took over his last command on 7 March 1918. He was Mentioned in Despatches and created a Companion of the Order of St. Michael and St. George. He was originally buried in the Military Cemetery. His brother, Brigadier General Ronald Campbell MacLachlan, DSO was killed in action on 11 August 1917 near Ieper and is buried at Loker Hospice Cemetery. Another brother Major Neil Campbell MacLachlan, was accidentally killed on the Mohmand Expedition on the North West Frontier of India on 24 May 1908.

Also here is Lieutenant William Ashcroft, 19th (3rd Liverpool Pals) King's (Liverpools), killed in action on 22 March 1918. His brother, 2nd Lieutenant Frederick Ashcroft, 18th (2nd Liverpool Pals) King's (Liverpools), was killed in action on 9 April 1917 and is buried in Neuville-Vitasse Road Cemetery. He had been in France since January 1917. Another brother, Lieutenant Edwin Stanley Ashcroft, 17th (1st Livepool Pals) King's (Liverpools), died of wounds in German hands and is buried in Harlebeke New British Cemetery.

Concentrated here:

Dallon German Cemetery – 3km south-east of here on the Somme Canal and north-west of the village. It contained the graves of 21 British men who died in March 1918.

Inniskillings Cemetery, Dallon - the cemetery was on the south side of a small wood, north of the St. Quentin-Savy road about 2km east of here. In April 1917 the 2nd Royal Inniskilling Fusiliers buried seventeen of their men here with three other British soldiers and a French Interpreter.

Lancashire Cemetery – located on the east side of Savy Wood about 1km north-east of here. It was made by the 16th Lancashire Fusiliers in April 1917, and contained the graves of 27 men of the 15th and 16th (1st and 2nd Salford Pals) Lancashire Fusiliers and nine other British soldiers.

St. Quentin—Roupy Road German Cemetery – Dallon is about 3km south-east of here and L'Epine-de-Dallon is on the north side of the village near the D930. Buried here were 232 British soldiers who died in March 1918.

Savy Communal Cemetery Extension – the Communal Cemetery is on the north side of the village on the west side of the road to Holnon. It was used in in April 1917 for the burial of fourteen British soldiers.

Savy Military Cemetery - close to Savy Church in the centre of the village. It was made in April and May 1917 for the burial of 39 British soldiers.

Savy Wood North Cemetery – the wood is about 1km north-east of the village and the cemetery was at the north-west corner of the wood. It was made by the 32nd Division in April and May 1917 for 44 British graves.

UK – 867   Ger – 1   Unnamed – 438
Area – 2555 sq mts

Special Memorials to 68 soldiers, mostly 19th (3rd Liverpool Pals) Kings (Liverpools) and the 17th (2nd Manchester Pals) Manchesters, buried by the Germans in St. Quentin-Roupy Road German Cemetery, whose graves were destroyed by shell fire.

LOCATION

Savy is situated about 5km west of St. Quentin and 1km south of the A29 Autoroute. This cemetery is south-west of the village on the road to Roupy. It is found on the west side of the road about 300m from the village centre.

SENLIS COMMUNAL CEMETERY EXTENSION

HISTORY

This Extension was begun in April 1918 after the fall of Albert and remained in use until August. It was enlarged after the war.

INFORMATION

The cemetery was begun by the 12th and 38th Divisions. The Communal Cemetery contained the graves of 174 French and 23 British soldiers who died from 5 to 9 April 1918. The British men have been moved here.

Among those buried here is Company Serjeant Major Percy Charles Hansford, DCM, 204th Field Company, Royal Engineers, killed in action on 9 April 1918 aged 31 years. An upholsterer before the war, the citation for his Distinguished Conduct Medal, won when he was an acting Sergeant in 1916 reads 'For conspicuous bravery and resource when superintending the construction of a new trench. His officers having been wounded he took control of the R.E. and Infantry parties which were waiting to commence work. He went out alone, laid the trench out under heavy shell fire, got his party to work and carried on for several hours until relieved by an officer. He showed great coolness in controlling a difficult situation.'

UK – 80   Aust – 23   SAfr – 1
Unnamed – 7   Area – 596 sq mts

Special Memorial to one Australian soldier who is believed to be buried among the unnamed graves.

LOCATION

Senlis-le-Sec is about 4km north-west of Albert. The cemetery is on the north side of the village on the west side of a dead end road leading from the road towards Hedauville. It is on a ridge 100m south of a water tower. The Extension is on the south side of the Communal Cemetery.

SERRE ROAD CEMETERY No. 1

HISTORY
The cemetery was created as part of the battlefield clearance that took place in February 1917. It was enlarged after the war.

INFORMATION
The French held the German advance here in 1914 and remained until 1915 when the area was handed over to the British. Serre was an objective to be taken on 1 July 1916, the attack to be made by the 31st Division, which was made up of Pals Battalions, north of this road, while the 4th Division attacked astride this road with some territorials from the 48th Division in support. The attack was an abject failure. Serre was an objective again in November 1916 the advance this time by 3rd and 31st Divisions. It did not fall on either occasion. The villages of Puisieux and Serre-les-Puisieux, commonly called Serre, were taken from the Germans on 28 February 1917, lost to them on 26 March 1918 and taken for the final time on 21 August 1918.

This cemetery is on the British front line of 1 July 1916. The approximate position of the German line is 100m north of the cemetery. The cemetery was made by V Corps when Plot I, Rows A to G were made. These are the burials furthest from the road and face the British line. The men in Plot I are men who died here on 1 July 1916 whose bodies could not be recovered until the German withdrawal to the Hindenburg Line in 1917. Many are West Yorkshires and Durham Light Infantry from 31st Division and Kings Own Lancashires, Essex and Rifle Brigade from 4th Division. There are also territorials of the Royal Warwickshires from the Brigade attached from the 48th Division who attacked with 4th Division on 1 July 1916.

The rest of the cemetery was made after the war. These burials were made such that they filled the space to the road. Over 71% of the graves are unidentified, one of the highest percentages on the Somme.

Among those buried here is 2nd Lieutenant Major William Booth, 15th (1st Leeds Pals) West Yorkshires killed in action on 1 July 1916 aged 29 years. He was a professional cricketer who played for Yorkshire and England, though his international career was restricted to the 1913-14 tour of South Africa. He played in the first test in December 1913 which England won, taking 2 for 38 in South Africa's first innings. He played in the last test, which England won by 10 wickets – the last overseas test before the war. He was in the first wave on 1 July 1916 and was wounded falling into a shell-hole. Soon after he was joined by Abe Waddington, who played cricket for Yorkshire and England after the war. Waddington held Booth until he died. Waddington was rescued later in the day, but Booth's body remained in the shell hole until the battlefield clearance by V Corps. He was identified by the MCC cigarette case in his pocket.

Also buried here are Lance Corporal Charles Guy Destrube, aged 27 years and his brother Private Paul Jean Destrube, aged 26 years, both 22nd (Kensington) Royal Fusiliers and both killed in action on 17 February 1917. The brothers were French Canadians and they are buried in the same grave. They were found in each other's arms.

Another 'man' buried here is Private Horace Iles, 15th (1st Leeds Pals) West Yorkshires, killed in action on 1 July 1916 almost at the location of this cemetery. He enlisted aged 14 years at Leeds Town Hall and was aged 16 years when he died. He had already been wounded in May. His sister wrote a letter to him asking him to admit his age and come home but it was returned with the words 'killed in action' stamped upon it.

Another here is Private Fred Walker, 2/6th West Yorkshires who died on 15 February 1917 aged 27 years. His brother, Private Arthur Walker, 8th York and Lancasters died on 9 April 1917 aged 21 years and is commemorated on the Menin Gate at Ieper. Another brother, Private Harry Walker, 'A' Company, 10th Sherwood Foresters (Notts and Derby Regiment), was killed on 6 May 1918 aged 24 years and is buried in Acheux British Cemetery which is about 6km south-west of here.

Among those buried here is Private Alfred Whibley, 22nd (Kensington) Royal Fusiliers who died on 17 February 1917. His brother, 2nd Corporal Jack Whibley, 61st Field Company, Royal Engineers, who died on 9 August 1915 aged 22 years is buried in Brandhoek Military Cemetery near Ieper. Another brother Carpenter Leo Whibley, died on the SS Orama with the Merchant Navy on 8 June 1940 aged 40 years and is commemorated on the Tower Hill Memorial in London.

There is a memorial to 12th York and Lancasters on the edge of Serre next to the road.

Concentrated here:

Acheux Communal Cemetery French Extension – about 6km south-west of here. Buried here were two British soldiers who died in April and May 1916.

Albert German Cemetery – there were eighteen British soldiers buried by and among the Germans in April and May 1918 while the Germans held the town.

Beaucourt-sur-Ancre British Cemetery – 2km south-east of here in the centre of the village. It was originally known as V Corps Cemetery No. 13. It contained the graves of 21 British men who died between November 1916 and February 1917.

Cerisy-Buleux Churchyard – the village is 15km south of Abbeville and is about 60km from here. It contained the grave of one British soldier buried in November 1916.

Puisieux Churchyard – 2km north-east of here. It contained the graves of two British soldiers buried by the Germans in September 1915.

Ten Tree Alley Cemetery No. 1, Puisieux – this was about 700m south-east of here. It was known as V Corps Cemetery No. 24. It was close to the present Ten Tree Alley Cemetery which was known as No. 2 before this cemetery was concentrated here. It contained the graves of 37 British soldiers who died from November 1916 to February 1917.

UK – 2125	Aust – 147	Can – 120
NZ – 27	SAfr – 6	NF – 1
Unnamed – 1728		Area – 6569 sq mts

Special Memorials to ten British men known or believed to be buried among the unnamed.

Special Memorials to twelve British men, three who were buried in Albert German Cemetery, seven who were buried in Beaucourt-sur-Ancre British Cemetery and two who were buried in Puisieux Churchyard, whose graves have been destroyed by shellfire.

LOCATION
Serre-les-Puisieux, commonly called Serre, is situated about 20km south of Arras and 5km west of Bapaume. The cemetery is 750m south-west of the hamlet on the north side of the D919 just within the boundary of the Department of the Somme. This is an impressive cemetery as it is situated on the slope of the valley up to the Cross of Sacrifice.

SERRE ROAD CEMETERY No. 2

HISTORY
The cemetery was created as part of the battlefield clearance that took place in 1917. It was significantly enlarged after the war.

INFORMATION
See Serre Road No. 1 Cemetery.

This cemetery is on the British front line of 1 July 1916. The approximate position of the German line is 200m north of the cemetery.

It is easy to identify the original cemetery, Plots I and II, as the graves are at a different angle to the concentrated burials. The concentrated burials were brought here over many years from 1922, when the area to the road was filled in, and 1924-36. The cemetery was formally opened in 1938, the last on the Somme. It is the largest CWGC cemetery on the Somme. The percentage of unidentified burials is 69%. There are very few officers and few gunners. Hence this is an infantry cemetery. Six French and two German burials have been removed.

Among those buried here is Lieutenant Colonel Charles Peter Marten, MiD, 1st West Yorkshires attached and commanding 18th (Arts and Crafts) King's Royal Rifle Corps, killed in action on 15 September 1916 aged 36 years. He was gazetted to the 3rd West Yorkshires in 1900. A year later he was appointed to the 1st Battalion at Karachi, India, (now Pakistan) and was Adjutant of that Battalion from 1907 to 1909 during which time he saw action in the Mohmand Expedition in 1908. In 1911 he was promoted to Captain, and in March 1912 was appointed Adjutant of his original Battalion which appointment he held until he was sent to the Front in 1915. In March 1916, he was appointed Second in Command of the 32nd (East Ham) Royal Fusiliers, and on 24 June he was promoted to command the 18th King's Royal Rifle Corps. He was killed by a high explosive shell during the advance on Flers and was buried close to the spot where he fell. Also killed were his Major and three Company commanders. He remains were concentrated here from Delville Wood British Cemetery in 1931.

Another here is Private Albert Edward Bull, 12th (Sheffield City Battalion) York and Lancasters, killed in action in front of Luke Copse on 1 July 1916 aged 22 years. There is now a memorial to him in the Sheffield Memorial Park. His body was discovered in 1928 and then buried here.

Also here is Private Arthur MacDonald Purkiss, 1st Royal Welsh Fusiliers, killed on 4 September 1916 aged 16 years originally buried between Delville Wood and Ginchy. Private Ernest Reeve, 8th Canadian Infantry, killed on 8 September 1916 aged 16 years was originally buried on the northern edge of Pozieres.

One of the original burials here is Private Reginald Luke Prince, DCM, 1st Somerset Light Infantry killed in action on 1 July 1916 aged 30 years. He was awarded the Distinguished Conduct Medal for actions on 8 March 1915 when he continued to operate a forward telephone post after being hit in the mouth by shrapnel. His brother, Lance Serjeant Joseph Ernest Prince, 1st Dorsets was killed in action on 30 September 1918 and is commemorated on the Vis-en-Artois Memorial. Another brother, Serjeant Bertie Leopold Prince, 1st Royal Munster Fusiliers, was killed in action on 20 November 1917 and is buried in Croisilles British Cemetery.

Another to lose two brothers, and also an original burial here, is Captain James Murray Round, MC, 13th Essex, killed on 13 November 1916 aged 22 years. His brother, Lieutenant Auriol Francis Hay Round, 2nd Essex, died, of tetanus in hospital in London while convalescing from wounds received at Le Cateau on 26 August, on 5 September 1914 aged 22 years and is buried in Witham (All Saints) Churchyard near the family home. He was a County cricketer for Essex. Another brother, Captain Harold Cecil Round, DSO, MC, MiD, 6th attached 9th Rifle Brigade, was killed in action on 24 August 1917 aged 21 years and commemorated on the Tyne Cot Memorial near Ieper. He was awarded the Distinguished Service Order as a 2nd Lieutenant near Cherisy on 3-4 May 1917. The citation says 'When our troops were forced to withdraw he collected a few men and made a strong-point within 70 yards of the enemy trench. This position he held for two days without supplies of any kind. He was finally able to get a valuable report through before being ordered to withdraw.'

There is a memorial nearby to 2nd Lieutenant Valentine A Braithwaite, MC, Twice MiD, 1st Somerset Light Infantry, killed in action here on 2 July 1916. He had served in Gallipoli and was killed with his adjutant and fourteen other officers of his battalion attacking the Quadrilateral Redoubt upon which the cemetery is now sited. Braithwaite's body was never recovered and he is commemorated on the Thiepval Memorial. He was the son of Major General, later Lieutenant General, Walter Pipon Braithwaite, commanding 62nd Division and in 1918 IX Corps. Braithwaite's son fought as a Company commander in Normandy in 1944.

It is known that the poet Wilfred Owen served in this area with the 2nd Manchesters. It is believed that somewhere between what is now the cemetery and the French Chapel near Serre Road No. 1 Cemetery is where Owen spent a period in a captured German bunker during January 1917. He wrote to his mother on 16 January 1917 describing the awful conditions of mud and rain while they occupied the line during which one of the sentries was blown down the steps by a bombardment. The soldier had been blinded and the incident may have inspired the poem 'The Sentry' though other locations may also be a suitable place to have been the inspiration.

Near the French Cemetery and Serre Road Cemetery No. 1 there is a small monument. It tells us that in October 2003 the remains of three soldiers were found in the field nearby.

- Wehrmann Jakob Hönes, 09 December 1880 – 13 June 1915, 121st (Württembergisches) RIR
- Vizefeldwebel Albert Thielecke, 31 December 1888 – 11 June 1915, 121st (Württembergisches) RIR
- An unidentified British soldier, died 1 July 1916, King's Own (Royal Lancaster) Regiment

The two German soldiers were reburied at Labry Deutscher Soldatenfriedhof near Verdun on 26 August 2004 while the unidentified British soldier is now buried here.

The cemetery was used in WW2 to hide escaping airmen who had been shot down.

Concentrated here:

Baizieux Communal Cemetery – about 15km south-west of here, the cemetery is on the north side of the village. One British soldier who died in March 1918 was buried here.

Boismont Churchyard – located at the mouth of the River Somme 7km north-west of Abbeville and 50km west of here. One British soldier who died in October 1914 was buried there.

Bucquoy Communal Cemetery – located 5km north of here with the cemetery on the north-east edge of the village. It contained 25 British graves dating from August 1918.

Ercheu Churchyard – located 35km south-east of here and 10km east of Roye. One British soldier who died in March 1918 was buried there.

Frettecuisse Churchyard – located about 45km south-west of here and 25km west of Amiens. One British soldier who died in September 1916 was buried there.

Hervilly Churchyard – located about 35km south-east of here and 10km north-west of St. Quentin. One British airman who died in September 1916 was buried here by the Germans.

Holnon Communal Cemetery - located about 40km south-east of here and 2km west of St. Quentin. It contained the graves of five British men who died in April 1917.

Laboissiere Churchyard - Laboissière-en-Santerre is located nearly 50km south of here and 10km south-west of Roye. One British soldier who died in April 1917 was buried there.

Le Sars German Cemetery – located about 6km south-east of here. One British soldier was buried there.

Madame Military Cemetery, Clery-Sur-Somme – located about 16km south-east of here and 3km north-west of Peronne. It contained three graves of British men who died in February 1917.

Meaulte Churchyard – situated 10km south of here. One British soldier who died in April 1916 was buried there.

Pozieres Communal Cemetery - situated 7km south of here. One Canadian soldier who died in September 1916 was buried there.

Remiencourt Communal Cemetery – located about 35km south-west of here and 10km south-east of Amiens. One British soldier who died in April 1918 was buried there.

Somme American Cemetery, Bony - located about 30km south-east of here and 15km north of St. Quentin. Among the Americans were two British men buried in July and October 1918, and one Australian buried in September 1918.

Voyennes Churchyard – located about 30km south-east of here and 3km east of Nesle. Seven British soldiers were buried in March 1918.

Ytres Churchyard – located about 15km east of here and 7km south-east of Bapaume. Buried here were fourteen British men and four New Zealanders dating from September 1918, mainly buried by the 15th Field Ambulance.

UK – 5971	Aust – 401	Can – 619
NZ – 73	SAfr – 34	NF – 28

Unnamed – 4944 (UK – 4287, Aust – 72, Can – 508, NZ – 29, SAfr – 24, NF – 24)

Ger – 13 (Unnamed – 6)   Area – 27500 sq mts

Special Memorials to 21 British soldiers whose graves are not exactly located in the cemetery.

LOCATION

See Serre Road No. 1 Cemetery. The cemetery is on the south side of the D919 200m south of No. 1 Cemetery.

SERRE ROAD CEMETERY No. 3

HISTORY
The cemetery was created as part of the battlefield clearance by V Corps that took place in 1917.

INFORMATION
See Serre Road No. 1 Cemetery.

This cemetery is in the no-mans's land of 1916. The approximate position of the German line is 100m north of the cemetery. In the spring of 1917, the battlefields of the Somme and Ancre were cleared by V Corps and a number of new cemeteries were made. You can see a string of small cemeteries across the ridges following the line of no-man's land of 1 July 1916.

The burials here are men of the 31st, 3rd and 19th Divisions who died in July and November 1916 and February 1917. Many of those buried here are Leeds and Bradford Pals who attacked the village over this spot on 1 July 1916.

The only officer buried here is Lieutenant Arthur Dudley Maitland, 14th attached 16th (1st Bradford Pals) West Yorkshires, killed in action on 1 July 1916 aged 21 years. The 14th Battalion was a reserve and training battalion. He was one of 22 officers and 493 men of the 1st Bradford Pals lost in the failed attack, many of them killed by German artillery and machine gun fire before they even left their trenches. He is believed to be buried here rather than confirmed.

UK – 81   Unnamed – 49   Area - 294 sq mts
Special Memorials to four British soldiers known to be buried among the unnamed.

LOCATION
Serre-les-Puisieux, commonly called Serre, is situated about 20km south of Arras and 5km west of Bapaume. The cemetery is situated on the Serre battlefield 750m south-west of Puisieux and south of the hamlet of Serre-les-Puisieux. The cemetery is only accessible on foot and is reached by a farm track which leads 200m from the D929 road to this cemetery and then on to the Sheffield Memorial park and several other burial grounds. It is best to park at the road and take a stroll to this cemetery, the other local burial grounds and the Memorial Park. This is not easy to reach if you are not very mobile.

SHRINE CEMETERY

HISTORY
The cemetery was begun in March 1917 and used again in August 1918. It was enlarged after the war as remains were concentrated here mainly from Le Barque and Eaucourt-l'Abbe.

INFORMATION
Bucquoy was in German hands until 1917, though it was an objective on 1 July 1916. It was taken by the 7th Division in March 1917 during the German withdrawal to the Hindenburg Line. It was attacked by the Germans in April 1918, but was partially held by the 62nd (West Riding), 37th and 42nd (East Lancashire) Divisions. It was cleared of Germans on the following 21 August.

The cemetery was named after a crucifix standing on a mound nearby. The cemetery was opened by the 46th (North Midland) Division.

Buried here is Captain Leslie Sayer, MC & Bar, 'A' Company, 16th (3rd Birmingham Pals) Royal Warwickshires, killed in action on 23 August 1918 aged 25 years. He was one of only two men from his school, King Edward's in Birmingham, to win a Bar to the Military Cross. Sayer rose from being a Private in the Royal Warwickshires, commissioned in January 1915, to Captain before he was killed. The other man to win a Bar to his MC from the school was Sayer's brother Alfred, who was also commissioned into the 3rd Birmingham Pals but who survived the war.

UK – 74   Aust – 8   NZ – 7
KUG – 1   Ger – 1   Unnamed – 41
Area – 380 sq mts

LOCATION
Bucquoy is situated about 5km north-west of Bapaume and midway between Albert and Arras. Shrine Cemetery is on the west edge of the village on the road to Hannescamps. The cemetery is partly hidden behind trees in a bend in the road by a shrine.

ST. AMAND BRITISH CEMETERY

HISTORY
The British Cemetery was begun in April 1916 and used until August 1918, though it was used very little in 1917.

INFORMATION
The cemetery was mainly used by the 37th and the 56th (London) Divisions.

Among those buried here is Serjeant James Frederick Norman, 'A' Company, 1/3rd Londons (Royal Fusiliers), killed in action on 29 May 1916 aged 22 years. His brothers were also killed in action. They are Rifleman William John Norman, King's Royal Rifle Corps attached 1/9th (Queen Victoria's Rifles) Londons, killed in action on 16 August 1917 aged 19 years at Langemark near Ieper and commemorated on the Tyne Cot Memorial and Gunner Sydney James Norman, 141st Heavy Battery, Royal Garrison Artillery, killed on on 1 July 1917 aged 27 years and buried at Hop Store Cemetery near Ieper.

UK – 222   NZ – 1   India – 1
Unnamed – 3   Area - 1232 sq mts

LOCATION
St. Amand is situated about 10km east of Doullens and 20km north of Albert. The cemetery is at the north-east corner of the village. The British Cemetery is next to, and on the east side of, the Communal Cemetery.

ST. LEGER BRITISH CEMETERY

HISTORY
The cemetery was opened in March 1917 and remained in use until March 1918. The Germans then used it when they were here from March to September 1918.

INFORMATION
St. Leger was in German hands from 1914 until occupied by British troops in the middle of March 1917 as the Germans retreated to their new Hindenburg Line defence system. It was retaken by the Germans during their advance in March 1918 despite attempts to hold it by the 40th and 34th Divisions. It fell for the final time in late August 1918, being captured by the 62nd (West Riding) and Guards Divisions. The cemetery was created by Field Ambulances when they were stationed here and by men of fighting units. The front row is made up of unidentified German burials and by the graves of two unidentified British soldiers with five men of the Royal Dublin Fusiliers.

Among those buried here is Captain Thomas Trelawny Beaty-Pownall, 3rd attached 2nd Borders, died of wounds on 24 March 1917 aged 35 years. He was brother of Lieutenant Colonel George Ernest Beaty-Pownall, DSO, 1st King's Own Scottish Borderers attached from 2nd Borders, who died of wounds on 18 October 1918 and is buried at Lijssenthoek Cemetery near Ieper. They were sons of Lieutenant Colonel George Albert Beaty-Pownall. Another brother, William Charles Beaty-Pownall, had died aged 21 years in South Africa in 1896 and another in 1903. Another brother served in the Royal Navy notably landing troops for the campaign in the Cameroons in 1914.

UK – 183   India – 1   Ger – 20
Unnamed - 3   Area – 1314 sq mts

Special Memorials to six British soldiers whose graves were destroyed by shelling.

LOCATION
St. Leger is located about 6km north of Bapaume and 10km south of Arras. The cemetery is in a valley north-west of the village and is best reached by walking from the town centre. By car access is by a track just on the western edge of the village leading north from the Rue de la Vallee which leads north-west from the road to Ervillers, but you cannot reach the cemetery without walking the last 300m. There is no turning space on the farm track that leads to the cemetery.

ST. MARTIN CALVAIRE BRITISH CEMETERY

The cemetery was named after a nearby calvary, or shrine, that was destroyed during the war. The cemetery was begun by the 30th Division. These burials make up Plot I. The later burials are what is now Plot II.

Among those buried here is Major Frank Harvey Bowring, 2nd attached 1/9th King's (Liverpools), died of wounds received at Hendecourt on 28 August 1918 aged 39 years. A stockbroker and solicitor from a wealthy family in Liverpool who had emigrated to Newfoundland, he was a keen cricketer and unmarried. He had enlisted in August 1914 as a Private and risen through the ranks. He had three brothers serving who all survived.

Also here is Private Albert McCullough, 7th/8th Royal Irish Fusiliers killed on 20 November 1917 aged 16 years in an action to capture Tunnel Trench.

UK – 228   Ger – 3   Unnamed – 5
Area – 1272 sq mts

HISTORY
The cemetery was opened in April 1917 and used until March 1918. Further burials were made in August and September 1918.

INFORMATION
The village was captured by the 30th Division on 9 April 1917. The Germans re-captured the village in March 1918 but lost it again in August 1918.

LOCATION
St. Martin-sur-Cojeul is about 10km south-east of Arras just west of the A1 Autoroute. The cemetery is in a valley south of the village on a road that leads from the village centre. It is on the south-west side of the Communal Cemetery.

ST. PIERRE (NEW) CEMETERY, AMIENS

the French forces at Amiens in 1918, and to French colonial troops. A memorial to the US 6th Engineers Regiment can also be found. These were 500 engineers who formed part of Carey's Force, a makeshift British group which held part of the line in front of Amiens at the end of March 1918. Finally, there is a memorial, which was added after 1945, to General LeClerc who landed with the French in Normandy. Further afield you will find a memorial on a bridge near the port to the 'Patriots of Amiens' who held the bridge against the Germans on 31 August 1944 to aid the British advance and avoid another 'Battle of Amiens'. In Place Rene Goblet is a memorial to the Picardy Martyrs. Amiens was the headquarters of the French II Corps and during part of August 1914 it was the British advanced base. It was captured by the Germans on 31 August 1914, retaken by the French on 13 September and remained in Allied hands for the rest of the war. Amiens was one of the objectives for the German spring offensive of 1918 but the Battles of Villers-Bretonneux in April 1918 held the German advance about 5km east of the city.

The 7th General Hospital was in Amiens in August 1914. It was followed by the 56th (South Midland) Casualty Clearing Station from April to July 1916, the New Zealand Stationary Hospital from July 1916 to May 1917, the 42nd Stationary Hospital from October 1917 to March 1919, and the 41st Stationary Hospital in March 1918, December 1918 and January 1919.

During the Second World War, Amiens was again a British base, with GHQ reserve south-west of the town. On 18 May 1940 the town was defended by the 7th Royal Sussex when it was attacked by the German 1st Panzer Division which had already routed the British territorial battalions at

HISTORY
The British first made burials here in September 1915 and the British Plot remained in use until October 1919. It was enlarged after the war by the concentration of a few graves from isolated positions near, or in, the city.

INFORMATION
Amiens is a Cathedral town on the left bank of the River Somme with a population of approximately 130,000. The beautiful 13th Century Cathedral of Notre Dame is the largest in France. Eleven memorials were placed in the Cathedral near the south door after the war. A plaque placed by the CWGC honours those from the armies of Britain and Ireland who died in France and Belgium. There are other memorials to the ANZACs, the Royal Canadian Dragoons, the South Africans, Newfoundlanders and to Raymond Asquith, son of the former British Prime Minister, killed in action on the Somme in 1916. French Memorials are to Marshal Foch, General Debeney who commanded

Albert and Doullens earlier in the day. There was heavy fighting in and around Amiens when the Germans broke through the Somme line and took the town. Much damage was done, but although all the houses to the west of the cathedral were completely destroyed by the bombardment, the cathedral survived.

Amiens Prison was attacked in Operation Jericho on 18 February 1944. The French Resistance had requested the raid as their members were being tortured in the prison and may be giving up vital information. By December 1943, twelve members of the Resistance had been executed at the prison and it was learned that more than 100 other members were to be shot on 19 February 1944. When two Allied intelligence officers were captured and sent to Amiens prison, a precision air attack on the prison was agreed. On a snowy day fourteen Mosquitoes of No. 21, No. 464 and No. 487 Squadrons flew to Albert and then along the main road to Amiens. The raid was successful as of the 717 prisoners, although 102 were killed and 74 wounded, 258 escaped, including 79 Resistance and political prisoners, though two thirds of the escapees were later recaptured. The only casualties among the airmen were the leader of the raid, Group Captain Pickard, and his observer, 'Bill' Broadley. Group Captain Percy Charles 'Pick' Pickard, DSO & two Bars, DFC, MiD, Czech Cross, was shot down towards the end of the raid. He was awarded the Distinguished Flying Cross in July 1940 while serving as a Flight Lieutenant in a bomber squadron. He was promoted to Squadron Leader with No. 311 (Czechoslovak) Squadron and was awarded a Distinguished Service Order in March 1941. In May 1942, as Wing Commander in charge of No. 51 Squadron, he was awarded a Bar to the DSO in recognition of his leadership in the Bruneval raid on 27 February 1942. In March 1943, while commanding No. 161 Squadron, which carried out operations in support of the Special Operations Executive in occupied Europe, he was awarded a second Bar to the DSO. He was the first RAF officer in World War II to be awarded the DSO and two bars. Flight Lieutenant John Alan Broadley, DSO, DFC, DFM, No. 487 (RNZAF) Squadron, Royal Air Force had joined up as a Sergeant and was promoted from the ranks. He was awarded the Distinguished Flying Medal as a Sergeant with No. 9 Squadron in September 1941 at which time he gained his commission. He was awarded the Distinguished Flying Cross in April 1943 and the Distinguished Service Order a few months later in October, both for exceptional service rather than one act. Pickard and Broadley are buried here.

Amiens was retaken by the British Second Army on 31 August 1944. Then No. 25 and 121 General Hospitals were posted here in October 1944, remaining until April 1945.

St. Pierre is one of the town's civil cemeteries. At the rear of the cemetery is a French National Cemetery containing almost 1400 French war graves, over 50% of whom died of wounds in 1916. There are civil graves on the edge of the French National Cemetery. Many of these are the dead of WW1, some from Verdun who died of their wounds here or who have been brought here.

Within the enclosure is also the British Plot used throughout the British occupation of the city during the war. After the war a further 33 graves were concentrated here. At the same time 28 graves of German Prisoners of War were removed elsewhere. It is possible to see where the WW2 burials filled in between the WW1 Plots. An attempt was made to bury the dead of the same plane together because you can identify plane types where a larger or smaller group are buried on the same day.

Among those buried here is Brigadier General Colquhoun Grant Morrison, CMG, General Staff, President of Claims Commission, late 1st (Royal) Dragoons, who died in a motor accident on 23 May 1916 aged 56 years.

Also in the town is St. Acheul French National Cemetery that contains British graves. La Madelaine Cemetery contained the grave of Driver A. Burden, Royal Army Service Corps attached 7th Cavalry Field Ambulance who died of wounds on 10 April 1918. He was moved to Terlincthun Cemetery in 1959. La Madeleine is not strictly within the area covered by this book as it is on the western side of the city. It was used by the Germans in 1870-71 and German prisoners were buried here from British hospitals late in the war. It contains the grave of the author, Jules Verne.

UK – 563	Aust – 95	Can – 10
NZ – 3	SAfr – 1	India – 2
Chinese Labour Corps – 1		KUG – 1
WW2 – 82		Area – 3774 sq mts

Special Memorial to one British soldier whose grave has been lost.

LOCATION

Amiens is the largest town in the area. It is at the western edge of the battlefield of the Somme. This cemetery is in the north-western, or St. Pierre, district of the city. The cemetery is on the north side of the D929 road to Albert about 2km from the city centre.

STE. EMILIE VALLEY CEMETERY, VILLERS-FAUCON

HISTORY

The cemetery was begun by the Germans who buried British soldiers in three groups at some time during the summer of 1918. The rest of the cemetery was made by the concentration of graves after the war.

INFORMATION

The original burials made by the Germans in March 1918 now comprise part of Plot I. They made three large graves after capturing this area. The original burials can be made out as the headstones are closer together.

A few graves were concentrated from another burial ground nearby that had the same name. In total 454 graves were concentrated here, mostly men from the 16th Division who died on 21 March 1918. There are also men of the 39th Division who were sent into action from reserve here on the afternoon of 21 March.

Ste. Emilie Roadside German Cemetery was situated about 1km north-east of here on the road from Ste. Emilie to Ronssoy. It was made by the British after the war for the burial of 791 German soldiers but it has been removed.

Among those buried here is Major John Bolle Tyndale Gough, 1/1st Hertfordshires, killed in action on 22 March 1918 aged 37 years. In 1905, he took a commission from the 1st Volunteer Battalion Bedfordshire Regiment. During the war he served in Mesopotamia attached to the Buffs (East Kents) from where he was invalided home. At his own request he was allowed to re-join the Hertfordshires in France in November 1917. He died while attempting to cover the retreat of the battalion.

Concentrated here:
Ste. Emilie Valley Old Cemetery - situated about 300m to the east of here further from the road. It was made by the 74th Division and by Field Ambulances located here in 1917 for the burial of 32 British soldiers.

UK – 484	Aust – 25	SAfr – 2
Can – 1	NZ - 1	Ger – 10
Unnamed – 222		Area – 1908 sq mts

Special Memorials erected to 21 British soldiers believed to be buried among the unnamed graves.

LOCATION
Ste. Emile is a hamlet situated about 10km north-east of Peronne and 2km east of Villers-Faucon. The cemetery is about 1km south of the village on the east side of the road from Epehy to Roisel.

STUMP ROAD CEMETERY

HISTORY
The cemetery was made as part of the battlefield clearances in the early part of 1917.

INFORMATION
The area was defended by the French in 1914 but fell to the Germans. Grandcourt was an objective on 1 July 1916 and was reached by men of the 36th Division but it could not be held. It was attacked again in November 1916 but was not taken until 7 February 1917 when it was captured by the 63rd Division. It was lost again in the German offensive in 1918 and taken for the final time in the summer of 1918. Stump Road was a sunken road running south from Grandcourt across the hills towards Poizieres.

Stump Road Cemetery was made by the 7th Buffs (East Kents). Many of the unnamed are probably men from the 18th Division. All died in the period July 1916 to February 1917. Each headstone bears two names.

Among those buried here is 2nd Lieutenant Ethelbert Horatio Nelson, 1/4th Queen's (Royal West Surreys), killed in action on 18 November 1916 aged 31 years. I think he has a wonderful name and is an interesting example of facts being lost over time and in the fog of war. He enlisted as a Private in the 1/20th (Blackheath and Woolwich) Londons in August 1914 from his job as clerk with the Central Mining and Investment Corporation. The 1/20th Londons had an association with his Rugby Club, Old Dunstonians. He was quickly promoted to Lance Corporal seeing action in France from March 1915 until the Battle of Loos. He was then commissioned into the Queen's (Royal West Surreys) as a 2nd Lieutenant in January 1916. It appears that his CWGC record as being in 1/4th Queen's is wrong as that Battalion served in India throughout the war. It was the 7th Queen's that attacked Desire Trench at Grandcourt on 18 November 1916 as part of 55th Brigade in 18th (Eastern) Division. In fact, De Ruvigny's Roll of Honour states that he was in 1/4th attached 7th Queen's (Royal West Surreys) joining them on 4 October 1916. However, there is no mention of him in the Battalion War Diary on 4 October or 18 November. The attack on Grandcourt was part of the opening phase of the Battle of the Ancre, one of the last acts of the Battles of the Somme. Despite heavy rain in late October and early November, which turned the already waterlogged battlefield into a quagmire, Haig wanted to try to break the German line astride the River Ancre. The attack was to be made first light on 18 November. The 55th Brigade, with a Canadian Brigade on their right, was to capture Desire Trench and Grandcourt Trench, just south of the village of Grandcourt. The weather was bitterly cold with snow flurries. The fighting raged at close quarters for eighteen hours. It is in this battle that 2nd Lieutenant Nelson was killed.

| UK – 237 | Can – 24 | KUG – 2 |
| Unnamed – 50 | | Area – 399 sq mts |

LOCATION
Grandcourt is in the valley of the River Ancre about 6km north-east of Albert and a similar distance south-west of Bapaume. The cemetery is in fields 2km south of the village. It is 500m from the Thiepval-Grandcourt road on the old 'Stump Road' which is now a farm track located just below the ridge between Grandcourt and Pozieres.

SUCRERIE BRITISH CEMETERY, GRAINCOURT-LES-HAVRINCOURT

HISTORY
The cemetery was opened and closed on 6 October 1918 by the Burial Officer of the 63rd (Royal Naval) Division for the burial of 57 officers and men killed in the battle to capture the village.

INFORMATION
The sucrerie, or sugar beet factory, after which the cemetery is named is in a dip in the main Bapaume-Cambrai road. The cemetery is north of the factory on the ridges above the road.

The village was captured by the 62nd (2nd West Riding) Division on 20 November 1917 during the Battle of Cambrai but it fell at the start of the German spring offensive in March 1918. The village was captured again, on 27 September 1918, by the 63rd Division during the final advance to victory.

The cemetery was made during that final advance when men of the Royal Naval Division were buried in one long row now on the north side of the cemetery.

Buried here is Private Albert George Taylor Osmond, 1st Royal Marine Battalion, Royal Marine Light Infantry, 63rd (Royal Naval) Division, killed in action on 28 September 1918 aged 21 years. He is commemorated by a Special Memorial as he is known to be here but not exactly where. He enlisted in September 1916 aged 18 years 8 months and joined the Royal Marine Light Infantry in November. He went to the front as a signaller in April 1918 when he was posted to the 2nd RMLI transferring to 1st RMLI within weeks. He was under medical care for Pyrexia (fever) until 8 September 1918 and was killed three weeks later.

UK – 57   Unnamed – 5   Area – 202 sq mts

Special Memorial to one British soldier known to be buried here but whose grave cannot now be located.

LOCATION
The cemetery is about 10km south-west of Cambrai and about 2km north of Graincourt-les-Havrincourt. It is on the ridges north of the village north of the Bapaume-Cambrai road. A farm track leads north to a CWGC path that runs 200m east to the cemetery.

SUCRERIE MILITARY CEMETERY, COLINCAMPS

HISTORY
The cemetery was begun by French troops in the early summer of 1915. It was used by the British from July 1915 until December 1918, though burials were limited during the period from the German retreat in 1917 until August 1918. Further burials have been concentrated here since the war.

INFORMATION
The cemetery was next to one of the main communication routes up to the front line when it was known as the 10th Brigade Cemetery. Grave trenches had been dug here in late June 1916 in preparation for the attack on 1 July 1916 so men passed by them on the way to the front-line.

The New Zealand Division was engaged in fighting here in 1918. Hence, the burials of April 1918 are mainly New Zealanders who halted the German advance nearby.

The first British burials are Privates W E Swainstone, William Tarver and E Williams of the 1st Royal Warwickshires killed on 26 July 1915. The early burials can be found in different sections of the cemetery. It is probable that different battalions had HQs along the track and buried their men together in small plots, but the spaces were filled in as time passed and the cemetery grew. Those of August 1918 are mainly men of 42nd (East Lancashire) Division who pushed the Germans back from where they had been halted. The 285 French and twelve German graves were removed to other cemeteries after the war.

Fifteen men of the 12th (Sheffield City Battalion) York & Lancasters killed in a German air raid in May 1916 are buried together in Plot I, Row G. Plot I Rows D and E are men killed on 1 July 1916. Plot I Row H are all officers. This includes two battalion commanders from 11th Brigade killed in action on 1 July 1916. They are Lieutenant Colonel The Honourable Lawrence Charles Walter Palk, DSO, Legion of Honour, 1st Hampshires, aged 45 years, son of the late Lawrence Hesketh Palk, 2nd Baron Haldon and Baroness Haldon; and Lieutenant Colonel John Audley

Thicknesse, 1st Somerset Light Infantry aged 46 years, son of the Right Reverend Dr F. H. Thicknesse, late Bishop of Leicester, also served on the North-West Frontier of India and in the South African War and whose son was killed in action in Holland in October 1944.

Among those here is Rifleman James Crozier, 9th Royal Irish Rifles, executed for desertion on 27 February 1916. He worked in the Belfast shipyards when he was recruited in 1914 by Major Crozier who went on to command James's battalion, signed the recommendation for execution, and was further promoted to be a Brigadier. It is reputed that Major Crozier promised James' mother he would look after him but Major Crozier wrote on James' recommendation for execution 'From a fighting point of view this soldier is of no value. His behaviour has been that of a "shirker" for the past 3 months.' He deserted near Serre and made his way to an advanced Dressing Station from which he was sent back and court-martialled on 14 February. He was executed in a villa in Mailly-Maillet and his body concentrated here after the war. On the night before the execution Rifleman Crozier was plied with drink whilst the officer in charge of the Execution Party was entertained by Major Crozier intending to prevent the young subaltern getting drunk. Feelings ran high amongst the ranks and the Military Police feared a mutiny with the firing squad refusing to shoot. Just before dawn the 9th Royal Irish Rifles paraded alongside the wall surrounding the chateau grounds. Private Crozier was carried unconscious to the place of execution where he was blindfolded and tied to the post. On the command the squad fired but Crozier was not dead so the subaltern took aim with his revolver and fired a bullet into Crozier's head. The wall surrounding the chateau prevented the whole battalion from seeing the execution.

Also here is Private Alexander McIntyre, 5th Cameron Highlanders attached 245th Prisoner of War Company, Labour Corps who was killed on Christmas Day 1918 aged 50 years while working with German prisoners clearing the battlefields of unexploded ordnance.

UK – 965	Aust – 29	NZ – 65
Can – 13	SAfr - 32	Unnamed – 219

Area – 6322 sq mts

Special Memorials to seven British soldiers known or believed to be buried among the unnamed.

LOCATION

Colincamps is located about 16km north of Albert. Sucrerie Military Cemetery is about 3km south-east of the village on the north side of the D919 road from Mailly-Maillet to Puisieux. It is about 250m from the sucrerie. Access is by a farm track from the D919 about 100m south-west of the sucrerie crossroads.

SUMMIT TRENCH CEMETERY

HISTORY

The cemetery was made at the end of August 1918 after the fighting here.

INFORMATION

The village was in German hands for most of the war. It was attacked by the British 7th Division in March 1917 but did not fall until an attack made in a blizzard on 2 April 1917. The Germans re-took the village on 21 March 1918. It fell for the final time, to the 56th (London) Division, on 28 August 1918 after heavy fighting. Summit Trench had fallen on 24 August 1918.

Summit Trench was a long trench on a low hill between Croisilles and Henin forming part of the Hindenburg Line. This cemetery is 90m west of the site of the trench. The cemetery was made by the 56th (London) Division and all are men of, or posted to, the London Regiment.

Buried here is 2nd Lieutenant George Houlden Merrikin, 1/2nd Londons (Royal Fusiliers), killed in action on 27 August 1918 aged 40 years. Before the war he was Chaplain at Wellingborough School, Curate at Dulwich College and Precentor at Bristol Cathedral. He enlisted as a Private and Stretcher Bearer in the Royal Army Medical Corps in October 1914 with whom he served until October 1917. He was then sent for training as an officer being commissioned in January 1918. He joined his battalion in France at the end of April and fought in the Second Battle of Arras. A letter home said of his death 'under most heroic circumstances he met his death at a spot between Croisilles and Henin-sur-Cojeul, while going out in broad daylight to the German trenches to rescue eight or nine of our own wounded. He succeeded in saving eight men, and when going to save the remainder was shot through the heart'.

UK – 74	Unnamed – 5	Area – 342 sq mts

LOCATION

Croisilles is located about 10km south-east of Arras and 7km north of Bapaume. It is on the east side of the A1 Autoroute. This is a strange place to access. A farm track leaves the Croisilles-Henin road on the east side of the motorway. The track heads north next to the northbound carriageway separated from it by a few bushes and a thin fence, so you almost feel you are on the motorway. The cemetery is on a ridge in fields with excellent views.

SUN QUARRY CEMETERY, CHERISY

HISTORY
The cemetery was opened after the village fell to the British advance in September 1918. It remained in use during the following month.

INFORMATION
The village was behind the German lines for most of the war. It was entered by the British 18th Division on 3 May 1917 but retaken by the Germans at the end of the day. It finally fell to the Allies on 27 August 1918 when it was captured by the Canadian Corps.

The cemetery was made on the site of a flint quarry. It contains the bodies of men who died during fighting in the area from 26 August to 28 September 1918.

If you look west across the valley you can identify Upton Wood (Bois de Hendecourt) and to its right a large hillock known as the Crow's Nest. This was the scene of an assault made by the 15th Canadian Infantry (48th Highlanders of Canada) on 1 September 1918. Their Battalion Headquarters was located at the Sun Quarry. You will find their monument to this action on the roadside at the base of the mound near the track leading to Upton Wood Cemetery.

Among those here is Private James Henry Birch Silcox, 31st (Alberta) Canadian Infantry, killed in action on 28 August 1918 aged 32 years. He was a farmer and was conscripted in January 1918.

Also here is Lance Sergeant Robert Henry Jackson, DCM, 3rd Canadian Infantry, killed in action on 30 September 1918 aged 30 years. Born in Ireland he was a carpenter when he enlisted into the 95th Canadian Infantry in January 1916. He went to France in September 1916, where he was promoted to Corporal in August 1917, the same year in which he attended a Lewis Gun course, and to Lance-Sergeant in mid-August 1918 shortly before his death. The citation for his Distinguished Conduct Medal won in 1918 just before he died reads 'When his platoon officer and sergeant had both been killed while attacking a machine-gun nest, he took command and, reorganising the men, clearly manoeuvered them and 18 men. He then led his platoon to the final objective saving casualties by his skillful handling. He was a splendid example to his men.'

UK – 31   Can – 160   Unnamed - 8

Area – 462 sq mts

LOCATION
Cherisy is situated about 30km west of Cambrai and 10km south-east of Arras. It is about 2km south of the Arras-Cambrai road. The cemetery is south-east of the village on the road to Hendecourt.

SUNKEN ROAD CEMETERY, BOISLEUX-ST. MARC

HISTORY
The cemetery was begun in May 1917 and used until July. Further burials were made in March 1918 and again in September and October 1918.

INFORMATION
The village was in German hands for much of the war and was captured from the Germans in March 1917 during the retreat to the Hindenburg Line. The Germans retook the village in early April 1918 before it fell for the final time at the end of August 1918. The 20th Casualty Clearing Station was here from 31 June 1917 to 28 March 1918. The 43rd CCS was here from 4 November 1917 to 3 March 1918. From September to the end of the war a number of CCS's were stationed here for brief periods – No.'s 38, 19, 1, 30, 33 and 22.

This cemetery was originally known as Boisleux-au-Mont British Cemetery. A nearby German cemetery containing 185 burials has been removed.

Among those buried here is Lieutenant Colonel Robert Romney Godred Kane, DSO and Bar, Legion of Honour, MiD, 1st Royal Munster Fusiliers, died of wounds on 1 October 1918 aged 29 years. He entered the Army in 1908, joining the 1st Royal Munster Fusiliers in India. The regiment was in Burma when war broke out, and moved towards Europe in January 1915 but was diverted with the 29th Division to Gallipoli. There Kane was liaison officer until he was badly wounded in July 1915. He was Mentioned in Despatches and received the Distinguished Service Order for his services in the Gallipoli campaign rather than for a single act. Afterwards he served on Staff in France, and was made Chevalier of the Legion of Honour. In February of 1918 he went back to his battalion as Lieutenant-Colonel, and was with them until his death. He was awarded a posthumous Bar to his DSO in the January 1919 New Years Honours List. His elder brother was killed in the Boer War.

Also here is Captain Henry Edward Stewart, MiD, 8th Royal Sussex, killed in action on 1 June 1917. He was grandson of the 14th Duke of Norfolk and nephew of the 15th Duke. His father was knighted for his work with Sir Fabian Ware in laying the foundations for the work of the CWGC.

UK – 398 Can – 14 NZ – 2
Indian – 1 Ger – 4 Unnamed – 1
Area – 1128 sq mts

LOCATION
Boisleux-St.-Marc is a village in the valley of the River Cojeul about 5km south of Arras. The cemetery is in fields on a ridge north-west of the village and north-east of Boislieux-au-Mont. Sunken Road leads north from the road between the two villages of Boisleux St. Marc and Boisleux-au-Mont at a point about 250m west of this village.

SUNKEN ROAD CEMETERY, CONTALMAISON

HISTORY
The cemetery was made during the period July–October 1916.

INFORMATION
Contalmaison was in German hands from 1914. It was a primary objective, and is believed to have been entered, on 1 July 1916 by small parties of the Tyneside Irish of the 34th Division. It was stormed by the 23rd Division on 7 July, and some men of the Northumberland Fusiliers captured several days earlier were released. It was lost on the same afternoon and not fully captured until the 8th and 9th Yorkshires cleared it on the 10 July. The Germans re-took the village in March 1918. It was finally recaptured by the 38th (Welsh) Division on the evening of 24 August 1918. The underground fortifications made by the Germans before 1916 played an important part in the defence of the village.

The cemetery was opened by front-line units who were fighting locally. Field Ambulances in the area continued to use the cemetery. The site was formerly wooded and Sunken Road Cemetery was created in the Bois Defriches. The graves of two German soldiers, buried by the Germans at the end of March 1918, have been removed.

The first man buried here is Private Wilfred Augustus Fraser who served as Hicks, 17th Australian Infantry, killed in action at Pozieres on 26 July 1916 aged 28 years. He enlisted on 7 March 1915 in the 17th Battalion Headquarters as a Driver.

Also buried here are several officers of Canada's famous 'Van-Doos' battalion, officially the 22nd Canadian Infantry, from Quebec. The battalion was created, after much pressure on the government who wanted to ban the teaching of French and had previously scattered French speakers among all battalions in the first contingent to go to Europe, as a place for Francophones to train and fight together. It was also thought an incentive for French-speaking Canadians to enlist in a war which was seen as an 'English' conflict. The 22nd Canadian Infantry went to France as part of the 5th Canadian Brigade, 2nd Canadian Division in September 1915. During the war 5584 soldiers served in the battalion and of that total 3961 were killed or wounded. Those buried here include Captain Maurice Edouard Bauset, killed on 16 September 1916 aged 27 years; Lieutenant Abel P. Beaudry, killed on 15 September 1916 aged 31 years; Lieutenant L R Lavoie, MM, killed on 15 September 1916 aged 27 years; and Major A L H Renaud, killed on 15 September 1916.

Can – 148 Aust – 61 UK – 5
Unnamed – 4 Area – 1106 sq mts

Special Memorials to three Australians who are believed or known to be buried here but whose graves cannot be found.

LOCATION
Contalmaison is a small village about 6km north-east of Albert. The cemetery is in fields north of the village north of the Contalmaison-Pozieres road. It is at the head of a valley running north-east from the road. A rough track leads 400m to the cemetery past 2nd Canadian Cemetery and the cemetery is on the east side of the track. The track can be impassable in winter, there is no turning area for vehicles and it will be necessary to reverse back up the track, so walking from the road is best.

SUNKEN ROAD CEMETERY, VILLERS-PLOUICH

HISTORY
The cemetery was used in December 1917, January and September 1918.

INFORMATION
The village was in German hands for much of the war. It was captured by the 13th East Surreys as part of the actions surrounding the German withdrawal to the Hindenburg Line. It fell to the Germans in March 1918 and was not recaptured until September 1918 when the 1st East Surreys were the first troops to enter the village.

Many of the burials are men of the 63rd (Royal Naval) Division. Among them is Sub-Lieutenant J Watkins, Hood Battalion, Royal Naval Division, Royal Naval Volunteer Reserve, who was killed on the last day of 1917. On the previous day Petty Officer Hilton Cummings Williamson, MM & Bar, 189th Stokes Trench Mortar Battery, Royal Naval Division, Royal Naval Volunteer Reserve was killed in action aged 21 years. He had been awarded his Military Medal in April 1917 as an Able Seaman and the Bar in July 1917 as a Leading Seaman.

UK – 51   Unnamed – 3   Area – 257 sq mts

LOCATION
Villers-Plouich is situated about 10km south-west of Cambrai and 2km west of the A26 Autoroute. The cemetery is north-west of the village on the edge of a sunken road running to Beaucamp. It is high above the road with good views.

SUZANNE COMMUNAL CEMETERY EXTENSION

HISTORY
The cemetery was begun by the French in 1914. It was used by the British from their arrival in August 1915 until the withdrawal of the Germans to the Hindenburg Line in 1917. The Germans made burials in 1918 when they held the area. The British used it again in August and September 1918.

INFORMATION
The village was in French or British hands for most of the war and was well behind the lines. It fell to the Germans in their advance in the spring of 1918 but was re-captured in August 1918. The British and Commonwealth burials were begun by the 5th Division which took over this area from the French. Many of the graves are men of the Liverpool and Manchester Pals of the 30th Division who held the line in the winter of 1915-16. There are fourteen Australians buried in late 1918. Unusually, every grave is identified.

The graves of 387 French and 71 German soldiers have been removed to other cemeteries.

Among those buried here is Lance Corporal David Logan, 18th (3rd Manchester Pals - Clerks and Warehousemen) Manchesters, killed in action on 4 February 1916 aged 22 years. The Battalion, part of the 30th Division, occupied a hazardously exposed position in the winter of 1915-16, along the Somme marshes on the extreme right of the British line near the village of Vaux, consisting of scattered posts and duckboard walkways in an area of marshland. Raids among the reed-beds and rivulets took a toll in killed, wounded and missing, Logan among them.

UK – 141   Aust – 14   Area – 981 sq mts

LOCATION
Suzanne is a village about 13km south-east of Albert and 8km west of Peronne. It is in the valley of the River Somme on the north side of the river. Suzanne Communal Cemetery is in a valley 350m north-west of the village on the west side of the road from Albert and the Extension is on the south-east side of the Communal Cemetery.

SUZANNE MILITARY CEMETERY No. 3

HISTORY
The cemetery was begun by the French in 1914-15. It was not used by the British during the war. So, this is a concentration cemetery made after the war.

INFORMATION
See Suzanne Communal Cemetery Extension.

When the French began this cemetery it was called Cimetiere Mixte No. 3 de Suzanne. However, the French burials have been removed. It was used by the British after the war for the concentration of graves from the battlefields north of the River Somme. There were not two other British military cemeteries in Suzanne, but there were two French cemeteries, this being the third, from which the No. 3 comes. The French have been removed.

Among those here is Private David Graham, 11th Royal Irish Rifles, killed in action on 1 July 1916 aged 21 years. The Battalion was part of 36th (Ulster) Division and sustained heavy casualties during the move forward from Thiepval Wood to assembly positions in no man's land at 7.15am. Thiepval is about 15km from here so he was one of those brought south from his original grave near Thiepval.

Three men buried here were executed during the war. They were buried in a small burial ground on the south-eastern edge of Suzanne, next to the River Somme about 1km south of here. Private Frederick Wright, 1st Queen's (Royal West Surreys), was executed for desertion on 28 January 1917. We know little of this man except that he served through the Battle of the Somme before deserting having been with the battalion for about a year.

Private Benjamin Albert Hart, 1/4th Suffolks, executed for desertion on 6 February 1917 aged 22 years. Benjamin Hart was a Territorial soldier who went to France in January 1916. Whilst serving near the Brickstacks at Cambrin near Béthune, Hart and others were buried alive by a German mine exploding under their position. Hart was severely shocked by the incident and from this moment began avoiding any service in the front lines by reporting himself as unfit for duty. Hence, he began to get a bad record. Over the months that his battalion was serving on the Somme Hart refused to go back to the Front or absented himself. He was charged on a number of occasions but managed to avoid a capital sentence. His Platoon commander 2nd Lieutenant Charles Stormont-Gibbs, MC had made him a servant in the hope of keeping him away from battle. Then on 13 December 1916 Hart absconded when his unit was sent to front-line trenches. He gave himself up at Bray-sur-Somme two days later and was placed in detention prior to a Court Martial for desertion which took place on 28 December. Hart's brother, Serjeant Ernest Hart, 11th Suffolks was killed near Passendale on 22 October 1917 and is commemorated on the Tyne Cot Memorial.

Private Frederick Stead, 2nd Duke of Wellington's, was executed for desertion on 12 February 1917 aged 20 years. Stead had joined the Army in 1913 and been sent to France at the end of 1914 fighting in the First Battle of Ypres. In 1915 he fell sick with diarrhoea but recuperated after a few days. His good health did not last long and he was returned to hospital in England. Sent back to France in May 1916 his poor health continued. In October 1916 he was admitted to a Casualty Clearing Station with a possibly self-inflicted gunshot wound to his right hand. His absence from his battalion coincided with their heavy losses in the attack against Le Transloy in the Battle of the Somme. In late October 1916 Stead deserted, but was captured and condemned to death. The sentence was suspended but a day after his release Stead deserted again. He was re-captured on 23 December and again sent for trial. His commanding officer suggested that he might have been mentally handicapped and Stead was sent for a medical examination at No. 21 Casualty Clearing Station but the Doctor could find nothing wrong with him. With his previous record the execution was confirmed.

UK – 102   Aust – 28   Can – 8
Ger – 1   Unnamed – 42   Area – 921 sq mts

LOCATION
The cemetery is about 2km north of the village in open fields on the east side of the road to Maricourt. It is 50m from the road and is reached by a CWGC path. It has excellent views.

TANK CEMETERY

HISTORY
The cemetery was begun in April 1917 and used until June.

INFORMATION
Guémappe was in German hands for much of the war. The village was captured by British troops on 23-24 April 1917 though it took until 28 April to clear nearby Cavalry Farm. It was lost on 23 March 1918 and retaken, by the Canadian Corps, on 26 August 1918.

The cemetery was damaged by shellfire in 1918. Row F is a mass grave of 64 men of the 7th Cameron Highlanders.

Among those here is 2nd Lieutenant Percy Cargill Reid, 16th (Queen's Westminster Rifles) Londons, killed in action leading his men in an attack on 6 May 1917 aged 33 years. He was educated at Wanganui College, New Zealand and then at Marlborough College. He went to Canada to work in banking, from where he returned with the Canadian

Expeditionary Force as a Private. He was commissioned into the Queen's Westminster Rifles in December 1916.

UK – 218 NF – 1 Unnamed – 25
Area – 742 sq mts

Special Memorials to five British soldiers known or believed to be buried among the unnamed.

Special Memorials to six men whose exact location of burial in the cemetery cannot be identified.

LOCATION
Guemappe is located 1km south-west of the road from Arras to Cambrai, and Wancourt is 1km south-west of Guemappe. The cemetery is about 700m north-west of Guemappe on the west side of the road leading from the Arras-Cambrai road to Wancourt. It lies 30m from the road in a small valley and is reached by a CWGC path.

TARGELLE RAVINE BRITISH CEMETERY

Among the 76 men of the 9th Highland Light Infantry buried here by their comrades is 2nd Lieutenant Andrew Moffatt Bruce, 9th (Glasgow Highlanders) Highland Light Infantry, killed in action on 29 September 1918 aged 21 years. After school he worked for an iron and steel merchants in Glasgow until the start of the war when he enlisted as a Private aged 17 years. He was kept in the UK for eighteen months due to his age until he went to France in 1916. He was soon home suffering from Trench Foot but upon his recovery was offered a commission. He returned to his battalion as an officer in April 1918 and saw action in the summer. He was killed, when shot through the head, leading his men into action when they were hit by a machine gun. His four brothers also served in the war with one other not returning home. 2nd Lieutenant Charles James Bruce, 52nd Division Cyclist Battalion, Army Cyclist Corps attached 1/5th Royal Scots Fusiliers, died of wounds in Palestine on 20 May 1917 aged 30 years and is buried in Cairo War Memorial Cemetery.

HISTORY
The cemetery was made in September and October 1918.

INFORMATION
Villers-Guislain was behind the German lines for much of the war. In the actions associated with the German retreat to the Hindenburg Line the village was attacked and captured by the British in April 1917. The Germans recaptured the village in November during the Battle of Cambrai and held it against an attack by the Tank Corps and Guards Division. The British did not regain the village until 30 September 1918.

UK – 114 Unnamed – 7 Area – 348 sq mts

LOCATION
Villers-Guislain is located about 15km south of Cambrai, a similar distance north-east of Peronne and 2km west of the A26 Autoroute. The cemetery is about 1.5km south of the village, on the north side of a shallow valley or ravine in open country reached by a farm track from the village.

TEMPLEUX-LE-GUERARD BRITISH CEMETERY

HISTORY
The cemetery was in use from April to August 1917 and September to October 1918. It was enlarged after the war.

INFORMATION
The village was behind German lines for much of the war. It was attacked and captured in April 1917 as part of the actions linked to the German withdrawal to the Hindenburg Line. It remained in Allied hands until 21 March 1918 when it was lost on the first day of the German spring offensive. The village was captured again on 18 September by the 15th Suffolks of the 74th (Yeomanry) Division.

The cemetery was begun by the 59th (2nd North Midland) Division. It was enlarged after the war by the concentration of 360 graves from the battlefields which saw the remains of men who died in April 1917, and March and September 1918 brought here. It is probable that men who died on 21 March 1918 make up many of the unnamed burials.

Many of the burials of men who died in the March 1918 fighting have 'attached' as part of their information. This reflects the re-organisation that was taking place in the British army at the time, a re-organisation that hindered the British when the Germans attacked. It also shows how close to the edge the British were when the Germans took their 'Gamble', which could have paid off.

Buried here is Reverend Alfred Ernest Goller, Chaplain 4th Class, Australian Army Chaplains Department, killed on 29 September 1918 aged 35 years. Chaplain Goller had spent the first years of the war breaking bad news to families in his parish. When he tired of being a 'messenger of death' he decided that he would be more useful at the Front. On 16 January 1917 he enlisted and, a month later, he sailed for France. As the ship passed through the English Channel a German torpedo hit the ship. Goller remained on deck until Royal Navy vessels had rescued everyone and he became one of the last to depart before the ship sank. In England, Goller was posted to training battalions but he wanted to be at the Front as this was where he felt he could do the most good. So, in September 1917, he was sent to France. Initially he was attached to the 2nd Australian General Hospital. He again requested to be at the Front rather than in a hospital and was posted to the 37th Australian Infantry. Like many battalions the 37th had suffered many losses and was significantly below strength, partly as Australia did not introduce conscription. Late in the war they were to be disbanded but the men refused the order, including Goller. The local commanders cut off the men's rations, but other units in the area gave up half of their food to feed the protesters. Supply units changed their routes and arranged for boxes of food to 'fall off' as they passed the 37th. The men got their way but were sent into action soon after against the Hindenburg Line. As the battalion reached the German wire, machine-guns opened fire killing most of the front ranks. The remainder of the battalion consolidated in a hollow and readied themselves for the next push. Goller crawled into the open to bring injured men back to safety. When the battalion again moved forward, he stopped at the bodies of three men from 'A' Company to collect their personal belongings, and offer a prayer at which time he was killed.

Also here is Lieutenant Colonel Robert Oswald Henderson, DSO, MiD, 39th Australian Infantry, killed in action on 29 September 1918 aged 43 years. He had previous military experience before enlisting in May 1916. His Distinguished Service Order was awarded five days before his death. The citation says 'For conspicuous gallantry and devotion to duty. When his battalion had reached its objective he personally supervised the digging in and remained in the shell holes with his men. On another occasion, when his battalion was brought up from reserve to replace casualties, he did excellent work in re-organising the various units under heavy fire after many officers had become casualties. He set a splendid example to his men.'

Another buried here is Major Valentine Fleming, DSO, twice MiD, 'C' Squadron, Queen's Own Oxfordshire Hussars, killed in action on 20 May 1917 aged 35 years. He was killed near Gillemont Farm which is between the villages of Vendhuille and Lempire about 5km north east of here. He was MP for South Oxfordshire and, possibly of greater note, he was the father of Ian Fleming, the creator of James Bond.

In 1930 two British cemeteries were concentrated here:
Gouy British Cemetery – Gouy is about 7km north-east of here. The cemetery was in the hamlet of Rue-Neuve (or Rue-du-Moulin), which is about 400m from the centre of Gouy, on the road from Gouy to Estrées. It stood in a paddock close to a farmhouse. It was made by the 50th Division in October 1918 after they captured Gouy and Le Catelet on 3 October for the burial of 127 British and one Australian soldiers. Almost all were men of the 50th Division and most died between 3 and 10 October 1918.

Ste. Emilie British Cemetery, Villers-Faucon – the village is about 7km south-west from here. The cemetery stood in the grounds of Ste. Emilie Chateau which is 500m north-east of the centre of the village. It was begun by the 42nd (East Lancashire) Division in May 1917, used by Cavalry, other units and Field Ambulances until March 1918, and again by British and American troops in September-November 1918. The American 27th and 30th Divisions, with Australian troops, attacked and carried the Hindenburg Line, a little east of Ste. Emilie, on 27–30 October 1918. The cemetery contained the graves of 196 British, 108 American, 22 Australian soldiers and one South African. The American graves, mainly of the 107th and 108th Infantry Regiments, were concentrated into the Somme American Cemetery, Bony, 5km to the east of this cemetery before 1922.

UK – 723   Aust – 45   Can – 1
SAfr – 1   India – 3   Unnamed - 188
Area – 2509 sq mts

Special Memorials to sixteen British soldiers, known or believed to be buried among the unnamed.

LOCATION
Templeux-Le-Guerard is a village located 25km east of Peronne and 15km north-west of St. Quentin. It lies in the valley of the River La Cologne. This cemetery is 200m south-east of the village in a small valley on the north side of the road to Hargicourt.

TEMPLEUX-LE-GUERARD COMMUNAL CEMETERY EXTENSION

HISTORY
The cemetery was used from April to October 1917 by the British and again in September and October 1918.

INFORMATION
This cemetery was begun by the 59th (North Midland) Division immediately after the capture of the village. It was used by the Germans to bury British dead in March 1918. The British used it again in September and October 1918.

The graves of four American soldiers, buried here in September and October 1918, and of seven German soldiers buried here in July 1917 and October 1918, have been removed.

Templeux-Le-Guerard Communal Cemetery German Extension was made of two sections, one on the south-west side of the Communal Cemetery and one on the north-west side. It contained the graves of 339 Germans, fifteen British who died in March 1918, and three French soldiers. The British graves were moved here in 1924.

Among those buried here is Serjeant P L Hill, DCM, 6th Siege Battery, Royal Garrison Artillery, killed on 8 October 1918. The citation for his Distinguished Conduct Medal reads 'When an enemy shell burst under his gun and destroyed half of his detachment this NCO, although knocked off his feet and badly shaken, collected the rest of his men and continued firing the gun. It was entirely owning to his example under this heavy fire that this section remained steady.'

UK – 111   Aust – 20
Unnamed – 5   Area – 729 sq mts

Special Memorial to one British soldier who is known to be buried among the unnamed.

Special Memorials to twelve British soldiers, buried in the German Extension, whose graves were destroyed.

LOCATION
This cemetery is north of the village on the north side of a narrow road leading north-east from the road to Ronssoy. The farm road becomes a track at the Communal Cemetery. The Extension is on the north side of the Communal Cemetery. It lies below the track in a small valley and is accessed through the Communal Cemetery. It is a pretty little cemetery finally reached by a set of steps.

TEN TREE ALLEY CEMETERY

HISTORY
Ten Tree Alley Cemetery was made by V Corps, as Ten Tree Alley Cemetery No. 2, V Corps Cemetery No. 24, in 1917.

INFORMATION
The French held the German advance here in 1914 and remained until 1915 when the area was handed over to the British. Beaumont was an early objective for 1 July 1916 but was not reached or even approached as the men who were cut down in what is now Newfoundland Park failed to get far from their own lines. Beaumont was attacked again, and taken, on 13 November 1916 by the 51st (Highland) and 63rd (Royal Naval) Divisions. On 10 February 1917 the 32nd Division again attacked the German positions, capturing Munich and Frankfurt Trenches. The 62nd (West Riding) Division went into the line here on 15 February 1917 and continued the efforts to push the Germans out. The villages of Puisieux and Serre were taken from the Germans on 28 February 1917, lost to them on 26 March 1918 and taken for the final time on 21 August 1918.

The cemetery stood beside a former German trench, captured by the 32nd Division on the night of 10-11 February 1917. The men buried here fell during fighting on 18 November 1916 or 10-18 February 1917.

Among those buried here is Captain Allan Gow Marshall, 17th (3rd Glasgow Pals) Highland Light Infantry, killed in action on 12 February 1917 aged 36 years. He enlisted as a Private in in the battalion in September 1914 and reached the rank of Lance Corporal in 'B' Company before being given a commission as a 2nd Lieutenant in May 1915. He was promoted to Lieutenant in September 1915 and Captain in November 1916 having gone to France in June 1916 joining 'C' Company in the 17th Highland Light Infantry. He was killed by a sniper once the position had been captured. His family had been responsible for the development and widespread sale of Semolina.

UK – 67   Unnamed – 24   Area – 250 sq mts

LOCATION

Serre-les-Puisieux village is situated about 5km west of Bapaume. The cemetery is 1km south-west of the village, which is commonly known as Serre, situated in open fields east of Serre on the Redan Ridge between the Serre battlefield and Beaumont. The cemetery is reached by using the small road that leaves the D919 in Serre opposite the 12th York and Lancasters Memorial or from Beaucourt-sur-l'Ancre. A track leads about 150m from the road to the cemetery on the edge of a valley. It is a very attractive small cemetery.

TERTRY COMMUNAL CEMETERY

HISTORY

The cemetery was used for burials from March to April 1917 and March and September 1918

INFORMATION

Of the fifteen buried here, nine are men of the 10th (Prince of Wales's Own Royal) Hussars killed in a German air raid at about 8.00pm on 9 March 1918. A bomb dropped on a large hut which was full of men sitting together in the centre around a stove on a bitterly cold night. Six men were killed instantly and 35 wounded, of whom four died later.

Also here is Captain Philip Henry Harcourt Beck, 2/6th Gloucesters attached 2/1st Oxford and Bucks Light Infantry, killed in action on 2 April 1917 aged 27 years. At the start of the war he was a student at Bristol University. He was commissioned in November 1914 into a territorial battalion of the Gloucesters, the 2/6th, which seems to have been confused in the CWGC records as the 2/6th Oxford and Bucks Light Infantry, a battalion which did not exist. He was then attached to the 2/1st Oxford and Bucks Light Infantry. On 24 June 1917 he was posthumously promoted to the rank of Lieutenant (temporary Captain) with precedence as from 1 June 1916.

UK - 15

LOCATION

Tertry is situated about 10km west of St. Quentin in the valley of the River l'Omignon about 2km north of the A29 Autoroute. The cemetery is on the northern edge of the village on the crest of a ridge as you leave the village on the east side of the road to Peronne. The graves are left of the entrance in what used to be a corner of the cemetery. But as the cemetery has grown down the hill and to the east (it is still possible to identify the original cemetery boundary), now the graves are nearer to the middle of the cemetery.

THIEPVAL ANGLO FRENCH CEMETERY

HISTORY

The cemetery was created after the war.

INFORMATION

Thiepval, situated on a ridge above the River Ancre, was once a thriving village serving a chateau. As with countless other places in France and Belgium, it was devastated in the war, notably during the course of the Battle of the Somme, and was reduced to rubble. Its commanding position sealed its fate as early as 1914 for, once their advance was held here by the French, the Germans saw that it was a strong defensive position capable of dominating the surrounding country. Inevitably, the British had to capture it before they could advance elsewhere but the attack on 1 July 1916 was a failure. After careful preparation, the British finally captured the village in a well-executed assault by the 18th Division, who have a memorial here, in September. However, this did not mark the end of the war for Thiepval, for it was fought over twice more in 1918 first during the German advance in April and then for the last time when the British passed back through it in August.

Thiepval did not recover after the war, partly due to its isolated position which made it a very low priority for redevelopment, and partly because the family who owned the chateau chose to not return.

Once this location had been chosen for the Memorial to the Missing of the Battles of the Somme, it was decided to create a small cemetery at the foot of the memorial containing British and Commonwealth dead alongside the dead of France. This would symbolise the common effort of the French and British armies, not only in the Battles of the Somme of 1916, but also on the wider battlefields of

Europe, Asia and Africa in all the years of the 'Great War'. The French Government and the Commonwealth War Graves Commission, formerly the Imperial War Graves Commission, have borne the cost equally, and the 600 who lie here represent the dead of the Commonwealth as well as those of France and her colonies.

The cemetery is approximately on the German line of 1 July 1916 attacked by the 15th and 16th (1st and 2nd Salford Pals) Lancashire Fusiliers. Bodies were brought in from small burial grounds and isolated graves on the battlefields in December 1931 and March 1932. Some were brought from as far north as Loos, or as far south as Le Quesnel, but the majority came from the battlefields of the Somme, July-November 1916. Of the 300 French dead, 253 are unidentified while 239 of the Commonwealth dead are unidentified.

The cemetery contains a Cross of Sacrifice, bearing the inscription, in English and French, 'That The World May Remember The Common Sacrifice Of Two And A Half Million Dead Here Have Been Laid Side By Side Soldiers Of France And Of The British Empire In Eternal Comradeship.' Among those buried here is Captain Ivan Provis Wentworth Bennett, 7th Queen's (Royal West Surreys), killed in action on 14 July 1916 aged 25 years. When war broke out he was studying to be a lawyer and was a keen golfer winning trophies at his local club. He was commissioned on 12 September 1914 and was promoted to Lieutenant in January 1915 going to France in June before he was promoted to Captain in November. The battalion remained in training until 1 July 1916 when they saw action for the first time. Bennett missed the attack on Montauban when his battalion suffered over 500 casualties as he was at the Army School. He returned on 4 July ready for the battalion's next action, an attack at Trones Wood on the evening of 13 July. The War Diary records 'The first line suffered immediate and heavy casualties. The second line reinforced at once but also suffered heavily and in spite of very gallant leading by Capt I P W Bennett and 2 /Lt P R Woollatt was unable to get to within 100 yards of Trones Wood.' They were among nearly 230 casualties. Bennett was shot in the head about 150m in front of the British trenches and died shortly afterwards. Private Courtman, his batman, went to him as soon as he was wounded and tried to bandage him. Courtman courageously stayed with him until he was wounded himself and had to withdraw. Bennet was originally buried on the north-western edge of Trones Wood and moved here in 1931 with an unidentified soldier from his battalion who still lies besides him.

| UK – 285 | Aust – 10 | Can – 4 |
| NZ – 1 | Fr – 300 | Unnamed – 239 |

THIEPVAL MEMORIAL TO THE MISSING OF THE SOMME

The Thiepval Memorial is situated near the south boundary of what was the park of the Chateau of Thiepval. Upon it are listed the names of approximately 72,000 British and South African officers and men who died from 1915, when the British arrived in the Somme, to 20 March 1918, and whose graves are not known. Over 90% of those commemorated died between July and November 1916. There is a memorial at Pozieres for the missing of the battles on the Somme after 20 March 1918.

The memorial, designed by Sir Edwin Lutyens, was built between 1928 and 1932 and unveiled by the then Prince of Wales on 1 August 1932 becoming the largest Commonwealth memorial in the world. Several battlefield cemeteries were cleared to create the park in which the cemetery and memorial stand. The monument is 44.2m high and is visible from much of the battlefield.

The site was chosen in 1926 but work did not begin for two years due to negotiations with the French authorities. Lutyens had originally proposed a very similar design for a memorial to be built across the Albert-Bapaume Road or at St. Quentin. He wanted it to be across a road in a similar fashion to the Menin Gate at Ieper, hence the narrow central arch we see today, but this was one of those objected to by the French, who were worried that there would be too many British memorials in France.

There are several men awarded the Victoria Cross commemorated on the memorial. Captain Eric Norman Frankland Bell, VC, 9th Royal Inniskilling Fusiliers attached 109th Light Trench Mortar Battery, killed in action on 1 July 1917 aged 20 years. Citation – 'For most conspicuous bravery. He was in command of a Trench Mortar Battery, and advanced with the Infantry in the attack. When our front line was hung up by enfilading machine gun fire Captain Bell crept forward and shot the machine gunner. Later, on no less than three occasions, when our bombing parties, which were clearing the enemy's trenches, were unable to advance, he went forward alone and threw Trench Mortar bombs among the enemy. When he had no more bombs available he stood on the parapet, under intense fire, and used a rifle with great coolness and effect on the enemy advancing to counter-attack. Finally he was killed rallying and reorganising infantry parties which had lost their officers. All this was outside the scope of his normal duties with his battery. He gave his life in his supreme devotion to duty.'

Private William Buckingham, VC, 1st Leicestershires, killed in action at Thiepval in the attack that captured the village from the Germans on 15 September 1916 aged 29 years. Citation – 'For conspicuous acts of bravery and devotion to duty in rescuing and rendering aid to the wounded whilst exposed to heavy fire, especially at Neuve-Chapelle on 10 and 12 March 1915.'

Lieutenant Geoffrey St. George Shillington Cather, VC, adjutant 9th Royal Irish Fusiliers, killed in action on 2 July 1916 aged 25 years. Citation – 'For most conspicuous bravery. From 7.00pm till midnight he searched 'No Man's Land', and brought in three wounded men. Next morning at 8.00am he continued his search, brought in another wounded man, and gave water to others, arranging for their rescue later. Finally, at 10.30am, he took out water to another man, and was proceeding further on when he was himself killed. All this was carried out in full view of the enemy, and under direct machine gun fire and intermittent artillery fire. He set a splendid example of courage and self sacrifice.'

Rifleman William Mariner, VC, 'B' Company, 2nd King's Royal Rifle Corps, killed in action on 1 July 1916 aged 34 years. Citation – 'During a violent thunderstorm on the night of 22 May, 1915, he left his trench near Cambrin, and crept out through the German wire entanglements till he reached the emplacement of a German machine gun which had been damaging our parapets and hindering our working parties. After climbing on the top of the German parapet he threw a bomb in under the roof of the gun emplacement and heard some groaning and the enemy running away. After about a quarter of an hour he heard some of them coming back again, and climbed up on the other side of the emplacement and threw another bomb among them left-handed. He then lay still while the Germans opened a heavy fire on the wire entanglement behind him, and it was only after about an hour that he was able to crawl back to his own trench. Before starting out he had requested a serjeant to open fire on the enemy's trenches as soon as he had thrown his bombs. Rifleman Mariner was out alone for one and half hours carrying out this gallant work.' He was killed near Loos, in an attack that was a diversion from the Battle of the Somme, when a shell exploded on him.

Rifleman William Frederick McFadzean, VC, 'C' Company, 14th Royal Irish Rifles, killed in action on 1 July 1916 aged 20 years. Citation – 'For most conspicuous bravery. While in a concentration trench and opening a box of bombs for distribution prior to an attack, the box slipped down into the trench, which was crowded with men, and two of the safety pins fell out. Private McFadzean, instantly realising the danger to his comrades, with heroic courage threw himself on the top of the bombs. The bombs exploded blowing him to pieces, but only one other man was injured. He well knew his danger, being himself a bomber, but without a moment's hesitation he gave his life for his comrades.'

Lieutenant Thomas Orde Lawder Wilkinson, VC, 7th Loyal North Lancashires, killed in action on 5 July 1916 aged 22 years. Citation – 'For most conspicuous bravery. During an attack, when a party of another unit was retiring without their machine-gun, Lieut. Wilkinson rushed forward, and, with two of his men, got the gun into action, and held up the enemy till they were relieved. Later, when the advance was checked during a bombing attack, he forced his way forward and found four or five men of different units stopped by a solid block of earth, over which the enemy was throwing bombs. With great pluck and promptness he mounted a machine-gun on the top of the parapet and dispersed the enemy bombers. Subsequently he made two most gallant attempts to bring in a wounded man, but at the second attempt he was shot through the heart just before reaching the man. Throughout the day he set a magnificent example of courage and self-sacrifice.'

Lieutenant Alexander Young, VC, 4th South African Infantry, killed in action on 19 October 1916 aged 44 years. Citation – 'Towards the close of the action at Ruiter's Kraal (South African War) on 13 August 1901, Sergeant-Major Young, with a handful of men, rushed some kopjes which were being held by the Boers. Sergeant Major Young then galloped on some 50 yards ahead of his party and closing with the enemy shot one of them and captured Commandant Erasmus, the latter firing at him three times at point blank range before being taken prisoner.'

There are three men who were executed commemorated on the Memorial. Private Peter Cairnie, 1st Royal Scots Fusiliers, executed at 7.00am near Bus-les-Artois for desertion on 28 December 1916. He deserted to avoid the attack by his unit at Serre on 13 November 1916 in which they suffered 200 casualties for no gains. He had been transferred to this battalion on 20 October 1916 having served with reserves in Scotland before that date. His first name is William but he was known as Peter.

Private Harry Farr, 1st West Yorkshires, executed for cowardice at 6.00am at Carnoy on 18 October 1916. He had enlisted in 1908 and suffered shell-shock in May 1915. He returned to Ieper five months later but repeatedly had time in medical units. He requested another visit to a Field Ambulance, which was denied, so he refused to move to the front-line at Guillemont on 17 September 1916. His court martial took place at Ville-sur-Ancre on 1 October and lasted twenty minutes.

Private Charles Walter F Skilton, 22nd (Kensington) Royal Fusiliers, executed for desertion on 26 December 1916, aged 20 years. He deserted before an attack by his battalion on the Quadrilateral near Serre in November 1916. His battalion commanding officer gave a damning report on his conduct and character. He was executed at Yvrench near Abbeville but the grave was lost.

Among many unhappy stories that come from the names on the memorial the following are all on Pier 15A, all are brothers and all were killed whilst serving in the 13th Royal Irish Rifles, 36th (Ulster) Division on 1 July 1916. They are Rifleman James Donaldson, 18960, aged 23 years, Rifleman Samuel Donaldson, 18959, aged 21 years and Rifleman John Donaldson 18958, aged 26 years. Note the consecutive service numbers. From this memorial you can see the hill up which the 36th (Ulster) Division attacked.

Other relatives who were in the 36th (Ulster) Division killed on 1 July 1916 commemorated on the memorial, and this is not a definitive list, include:

- Private Andrew Hobbs, 14259, Private David Hobbs, 14305 and Sergeant Robert Hobbs, 14302, all 9th Royal Irish Fusiliers.
- Lieutenant Arthur Hollywood, 9th Royal Irish Fusiliers aged 24 years and 2nd Lieutenant James Hollywood, 18th attached 12th Royal Irish Rifles, aged 23 years.
- Rifleman George Larmour, 16674, 14th Royal Irish Rifles, aged 25 years and Rifleman William Larmour, 16675, 9th Royal Irish Rifles, aged 29 years.
- Rifleman James McGowan 6190, aged 19 years and Rifleman John McGowan 19687, aged 18 years, 12th Royal Irish Rifles.

The list above is just a surface look at how families were affected by the war as are the following. Arthur Gilbert Decimus Dorman, 24th (Sportsmen) Royal Fusiliers, killed in action on 13 November 1916 at Boom Ravine near Grandcourt aged 20 years. Lieutenant Anthony Godfrey Dorman, MC, 13th East Yorkshires, was killed on the same day near Serre.

Corporal Charles Freeman and his brother Sergeant James Freeman, MM, both of 1/4th King's Shropshire Light Infantry were killed in action on the same day in the Battle of Cambrai, 30 December 1917. James is buried at Fifteen Ravine Cemetery while Charles's body was not identified. Their sister Mrs W Hawkins also lost her husband Pte W H Hawkins, 1st King's Shropshire Light Infantry who died of wounds on 27 June 1915 while at home.

Notably commemorated here is one of a family who lost five sons in the war. The family came from Great Rissington which is found between Oxford and Cheltenham. Private Frederick George Souls, 16th Cheshires, killed in action on 19 July 1916 aged 30 years, is commemorated here. Lance Corporal Arthur William Souls, MM, 16th Cheshires attached 7th Queen's Own (Royal West Kents), killed in action on 25 April 1918 aged 31 years (twin of Alfred Souls) is buried in Hangard Communal Cemetery Extension. Private Alfred Souls, 11th Cheshires, killed in action on 20 April 1918 aged 31 years (twin of Arthur William Souls), is buried in Strand Military Cemetery, Ploegsteert Wood. Private Albert Souls, Machine Gun Corps, killed in action on 14 March 1916 aged 20 years, is buried at Bully-Grenay Communal Cemetery. Private Walter Davis Souls, Machine Gun Corps, died of wounds on 2 August 1916 aged 24 years, is buried in St. Sever Cemetery, Rouen.

Also here is a member of one of the other families to lose five sons. Corporal George Henry Smith, 1/6th Durham Light Infantry was killed on 5 November 1916 aged 26 years. His brother, Private Robert Smith, 1/6th Durham Light Infantry was killed on 19 September 1916 and is buried in Dernancourt Communal Cemetery Extension. A third brother, Private Frederick Smith, 20th Durham Light Infantry, was killed on 31 July 1917 and is commemorated on the Menin Gate Memorial at Ieper. Another brother, Private Alfred Smith, 9th Durham Light Infantry, died on 22 July 1918 and is buried in Terlincthun British Cemetery. The last sibling, a half brother John William Stout, 1/5th West Yorkshires, was killed in action on 9 October 1917 and is commemorated on the Tyne Cot Memorial near Ieper.

We know of three families from the United Kingdom to lose five sons, the Souls, the Smiths and the Beecheys (see Villers-Bretonneux Memorial).

Another man here is Private George Colclough, 7th Loyal North Lancashires, killed in action on 14 November 1916, aged 17 years. He was the son of Private Joseph Colclough who died on 22 November 1915, and is buried at Hedge Row Trench Cemetery, near Ieper. He went to war after three girls who lived in his street sent him a white feather. He was only at the front a few weeks when he was killed.

Also commemorated on the memorial is Lieutenant George Sainton Kaye Butterworth, MC, MiD, 13th Durham Light Infantry, killed in action on 5 August 1916 aged 31 years. At the outbreak of the war, Butterworth joined up as a Private in the Duke of Cornwall's Light Infantry, but he soon became a 2nd Lieutenant in the 13th Durham Light Infantry, and he was later promoted to Lieutenant. The 13th Durham Light Infantry fought at Contalmaison and Pozieres in July 1916 capturing a series of trenches near Pozieres on 16–17 July. Butterworth was wounded in the action for which he was awarded the Military Cross. During the night of 4 August 1916 Butterworth and his men captured and held a communication trench known as Munster Alley suffering severe losses. At 4.45am on 5 August, during German attempts to recapture the position, Butterworth was shot through the head by a sniper. He was buried by his men in the side of the trench, but his body was lost. He was regarded as potentially a great composer. Butterworth's 'The Banks of Green Willow' have come to symbolise the sacrifice of his generation and has been seen by some as an anthem for all 'Unknown Soldiers' while his works based on A. E. Housman's collection of poems 'A Shropshire Lad' are among the best known of his music.

A well-known journalist and author on the memorial is Lance Serjeant Hector Hugh Munro, 'A' Company, 22nd (Kensington) Royal Fusiliers, killed on 14 November 1916 aged 45 years. He was known as 'Saki'. He was killed by a sniper while sheltering in a crater.

There are four members of the Heart of Midlothian Football Club commemorated here who volunteered together in 1914. Sergeant Duncan Currie, Private Ernest Edgar Ellis and Private Henry Wattie died between Contalmaison and La Boiselle on 1 July 1916. The battalion suffered nearly 600 casualties in the attack. Lance Corporal James Boyd was killed on 3 August 1916, a 'quiet day' following yet another failed attempt to take an enemy trench in full daylight.

Private James Smith, 7th East Lancashires, was killed in action 5 July 1916. He had been married since April 1916 and at the front for less than three weeks.

There are many sportsmen commemorated here and this list is not definitive. One is Sergeant Tom McCormick, 12th Manchesters who was killed in action at Fricourt on 6 July 1916. By 1914 he had become British, European and World Welterweight Boxing Champion. Corporal Jeremiah Delaney, MM, 23rd (1st Sportsmens) Royal Fusiliers was a professional boxer and Lightweight Champion killed in action on 27 July 1916 at Delville Wood. Company Sergeant Major William Philo, 8th Royal Fusiliers, killed in action at Ovillers on 7 July 1916, aged 36 years won the Middleweight Boxing Bronze at the 1908 Olympics.

Lance Corporal Leigh Richmond Roose, who served as Leigh Rouse, MM, 9th Royal Fusiliers, killed in action on 7 October 1916 aged 38 years was a footballer and Welsh International goalkeeper. Corporal Dan Dunglinson, 16th Northumberland Fusiliers was killed just south of Thiepval on 1 July 1916 aged 26 years. Killed alongside Dan was Private Thomas Goodwill. They were both pre-war footballers with Newcastle United. Dunglinson's brother, William, was killed in 1918 and is buried at Bienvillers. Private Walter Gerrish, 17th (Footballers) Middlesex, was an Aston Villa and Bristol Rovers player who died on 8 August 1916 near Waterlot Farm aged 27 years. He is reported to have lost both his legs before he died. With him was Private Oscar Linkson, a Manchester United star full-back who had won the FA Cup in 1909 and League in 1911.

Olympian Alfred Edward Flaxman, 1/6th South Staffordshires, killed in action on 1 July 1916 at Gommecourt was an athlete who represented Great Britain at the 1908 summer Olympics. Captain John Robert Somers-Smith, 1/5th (London Rifle Brigade) Londons, also killed in action at Gommecourt was a member of the Gold Medal winning Rowing Coxless Fours at the 1908 Olympics. Somers-Smith won a Military Cross in 1916 for his bravery at Ieper the previous year. He was killed exactly one year and one day after his brother lost his life. Another Olympian, Captain Robert M Finden Davies, 1/9th (Queen Victoria's Rifles) Londons was lost on 9 September 1916. He was in the British Shooting team in the 1912 Olympics. Captain Rowland Fraser, 6th attached 1st Rifle Brigade and Scottish Rugby Union international was killed on 1 July 1916 aged 26 years. Lieutenant Eric Milroy, 8th Black Watch, was killed on 18 July 1916 in Delville Wood. He had been captain of Scotland's Rugby Union team. Company Sergeant Major 'Dick' Thomas, 16th Welsh, Welsh Rugby Union international was killed on 7 July 1916. Soon after, another Welsh international, Captain John Lewis "Johnnie" Williams, 16th Welsh was killed in action at Mametz Wood on 12 July 1916. He played seventeen times for his country losing only twice winning the 'Triple Crown' on three occasions. Two days later another Welsh international, who played for his country on four occasions, Corporal David Watts, 7th King's Shropshire Light Infantry was killed in action. Another Welsh Rugby Union international is 2nd Lieutenant Horace Wyndham Thomas, 14th attached 16th Rifle Brigade, killed in action at Guillemont on 3 September 1916. Two men who served in the 1/10th King's (Liverpools) and represented England at Rugby Union were killed attacking Waterlot Farm and Guillemont on 9 August 1916. Lance Corporal John Abbott King had won twelve caps for England at rugby. 2nd Lieutenant Lancelot Andrew Noel Slocock had played for England on eight occasions. Lieutenant Alfred Frederick Maynard, Howe Battalion, Royal Naval Division was an England rugby international killed at Beaumont on 13 November 1916.

The Reverend Rupert Edward Inglis, Chaplain 4th Class, Army Chaplains' Department, killed in action on 18 September 1916 aged 53 years was an England international rugby player who later became a Church of England rector in 1889. He made three appearance for England in 1886 winning the Home Nations Championship.

In 1915, Inglis decided that, if he was to encourage the young men of his village to sign up, he would also have to volunteer which he did at the age of 51. He spent much of his service with Medical Units. By mid-September, he was at Ginchy on the Somme where, on 18 September, he joined a party of stretcher-bearers to bring in the wounded. While doing this, he was struck by a fragment of shell and while his wound was being dressed a second shell killed him. His father commanded the British during the Siege of Lucknow in 1857 where his wife was by his side. Lieutenant Kenneth Lotherington Hutchings, 4th attached 12th The King's (Liverpools), killed in action when struck by a shell on 3 September 1916 was an English international cricketer. Hutchings was a member of the Kent team that won the County Championship in 1906, 1909 and 1910. He played seven Test matches for England, with a highest score of 126 at Melbourne on the 1907-08 tour of Australia. In that innings, he reached his hundred in 126 minutes, his second fifty taking only 51 minutes.

Another name of note on the memorial is Major Cedric Charles Dickens, 1/13th (Kensington) Londons, killed in action on 9 September 1916 attacking Louze Wood aged 27 years. He had been in the army since 1915, when he was wounded, and survived the attack at Gommecourt on 1 July 1916. On the road from Guillemont to Combles is a well-marked track leading north to a place know as Dickens Cross. It is a memorial to Major Cedric Charles Dickens, grandson of the author, Charles Dickens. His men had put up a cross in 1917 where they believed he was buried. After the war the Dickens family tried to rebury their relative but his body could not be found. The grave had been clearly marked so it is probable that it had been disturbed in 1918 and the original markers were put back out of position. In 1979 a farmer ploughed up some officer's equipment nearby. In the 1990's, the memorial cross was moved to a new and more accessible site nearer the road.

LOCATION
Thiepval is a small village 5km north of Albert on ridges above the valley of the River Ancre. There are many routes to Thiepval, from Authuille and Aveluy, or via the D50 on the north side of the Ancre, or on a road from Pozieres or others. Whichever way you come you will be able to see the Thiepval Memorial to the Missing from some distance. The cemetery lies at the foot of the Memorial.

THILLOY ROAD CEMETERY, BEAULENCOURT

HISTORY
The cemetery was only used from September 1918 until the early part of October 1918.
INFORMATION
Ligny-Thilloy was held by the Germans for much of the war. It was taken from them during the German retreat to the Hindenburg Line in March 1917 when nearby villages were also taken. The villages were lost again to the Germans on 25 March 1918 and were not recaptured until August 1918 when they fell after fierce fighting.
The cemetery was opened by the 53rd Field Ambulance and was used during the next six weeks by the 3rd, 4th and 43rd Casualty Clearing Stations.

It was situated next to a larger German cemetery made in early 1918. This was removed soon after the war when over 200 German graves were taken to larger cemeteries and the seven British graves were moved to Favreuil British Cemetery. Of the ten Germans who are still here, nine are unidentified.
Among those buried here is Major William Guthrie Forbes, MC, 135th Heavy Battery, Royal Garrison Artillery, died of wounds on 26 September 1918 aged 28 years. William was a banker and joined the Royal Naval Volunteer Reserve. He served as an Able Seaman in the London Anti-Aircraft section, but later obtained a commission in the Royal Garrison Artillery. He went to France in September 1916,

was promoted to Captain in September 1917 and Major in July 1918. On 25 September 1918 Major Forbes was wounded and died the following day.

UK – 230 NZ – 9 BWI – 1
Ger – 10 Area – 673 sq mts

LOCATION
Beaulencourt lies on the Bapaume-Peronne road about 3km south-east of Bapaume. This cemetery can be found on the north side of the road to Ligny-Thilloy almost 3km directly south of Bapaume, 1km west of the Autoroute and just on the north side of the border of the Department of the Somme. It is in open fields east of Beaulencourt midway between the village and Ligny-Thilloy. A farm road leads 100m to the cemetery.

THISTLE DUMP CEMETERY

Among those here is Major Ivan Brunker Sherbon, MC, 19th Australian Infantry, killed, leading an attack on a German position, on 14 November 1916 aged 23 years. He was awarded the Military Cross while still a Captain for his work at Pozieres particularly for leading the 28th Australian Infantry into position under fire on 28 July. He had obtained a commission in 1913 and left Australia for Europe in June 1915 as a Captain. Between these events he had been involved in the campaign to occupy the German possessions in the Pacific and been promoted to Lieutenant. He served through the latter part of the Gallipoli campaign, and then France.

UK – 122 NZ – 38 Aust – 36
Ger – 7 KUG – 12 Unnamed – 59
Area - 1118 sq mts

Special Memorials erected to three British soldiers and one from New Zealand who are known to be buried among the unnamed graves.

HISTORY
The cemetery was opened in August 1916 and remained in use until February 1917. The cemetery was enlarged after the war by the concentration of 56 graves from isolated positions on the surrounding battlefields.

INFORMATION
Thistle Dump was a small camp for munitions and rations from August 1916 and was therefore used for the burial of dead men brought back from the nearby front-line who did not survive to reach a dressing station. It was used by the Germans for the burial of five men in March and April 1918.

LOCATION
The cemetery is situated in a valley that runs north of, and parallel to, the Contalmaison-Longueval road. It is about 1km west of Longueval and is reached from the road by means of a small track. It may be best to park at Caterpillar Valley Cemetery and walk to this cemetery.

TIGRIS LANE CEMETERY

HISTORY
The cemetery was opened in May 1917 by the 14th (Light) Division, naming it after a local trench line, and used again in August-September 1918.

INFORMATION
Wancourt was captured by British troops on the 12 April 1917. At the end of March 1918 the village and its neighbourhood were lost, but they were recovered by the Canadian Corps on the following 26 August. Neuville-Vitasse was attacked by the 56th (London) Division on 7 April 1917 and captured by the same Division on 9 April. The village was almost entirely lost at the end of March 1918 but regained at the end of the following August. The location of this cemetery came and went under British

control on the same dates as the local villages. The cemetery is named after a trench.

Among those buried here is Lieutenant Leroy Eaton Awrey, 1st Battalion, Canadian Machine Gun Corps, killed in action on 30 August 1918 aged 29 years. Leroy was a lawyer who had been a local football quarterback star for the Hamilton Tigers in Canada. He had enlisted in 1916 and only arrived in France in the spring of 1918.

UK – 86   Can – 33   Unnamed – 9

Area – 668 sq mts

LOCATION

The cemetery is located about 5km south-west of Arras 1km south of the Arras-Cambrai road. It is 2.5km west of Wancourt and a similar distance north-east of Neuville-Vitasse. It lies in open countryside on the north side of the road between Wancourt and Tilloy lès Mofflaines. The graves are located in clusters.

TILLOY BRITISH CEMETERY

HISTORY

The cemetery was in use by the British from April 1917 until March 1918 and again in August 1918. After the war it was used as a concentration cemetery for the burial of men brought in from smaller burial grounds and isolated locations on the battlefields east of Arras.

INFORMATION

Tilloy was in German hands for much of the war. It was captured by the British on 9 April 1917 but partly retaken by the Germans again from March to August 1918.

Rows A to H in Plot I represent for the most part burials from the fighting to take the village from the Germans in early 1917. The remaining graves in Plot I, and the first three rows of Plot II, represent the remaining war-time burials. The other Plots were formed after the war.

Among those here is Major James Donaldson Dulany Brancker, DSO, 116th Siege Battery, Royal Garrison Artillery, killed in action on 1 May 1917 aged 39 years. He was the son of the former British Vice-Consul in Baltimore, Maryland, USA and held American citizenship. An elder brother was killed in the South African Wars in 1900. By that time, James was already in the Royal Artillery serving as a Lieutenant. He saw time in India before visiting the USA briefly and then returned to service in England. He was killed with several men from his Battery and posthumously awarded the Distinguished Service Order for his actions.

Also here is Lance Corporal William Swift, 8th King's Own (Royal Lancasters), killed in action on 9 May 1917 aged 19 years. He had been sentenced to three years youth detention in June 1915 but was allowed to join the army, though underage, to avoid prison.

Also here is Lance Corporal William Henry Jeffery, 2nd Yorkshires, killed in action on 2 April 1917. His brother, Private George David Jeffery (recorded as Jeffrey), 2nd Lincolnshires, was killed in action on 21 March 1918 and is commemorated on the Pozieres Memorial. Another brother, Private Lawrence Frederick Jeffery (recorded as Jeffrey), 10th East Yorkshires, was killed in action on 29 October 1916 and is commemorated on the Thiepval Memorial.

Another of note is 2nd Lieutenant Cecil Fred Rowland, 231st Siege Battery, Royal Garrison Artillery killed in action on 21 March 1918 aged 35 years. He was an organist at Gloucester Cathedral.

Concentrated here:

Artillery Track Cemetery, Arras – it contained 39 British soldiers killed in action on 9 and 10 April 1917.

Chapel Road Cemetery, Wancourt – about 1.5km east of here midway between Feuchy Chapel on the Arras-Cambrai road and Neuville-Vitasse, where 34 British soldiers were buried in April 1917.

Harp Redoubt Cemetery, Tilloy-Les-Mofflaines – located near a German redoubt on the south side of the village which was taken by the 14th (Light) Division supported by tanks on 9 April 1917. It contained 87 British soldiers, of whom 36 were from the King's Royal Rifle Corps.

Maison-Rouge British Cemetery, Tilloy-Les-Mofflaines – situated about 500m north of here on the road to Cambrai. It contained the graves of 89 British soldiers, 14 South Africans, one Canadian and one from New Zealand. There were also thirteen German soldiers. The cemetery was used in 1917 and again in March, April and August 1918.

Tees Trench Cemeteries No. 1 and No. 2, St. Laurent-Blangy - roughly 4km north of here, near the D60 road to Bailleul-sir-Berthoult. They contained 32 British soldiers who were killed, with two exceptions, on 9 April 1917.

Telegraph Hill British Cemetery, Neuville-Vitasse – located about 1km south of here on the south-western slopes of the hill between Tilloy and Neuville-Vitasse that was captured by the 14th Division on 9 April 1917. The cemetery contained the graves of 147 British soldiers, most of whom were men of the 14th Division killed in April 1917.

Tilloy Wood Cemetery – found on the western side of the village about 500m from here. It contained the graves of 80 British soldiers who died in April 1917.

White House Cemetery, Tilloy-Les-Mofflaines - situated about 500m north of here on the main road to Cambrai. It contained the graves of 22 British and two German soldiers who died on 11 and 12 April 1917.

UK – 1447   Aust – 91   Can – 57
SAfr – 15   NF – 4   NZ – 3
Ger – 2   Unnamed – 610

Area – 5388 sq mts
Special Memorials to fourteen British soldiers known or believed to be buried among the unnamed.
Special Memorials for eleven men of the 6th King's Own Scottish Borderers, buried in Tees Trench Cemetery No. 2, whose graves were destroyed by shell fire.

LOCATION
Tilloy-les-Mofflaines is on the south-eastern edge of Arras with just a very short area of open space between Arras and the village. The cemetery is on the south-east side of the village on the north side of the road to Wancourt next to the civilian cemetery and opposite a sports centre.

TINCOURT NEW BRITISH CEMETERY

HISTORY
The cemetery was opened in June 1917 and remained in use until March 1918. The British made further burials in September 1918 and continued to use the cemetery until September 1919. It was enlarged by the burial of soldiers concentrated from isolated positions or smaller cemeteries on the surrounding battlefields.

INFORMATION
Tincourt was behind the German line for most of the war. It was taken by the British in the actions following the German retreat to the Hindenburg Line in March 1917 but fell again to the Germans on 23 March 1918. The village was retaken by the Allies, having been destroyed by shell-fire, on 6 September 1918.

The village was a centre for Casualty Clearing Stations when it was in British hands. It is from these that many of the burials were made here. The German burials, made during their occupation of the village, are in Plot VI, Row A. The graves of 136 American soldiers, buried here in late 1918, have been removed, as have those of two Italian soldiers.

Among those here are Company Serjeant Major John Pollard, DCM, 9th King's Own Yorkshire Light Infantry, killed in action on 30 December 1917 aged 41 years. His citation for the award of the Distinguished Conduct Medal reads 'For conspicuous gallantry and devotion to duty. During five nights he took up rations to the front line and showed unfailing resolution and devotion to duty in bringing his parties repeatedly through the zone of the enemy's barrage. His example was a fine incentive to his men.'

The 'civilian' buried here is Paul Murphy, 13th (Civilian) Labour Company, Labour Corps who died on 29 July 1917. Three Civilian Labour companies were sent to France in 1917 – 11th, 12th and 13th Civilian Platelayer Companies. Their role was to provide professional expertise in the laying of broad and narrow gauge railway track in the British sector. Tincourt was important for narrow gauge railways as a whole system of trench railways was established to serve the front line beyond Hargicourt.

Lieutenant Colonel H H F Turner, 2nd Lancers (Gardner's Horse), killed in action on 1 December 1917 lies here. He was killed at the site of Pigeon Ravine Cemetery near Epehy 8km north-east of here. A cavalry charge was led by the Indian Army 2nd Lancers on 1 December 1917 to halt the German advance from Cambrai. The commanding officer, Lieutenant Colonel H H F Turner, led an attack along a shallow valley under intense fire from German machine guns. His Lancers were supported by the 6th Inniskilling Dragoons and a mounted machine gun section. The 2nd Lancers lost two British officers, including Turner, one Indian officer and six Indian other ranks killed. One Victoria Cross, one Distinguished Service Order and one Bar, three Military Crosses, two Indian Order of Merit (2nd Class), seven Indian Distinguished Service Medals and one Bar were awarded. Turner was the third cavalry commanding officer to die on that day.

Also here is Captain D'Urban Victor Armstrong, DFC, No. 151 Squadron, Royal Air Force, killed on 13 November 1918 aged 21 years. Armstrong joined the Royal Flying Corps in 1915 and was assigned to No. 60 Squadron the following year. While with them, he scored his first victory on 9 November 1916 shooting down an Albatros DI near Havrincourt. His next posting was to No. 44 Squadron on home defence duties. In 1917, he was transferred to No. 78 Squadron to lead a flight. His final assignment was with No. 151 Squadron. He was one of the first to achieve a victory at night in aerial warfare, as No. 151 Squadron was the Royal Air Force's first night fighter squadron. Armstrong was credited with four night-time victories between 29 June and 17 September 1918, including a Gotha G bomber on 24 August. Two days after the end of the war, Armstrong was killed in a flying accident while performing aerobatics in his Sopwith Camel. The citation for his Distinguished Flying Cross, awarded posthumously, reads 'A brilliant pilot of exceptional skill. His success in night operations has been phenomenal; and the services he renders in training other pilots is of the greatest value, personally supervising their flying and demonstrating the only successful method of attack by night. On the night of 10-11th September, learning that an enemy aeroplane was over our front, he volunteered to go up. The weather conditions were such as to render flying almost impossible, the wind blowing about fifty miles an hour, accompanied by driving rainstorms; despite this, Capt. Armstrong remained on patrol for over an hour, his machine at times being practically out of control. The foregoing is only one

of many instances of this officer's remarkable skill and resolution in night operations.'
Concentrated here:

Barleux French Military Cemetery No. 2 - situated about 8km south-west of here, and just south-west of Peronne, between that village and Belloy-en-Santerre. Among the French graves it contained the graves of two British soldiers of the 1st Loyal North Lancashires killed in February 1917.

Bernes Churchyard - situated in the village which is about 4km south-east of here. It contained the graves of eighteen British soldiers and one Canadian among the 38 German graves.

Howitzer Wood Cemetery, Clery-Sur-Somme - situated about 8km west of here and just north-west of Peronne. This French Cemetery was in the wood called the Bois des Ourages south of the village. It contained the graves of three British soldiers and an Australian among the French.

Jeancourt Indian Cemetery - situated in the village about 6km south-east of here. It was near the present Communal Cemetery on the west edge of the village. It contained the graves of fifteen Indian cavalryman buried in 1917. After the war 541 German graves were concentrated into a cemetery on the edge of the Indian burial ground but these have also been removed.

Le Mesnil Churchyard German Extension - situated in the village about 5km south-west of here and 3km south of Peronne. It contained the graves of ten British soldiers among the 150 Germans.

Le Verguier German Cemetery - near the church in the village 9km east of here. It contained the graves of five British soldiers, killed in April 1918, among the 292 Germans.

Longavesnes British Cemetery - situated on the west side of the village about 4km north of here. It contained the graves of nineteen British soldiers who died in September and October 1918. Three American soldiers buried here have been removed.

Magny-La-Fosse Churchyard Extension - situated about 15km east of here. It was made by an advanced Dressing Station in October 1918 to contain the graves of seven British soldiers, three men of the Chinese Labour Corps and an Australian.

Manancourt Churchyard - situated on the Canal du Nord about 15km north of here. The churchyard had been closed in 1865 but was used by the Germans and the Allies during the war. It contained the graves of ten British soldiers with one South African serviceman.

Marquaix German Cemetery - situated on the north side of the village that is about 2km east of here. It contained the graves of ten British and 338 German soldiers with one French military burial.

Peronne Communal Cemetery German Extension - in the centre of the town and now removed it contained the graves of 25 British and 824 German soldiers.

Ramicourt Communal Cemetery Extension - situated south of the village about 20km east of here. It was begun by the Germans and in October 1918 the British buried ten Australians and a British soldier.

Suzanne French Military Cemetery No. 1 - situated in the chateau near the village about 15km west of here. It contained the graves of one British, one Australian and one German soldier among the 255 French burials.

Tincourt German Cemetery - situated on the south-west side of the village where the Germans had located hospitals. It was used during the German occupation in 1918. Among the German graves were buried thirteen British and three Canadian soldiers with an Australian.

Vraignes Churchyard - situated in the village of Vraignes-en-Vermandois about 5km south of here. It contained the graves of three British soldiers buried by the Germans in March and April 1918.

Vraignes Communal Cemetery German Extension - on the north side of the village next to the present Communal Cemetery. It contained the grave of a British soldier among the 117 German burials.

UK – 1562	Aust – 226	Can – 45
SAfr - 39	Indian – 20	RGLI – 6
NF – 2	UK Civ – 1	Ger - 152
Chinese Labour Corps – 58		Unnamed – 251
Area – 6149 sq mts		

Special Memorials erected to seven British soldiers and one Australian known, or believed, to be buried among the unnamed graves.

Special Memorials erected to 21 British and two Canadian soldiers, one Australian and one South African, buried in other cemeteries, whose graves were destroyed by later shell-fire.

LOCATION
Tincourt-Boucly is situated in the valley of the River Cologne about 6km east of Peronne. The cemetery is on a ridge on the north side of the village about 50m from the road and reached by a farm track.

TORONTO CEMETERY, DEMUIN

HISTORY
The cemetery was made in August 1918 after the Allied advance in this area.

INFORMATION
Demuin was behind Allied lines for most of the war. However, it fell to the Germans on 30 March 1918, before brief recapture, and again on 31 March 1918. The 58th Canadian Infantry retook the village on 8 August 1918.
The cemetery was made by the 3rd Canadian Infantry and remained in use throughout August 1918 for the burial of dead from various Canadian units in action in the area. Some burials were also made of British troops who had been killed in March 1918.

The cemetery contains four Lieutenants of the 14th Canadian Infantry and two of the 3rd Canadian Infantry killed in action on 8 August 1918. There is also a Captain of the 3rd Canadian Infantry killed with them buried here.

Also buried here is Lance Corporal Frederick John Spratlin, MM & Bar, 3rd Canadian Infantry, killed in action on 8 August 1918 aged 36 years. A man of strong Presbyterian faith though not opposed on conviction to the war, he had gone to war as a stretcher bearer, as he was considered unfit for front-line duty due to varicose veins, in December 1915. He was awarded the Military Medal for his action during the attack on Fresnoy on 3 May 1917 where he spent much time in no-man's land rescuing men under sniper fire. He was one of the last medics to return to his trenches. His Bar was awarded in November 19197 at Passendale. The citation reads 'This man is recommended for most remarkable gallantry during the attack on PASSCHENDALE RIDGE on November 6th, when he went out from t h e vicinity time after time under an exceptionally heavy barrage and a very heavy snipers fire, and dressed wounded and dragged them to shelter from whence as soon as darkness permitted he collected them and dispatched them to the Dressing Station. His work throughout the entire engagement was absolutely marvellous and has been the comment of all his company.' Spratlin was killed in an attack near the Bois Morgemont that took place in heavy fog which hid the German machine-guns and pockets of resistance until the Canadians were on top of them. He was among 37 men killed in the attack and buried here. His Bible was one of the few possessions recovered and sent to his family. It was full of comments and notations about Spratlin's attitude towards the war, his motivations, his job as a stretcher-bearer and how to cope with what he had to see every day.

UK – 22   Can – 74   Aust – 1
Ger – 4   Unnamed – 22
Area – 390 sq mts

LOCATION
Demuin is a small village on the north side of the Amiens-Roye road about 15km south-east of Amiens. The cemetery is in the fields on a ridge to the north-east of the village on the east side of the road to Villers-Bretonneux. It is marked from the road and is reached by means of a farm track leading nearly 500m from the road. It is not advisable to take cars along the track, especially in winter, so this is a 200m walk from the last suitable parking space.

TOUTENCOURT COMMUNAL CEMETERY

HISTORY
The cemetery was used for British burials from October 1915 to August 1918.

INFORMATION
The village was behind Allied lines throughout the war. There are two groups of British graves which include one Australian officer who died of accidental injuries while serving with the 5th Australian Pioneers. Most of the dead here were serving with units other than front-line formations, though several were killed in action. There are three men of the Labour Corps, one of the Army Service Corps and three of Divisional Ammunition Columns reflecting the location behind the lines.

The Reverend Alfred Heath, Chaplain 4th Class attached 9th Duke of Wellington's killed in action on 30 June 1918 aged 39 years, is buried here, as are Lieutenants F. Crathorne and Thomas Alington Royds, both of the General List who died while attached to units, Crawthorne to the 252nd Tunnelling Company, Royal Engineers and Royds to No. 59 Squadron, Royal Air Force.

Driver Baker has a memorial next to his headstone from his comrades in the 4th Divisional Ammunition Column.

Among those here is Sapper Robert Bell, 123rd Field Company, Royal Engineers, executed for murder at 4.12am on 22 May 1918 aged 29 years. He shot 2nd Lieutenant Wynell Lloyd (buried in Warloy-Baillon Communal Cemetery Extension) on 17 April 1918. There seems to have been no motive other than a reprimand from the officer for Bell not wearing his putties on parade. Bell claimed to have slipped when climbing from his trench to return to parade having been sent for his putties and that his rifle had fired accidentally. He was court-martialled on 4 May and kept in a German Prisoner of War Camp until the execution took place.

UK - 22   Aust - 1

LOCATION
Toutencourt is about 20km north-east of Amiens and 15km west of Albert. The cemetery is on the western edge of the village on the south side of the road to Puchevillers and Doullens. The graves are in clusters in the western corner of the cemetery furthest from the gate.

TREFCON BRITISH CEMETERY

HISTORY
The cemetery was used in September 1918.

INFORMATION
The village was in German hands for much of the war. It was taken in 1917 by the British and fell again to the Germans in the spring offensive on 22 March 1918. The British recaptured the village in September 1918.

The cemetery was made by IX Corps (6th and 32nd Divisions) within the grounds of Caulaincourt Chateau. At that time it was called Caulaincourt Military Cemetery.

The WW2 casualty buried here is Pilot Officer Alexander Francis Burnett Ramsay, No. 4 Squadron, Royal Air Force, died on 21 April 1940 aged 19 years. He died in the French Military Hospital in Marcoing. It is unclear how he came to be there but Lysander L4741 of No. 4 Squadron was written-off when it crashed on approach to Mons-en-Chausee on 18 April 1940. Is it possible this incident involved Ramsay who had been with the Squadron since 23 March 1940.

Also buried here is Lieutenant Colonel Reginald Thomas Collins, DSO, MiD, Croix de Guerre, 17th Field Ambulance, Royal Army Medical Corps, killed in action on 18 September 1918. He entered the RAMC as a Lieutenant on 31 August 1903, became a Captain in 1907, Major in February 1915, and Lieutenant Colonel in September 1916. He received the Distinguished Service Order on 1 January 1918 in the New Year Honours List for his service rather than for a single act.

The nearby village of Caulaincourt was the scene of a battle in July 1871 during the Franco-Prussian War. There is a monument to this in the Communal Cemetery.

| UK – 282 | India – 1 | Unnamed – 13 |
| WW2 – 1 | | Area – 977 sq mts |

LOCATION
Trefcon is located about 14km west of St. Quentin on the south side of the N29 Amiens-St. Quentin road and north of the A29 Autoroute. The cemetery is north-east of the village on the D34 Caulaincourt to Beauvois-en-Vermandois road. It is a beautiful and tranquil spot.

TRIANGLE CEMETERY, INCHY-EN-ARTOIS

HISTORY
The cemetery was made in late September and early October 1918 after this area had been captured from the Germans in the final advance to victory.

INFORMATION
This area had been behind the German lines for most of the war. It was captured by the 4th Canadian Division on 27 September 1918 and the cemetery was made soon after. The cemetery gained its name from its triangular shape next to the road which makes it a very attractive cemetery. Among those here is 2nd Lieutenant The Honourable Richard Gerald Ava Bingham, No. 209 Squadron, Royal Air Force, killed in an air accident on 8 October 1918 aged 22 years. His Sopwith Camel collided with Captain Dudley George Antoine Allen of the same Squadron at about 3.00pm near Bourlon. Allen is also buried here. Bingham was son of the 5th Baron Clanmorris and younger brother of the 6th Baron. He was one of five brothers who fought in the war, one of whom, Commander (later Rear-Admiral) the Honourable Barry Bingham, won the Victoria Cross at the Battle of Jutland though he was taken prisoner by the Germans. Another brother, Lieutenant-Colonel The Honourable John Denis Yelverton Bingham, 15th/19th Hussars, won the Distinguished Service Order and the Legion d'Honeur. The Honourable Hugh Terence de Burgh Bingham served with the Indian Defence Forces. Squadron Leader The Honourable George Roderick Bentinck Bingham served as a Captain in the Royal Welsh Fusiliers and in the Waziristan Campaign in 1921. He fought in WW2 with the Royal Air Force Volunteer Reserve where he became a Squadron Leader.

| UK – 19 | Can – 69 | KUG – 2 |
| Unnamed - 9 | | Area – 472 sq mts |

LOCATION
Inchy-en-Artois is situated about 10km west of Cambrai and about 2km north of the Bapaume-Cambrai road. The cemetery is on the south-eastern edge of the village at a bend in the road to Moeuvres.

UNICORN CEMETERY, VEND'HUILE

HISTORY
Unicorn Cemetery was begun in October 1918 for the burial of a few men. Most of the cemetery was made after the war as a concentration cemetery.

INFORMATION
This area was behind German lines from 1914 until it was captured in early 1917. The Germans re-took this location during their offensive in March 1918. The area was attacked in late September 1918 by the American 27th and 30th Divisions with the British 50th Division in support. The British 12th and 18th Divisions cleared the area in taking the Hindenburg Line on 30 September when they made Row A of this cemetery. The cemetery lies on the American side of the Corps boundary between the British III Corps and the US II Corps during the final advance in 1918.

The name of the cemetery comes from the symbol of the 50th Division who made the first burials here. It is mainly burials of men of the 18th and 50th Divisions. The large part of the cemetery was concentrated here after the war when graves from smaller cemeteries, made in 1917 and 1918, and isolated positions on the surrounding battlefields were brought in.

Among those buried here is Corporal Lawrence Carthage Weathers, VC, 43rd Australian Infantry, died of wounds on 29 September 1918. A New Zealander, the citation for his Victoria Cross reads 'For most conspicuous bravery and devotion to duty on 2 September 1918, north of Peronne, when with an advanced bombing party. The attack having been held up by a strongly held enemy trench, Cpl. Weathers went forward alone under heavy fire and attacked the enemy with bombs. Then, returning to our lines for a further supply of bombs, he again went forward with three comrades, and attacked under very heavy fire. Regardless of personal danger, he mounted the enemy parapet and bombed the trench, and, with the support of his comrades, captured 180 prisoners and three machine guns. His valour and determination resulted in the successful capture of the final objective, and saved the lives of many of his comrades.' Shortly afterwards, Weathers was promoted to Corporal but less than a month later, he received serious wounds north-east of Peronne during an artillery barrage. He died three days afterwards without knowing he would receive the Victoria Cross, the award of which was gazetted on 24 December 1918.

Also here is Lieutenant Colonel Ralph Hindle, DSO, 4th Loyal North Lancashires, killed in action on 30 November 1917 aged 35 years. He commanded the battalion from February 1915 until wounded in action at Festubert. He took command again from August 1915, receiving the Distinguished Service Order for his leadership at Ieper in 1917. He was killed in action leading his men into attack at Vaucellette Farm. Their orders were to clear Villers Hill which they were achieving until ammunition ran low and a large German counter-attack was encountered. He and all his Company commanders in the attack were killed.

Another battalion commander here is Lieutenant Colonel Edward Hills Nicholson, DSO & Bar, three times MiD, 3rd Royal Fusiliers, killed in action on 4 October 1918. He joined the Royal Fusiliers as a 2nd Lieutenant in 1900 and served in the South African War. He was promoted to Captain in 1909. After the start of the war he was employed as Adjutant of the East India Railway. He then served in France from September 1915, when he was made a Major, before being sent to Salonika in October, where he became a Lieutenant Colonel in 1916. He returned to France in 1917, took command of 3rd Royal Fusiliers on 25 April 1918, and was killed near Le Catelet on the Hindenburg Line as his unit took Richmond Copse and 300 German prisoners at high cost. He was awarded the Distinguished Service Order in the Birthday Honours List for services in the field on 1 June 1918. He was posthumously awarded a Bar to his DSO in the New Years Honours List in January 1919 for his services in Salonika. He came from the family that had been involved in the invention and manufacture of linoleum, his father being Chairman of the company at his death in 1908. His brother Walter served with the Royal Fusiliers winning the Military Cross. Walter joined the RAF in WW2 and was killed as a Flight Lieutenant in February 1943 and is buried in Harwell Cemetery near Didcot, Oxfordshire. Another brother 2nd Lieutenant Bruce Hills Nicholson, served as a Trooper with the County of London Yeomanry at Gallipoli before becoming an officer with the 6th Royal Fusiliers in 1916. He went to France in early 1917, was killed near Arras on 3 May 1917 aged 20 years and is commemorated on the Arras Memorial. A third brother Sub-Lieutenant Victor Hills Nicholson joined the Royal Navy and died on 9 August 1917 aged 20 years when his ship, HMS Recruit was torpedoed and sunk. He is commemorated on the Plymouth Naval Memorial.

Concentrated here:

La Paurelle British Cemetery, Ronssoy - situated about 1km north of here. It was begun in April 1917 by the 1/5th Gloucestershires and remained in use until February 1918. It was used again in September 1918 by the 6th Northamptonshires after the 18th Division had recaptured Ronssoy. It contained 110 British men.

Basse-Boulogne British Cemetery, Lempire - situated about 1km west of here on the eastern edge of the former hamlet of Basse-Boulogne. It was made by the 103rd Labour Company after the capture of the hamlet by the 6th Northamptonshires and contained 67 British and Australian soldiers.

Lempire British Cemetery - situated on the eastern edge of the village about 200m west of this cemetery. It was made by the 18th Division after they had cleared the village on 19 September 1918. It contained 118 British, one Australian, 40 American and 40 German soldiers.

Lempire Communal Cemetery Extension - situated on the edge of the cemetery that is behind the present church that is at the south-western edge of the village at the boundary with Ronssoy. It contained seven British soldiers buried in late 1918.

Vend'huile Communal Cemetery Extension - situated on the edge of the present Communal Cemetery that is in the centre of the village which is 4km to the east of here. It contained six British soldiers buried in late 1918. The Communal Cemetery now contains two British soldiers, one buried in 1914.

UK – 689	Aust – 78	Can – 1
India – 2	KUG – 218	Unnamed – 409
Indian Labour Corps – 2		Area – 3859 sq mts

Special Memorials to ten British soldiers known, or believed, to be buried among the unnamed.

Special Memorials to eight British soldiers buried in Lempire British Cemetery whose graves could not be found at the time of concentration.

LOCATION
Unicorn Cemetery lies on the north side of the road from Ronssoy and Lempire to Vend'huile. It is on the west side of the Autoroute and the noise of traffic can be intrusive. However, the graves lie across the crest of the ridge which makes this an 'inviting' cemetery.

UPTON WOOD CEMETERY

HISTORY
The cemetery was made in September 1918.

INFORMATION
The village of Hendecourt-les-Cagnicourt was in German hands from 1914 until captured by the 57th (West Lancashire) and 52nd (Lowland) Divisions on the night of 1-2 September 1918. The wood was captured on 30 August 1918 by the 1st Canadian Division though the fighting continued over the next two days. It was vital that the wood be secured before the attack on the Drocourt-Queant Line began.

The cemetery was made by the Canadians, mostly for the burial of their own dead. The name comes from the nearby wood, though it was known to the French as the Bois d'Hendecourt.

Among those here is Private Robert Scott Chalmers, 5th (Saskatchewan) Canadian Infantry killed in action on 1 September 1918 aged 37 years. His headstone says that he was 'One of six brothers in all answered the call. One crippled, three killed.' One brother was Major John Stuart Chalmers, graduate of Glasgow University, 9th (Glasgow Highlanders) Highland Light Infantry, killed in action by shellfire near Ieper on 17 April 1918 aged 36 years and commemorated on the Ploegsteert Memorial. I have failed to identify the other brother to be killed but I believe it may be Assistant Steward David Blair Chalmers, Mercantile Marine, killed when the SS Ava was lost on route from Liverpool for Rangoon via Dakar on 26 January 1917 aged 26 years and commemorated on the Tower Hill Memorial in London. The crew of 92 died.

Also of note is Private Tokutoro Iwamoto, MM, 10th Canadian Infantry, killed in action on 2 September 1918 aged 38 years. He was one of several men of Japanese heritage who served with the Canadians in the war. His Military Medal was awarded for his work at Hill 70 on 15-16 August 1917. His father still lived in Kobe, Japan.

UK – 9	Can – 216	Unnamed – 9
KUG – 1	Area – 577 sq mts	

Special Memorial to one Canadian soldier believed to be buried among the unnamed.

LOCATION
The village of Hendecourt-les-Cagnicourt lies midway between Cambrai and Arras about 15km south-east of Arras and 4km south of the Arras—Cambrai road. The village is on the Bapaume-Douai road. The wood is situated about 1.5km north of the village and the cemetery is on the southern edge of the wood on a ridge between the Arras-Cambrai road and the village. The cemetery is about 300m north of the D956, can be seen from some distance, and is reached by a farm track from the road.

VADENCOURT BRITISH CEMETERY

HISTORY
The cemetery was opened in August 1917. It was used until March 1918 and again in October and November 1918. It was enlarged after the war.

INFORMATION
This area was in German hands from 1914. The British captured it in 1917 during the German withdrawal. The Germans recaptured it on 21 March 1918, though it was vigorously defended by the 24th Division and 2/4th Royal

Berkshires. The 1st Division took the area for the final time on 15 September 1918. Please note the hamlet is spelt differently from the name of the cemetery – an error made at the time and not corrected.

At the beginning of October 1918, the IX Corps Main Dressing Station was at Vadancourt. It, the 5th, 47th and 61st Casualty Clearing Stations and other Field Ambulances used the cemetery.

The cemetery was first known as Vadencourt New British Cemetery. The original graves are in Plots I-III. After the war those plots were enlarged, and Plots IV and V laid out, as 472 sets of remains were brought in from the surrounding battlefields and from a few smaller burial grounds. These burials were mainly of men who died in April 1917 and March, April, September and October 1918. Many of these were men of the 59th (North Midland) Division. When the cemetery was enlarged after the war, four French, 31 American and 28 German graves, all made in October 1918, were removed to other cemeteries.

Among those buried here is Lieutenant Colonel John Henry Stephen Dimmer, VC, MC, twice MiD, Kings Royal Rifle Corps attached and commanding 2/4th Royal Berkshires, killed in action on 21 March 1918 aged 35 years. Dimmer was a 31 year old Lieutenant in the 2nd Kings Royal Rifle Corps, when he was awarded the Victoria Cross for his actions on 12 November 1914 at Klein Zillebeke, near Ieper. He had been with the regiment since 1900, serving in Africa for several years, and becoming an officer during the Haldane Reforms in 1908. He received the Military Cross for his actions at Gheluvelt between 29 and 31 October 1914 being on the first list of recipients of awards in WW1. The Victoria Cross came soon after, the citation succinctly saying 'This officer served his Machine Gun during the attack on the 12th November at Klein Zillebeke until he had been shot five times – three times by shrapnel and twice by bullets, and continued at his post until his gun was destroyed.' Dimmer learned about his award from reading a British newspaper while recovering in a French hospital at Wimereux before he was evacuated to England and promoted to Captain in April 1915. He filled various appointments in England until May 1916 when he was sent to Salonika as a Company commander, and acting Major, with the 3rd Kings Royal Rifle Corps. Soon afterwards he was appointed machine-gun officer in the 10th (Irish) Division and qualified as an observer in the Royal Flying Corps. In October 1917 he was promoted to Lieutenant-Colonel commanding 2/4th Royal Berkshires in France. He was Mentioned in Despatches during the Battle of Cambrai in 1917. Two months later Dimmer was killed leading his battalion while on horseback in a counter-attack about 3km south of here at Marteville. He was subsequently awarded a posthumous Mention in Despatches.

Also here is Brigadier General Sir William Algernon Ireland Kay, CMG, DSO, six times MiD, General Staff, commanding 3rd Infantry Brigade late King's Royal Rifle Corps, died on 4 October 1918 aged 42 years. He was the 6th Baronet Kay, son of Lieutenant-Colonel Sir William Kay, 5th Baronet, and Lady Kay. He served in Sierra Leone from 1898-1899 and the South African Wars 1899-1902. He was awarded the Distinguished Service Order as a Major in 2nd Kings Royal Rifle Corps scouting the German line on 1 October 1914 and was, like Dimmer, on the first list of recipients of awards in WW1. He was severely wounded in October 1914 at Hooge near Ieper and at the same time inherited his title. He took command of 2nd Brigade in March 1918 and was wounded soon after. After recovery he was made a Companion of the Order of St. Michael and St. George (CMG) and then he took command of the 3rd Brigade in April 1918. He was killed by a gas shell while reconnoitring the German positions with his aide, Captain William Fulton Somervail, DSO, MC, MiD, 2nd Cameronians (Scottish Rifles). Somervail had won the Military Cross for taking command of his battalion for two days as a 2nd Lieutenant at the Battle of Neuve Chapelle. In July 1917. He took command of his battalion again, though formally, and was awarded the Distinguished Service Order for his leadership rather than for a single act. The two men are buried side by side.

Concentrated here:

Maissemy Churchyard – destroyed in the war it was located in the centre of the village on the south side of the river from here. It contained the graves of five British soldiers who died in April and May 1917 and were buried by their comrades near the south side of the churchyard.

Vadencourt Chateau Cemetery – situated about 200m west of here, in which nine British soldiers and six Canadians were buried in April-August 1917.

Vendelles Churchyard Extension – located about 2.5km north-west of here. It was made by the 59th Division in April 1917 and contained the graves of 36 British soldiers.

UK – 726	Aust – 11	Can – 7
Chinese Labour Corps – 4		Indian – 2
Unnamed – 214		Area – 2953 sq mts

Special Memorials to five Indian cavalry soldiers whose bodies were cremated.

LOCATION

Vadancourt is a small hamlet about 8km north-west of St. Quentin. It is in the valley of the River L'Omignon on the opposite side of the river from Maissemy. It is about 3km north of the Amiens to St. Quentin road and a similar distance west of the A26 Autoroute. The cemetery is on the north side of the Vermand to Bellenglise D33 road in a dip on the south side of the hamlet after which it is named. Please note the hamlet is spelt differently from the name of the cemetery – an error made at the time and not corrected.

VALLEY CEMETERY, VIS-EN-ARTOIS

HISTORY
The cemetery was opened on 30 August 1918 and closed soon after once this area had been taken from the Germans. The cemetery was enlarged after the war by the concentration of a small number of graves.

INFORMATION
Vis-en-Artois was in German hands from 30 September 1914 until taken by Canadian forces on 24 August 1918.

The 3rd Canadian Infantry began this cemetery when they buried 31 men in what is now Row A who had been killed in the capture of Orix Trench on 30 August 1918. The men share the same grave reference so it seems to have been a communal burial of the 31 men. Row A was completed in September when the original cemetery was closed. In 1924-25 Rows B and C were added as 27 British graves were concentrated from Thilloy German Cemetery.

Among those buried here is Lieutenant Edward Slattery, DCM, MM and two Bars, 3rd Canadian Infantry, killed in action on 30 August 1918 aged 23 years. The eldest of twelve children from Newfoundland, he had been promoted through the ranks and became a Lieutenant in January 1918. At that time he had already received his four decorations - the Distinguished Conduct Medal for gallantry at Fresnoy in 1917, the Military Medals for bravery at the Somme in September 1916, Vimy Ridge in April 1917 and Passendale in November 1917. His brother Private Michael Slattery, MM, 87th Canadian Infantry was killed in action on 14 August 1917 and is buried at Villers Station Cemetery west of Vimy Ridge.

Concentrated here:

Thilloy German Cemetery - situated close to the Albert-Bapaume road on the south-western edge of Bapaume about 1km north of Thilloy village. It was located next to a Dressing Station and contained approximately 300 Germans with four Australian and three British soldiers.

UK – 24   Can – 37   Aust – 7
Unnamed - 16   Area – 275 sq mts

Special Memorial to a British soldier, buried in Thilloy German Cemetery, whose grave could not be identified at the time of concentration.

LOCATION
Vis-en-Artois lies on the Arras-Cambrai road about 10km to the south-east of Arras. Valley Cemetery is situated on the open farmland 1km south of the village and 1km north of Cherisy. The cemetery is in a quiet valley running between Vis-en-Artois and Cherisy. It is on the south side of the River Sensee and reached from the D9 by a small road leading south that becomes a farm track. You must park and walk the final 100m along the CWGC path to the entrance.

VARENNES MILITARY CEMETERY

HISTORY
This cemetery was first used in October 1916, though the area had been allocated for burials in August. It remained in use until May 1917 when the first stage of burials was ended. It was used again from April to September 1918.

INFORMATION
The village was behind French and British lines. The 39th Casualty Clearing Station prepared the ground for use in August and September 1916. However, it was first used by 4th and 11th Casualty Clearing Stations from October 1916 to May 1917 with the 47th CCS joining them in December 1916. Plots II and III were created by the 17th and 38th (Welsh) Divisions in 1918. The last burials were made by the 3rd Canadian and 59th CCS in late 1918.

A Russian officer who was attached to II Corps Staff is buried here though 42 German and one French burial have been removed.

Among those here is Brigadier General George Bull, DSO, four times MiD, General Staff commanding 8th Infantry Brigade, 3rd Division, formerly Royal Irish Fusiliers, died of wounds on 11 December 1916 aged 39 years. He served with the 5th Royal Irish Rifles in the South African War. He joined the Leinster Regiment in 1905 and transferred to the Royal Irish Fusiliers in 1907. He went to France as a Captain in the 1st Royal Irish Fusiliers in 1914. In November 1915 he took command of the 12th Royal Irish Rifles and was awarded the Distinguished Service Order for gallantry and devotion to duty in the field. On 3 December 1916 he was appointed Brigadier General commanding 8th Infantry Brigade. On 6 December he had gone to Bus-les-Artois to visit the 7th King's Shropshire Light Infantry and then proceeded on a tour of the trenches when he was wounded by a German sniper. He later died of his wounds.

Also here is Brigadier General Philip Howell, CMG, General Staff, II Corps formerly 4th (Queen's Own) Hussars, killed in action by a shell near Authuille on 7 October 1916 aged 37 years. In 1897 he entered the Indian Army serving with the Queen's Own Corps of Guides, a regiment serving mainly on the North West Frontier, but in 1913 he became a Major in the 4th (Queen's Own) Hussars. He went to France with the Hussars in 1914 as part of 2nd Cavalry Division which, on 31 October 1914, was holding a line between Wytschaete and the Comines Canal. A large body of German infantry tried to advance from Hollebeke to the bridge north of the village which, owing to lack of explosives, had not been blown up. The 4th Hussars under Howell enfiladed the German advance and, in spite of regular and continuous shelling from four German Batteries, inflicted such heavy losses that the advance was abandoned. In 1915 he was made a Companion of the Order of St. Michael and St. George (CMG) and appointed Brigadier General, General Staff of II Corps in June 1916. At the time of his death his men were trying to capture the Schwaben Redoubt.

Also here is Lieutenant Colonel Gerald Ponsonby Sneyd Hunt, CMG, DSO, four times MiD, 1st Royal Berkshires, killed in action on 23 March 1918 aged 40 years. He joined the Royal Berkshires as a 2nd Lieutenant in 1897 and saw service in the South African Wars from 1899 to 1902. He was promoted to Captain in 1905 while in Egypt, then went to India, and was at Jhansi when the war began. He went to France in November 1914 and was wounded early in 1915. When the former commanding officer of his old battalion, the 2nd Royal Berkshires, was killed in May 1915 Captain Hunt took over and was promoted to Major. He was with them at Bois Grenier in the Battle of Loos. In December 1915, he was appointed to command a Territorial Infantry Brigade, with the rank of Brigadier-General, and shortly afterwards he was made Companion of the Order of St. Michael and St. George (CMG). He then returned to command of the 1st Royal Berkshires. He was awarded the Distinguished Service Order and was Mentioned in Despatches in 1916. His DSO citation says 'He established and organised the line after an attack by siting a series of posts on commanding ground. During an enemy attack he held his position against repeated thrusts by the enemy, although his right flank was exposed, and when touch was lost with the brigade on his right he re-established communication. He showed splendid leadership and courage.' He was recommended for the Victoria Cross for the actions near Manancourt in which he was killed. His brother 2nd Lieutenant John Henry Sneyd Hunt, 23rd (1st Sportsmen) Londons, was killed in action near High Wood on 16 September 1916 aged 42 years. He is listed on the Thiepval Memorial.

Also here is Lieutenant Colonel Arthur S Tetley, twice MiD, Croix de Guerre with Palm (France), Drake Battalion, 63rd (Royal Naval) Division, Royal Naval Volunteer Reserve, killed in action in the attack on Beaucourt on 15 November 1916 aged 36 years.

Another burial of note is Regimental Sergeant Major Henry George Congdon, Long Service and Good Conduct Medal, Croix de Guerre (Belgium), HQ 12th Division, Royal Engineers, killed on 28 May 1918 aged 51 years. A professional soldier until his retirement, he then kept a pub before returning to the colours.

Concentrated here:

Varennes Communal Cemetery - two British soldiers who were buried in the Communal Cemetery opposite were concentrated in the Military Cemetery in October 1934.

| UK – 1191 | NZ – 16 | Can – 5 |
| Aust – 2 | SAfr – 4 | Russia – 1 |

LOCATION

Varennes is a small village between Albert and Doullens about 20km north-east of Amiens and 7km north-west of Albert. The cemetery is about 500m north-west of the village, almost opposite the Communal Cemetery, on the north side of the road to Lealvillers.

VAULX AUSTRALIAN FIELD AMBULANCE CEMETERY

HISTORY

The cemetery was used from April 1917 to February 1918 by the British. It was then used by the Germans until August 1918. It was also used for one British burial, made by the Germans, in August 1918.

INFORMATION

The village was behind German lines from 1914 until the German retreat to the Hindenburg Line in March 1917. It was retaken, after heavy fighting, by the Germans in March 1918 at the start of their offensive. It fell for the final time in September 1918.

The CWGC cemetery is notable in that it contains more German graves than Allied burials.

Among those buried here is Major Alistair Cosmo Burton Geddes, MC, Cross of the Legion of Honour (France), 17th Kite Balloon Company, Royal Flying Corps, killed in action on 19 April 1917 aged 25 years. He joined the Royal Naval Air Service in July 1915 and served in the kite balloon section until May 1916 when he transferred to the Royal Flying Corps. He was awarded the Military Cross for observing on the action at Thiepval and reporting from his balloon over fourteen hours in September 1916. He was promoted to Major in December 1916. He had to parachute from his balloon on 3 April 1017 as it was shot down. He was killed by shellfire walking back to his billet in Vaulx-Vraucourt after visiting the artillery battery at Lagnicourt with whom his balloon was linked. He was the most senior British kite balloon officer to be killed in the war.

Aust – 32   UK – 20   Ger – 61
Unnamed – 1   Area – 582 sq mts

LOCATION
Vaulx-Vraucourt is situated about 5km north-east of Bapaume. It is in the valley of the River L'Hirondelle almost at the head of the river. The village is about 2km east of the A1 Autoroute and a similar distance north of the Bapaume to Cambrai road. The cemetery is 2km south of the village on the west side of the road to Beugnatre and Bapaume. A path leads 70m from the road to the cemetery.

VAULX HILL CEMETERY

HISTORY
The cemetery was used in September 1918. Most of the cemetery is a concentration cemetery made after the war when bodies were brought in from isolated positions on the surrounding battlefields.

INFORMATION
See Vaulx Australian Field Ambulance Cemetery.

The cemetery consists of seventeen burials made in September 1918, now Plot I, Rows A and B, while the others were made after the war. A German burial ground next to the churchyard in the village has been removed.

Among those buried here is Lieutenant Cecil Harold Sewell, VC, Queen's Own (Royal West Kents) and 3rd (Light) Tank Battalion, Tank Corps, killed in action on 29 September 1918 aged 23 years. The citation for his Victoria Cross reads 'When in command of a section of Whippet Light Tanks in action this officer displayed most conspicuous bravery and initiative in getting out of his own Tank and crossing open ground under heavy shell and machine-gun fire to rescue the crew of another Whippet of his section which had side slipped into a large shell-hole, overturned and taken fire. The door of the Tank having become jammed against the side of the shell-hole, Lt. Sewell, by his own unaided efforts, dug away the entrance to the door and released the crew. In so doing he undoubtedly saved the lives of the officer and men inside the Tank as they could not have got out without his assistance. After having extricated the crew, seeing one of his own crew lying wounded behind his Tank, he again dashed across the open ground to his assistance. He was hit in doing so, but succeeded in reaching the Tank when a few minutes later he was again hit, fatally, in the act of dressing his wounded driver. During the whole of this period he was within full view and short range of the enemy machine guns and rifle-pits, and throughout, by his prompt and heroic action, showed an utter disregard for his own personal safety.' His brothers were Lieutenant Harry Kemp Sewell, 21st Battery, Royal Field Artillery formerly West Kent Yeomanry (Queen's Own), who died of sickness on 20 August 1917 after being wounded in action aged 32 years and is buried in Charlton Cemetery, Greenwich; and 2nd Lieutenant Herbert Victor Sewell, 186th Brigade, Royal Field Artillery, killed in action on 13 November 1916 aged 27 years, commemorated on the Thiepval Memorial.

Also here is Lieutenant Colonel Bertram Alexander Gordon Watts, DSO, twice MiD, 4th Brigade, Australian Field Artillery, killed in action on 10 April 1917 aged 37 years. He served in the ranks during the South African Wars and was commissioned into the Royal Australian Garrison Artillery in 1906, being promoted to Captain five years later. He held the position of adjutant RAGA from May 1911 to June 1913. At the start of war he was attending a gunnery staff course in England where he became a Lieutenant Colonel in 1914. He was one of the first to go to the Front, being Mentioned in Despatches in January and June 1916, and awarded the Distinguished Service Order in the Birthday Honours List in June 1916.

The men buried here who died earliest are Captain George Edward Cockerill, 1/16th (Queens Westminster Rifles) Londons and Private George William Wright, 1/5th Sherwood Foresters, both died of wounds in German hands on 3 July 1916. They had both been in the attack at Gommecourt on 1 July 1916 but were buried by the Germans on the north-west edge of Vaulx before being moved here in November 1919.

Another of note is 2nd Lieutenant Charles Gustave Rochefort MacKintosh, No. 18 Squadron, Royal Flying Corps, killed in action on 5 April 1917 aged 38 years. He was a fluent German and French speaker so he was employed as a sports journalist for the Daily Mail and winters sports representative for the Royal Automobile Club (RAC) in Switzerland. He, with several other journalists, was accused of spying, imprisoned and tried by Court Martial, but was found not guilty and released.

Concentrated here:

Chafours Wood Cemetery, Morchies – about 2km south-east of here and about 500m south of Morchies village centre. It contained seventeen Australian and five British graves dating from 1917.

Lagnicourt Australian Cemetery – about 1km north-east of here. The burial ground contained seven Australian graves of 1917 and 27 British burials of September 1918.

New Zealand Cemetery No. 17, Favreuil – about 4km south-west of here. Here were buried in August 1918 22 men of the 2nd New Zealand Rifles Brigade.

Sunken Road Cemetery, Beaumetz-Les-Cambrai – about 4km south-east of here. It contained 23 Australian and five British graves dating from May 1917.

Vraucourt Churchyard Extension - which was across the road from the church in the centre of the village. Buried here were 185 British and seven Australian graves of 1917 and 1918.

UK – 658   Aust – 106   NZ – 58
Can – 1   Unnamed – 258
Area – 2752 sq mts

Special Memorials to 28 British soldiers and one Australian believed or known to be among the unnamed.

Special Memorials to three Australian and one British men, buried in other cemeteries, whose graves were destroyed by shellfire.

LOCATION
See Vaux Australian Field Ambulance Cemetery. The cemetery is about 1km north-east of the village centre on the north side of the road to Lagnicourt. It is opposite the Communal Cemetery.

VERMAND COMMUNAL CEMETERY

HISTORY
The cemetery was used in April and May 1917 and March and September 1918.

INFORMATION
The area was in German hands for much of the war. There is one main plot and several burials spaced out among civilian graves. Ten of the men here are from the Royal Berkshires. Two of the three officers buried here are of the 15th Sherwood Foresters killed in action in April 1917.

Among those here is Lance Serjeant Francis Hugh Silvester Smith, 2/4th Oxford and Bucks Light Infantry, killed in action on Good Friday 6 April 1917 aged 22 years. He was killed in an attack on German trenches running between Le Verguier and the River L'Omignon. It was snowing, the German wire was uncut and British shellfire was falling short hitting their own troops. The German machine-guns also took their toll one of whom was Smith.

UK – 42   Area – 228 sq mts

LOCATION
Vermand is located about 5km north-west of St. Quentin on the Amiens to St. Quentin road in the valley of the River L'Omignon. The Communal Cemetery is on the south-western edge of the village at the end of a small road, though there are municipal signs to show the way.

VILLERET OLD CHURCHYARD

HISTORY
The British burials were made in August 1914, September 1917 and March 1918. The Indian cavalryman was buried in February 1918.

INFORMATION
The Hindenburg Line ran very close to this village which was in German hands for most of the war. The old church is now gone, though the churchyard remains. Therefore, it has become a communal cemetery. There are a Company commander and ten men of the Manchesters killed, with one exception, in the German advance in late March 1918. The officer buried here is Captain Henry Leater, MiD, 2/9th Manchesters, killed in action on 21 March 1918 aged 25 years. Prior to the war he was a tutor at Manchester Technical College, now part of Manchester University. He was posthumously Mentioned in Despatches and gazetted on 24 May 1918 as a 2nd Lieutenant. A week earlier the London Gazette had indicated both that he had relinquished his post of Acting Captain and subsequently been killed in action.

Also worth a visit, though not strictly within the area covered by this book, is the Ricqueval Bridge across the St. Quentin Canal which is about 2km south-east of here and just north of the village of Ricqueval. This bridge was captured intact by Captain Arthur Humphrey Charlton and his men of the 6th North Staffordshires on 29 September

1918. After the battle, a famous photo was taken of Brigadier General John Vaughan Campbell, VC, addressing the 137th Brigade on the canal bank. The American 27th and 30th Divisions were also involved in capturing parts of the canal in this area.

UK – 18   India – 1   Unnamed – 5

LOCATION
Villeret is about 15km north of St. Quentin and 20km south of Cambrai. It is a small hamlet about 1km south-east of Hargicourt and 500m west of the A26 Autoroute. The old churchyard lies on the western edge of the village on a road called Rue Neuve. It can be accessed from a small road opposite the current church at the north end of the village. Almost all of the burials are on the left of the main path near the rear of the cemetery, though one single grave is located on the right side midway down the cemetery.

VILLERS HILL BRITISH CEMETERY, VILLERS-GUISLAIN

HISTORY
The cemetery was opened on 3 October 1918 and remained in use for the following two weeks. It was greatly enlarged after the war.

INFORMATION
Villers-Guislain was behind the German lines for much of the war. In the actions associated with the German retreat to the Hindenburg Line the village was attacked and captured by the British in April 1917. The Germans recaptured the village on 30 November during the Battle of Cambrai and held it against an attack by the Tank Corps and Guards Division on the following day. The British did not regain the village until 30 September 1918.

The cemetery was begun by the 33rd Division and named the Middlesex Cemetery, Gloucester Road. At the end of the war the cemetery contained 100 graves, now Plot I, of which 50 were men of the 1st Middlesex, hence the name, and 35 were men of the 2nd Argyll and Sutherland Highlanders. There were also twelve German graves. After the war 628 graves were concentrated here.

Among those buried here are 2nd Lieutenant Patrick Alfred Russell, No. 22 Squadron, Royal Flying Corps aged 27 years when he died, and Lieutenant Henry Loveland, 78th Canadian Infantry attached. No. 22 Squadron, Royal Flying Corps. They were killed in action when their FE2b fighter was shot down in flames near Gouzeaucourt Wood on 2 April 1917. They are buried side by side.

Also here is Major Isham Percy Smith, DSO, 102nd Siege Battery, Royal Garrison Artillery, killed on 30 November 1917 aged 27 years. He was commissioned in 1910 and served in Bermuda until 1914. He went to the Front in April 1915, and in the following June was very severely wounded at Givenchy, so was invalided home. He was promoted to Captain in December, returned to France in May 1916, and was promoted to Major in October. He was off duty when the German attack began on 30 November 1917 but he went to his guns without putting on his uniform. He set about dismantling his guns, sent his men back, and then, borrowing a rifle, rallied the retreating infantry, and by his leadership held the line against the advancing enemy. He was wounded, but refused to leave his post, and was later killed. He was posthumously awarded the Distinguished Service Order in the New Year's Honours List in January 1918 for his actions during the Battle of Arras.

Concentrated here:

Gonnelieu Communal Cemetery German Extension - situated about 2km north of here on the north side of the village next to the road to Villers-Plouich. It contained eight British soldiers who were killed on 6 May 1917 among the, now removed, 400 German graves. Seven graves that could not be identified are now represented in Villers Hill British Cemetery by Special Memorials.

Honnecourt German Cemetery - situated about 2km east of here next to the Gonnelieu-Honnecourt road. It contained twenty German and three British graves.

Villers-Guislain German Cemetery - on the north-west side of the village opposite the present Communal Cemetery on the north side of the road that was called 'Cemetery Road'. It contained one British soldier who was killed in April 1917 and 21 British men who were killed in September and October 1918. The 600 German graves were removed in 1922.

UK – 702   NZ – 23   Can – 5
Aust – 1   SAfr – 1   Ger – 13
Unnamed - 350   KUG – 1
Area – 2948 sq mts

Special Memorials erected to seven British soldiers known, or believed, to be buried among the unnamed graves.
Special Memorials erected to seven British soldiers buried in Gonnelieu Communal Cemetery German Extension and three British soldiers buried in Honnecourt German Cemetery whose graves could not be found at the time of concentration.

LOCATION
Villers-Guislain is located about 15km south of Cambrai, a similar distance north-east of Peronne and 2km west of the A26 Autoroute. The cemetery is about 1km south-east of the village on the south-west side of the farm track that was known as 'Gloucester Road'. It is on the crest of Villers Hill.

VILLERS-BOCAGE COMMUNAL CEMETERY EXTENSION

HISTORY
This cemetery was used from October 1915 to February 1917.

INFORMATION
The village was behind Allied lines throughout the war. The old Communal Cemetery, not to be confused with the new one, is still here on the north side of the Extension. At one time it contained thirteen British burials of men who died between August 1915 and April 1916. They have been concentrated elsewhere.
The 51st (Highland) Casualty Clearing Station was posted near the village in April and May 1916 and men were buried from it into the Communal Cemetery and Extension. However, most men buried here died of illness or accidents rather than as the result of war wounds.

Notably, there are no officers buried here. The Australian buried here is Private Herman Sweeney, 23rd Australian Infantry, who died on 14 December 1916 aged 41 years. He left a wife in Richmond, Victoria. He had enlisted on 14 February 1916 and arrived in France in April dying of disease.

The two men who were buried here in WW2 are a Pioneer Corps soldier named Thomas Turley who died on 3 March 1940 and a Spitfire Pilot, Flight Sergeant Cyril Woodall, No. 129 Squadron, Royal Air Force Volunteer Reserve, shot down on 4 July 1943. His squadron was based in Hornchurch, Essex.

UK – 59   Aust – 1   WW2 – 2
Area – 933 sq mts

LOCATION
The village is situated on the road between Doullens and Amiens about 10km north of Amiens and 20km south of Doullens. The Communal Cemetery is on the north east edge of the village on the south side of the road to Rubempre. This is the new Communal Cemetery. The CWGC Extension to the old Communal Cemetery is on the small track running north opposite this new Communal Cemetery. It is about 200m north on the east side of the track.

VILLERS-BRETONNEUX COMMUNAL CEMETERY

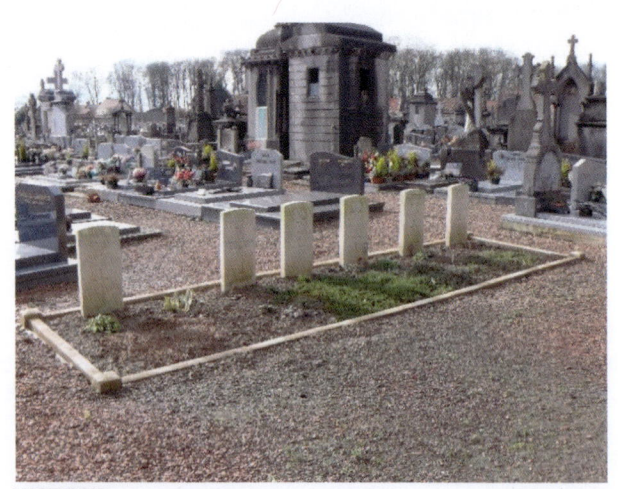

INFORMATION
See Villers-Bretonneux Military Cemetery.
Among those buried here is Lance Corporal William James Connaughton, MM, 48th Australian Infantry, killed in action on 14 May 1918 aged 23 years. He was a mill hand from Western Australia who enlisted into the 16th Australian Infantry in late 1915 and left Australia in May 1916. He was recommended for the Military Medal in April 1918 and awarded the decoration posthumously.

UK – 2   Aust – 10   Fr - 42

LOCATION
Villers-Bretonneux is about 10km east of Amiens. The Communal Cemetery is on the south side of the Amiens-St. Quentin road a little distance east of the junction where you turn to the Military Cemetery and Memorial. The CWGC burials are in three groups - one in the north-west corner, one in the north-east corner and one group on the west side of the cemetery.

HISTORY
The cemetery was used for British and Australian burials from March to August 1918 when significant battles were taking place in this area.

VILLERS-BRETONNEUX MILITARY CEMETERY

HISTORY

The cemetery is a concentration cemetery made entirely after the war.

INFORMATION

Fifth Army HQ was moved here on 24 March 1918 and moved again the following day, by which time the Germans were approaching the area. Decisions had already been taken that, should Amiens be threatened or fall, the British would withdraw from the war. The German advance since 21 March 1918 had been so quick that General Gough decided to use an old French position dating from 1915 called the 'Amiens Defence Line'. It was situated on the western edge of Lamotte-Warfusee and ran for 12km north to south. It was occupied on the night of 25-26 March 1918 by a group simply called 'Carey's Force' under Major General George Glas Sandeman Carey, an artilleryman and commander of 139th Brigade. The retreat was so chaotic that Divisions had been reduced to composite battalion status. 'Carey's Force' included two Companies of engineers from the US 6th Regiment, US 3rd Division. These 500 men held the position north of the Amiens-St. Quentin road. The Germans attacked during the night of 27 March but were held for a week by Carey's men.

The German attack with fifteen Divisions towards Amiens, now known as the First Battle of Villers-Bretonneux, began at dawn on 4 April 1918. The town was defended by the British 14th and 18th Divisions who had been in the line since the start of the campaign. With them were the Australian 9th Brigade. There was heavy fighting all day in which Brigadier General George Norman Bowes Forster was killed. His body was lost and he is named on the Pozieres Memorial. The Germans made progress as the 9th Australian Brigade and the British 18th Division, which were holding the northern sector, were driven back to the outskirts of Villers-Bretonneux. Adjacent German attacks captured Hamel and Hangard Woods. A counter attack at dawn by the 36th Australian Infantry halted the German advance but the action cost the 9th Brigade 660 casualties. By 18 April 1918 the signs of a coming attack were unmistakable. Australian troops were relieved, from positions at Villers-Bretonneux to the flank of the French at Hangard in the south, by troops from the British 8th Division. On 21 April, German deserters revealed that preparations were nearing completion for another German attack. The attack would commence early on 24 April, with the first two to three hours consisting of gas shelling. British aerial observations revealed German troops massing in trenches in Hangard Wood.

On the night of 22-23 April, British and Australian artillery shelled German mustering areas. At dawn the infantry was standing ready but no attack came. Most of the activity on this day was in the air as planes from both sides criss-crossed the battlefield, bombing, strafing and engaging in dogfights. It was during one of these dogfights that the German 'Red Baron', Baron Manfred von Richthoffen, was shot down over Australian lines, north of Villers-Bretonneux at Corbie. On the afternoon of 23 April, heavy shelling, mainly mustard gas, fell on the area just beyond Villers-Bretonneux, just as the German deserters revealed. The Germans attacked on 24 April, in the Second Battle of Villers-Bretonneux, with four Divisions and fifteen tanks with a Jaeger Division in Reserve. Wherever they attacked the Germans broke through immediately. The British troops defending the area mostly fell back before strong German attacks. Though the 8th and 58th Divisions defending Villers-Bretonneux had been involved in most of the campaign the majority of the British troops were composed of new conscripts who were 18 and 19 years of age and who were not ready for battle. The Germans took over 2400 prisoners during the engagement. Before the sector commander, Lieutenant General Sir Richard Harte Keatinge Butler, KCB, KCMG of III Corps, had even heard of the attack, Villers-Bretonneux and Abbey Wood to the west of the town had been lost to the Germans, along with Hangard village and Hangard Wood. They set a new line west of the village. Amiens was almost under threat.

It was at this time that the first tank versus tank battle in history took place when three British Mark IV's fought three German A7V's. One of the British tanks was commanded by Lieutenant Frank Mitchell, No. 1 tank, 1st Section, 'A' Company, 1st Tank Battalion who destroyed one of the German tanks and received a Military Cross for his actions. Even though the battle was even the Germans were the first to withdraw.

The main counter attack came overnight on 24-25 April 1918. Major General Heneker, commanding 8th Division used his Division and a Brigade of 18th Division consisting of 7th Royal Warwickshires, 7th Bedfords and 9th Londons to attack. Most important, though, were two Brigades of the Australian 5th Division, the 15th Brigade north of the village under Harold 'Pompey' Elliott and the 13th Brigade south of the village under Thomas William Glasgow. The attack, which commenced at 10.00pm, swept from the north around the town while the southern attack by the 13th Brigade was also successful but could not find the 15th east of the town and had to pull back slightly, leaving a gap through which the Germans retreated. The fighting during the night was vicious and intense with heavy casualties on all sides. After the battle, the bodies of Australians were found heaped amongst the barbed wire. It was in the attack by the 13th Brigade that Lieutenant Clifford Sadlier, 51st Australian Infantry, won his Victoria

Cross and Sergeant Charles Albert Stokes a Distinguished Conduct Medal. The citation for Sadliers VC reads 'For conspicuous bravery during a counterattack by his Battalion on strong enemy positions. Lieutenant Sadlier's platoon, which was on the left of the Battalion, had to advance through a wood, where a strong enemy machine gun post caused casualties and prevented the platoon from advancing. Though badly wounded, he at once collected his bombing section, led them against the machine guns and succeeded in killing the crew of four and taking the gun. In doing so, he was again wounded. The very gallant conduct of this officer was the means of clearing the flank and allowing the Battalion to move forward, thereby saving a most critical situation. His coolness and utter disregard of danger inspired all.'

After dawn, the town was cleared but the capture of Villers-Bretonneux was not considered complete until 27 April when the 60th Australian Infantry straightened the Australian line east of the town. The German advance was effectively over and the next time the Germans threatened Amiens was in 1940. Gough, whose father, uncle and brother all won Victoria Crosses, was relieved of command and never given another post except in the Home Guard during WW2. He was a controversial commander, like many in WW1, but is now being seen as possibly the wrong person in the wrong place at the wrong time and opinions of him are being revised or, at least, re-considered.

This cemetery stands on a ridge with excellent views. Amiens can just be made out to the east - look for the tall radio tower. Plots I to XX in the cemetery were completed by 1920 and contain mostly Australian graves, almost all from the period March to August 1918. Plots IIIA, VIA, XIIIA and XVIA, and Rows in other Plots lettered AA, were completed by 1925, and contain a much larger proportion of unidentified graves brought in from a wider area. Later still, 444 graves were brought in from Dury Hospital Military Cemetery. This reflects the Australian policy after the war to bring their men from small burial grounds together into large concentration cemeteries. By contrast, the Canadian policy was to leave their men in place with concentration only when necessary.

Within the village is a museum and school built in 1923 with money donated by the people of Victoria, Australia from which the 13th Australian Brigade had come. Several locations in the school contain signs that translate as, or say, 'Do not forget Australia'.

Also in the village are memorials to victims of WW2 – men of the Resistance executed in the village, local politicians sent to die in concentration camps and forced labour as well as the liberators of the village who arrived on 31 August 1944.

Buried here is Lieutenant John Brilliant, VC, MC, 22nd (Canadien Francais, Quebec Regiment) Canadian Infantry, killed in action on 10 August 1918. His citation reads 'For most conspicuous bravery and outstanding devotion to duty when in charge of a company which he led in attack during two days with absolute fearlessness and extraordinary ability and initiative, the extent of the advance being twelve miles. On the first day of operations shortly after the attack had begun, his company's left flank was held up by an enemy machine gun. Lt. Brillant rushed and captured the machine-gun, personally killing two of the enemy crew. Whilst doing this, he was wounded but refused to leave his command. Later on the same day, his company was held up by heavy machine-gun fire. He reconnoitred the ground personally, organised a party of two platoons and rushed straight for the machine-gun nest. Here 150 enemy and fifteen machine-guns were captured. Lt. Brillant personally killing five of the enemy, and being wounded a second time. He had this wound dressed immediately, and again refused to leave his company. Subsequently this gallant officer detected a field gun firing on his men over open sights. He immediately organised and led a "rushing" party towards the gun. After progressing about 600 yards, he was again seriously wounded. In spite of this third wound, he continued to advance for some 200 yards more, when he fell unconscious from exhaustion and loss of blood. Lt. Brillants wonderful example throughout the day inspired his men with an enthusiasm and dash which largely contributed towards the success of the operations.' His headstone is in French.

Also buried here is Lieutenant Eric Henry Drummond Edgerton, DSO, MM and Bar, MiD, 24th Australian Infantry, killed in action on 11 August 1918 aged 21 years. He received the Military Medal and Bar before becoming an officer in which position he won the Distinguished Service Order. Edgerton was born at Moonee Ponds, Victoria in 1897 and prior to the war he spent seven years as a cadet. Edgerton was aged 18 and a student when he joined the 24th Australian Infantry on 14 April 1915. On 25 June 1915, he departed from Melbourne aboard HMAT Ceramic. Serving at Gallipoli, Edgerton was promoted to Corporal in November 1915. Edgerton was awarded the Military Medal on 27 October 1916 and promoted to Sergeant in November. On 11 May 1917 he gained a Bar to his Military Medal and promotions to 2nd Lieutenant in March and Lieutenant in September 1918 followed. On 16 September 1918 Edgerton was awarded the Distinguished Service Order for 'conspicuous gallantry and devotion to duty' in capturing several German machine gun positions. His death was Mentioned in the Despatches of Field Marshal Douglas Haig on 8 November 1918. Two of Edgerton's cousins also served in the First World War, Private Percival John Young and 2nd Lieutenant Harry Leslie Killingsworth, and a relative had fought at Waterloo.

A fighter ace buried here is 2nd Lieutenant Francis James Ralph, DFC, No. 20 Squadron, Royal Air Force, who had claimed thirteen victories before he was shot down in his Bristol F2B and killed on 3 September 1918 aged 25 years. He had been awarded the Distinguished Flying Cross for actions in late 1918 just before his death. The citation reads 'A brave and skilful observer who has taken part in many combats with enemy aircraft, invariably displaying cool courage and presence of mind. On a recent occasion our patrol of eleven machines, after bombing a railway junction, was attacked by fifteen enemy scouts. One of these, which was engaged by this officer's pilot, crumpled and fell. The formation was then attacked by seven Fokkers from above, one of which was shot down by 2nd Lieutenant Ralph'. He was one of those moved from Dury Hospital Military Cemetery.

Buried here is Captain Neville Wallach, MC, 13th Australian Infantry, died on 1 May 1918 aged 21 years. He was awarded the Military Cross in April 1917 for his actions during the Battle of Bullecourt. He was killed by shrapnel to the head when a shell hit his Company headquarters as the officers were sitting down to tea. While he was a good rugby player, his brother, Captain Clarence Wallach, MC, 19th Australian Infantry, killed in action on 22 April 1918 aged 28 years and buried in Etretat Churchyard Extension represented Australia on five occasions. Four other brothers served and survived the war.

Nearby is Gunner William George Tasker, 13th Brigade, Australian Field Artillery who died on 9 August 1918 aged 26 years. He was severely wounded at Quinn's Post at Gallipoli and invalided back to Australia. In 1916 he re-enlisted with the 116th Howitzer Battery. He was twice wounded before his death from wounds at Harbonnieres. He played for Australia six times against New Zealand at Rugby Union in 1913-14.

An interesting (though they are all interesting) headstone here is that of Sergeant Philip Ball, MM, 43rd Australian Infantry, killed in action on 28 March 1918. His family chose the words 'I Died in the Great War to end all wars. Have I died in vain?'

The WW2 airmen buried here are Squadron Leader (Pilot) Ian George Medwin, aged 27 years and Pilot Officer (Navigator) A J Coe aged 25 years. They were both from No. 487 Squadron, Royal New Zealand Air Force and were killed on 6 April 1945 when their Mosquito aircraft crashed on take-off from an airfield at Rosieres.

Concentrated here:

Blangy-Tronville Australian Cemetery – located about 5km east of here and 1km north of the road to Amiens. It contained about 100 Australian burials and thirteen British graves made between April and August 1918.

Card Copse Cemetery, Marcelcave – located just north of here on the road to Fouilloy. It contained the graves of 35 Australian soldiers buried by the 2nd Australian Division in July and August 1918.

Dury Hospital Military Cemetery - this is located about 10km west of here on the southern edge of Amiens. The asylum was used by British medical units from August 1918 to January 1919. The cemetery was next to an existing French Military Cemetery also now removed. The British cemetery contained the graves of 195 Canadian and 185 British men, 63 Australian soldiers, one South African man of the Cape Auxiliary Horse Transport Corps, and one French soldier and one American soldier. The latter two graves have been removed elsewhere.

High Cemetery, Sailly-le-Sec – located about 10km north-east of here on the ridge north of the village on the road to Ville-sur-Ancre. Buried here in June-August 1918 were eighteen British and eleven Australian soldiers.

Kangaroo Cemetery, Sailly-le-Sec – located close to High Cemetery on the Ville-sur-Ancre road, but nearer to Sailly-le-Sec. It contained thirteen Australian soldiers buried by the 41st Australian Infantry in March and April 1918, and fourteen men of, and buried by, the 58th (London) Division in August 1918.

Lamotte-en-Santerre Communal Cemetery Extension – the village is now the southern part of Lamotte-Warfusee, a political construct created in 1974. The village was captured by Australian troops on 8 August 1918. The cemetery was on what is now the southern edge of the village about 5km east of Villers-Bretonneux, and the Extension contained the graves of 56 Australian and twelve British soldiers who died in August and September.

La Neuville-les-Bray Communal Cemetery – located on the southern edge of Bray-sur-Somme in the valley of the River Somme about 15km north-east of here. It contained the grave of one Australian soldier who died in August 1918.

Le Hamelet British Cemetery – located about 1.5km north of here and found behind the church. It contained the graves of 25 Australian soldiers who died in April-July 1918.

Le Hamelet Communal Cemetery Extension – located with the British Cemetery in the village. Buried here were 27 Australian soldiers and one British man who were buried in July and August 1916.

Midway Cemetery, Marcelcave – this is about 3km south-east of here. It contained the graves of 53 Canadian and three British soldiers buried by the Canadian Corps in August 1918.

Vaux-sur-Somme Communal Cemetery – located about 4km north-east of here. It contained three Australian graves dating from March-April 1918, and two British men buried in 1916 and 1917.

Vaux-sur-Somme Communal Cemetery Extension – next to the Communal Cemetery. It was made in May-August 1918, and contained the graves of 130 Australian soldiers and 105 British men, mainly 58th Division or artillerymen.

Warfusée-Abancourt Communal Cemetery Extension - the village is now the northern part of Lamotte-Warfusee, a political construct created in 1974. It contained the graves of five Australian soldiers who were buried by the 12th Australian Field Ambulance in August 1918.

UK – 1089	Aust – 779	Can – 267
SAfr – 4	NZ – 2	Unnamed – 607
WW2 – 2		Area – 15437 sq mts

Special Memorials to four British men and one Australian known or believed to be among the unnamed graves.

Special Memorials to seven British, six Australian and two Canadian men buried at Lamotte-en-Santerre Communal Cemetery Extension, Vaux-sur-Somme Communal Cemetery and Extension and Dury Hospital Military Cemetery whose graves could not be identified.

AUSTRALIAN NATIONAL MEMORIAL

This is situated at the 'rear' of the cemetery. It was erected to commemorate all Australian soldiers who fought, and especially those who died, in France and Belgium during the First World War. On it are commemorated the names of those who fell in France and whose graves are not known. The Australian servicemen named on the memorial mainly died in the battlefields of the Somme, Arras, the German advance of 1918 and the advance to Victory. There are approximately 5000 Australians named on the Menin Gate at Ieper who died and have no known grave in Belgium and another 1298 names at VC Corner Cemetery near Fromelles. The Memorial was unveiled by King George VI on 22 July 1938. It was the last memorial to be finished before WW2 began. There were problems due to funding so a planned impressive archway was not built.

The top of the 100ft or 30m high tower, a considerable climb, has an orientation table which makes the climb well worth the effort. In June 1940 Senegalese troops had a machine gun set up at the top of the tower when they were attacked by a German tank and a Messerschmitt 109. The damage to the memorial and cemetery was repaired after the war but some battle scars can still be identified.

The lawn in front is where King George opened the memorial. The lawn is also the site for a moving Dawn Service held each year on 25 April, the anniversary of the battle here in 1918 and the landings at Gallipoli in 1915.

Of the 10982 names displayed at the unveiling of the Villers-Bretonneux Memorial the burial places of many have since been identified for example there are six names who are now found and buried in Fromelles (Pheasant Wood) Cemetery. There are now 10739 Australian servicemen officially commemorated by this memorial and named within the register, though that will have changed since this book was printed.

Commemorated on the memorial is Private Thomas Cooke, VC, 8th Australian Infantry, killed in action at Pozieres on 28 July 1916 aged 35 years. His citation reads 'For most conspicuous bravery. After a Lewis gun had been disabled, he was ordered to take his gun and gun-team to a dangerous part of the line. Here he did fine work, but came under very heavy fire, with the result that finally he was the only man left. He still stuck to his post, and continued to fire his gun. When assistance was sent he was found dead beside his gun. He set a splendid example of determination and devotion to duty.' He was a native of New Zealand.

Also commemorated here is Major Percy Charles Herbert Black, DSO, DCM, 16th Australian Infantry, killed in action at Bullecourt on 11 April 1917. He had won the Distinguished Conduct Medal at Gallipoli and the Distinguished Service Order at Pozieres in 1916. He died trying to cut his way through the German wire during the disaster that was the First Battle of Bullecourt.

And also on the memorial is Sergeant James Lihou, DCM & Bar, MM, 13th Australian Infantry, died of wounds on 18 September 1918. He was a Lewis Gunner and won the Distinguished Conduct Medal in the attack at Le Hamel on 4 July 1918. He won the Military Medal in August. At Le Verguier in September, thick fog led to his group getting lost and reaching the German line ahead of their comrades. Lihou attacked a German machine-gun on his own, killing three Germans and capturing the position. His group pushed on reaching their objective well ahead of the rest of his battalion. The Germans opened fire and Lihou attacked alone again to cover his pals. Lihou spotted another machine gun position which he attacked once more alone. He was shot and died later in the day. He was awarded a Bar to his DCM for his actions.

Notable here is Lance Corporal Harold Reeve Beechey, 48th Australian Infantry, who was killed on 10 April 1917 aged 26 years. He had emigrated to be a farmer in Western Australia but enlisted at the start of the war. He fought at Gallipoli and Pozieres being wounded and invalided with disease. He was killed by a shell at Bullecourt but his body was not identified. He is one of five brothers to be killed in service during the war. Serjeant Bernard Reeve Beechey, 2nd Lincolnshires, killed in action on 25 September 1915 aged 38 years is commemorated on the Ploegsteert Memorial near Ieper. He was the first of the brothers to die and was killed charging to his death in the Battle of Loos. Private Charles Reeve Beechey, 25th (Frontiersmen) Royal Fusiliers, was killed in action by machine-gun fire on 20 October 1917 aged 39 years while defending Lukeledi Mission in East Africa against a German assault. He is now buried in Dar Es Salaam War Cemetery in Tanzania. 2nd Lieutenant Frank Collett Reeve Beechey, 13th East Yorkshires, died of wounds at Serre in some of the last acts of the Battles of the Somme on 14 November 1916 aged 30 years. A shell took Frank's legs off during the attack on 13 November and he lay in no-man's land under fire from dawn until dusk before an army doctor risked his life to crawl out and administer morphine. He is buried in Warlincourt Halte British Cemetery. Rifleman Leonard Reeve Beechey, 18th (London Irish Rifles) Londons, died of wounds on 29 December 1917 aged 36 years. He was gassed and wounded at Bourlon Wood and is buried in St. Sever Cemetery Extension, Rouen. Another brother, who had emigrated to Australia with Harold, Christopher William Reeve Beechey, was wounded at Gallipoli serving as a stretcher bearer with the 4th Field Ambulance. He was unable to walk for any great distance for the rest of his life. Two other brothers, Samuel St. Vincent Reeve Beechey and Eric Reeve Beechey served and survived the war.

We know of three families from the United Kingdom to lose five sons, the Souls (see Hangard Communal Cemetery Extension and the Thiepval Memorial), the Smiths (see

Dernancourt Communal Cemetery Extension and the Thiepval Memorial) and the Beecheys.

A 'man' remembered here is Private Leslie Thomas Prior, 23rd Australian Infantry, who was a labourer from Carlton, Melbourne. He was killed in the Second Battle of Bullecourt on 3 May 1917. His mother wrote that he was 15 years 3 months of age at the time of death.

Several 16 year old 'men' are on the memorial. Private Stanley John Adams, 4th Australian Infantry, from Sydney, who was a plumber before the war, lied claiming to be 18 years old when he enlisted in January 1916. Stanley was killed by a shell at Mouquet Farm on 16 August 1916 and was buried between Mouquet Farm and Pozieres but the grave could not be located after the war. Stanley's brother, Corporal J.W. Adams of the 1st Australian Infantry, served in both Gallipoli and France. Private Edward Sydney Cawe, 20th Australian Infantry, from New South Wales, who had been a railway porter, was killed in action at Pozieres on 26 July 1916, one year to the day after his enlistment. Private Alfred Kerfoot, 20th Australian Infantry, was born in Newton Heath, Manchester, England and moved to Australia at the age of 8 years. Before enlisting, Alfred was working as a newsagent. He was killed in action near Flers on 10 November 1916. Private Roy Harry Robertson, 3rd Australian Infantry, was a letter carrier from Gordon, New South Wales. He was killed in action at Flers on 5 November 1916. Private Frederick Clive Collins, 11th Australian Infantry was born in Godalming, England, moved to Australia at the age of 14 years and was 15 years 4 months when he enlisted. Fred was killed in action near Pozieres on 25 July 1916 at the age of 16 years 2 months. Fred's father Private Lewis Frank Collins served in the 48th Australian Infantry and died in January 1918 in Freemantle, Australia as a result of wounds received at Mouquet Farm in August 1916. Fred's brother Driver Frank Collins served in the 16th Australian Infantry and was also wounded near Pozieres in August 1916. Private Arthur Hill, 29th Australian Infantry, was a farm labourer from Victoria. He had been a bugler with the Australian Citizen Military Forces before enlisting in September 1915. Arthur was killed in action near Flers on 27 October 1916 aged 16 years 4 months only twelve days after joining his battalion. Arthur's father, Private Thomas Hill, served with the 4th Australian Division Headquarters. Private Harry Fox, 2nd Australian Infantry, from New South Wales, enlisted on 14 February 1916 while he was still a student at the Technical High School in Ultimo. Harry was killed on 4 May 1917 during the Second Battle of Bullecourt aged 16 years 7 months. Harry's brother George served with the Australian Railway Troops. Private John Morgan Jenkins, 21st Australian Infantry, was born on 8 December 1899 in New South Wales. He was working as a blacksmith when he enlisted in May 1915 in Victoria, under the name of John Thomas Jenkins. John was killed in action on 1 August 1916 at Pozieres aged 16 years 8 months. Private Ernest Lachlan Powter, 53rd Australian Infantry, was born in New South Wales. He was working as a junior clerk when he enlisted in September 1915. He died on 1 November 1916 aged 16 years 8 months of wounds received in action near Flers. Ernest's brother Gunner Claude Jabez Powter was awarded a Distinguished Conduct Medal. Private Maurice Challis Redwood, 18th Australian Infantry, who was a clerk in New South Wales when he enlisted on 19 June 1915 with his mother's consent, giving his age as 18 years 4 months. He was killed in action at Pozieres on 5 August 1916 aged 16 years 10 months. These are but a sample as there are many other teenagers commemorated on the memorial.

Another teenager here is Private Reg Crowley, 34th Australian Infantry, killed in action 4 April 1918 aged 18 years. He had enlisted at 16 and was, according to reports, about to bayonet a German officer who begged for mercy. Crowley hesitated and the German shot him dead. Crowley's uncle had died of wounds at Gallipoli and his father had been killed on the Broodseinde Ridge at Ieper aged 52 years in 1917.

LOCATION

The Military Cemetery is about 1.5km north of the town on the east side of the road to Fouilly. There is good parking.

VILLERS-FAUCON COMMUNAL CEMETERY

HISTORY

The Communal Cemetery was first used by the British Army in February 1917 when the Germans withdrew to the Hindenburg Line. It remained in use until August 1917. Two further burials were made in September 1918.

INFORMATION

Villers-Faucon was behind the German lines for much of the war. When the Germans retreated on 27 March 1917 the village was occupied by the 5th Cavalry Brigade. The Germans recaptured the village in their offensive on 22 March 1918 but it fell for the final time on 7 September 1918 when it was captured by III Corps.

The British graves were mostly made by cavalry units or by the 42nd Division. There is a large Plot of German graves among the British burials. Row A is mainly officers.

It is hard to distinguish between the Communal Cemetery and the Extension. The demarcation can be identified though it is essentially artificial.

Among those buried here are two holders of the Victoria Cross. 2nd Lieutenant John Spencer Dunville, VC, 1st Royal Dragoons, died of wounds on 26 June 1917 aged 21 years.

The citation for his Victoria Cross reads 'For most conspicuous bravery. When in charge of a party consisting of Scouts and Royal Engineers engaged in the demolition of the enemy's wire, this officer displayed great gallantry and disregard of all personal danger. In order to ensure the absolute success of the work entrusted to him, 2nd Lt. Dunville placed himself between the N.C.O. of the Royal Engineers and the enemy's fire, and thus protected, this N.C.O. was enabled to complete a work of great importance. 2nd Lt. Dunville, although severely wounded, continued to direct his men in the wire-cutting and general operations until the raid was successfully completed, thereby setting a magnificent example of courage, determination and devotion to duty, to all ranks under his command. This gallant officer has since succumbed to his wounds.'

2nd Lieutenant Hardy Falconer Parsons, VC, 14th Gloucestershires, died of wounds on 21 August 1917 aged 20 years. The citation for his Victoria Cross reads 'For most conspicuous bravery during a night attack by a strong party of the enemy on a bombing post held by his command. The bombers holding the block were forced back, but Second Lieutenant Parsons remained at his post, and, single-handed, and although severely scorched and burnt by liquid fire, he continued to hold up the enemy with bombs until severely wounded. This very gallant act of self-sacrifice and devotion to duty undoubtedly delayed the enemy long enough to allow of the organisation of a bombing party, which succeeded in driving back the enemy before they could enter any portion of the trenches. The gallant officer succumbed to his wounds.'

At the back of the cemetery are a group of officers killed when the Battalion HQ of the 1/6th Gloucestershires, in a cellar at Villers-Faucon, was destroyed on 18 April 1917 by a German delayed action fuse mine. The following were killed: commanding officer Lieutenant Colonel Thomas Walker Nott, DSO, aged 28 years; second in command Major Robert Finlay Gerrard, MiD, attached from 4th Gloucestershires aged 29 years; Adjutant and Captain Louis Nott, MC, brother of Colonel Nott aged 23 years; Chaplain Matthew Burdess, attached from the Army Chaplains Department, aged 39 years; Medical Officer Captain Everard Harrison, attached from the Royal Army Medical Corps aged 37 years and Lieutenant Leonard King, MC aged 27 years. A third Nott brother, Lieutenant Henry Paton Nott, MiD, 1/6th Gloucestershires, was killed on 27 April 1916 aged 21 years and is buried at Hebuterne Military Cemetery.

The German plan for early 1917 envisaged a controlled retirement to the Hindenburg Line. The whole zone between the original line and the new fortified line was to be made a desert. Not only were all military buildings to be dismantled but railways were to be torn up, craters blown in the roads or roads mined, every town and village and buildings in them were to be destroyed by fire or explosives, watercourses dammed, even fruit trees cut down or 'ringed' to ensure they died, civilians removed, wells to be filled up or polluted, cellars to be made into death traps with concealed bombs, buildings mined, and seemingly innocent deposits of materials or tools made into booby traps or left with delayed action charges.

Also buried here is Brigadier General Vincent Alexander Ormsby, CB, MiD, General Staff, Commanding 127th Infantry Brigade in the 42nd (East Lancashire) Division late 3rd Queen Alexandra's Own Gurkha Rifles, killed when he bled to death having been hit by a shell fragment near Epehy on 1 May 1917 aged 51 years. He had just arrived in France from Egypt.

UK – 226   India - 1   Ger – 90
Unnamed – 5   Area – 960 sq mts

LOCATION

Villers-Faucon is situated about 15km north-east of Peronne. The Communal Cemetery is on the north-west side of the village just off the road to Guyencourt-Saulcourt on a hill above the village. The British graves in the Communal Cemetery are at the furthest end, and clearly visible, from the entrance.

VILLERS-FAUCON COMMUNAL CEMETERY EXTENSION

HISTORY

The Communal Cemetery was in use until August 1917 and shortly after the Extension was begun. It remained in use by the British until the Germans captured the village in March 1918. German burials were made during the period of German occupation in the summer of 1918 and further British burials were made in September and October 1918. After the war the Extension was enlarged as 118 graves were concentrated here.

INFORMATION

Among those buried here is Major Frederick St. John Atkinson DSO, 9th Hodson's Horse who died on 30 November 1917 aged 35 years. Hodson's Horse was a regiment of Lancers of the Indian Army which went to France in November 1914 and served there until February 1918 when it was sent to Palestine. At dawn on 30 November 1917, during the Battle of Cambrai, the German counter-attack to re-take ground lost in the British offensive of 20 November 1917 commenced. Just over 8km to the north of Villers-Faucon is the village of Villers-Guislain which had been occupied by Commonwealth forces since April 1917 until it fell in the German counter-attack. The 5th Cavalry Division advanced in a northerly direction towards Villers-Guislain but a mounted attack failed under heavy German artillery and machine-gun fire. A Squadron of the 8th Hussars reinforced by the 9th Hodsons's Horse tried a dismounted attack which fared little better until eventually a line was secured along a sunken road west of the railway with Hodson's Horse on the left. Hodson's Horse had two Squadron commanders killed and lost 50 men and 70 horses. Major St. John Atkinson was one of those Squadron commanders killed. With him is his brother officer Major Arthur Ion Fraser DSO, MiD, 9th Hodson's Horse killed aged 37 years in the same action as Atkinson. He was born in London, had seventeen years service in the Indian Army, and went to France with the 1st Indian Cavalry Division from Ambala in 1914. Another officer killed in the attack and buried here was Major The Honourable Robert Nathaniel Dudley Ryder, 8th (King's Royal Irish) Hussars aged 34 years. He served with the Hussars in the South Africa Wars from 1900–1902. In October 1914 he was made Captain of 'A' Squadron and was later promoted to Major. The Hussars were pushing on towards Gauche Wood where they were to stop the German advance and link up with the Guards Division who were attacking the villages of Gouzeaucourt and Gonnelieu. But the enemy were well positioned and the Hussars, like Hodson's Horse, only got to the sunken road where in the dismounted fight with the enemy, Ryder was killed with another officer, 36 men and 73 horses. He was the son of the 4th Earl of Harrowby.

UK – 432	Aust – 10	India – 8
NZ – 2	SAfr - 1	Ger – 66
Unnamed – 144		Area – 1725 sq mts

Special Memorials are erected to six British soldiers who are believed to be buried among the unnamed graves.

LOCATION
The Extension is to the west side of the Communal Cemetery to the left of the main path.

VILLERS-GUISLAIN COMMUNAL CEMETERY

HISTORY
The cemetery was used by the British in 1917 and 1918.

INFORMATION
Villers-Guislain was behind the German lines for much of the war. In the actions associated with the German retreat to the Hindenburg Line the village was attacked by the British in April 1917. The Germans recaptured the village in November during the Battle of Cambrai and held it against a counter-attack by the Tank Corps and Guards Division on the following day. The British did not regain the village until 30 September 1918.

Among those buried here are four Privates of the 23rd Manchesters, H Bell, James Leigh, R Taylor and H Whitehouse killed in action on 27 June 1917 while their battalion was 'holding the line'. They were among five men killed by enemy shelling. Only four are named here so it may be that one has been totally lost as there are eighteen men, three of them among the four men of the Manchesters, who have Special Memorials here.

| UK – 51 | Unnamed – 7 | Area – 202 sq mts |

Special Memorials to five men known, and thirteen men believed, to be buried here but whose graves have been destroyed by shell-fire.

LOCATION
Villers-Guislain is located about 15km south of Cambrai, a similar distance north-east of Peronne and 2km west of the A26 Autoroute. The cemetery is at the north-eastern edge of the village on the south side of the road to Gouzeaucourt. The British plot is in the south-west corner of the cemetery which is the far right corner from the entrance. A further three graves, two men of the 2nd Gloucestershires killed on 1 July 1916 and one unnamed soldier, are to the left of the main path separate from the others.

VILLERS-PLOUICH COMMUNAL CEMETERY

HISTORY
The cemetery was used from November 1917 to January 1918.

INFORMATION
The village was in German hands for much of the war until it was captured by the 13th East Surreys as part of the actions surrounding the German withdrawal to the Hindenburg Line. It fell to the Germans in March 1918 and was not recaptured until September 1918 when the 1st East Surreys were the first troops to enter the village.

There are two graves outside the main British plot. One is a man of the East Lancashires buried in October 1916 and the other is Captain Tom Rees, No. 11 Squadron, Royal Flying Corps, formerly 14th Royal Welsh Fusiliers, who died on 17 September 1916 aged 21 years. He was the observer in the first Royal Flying Corps aircraft to be shot down by the 'Red Baron', Baron Manfred von Richthofen. Rees' pilot was 2nd Lieutenant Lionel Morris, formerly 3rd Queens (Royal West Surreys) aged 19 years. He is buried in the Porte de Paris Cemetery in Cambrai.

UK – 50   NF – 1   Unnamed - 8
Special Memorials to two men known to be among the unnamed.

LOCATION
Villers-Plouich is situated about 10km south-west of Cambrai and 2km west of the A26 Autoroute. The cemetery is on the north-east edge of the village on the east side of the road to Marcoing. It is next to a railway crossing in a valley. The British plot is at the north-east corner of the cemetery on the edge of the valley.

VILLE-SUR-ANCRE COMMUNAL CEMETERY

INFORMATION
The village was in Allied hands for most of the war. In 1916 the village was used occasionally by Field Ambulances. It was captured by the Germans at the end of April 1918, and retaken by the 2nd Australian Division on 19 May.
Most of the burials here are Royal Engineers. They are buried together. Many were killed when a shell hit their billets in the village. The Australians are a little apart and the WW2 burials are in a communal grave.
Among those here is Corporal Duncan Alexander McGregor, 21st Australian Infantry, killed in action attacking a machine gun position in front of the village on 19 May 1918 aged 20 years.
UK – 20   Aust – 4   Fr – 1
WW2 – 4 (1 unnamed)

LOCATION
Ville-sur-Ancre is in the valley of the River Ancre about 2km south of Albert. The Communal Cemetery is on the south-west edge of the village on the south-east side of the road to Treux. The British graves are at the rear of the cemetery.

HISTORY
The Communal Cemetery was used for burials during 1916 before the Battle of the Somme though there are four burials of Australians from 1918 and four men of the 7th Queen's Own Royal West Kents buried on 21 May 1940.

VILLE-SUR-ANCRE COMMUNAL CEMETERY EXTENSION

INFORMATION
Among those buried here is Captain Clarence Daniel Henry Wooster, MC, 6th Queens (Royal West Surreys), killed in action after the capture of Morlancourt on 9 August 1918 aged 27 years. He joined up in August 1914 and became an officer on 22 August. He went to France in May 1915 and served as Transport Officer, first for his battalion and then for his Brigade. He became a Captain in September 1917. He gained his Military Cross in 1917 for rescuing a man from a burning arms store, saving his life.
Concentrated here:
Beaumont-Hamel German Cemetery – located on the south-west side of Beaumont village. It contained one British soldier.
UK – 106   Unnamed – 54   Area – 323 sq mts

LOCATION
Access to the Extension, which is at the southern edge of the Communal Cemetery, is through the Communal Cemetery.

HISTORY
The Extension was begun in August 1918 by the 12th Division. It was extended after the war as graves were brought in from the battlefields of the Somme and Ancre.

VIS-EN-ARTOIS BRITISH CEMETERY, HAUCOURT

HISTORY

The cemetery was begun at the beginning of September 1918 and used until the middle of October 1918. It was greatly enlarged after the war.

INFORMATION

The villages of Vis-en-Artois and Haucourt were behind the German lines for almost the entire war. They were captured, for the only time, by the Canadian Corps on 27 August 1918.

The cemetery was begun immediately afterwards. It was used by fighting units and Field Ambulances until the middle of October. At the end of the war the cemetery contained 430 graves now in Plots I and II. Over 50% of the men were Canadian and 55 were from the 2nd Duke of Wellington's. After the war 1901 graves were concentrated from isolated positions on the battlefields or smaller cemeteries in the surrounding area. Many of the graves dated from the battles of April to June 1917 or August and September 1918.

Among those buried here is Captain Edmond William Claude Gerard de Vere Pery, No. 32 Squadron, Royal Air Force, killed in action on 18 May 1918 aged 24 years when shot down in combat over Etaing. He was Viscount Glentworth, eldest and only son of the 4th Earl of Limerick. Also here is Major George Henry Musgrove, DSO, MiD, 20th Canadian Infantry, killed in action on 28 August 1918 aged 36 years. He was a veteran of the Boer War and lost an arm in 1915 near Festubert before winning his Distinguished Service Order and subsequent death, the DSO being awarded posthumously. The citation of his DSO reads 'For conspicuous gallantry and devotion to duty in action. In the preparatory stages of a raid on the enemy defence, he, by his personal courage and example, inspired all ranks, and was able to develop an intensity of observation and a patrol reconnaissance, which was largely responsible for the clear appreciation of the ground gained. Later, under the handicap of only one arm, the other having been lost in previous operations, he personally supervised the forming up of assaulting parties under heavy fire, and returned to his post, keeping the battalion headquarters fully informed as to each stage of the fighting. His keen sense of duty, fearless conduct in the open, and great energy in all preparations contributed in a large measure to the success of the operations'. He was killed when shot in the throat.

Also of note is Private Joseph Millard Sears, 18th Canadian Infantry, killed in action on 28 August 1918 aged 36 years. He had previously served with the United States Coastal Artillery and the United States Marine Corps.

Another of note is 2nd Lieutenant Eric Thomas Somervelle Salvesen, 7th attached 13th Royal Scots, killed in action on 23 April 1917 aged 19 years. He was a member of the family who owned the Salvesen shipping company. His brother, Lieutenant Christian Raymond Salvesen, 7th Royal Scots was killed in the Quintishill rail disaster in Scotland on 22 May 1915 with 230 others.

One airman is buried in the nearby Communal Cemetery which is just outside of the area covered by this book. From the main road through the village travelling towards Arras, take the right fork towards the end of the village and keep left at the next fork on to the Rue de l'Offussé. Here, buried by the Germans, is 2nd Lieutenant Roland Murray Wilson-Browne, No. 12 Squadron, Royal Flying Corps. He was shot down in his BE2c by two German Fokkers and died as a Prisoner of War on 21 July 1916, aged 19 years.

Concentrated here:

Bois-du-Sart British Cemetery, Pelves - situated about 5km north of here at the north-western edge of the Bois-du-Sart. It contained the graves of ten British and nine Canadian soldiers who were killed in August and September 1918.

Dury German Cemetery - situated about 5km east of here on the south-eastern edge of the village near the present British Cemetery. It contained four British soldiers buried among the 49 German graves that have now been removed.

Ecourt-St. Quentin German Cemetery - still in existence, but outside of the area covered by this book, this is situated about 10km east of here on the western edge of the village on the east side of the road to Lecluse opposite the Communal Cemetery. It contained the graves of sixteen British soldiers.

Etaing Communal Cemetery German Extension - situated on the north-eastern edge of the village which is about 5km north-east of here. It contained the graves of six British men who died in 1917 and 1918. Also in the Extension, now removed, were 331 Germans and two Russian prisoners.

Lecluse German Cemetery - situated on the west side of the village which is about 8km north-east of here. Among the 476 German graves were those of eleven British soldiers killed in 1917 and a Russian Prisoner of War.

Monchy Quarry Cemetery - the village of Monchy-le-Preux is about 5km north-west of here just north of the Arras road. The Quarry Cemetery was situated about 1km south-east of the village. It contained the graves of 22 British soldiers killed in July 1917.

Pelves Canadian Cemetery - situated in the fields about 2km south of the village which is about 5km north of here. It contained the graves of 39 Canadian soldiers killed in August and September 1918.

Pelves Communal Cemetery German Extension - now removed it contained the graves of two British soldiers killed in 1917.

Rumaucourt German Cemetery - still in existence on the southern edge of the village which is about 10km east of here but outside of the area covered by this book. It contained the graves of 21 British and six Australian soldiers.

Sailly-en-Ostrevent Communal Cemetery - situated on the north side of the village, which is about 7km north-east of here, on the east side of the road to Vitry-en-Artois. It contained the graves of three British soldiers but it was destroyed by shell-fire during the war. Two graves could be identified but one is now marked by a Special Memorial.

Vis-en-Artois Communal Cemetery German Extension - situated in the centre of the village it was badly damaged by shell-fire during the war. It contained the graves of fourteen British soldiers among the now removed 621 Germans. Also concentrated elsewhere were eight French and two Russian graves.

UK – 1736	Can – 572	Newf – 9
Aust – 6	SAfr – 2	KUG – 6
Unnamed – 1461		Area – 6577 sq mts

Special Memorials erected to seven British soldiers and one Canadian known, or believed, to be buried among the unnamed graves.

Special Memorials erected to four British soldiers, buried in other cemeteries, whose graves could not be located at the time of concentration.

VIS-EN-ARTOIS MEMORIAL

This memorial was created to commemorate the names of over 9000 British and South African men who died in the period from 8 August 1918 to 11 November 1918 in the advance to Victory in Picardy and Artois, between the Somme and Loos, and who have no known grave.

The memorial consists of a screen wall in three sections upon which are the names of the missing. The middle section is 8m high flanked by pylons 20m high. The Stone of Remembrance stands exactly between the pylons and behind it, in the middle of the screen, is a relief representing St. George and the Dragon. The flanking sections form the back of a roofed colonnade, and at the far end of each is a small building.

Three holders of the Victoria Cross are listed on the Memorial. Corporal Allan Leonard Lewis, VC, 6th Northamptonshires, killed in action on 21 September 1918, aged 23 years. His citation reads 'For most conspicuous bravery at Ronssoy on the 18th September, 1918, when in command of a section on the right of an attacking line held up by intense machine gun fire. L./Cpl. Lewis observing that two enemy machine guns were enfilading the line, crawled forward singlehanded, and successfully bombed the guns, and by rifle fire later caused the whole team to surrender, thereby enabling the line to advance. On 21st September, 1918, he again displayed great powers of command, and, having rushed his company through the enemy barrage, was killed whilst getting his men under cover from heavy machine gun fire. Throughout he showed a splendid disregard of danger, and his leadership at a critical period was beyond all praise.'

Chief Petty Officer George Prowse, VC, DCM, Drake Battalion, Royal Naval Volunteer Reserve, 63rd (Royal Navy) Division, killed in action on 27 September 1918, aged 32 years. His citation reads 'For most conspicuous bravery and devotion to duty when, during an advance, a portion of his company became disorganised by heavy machine gun fire from an enemy strong point. Collecting what men were available he led them with great coolness and bravery against this strong point, capturing it together with twenty-three prisoners and five machine guns. Later, he took a patrol forward in face of much enemy opposition, and established it on important high ground. On another occasion he displayed great heroism by attacking single-handed an ammunition limber which was trying to recover ammunition, killing three men who accompanied it and capturing the limber. Two days later he rendered valuable services when covering the advance of his company with a Lewis gun section, and located later on two machine gun positions in a concrete emplacement, which were holding up the advance of the battalion on the right. With complete disregard of personal danger he rushed forward with a small party and attacked and captured these posts, killing six enemy and taking thirteen prisoners and two machine guns. He was the only survivor of the gallant party, but by this daring and heroic action he enabled the battalion on the right to push forward without further machine gun fire from the village. Throughout the whole operations his magnificent example and leadership were an inspiration to all, and his courage was superb.' Although serving in a naval unit, his service was entirely on land, being wounded twice and earning a Distinguished Conduct Medal, awarded posthumously, for action at Longeast Wood, on 21-22 August 1918. His wife received his VC from King George V in a ceremony at Buckingham Palace on 17 July 1919. It was the last VC to be awarded with a blue ribbon to signify naval service.

Serjeant Frederick Charles Riggs, VC, MM, 6th York and Lancasters, killed in action on 1 October 1918, aged 29 years. His citation reads 'For most conspicuous bravery and self-sacrifice on the morning of 1st Oct., 1918, near Epinoy, when, having led his platoon through strong uncut wire under severe fire, he continued straight on, and although losing heavily from flanking fire, succeeded in reaching his objective, where he rushed and captured a machine gun. He later handled two captured guns with great effect, and caused the surrender of fifty enemy. Subsequently, when the enemy again advanced in force, Serjt. Riggs cheerfully encouraged his men to resist, and whilst exhorting his men to fight on to the last, this very gallant soldier was killed.'

Also commemorated on the memorial is Private Frederick Charles Butcher, 7th Buffs (East Kents), executed for desertion on 27 August 1918, aged 23 years. He was from Folkestone and had enlisted in 1915.

UK - 9814   SAfr - 16

LOCATION

Vis-en-Artois and Haucourt are villages on the Arras-Bapaume road about 10km south-east of Arras. The cemetery is situated between the two villages on the north side of the road.

VRAUCOURT COPSE CEMETERY

HISTORY
The cemetery was begun in April and May 1917, used by the Germans in March 1918, and used again by Commonwealth troops in September 1918. It was used after the war in 1928.

INFORMATION
The village was behind German lines from 1914 until the German retreat to the Hindenburg Line in 1917. It was retaken by the Germans, after heavy fighting, in March 1918 at the start of their offensive. It fell for the final time in September 1918.

The copse from which the cemetery is named lies to the north. The cemetery originally contained 43 graves of men who died on 2-3 September 1918, mainly from the 3rd Division, but in 1928, Plots II and III were made when graves were brought, many from Vaulx ADS Cemetery, in to the space between Plot I and the road.

Buried here is Private Hugh McIver, VC, MM and Bar, 'B' Company, 2nd Royal Scots, killed in action on 2 September 1918. His citation for Victoria Cross awarded for his action on 23 August 1918 reads 'For most conspicuous bravery and devotion to duty when employed as a company runner. In spite of heavy artillery and machine-gun fire he carried messages regardless of his own safety. Single-handed he pursued an enemy scout into a machine gun post and having killed six of the garrison captured twenty prisoners with two machine guns. This gallant action enabled the company to advance unchecked. Later he succeeded at great personal risk in stopping the fire of a British Tank which was directed in error against our own troops at close range. By this very gallant action Pte. McIver undoubtedly saved many lives.' Private McIver was awarded the Military Medal for actions on 14 July 1916, followed by a Bar for actions on 1 July 1918.

Also buried here is 2nd Lieutenant Richmond Gordon Howell-Price, MC, 1st Australian Infantry, killed in action on 4 May 1917 aged 20 years. A bank clerk before enlisting in December 1915, he served in the ranks in the Middle East until commissioned as a 2nd Lieutenant in the 1st Australian Infantry on 31 December 1916. On 4 May 1917 he was wounded at Bullecourt, and died later that day. Three days later it was announced that he had been awarded the Military Cross. He had three brothers, Lieutenant John, RN, DSO, DSC; Major Frederick, DSO, twice MiD, 6th Company, Australian Army Service Corps; Lieutenant-Colonel Owen, DSO, MC, twice MiD, 3rd Australian Infantry, died of wounds on 4 November 1916 and buried at Heilly Station Cemetery; Major Philip, DSO, MC, MiD, 1st Australian Infantry, killed in action at Broodseinde near Ieper on 4 October 1917 and commemorated on the Menin Gate. The family accrued one DSC, four DSO's, three MC's and were five times MiD. Three were killed. This is a considerable contribution well worth commemoration. For more details on each brother please see Heilly Station Cemetery.

UK – 66   Aust – 38   Unnamed - 6
Area – 396 sq mts

LOCATION
Vaulx-Vraucourt is situated about 5km north-east of Bapaume. It is in the valley of the River L'Hirondelle almost at the head of the river. The village is about 2km east of the A1 Autoroute and a similar distance north of the Bapaume to Cambrai road. The cemetery is beyond the northern edge of the village on the east side of an old road to Noreuil that is little more than a track.

VRELY COMMUNAL CEMETERY EXTENSION

HISTORY
The Communal Cemetery Extension was made by the Canadian Corps Burial Officer in August 1918.

INFORMATION
The area was the scene of heavy fighting between the French Sixth Army and the German First Army at the end of August 1914. The village was in German hands until it fell to the British in February 1917. It was taken by the Germans on the evening of 27 March 1918 and taken back by the 2nd Canadian Division on 9 August 1918.

Most burials here are men of the 22nd (Canadien Francais, Quebec Regiment), 24th and 25th Canadian Infantry. The graves are in two rows and include Tank Corps and cavalry killed in August 1918. A German burial ground has been removed.

Among those buried here is Sergeant Rene Desmarais, MM & Bar, 25th Canadian Infantry, killed in action when shot by a German machine gun during the advance on Vrely on 9 August 1918 aged 26 years. He enlisted in February 1916 with the 9th Canadian Infantry, transferred while in England to the 17th Canadian Infantry in July 1916 and joined the 25th Canadian Infantry in France in September 1916. He became a Lance Corporal in November 1917, Corporal in February 1918, and Sergeant in March 1918. When promoted to Sergeant he was awarded the Military Medal for services in the field. The Bar was awarded posthumously.

UK – 4   Can – 39   Unnamed - 4
Area – 199 sq mts

LOCATION

Vrely is located about 25km south-east of Amiens and 8km north-west of Roye. It is on the high heath south of the road from Amiens to St. Quentin and 1km south of Rosieres-en-Santerre. The Communal Cemetery is at the western edge of the village on the north side of the Rue du Caix. The Extension is at western end of the Communal Cemetery. There is no access through the civilian cemetery. A small CWGC path leads from the road at the west end of the civilian cemetery to the Extension.

WAGGON ROAD CEMETERY, BEAUMONT-HAMEL

HISTORY

The cemetery was only used in early 1917.

INFORMATION

Beaumont was in German hands from 1914. It was an objective for the 29th Division on 1 July 1916 but their attack failed. It was attacked again, and taken, on 13 November 1916 by the 51st (Highland) and 63rd (Royal Naval) Divisions. Most of the dead buried here were killed in November 1916 and most are men of the Highland Light Infantry.

When the Germans withdrew to the Hindenburg Line in early 1917 the British had the opportunity to bury the dead who had fallen during the Battle of the Ancre in November 1916. The V Corps created a number of cemeteries in this area at that time.

This cemetery was originally known as V Corps Cemetery No. 10. It gained its present name after the war and was named after the road that ran from Beaumont to Serre. 49 of the graves are men of the 11th (Lonsdale) Borders who attacked here in both July and November 1916.

Among those buried here is Lieutenant George Neale Higginson, MiD, 16th (1st Salford Pals) Lancashire Fusiliers, killed in action on 23 November 1916 aged 30 years. He, with eleven of his men, led an attack to rescue men of the 16th (2nd Glasgow Pals) Highland Light Infantry and 11th Borders. It failed and the trapped men who survived were eventually taken prisoner by the Germans. Those who died are buried in local cemeteries. His brother, Captain Tom Arthur Higginson, 6th King's Shropshire Light Infantry, was killed in action on 19 September 1915 and is buried at Royal Irish Rifles Graveyard, Laventie.

UK – 195   Unnamed – 36   Area - 622 sq mts

LOCATION

Beamont lies on the ground above the River Ancre about 8km north of Albert. The cemetery can be found in the area north of the village between it and Serre on the east side of the track from Beaumont to Serre near, and on the same farm track, as Munich Trench Cemetery though this is 100m closer to the village and the road. It lies on the ridge at the head of the valley. This is not an easy cemetery to reach but there are excellent views of the battlefield.

WAILLY ORCHARD CEMETERY

HISTORY

The cemetery was begun in May 1916 as a front-line cemetery and was used regularly throughout 1916. In 1917 very few burials were made here but during the German offensive of 1918 it came back into use. It was closed at the end of August 1918.

INFORMATION

The village was behind Allied lines throughout the war. The cemetery was opened by the Liverpool battalions of the 55th (West Lancashire) Division in a location hidden from the enemy by a high wall.

The Canadians made many burials here in 1918 when the area was defended by the Third Army. Of the Canadians buried here, 60 belonged to the 22nd (Canadien Francais, Quebec Regiment) Canadian Infantry.

Among those buried here is Captain Herbert Norris, DSO, twice MiD, 31st Canadian Infantry, killed in action on 25 June 1918 aged 36 years. He served with 2nd Queen's in the South African War from 1901-02, emigrated to Canada in 1905 and married Hilda Clements in 1907. He enlisted on 16 November 1914, was wounded St. Eloi in April 1916, and was awarded the Distinguished Service Order for gallantry at Courcelette in September 1916. He, with two other officers, were killed in a trench raid at Neuville-Vitasse.

Also here is Private Thomas John Wellington, 24th Canadian Infantry, killed in action on 27 May 1918 aged 34 years. The epitaph at the foot of his headstone reads 'This grave I may never see, Will some kind friend Place a flower for me, Mother'. I find this type of wording some of the most touching as their family accepts that they will never visit the grave due to distance. I try to spend a few minutes at graves with this type of request.

UK – 162   Can - 189   KUG – 15
Area – 1634 sq mts

LOCATION

Wailly lies about 6km south-west of Arras in the valley of the River Crinchon. It is easy to get lost in the narrow roads of this valley, hence it may take some time to orientate yourself. The cemetery is on the high ground above the village, in part of an old orchard, on the north-western outskirts of the village in a housing estate on Rue des Allies.

WANCOURT BRITISH CEMETERY

HISTORY

The cemetery was opened in late April 1917 after the village had been captured by the British. It remained in use until March 1918 when the area fell to the Germans and then it was used again from August to October 1918. At the end of the war it contained 410 graves, when Row D of Plot III was the last row, but it was greatly enlarged by the concentration of 1429 graves from isolated positions in the surrounding battlefields or from smaller graveyards.

INFORMATION

Wancourt was captured on 12 April 1917 and the surrounding area soon after. The cemetery was begun by units from the north of England to bury their dead from this battle. The 72nd (Seaforth Highlanders) Canadian Infantry, have buried 60 men in this cemetery. When relieved from the front line near Triangle Wood on 5 September 1918 the battalion retrieved all its casualties from no-man's land and buried them here. The cemetery was originally called Cojeul Valley Cemetery and then River Road Cemetery. During the German advance in 1918 the cemetery and village fell into German hands though it was recaptured by the Canadian Corps on 26 August.

Among those here is Captain Montagu Locke Yeatherd, 12th (Prince of Wales's Royal) Lancers, killed in action on 11 April 1917 aged 33 years. Montagu Yeatherd obtained his commission in April 1903 in the 7th Queen's Own Hussars and saw service with them in South Africa and India. In 1913 was appointed Adjutant of Yeomanry (Yorkshire Dragoons). He departed for France early in the war but had to return home due to illness, and then re-joined his own regiment in India. He was, however, anxious to be at the Front and in October 1916 obtained a transfer to the 12th Lancers but he was killed at Wancourt during the Battle of Arras. He was elder son of Lieutenant Colonel Ernest Walter Yeatherd, King's Own Royal Lancashire Regiment, who died at the Relief of Ladysmith in 1900, and brother of Lieutenant Raymond Gilbert Hooker Yeatherd, Dragoon Guards, who died at Ginchy on the Somme on 15 September 1916 and is commemorated on the Thiepval Memorial.

Also here is Lieutenant Colonel Archibald Ernest Graham McKenzie, DSO and Bar, MiD, 26th Canadian Infantry, killed in action on 28 August 1918 aged 39 years. He had prior service in the 73rd Regiment of Militia and was the first commanding officer of the 26th Canadian Infantry. He was killed by machine gun fire leading his battalion in an attack near Cambrai trying to break the Frenes-Rouvroy Line. The day that McKenzie was killed, 56 other members of his battalion died with him. He was awarded the Distinguished Service Order for his leadership, particularly at Courcelette, during the Canadian involvement on the Somme in 1916. He received a posthumous Bar in October 1918 for 'skill, leadership, and courage at Amiens'.

Concentrated here:

Fontaine Road Cemetery, Heninel - situated on the ridge between Wancourt and Cherisy about 100m north of Signal Trench Cemetery. It was used for the burial of seventeen British officers and men, fifteen of the 2nd Royal Welsh Fusiliers, who died in April 1917.

Henin North Cemetery, Henin-Sur-Cojeul - situated about 1.5km north of the village on the road to Neuville-Vitasse. It contained 29 British soldiers, mostly of the 2nd Wiltshires or 18th King's (Liverpools), who died on 9 April 1917.

Heninel-Cherisy Road West Cemetery, Heninel - situated on the road between the villages about 1km east of

Heninel. It contained 25 British soldiers who were buried in April 1917.

St. Martin-Croisilles Road Cemetery - situated where the Autoroute now crosses the road between the two villages. It was used to bury fifteen British officers, thirteen of the 1st East Yorkshires, who died from 9-13 April 1917.

Shaft Trench Cemetery - about 1.5km south of Heninel on the road to Croisilles. It was used for the burial of nineteen British soldiers of the 50th Division who died from April to June 1917.

Signal Trench Cemetery, Heninel - situated on the ridge between Wancourt and Cherisy. It was used for the burial of 22 British soldiers who died in April and May 1917.

The Lincolns Cemetery, St. Martin-Sur-Cojeul - situated about 1.5km south-east of the village near to the site of the present Autoroute. It was used for the burial of 22 men of the 1st Lincolns who died on 11 April 1917.

UK – 1026   Can – 246   Bermuda – 1
KUG – 566   Unnamed - 262 (238 UK and 24 Can)
Area – 5421 sq mts

Special Memorials to 76 British soldiers known, or believed, to be buried among the unnamed.

Special Memorials to 20 British soldiers who were buried in Signal Trench Cemetery whose graves were destroyed in later battles.

LOCATION

Wancourt lies in the valley of the River Cojeul south of the Arras-Cambrai road and about 7km south-east of the centre of Arras. This cemetery is on the hillside south-east of the village, across the river.

WARLENCOURT BRITISH CEMETERY

HISTORY
The cemetery was made in late 1919 as a concentration cemetery after the war.

INFORMATION
The village of Warlencourt-Eaucourt is at the limit of the British advance during the Battles of the Somme in 1916. Eaucourt-l'Abbaye was a hamlet situated about 2km south-east of Warlencourt and 1km east of Le Sars on the road to Gueudecourt. The Butte de Warlencourt, a chalk mound created during Roman times, and situated about 500m from the village of Warlencourt on the south-east side of the Albert-Bapaume road about 5km south-west of Bapaume, is nominally the point that marks the limit of the advance here. Haig decided that he wanted this ridge captured before winter set in. The 23rd and 47th Divisions in mid-October, and the 48th and 50th Divisions in late-October to early November, carried out attacks here but failed to gain the ridge north of Le Sars. Eaucourt was captured by the 47th Division in early October. The Butte never fell, though British troops gained and lost a foothold several times, but was abandoned by the Germans in February 1917 during their retreat to the Hindenburg Line. The Germans retook the area on 25 March 1918 in their spring offensive despite strong defence by the 51st Division. The 42nd Division captured the ground for the final time on 25 August 1918.

The Western Front Association purchased the Butte in 1990. The Butte also played a significant role during the Franco-Prussian War of 1870-71.

The cemetery lies in the area that became no-man's land by the end of 1916. It contains many of the dead who died attacking the Butte as well as those concentrated from south of this location. It also contains many of the dead who were killed 'holding the line' here in the winter of 1916-17. Approximately 50% of the graves are unidentified.

Among those buried here is Serjeant Donald Forrester Brown, VC, 2nd Otago Regiment, New Zealand Expeditionary Force, killed in action on 1 October 1916 aged 26 years. The citation for his Victoria Cross reads 'For most conspicuous bravery and determination in attack (south-east of High Wood, France, on September 15, 1916), when the company to which he belonged had suffered very heavy casualties in officers and men from machine gun fire. At great personal risk this N.C.O. advanced with a comrade and succeeded in reaching a point within 30 yds. of the enemy guns. Four of the gun crew were killed and the gun captured. The advance of the company was continued until it was again held up by machine gun fire. Again Serjt. Brown and his comrade, with great gallantry, rushed the gun and killed the crew. After this second position had been won, the company came under very heavy shell fire, and the utter contempt for danger and coolness under fire of this N.C.O. did much to keep up the spirit of his men. On a subsequent occasion in attack, Serjt. Brown showed most conspicuous gallantry. He attacked, single handed, a machine gun which was holding up the attack, killed the gun crew, and captured the gun. Later, whilst sniping the retreating enemy, this very gallant soldier was killed.' Initially, Brown's Company commander had recommended him for a Distinguished Conduct Medal although his battalion commander had written to Brown's father indicating that he had hoped that Brown's recommendation would be upgraded to a Victoria Cross. However, with Brown's death the officers of his battalion started pushing for a Victoria Cross. Brown's VC was the first earned by a soldier of the New Zealand Expeditionary Force on the Western Front.

One of the men lost at Hexham Road Cemetery, and now commemorated by a Special Memorial here, is Major Julius August William Kayser, 12th Australian Infantry, killed in action on 16 February 1917 at Gueudecourt. He enlisted soon after the outbreak of war and served at Gallipoli where he was severely wounded. He returned to Australia thinking his war had ended. However, he recovered and returned to his battalion with whom he was wounded again, this time at Pozieres in July 1916. Once more he recovered and returned to his battalion before he was killed by a German mortar.

There were two soldiers buried in an isolated grave located on the road from Le Barque to the Abbey about 2km south of here. The two officers of the 9th Trench Mortar Battery who died on 16 October 1916 are 2nd Lieutenants Edward Montgomery and John Tarras. In May 1930, according to CWGC records, they were moved to Serre Road No. 2 Cemetery.

Concentrated here:

Hexham Road Cemetery, Le Sars - situated on the western edge of the Abbey about 2km south of here. Hexham Road was the name given by the British Army to the road, now a farm track, from Warlencourt to the Abbey. The cemetery was opened in November 1916 and remained in use until October 1917. It contained the graves of seventeen British and thirteen Australian soldiers.

UK – 2765	Aust 461	SAfr – 121
NZ – 79	Can - 4	Fr – 2
Unnamed – 1825		Area – 10300 sq mts

Special Memorials erected to 44 British, nine Australian and two South African soldiers known, or believed, to be buried among the unnamed graves.

Special Memorials erected to eight British and seven Australian soldiers, buried in Hexham Road Cemetery, whose graves were destroyed by shell-fire.

LOCATION
Warlencourt is situated to the north of the Albert-Bapaume Road about 5km from Bapaume and 15km from Albert. The cemetery is on the south-east side of the Albert-Bapaume road 5km from Bapaume.

WARLOY-BAILLON COMMUNAL CEMETERY

HISTORY
The Communal Cemetery was used from October 1915 to 1 July 1916.

INFORMATION
The village was behind Allied lines for most of the war. It fell to the Germans in April 1918 and was soon won back. The dead in the Communal Cemetery date from the period when the British were merely 'holding the line'. The first Commonwealth burial took place in the Communal Cemetery in October 1915 and the last on 1 July 1916. By that date, Field Ambulances had come to the village in readiness for the attack, and the Extension was begun on the eastern side of the cemetery. Two IWGC workers are buried here, one in 1940 and one in 1947.

Among those buried here is Lieutenant Colonel Thomas Mowbray Martin Berkeley, MiD, Camp Commandant, VIII Corps, Staff Deputy Assistant Quartermaster General (DAQMG), late Black Watch (Royal Highlanders), killed in action on 20 May 1916 aged 56 years. He arrived in France on Sunday 23 April 1916 so had been at the Front for only four weeks. He had fought in the Boer War, where he was wounded at Magersfontein and Paarderburg, and was Mentioned in Despatches. He also served in the Nile Expedition of 1884-5. He was grandson of the 3rd Earl of Kenmore.

Also here is Lieutenant Colonel Percy Wilfrid Machell, CMG, DSO, 11th (Lonsdale) Borders, killed in action on 1 July 1916 aged 54 years. He was married to Countess Victoria known as Lady Valda Gleichen, daughter of Admiral Prince Victor of Hohenlohe-Langenburg and great-niece of Queen Victoria. In 1884-5 he served in the Nile Expeditionary Force while with the 56th Regiment (Essex Regiment). He was then attached to the Egyptian Army in 1886, and was in command at the capture of Fort Khor Moussa, for which he was awarded the Order of the Osmanieh, 4th Class. He was then involved in operations at Suakin and Gemaizahin in 1888 in which his horse was shot from under him. In the Sudan in 1889-91 he took part in the Toski Expedition as Brigade-Major of No. 2 Column and took part in the capture of Tokar for which he was awarded the Bronze Star, Medjidie, 4th class. He helped to raise, and commanded from 1891-95, the 12th Sudanese Battalion, became Inspector General of the Egyptian Coastguard in 1896, and Adviser to the Ministry of Interior, Egypt from 1898-1906 for which he gained the Grand Cordon of the Medjidie in 1902. He was made a Companion of the Order of St. Michael and St. George (CMG) in the Birthday Honours List in June 1906 for his work in Egypt and the Distinguished Service Order in the June 1916 Birthday Honours List for service in the field. He raised, trained, as a Captain, and then commanded the 11th (Lonsdale) Borders leading them into attack at the Leipzig Salient near Thiepval on the first day of the Battle of the Somme. He was killed in the attack and his men brought him here for burial.

Another 'man' here is Private Henry William Cox, 47th Australian Infantry, who was a labourer from New South Wales. He first enlisted at Lismore in August 1915, but was discharged on 19 October 1915 due to his age. The following day he enlisted at Brisbane. He died of wounds received in action at Pozieres on 12 August 1916 aged 16 years 9 months.

UK – 46   Fr - 158

LOCATION
Warloy-Baillon is about 5km west of Albert. The Communal Cemetery is on the north-eastern edge of the village, on the north side of the road to Mailly-Maillet and Arras. The burial grounds are above the level of the road. The separation between Communal Cemetery burials and the Extension is less clear than in the past. The French WW1 graves are now the primary separation between the two CWGC cemeteries.

WARLOY-BAILLON COMMUNAL CEMETERY EXTENSION

HISTORY
The Extension was opened in July 1916 and it remained in use until November 1916 though there are also a small number of burials dating from the spring of 1918.

INFORMATION
Field Ambulances came to the village in June 1916 in preparation for the large number of casualties expected from the Battle of the Somme. It was known as an 'Advanced Operating Centre'. Burials between July and November 1916 account for the majority of the dead.

Among those buried here is Major General Edward Charles 'Inky-Bill' Ingouville-Williams, CB, DSO, four times MiD, General Staff commanding 34th Division, formerly Worcestershire Regiment, killed in action on 22 July 1916 aged 55 years. The General and his aide-de-camp had been reconnoitring the area near Mametz Wood. He was killed at Queen's Nullah, south-west of Mametz Wood, after having walked from Contalmaison around the south side of the wood to meet his car which was at Montauban. He had served in the Nile Expedition, the Battle of Atbara and the Battle of Khartoum, as well as the Boer Wars where he was at the Relief of Ladysmith. His Distinguished Service Order was for service during that conflict. He was appointed a Companion of the Order of the Bath in 1910.

Also here is Lieutenant Colonel Albermarle Cator Annesley, DSO, MiD, commanding 8th Royal Fusiliers, killed in action on 7 July 1916 at Ovillers. He fought in the Boer War between 1899 and 1901, where he was Mentioned in Despatches. When the attack got under way, the 8th Royal Fusiliers was led from the front by Annesley, waving his stick. Although they carried the first three enemy lines at Ovillers, and even managed to gain a footing at the village, due to the high number of casualties they were unable to consolidate their gains, and were eventually forced to fall back to the former German second line. Of the 800 officers and other ranks who took part in the attack on Ovillers, 640 were casualties by the end of the day, and amongst the dead was Lieutenant-Colonel Annesley who had died in the medical centre here, having carried on fighting although wounded on three separate occasions. He was awarded the Distinguished Service Order in April 1916. The citation reads 'For conspicuous ability and energy when in command of his Battalion during an attack. The success of the attack and the subsequent defeat of counter-attacks were due to his foresight, energy, and example.'

Another buried here is Lance Corporal George Edward Hughes, 7th King's Own (Royal Lancasters), executed for desertion on 23 November 1916. Hughes was from Manchester and is believed to have been a volunteer, and it is known that he deserted on the Somme.

Also here is 2nd Lieutenant Wynell Hastings Lloyd, 123rd Field Company, Royal Engineers, who died on 17 April 1918 aged 23 years. Lloyd was murdered by Sapper Robert Bell. At the trial it was stated that the events leading to his murder were that Lloyd had ordered Bell to get his puttees while on parade as Bell was not wearing them. While inspecting the rear of the two ranks, Lloyd was shot in the forehead and fell to the ground. Company Sergeant Major Foster said that Bell told him "When I set out to accomplish a thing, I do it, there it is. I have done the Section a good turn. You'll think of Bob Bell in years to come." Bell stated that he slipped when getting out of the trench to re-join the parade, after failing to find his putties. His rifle flew forward and exploded. He had forgotten to remove the round placed in the barrel earlier in the day, when he went hunting for hare or partridge. Sapper Robert Bell was found guilty of the murder of 2nd Lieutenant Lloyd and was sentenced to death with no recommendation for mercy. He was executed at 4.12am on 22 May 1918. Bell was the last Royal Engineer to be executed during World War One and is buried in Toutencourt Communal Cemetery.

A British and an Australian soldier were concentrated into the Extension from Baizieux Communal Cemetery 1km to the south of here in 1934.

UK – 857   Aust – 319   Can – 152
Ger – 18   KUG – 3   WW2 - 2

LOCATION
See the Communal Cemetery. The Extension is on the eastern side of the Cemetery.

WARRY COPSE CEMETERY

HISTORY
The cemetery was in use from 21-23 August 1918.

INFORMATION
Courcelle-le-Comte was taken by the 3rd Division on the 21 August 1918 and the cemetery was made by the 3rd Division soon after.

Among those buried here is Captain Reginald James Barrett, MC, 6th King's (Liverpools), killed in action on 21 August 1918 aged 26 years. The citation for his Military Cross gained in late 1917 reads 'For conspicuous gallantry and devotion to duty. He led a counter attack with great dash and determination and drove out the enemy from a post they had taken. He did fine service.'

Also here is Lance Serjeant Charles Napier Mitchell, MM & Bar, 13th King's (Liverpools), killed in action on 21 August 1918 aged 23 years. Before the war he worked for the Lancashire and Yorkshire Railway. He enlisted in November 1914, and went to France a year later. He had been wounded three times and was posthumously awarded the Military Medal, 29 August, and Bar, 7 October, for bravery in the field.

UK – 40   Unnamed – 2   Area - 280 sq mts

LOCATION
The village of Courcelle-le-Comte is about 4km north-west of Bapaume and 20km south of Arras. The cemetery is about 1km south-east of the village, on the east side of the railway line, and 50m north-west of the small copse from which it takes its name.

WARVILLERS CHURCHYARD EXTENSION

HISTORY
The Extension was opened and closed during the fighting in this area in August 1918.

INFORMATION
The Extension was made by front-line units attacking the Germans during August 1918. It looks over the fields where the Canadians advanced in August 1918. Of the original burials here, eleven of the twelve British graves were men of the Tank Corps or Cavalry units. One British grave was concentrated here from Rouvray-en-Santerre Communal Cemetery in 1934. It is Private William Jackson who is now in Row A, Grave 1A.

Among those buried here is the famous French Cree marksman Private Henry Norwest, MM and Bar, 50th (Alberta) Canadian Infantry, killed in action on 18 August 1918 aged 30 years. He worked as a ranch hand and rodeo performer before joining the battalion in 1915. His ability to be still for hours and his camouflaging techniques made him suited to the task of sniper. He felt that it was his duty to take such a dangerous role, often well out in front of his own trenches. At the Pimple during the Canadian victory at Vimy he killed so many German snipers that he won a Military Medal. In 1918 he won Bar to his Military Medal, again as a marksman and making himself the battalion record holder at 115 confirmed kills.

UK – 13   Can – 35   Unnamed – 3
Area – 322 sq mts

LOCATION
Warvillers is situated about 10km north-west of Roye. It lies on the road from Bouchoir to Rosieres-en-Santerre midway between the two villages. The Extension is found on the eastern edge of the village and is hidden behind the church, in a field, and separated from the churchyard by 10m. It is reached through the churchyard.

WINDMILL BRITISH CEMETERY, MONCHY-LE-PREUX

HISTORY
The cemetery was begun in May 1917. It remained in use until March 1918 when the area fell to the Germans. It was used again from August to October 1918.

INFORMATION
The villages nearby were captured during the Battles of Arras on 23 April 1917 and, although Guemappe was lost briefly, it was soon recaptured.

The cemetery got its name from a windmill that used to be here before the war. The cemetery was begun in early May to bury the dead of the 1917 battles. In Plot II there are 23 officers and men of the 1st King's Own (Royal Lancasters) who were killed in the Battle of the Drocourt-Queant Line during September 1918.

Among those buried here is Major James Christian Lawrence Young, Regimental Depot, (Alberta), seconded to 1st Canadian Divisional HQ who died on 13 October 1918. He had previously served with the 4th Gloucestershires before joining the Territorial Force. He attested to the 202nd Battalion on 4 October 1916 at Sarcee Camp, Alberta.

UK – 320	Can – 61	Newf – 4
SAfr – 1	Ger – 1	
Unnamed – 17	KUG - 15	

Area – 1112 sq mts

Special Memorial to a British soldier who is believed to be buried among the unknown graves.

LOCATION
The cemetery is on the northern side of the Arras-Cambrai road close to a road, known during the war as Hussar Lane, that leads to Monchy. It is about 7km south-east of the centre of Arras.

WOOD CEMETERY

HISTORY
Wood Cemetery was made by the Canadian Corps in August 1918.

INFORMATION
The cemetery is a small pretty battlefield cemetery in the middle of fields and in the middle of the area over which the Canadians advanced on 8 August 1918 in capturing Marcelcave. The graves are in two rows with one isolated burial. The Canadians are mostly from the New Brunswick, Quebec and Central Ontario battalions.

Among those buried here is Private Theophilus Ellery Underhill, 26th (New Brunswick) Canadian Infantry, killed in action on 8 August 1918 aged 22 years. He was a teacher who enlisted in March 1915. Four other men in his battalion and from his locality were killed on 8 August 1918.

| UK – 9 | Can – 41 | Unnamed – 3 |

Area – 272 sq mts

LOCATION
Marcelcave is situated about 10km east of Amiens and 1km south-east of Villers-Bretonneux. The cemetery is about 1.5km south-east of the village on a farm road that becomes unpaved soon after the cemetery. There is a CWGC path that leads about 150m from the road to the cemetery.

'Y' RAVINE CEMETERY

HISTORY
The cemetery was in use for a brief period in early 1917.

INFORMATION
Beaumont was in German hands from 1914. It was an objective for 29th Division on 1 July 1916. The German regiment in the line at Beaumont was the 119th Reserve Infantry Regiment. The regiment had taken this area from the French in late September 1914, and had been in place for nineteen months as part of the 26th Reserve Division building defences. In August 1915 the French Army left and the British took over.

'Y' Ravine runs east to west about 1km south of Beaumont at the north end of Newfoundland Park. It was a deep ravine with steep sides clearly shaped like a 'Y' on trench maps. Many of the men in 119th Reserve Infantry Regiment were miners so had skills that they employed in building a series of deep bunkers in the hillside of 'Y' Ravine. The Germans called these 'Stollen' or 'Feste'. One of the large bunkers was the Leiling Stollen named after Hauptmann Leiling, one of the German Captains in the regiment and designer of the bunker. In spite of the British artillery bombardment, which lasted for seven days before the attack on 1 July, most of the German soldiers had survived by sheltering in their protective bunkers so casualties were relatively light.

When the British artillery fire was lifted off the German front line trenches a few minutes before Zero Hour at 7.30am, the German soldiers at 'Y' Ravine were able to quickly enter their trenches and man their machine guns. The British battalions making their way down the slope towards them were plain to see and were fired on by the German defenders as they approached. The attack failed with heavy casualties. This area was not captured until 13 November 1916 when the 51st (Highland) took it with 63rd (Royal Naval) Divisions nearby.

The cemetery was made by V Corps in the spring of 1917, when these battlefields were cleared. It was originally called 'Y' Ravine Cemetery No. 1. 'Y' Ravine No. 2 Cemetery was concentrated after the war into Ancre British Cemetery. The majority of the burials are in four straight rows in the centre of the cemetery. Many of the headstones commemorate two soldiers, which reflects the fact that the cemetery is more of a mass grave than individual burials. Some headstones have two names inscribed, but sometimes one of the burials is known and one unknown.

On the headstone of Private Charles Taylor, one of the Newfoundlanders who died on 1 July, the inscription reads 'His last words when leaving home were "I have only once to die"'.

Among those buried here is Company Serjeant Major Joseph Sydney Fairbrass, 2nd South Wales Borderers, killed in action on 1 July 1916 aged 27 years. He had served at Gallipoli in 1915 and was one of six brothers who served during the war, three of whom were killed. His two brothers who died in the war were Private William Samuel Fairbrass, 7th Field Ambulance, Royal Army Medical Corps, who died on 25 April 1917 aged 30 years and is buried at Duisans British Cemetery; and Ordinary Seaman Walter Daniel Fairbrass HMS Pembroke I, Royal Navy who died on 3 November 1918 aged 18 years and is buried at Leigh-on-Sea Cemetery. HMS Pembroke was the shore base at Sheerness and it is possible that he was one of the 242 servicemen who succumbed there to Spanish Flu between 1918 and 1921.

UK – 328   NF – 38   Unnamed - 151
Area – 1166 sq mts

Special Memorials are erected to 53 British men and eight from Newfoundland, known or believed to be buried among the unnamed.

Newfoundland Park

This is one of the more frequently visited places on the Western Front. It contains preserved trenches, monuments, three cemeteries, and a visitor centre with toilets. Newfoundland, an independent territory until it joined Canada in 1959, purchased the 84 acres in 1921. The park was opened by Haig on 7 June 1925.

The 29th Division Memorial, is near the entrance. The magnificent Caribou Memorial stands above the front-line of 1 July 1916. The 51st (Highland) Division, who captured the German line on 13 November 1916 and continued into Beaumont, Memorial is situated on the German line near Y Ravine. It faces in the direction of the Division's attack and bears the Gaelic inscription 'Friends are good on the day of battle'.

The Newfoundlanders were one of the reserve units for the 29th Division on 1 July 1916. When called to move forward they felt the urgency of the situation and, as the communication trenches were in chaos, they moved from the reserve line to the front line by crossing the open ground between the lines. The 1st Essex were given the same order, but as 'regular' experienced soldiers, unlike the volunteer Newfoundlanders, they stuck to the communication trenches and took time to reach the front line. So, after the failure of the initial attack, the Newfoundlanders found themselves the only things moving on the horizon. It was said of them that 'The only visible sign that the men knew they were under this terrific fire, was that they all instinctively tucked their chins into an advanced shoulder as they had so often done when fighting their way home against a blizzard in some little outpost in far off Newfoundland'. Of the 801 Newfoundlanders who attacked that day, only 68 did not become casualties. This includes three men, two brothers and a cousin, of the Ayres family.

LOCATION

'Y' Ravine Cemetery is in the north-east corner of Newfoundland Park and access is best through the park, (though there is a path from Beaumont), which is on the north side of the Auchonvillers-Hamel road. There is good parking available outside Newfoundland Park, but the car park closes at 5.00pm promptly. From here you cross the road and follow the paths through the park to the cemetery. It cannot be guaranteed that the paths through the park will be open at all times of the year. They are frequently closed in winter.

SMALL CEMETERIES (Ten Burials or Less)

ABLAINZEVELLE COMMUNAL CEMETERY

The Communal Cemetery contains, near the north corner, the grave of one unidentified British soldier. Eighty-one German graves, and the German Extension on the east side, have been removed and the body of one British soldier, buried among the German graves, is now in Filliévres British Cemetery.

UK – 1 KUG

Location

Ablainzevelle is nearly 5km north-west of Achiet-le-Grand. The cemetery is on the eastern edge of the village on the north side of the road to Courcelles-le-Comte. It is next to the crossroads with the Ayette-Achiet road.

ACHIET-LE-GRAND COMMUNAL CEMETERY

The Communal Cemetery contains four CWGC graves. Three burials date from early 1917 while one is from August 1918. There are two British soldiers, a member of the Royal Flying Corps and Flight Commander Colin Roy Mackenzie, DSO, twice MID, French Croix de Guerre who was killed in January 1917 aged 24 years. In 1914 he was with the Royal Naval Medical Service. However, in 1915 he transferred to the Royal Naval Air Service and was commissioned as a Flight Sub-Lieutenant. He was awarded the Distinguished Service Order and the Croix de Guerre for 'his skill and gallantry in destroying a German kite balloon on 7 September 1916 under very severe anti-aircraft fire.' By January 1917 Mackenzie was flying a Sopwith Pup aircraft and commanded 'A' Flight, 'Royal Naval Air Service Squadron on detachment to the Royal Flying Corps', soon re-named No. 8 Squadron, Royal Naval Air Service in February 1917. He was shot down and killed at Bihucourt, near Bapaume, on 24 January 1917.

UK - 4

Location

Achiet-le-Grand can be found about 3km north-west of Bapaume. It is on the Amiens-Arras railway and has a railway station. The cemetery is on the north-west edge of the village. The road upon which it stands is a dead-end and the cemetery can be difficult to locate.

ACHIET-LE-PETIT COMMUNAL CEMETERY

The cemetery contains the CWGC graves of seven WW2 airmen. The men are the crew of a Lancaster Bomber from No. 550 Squadron, from North Killingholme in Lincolnshire, that went down on the night of 10-11 April 1944. They are five men of the Royal Air Force Volunteer Reserve and two men from the Royal Canadian Air Force. Among the crew are two holders of the Distinguished Flying Medal and two holders of the Distinguished Flying Cross.

WW2 – 7

Location

The village is about 3km north-west of Bapaume and just south of Achiet-le-Grand. The cemetery is on the eastern edge of the village on Rue du Cimetiere. The graves are located near the centre of the eastern boundary of the cemetery.

AILLY-SUR-NOYE CHURCHYARD

This is one of 23 burial grounds located in the western part of the Somme. Men were mostly buried by their own units though, in 1918, may have been buried by French medical units. The two men buried here died in late March 1918.

UK - 2

Location

The village is about 10km south of Amiens. It is on the western edge of the area covered by this book. The cemetery is in the centre of the village at the main church at the junction of the D26, D188 and D920 roads. The graves are at the rear of the cemetery, one by the French memorial and one in the south-east corner.

AIZECOURT-LE-BAS CHURCHYARD

The Churchyard contains the graves of two Royal Flying Corps officers of No. 13 Squadron killed on 20 February 1916 and buried by the Germans. There is also an officer of 181st Brigade, Royal Field Artillery who died in March 1917 aged 19 years.

UK - 3

Location

The village is about 8km north-east of Peronne. This is a very small village on a minor road between Lieramont and Templeux-la-Fosse. The church is on the west side of the village on the road to Nurlu. The graves are together to the right of the entrance to the churchyard next to the road. It is easy to miss them.

AMPLIER COMMUNAL CEMETERY

Both men buried here died in August 1916, one of drowning. Both served with the Durham Light Infantry though in different battalions.

UK – 2

Location

Amplier is a small village located about 5km south-east of Doullens. It is on the north side of the River Authie on the D24 and north of the D938 that runs between Doullens and Albert. The cemetery is north of the village and can be found by taking the Rue Hector Daillet north from the village centre. The cemetery is about 300m from the village centre on the west side of the track. The British graves are opposite each other near the entrance.

ANDECHY COMMUNAL CEMETERY

This is one of 23 burial grounds located in the western part of the Somme. Men were mostly buried by their own units though, in 1918, may have been buried by French medical units. There is one unidentified soldier from Canada buried here. He had been in the Fort Garry Horse and is buried to the left or north of the central path.

Can – 1   Unnamed - 1

Location

Andechy is on the southern edge of the Department of the Somme about 5km west of Roye. The cemetery is on the south-east edge of the village, on the north side of the road that leads from the centre of the village at the church to the D54 road to Roye.

AUTHIE CHURCHYARD

The churchyard was used for two British burials on 19 May 1940 when No. 26 Squadron, Royal Air Force was stationed in Authie. The squadron had been here for a week and moved back to England on 19 May. The men had been flying a Westland Lysander II on a tactical reconnaissance mission when they crashed west of Authie at 5.30am.

WW2 – 2

Location

Authie is a village 12km south-east of Doullens and 18km north-west of Albert. The churchyard is on the north side of the village and on the north side of the church. Access is from the church or the road to Pas-en-Artois on the north side of the churchyard as the road turns north-east and climbs out of the village. The two British graves are near the south-eastern corner of the churchyard.

BAILLEULVAL COMMUNAL CEMETERY

The burials were made at different times during the period British troops were here. They are a Private of the Manchesters who died in an accident in November 1916 and a Non-Commissioned Officer of the Leicestershires who died in April 1917.

UK – 2

Location

Bailleulval is a village located about 500m south of the Doullens-Arras road. The village is on the D1 about 10km south-west of Arras. The cemetery is on the north side of the village and on the north side of the church at the end of a dead end road. The two British graves are on the east side of the cemetery.

BANCOURT COMMUNAL CEMETERY

Bancourt Communal Cemetery contains the graves of six officers of the Royal Flying Corps, one of them unidentified, buried by the Germans in the autumn of 1916. It was later used by the Allies for the burial of one soldier from New Zealand who had served at Gallipoli and who died in September 1918.

UK – 5   NZ – 1   Aust – 1

Special Memorial to an Australian soldier, buried in the cemetery in April 1917 having died of sickness, whose grave was later destroyed by shell fire.
Special Memorial to an unidentified officer of the Royal Flying Corps.

Location

Bancourt is located about 4km east of Bapaume. The Communal Cemetery is situated on the eastern edge of the village opposite the British Cemetery. Both are found on a road that runs from the D7 Bapaume-Haplincourt road to the D930 Bapaume-Cambrai road. This small road is easy to miss. The graves are in several small plots in the cemetery.

BAZENTIN-LE-PETIT COMMUNAL CEMETERY

The cemetery was used during battles nearby in August 1916. It contains the graves of two men who died in August 1916 buried here after the capture of the village.

UK – 2

Location

Bazentin-le-Petit is located about 10km north-east of Albert and a little more than 10km south-west of Bapaume. The Communal Cemetery is on the east side of the village in a valley at the end of a farm road from the centre of the village. The graves are in the centre of the cemetery.

BEAUMETZ COMMUNAL CEMETERY, CARTIGNY

The cemetery was used by the Germans to bury three officers and a Sergeant of the Royal Flying Corps lost in action on 2 August 1916. The men were two pilots and two observers of No. 60 Squadron which had been formed in April 1916. While it is recorded by CWGC that all died on 2 August it is believed that the Canadian, Lieutenant Ormsby, may have survived the action but died of his wounds a few days later as a Prisoner of War.

UK – 4

Location
Beaumetz is a village near Cartigny between Peronne and St. Quentin. The cemetery is on the west side of the only road leading north from the village, about 200m south of the D194. The graves are at the rear of the cemetery.

BEHENCOURT CHURCHYARD

This is one of seven burial grounds north of the River Somme and behind the line for most of the war that contain a very few Allied military burials. This churchyard contains two artillerymen and a man of the Royal Army Service Corps. Two were buried at different dates in 1916 and one in 1918.

UK – 2   Aust - 1

Location
Behencourt is between Amiens and Albert. The churchyard lies on the D115 which leads from the D929 approximately 10km north of Corbie. The church is on the western edge of the village on the north side of the road to Montigny. The graves are together to the left of the entrance.

BERTRANCOURT COMMUNAL CEMETERY

The cemetery contains one burial, that of a soldier from New Zealand, killed in 1918.

UK – 1

Location
Bertrancourt is situated about 5km north-west of Albert. The cemetery is north of the village on the road to Courcelles-au-Bois about 200m from its junction with the road to Coigneux. The grave is in the south part of the cemetery.

BEUGNATRE COMMUNAL CEMETERY

The Communal Cemetery was used by the Allies for burials in one week in April and three days in May 1917. Two men buried here were members of No. 4 Squadron, Royal Flying Corps and were killed in an accident on 24 March 1917. 2nd Lieutenant Eustace Bertram Low was aged 18 years when he died while 2nd Lieutenant Albert Fisher Gibson died on his 21st birthday. They are together. The other graves are three men of the 2/10th (Hackney Rifles) Londons killed on the same day and buried together seperate from the others while the remainder are five Australians.

UK – 5   Aust - 5

Location
Beugnatre is located about 2km north of Bapaume just east of the A1 Autoroute. The cemetery is on the northern edge of the village.

BIHUCOURT COMMUNAL CEMETERY

The graves of 47 German soldiers have been removed. The burials here are of one Rifleman of the 1/12th (The Rangers) Londons who died on 3 July 1916 and an unidentified New Zealander.

UK – 1   NZ – 1   Unnamed - 1

Location
Bihucourt is a small village located about 3km north-west of Bapaume. The cemetery is on the eastern edge of the village on the Rue du Bapaume. The cemetery is 100m north of the Achiet-Bapaume road on a side-road. The British grave is in the north-west corner while the New Zealand grave is in the south-west corner.

BLAIRVILLE CHURCHYARD

This churchyard contains two British Privates who died in early 1918.

UK – 2

Location
Blairville is a small village about 10km south of Arras. The church is in the centre of the village about 50m south of the road to Hendecourt. The graves are at the rear of the churchyard at the south-east corner of the church.

BOISLEUX-AU-MONT COMMUNAL CEMETERY

The cemetery was used in March, April and August of 1918. The cemetery only contains graves of men from the Grenadier Guards, five of 1st Battalion and one of 2nd Battalion. However, two WW2 burials were added later during the retreat in May 1940. A German extension has been removed. In addition 149 German and seven French graves were removed and re-buried in 1923.

Buried here is The Reverend Edward Reginald Gibbs, a Chaplain attached to the 1st Grenadier Guards. He had been Chaplain to the Archbishop of York and was killed just after conducting a funeral service for a soldier. His brother, Lieutenant Colonel William Beresford Gibbs, 3rd Worcestershires, was killed by shellfire on 3 September 1916 aged 35 years and is buried in Blighty Valley Cemetery.

Also here is The Honourable Harold Fox Pitt Lubbock, son of the 1st Baron Avebury. For some years before the outbreak of the war he had held a commission in the Queen's Own Royal West Kent Yeomanry. After the outbreak of the war, he served with the Yeomanry in Kent, then Egypt and then as a dismounted force in Gallipoli until the evacuation, when the unit was sent to Palestine. He acted as Adjutant during most of the time when abroad and was promoted to Captain in January 1917. Being anxious to serve in France, he obtained a transfer to the Grenadier Guards in July 1917, and after some months with the Regiment in England served in France from January 1918 until he met his death. He had been slightly gassed, but had not previously been wounded. He was killed by a shell on 4 April 1918 aged 29 years. His brother, Captain The Honourable Eric Fox Pitt Lubbock, MC, was killed in action on 17 March 1918, aged 23 years, as Flight Commander with No. 45 Squadron, Royal Flying Corps and is buried in Lijssenthoek Military Cemetery near Ieper. His wife, daughter of Lord Forster, also lost both of her brothers in the war.

Also here is Captain Lionel de Jersey Harvard, 1st Grenadier Guards, killed in action on 30 March 1918. He is a descendant of John Harvard who founded the University in Massachusetts in 1663. His brother, Lieutenant Kenneth O'Gorman Harvard, 2nd Grenadier Guards was killed in action on 1 August 1918 aged 20 years and is buried in Artillery Wood Cemetery near Ieper.

UK – 6   WW2 - 2
Location
Boisleux-au-Mont is a village about 5km south of Arras. It lies in the valley of the River Cojeul. The Communal Cemetery is north-west of the village on the D36 road which leads to the village of Ficheux. The cemetery is on the west side of the road and the burials are in the south-east corner of the cemetery.

BOUVINCOURT COMMUNAL CEMETERY
The cemetery was used in 1917 and 1918. Most of the men were buried by Field Ambulances while one was buried by the Germans.
UK – 6
Location
Bouvincourt-en-Vermandois is a small village mid-way between Peronne and St. Quentin. The cemetery is on the eastern edge of the village opposite the church. The British graves are at the rear on the western edge of the cemetery.

BRAY-SUR-SOMME COMMUNAL CEMETERY
The Communal Cemetery was used for three burials in 1916 and was also used for the burial of seven British soldiers buried by the Germans in 1918. They have been moved to Bronfay Farm Military Cemetery and Bray Military Cemetery. One of the original burials here, unidentified at the time, has subsequently been identified as Private Richard Parr Morris, 1/4th Loyal North Lancashires, who drowned on 29 July 1916 aged 23 years. Captain John Percival Longfield, MVO, 3rd Norfolks, who died on 30 September 1915, aged 29 years was son of Lieutenant Colonel Augustus Henry Longfield, commanding officer of the 1st Norfolks.

UK - 3
Location
Bray-sur-Somme lies on the north bank of the River Somme about 8km south-east of Albert and 30km east of the centre of Amiens. The Communal Cemetery is on the north side of the village next to the French National Cemetery so is easily identified by the French flags at the roadside. It is on the west side of the road to Albert. Longfield and Morris are buried together on the western edge of the cemetery. Quinn is alone on the eastern edge of the cemetery near the road.

BUCQUOY COMMUNAL CEMETERY

The cemetery was used in 1914-16 by the Germans to bury 558 of their men. A monument was erected to these men by the 55th Reserve Infantry Regiment. The Germans also buried nine Allied men. The Royal Naval Division also made burials here in August 1918. All of these graves have been removed leaving eight identified and 2 unidentified burials.
UK – 8   KUG - 2
Location
Bucquoy is located about 10km south of Arras and 7km west of Bapaume. It lies on a line between Bapaume and Doullens. The Communal Cemetery is north-east of the village and the burials are by the entrance.

BUIRE COMMUNAL CEMETERY
The communal cemetery was used for the burial of two British artillerymen on 22 March 1918 and for six Australian soldiers between 6 and 13 September 1918.
UK – 2   Aust - 6
Location
Buire can be found about 4km east of Peronne. It lies on the northern side of the valley of the River Cologne. The cemetery is 100m from the eastern edge of the village south of the road to Tincourt on a small dead-end road from the main road leading towards the river. It is near a small wood with good parking and turning. It is possible to see the cemetery in the valley from the main road. The graves are in three groups, one on the west side of the cemetery and the other two on the east side.

BUIRE-SUR-L'ANCRE COMMUNAL CEMETERY
The Communal Cemetery was used for the burial of five soldiers in 1916 and one in 1918. The village had two communal cemeteries. The other one contained the graves

of four British soldiers but they were removed after the war.

The main railway line nearby was a vital means of communication and supply during the war especially during June-November 1916 when it fed food and supplies to the great battle and took the wounded away. The village was the last 'safe' stop on the line and therefore was a major railhead. Additionally, leave trains left from extra sidings built during the war.

UK – 4   Aust - 2

Location

Buire-sur-l'Ancre lies about 4km south-west of Albert on the north side of the River Ancre. This cemetery is on the northern edge of the village on the east side of the road that runs from the church to the Amiens-Albert road. The graves are together on the southern edge of the cemetery.

BUS-LES-ARTOIS COMMUNAL CEMETERY

This area behind the lines was well known for its Divisional Camps and Medical Units. The Communal Cemetery was used for the burial of two British soldiers on 21 August 1916. One of those here is Corporal Albert E Worricker, 13th Essex, who died of wounds. Sadly, Albert's story is not an unusual one for any war. When home on leave Albert found his wife had been unfaithful to him. He told close relatives and friends that he would not be returning again from France. He 'went over the top' of his own volition and was mortally wounded.

UK – 2

Location

The village is about 10km north-west of Albert, 15km west of Bapaume and 3km east of Louvencourt. The Communal Cemetery is on the road heading east from the centre of the village at the church to Bayencourt, north-east of the village. The two graves are near the east end of the cemetery.

BUSSY-LES-DAOURS COMMUNAL CEMETERY

The cemetery was used for one burial in 1916 and one in 1918. This is one of several cemeteries in the area of Amiens which contain graves of men who died by accident or of illness rather than in battle. One of those here died in an air raid.

UK – 2

Location

The village is about 5km east of Amiens mid-way between Amiens and Corbie. The cemetery is at the south-west corner of the village and reached by a road from the church. The graves are together in the south-east corner of the cemetery near the road.

CACHY COMMUNAL CEMETERY

The communal cemetery was used for the burial of Lieutenant Harold Hubert Thompson, 18th Australian Infantry, who died of wounds on 15 April 1918 aged 29 years. He was from Macleay River, New south Wales. He joined up in February 1915, leaving Australia in August 1915, and rose through the ranks from enlistment as a Private.

A memorial here was erected to the men of the French 4th Regiment and to a cavalry officer who were killed here in September 1870 in the Franco-Prussian War. The memorial was then additionally used to commemorate local people who died in both World Wars including men of the French 4th Colonial Division who fought and died nearby in May and June 1940.

Aust - 1

Location

Cachy is about 5km east of Amiens and 1km south-west of Villers-Bretonneux. The Communal Cemetery is on the edge of town on the road to Gentelles and Boves about 500m from the town centre and church. The CWGC grave is visible from the entrance near the north-east side of the central path.

CAGNICOURT COMMUNAL CEMETERY

The cemetery was used for the burial of one British airman killed in 1944. He was was a member of No. 426 Squadron which was formed at Dishforth, Yorkshire, on 15 October 1942, as a bomber unit in No. 4 Group. Early in January 1943, it joined No. 6 (Royal Canadian Air Force) Group with which, during the next 28 months, its Wellington, Lancastes and Halifax aircraft played their part in attacking Hitler's Europe. In June 1943, it moved to Linton-on-Ouse which was to be its home for nearly two years. The squadron flew 261 missions involving 3213 sorties, and in doing so lost 88 aircraft. The airman's Halifax crashed near Villers-les-Cagnicourt on 13 June 1944. Of the eight crew, Sergeant (Flight Engineer) Eric White is buried here and Squadron Leader Ian McKenzie McRobie is commemorated on the Runnymede Memorial. Two airmen, Flying Officer G. W. Bedford and WO 2nd Class M A Brazey were taken prisoner. Flight Sergeant A H Hammond, WO 2nd Class C A McLeod and Flight Sergeant Bremrose evaded capture, possibly with the help of local people.

WW2 - 1

Location
Cagnicourt is about 15km south-east of Arras and 10km north-west of Cambrai south of the Arras–Cambrai road. The cemetery is on the north-east corner of the village on the east side of the road to Villers-les-Cagnicourt.

CLERY-SUR-SOMME COMMUNAL CEMETERY
The Communal Cemetery was used for one burial in August 1918. A large French National Cemetery is near the village.
Aust - 1
Location
Clery-sur-Somme is 3km north-west of Peronne in the valley of the River Somme. The cemetery is on the south side of the road in the river valley at the south-west corner of the village. The grave is in the south-east corner of the cemetery.

COLINCAMPS COMMUNAL CEMETERY
The cemetery was used in April and May 1918. The nine men buried here are all from the 1st Canterbury Regiment, NZEF, eight buried between 23 and 27 April 1918 with one added on 25 May 1918.
NZ - 9
Location
Colincamps is about 12km north of Albert. The cemetery is on the southern edge of the village on the east side of the road to Mailly-Maillet 100m south of the nearest house. The graves are to the right of the entrance.

COUIN COMMUNAL CEMETERY

The Communal Cemetery was used for the burial of Sergeant Victor Alexander Douglas Mcphee, 4th Field Ambulance, Australian Army Medical Corps, killed in action on 10 April 1918. He enlisted in September 1914 and left Australia in December. He had been in hospital several times during 1915 in and around Gallipoli. He received his promotions from Private in 1916 having moved to France.
Aust - 1
Location
Couin is a small village about 15km east of Doullens and 30km south-west of Arras. The cemetery is on a small road south-west of the village. There is a crossroads south of the village where the Coigneux-St. Leger road meets the Couin to Bus-les-Artois road. The cemetery is 200m west of the crossroads. The grave is in the north-east corner of the cemetery near the entrance.

DAOURS COMMUNAL CEMETERY
The Communal Cemetery was used for two burials, one in February 1916 and one in May 1916. In June 1916 the 1/1st (South Midland), 21st, 34th, 45th and Lucknow Casualty Clearing Stations were all grouped in the village in readiness for the coming battles so burials in the Communal Cemetery ended as an Extension was opened. The two men, Private C. Reynolds of the 8th Norfolks and Sapper A. Scott of the 2/2nd (Highland) Field Company, Royal Engineers, are in the north-west corner of the cemetery.
UK - 2
Location
Daours is a village about 10km east of Amiens lying on the north bank of the River Somme. The cemetery is about 300m north of the village on the west side of the road to La Neuville and Pont Noyelle.

DEMICOURT COMMUNAL CEMETERY
Although the village was in German hands for much of the war, it was behind the lines by late 1917 and had become an important artery for supplies. Hence, it also became a target for German shelling. The village was evacuated when the cookhouse was hit by a shell. The cemetery was used in September and October 1918. The men buried here are mostly Guards or artillerymen.
UK - 10
Location
Demicourt is a small village about 20km north-east of Bapaume about 1km south of the Bapaume-Cambrai road. The cemetery is on the eastern edge of the village just off the main road through the village. The graves are together in one row near the gate at the eastern edge of the cemetery.

DOULLENS COMMUNAL CEMETERY
This cemetery was used for burials in WW2. The men buried here were killed in the retreat, or during flying missions, in May 1940.
WW2 – 10 (4 unnamed)
Location
Doullens lies at the western edge of the area covered by this book. It is 28km north of Amiens and a similar distance north-west of Albert. It is 36km south-west of Arras. The Communal Cemetery and the Extensions are on the eastern edge of the town. About 100m north of the road to the hospital is a small road leading east to the cemetery behind high walls. There is parking by houses at the old and main entrance on the south side of the cemetery.

DURY COMMUNAL CEMETERY
This cemetery was used for a burial of one man killed in the advance in 1944 in WW2.
WW2 - 1
Location
Dury is about 5km south of Amiens. The cemetery is 1km north of the village on the road from the village to Amiens. It is next to a radar tower and 100m south of a monument. The one British grave is in the south-eastern corner.

EPEHY COMMUNAL CEMETERY

The cemetery was used for one burial, an officer of No. 19 Squadron, Royal Flying Corps shot down near Bapaume while flying a BE12 on offensive patrol in 1916 and buried by the Germans.

UK – 1

Location

Epehy is situated about 20km north-west of St. Quentin and a similar distance north-east of Peronne. It is now a little to the west of the A26 Autoroute. The Communal Cemetery is at the south end of the village between the main road and the railway. The single grave is at the right side of the entrance.

ETREILLERS COMMUNAL CEMETERY

The cemetery was used for the burial of a man of the Cyclist Corps In March 1917.

UK – 1

Location

The village is situated about 8km west of St. Quentin and 1km south of the Autoroute between St. Quentin and Amiens. The cemetery is on the west side of the village on the south side of the road to Vaux-en-Vermandois. The British grave is to the right of the central path near the gate.

ETRICOURT COMMUNAL CEMETERY

The cemetery was used for the burial of four men from, or attached to, the Royal Army Service Corps and Labour Corps accidentally killed on 28 September 1922. They are not registered as WW1 war dead as they died after 1921, the official cut off date for WW1 burials. They are

- Private J H Lester, Royal Army Service Corps, died 23 September 1922, aged 35 years.
- Sergeant W G Prior, Labour Corps, died 23 September 1922, aged 48 years.
- Private A E Scott, 4th Hussars, died 23 September 1922, aged 46 years.
- Sergeant W H White, Royal Army Medical Corps, died 23 September 1922, aged 52 years.

On a hillside 600m south-west of Etricourt-Manancourt Communal Cemetery is buried a British airman, Captain Cecil Robert Tidswell, 1st Royal Dragoons and No. 19 Squadron, Royal Flying Corps killed on 16 October 1916 aged 36 years, whilst flying over German lines and buried by the Germans beside his machine. The grave is reached by a track from the road.

UK – 4   Isolated UK Grave - 1

Location

Etricourt is about 10km north of Peronne and 10km south-east of Bapaume. It can be found 1km south of the D172. The cemetery is on the north-west edge of the village on a ridge. It is on the Rue Cimetiere and is visible from the village centre.

FLUQUIERES COMMUNAL CEMETERY

The cemetery was used for one burial on 1 April 1917 and two burials on 3 April 1917. These are two men of the 2nd Manchesters and a driver of the Royal Field Artillery. The two men of the Manchesters seem to have been killed when 'C' Company came under intense shelling while removing captured German guns.

UK – 3

Location

Fluquieres is a village situated just north the road from Ham to St. Quentin. The cemetery is on the western edge of the village. The burials are in the south-west corner of the Communal Cemetery to the left of the entrance.

FOLIES COMMUNAL CEMETERY

The cemetery was used for two burials, one British and one Canadian soldier, on 10 August 1918 though it had previously been used by French and German troops. An Extension was created by Canadian troops in August 1918 but it has since been removed to Bouchoir New British Cemetery.

UK – 1   Can – 1

Location

Folies is on the north-east side of the Amiens-Roye road about 500m from the D934. There is a small road leading south-east from the centre of the village. It lies on the southern edge of the village about 200m from the churchyard. The graves are to the left of the entrance against the wall.

FONCHETTE CHURCHYARD

The cemetery was used for one burial on 30 August 1918.

UK - 1

Location

Fonchette is a very small village 2km east of the A1 Autoroute about 10km north of Roye and 20km west of Ham. The churchyard is in the centre of the village.

FOUCAUCOURT COMMUNAL CEMETERY

Near the south-west corner of the Communal Cemetery are the graves of one British soldier, buried by the Germans in March 1918, and seven men buried by the British in August and September 1918.

The village is actually called Foucaucourt-en-Santerre. Santerre comes from the Latin for 'sanis terrain' or 'fertile land' or from 'sanguis terrain' which means 'bloody land'. I know which I think is more appropriate.

Nearby, in a dip in the road, is a memorial to Colonel Rabier of the French 33rd Brigade killed here in September 1914.

UK – 8

Location
Foucaucourt is on the road from Amiens to St. Quentin about 15km east of Amiens. The cemetery is about 300m west of the village. The British graves are near the right hand corner of the cemetery, though the March and August/September burials are separate.

FOUQUESCOURT OLD CHURCHYARD (COMMUNAL CEMETERY)
The village was captured by the 10th Canadian Infantry Brigade on 10 August 1918. The cemetery was then used for the burial of one man aged 19 years.
Can – 1
Location
Fouquescourt is situated about 35km east of Amiens and 8km due north of Roye. Fouquescourt Old Churchyard is in the centre of the village opposite the new church. It is now the Communal Cemetery. The single grave is at the rear of the cemetery, on the top of a rise, behind the town war memorial.

FRAMERVILLE COMMUNAL CEMETERY
The village was the scene of severe fighting in March 1918 and it was retaken by the 2nd Australian Division on 9 August 1918. The Communal Cemetery was used for one burial in October 1915 and four burials in August 1918.
UK – 4   Aust - 1
Location
Framerville is found a little south of the road from Amiens to St. Quentin. The cemetery is at the southern limit of the village on the west side of the road to Rosieres. The graves are in two plots, one group of three almost hidden by a large family mausoleum at the rear of this little cemetery.

FRANVILLERS COMMUNAL CEMETERY
The Communal Cemetery was used, at infrequent intervals, for the burial of four British soldiers, three from Australia and a Canadian between May 1916 and May 1918. The Australians and a British soldier date from the fighting in April 1918 while the others from various dates in 1916.
The Roman road was used to supply the font-line. Gough's 'Mobile Army' waited astride the road on 1 July 1916 waiting for the breakthrough that never came. The road was used in May 1940 by the 1st Panzer Division. It was also used as a guide by the Mosquito Squadrons that bombed Amiens prison in February 1944.

UK - 4   Aust - 3   Can - 1
Location
Franvillers lies on the north side of the Albert-Amiens road midway between the two towns. This is the old Roman road and hence, it is very straight except where a local aristocrat had it diverted around his new chateau. The Communal Cemetery and the Extension are south-east of the village about 200m from the main road. In the Communal Cemetery, Callaghan is near the entrance while the others are in the north-west corner close to the access to the Extension.

FRESNOY-LES-ROYE COMMUNAL CEMETERY
The Communal Cemetery was used for one burial on 16 August 1918. Private Ashton Moore, 43rd Canadian Infantry joined up in January 1918 from Manitoba. He was killed by shell-fire on 16 August 1918 aged 21 years as the Germans attacked and briefly took the village.
Can - 1
Location
Fresnoye-les-Roye is situated about 2km north of Roye and on the west side of the A1 autoroute. The cemetery is on the northern edge of the village on the road to Lihons. The single grave is isolated at the rear right corner of the cemetery. The cemetery has a pretty shaded entrance.

FRICOURT COMMUNAL CEMETERY
This cemetery was used in WW2. There are three airmen, the crew of a Blenheim airplane of No. 59 Squadron shot down by a Royal Air Force Spitfire on 22 May 1940. They are in the south-east corner. Also buried here is an IWGC worker who died in 1926. He is in the south-west corner.
WW2 – 3   Other – 1
Location
Fricourt is a village located about 5km east of Albert. The Communal Cemetery is on the southern edge of the village on the road to Bray.

FRISE COMMUNAL CEMETERY
The cemetery was used for the burial of Major George Edmund Borlase Watson, DSO, MC, Royal Horse Artillery, commanding 'O' Battery (The Rocket Troop), who died on 29 August 1918, aged 33 years. He was awarded his Distinguished Service Order in the Birthday Honours List in June 1917 and his Military Cross in the 1916 Birthday Honours List. His brother, Major Francis Shuldham Watson, DSO, MC, twice MiD, 276th Siege Battery, Royal Garrison Artillery, died of wounds on 2 May 1918, his 38th birthday, and is buried in Doullens Communal Cemetery Extension No. 2. Another brother, Captain Charles Reginald Watson, 28th Punjabis, Indian Army, was killed in action on 6 April 1918 aged 28 years and is commemorated on the Basra Memorial.
UK – 1
Location
Frise is a small village in the valley on the south side of the River Somme about 5km west of Peronne. The cemetery is on the south-west edge of the village on the south side of the road to Eclusier and Cappy that follows the edge of the River Somme. The grave is visible from the entrance to the left of the path.

GLISY COMMUNAL CEMETERY

The village was always behind the front-line but came close to the line at the limit of the German advance in the spring of 1918. Hence, the cemetery was only used in April and May 1918.

UK – 4   Aust – 3   Unnamed - 1

Special Memorials to one man known to be buried here whose grave location has been lost.

Location

Glisy is on the eastern edge of Amiens just north of the airfield. The cemetery is on the western edge of the village on a ridge overlooking the River Somme. The cemetery is 20m north of the road to Longueau. Access is by a track. The known graves and the Special Memorial are on the west side of the cemetery. The unidentified grave is alone on the eastern edge of the cemetery.

GONNELIEU COMMUNAL CEMETERY

The village was the scene of bitter fighting during the Battle of Cambrai. The Communal Cemetery was used for one burial on 1 December 1917. The graves of seven British soldiers have been lost during fighting in 1918. They are now represented by Special Memorials at Villers Hill British Cemetery.

UK – 1

Location

Gonnelieu is about 12km south-west of Cambrai. The cemetery is on the north edge of the village on the east side of the road to Villers-Plouich. The old boundary wall has been removed to make way for new burials. The British grave is at the south edge of the cemetery to the right of the entrance gates.

HAILLES COMMUNAL CEMETERY

The village was always behind the front-line but came close to the line at the limit of the German advance in the spring of 1918. Hence, the cemetery was only used in March 1918.

Buried here is Major Claud Frederick Thomas Lindsay, 33rd Battery, Royal Horse Artillery. He was Mentioned in Despatches and killed in action on 31 March 1918. He came from a line of military men.

UK - 1

Location

Hailles is on the south-eastern edge of Amiens 7km from the city centre. It is about 5km south-east of Villers-Bretonneux and on the southern side of the River L'Avre. The cemetery is south of the village on the road to Rouvrel and Castel where the road forks. This is a triangular cemetery. The British burial is in the centre near the cross.

HALLOY COMMUNAL CEMETERY

The Communal Cemetery was used for two burials of men killed in the retreat in May 1940. One is unidentified.

UK – 2 WW2   KUG - 1

Location

Halloy is 2km east of Doullens. The cemetery is on the west edge of the village on a road that leads directly opposite the church called Rue du Cimetiere. The graves are near the main path and visible from the gate.

HERLEVILLE CHURCHYARD

The men were buried in October 1915 when the British army began to take this area over from the French.

UK – 2

Location

Herleville is located about 2km south of the Amiens-St. Quentin road about midway between the two towns. It is 3km west of the A1 Autoroute. The church is on the west side of the village. There are steps at the west end of the church leading to the graves at the rear west corner.

HEUDICOURT COMMUNAL CEMETERY

The Communal Cemetery contains four graves of Allied serviceman including Private David Schalk Ulundi Ross, 2nd South African Infantry who died of wounds on 25 March 1918 aged 14 years and 3 months, the youngest casualty known to have been killed on the Western Front. He enlisted on 5 February 1917 claiming to be 18 years and 6 months of age. He was on his way to France in April and was involved in the Battle of the Menin Road at Ieper on 20 September 1917 where he received a gunshot wound to the leg. When recovered he returned to France and died as a Prisoner of War having been captured at Gauche Wood on 21 March 1918.

UK – 3   SAfr - 1

Location

Heudicourt is about 10km north-east of Peronne and 15km south-west of Cambrai. The Communal Cemetery is on the eastern edge of the village. The graves are in two places in the cemetery, three including Ross together by the boundary and one separate from the others.

HUMBERCAMPS COMMUNAL CEMETERY

The two men buried here were casualties in September 1915 during the period when the British moved to take over this area from the French. They both died of wounds.
UK - 2
Location
Humbercamps is situated 20km south-west of Arras. The Communal Cemetery is on the northern edge of the village, and in its north-western corner are the graves of two British soldiers.

IGNAUCOURT CHURCHYARD

This churchyard contains the grave of Lieutenant Colonel Henry Kelso Utterson, DSO, three times MiD, 2nd Dorsetshires attached 15th (1st Salford Pals) Lancashire Fusiliers, killed in action on 10 August 1918, aged 40 years. Son of a Major General, he had twice previously been wounded. The citation for his Distinguished Service Order, which was awarded in 1916, reads 'He led his men with marked coolness and skill when assaulting a strong redoubt. He behaved very gallantly in several engagements, during one of which he took command of his battalion when all the senior Officers had been killed or wounded, and led a successful charge resulting in the capture of the German's trenches.' He was in command of his battalion from 31 October 1917 to 13 April 1918 and 31 May to 10 August 1918.
UK - 1
Location
Ignaucourt is in the valley of the River Luce about 10km south-east of Amiens and 3km south-east of Villers-Bretonneux. The churchyard is behind the church in the centre of the village. The grave is near the gate on the south-west side of the churchyard.

LA HERLIERE COMMUNAL CEMETERY

There are a two British men buried here who were killed in May and June 1916. There is also a soldier killed in May 1940, a Private of the 5th Buffs, killed aged 34 years.
UK – 2   WW2 – 1
Location
La Herliere is just south of the Doullens–Arras road midway between the two towns. The cemetery is on the southern edge of the village on the east side of the road to Humbercamps.

LA MOTTE-BREBIERE COMMUNAL CEMETERY

The Communal Cemetery was used for nine burials between 25 May and 1 July 1918. This is one of several cemeteries in the area of Amiens which contain graves of men who died by accident or of illness rather than in battle, though some are shown as 'killed in action' on their records.
UK – 5   Aust - 4
Location
The village is on the eastern edge of Amiens just in the countryside beyond the city and is located on the north bank of the River Somme. The cemetery is on a ridge above, and north of, the village. The nine graves are located in several places in the cemetery.

LAVIEVILLE COMMUNAL CEMETERY

The cemetery was used for the burial of one British artilleryman in January 1917 and six Australians in April 1918. Among them is Lieutenant Arthur Barker, 22nd Australian Infantry, killed in action on 24 April 1918 when his patrol ran into a group of Germans in no man's land. He had served in Gallipoli being wounded by a grenade. Also here are Lance Corporal Tom Part and Sapper William Newbigging of 2nd Division Signal Company, Royal Engineers killed by the same shell nearby on ANZAC Day 1918 and buried side by side. Part was a Gallipoli veteran and one of four brothers to serve in the war.
A casualty of WW2, a Corporal in the Royal Horse Guards killed on 1 September 1944 when his armoured car was hit during the Guards Armoured Division advance, is also buried here.
UK – 1   Aust – 6   WW2 - 1
Location
Lavieville is a village just north of the Amiens-Albert road about 7km from Albert. The cemetery is 100m north of the village on the east side of the road to Henencourt. The graves are in four separate plots on the southern side of the cemetery.

LE HAMEL COMMUNAL CEMETERY

This is one of seven burial grounds north of the River Somme and behind the line for most of the war that contain a very few Allied military burials. This cemetery contains one British grave of a Royal Engineers driver killed on 1 August 1916.
UK – 1
Location
Le Hamel is situated about 17km east-north-east of Amiens. To get to the Communal Cemetery, take the road behind the church, Rue 11 Novembre 1918, and at the T-junction turn to the right. Head west and you will find the cemetery behind high walls. The graves are at the rear of the cemetery at the north end.

LE SARS COMMUNAL CEMETERY

The cemetery was used for the burial of one man killed during the British advance in September 1944.
WW2 UK - 1

Location
Le Sars is situated on the Albert-Bapaume road about 5km south-west of Bapaume almost at the limit of the British advance at the end of the Somme battles in 1916. The cemetery is on the north-east edge of the village on the south-east side of the main road.

LE VERGUIER CHURCHYARD
The churchyard contains the graves of two Australians and one British soldier killed in September 1918 during the recapture of Le Verguier.

UK – 1 Aust - 2

Location
Le Verguier is situated about 5km north-west of St. Quentin about 3km east of the A26 Autoroute. The church is in the centre of the village. The entrance to the churchyard is behind the town war memorial on the east side of the church. The CWGC graves are on the left of the entrance against the wall of the churchyard in the north-west corner.

LONGUEAU COMMUNAL CEMETERY
The cemetery was used for the burial of four British soldiers, three who died in 1918 and one in 1919. None were infantry.

UK – 4 Unnamed – 1

Location
Longueau is a suburb of Amiens to the south-east of the city centre. The cemetery is east of the village, on the south side of the road to Glisy. It is not easy to find. It is best approached on the road, Rue Paul Baroux, opposite the school Paul Baroux. The cemetery is on the left 150m from the school.

MANANCOURT COMMUNAL CEMETERY
The cemetery was used for the burial of one man killed during the British advance in September 1918. At the end of the war the commune of Manancourt contained over 1000 graves in German cemeteries. With them were a few British. Now there is one grave on the north-west side of the Communal Cemetery.

UK - 1

Location
Manancourt is about 10km north of Peronne and 10km south-east of Bapaume. It is found on the D34 1km south of Etricourt-Manancourt.

MARIEUX COMMUNAL CEMETERY
The cemetery was used for the burial of one man who died on 5 October 1939 aged 19 years.

WW2 UK - 1

Location
Marieux is 6km south-east of Doullens and 15km north-west of Albert. The cemetery is north of the village and 100m north of the Doullens-Albert road. It is accessed by a track from the Doullens-Albert road about 50m east of the Amiens to Pas-en-Artois road. The grave is found in the rear north-west corner of the cemetery.

MARTINPUICH COMMUNAL CEMETERY
The Cemetery was used for the burial of two men in late 1916 and further burials were made later. Two men known to be buried here are artillerymen. A soldier of the Royal Warwickshires is represented by a Special Memorial as is a man of the Royal Naval Division who was buried in Martinpuich German Cemetery but whose grave has been lost. There is also an unidentified British soldier.

In 1931 the graves of ten British soldiers who were buried by the Germans in the Communal Cemetery were rediscovered and concentrated in the British cemetery. A German Military Cemetery has been removed from the village.

UK – 5 Unnamed - 1

Special Memorials erected to a man of the Royal Naval Division who was buried in Martinpuich German Cemetery but whose grave has been lost and to a man believed to be buried here but whose grave has been lost.

Location
Martinpuich is situated 1km south of the Albert-Bapaume road about 10km from each town. The Communal Cemetery is on the southern edge of the village on the road to Longueval. The graves are on the southern side of the cemetery.

MESNIL ST. NICAISE CHURCHYARD
The cemetery was used for one burial, a British Private in the 16th Cheshires who died in March 1917.

UK – 1

Location
Mesnil St. Nicaise is a small village less than 1km north of Nesle. The churchyard is in the centre of the village. The burial can be found at the north-west corner of the churchyard 'behind' the church.

MOLLIENS-AU-BOIS COMMUNAL CEMETERY
The cemetery was used for the burial of six men, three of whom died in February and March 1917 and three in March to May 1918.

UK - 6

Location
Molliens-au-Bois is situated 14km north-north-east of Amiens and 2km east of the Amiens-Thievres road. The cemetery is on the southern edge of the village near a crossroads of the roads to Pierregot and Villers-Bocage but it is behind a hedge and easy to miss. The graves are in two groups of three, each group being the burials of 1917 and 1918 respectively.

MONS-EN-CHAUSSEE COMMUNAL CEMETERY
Five of the men buried here, including the Canadian, died in 1917. One man died in an accident in 1918. The other, Christopher Monckton, was attached to No. 13 Squadron, Royal Flying Corps and was killed on 1 July 1916 in combat over St. Quentin in the late afternoon. He was buried by the Germans.
WW2 UK – 6   Can - 1
Location
Mons-en-Chaussee is part of Estrees-Mons and is found on the Amiens-St. Quentin road some 6km south-east of Peronne and 12km from St. Quentin. The cemetery is at the west edge of Estrees-Mons 200m north of the main road on a side road opposite the church. The cemetery is on the east side of the road.

MORCHIES COMMUNAL CEMETERY
The cemetery was used by the Germans for the burial of British, Canadian and an unidentified Australian soldier who died in September and October 1916. They also used the cemetery for the burial of 662 Germans who have since been removed.
UK – 5   Aust – 1   Can – 2
Unnamed - 3
Location
Morchies is situated between Bapaume and Cambrai and is about 2km north of the road between the two towns. The Communal Cemetery is on the northern edge of the village, on the west side of the road to Lagnicourt, beyond the boundary of the village and the Military Cemetery. The CWGC graves are spread throughout the cemetery.

MORVAL COMMUNAL CEMETERY
This cemetery was used for the burial of a pilot and observer of a Blenheim Bristol 142M/L, Mk.1V of No. 15 Squadron, Royal Air Force shot down on 23 May 1940. The cause of loss has not been established but the plane crashed near this village with the loss of three crew. Pilot Officer Masters, aged 19 years and Flight Sergeant Tucker aged 24 years are here. The other crew member, Flight Sergeant Clifford W Thompson, aged 19 years is buried in London Cemetery near High Wood.
WW2 UK - 2
Location
Morval is situated about 10km south of Bapaume just west of the Autoroute. The Communal Cemetery is on the west side of the village 50m from the road. It is behind a grassy area in the centre of the village. The men are buried near the gate.

ORVILLE COMMUNAL CEMETERY
The cemetery was used for the burial of one soldier who died on 31 August 1944 in the advance from Normandy. He is Trooper Vincent Fletcher Gold of the Royal Armoured Corps and The Inns of Court Regiment. He had worked for the Union Assurance Company before the war.
WW2 - 1
Location
Orville is about 3km south-east of Doullens. The cemetery is on the northern edge of the village on a ridge overlooking the village on the road to Amplier. This is a large cemetery 200m from the church. You will find the CWGC grave on the eastern edge of the cemetery to the right of the entrance. You can just see it from the gate.

PAS-EN-ARTOIS COMMUNAL CEMETERY
The cemetery was used for the burial of one man who died in 1915 and again in 1944 for the burial of a soldier killed during the advance to Germany.
UK – 1   WW2 - 1
Location
Pas-en-Artois is 6km east of Doullens. The cemetery is in the northern part of the village at the junction of the roads to Mondicourt and Warlincourt. The cemetery is behind a hedge above the level of the road. The two CWGC graves are together.

PONT-NOYELLE COMMUNAL CEMETERY
The cemetery was used for the burial of three men of 1st Cavalry Brigade, two who died in July 1916 when Fourth Army HQ was in Querrieu, and one in March 1918. One drowned and one died of accidental injuries. The burials of 1916 are together on the south-west wall next to the memorial here to the battle of 1870. The 1918 burial is on the west side opposite the gate.
UK - 3
Location
Pont-Noyelle is next to Querrieu about 10km south-west of Albert and 7km north-east of Amiens. It is in the valley of the River Hallue. The cemetery is on the north side of the old main road, though there is now a bypass.

PUISIEUX COMMUNAL CEMETERY

The cemetery was used for the burial of three men killed in May 1940. Two are troopers from the Royal Armoured Corps. The third is Captain Philip Arthur Batty who was on the General List. He had served with Royal Field Artillery in France and Belgium during WW1. He went to Cambridge after WW1 and played rugby for the University and 'The Rest' against England.

WW2 - 3

Location

The village is situated about 5km west of Bapaume. The cemetery is on the south-eastern edge of the village on the south side of the road to Miraumont. It is on a ridge as you head out of the village next to the sports stadium. There is a large parking area. The graves are to the south-east of the entrance and can be seen from the entrance.

RAINCHEVAL COMMUNAL CEMETERY

The cemetery was used for the burial of one man who died in April 1918.

UK – 1

Location

Raincheval lies between Doullens and Albert about 10km south-east of Doullens. The cemetery is on a hill on the east side of the village with excellent views. It is at the end of a long dead-end road. The grave is in the north-west corner of the cemetery.

RIENCOURT-LES-CAGNICOURT COMMUNAL CEMETERY

The cemetery was used for the burial of Pilot Officer Frederick William Ratford, No. 253 Squadron, Royal Air Force, shot down in his Hurricane on patrol over Arras on 19 May 1940.

WW2 - 1

Location

Riencourt-les-Cagnicourt is a small village situated about 15km west of Cambrai and a similar distance south-east of Arras. The cemetery is on the northern edge of town on the north side of the road to Cagnicourt.

ROISEL COMMUNAL CEMETERY

The cemetery was used by British units and Field Ambulances from April 1917 to March 1918, by German medical units in March and April 1918, and by British units again in September and October 1918. At the end of the war, besides German graves, those of 94 British and 24 Australian soldiers were buried here with one man of the United States Army. All of the graves, except that of Coules, have been removed into the Extension.

This cemetery now contains the burial of 2nd Lieutenant Eric Allan Gifford Coules, 129th Field Company, Royal Engineers, who died on 28 October 1917, aged 19 years. He does not have a CWGC headstone but a private memorial. He passed out of Woolwich Royal Military Academy second on the list. He joined his unit, who spent much of their time improving the front line around Hargicourt, on 12 October 1917 and was killed by a sniper having been at the Front for just over two weeks. In 1921, the Imperial War Graves Commission wished to have his body moved to the Communal Cemetery Extension. His father refused this request on the grounds that, as his son had been buried without a coffin, he would not risk any part of his body being left behind. He therefore purchased three grave spaces, and erected the large stone we see today, to ensure all of the body was within the plot. His inscription reads "Never mind me, get on with the work".

UK - 1

Location

Roisel is a small village about 8km east of Peronne and 15km north-west of St. Quentin. The Communal Cemetery is on the north-west of town on the east side of the road to Villers-Faucon and Nurlu. The grave is on the right of the first entrance into the cemetery approaching from the town centre.

ROUVREL COMMUNAL CEMETERY

The cemetery was only used for the burial of Lieutenant Colonel The Honourable Ralph Gerard Alexander Hamilton, three times MiD, Croix de Guerre (France), 'C' Battery, 108th Brigade, Royal Field Artillery, killed in action by a shell on Easter Monday 31 March 1918 at Castel near Amiens defending the ridge where the German advance was finally halted. Before the war he had been a Lieutenant in the 3rd King's Own Hussars and Major commanding the Essex Royal Horse Artillery as well as an Honorary Attaché in the Diplomatic Service. He served with the 7th Division in Flanders in 1914 and in August 1915 he took out his Battery to France. He fought in the First, Second and Third Battles of Ypres, the Battle of Loos, the Somme Offensive and the Battle of Messines. The location of his death is believed to have been in the woods 2km west of Moreuil. He was wounded twice. He was Master of Belhaven from 1893, only son of the 10th Lord Belhaven & Stenton.

UK – 1

Location

Rouvrel is about 20km south-east of Amiens. The cemetery is located just north of the D920 between Ailly-sur-Noye and Moreuil on the road to Dommartin. The burial is at the rear of the cemetery.

ROUY-LE-GRAND CHURCHYARD

The churchyard contains one burial. We do not know who it is or when the burial was made.

UK – 1   Unnamed - 1

Location
Rouy-le-Grand and Rouy-le-Petit are two small villages (le-Grand is now the smaller village) on the canal that joins the River Somme and River l'Oise at Sempigny. They are 4km north-east of Nesle and lie either side of the canal with le-Grand on the north side of the canal. The ruined churchyard, no longer with a church, is in the centre of the village on Rue de Cimetiere. There is a single burial here, an unidentified British officer of the Rifle Brigade, in the north-west corner.

ROUY-LE-PETIT CHURCHYARD
The churchyard contains two burials made in March 1918. They are close together.
UK – 2
Location
See Rouy-le-Grand Churchyard.
The churchyard is in the centre of the village at a bend in the main road through the village and close to the canal. The two graves are to the left of the church from the entrance against the north-eastern wall of the church.

RUBEMPRE COMMUNAL CEMETERY
The cemetery was used for the burial of two soldiers from separate battalions of the Highland Light Infantry killed on 5 January 1917 and one soldier from the Yorkshire Hussars Yeomanry killed on 11 March 1916. One of these is Private James Henry Kean, 16th (2nd Glasgow Pals) Highland Light Infantry who was murdered by Private Alexander Reid during a fight in their barracks.
UK – 3

Location
Rubempre is about 10km north of Amiens and 15km south of Doullens. It is about 4km east of the N25 between Amiens and Doullens. The cemetery is at the eastern edge of the village on the north side of the road to Herissart. The three graves are together near the road on the south side of the cemetery to the right of the main path.

SAINS-LES-MARQUION CHURCHYARD
This cemetery contains the grave of Pilot Officer Iain Colin Moorwood, No. 111 Squadron, Royal Air Force, killed in action on 19 May 1940 aged 21 years. He was one of two pilots of this Squadron shot down in Hurricanes over France on this day.
WW2 - 1
Location
Sains-les-Marquion is 8km west of Cambrai. It is at the eastern edge of the area covered by this book. The village is 1km south of the Arras-Cambrai road. The churchyard is in the centre of the village.

ST. FUSCIEN COMMUNAL CEMETERY
This is one of seven burial grounds north of the River Somme and behind the line for most of the war that contain a very few Allied military burials. This cemetery contains three British burials, two dating from 21 April and one from 29 April 1918.
UK - 3
Location
St. Fuscien is situated about 4km south of Amiens. The cemetery is west of the village on the village side of the D7 at a large roundabout. There is good parking. The three graves are in the middle of the cemetery.

SAUVILLERS-MONGIVAL COMMUNAL CEMETERY
This cemetery was used once, for the burial of five British WW2 airmen. They are a sailor, who was attached to this aircrew, and four airmen, members of a Lancaster crew of No. 106 Squadron, RAF, shot down on 15 April 1943. The Lancaster ED752 ZN*H was returning to Syerston from a raid on Stuttgart when it came down, cause unknown, at Sauvillers-Mongival. The Pilot was Squadron Leader Jerrard Latimer, DFC. The other crew members who were killed and buried here are Sergeant G W Hancock, Lieutenant G. Muttrie, RNVR, Sergeant H Buxton and Sergeant W T McLean. Due to a shortage of trained navigators naval personnel were attached in this role and this aircraft carried Lieutenant G Muttrie, attached from HMS Daedalus. Also in the aircraft, and taken prisoner, were Sergeant H Jones, Flight Lieutenant L C J Brodrick, Pilot Officer J A Burns RCAF. Flight Lieutenant L C J Brodrick was the 52nd escapee in the 'Great Escape' from Sagan, though he was recaptured and survived the war.
WW2 - 5
Location
Sauvillers-Mongival is towards the south of the area covered by this book. It is about 20km south-east of Amiens and a similar distance west of Roye. The cemetery is north of the village on the road to Moreuil and Mailly-Raineval. The British graves are together at the southern edge of the cemetery.

SAVY COMMUNAL CEMETERY

The cemetery was used for the burial of two men of 'A' Battery, 161st Brigade, Royal Field Artillery killed on 2 April 1917 and one man of 182nd Company, Machine Gun Corps killed on 24 April 1917.

UK – 3

Location

Savy is a village situated about 5km west of St. Quentin and 1km south of the A29 Autoroute. The Communal Cemetery is on the north side of the village on the west side of the road to Holnon. The British graves are at the rear in the right hand corner from the main entrance.

SOUASTRE CHURCHYARD

This cemetery was used for the burial of one artilleryman who died on 27 March 1918.

UK - 1

Location

Souastre is about 10km east of Doullens and 2km east of Pas-en-Artois. It is south of the Doullens-Arras road. The church is on the south side of the road to Bienvillers towards the east end of the village. The grave is at the rear of the south side of the church.

TALMAS COMMUNAL CEMETERY

The Communal Cemetery was used for two burials, one in February and the other in September 1916. It was used again on 31 May 1940 for the burial of two unidentified soldiers of the Queens Own Royal West Kents.

UK – 2   WW2 - 2

Location

Talmas is about 8km north of Amiens just east of the main road to Doullens. The cemetery is on the northern edge of the village on Rue de Cimetiere. The burials are in the south-east corner of the cemetery.

TERRAMESNIL COMMUNAL CEMETERY

The Communal Cemetery was used for the burial of a gunner of the 4th Division Ammunition Column who was buried here in July 1915 soon after the British took over the area from the French. A further two burials were made in WW2. They are two members of a Lancaster crew from No. 617 Squadron – the Dambusters. The men were killed when their aircraft crashed after dropping supplies to SOE members. Four other members of the crew were taken prisoner while a fifth evaded capture.

The village of Beauquesne just south of Terramesnil had two WW1 burials in their Communal Cemetery. They were moved to Gezaincourt Cemetery Extension in 1935.

UK – 1   WW2 - 2

Location

Terramesnil is 4km south of Doullens on the D23 from Doullens to Puchevillers and Franvillers. The cemetery is at the south-east edge of the village. The Rue de Cimetiere leads east from the D23 about 400m south of the village centre. The three CWGC graves are together in a plot in the north-west corner of the cemetery by the entrance.

TINCOURT CHURCHYARD

The burials here date from September 1918, all men of the Royal Garrison Artillery, two of the 137th Heavy Battery buried on 14 September and another gunner from the 283rd Siege Battery buried on 11 September.

UK - 3

Location

Tincourt-Boucly is situated in the valley of the River Cologne about 6km east of Peronne. The churchyard is to the south of the road to Buire-Courselles. It is easily reached by the road opposite the road to Tincourt New British Cemetery from the middle of the village. It lies between the D199 and the river. The graves of two of the soldiers are to the rear of the church in the south-west corner. The third grave is to the left of the entrance in the south-east corner opposite.

TRESCAULT COMMUNAL CEMETERY

The cemetery was used by the Germans for the burial of seven British men who died as prisoners from January to April 1917. They were buried among 37 German dead who have been removed.

UK - 7

Location

Trescault is located 22km east of Bapaume and 10km south-west of Cambrai. It is about 2km south-east of the A2 Autoroute. The cemetery is located by taking a small road to the left of the village war memorial, opposite the Mairie. It is found on the eastern outskirts of the village north of the road to Ribecourt. It is behind trees and can be easily missed. Six graves are on the left hand side towards the centre of the cemetery, and one is in the rear right hand corner, down the slope in the north-east corner of the cemetery.

UGNY-L'EQUIPEE CHURCHYARD

The cemetery was used for the burial of two men of the 2/4th Royal Berkshires killed on 21 March 1918, the first day of the German offensive.

UK - 2

Location

The village is located about 10km west of St. Quentin and about 2km south of the A29 Autoroute. The churchyard is in the centre of the village and can be seen from some distance. The two CWGC graves are against the west end of the church and they can be seen from the gate directly in front of you. It is interesting that there is no CWGC sign at the gate as it is located above the graves on the wall.

VAIRE-SOUS-CORBIE COMMUNAL CEMETERY
The Communal Cemetery was used for the burial of four Australian artillerymen of 10th Brigade, Australian Field Artillery killed on 8 August 1918.
Aust – 4
Location
Vaire-sous-Corbie is on the south side of the valley of the River Somme about 20km east of Amiens and 3km north-east of Corbie. The cemetery is on the southern edge of the small village on the east side of the road to Corbie. It can be seen from the centre of the village. The graves are in an isolated position against the south wall.

VENDELLES CHURCHYARD (COMMUNAL CEMETERY)
This used to be a churchyard but the church and burial ground was mostly destroyed in the war. It is now a Communal Cemetery though there is a chapel in the village. The churchyard was used for the burial of five Allied soldiers killed from 31 March to 12 April 1917. Four of them are Sherwood Foresters. The other burial, an Australian Pioneer, was made in September 1918.
UK – 5   Aust - 1
Location
Vendelles is about 10km north-west of St. Quentin and 2km north of the Amiens-St. Quentin Road. It lies on the west side of the village near the road to Vermand. The graves are in several plots to the rear of the burial ground.

VILLERS-CARBONNEL COMMUNAL CEMETERY
The cemetery was used for the burial of three men of the Chinese Labour Corps who died in late 1918 and 1919, probably of the influenza epidemic.
CLC - 3
Location
The village lies on the Amiens-St. Quentin road about 5km south of Peronne 1km west of the valley of the Somme and 15km west of St. Quentin. The cemetery is next to the French National Cemetery on its eastern edge 100m west of the roundabout that is the junction of the road with the D1017. The three CWGC graves are at the rear left corner from the entrance.

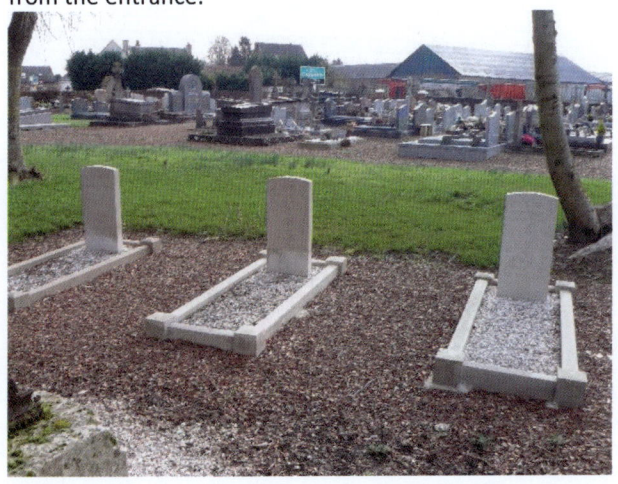

VILLERS-LES-CAGNICOURT COMMUNAL CEMETERY
The cemetery was used for the burial of two men killed on 24 May 1940. They are both in their 30's, one a Private from the Wiltshires and one a WO2 from the Royal Armoured Corps 2nd Armoured Reconnaissance Brigade.
WW2 - 2
Location
Villers-les-Cagnicourt is at the north-east corner of the area covered by this book. It is, as the name suggests, close to, and north of, the village of Cagnicourt. It is almost midway between Arras and Cambrai and 2km south-east of Vis-en-Artois. The cemetery is north of the village on the west side of the Cagnicourt-Saudemont road and 50m south of the Arras-Cambrai road.

VOYENNES COMMUNAL CEMETERY
The CWGC burial here is 2nd Lieutenant Robert Leslie Fairclough, 218th Company, Royal Engineers who died on 5 May 1917 aged 27 years.
UK - 1
Location
Voyennes is in the valley of the River Somme about 15km south-west of St. Quentin and a similar distance south of Peronne. The cemetery is in northern edge of the village on the Rue du Cimetiere that runs from next to the church in the middle of the village. The British grave is in the first plot to the left of the entrance among the civilian graves.

VRAIGNES COMMUNAL CEMETERY
This area came under Allied control when the Germans withdrew in early 1917. It fell to the Germans again in March 1918 and was retaken in the summer of 1918. Most of the men buried here are artillerymen and most fell during the fighting in late 1918.
UK – 6   Aust – 1   Unnamed - 1
Location
Vraignes-en-Vermandois is situated on the main road from Amiens to St. Quentin. It is about 10km north-east of St. Quentin and a similar distance south-east of Peronne. The cemetery is on the northern edge of the village on the west side of the road to Haucourt. The British graves are together at the rear to the right of the main path.

WAILLY COMMUNAL CEMETERY
Buried here are two men of the 7th Royal Tank Regiment, Royal Armoured Corps killed in action on 21 May 1940. With them is an unidentified officer killed in May 1940. These soldiers died during the Battle of Arras.
WW2 - 2
Location
Wailly is about 3km south-west of Arras and 1km south of the road between Arras and Doullens. It is almost a suburb of Arras. The cemetery is north-west of the village on a ridge above the River Crinchon. It is on the north-east side of the road to Berneville about 400m from the centre of Wailly. The graves are in the north-west corner of the cemetery.

WANCOURT COMMUNAL CEMETERY

The cemetery was used for the burial of six men in May 1940. Only three are identified. One is a pilot shot down in his Hurricane over Arras by German Me109 fighters. The others were shot by a German machine-gun when leaving a café in Wancourt in May 1940.

WW2 – 6 (Unnamed – 3)

Location

Wancourt lies in the valley of the River Cojeul south of the Arras-Cambrai road and about 7km south-east of the centre of Arras. This cemetery is on the western edge of the village on the east bank of the Autoroute. It is 50m south of the road to Thilloy. The burials are next to the entrance on the east side of the cemetery.

SOMME AMERICAN CEMETERY, BONY

HISTORY

The cemetery was established as a temporary burial site by the American War Graves Registration Service during the war. It was redesigned in the 1930's, including the building of a Memorial Chapel, so that the cemetery was formally opened on 30 May 1937.

INFORMATION

This cemetery is not strictly within the defined parameters of this book being just east of the A26 Autoroute between Cambrai and St. Quentin. However, it is an excellent contrast to the cemeteries covered in the book, is one of the few American cemeteries on the WW1 battlefields, and refers to itself as a cemetery of the Somme. It certainly contains Americans who fell during fighting on the Somme and has a justifiable place in this book.

In 1918 it was called by the American Expeditionary Forces Somme Cemetery No. 636. After the end of the war the next of kin of American Servicemen were asked if they wished their relative to be returned to the United States for burial. If the authorities received no reply, or a negative reply, then the bodies from this area were brought here for burial. It contains 1830 graves, mainly of the American 1st, 27th, 30th, 33rd and 80th Divisions, and is particularly connected with the advance of the 27th and 30th Divisions, with the 3rd and 5th Australian Divisions, at the end of September 1918.

The chapel is situated at the south-east corner. There is a large bronze double door on which are 48 stars, each representing one of the States in 1937. Over 300 names of those missing in action who have no known grave are engraved on the walls of the chapel. An inscription reads 'The Names Recorded On These Walls Are Those Of American Soldiers Who Fought In This Region Who Sleep In Unknown Graves'.

There are three recipients of the Medal of Honor, the highest military award by the United States for an act of valour. Robert Lester Blackwell, born 4 October 1895, was from North Carolina and his father was a Confederate army veteran. He was one of two soldiers from North Carolina to be awarded the Medal of Honor for service in the First World War. He served with Company 'K', 119th Infantry, 30th Division and was killed in action on 11 October 1918. The citation for his medal reads 'When his platoon was almost surrounded by the enemy and his platoon commander asked for volunteers to carry a message calling for reinforcements, Pvt. Blackwell volunteered for this mission, well knowing the extreme danger connected with it. In attempting to get through the heavy shell and machinegun fire this gallant soldier was killed.' A statue to honor his heroism stands today in Roxboro, North Carolina. Thomas E. O'Shea, born 18 April 1895, and from New York City, was a Corporal in Machine Gun Company, 107th Infantry, 27th Division. He was killed while trying to rescue others near Le Catelet on 29 September 1918. His citation reads 'Becoming separated from their platoon by a smoke barrage, Cpl. O'Shea, with 2 other soldiers, took cover in a shell hole well within the enemy's lines. Upon hearing a call for help from an American tank, which had become disabled 30 yards from them, the 3 soldiers left their shelter and started toward the tank under heavy fire from German machineguns and trench mortars. In crossing the fire-swept area Cpl. O'Shea was mortally wounded and died of his wounds shortly afterwards.'

William Bradford Turner, born 1892, and from Boston, Massachusetts was a First Lieutenant with the 105th Infantry Regiment, 27th Division when he won his medal near Ronssoy. His citation reads 'He led a small group of men to the attack, under terrific artillery and machinegun fire, after they had become separated from the rest of the company in the darkness. Single-handed he rushed an enemy machinegun which had suddenly opened fire on his group and killed the crew with his pistol. He then pressed forward to another machinegun post 25 yards away and had killed 1 gunner himself by the time the remainder of his detachment arrived and put the gun out of action. With the utmost bravery he continued to lead his men over 3 lines of hostile trenches, cleaning up each one as they advanced, regardless of the fact that he had been wounded 3 times, and killed several of the enemy in hand-to-hand encounters. After his pistol ammunition was exhausted, this gallant officer seized the rifle of a dead soldier, bayoneted several members of a machinegun crew, and shot the other. Upon reaching the fourth-line trench, which was his objective, 1st Lt. Turner captured it with the 9 men remaining in his group and resisted a hostile counterattack until he was finally surrounded and killed.'

Among those buried here is Nurse Helen Fairchild, a volunteer who served with the US Army Reserve in France and Belgium from June 1917. In late July 1917 she moved to No. 4 Casualty Clearing Station at Dozinghem near Ieper in Belgium. It was one of the field hospitals dealing with the wounded from the Third Battle of Ypres. Following an aerial bombing on 17 August the CCS was evacuated. A few weeks later Helen fell ill with tonsillitis. She died a few weeks after this on 1 January 1918 from complications considered to be as a result of exposure to Mustard Gas from the bombing attack in August.

The cemetery contains three CWGC graves - two Royal Air Force Officers and one New Zealand soldier who died in June-August 1918. However, they are all Americans. The other British graves formerly here have been removed to Unicorn Cemetery, Vendhuile.

One of the RAF Officers is Lieutenant James Grantley Hall, No. 60 Squadron, Royal Air Force, killed in action in combat over Foucaucourt-Wancourt area on 8 August 1918, the first day of the Battle of Amiens, aged 22 years. He was from Los Angeles, California. After America's entry into the war, Hall abandoned his studies at Burdett Business College to enlist but was too short. Spurred by that rejection, in July 1917 Hall joined the Royal Flying Corps at Boston and trained in Canada and Texas. He was commissioned as a 2nd Lieutenant in November 1917 and went to England in December. Hall was first posted, in March 1918, to No. 92 Squadron before joining the SE5-equipped No. 60 Squadron. He arrived on the Western Front on 11 June just two months before his death.

The other officer is Lieutenant Theodore Rickey Hostetter, No. 3 Squadron, Royal Air Force, killed in action when his Sopwith Camel was shot down at about 8.30am near Masnieres on 27 September 1918, the first day of the Battle of the Canal du Nord. He was a member of a wealthy family from Long Island, New York who had made their money first in patent medicines and later in oil and gas. Hostetter's will left $2,261,056.00, half of which went to his sister. He had died on her birthday, and she was to die a month later.

The 'New Zealander' is Rifleman Samuell Douthitt Hill, 4th Battalion, 3rd New Zealand Rifle Brigade, killed in action on 30 June 1918 aged 26 years. He was from New Castle, Kentucky, and had been acting as American Consular Officer in Auckland, New Zealand when he joined up in 1917. He was promoted to Lance Corporal on 17 August 1917 and Corporal on 9 October 1917 before departure from New Zealand on 13 October. He went to France on 14 April 1918. In April and May the Rifle Brigade was twice in the line, participating in raids but no major engagements. Lorries arrived with a shipment of greatcoats on 30 May 1918 and Hill was accidentally killed when run over by one of the trucks.

US – 1830 UK – 2 NZ - 1

LOCATION

Bony lies midway between Cambrai and St. Quentin about 15km from each town and about 2km east of the A26 Autoroute. The cemetery is on the north side of the road between Bony and Hargicourt about 400m east of the boundary of the Somme and the Aisne Departments just into the Aisne.

FRENCH NATIONAL CEMETERIES

ALBERT FRENCH NATIONAL CEMETERY

HISTORY
This is a concentration cemetery made entirely after the war by collecting remains from isolated graves and military cemeteries on the battlefield of the Somme. The main dates of activity were 1923, 1928 and 1935.

INFORMATION
There are over 6000 French soldiers buried or commemorated in the cemetery. There is also the grave of a Chinese Labour Corps man, Wing Yuk Shan who died on 5 December 1918.
French – 6290 (3409 in individual graves and 2881 in ossuaries)
CLC – 1   Area – 18318 sq mts

LOCATION
Albert French National Cemetery is on the south-east side of the town on the north side of the D938. It is about 350m east of Albert Communal Cemetery. At the back are four walled beds, mass graves containing around 3000 men, and there is a list of names on a series of tablets. The single Commonwealth grave, marked by a standard CWGC headstone, is located in the rear right quarter of the cemetery.

BEUVRAIGNES FRENCH NATIONAL CEMETERY

HISTORY
The cemetery was opened in 1914 and used throughout the war. However, much of it is a concentration cemetery made after the war mainly in 1921, 1929 and 1936.

INFORMATION
Roye with Beuvraignes fell to the Germans on 30 August 1914. It remained in their hands until the French captured the town on 17 March 1917. It fell again to the Germans on 28 March 1918 before the French took it for the final time on 27 August 1918.
Of those buried here, 1203 were buried in graves during WW1, three date from WW2 and 654 are buried in four ossuaries. It is probable that a nearby abbey was used as a field hospital and those buried here came from it.
French – 1857 (1203 in individual graves, 654 in four ossuaries, 3 burials from WW2)
Area – 6050 sq mts

LOCATION
Roye is at the southern edge of the area covered by this book. It is about 25km south-east of Amiens and a similar distance south-west of St. Quentin. Beuvraignes is about 3km south of Roye. The cemetery is on the north-eastern edge of the village on the south side of the road to Amy.

BIACHES FRENCH MILITARY CEMETERY

HISTORY
This is one of the smaller French National Cemeteries. It was created in 1920 to bury the dead from small local burial grounds who died during the Battle of the Somme. It was extended mainly in 1936.

INFORMATION
Biaches was captured by the Germans on 28 August 1914. It fell to the French 72nd Infantry Division, with the Légion Etrangère (Foreign Legion), and the 1st Colonial Corps as auxiliaries on 10 July 1916. This was after an intense struggle at the Herbecourt Redoubt which was taken by a Captain and eight men who captured 114 Germans. The Germans re-captured the village on 17 July but the French re-occupied it on 19 July though this marked the limit of the French advance in 1916. Once within sight of Peronne however the French had to hold back, conscious that their left flank was exposed given the lack of progress by the British. The French stayed until January 1917.

During the German withdrawal to the Hindenburg Line the British 40th and 48th Divisions entered Peronne which had been set on fire by the Germans. In the German advance of 1918 on 23 March the Germans recaptured the town when the remnants of the 66th Division retreated through the town. On 30 August to 1 September 1918, the 2nd Australian Division took Mont-St. Quentin, north of Peronne, commemorated by the 2nd Australian Division Memorial, and on 1 September they entered Peronne.
The nearby hamlet of la Maisonette was the scene of bitter fighting in October 1916. French troops captured the village early in the month but the Germans retook it later because it had good observation of the battlefield. South of the village is a memorial to the 56th Battalion of Chausseurs a Pied who were in action here in July 1916. The unit was led by Lieutenant Colonel Emile Driant who had previously led the 56th and 58th regiments in a stand against the German advance at Verdun in February 1916.

Driant and most of his men were killed but halted the Germans for a period.

On the Biaches-Flaucourt road is a memorial to the 'Colonials' who died here in 1916. Nearby is the grave of Sous-Lieutenant Marcel Brocheriou of the 22nd Colonial Infantry who was killed in August 1916. Just outside Flaucourt on the road to Bray was a large German cemetery which has now been removed. It is still possible to identify the brick memorial, the only relic of the cemetery that was in the German reserve lines.

Fr – 1361 (1040 in individual graves, 322 in two ossuaries)
Area – 5900 sq mts

LOCATION
Biaches in on the western bank of the River Somme opposite Peronne. It is now little more than a suburb of Peronne. The cemetery is on the Peronne-Bray road about 2km west of Biaches. It is on the south side of the road on a ridge above the River Somme.

BRAY-SUR-SOMME FRENCH NATIONAL CEMETERY

HISTORY
The cemetery was created in 1923 and extended in 1935 by the concentration of several smaller French military Cemeteries between Bray and Suzanne.

INFORMATION
Bray fell to the Germans in March 1918 but it was recaptured by the 40th Australian Infantry on 24 August.

In addition to the French graves Corporal Albert Edward King of the 155th Heavy Battery, Royal Garrison Artillery, who was killed on 14 October 1916 is buried here in grave number 582.

Fr – 1045 (943 in individual graves, 102 in an ossuary)
UK – 1   Area - 4306 sq mts

LOCATION
Bray-sur-Somme lies on the north bank of the River Somme about 8km south-east of Albert and 30km east of the centre of Amiens. The French National Cemetery lies on the south side of the Communal Cemetery which can be found north of the village on the east side of the road to Albert.

CERISY-GAILLY FRENCH NATIONAL CEMETERY

HISTORY
The cemetery was created next to the village Communal Cemetery by a French Tenth Army Casualty Clearing Hospital in February 1916. Most of the casualties buried here died during the Battles of the Somme in 1916.

INFORMATION
The cemetery was redesigned in 1923. 158 French and 35 German graves were removed from the British section after the war.

Fr – 990   UK – 342   Canada – 4
Australia – 44   NZ – 1   RGLI – 1
Unnamed – 296   Area - 5122 sq mts

LOCATION
Cerisy is found in the valley of the River Somme about 10km south of Albert. The cemetery is near the British Military Cemetery. It lies on the west side of the village at the end of Rue du Cimetiere which leads to the Communal Cemetery. It is about 150m north of the road to Hamel and next to the Communal Cemetery on its south side. A British Cemetery is at the western end of the French National Cemetery.

CLERY-SUR-SOMME FRENCH NATIONAL CEMETERY

HISTORY
This cemetery was built in 1920 as a concentration cemetery and extended in 1936.

INFORMATION
The cemetery is also called 'Le Bois Des Ouvrages' which was a thin strip of woodland that lay mid-way between the Bois de Hem and the Bois Croisette. Known as Earthworks Copse to the British, it was in the field between the present Clery French cemetery and the A1 Autoroute, marked only by a little ridge and depression in the field today.

The burials came from Monacu's Farm, Mill Fargny and Berlingots Woods. The military sections of the civil cemeteries at Morlancourt and Vaires-sous-Corbie were also cleared into here at that time. Seven British soldiers and one Canadian were buried here and have since been moved to Hem Farm Military Cemetery.

There is a memorial at the entrance to the French 363rd Regiment of Infantry and 'those Victorious Combatants of 7 August 1916 and 2 September 1916'.

Fr – 2332 (1203 in individual graves, 1129 in two ossuaries)
Area - 9575 sq mts

LOCATION
Clery-sur-somme is 3km north-west of Peronne in the valley of the River Somme. The cemetery is located west of the village on the road to Albert next to the A1 Autoroute and the railway. It is just west of the roundabout junction for the Autoroute, 100m north of the Albert to Peronne road and reached by a track.

COTE 80 FRENCH NATIONAL CEMETERY

HISTORY
In June-October 1916 two French Field Ambulances made this cemetery and another nearby at Cote (Point) 77. In 1923 the French authorities moved the French graves from Cote 77 into Cote 80.

INFORMATION
The village of Etinehem was in Allied hands for most of the war until the German advance of March 1918. It was retaken by the 50th Australian Infantry on 10 August 1918. Cote 80 French National Cemetery, called originally Cote 80 French Military Cemetery, was named from a road crossing nearby. It was known to the French as Etinehem Cimetiere Militaire. In 1916, the famous French author, Georges Duhamel, worked here as a surgeon.

In the middle of the cemetery at Cote 80, the French buried twelve British soldiers, mostly artillerymen, and in August 1918, Australian troops added burials to the existing Commonwealth ones so that most of the CWGC graves are of Australian men.

Among those buried here is Driver James Spencer, 65th Battery, 8th Brigade, Royal Field Artillery, executed for desertion on 29 September 1915. He deserted on 12 June and was arrested on 4 August. His trial was held on 9 September 1915.

Also buried here is Private Sidney Francis Hatch, 35th Australian Infantry, killed in action on 22 August 1918, aged 21 years. He enlisted in June 1917. In April 1918 he was severely gassed and after a few months in hospital returned to the front. He was acting as a stretcher-bearer when he was killed.

Fr – 1004   UK – 19   Canada – 1
Australia – 29   Unnamed – 5
Area – 4240 sq mts

LOCATION
Etinehem is about 7km south of Albert. It is near the River Somme in a large meander about 2km west of Bray-sur-Somme. The cemetery is in open fields on a ridge north of the village above the valley of the River Somme. It is about 100m east of the narrow road from Etinehem to Albert via Meaulte that runs past the west end of the airfield. It can be seen from the D1.

DOMPIERRE-BECQUINCOURT FRENCH NATIONAL CEMETERY

HISTORY
The cemetery was created in 1920 as a concentration cemetery. Further development was undertaken in 1935 and 1936 as bodies exhumed from communal cemeteries of the Somme were concentrated here. From 1948-1985 it was used for the burial of French bodies found on the battlefields.

INFORMATION
It lies on or near the trenches which became established here in late 1914 as the Germans had been halted by the French. The French attacked from here on 1 July 1916, pushed the Germans back and held the area until handing over to the British. The British XIX Corps were pushed out by the Germans in March 1918. It was captured for the final time in August 1918.

Of those buried here 75% of the graves are of men who fell in the 1916 battles nearby. The remainder date from the period when the line here remained static in 1914-15.

An Italian Memorial in north-west corner of cemetery was made by Italian stonemasons who came to this part of France to help with reconstruction.

Fr - 7034 (5363 in individual graves, 1671 in four ossuaries, 1 WW2 burial)
Ger – 1   Area – 20975 sq mts

LOCATION
Dompierre-Becquincourt is about 5km west of Peronne on the west side of the valley of the River Somme. The cemetery is on the south-west edge of the village on the south side of the road to Chuignies and Chuignolles. It is next to the Communal Cemetery.

HATTENCOURT FRENCH NATIONAL CEMETERY

HISTORY
The cemetery was created in 1920 as a concentration cemetery. From 1934 to 1936, and again in 1951, it was used for the concentration of military graves from local communal cemeteries. From 1960-61 it was used for the burial of bodies found on the battlefields.

INFORMATION
Hattencourt was near the front-line for much of the war, but most of the burials are men who fell in 1917 and 1918.

Fr – 1949 (1282 in individual graves and 667 in four ossuaries, also 5 burials from WW2)
Russian – 2   Area – 6160 sq mts

LOCATION
Hattencourt is to the south of the area covered in this book. It is about 5km north of Roye, roughly midway between Amiens and St. Quentin but about 7km south of the road between them. The cemetery is about 1km south of the centre of Hattencourt on the road to Fresnoy-les-Roye. It is on the east side of the road about 400m west of the A1 Autoroute.

LIHONS FRENCH NATIONAL CEMETERY

HISTORY
The cemetery was begun in 1915 and used after the war as a concentration cemetery with the main dates of redevelopment as 1919, 1935 and 1936.

INFORMATION
The cemetery lies just west of the old front line established here in August 1914 and some of the graves date from that time. It was originally known as the as the 'Cimetiere des Pommiers'.

A communal grave on the right of the entrance contains the remains of American poet Alan Seeger. He was from New York, educated at Harvard, and living in Paris when the war began. He joined the French Foreign Legion with forty other Americans and served on the Western Front until killed on 4 July 1916 reputedly cheering on his fellow soldiers in a successful charge after he had been hit several times by machine gun fire. He was buried in a communal battlefield grave and thought lost. Recent research discovered his body is in mass grave Ossuaire No. 1 at this cemetery. He is most well known for having authored the poem, 'I Have a Rendezvous with Death'.

The cemetery contains the graves of five British soldiers and one from Canada who died in March and August 1918. Two of the British graves are unnamed.

North of the village is the grave of, and memorial to, Marechal de Logis Louis Murat of the French 5th Regiment of Chasseurs, killed in action on 21 August 1916. He was the son of Prince Murat of Pontecorvo and grand-nephew of Napoleon. His grandfather was Marshal Joachim Murat, Napoleon's brother-in-law and a cavalry commander in Napoleon's later campaigns, notably leading the breakthrough at the Battle of Jena.

Fr – 6587 (4949 in individual graves, 1638 in four ossuaries)
UK – 5 including 2 Unnamed   Can - 1
Area – 25857 sq mts

LOCATION
Lihons is midway between St. Quentin and Amiens. It is about 3km south of the A29 Autoroute and 10km south-west of Peronne. The cemetery is on the Harbonnieres to Chaulnes roads about 1km west of the village of Lihons. It lies on the north side of the road. The cemetery is long and next to a wood.

MARCELCAVE 'LES BUTTES' FRENCH NATIONAL CEMETERY

HISTORY
The cemetery was begun in 1916 during the Battles of the Somme. It was used after the war, particularly in 1922 and 1936, for the concentration of graves from across the Somme.

INFORMATION
Most of the burials here came from a nearby Field Hospital, Evacuation Hospital No. 13, which was situated next to the railway line that used to be near the village. This cemetery contained one British burial which has been moved to Cayeux Military Cemetery.

Fr – 1610   Area – 11746 sq mts

LOCATION
Marcelcave is about 15km east of Amiens. It is 1km south of the A29 Autoroute and 2km south of the road from Amiens to St. Quentin. The cemetery is north-west of the village on the north side of the A29 and can be found about midway between Marcelcave and Villers-Bretonneux.

MAUCOURT FRENCH NATIONAL CEMETERY

HISTORY
The cemetery was used after the war as a concentration cemetery for the burial of men killed during the Battle of the Somme in 1916. It was used in 1920, in particular for those buried in the military cemetery at Méharicourt, 1935 and 1936. After WW2 it was used from 1949 to 1953 for the burial of men killed in that conflict.

INFORMATION
The village of Maucourt was destroyed during the Battle of the Somme when it was taken by soldiers of the French Tenth Army on 4 September 1916.

The British graves are the crew of an RAF Halifax bomber of No. 51 Squadron shot down on 17 April 1944 when on an operation to Plzen (Pilsen) in what is now the Czech Republic. They are in the south-west corner of the cemetery. There was one survivor, Warrant Officer W. R. Keirnan, DFM, who was taken Prisoner of War.

Fr – 5302 (3768 in individual graves and 1534 in six ossuaries) 24 are WW2 burials
UK – 5   Can – 1   Area – 17520 sq mts

LOCATION
Maucourt is midway between Amiens and St. Quentin about 5km south of the road between the two. It is about 2km west of the A1 Autoroute. The cemetery is next to the Bois Merlette 500m north of the village on the east side of a small road that leads to Lihons

MAUREPAS FRENCH NATIONAL CEMETERY

HISTORY
The cemetery was begun in 1916 and redesigned and extended in 1921 as a concentration cemetery. In 1936 further redevelopment took place to concentrate graves from local cemeteries, including those around Suzanne and Albert.

INFORMATION
The village was in German hands until the French 1st Infantry Regiment entered it on 12 August 1916. However, as it was strongly fortified by the Germans, it was not cleared until 24 August. The final clearance of the village was achieved with British help.

The burials in this cemetery are nearly all of men who died in this area during the Battles of the Somme as this area was, for the first part of the battle, a French sector.

There are several French memorials nearby. South of the village on the south side of the road to Hardecourt is a memorial to Gaston Chomet of the 160th Regiment of Infantry killed here on 30 July 1916. In the village is a memorial to the men of the 1st Infantry Regiment who died liberating Maurepas in 1916. East of the Autoroute and south of Le Foreste is a memorial to Edward Naudier who died of his wounds in 1916. He possibly died in the nearby farm known as the Ferme d'Hopital which must have been a field station in the war.

Fr – 3657 (2069 in individual graves, 1588 in two ossuaries), 1 French Civilian
Romanian – 1   Russ – 19
Area – 13700 sq mts

LOCATION
Maurepas is about 12km east of Albert and a similar distance south of Bapaume on the north side of the valley of the River Somme. The cemetery is in a valley on the east side of the village at the junction of the D146 to Herbecourt and a small road to the hamlet of Le Forest. It is on the north side of the road to Le Foreste.

MOISLAINS FRENCH NATIONAL CEMETERY

HISTORY
The cemetery was made for the dead of the Battle of Moislains on 28 August 1914. It was begun by the Germans after the battle and formally opened as a National Cemetery on 24 August 1924.

INFORMATION
This is the smallest French National Cemetery on the Somme and is also sometimes called 'Charentais Cemetery'. This cemetery contains the bodies of soldiers from the 123rd and 124th Infantry Brigades, mainly of young men from the department of Charente killed on 28 August 1914. A surprise bayonet charge attack by the 307th and 308th Infantry Regiments was cut down by German machine guns. The cemetery contains a memorial to the dead of the Charente 1914-18, and those who died on 28 August 1914. The monument has this inscription "The Charente, her children dead for France on August 28, 1914."

Fr – 465 (99 individual graves, 366 in an ossuary)
Area – 1688 sq mts

LOCATION
Moislains is 5km north of Peronne and about 10km south-east of Bapaume. The cemetery is north of the village on the east side of the road to Sailly-Saillisel. It is in a small copse next to the road as it climbs out of the village. It is a very attractive small cemetery.

MONTDIDIER COMMUNAL CEMETERY

HISTORY
The cemetery was in use throughout the war and for concentrated burials soon after the war.

INFORMATION
Montdidier was always in the French rear until the German advance in 1918 when the Germans arrived at Montdidier on 27 March 1918. The Germans almost forced a break in the French and British armies at this point, but the line was stabilised west of Montdidier until French troops recaptured the town in August 1918.

The cemetery, also known as the 'National Equality Necropolis', is at the rear, or west end, of the Communal Cemetery. The German Military Cemetery is also here. This is not a 'National' cemetery. Most of the soldiers buried in this place died of their wounds in military hospitals.

Fr – 745

LOCATION
Montdidier is at the southern edge of the area covered by this book being just north of the boundary of the Department of the Somme. It is about 30km south-east of Amiens and 15km west of Roye. This cemetery is on the north side of the town on the road to Albert at the east end of the Communal Cemetery. The French National and the German Military cemeteries are together within the same boundary. Access is from either north or south end or through the Communal Cemetery.

MONTDIDIER FRENCH NATIONAL CEMETERY

HISTORY
The cemetery was opened in 1914 and used throughout the war. It was redesigned in 1924 and further burials were made in 1935-6.

INFORMATION
The cemetery was once in open fields but is now surrounded by modern development. Most of the burials are of men who fell in the battles of 1918.

The British burials are men of four RAF planes including three men of No. 418 (Canadian) Squadron killed when their Boston night fighter was shot down attacking the airfield at Montdidier on 3 April 1942. The others are the crews of three Lancasters, one each from No.'s 35, 405 and 582 Squadrons killed during a mission on 4 May 1944 as part of the preparations for D-Day. Montdidier airfield, which was in the fields north of the Communal Cemetery, was an important German bomber base and had to be destroyed. RAF Bomber Command mounted its first attack on Luftwaffe airfields within fighter range of the beaches selected for the invasion of Normandy, when 84 Lancasters and eight Mosquitoes attacked the airfield at Montdidier. The May 1944 raid was successful, but four Lancasters were shot down, three nearby. The planes from No. 35 and 582 squadrons were recorded as intercepted by night fighters and exploded in mid-air. This set of graves, many of whom are in collective graves, is the largest group of British WW2 graves on the Somme.

There are a series of memorials nearby. First, near Assainvillers on the road to Compiegne is a memorial to General La Tours of 169th Infantry Division. It was erected in 1921, destroyed in 1940 and re-erected in 1955. Second, south of Montdidier on the road to Rubescourt is a memorial to American Corporal Pilot H H Houston Woodward, from Philadelphia, who went to France in 1917 to join a US Ambulance unit and then transferred to the French Air Force. He was shot down on 1 April 1918 flying a Spad of the 94th Lafayette Flying Corps. A plaque in Rubescourt church records a clock and bell given by the Woodward family. This is the most southerly memorial on the Somme. Woodward is buried in the American Cemetery in Paris.

North of Montdidier on the road to Amiens near an airfield is a memorial to the 19th Battalion of Chasseurs a Pied. The plaque lists the battle honours from 1854 to 1945. North-west of Montdidier on the road to Cantigny and Amiens is a memorial to the US 1st Division who were responsible for the first action by a complete American Division in WW1 when they re-captured Cantigny on 28 May 1918. The Division suffered 199 killed and 867 wounded. In Cantigny is a larger memorial opposite the village green to the same action.

Further north-west and north-west of the village of Grivesnes on the road to Aubvillers is a memorial to the French 125th and 325th Infantry Regiments which halted the German advance nearby in 1918.

Fr – 7432 (5815 in individual graves, 1617 in two ossuaries), 24 men of WW2

UK WW2 – 24   Belg – 1   Italian – 1

Area – 26100 sq mts

LOCATION
This cemetery is on the eastern edge of the town just north of the road to Roye on the Rue de Roye. It is an open formal and typical French National Cemetery.

RANCOURT FRENCH NATIONAL CEMETERY

HISTORY
This cemetery was begun in 1920 and finished in 1921 as a concentration cemetery for burials from the battlefields at Curlu and Clery-sur-Somme. It was later used from 1945-73 for the burial of bodies found on the battlefields. In 1980 a further concentration was undertaken from isolated graves or military burials in communal cemeteries at Flixecout, Bus-la-Mésière and other small villages.

INFORMATION
The village and area fell to the Germans in 1914. Rancourt was captured by the French on 26 September 1916 and handed over to the British soon after. The capture of this village was crucial to break the important German communication lines along the Bapaume-Peronne road. The assault was carried out by the French XXXII Army Corps. St. Pierre-Vaast Wood was taken by the British in March 1917 during the German retreat to the Hindenburg Line. It soon came to be far behind the front-line during the German retreat in 1917. However, the village fell to the Germans again in the early stages of their advance in 1918 and was not recaptured until 1 September 1918 when the 47th (London) Division attacked in this area. This village was completely destroyed during the war.

Rancourt contains French, British and German military cemeteries. It is also the location at which the French commemorate their participation in the Battle of the Somme each year. Rancourt cemetery is the largest French war cemetery on the Somme.

The chapel was a private memorial built in 1920 in memory of Lieutenant Jean du Bos and his comrades killed in action on 25 September 1916. Inside are other memorials, including those to Lieutenant Alan Humphrey Cheetham, 2nd Duke of Wellingtons, killed in action near Sailly-Saillisel on 15-16 December 1916 aged 20 years, commemorated on the Thiepval Memorial; and Lieutenant Neil Shaw-Stewart, 1st attached 3rd Rifle Brigade, killed in action leading 'D' Company at Guillemont on 22 August 1916 aged 22 years, buried at Delville Wood Cemetery.

Outside there is a memorial that contains a list of all infantry, artillery and cavalry units that fought for the French on the Somme during the war. There are also several memorials of British and Commonwealth interest:

- Captain Guy Drummond, 13th Canadian Infantry who died of gunshot wounds to the neck at St. Juliaan during the gas attack at Ieper on 22 April 1915, buried at Tyne Cot Cemetery. He relinquished the rank of Captain in the Canadian Militia, which he held prior to the outbreak of war, in order to get to France.
- 2nd Lieutenant Spencer Lort Mansel Mansel-Carey, 8th attached 9th Devonshires, killed in action on 24 February 1916. Spencer Mansel-Carey has the unusual distinction of having part of the Somme battlefield named after him – Mansel Copse from which the 9th Devonshires attacked on 1 July 1916 and which now contains Devonshire Cemetery.
- 2nd Lieutenant Henry Coxe, a BE2c pilot of No. 6 Squadron, Royal Flying Corps, killed in action over Cambrai on 1 July 1916 and buried at Point-du-Jour Cemetery near Arras.
- Captain Percy Robert Herbert, Viscount Clive, 1st Welsh Guards, son of the Earl of Powis, died of wounds on 13 October 1916 aged 23 years and is buried in Wales. His brother, Squadron Leader Mervyn Horatio Herbert, died on 23 March 1943 aged 38 years serving with No. 157 Squadron. He was also Viscount Clive. They are buried together.
- Corporal A G Leeson, 102nd Canadian Infantry, killed in action at Regina Trench on 21 October 1916 and commemorated on the Vimy Memorial.

South of the cemetery is the village of Bouchavesnes in which there is a statue of Marshal Foch, leader of French Forces at the end of the war. At the side of the road to Clery-sur-Somme from Bouchavesnes is a memorial to Gustave Fumery, aged 20 years, a Private in the 132nd Infantry Regiment and his 150 comrades killed nearby on 4 October 1916. A memorial to Aspirant Philippe Louis Calle of 106th Infantry Regiment killed on 25 September 1916 is also nearby.

Fr – 8567 (5327 in individual graves, 3240 in four ossuaries), 1 WW2 burial, 3 civilian graves
Area – 28110 sq mts

LOCATION
Rancourt lies astride the Arras-Peronne road about 10km south-east of Bapaume and a similar distance north of Peronne. This cemetery lies on the west side of the road about 1km south of the village. As it is a French Cemetery, and a bit off the 1916 battlefields, this is rarely visited by British and Commonwealth visitors, but it is well worth the effort and time.

SERRE-HÉBUTERNE FRENCH MILITARY CEMETERY

HISTORY
A burial ground of bout 150 French men, killed in an attack on Touvent Farm near the site of Luke Copse, had been made here during the battlefield clearances by V Corps in early 1917. They are in what is now the last seven rows. Any other French bodies subsequently found by the British during the war in this area were brought here. This cemetery, as we see it today, was created between 1919 and 1923 for the dead of the French 243rd Infantry Regiment killed in action during fighting against the German front line at Hébuterne from 10-13 June 1915. It was enlarged in 1923 for the dead of the 233rd and 327th Infantry Regiments from the same battle.

INFORMATION
The French held the German advance here in 1914 and remained until 1915 when the area was handed over to the British. Over three days in June 1915 seven hundred French soldiers, who were mostly reservists, were killed in the Battle of Serre-Hébuterne during an operation to divert attention away from the main French offensive, the Second

Battle of Artois, which had begun on 9 May 1915 and continued until 24 June 1915 under the command of General Foch. The battle here was led by the French 101st Brigade made up of 243rd, 233rd and 327th Regiments, under the command of General Petit, part of the 51st Division commanded by General Boudegourd. During the fighting the French pushed the Germans back but took heavy casualties. Soon after, the sector was handed over to the British though the men who survived the attack vowed to return to recover the remains of their comrades and ensure their burial.

Serre was an objective to be taken on 1 July 1916, the attack to be made by the 31st Division, which was made up of Pals Battalions, north of this road, while the 4th Division attacked astride this road with some territorials from the 48th Division in support. The attack was an abject failure. Serre was an objective again in November 1916 the advance this time by 3rd and 31st Divisions. It did not fall on either occasion. The villages of Puisieux and Serre-les-Puisieux, commonly called Serre, were taken from the Germans on 28 February 1917, lost to them on 26 March 1918 and taken for the final time on 21 August 1918.

In 1917 a memorial was erected and a new one unveiled on 14 June 1925. Beginning in 1919, the survivors of the 243rd Regiment formed a committee, which was in existence from 1919-33, to carry out the recovery of their friends. They also began an annual pilgrimage on the anniversary of the battle. Between 1919 and 1922, more than 500 officers and men were discovered, of which one-third could be identified. They bought the land and created the cemetery which was subsequently taken over by the government on 11 June 1933 and became a National Cemetery. The chapel was built in 1936. A few graves were concentrated here from other areas and some British cemeteries.

Serre-Hébuterne French War Cemetery and the nearby Commonwealth Cemeteries provide a fascinating insight into how the countries commemorate their dead. The French wished to emphasise the sacrifice made by their men so concentrated their war dead symbolically in mainly large, though some are huge, 'National' cemeteries. The British preferred, if possible, to bury their soldiers close to the battlefields where they lost their lives though they also recognised the practicalities of using large concentration cemeteries where required.

Fr – 834 (594 in individual graves, 240 in an ossuary)
Area- 5593 sq mts

LOCATION

Serre-les-Puisieux, commonly called Serre, is situated about 20km south of Arras and 5km west of Bapaume. The cemetery is 1km south-west of the hamlet on the north side of the D919 just within the boundary of the Department of the Somme next to Serre Road No. 1 Cemetery.

ST. ACHEUL FRENCH NATIONAL CEMETERY, AMIENS

HISTORY

The Cemetery was used by the French throughout the war for the burial of military dead. From August 1914 to September 1915 a few burials were made here of British soldiers. It was enlarged in 1921 and 1935.

INFORMATION

Amiens is a Cathedral town on the left bank of the River Somme with a population of approximately 130,000. The beautiful 13th Century Cathedral of Notre Dame is the largest in France. Eleven memorials were placed in the Cathedral near the south door after the war. A plaque placed by the CWGC honours those from the armies of Britain and Ireland who died in France and Belgium. There are other memorials to the ANZACs, the Royal Canadian Dragoons, the South Africans, Newfoundlanders and to Raymond Asquith, son of the former British Prime Minister, killed in action on the Somme in 1916. French Memorials are to Marshal Foch, General Debeney who commanded the French forces at Amiens in 1918, and to French colonial troops. A memorial to the US 6th Engineers Regiment can also be found. These were 500 engineers who formed part of Carey's Force, a makeshift British group which held part of the line in front of Amiens at the end of March 1918. Finally, there is a memorial, which was added after 1945, to General LeClerc who landed with the French in

Normandy. Further afield you will find a memorial on a bridge near the port to the 'Patriots of Amiens' who held the bridge against the Germans on 31 August 1944 to aid the British advance and avoid another 'Battle of Amiens'. In Place Rene Goblet is a memorial to the Picardy Martyrs. Amiens was the headquarters of the French II Corps and during part of August 1914 it was the British advanced base. It was captured by the Germans on 31 August 1914, retaken by the French on 13 September and remained in Allied hands for the rest of the war. Amiens was one of the objectives for the German spring offensive of 1918 but the Battles of Villers-Bretonneux in April 1918 held the German advance about 5km east of the city.

From August 1914 to September 1915 eleven British soldiers were buried in the Communal Cemetery. They include 2nd Lieutenant Evelyn Walter Copland Perry, Royal Flying Corps, who was accidentally killed while flying on 16 August 1914. Killed with him was Air Mechanic Herbert Edward Parfitt, aged 21 years. Another British soldier, Gunner W. M. Smith, was buried in the Extension on 6 April 1918. The graves were concentrated together in 1921 in one Plot on the edge of the French National Cemetery on the left-hand side of the main entrance.

Fr – 2751 (including 12 WW2 burials)
Belg – 10   Russ – 1   UK – 12
Area – 15170 sq mts

LOCATION
Amiens is the largest town in the area. It is at the western edge of the battlefield of the Somme. This cemetery is in the south-east corner of the city on the road from Longueau to the centre of the city. The National Cemetery is on a side road at the western edge of the Communal Cemetery.

ST. PIERRE AMIENS FRENCH NATIONAL CEMETERY

HISTORY
French military burials here began in September 1915 and used until 1919. It was used after the war in 1921 and 1934 for the concentration of French graves from other cemeteries in Amiens.

INFORMATION
See St. Acheul French National Cemetery.
St. Pierre is one of the town's civil cemeteries. At the rear of the cemetery is a French National Cemetery containing almost 1400 French war graves, over 50% of whom died of wounds in 1916. There are civil graves on the edge of the French National Cemetery. Many of these are the dead of WW1, some from Verdun who died of their wounds here or who have been brought here. The British first made burials in September 1915 and the British Plot remained in use until October 1919. It was enlarged after the war by the concentration of a few graves from isolated positions near, or in, the city.

Fr – 1372   Bel – 25   Area – 6830 sq mts

LOCATION
This cemetery is in the north-western, or St. Pierre, district of the city. The cemetery is on the north side of the D929 road to Albert about 2km from the city centre. There is clear parking here – and toilets.

VILLERS CARBONNEL FRENCH NATIONAL CEMETERY

HISTORY
The cemetery was begun in 1920 with further burials being made between the wars.

INFORMATION
The burials here are of men killed in the area in 1916.
Fr – 2297 (1008 in individual graves, 1289 in two ossuaries)

LOCATION
The village lies on the Amiens to St. Quentin road about 5km south of Peronne, 1km west of the valley of the River Somme and 15km west of St. Quentin. The cemetery is next to the Communal Cemetery on its eastern edge 100m west of the roundabout that is the junction of the road with the D1017.

GERMAN MILITARY CEMETERIES

ACHIET-LE-PETIT GERMAN MILITARY CEMETERY

HISTORY
The cemetery was started in the autumn of 1914. Burials continued here until March 1917 when the German forces withdrew from this area, but the cemetery was used again by the Germans from March until August 1918 when they briefly retook the territory.

INFORMATION
In 1924 the French authorities brought the remains of over 300 German servicemen to this cemetery from graves and small burial plots in the surrounding area. Most of the casualties buried in the cemetery were killed during the Battles of the Somme in 1916. Further developments took place in 1927, 1966 and 1978.

The cemetery at Achiet-le-Petit contains a number of German soldiers who died on their way to Field Hospitals at Vaulx-Vraucourt and Fremicourt.

Among those buried here is Paul Ernst Wachsmuth. He was a member of the Leipzig Branch of the Church of Latter Day Saints (Mormons), trained as an organist, and was killed in action on 25 August 1916. He was born on 16 June 1896 in Leipzig and baptized on 6 May 1910. He had been just a short time at the Front and was killed by a grenade.
Ger - 1314

LOCATION
Achiet-le-Petit is located about 19km south of Arras, 3km north-west of Bapaume and just south of Achiet-le-Grand. The cemetery is on the eastern edge of the village on Rue du Cimetiere on the north side of the Communal Cemetery.

ANDECHY GERMAN MILITARY CEMETERY

HISTORY
The cemetery was created after the war as a concentration cemetery when the French brought graves of German soldiers here from the surrounding area.

INFORMATION
Most of the casualties were killed locally in the March 1918 German advance and then during their retreat. The Amiens-Roye road marked the boundary between French and British forces in the August 1918 attack, so this cemetery was just in the French sector.

Ger - 2251

LOCATION
Andechy is at the southern edge of the area covered by this book. It is south of the road from Roye to Amiens and about 4km west of Roye. The cemetery is on the western edge of the village on the north side of the road to Erches. The trees clearly mark this as a German cemetery so it can be seen from some distance.

BETHENCOURT-SUR-SOMME GERMAN MILITARY CEMETERY

HISTORY
The cemetery was created by the French in 1922 for the collection of graves from a wide range of cemeteries and burial sites.

INFORMATION
A German hospital was posted in the village of Bethencourt in August and September 1914. But, nearly all of the men here died during the battles in 1918.

In 1415, Henry V and his army crossed the Somme here before heading to Agincourt.
Ger - 1242

LOCATION
Bethencourt-sur-Somme is in the valley of the River Somme about 15km south of Peronne. This small cemetery is on the northern edge of the village on the road to Pargny. It is on the west side of the road near the Communal Cemetery.

BRAY-SUR-SOMME GERMAN MILITARY CEMETERY

HISTORY
The cemetery was begun in 1918 but used again after the war as a concentration burial ground.

INFORMATION
The German Army initially occupied Bray in late August 1914, but as the Germans continued their thrust during the Battle of Albert from 25-29 September 1914, Bray attracted heavy bombing, forcing the Germans to evacuate on 4 October. As a result, the frontline reformed to the north and east of the town though the French resisted a strong German attack on 17 March 1915. For the next 28 months Bray served as an important centre for rest and recuperation for the French and British Armies. Bray became an important supply dump for munitions and equipment during the build-up and throughout the Battle of the Somme in 1916. But through 1916 and 1917 this was an area in the British sectors behind the front lines.

On 21 March 1918 the Germans launched a massive spring offensive in which Bray and its key river crossings were abandoned to the Germans. By the fourth week of August 1918, in what proved to be the most sweltering heat of the year, the Hundred Days Offensive brought Bray-sur-Somme back into the immediate frontline for the final time, this time defended primarily by remnants of the German 43rd Reserve Infantry Division, a veteran unit recruited from the reserve of the elite Prussian Guard, which had served on numerous Fronts since 1914. However, as a result of losses the Division had been rated third class. Despite this, on 22 August using a combination of machine gun fire, shelling and poison gas the Division managed to break up a night attack by the 33rd, 34th and 35th Australian Infantry and 3rd Australian Pioneers, who had tried to capture Bray from the north. Early on the night of 24 August, the 3rd Australian Pioneers and men of the 37th and 40th Australian Infantry began a fresh push into the town from the west behind a rolling artillery barrage. As was typical all along the Western Front, highly trained German machine gunners, shelling and poison gas were used once again in an attempt to repel the Australians. By the end of the day, however, the devastated town was finally liberated by the 40th Australian Infantry who had managed to infiltrate the town from three directions, using Stokes mortars to suppress German machine guns, most notably at Bray's railway yard.

The French brought in 200 graves in 1924. Further work to improve the burial ground took place between 1926 and 1929 but this ended due to the Depression and WW2. Further extension took place in 1966 and the latest work was in 1977 to bring it to its current state. This is the smallest German Military Cemetery in the Somme area. Most of the burials date from 1918 and many were made from German Medical Units stationed in the town.
Ger - 1119

LOCATION
Bray-sur-Somme lies on the north bank of the River Somme about 8km south-east of Albert and 30km east of the centre of Amiens. The cemetery is on the eastern edge of the village on the north side of the road to Corbie. Access to the small cemetery is from Rue des Fosses and up some steps. It is on the edge of a petanque arena and has a feeling of intimacy.

CAIX GERMAN MILITARY CEMETERY

HISTORY
The cemetery was created by the Germans in March 1918. From 1922 the French authorities extended the cemetery so it is mostly a concentration cemetery in which remains were brought in from the battlefields from up to 30km distance.

INFORMATION
The village was taken by British troops in March 1917 during the German retreat to the Hindenburg Line. The Germans re-captured the village in March 1918. The Canadian Corps finally re-took the village on 8 August 1918. Approximately 30 of the men buried here died from 1918 to 1919 as Prisoners of War.
Ger - 1264

LOCATION
The village of Caix is situated about 28km south-east of Amiens, midway between the N29 Amiens-St. Quentin road, and the D934 Amiens-Roye road. The Cemetery is south of the village. From the centre of the village head south towards Le Quesnel. About 200m along this road is the Communal Cemetery. There is easy access from the entrance opposite the Communal Cemetery.

FRICOURT GERMAN MILITARY CEMETERY

HISTORY
This is a concentration cemetery built entirely after the war.

INFORMATION
The cemetery was begun by the French in 1920 who brought bodies in from the battlefields north of the River Somme.

In 1929, the German War Graves Commission started working on the German military graves registration service and landscaping the cemetery. They created a new entrance with stairs and wrought-iron gate, and trees and bushes were planted. Work was suspended in 1939 and began again in 1966.

After the conclusion of the French-German War Graves Agreement, from 19 July 1966 the German War Graves Commission could begin the final organisation of the German cemeteries in France dating from the First World War. Starting from 1977, the provisional wooden grave markers were exchanged with those made of metal where possible. The German Federal Armed Forces took over the construction of the concrete foundations necessary for setting up the crosses, and they were helped by participants in youth camps.

Some 5057 soldiers are buried here in single graves, of whom 114 are unidentified. These soldiers are generally buried in a double grave at the foot of each cross. Four communal graves contain 11970 burials. There are fourteen graves for Jewish soldiers marked with a headstone instead of a cross. The Hebrew characters mean 'XXX rests buried' and 'their soul may be enwoven into the circle of the living persons.'

Most of those buried here were members of the Imperial German 2nd Army. Of the 17000 burials, about 1000 died in the autumn of 1914 and the subsequent trench warfare, about 10000 fell during the Battles of the Somme from July to November 1916, and the final 6000 in 1918.

The German pilot Baron Manfred von Richthofen, known as the 'Red Baron', who was shot down and killed on 21 April 1918, was first buried in the civilian cemetery at Bertangles. His body was later moved to Fricourt German Military Cemetery but again in 1925 he was exhumed and the body was taken to Germany for reburial.

The names of those who are known to be buried in the communal graves are inscribed on metal tablets at the rear of the cemetery.

Ger – 17027 (11970 in communal graves)

LOCATION
Fricourt is a village located about 5km east of Albert. The cemetery is north of the village on the east side of the road to Contalmaison. There is parking opposite and entry is by a set of stairs and a heavy iron gate.

HAM (MUILLE-VILLETTE) GERMAN CEMETERY

HISTORY
It was during the German occupation of the area in the spring of 1918 that they began this cemetery. French authorities extended the cemetery in 1922. The Germans took on the work in 1926 and again in 1964 with major work done in 1971.

INFORMATION
The Germans held this area from 1914 until spring 1917 when they withdrew. In that time they created several burial grounds as this was an important end point of supply transports by rail for the front between Chaulnes and Noyon and the repatriation of the seriously wounded. The local makeshift burial grounds were for those who died from injuries, accidents and diseases as well as wounded who did not make it any further. While the Allies were here this became an important base area for them. On 23 March 1918 the Germans, in their advance towards Amiens, crossed the Somme at Ham capturing the town. When the Fifth Army attempted to halt the German advance on 23-25 March 1918, the men of the 17th, 18th and 19th Kings (Liverpools) of 30th Division formed a defensive position on the north side of Ham. They believed the marshes of the River Somme on the south side of Ham would halt the

Germans. However, the Germans crossed the river east of Ham on 23 March 1918, captured the railway bridge over the canal, which was only held by the 21st Entrenching Battalion, and then moved to Ham. They fired on the Liverpool battalions from the rear at the same time as other Germans launched a frontal attack. The Germans captured three bridges which allowed their continued advance. This was all achieved in just three hours. The town remained in German hands until the French First Army re-took it on 6 September 1918.

Ger – 1534 (420 are unnamed)

LOCATION

Ham is a small town close to the Department of the Somme's southern boundary in the valley of the River Somme and at the limit of the area covered by this book. It is about 20kms south-west of St. Quentin at the crossroads of the St. Quentin-Roye and the Peronne-Chauny roads. The cemetery is in the neighbouring village of Muille-Villette on the southern edge of Ham. The German cemetery is at the front of a British cemetery.

MAISSEMY GERMAN MILITARY CEMETERY, VADANCOURT

HISTORY

The German military cemetery was created in 1924 by the French as a result of concentrating burials from approximately a 30km radius. Further work took place in 1929 and 1934-5 including work on the mass graves and the memorial hall which was opened on 12 July 1935. After WW2 work was renewed notably since 1972.

INFORMATION

This area was in German hands from 1914. The British captured it in 1917. The Germans recaptured it at the start of their spring offensive on 21 March 1918, though it was vigorously defended by the 24th Division and 2/4th Royal Berkshires. The 1st Division took the area for the final time in the war on 15 September 1918.

This is the second largest German military cemetery of the First World War in France (the largest is Neuville-St.Vaast near Arras with 44833 dead). The majority of the victims lost their lives during the battles on the Somme in 1916.

Among those buried here is Kannonier Xaver Wittkopf, Royal Bavarian 1st Foot Artillery Battalion. He was from Schiltberg, Bavaria, and a farmer before enlistment. He was already a serving soldier at the time of the outbreak of war and saw action in the Battle of the Frontiers, Artois, Verdun and the Somme, where he was killed in action by shellfire on his Battery on 24 September 1916.

Ger – 30481 (15481 in individual graves and 15000 in mass graves of which only 967 are known by name)

LOCATION

Vadancourt is a small hamlet about 8km north-west of St. Quentin. It is in the valley of the River L'Omignon on the opposite side of the river from the village of Maissemy. It is about 3km north of the Amiens to St. Quentin road and a similar distance west of the A26 Autoroute. The cemetery is on the north side of the Vermand-Bellenglise D33 on the hill above Vadancourt. It is about 1.5km north of Maissemy and 500m north-east of Vadancourt. This is a deceptively large, but very interesting cemetery.

MANICOURT GERMAN MILITARY CEMETERY

HISTORY

The German military cemetery was created in September 1914 when this area was in the German rear and remained in use until 1917. In 1922, the French greatly expanded the cemetery by the concentration of graves from large areas across the battlefields. Initial work on the improvement of the cemetery took place in 1931 and further work in 1973.

INFORMATION

The area was captured by the Germans in 1914 and held until their withdrawal in 1917 when it fell to British and French cavalry on 18 March. The Germans re-took the area as part of their advance in 1918 reaching it on 25 March. The area fell for the final time on 28 August 1918 when the French re-took it.

The first casualties were buried in the fighting during the so-called 'Race to the Sea' in 1914. More burials were added of men who died during the trench warfare in winter 1914-15. Most of the deaths took place here during the Somme battles in 1916 though in 1918 more burials were added of men who were brought here to medical units and then died of his wounds.

Among those believed to be buried here is Fusilier Abraham Rosenthal. He was fighting as a light infantry foot soldier in this area when he was shot in the stomach. His official Death Notice says that he died in Mobile Military Surgical Hospital No. 9 of the 18th Army Corps in Nesle at 10:30am on 24 July 1915. His grave cannot be found but it is known that German Soldiers who were buried in Nesle were moved during the 1920's to Manicourt. Only burials that were identified received individual graves. If identification was missing, or if soldiers shared a grave, these remains were placed in the mass graves. Hence, it is believed he is here but this shows the problems suffered by the losers in war and how difficult it is for us, as historians, to tell a full and complete picture of history, even the history of only 100 years ago.

Ger – 7326 (4225 in individual graves, 3101 in mass graves)

LOCATION

Manicourt is a tiny hamlet in the southern part of the area covered by this book. It lies 200m south of the road between Nesle and Chaulnes. The cemetery is on the north-western edge of the village on the south side of a minor road to Curchy. There are signs from the Nesle-Chaulnes road.

MONTDIDIER GERMAN MILITARY CEMETERY

HISTORY
The cemetery was opened in 1920 by the French as a post-war concentration cemetery bringing in German burials from a wide area. Over the next fifteen years a further 1000 graves were concentrated here, primarily during the battlefield clearances of the Somme. Many died in the German Spring Offensive in March 1918, when Montdidier was first occupied. Further work took place in 1927 and 1974.

INFORMATION
Montdidier was always in the French rear until the German advance when the Germans arrived at Montdidier on 27 March 1918. The Germans almost forced a break in the French and British armies at this point, but the line was stabilised west of Montdidier until French troops recaptured the town in August 1918.

Ger – 8051 (4351 in individual graves, 3700 in mass graves, 801 of them are unidentified)

LOCATION
Montdidier is at the southern edge of the area covered by this book being just north of the boundary of the department of the Somme. It is about 30km south-east of Amiens and 15km west of Roye. This cemetery is on the north side of the town on the road to Albert at the east end of the Communal Cemetery. The French Military and the German Military cemeteries are together within the same boundary. Access is from either north or south end or through the Communal Cemetery.

MORISEL GERMAN MILITARY CEMETERY

HISTORY
The cemetery was created in 1920 by the French as a concentration cemetery to bring in German burials from a 15km radius. Further work took place in 1926 and from 1964, often by youth groups.

INFORMATION
The cemetery contains the remains of a few men who fell in the 1916 Battles of the Somme and a few killed in 1914, but the majority of burials here are of men who fell in the last stages of the German advance in 1918. By the end of April 1918 the Germans held a small bridgehead here. The French advance on 8 August started from a line that was approximately at this cemetery running north to south-east along the valley of the River l'Avre.

Ger – 2640 (2605 in individual graves, 35 in a mass grave)

LOCATION
Morisel lies in the valley of the River l'Avre about 15km south-east of Amiens. The cemetery is on the eastern edge of the village on the south side of the road to Ailly-sur-Noye.

PROYART GERMAN MILITARY CEMETERY

HISTORY
This cemetery was created by the Germans during their offensive in 1918. After the war the French used this as a concentration cemetery for men brought in from the battlefield clearances. Further concentrations took place in the 1930's. Work to improve the cemetery took place in 1978.

INFORMATION
Proyart saw fierce fighting on 29 August 1914 and the village was briefly occupied as the German Army quickly overran the French who tried to stand firm and showed great resistance but with no success. In September, the French and British Armies pushed back the German troops during the Battle of the Marne. Proyart was no longer occupied and with the front line stabilising to the east, the village was now located behind Allied lines. Proyart saw fighting once more in 1918 as the Germans retook the whole of the Santerre plateau. Proyart was finally liberated on 9 August 1918.

Of those buried here, some died as Prisoners of War, some in British military medical units and some were brought from 27 'temporary' cemeteries.

Ger – 4643 (includes 1 unknown man of the Austro-Hungarian army)

LOCATION
Proyart is to the south of the River Somme. It lies just north of the road from Amiens to St. Quentin about 25km east of Amiens and 30km west of St. Quentin. The cemetery is north of the village in open countryside on a ridge overlooking the village. It is on the north side of the Communal Cemetery.

RANCOURT GERMAN MILITARY CEMETERY

HISTORY
This cemetery was begun by the French in 1920. The Germans undertook redevelopment from 1929 and the cemetery was officially opened on 17 September 1933. Further work has taken place since 1972.

INFORMATION
The village and area fell to the Germans in 1914. Rancourt was captured by the French on 26 September 1916 and handed over to the British soon after. The capture of this village was crucial to break the important German communication lines along the Bapaume-Peronne road. The assault was carried out by the French 32nd Army Corps. St. Pierre-Vaast Wood was taken by the British in March 1917 during the German retreat to the Hindenburg Line. It soon came to be far behind the front-line. However, the village fell to the Germans again in the early stages of their advance in 1918 and was not recaptured until 1 September 1918 when the 47th (London) Division attacked this area. This village was completely destroyed in the war.

A small chapel made from red Vosges sandstone lies within the cemetery. Most of the burials share a grey stone cross with the names of four soldiers upon them. Some of those buried here are women, probably nurses working near the Front.

Only a few of the burials are from the period 1914 to 1 July 1916, almost two thirds are from the 1916 Battles of the Somme and most of the remaining burials died during the fighting in 1918.

Ger – 11422 (3930 in individual graves, 7492 in mass graves)

LOCATION
Rancourt lies astride the Arras-Peronne road about 10km south-east of Bapaume and a similar distance north of Peronne. This cemetery is south-west of the village on the south side of the road to Combles. It is about 200m west of the French and British cemeteries.

ROYE-ST. GILLIES GERMAN MILITARY CEMETERY

HISTORY
The cemetery was created in 1920 by the French as a concentration cemetery for the burial of men from a wide area on the surrounding battlefields. Work continued by the Germans in the 1930's and after 1945.

INFORMATION
Roye fell to the Germans on 30 August 1914. It remained in their hands until the French captured the town on 17 March 1917. It fell again to the Germans on 28 March 1918 before the French took it for the final time on 27 August 1918.

Over 2000 of those buried here died during the fighting in autumn 1914 and spring 1915, but the majority are from the fighting in the spring and summer of 1918.

Ger – 6535 (3755 in individual graves, 2780 in mass graves)

LOCATION
Roye is at the southern edge of the area covered by this book. It is about 25km south-east of Amiens and a similar distance south-west of St. Quentin. This cemetery is south of the town 100m south of the N17 or D1017 bypass. There is a sign from the bypass down a track to this cemetery. It is a very attractive cemetery lying in open fields with oaks throughout the burial ground. It can be easily seen from the bypass.

SAPIGNIES GERMAN MILITARY CEMETERY

HISTORY
The cemetery was opened by the Germans in 1916 and used until March 1917, though primarily during the fighting between July and November 1916 in the Battles of the Somme. It was used by the Germans again between March and August 1918 during the German offensive. In 1924, the French authorities moved more than 400 German soldiers here from the surrounding civil cemeteries. Further redevelopment took place in the 1930's and after 1945.

INFORMATION
Two men killed in the fighting at Arras in early October 1914 was transferred here from the Sapignies civil cemetery.

Ger - 1550

LOCATION
Sapignies is a small village found about 3km north of Bapaume on the road between Bapaume and Arras. In the centre of the village about 200m west of the main road is the village church. 100m south of the church on the west side of a small road and above the level of the road is the German Military Cemetery.

VERMANDOVILLERS GERMAN MILITARY CEMETERY

HISTORY
The cemetery was made as a concentration cemetery by the French in 1920 to bring together German dead from the area south of the Somme.

INFORMATION
Many of the dead were first found during the clearing of the old battlefields. However, some of those buried here died of the influenza epidemic while in British hands in 1919. Today, the remains of German soldiers found on the battlefields in this part of the Somme are brought here for burial.

Apart from a few soldiers who died in 1914, most of the men buried here fell in the Battles of the Somme in 1916 and the battles in March 1918. The cemetery lies in the no-man's land of 1914-16.

Two famous German literary figures are buried here. Reinhard Sorge was a dramatist and poet best known for writing the Expressionist play The Beggar (Der Bettler), which won the Kleist Prize in 1912. Sorge was drafted in 1915 and was mortally wounded on 20 July 1916 and died at a field dressing station near Ablaincourt. Another German Expressionist writer was Alfred Lichtenstein who was killed in action on 25 September 1914. They are both recorded as being in one of the mass graves.

Also here are three German fighter aces. Leutnant Edgar Scholtz who scored one victory with Kest 10 before joining Jasta 11 in January 1918. After scoring five more victories he was killed when he was shot down by planes from No. 209 Squadron, RAF on 2 May 1918. Leutnant Hans Weiss had sixteen victories before he was shot down over Méricourt by Canadian ace Merrill Taylor also on 2 May 1918. Leutnant Hans Joachim Wolff was wounded on 14 August 1917 and again on 23 November 1917. He had his first confirmed victory on 18 March 1918 when he shot down John McCudden, MC, brother of James McCudden, VC, in an SE5a. Two months later, after ten victories, Wolff was killed on 16 May 1918 near Lamotte.

Ger – 22655 (9455 in individual graves, 13200 burials in a mass grave)

LOCATION
Vermandovillers is a small village that lies on the high heath south of the River Somme. It is midway between Amiens and St. Quentin about 1.5km south of the road between the two. The cemetery is north of the village on the east side of the road to Foucaucourt. It is visible from a great distance, notably from the A29.

VILLERS-AU-FLOS GERMAN MILITARY CEMETERY

HISTORY
The cemetery was opened in October 1914 by German units fighting in this area. It was in use throughout the war whenever the Germans were here. After the war about 800 graves were moved here from the area around Bapaume.

INFORMATION
The area was occupied by the British Army when the Germans withdrew to the Hindenburg Line in March 1917. The Germans took the area again during their Spring Offensive in March 1918 but it was captured for the final time, by the New Zealand Division, largely the 2nd Auckland Battalion, on 30 August 1918.

The cemetery contains a memorial to 14th Reserve Corps. Among those buried here is one man known to have taken part in the Christmas Truce 'football match' in 1914 at Frelinghien on the French-Belgian border just north-east of Armentieres. Men of the 2nd Argyll and Sutherland Highlanders and the 9th Saxon Infantry Regiment, or 133rd German Infantry Regiment met in no man's land, exchanged pleasantries, and played football. Among those at Frelinghien was Albert Schmidt, an inside right for the third team of Fussballclub 02 Schedewitz, a small town in eastern Germany. He was later killed on 20 August 1916 when his battalion was sent from reserve to counter a night-time attack by Australian units. On the opposing side was Sergeant James 'Jimmy' Coyle, Captain of the 2nd Argyll and Sutherland Highlanders football team and an inside left for Scottish league side Albion Rovers. He survived the war and was awarded the Military Medal.

Ger - 2449

LOCATION
Villers-au-Flos is located about 3km south-east of Bapaume 1km east of the Bapaume to Peronne road. The cemetery is on the north side of the village on the road that leads from the church through winding turns to the Rue Lacomte and the cemetery on the north side of the road. There is a small entrance behind a hedge so it is easy to miss. A path leads from the road 50m to the cemetery. It is a very quiet and peaceful location.

COMMONWEALTH WAR GRAVES COMMISSION

During the first months of the War in 1914 the dead were buried by their comrades, or by local inhabitants, in communal cemeteries, and burial returns were made by chaplains or serving officers. The Royal Engineers were involved in fighting so they could not perform the task as they had done in the South African Wars.

General Fowke, Engineering Adviser to the British Expeditionary Force, was happy to hand over the task of marking and registration of graves to Fabian Ware. He had volunteered his ambulance unit for the job at the end of October 1914 before Lord Kitchener, Minister of War, sanctioned the development. The unit was officially appointed by Sir John French, Commander-in-Chief, in February 1915 and was given the title of Graves Registration Commission. It was still a civilian group, manned by the Red Cross but became a military unit in October 1915 with Army officers in charge of Graves Registration Units (GRU's).

The Commission's task was the systematic marking and registration of all graves in France and Flanders. To achieve this the British zone of warfare was divided into seven areas in which all known graves were located with an appropriate religious marker, and photographs taken of every grave. Late in 1915 the French Government donated land for cemeteries to Britain and the Dominions. At the same time the British Government set up a national committee to make provision for the care of all graves in France and Flanders.

The committee, called the Commission of Graves Registration and Enquiries, headed by the Prince of Wales, was to arrange for the care of the graves, acquire land and provide a service for the relatives of the dead. It set up units in each sector to care for thirty-three cemeteries and 49,413 graves then identified. In May 1916 the Commission suggested that identity disks should be made of metal and that each man have two to replace the leather disks used previously.

Usually up to 1916 the dead were buried where they fell or in scattered graves in the rear. However, it became normal for trenches to be pre-dug before battles in preparation for the dead, a system that eased the job of identification and continued until the end of the War.

The Commission received a Royal Charter on 21 May 1917 and its membership represented all the countries of the Empire and Dominions who were taking part in the War and had dead buried on the battlefields. In 1919 the Commission announced that, despite many families wanting the remains of the dead to be repatriated, the bodies would remain where they fell and would not be returned to Britain. The main reason for this was the expense, though the care lavished on the cemeteries over the century has outstripped the cost of removal to Britain, and the effect has been a much more effective memorial to the fallen of the Great War.

The Imperial (now Commonwealth) War Graves Commission took over from the Empire War Office in 1921. The cost of its work is shared by those countries who have dead in Commission Cemeteries and in proportion to the number of dead from each country.

The main objective of the Commission at the end of the War, in caring for what French lamented as the 'Silent Army' of the dead, was to commemorate each individual equally. Thus, all men received the same tribute in the form of a headstone or as a line on a Memorial such as the Menin Gate. Each headstone is 2ft 8ins in height and 1ft 3ins wide, upon which is carved the badge of the regiment or unit, rank, name, date of death and age with an appropriate religious symbol. At the foot of the stone relatives were allowed to have a small inscription at their own expense. Exceptions to this design are for the few men who were awarded the Victoria Cross or the headstones that bear an inscription such as 'Known (or Believed) to be buried in this Cemetery' when the exact place of burial is lost. For bodies that could not be identified the headstone bears the simple, but effective, words, chosen by Rudyard Kipling, 'Known unto God'.

Each cemetery has a character of its own though a number of features, particularly the Cross of Sacrifice set upon an octagonal base and bearing a crusaders sword of bronze, are common to almost all. The larger cemeteries also have the War Stone, a plinth that looks like an altar and bears the words 'Their Name Liveth for Evermore', chosen by Rudyard Kipling, from the Book of Ecclesiastes. Most headstones are set in rows or narrow borders planted with a variety of flowers and shrubs.

The developmental work of the Commission was completed in 1938 with the unveiling of the Australian National Memorial in France. The area of the front had been divided into squares, each searched six times for bodies, between 1921 and 1928 nearly 30,000 corpses, of which only 25% could be identified, were re-buried. Even today when remains are still being found and interred in the War Cemeteries, there are still over 500,000 missing on the Western Front.

The work of the Commission is protected by international agreements. It is a shame that the registers of each cemetery cannot be equally well protected. A record for each cemetery is held at the offices of the Commission in Maidenhead, Ypres and at Beaurains, France, but there used to be a relevant copy stored in most cemeteries. Found in small repositories usually near the entrance, too many have been removed for the Commission to afford constantly replacing them. My finding three registers to be missing in one day is part of the inspiration for these books. I cannot thank the officers of the Commission enough for their help in compiling this book. Their advice, information and immense efforts over the years has eased my work and research on innumerable occasions.

THE BATTLES ON THE SOMME

THE BATTLE OF THE SOMME 1916

First phase: 1–17 July 1916
    First day on the Somme   1 July
    Battle of Albert   1–13 July
    Battle of Bazentin Ridge   14–17 July
    Battle of Fromelles   19–20 July

Second phase: July – September 1916
    Battle of Delville Wood   14 July–15 September
    Battle of Pozières Ridge   23 July–7 August
    Battle of Guillemont   3–6 September
    Battle of Ginchy   9 September

Third phase: September–November, 1916
    Battle of Flers–Courcelette   15–22 September
    Battle of Morval   25–28 September
    Battle of the Transloy Ridges   1 October–11 November
    Battle of Thiepval Ridge   26–28 September
    Battle of the Ancre Heights   1 October–11 November
    Battle of the Ancre   13–18 November

Background

British and French strategy to win the war had been agreed at a conference in 1916. Soon after the conference Haig became commander of the British army and wanted different objectives. However, by February 1916 he had agreed to a joint attack on the Somme. This strategy was disrupted by a German initiative to win the war in 1916 by splitting the entente. The Germans attacked at Verdun to 'bleed France white'. The consequence was that France had to play a lesser role on the Somme. Additionally, the Russian Brusilov Offensive was taking place which needed some visible support from the Allies in the west.

The original plan was for a joint offensive by the British and French along a 70km front. After the German attack on the French at Verdun in February 1916, this was reduced to a 40km front, of which the British were to have 29km. The main attack was to be carried out by Rawlinson's 4th Army. He mistrusted the ability of his infantry, because of its lack of experience, Much of the army that would attack on 1 July was made up of the 'New Armies'. The attack was to be the first major test of Kitchener's Army of volunteers, raised in 1914 and under training ever since. In the industrial North, the City Battalions were often known as Pals Battalions, e.g. Accrington Pals, Grimsby Chums. Some were drawn from specific occupations, e.g. Glasgow City Tramways Battalion. In some, e.g. Liverpool Commercials, companies could also have a common link, one being made up of clerks from the White Star Shipping office, another from Cunards. Rawlinson, and many of the other Generals, saw them as amateurs and incapable of complicated military skills when under fire.

So, Rawlinson created a simple plan which relied on a heavy preparatory bombardment. A week-long bombardment would destroy the German defences, break down the barbed wire and kill all the defenders. There was one artillery piece for 10m of front, in the week before the attack they fired more shells that had been fired in the first year of the war, about 1 1/2 million. The job of cutting the wire was given to the 18lb shrapnel shells. The infantry would simple walk across no-man's land and occupy the German front line. Reserves would move through them to the German second line. Once they were secure, the artillery would move up and repeat the process on the German third and fourth lines. The men would leave their trenches, form into open order and walk. Each battalion was divided into nine waves, each one minute apart.

The final destruction of strong points on the German line was to be achieved using mines. There were seven small ones, and three larger ones, two of which were at La Boisselle. These were to be blown two minutes before zero, with the exception of Hawthorn Redoubt mine at Beaumont Hamel which was blown ten minutes before so that a cameraman who film the explosion.

1 July 1916

By 4.00am it was getting light. 1 July was a gloriously hot summer day, 60,000 British troops were in the front line trenches, each carrying with 60-80lb equipment. At 6.25am the final barrage started. At 7.20 the Hawthorn mine was blown, followed by the others at 7.30. The barrage lifted and the infantry attack began. The men left the trenches and grouped to get though the gaps in the British wire, before they began to cross No-Man's land. The attack went disastrously wrong within moments. The German wire had been destroyed in very few places so once across no-man's land, the British in many places grouped again to get through the few gaps in the German wire. German machine gun crews, who had survived the artillery barrage, emerged from their dug outs and were presented with perfect targets. As they cut down the attacking troops, German artillery batteries, thought by the British to have been knocked out, opened fire causing further confusion to men in the open and heavy casualties in the reserve trenches.

The pattern was the same more or less all along the line, and was repeated many times throughout the day. Some 40,000 more troops were committed as the day went on, as plans were rigidly followed, by Generals incapable of showing initiative and flexibility, despite the inevitable slaughter and failure. Orders had be shared with officers and once they were killed, the men had little idea of objectives, alternatives and strategy. By the end of the day there had been some slight gain to the south of the Albert-Bapaume Road, but in the centre and the north nothing had been gained at all. At no point had the German second line been breached. These slight gains were made at a terrible cost, the British Divisions suffered 60,000 casualties of whom nearly 20,000 were killed. Many other died of the wounds in the following days and weeks. It was the worst day in the British Army's history.

The Continued Battle of 1916

Haig persisted with the offensive to draw German strength off from Verdun. He concentrated on the successful sectors which were mainly on the south of the initial battlefield. The German second line in those areas was breached by a night attack in which the men were guided in the dark by white tapes.

High Wood was taken but, through delays in bringing up reinforcements, it was lost and a breakthrough not made. Haig tried to wear down the Germans by attrition. Falkenhayn, the German Commander, poured in troops and these were consumed in the struggle, as Falkenhayn ordered, for every metre of land. Slow progress was made during the months of continuous fighting of July to September as the British painfully conquered the sites of pulverised villages and destroyed woods. Pozieres was taken with appalling losses by the Australians. "We have just come out of a place so terrible that ……. a raving lunatic could never imagine the horror …" said one of them. It cost 3000 South Africans to capture Delville Wood. The Canadians suffered at Courcelette and the surrounding area.

In a huge onslaught to breach the original German third line, the weary infantry were heartened by the help of a few tanks. These, appearing for the first time in war, were a surprise for the Germans. They helped make better progress in late September and the top of the ridge was a last taken. The German defence was brought to the point of collapse. It was their worst crisis until 1918. But the British were also utterly exhausted and in impossible November weather the battle ground to a halt. Many of the first day objectives such as Serre didn't fall while others, including Beaumont and what is now Newfoundland Park, were taken in the snow of November. Haig's maximum advance was only 11km, but the German line had been weakened and it was withdrawn in 1917. In February 1917 the Germans voluntarily withdrew to a line of defences that they had been building for months, the Hindenburg Line, and in so doing they gave up ten times the ground that the Allies had taken from them in 1916. Total losses in the Battle were over a million : 420,000 British and Empire, 200,000 French and 450,000 German. Falkenhayn was replaced by Hindenburg and Ludendorff. After the war, the German commanders agreed the Haig's policy of attrition cost the Germans the men they needed in 1918 to complete the 'gamble' to win the war before the Americans arrived.

So, the Somme in 1916 served several purposes. First, it showed Britain was committed to large scale involvement in the war on a scale considerable greater than the battles of 1914 and 1915. Second, it wore down the German army. Third, it may have taken some of the pressure off the French at Verdun. Most importantly, the British army learned many things. New technology such as tanks were introduced and then improved over the next 24 months. Tactics were refined so that attacks were never as simplistic as 1 July 1916 again, all men knew what to do under fire, not just Battalion and Company commanders and skills were developed that by 1918 what we today would call 'combined ops', the linking of infantry, armour, air power and artillery with good intelligence and communications was implemented at Le Hamel in July 1918. Poor leaders were replaced with men who could 'do the job'. This learning process continued in 1917 and early 1918. Hence, by the summer of 1918, the army had everything it needed to win the war. The Battle of the Somme in 1916 is seen as a time when the phrase 'Lions led by Donkeys' was most appropriate. But, this misses the value of the battle as a Victorian army changed into one that could win wars in the 20th Century. The Somme in 1916 was a significant battle from which the British army gained much and should not be dismissed as a 'waste'.

RETREAT TO THE HINDENBURG LINE (OPERATION ALBERICH) AND OTHER BATTLES IN 1917

Operations on the Ancre, January–March 1917
Pursuit of the German retreat to the Hindenburg Line
Battle of Arras
First Battle of Bullecourt
Battle of Lagnicourt
Second Battle of Bullecourt, 3–17 May 1917
Battle of Cambrai

Actions on the Somme continued through the harsh winter of 1916-17, though the Battle of the Somme 1916 had ended. Much of this action took place along the valley of the River Ancre and involved taking several German trenches that had been attacked earlier. The Germans planned to withdraw only if the British succeeded in breaking through the existing front line, but on 4 February 1917 the order was given to start to prepare for the withdrawal to the defensive position called the Hindenburg Line. During the withdrawal the Germans were to implement a 'scorched earth' policy whereby nothing of possible use to the Allies was to be left behind. A fighting withdrawal would be taken in places, with traps for the advancing soldiers in others. This was not an easy advance for the British, Canadians and ANZAC's. In many places the German front-line, and even the remains of entire villages, were found to be empty, the Germans waiting to surprise the advancing troops behind the German lines. This 'withdrawal, with the pursuit by the British and their Dominion troops, who often bore the full might of German counter-measures, took from February until mid-April 1917.

By this time other battles had become part of the events surrounding the German 'withdrawal'. They are represented by the cemeteries covered by this book and, hence, are listed above, though I will not cover them in any details. I would draw attention to the attacks at Bullecourt, and the German counter-attack at Lagnicourt, for which the Australians paid a heavy price. These also form part of the Battle of Arras 1917 which covered a line from north of the city to part of the area covered by this book. Some of the men killed in the actions that formed part of the battle are buried in cemeteries covered by the book.

Finally, in late 1917, following the events at Ieper, the British attacked at Cambrai using infantry with tanks, in an independent battle that initially was very successful. However, the use of infantry with armour was not yet fully understood by all the British commanders. So a German counter attack pushed the British back almost to the line from which they had first advanced.

Nonetheless, these events of 1917, which brought the two sides to a line roughly north-south close to the route of the current A26 autoroute, which is the eastern boundary for this book, also bring us to the line from which the 1918 campaigns on the battlefields of the Somme, knowns as the Battles of the Somme 1918, mean it would be difficult to justify not covering these cemeteries in this book. While many have burials of men who died in 1917, they all have men who died in the 1918 battles. There are, I agree, a few cemeteries that contain the graves only of the dead of 1917, but I cannot feel right in leaving them out.

BATTLES OF THE SOMME 1918

Battle of St. Quentin	21–23 March
Actions at the Somme crossings	24–25 March
First Battle of Bapaume	24–25 March
Battle of Rosières	26–27 March
First Battle of Arras	28 March
Battle of the Avre	4 April 1918
Battle of the Ancre	5 April
First Battle of Villers-Bretonneux	30 March–5 April 1918
Second Battle of Villers-Bretonneux	24–27 April 1918

Following the withdrawal of the Russians from the war, and with the threat of the Americans arriving in strength, the German strategy for a Spring Offensive in 1918 was to attack the British and push them out of the war before dealing with the French. This attack, known as Operation Michael, became called the Kaiser's Battle and the 'Great Gamble'. It was not known to the Germans that the British knew they had problems, and were willing to pull back from France should the city of Amiens be threatened or fall to the Germans. However, the Allies now had a unified command structure that placed the British and French armies under one leader – Supreme Allied Commander Marshal Foch.

When the German attack began on 21 March 1918 the British were in the process of restructuring the army from four battalion Brigades to three battalion Brigades to cope with a manpower crisis. In this way understrength battalions could be brought back up to fighting strength as men were re-assigned. However, it also meant that some men were new to their platoons when the fighting began so did not know the men in their own unit. Similarly, some command positions were newly filled or not filled at all. This was a time of confusion and one of the worst times to face a major attack. On the other hand, in some ways it brought out the best in some men who made the best of the situations in which they found themselves to fight as well as could be imagined against the weight of German troops coming at them. For example, the 39th Division, was officially designated a 'composite battalion' due to its losses meaning that a structural unit of 16-20000 men was, during the battles in March and April 1918, composed of about 1000-1500 men. Even so, the Germans advanced up to 65km in a few days in some areas on the Somme. In our terms they moved from the east to the west of the area covered by this book.

In addition to structural issues, the Germans took advantage of fog on the 21 March, which meant the defenders of the British line, only recently taken over from the French and comprising little more than a series of shell-holes linked by limited lines of barbed wire, were unable to see the advancing Germans until they were upon the British. They forged crossings over the River Somme behind the British defenders. Consequently, this was a battle in which the number of casualties taken as prisoners was as great as those killed and wounded. In many ways, this was not the stereotype that we have of WW1.

Despite the actions of troops such as the New Zealanders near Colincamps, and British battalions along the valley of the River Somme, the actions at Villers-Bretonneux are seen as being the zenith of the German advance on the Somme in 1918. There were two battles told in details in the entry for the Villers-Bretonneux Military Cemetery.

Once the German advance had been held short of a ridge from whence Amiens could be threatened by German artillery, their advance had failed as had the 'gamble'. After a short period of consolidation in which some minor actions took place, the Allies prepared for their advance on 8 August 1918.

FINAL BREAKOUT 1918 (100 DAYS OFFENSIVE)

Battle of Amiens	8-12 August
Battle of Montdidier	9 August
Second Battle of the Somme	21 August–2 September
Second Battle of Noyon	17 August
Battle of Albert (1918)	21–29 August
Second Battle of Bapaume	31 August-3 September
Battle of Mont Saint-Quentin	31 August–3 September
Battle of the Drocourt-Quéant Line	2 September
Advance to the Hindenburg Line	
Battle of Havrincourt	12 September
Battle of Épehy	18 September
Battle of Canal du Nord	27 September - 1 October
Battle of the St. Quentin Canal	29 September - 2 October

The Germans regard 8 August 1918 as the 'Black Day' for the German army. Following actions such as that at Le Hamel on 4 July in which tactical plans had been tested, and success elsewhere including American involvement, the plans for an attack on the Somme were developed by Haig and Rawlinson and submitted to Foch for approval. He insisted on French involvement so a revise plan was created for implementation on 8 August 1918. The Battle of Amiens or Third Battle of Picardy was an attack launched in fog on a 22km front by 11 British divisions and the left wing of the French First Army on their right flank. Canadian forces would attack in the center. Due to the need for secrecy there was to be no artillery bombardment so an attack by 435 tanks took place ahead of the infantry assault. The swift advance by the British and French divisions caught the Germans by surprise so that by the end the day the British had pushed the Germans back by about 16km. By the end of the second day 30,000 German prisoners had been captured and 300 artillery pieces. On 9 August the French Third Army launched attacks in the southern sector of the advance. Montdidier was re-captured and the Paris-Amiens railway line was once again in Allied hands. On 12 August the first phase of the battle ended.

The second phase of the offensive, the Second Battles of the Somme 1918, began on 21 August. The French Tenth and Third Armies, with the British Third and First Armies attacked. The ANZACs captured ground north of the Somme at Péronne and Mont St. Quentin. Canadian forces captured ground near Quéant. By 4 September the German forces had withdrawn to the Hindenburg Line, the position from which they had advanced in the earlier part of the year.

On 15 August 1918, Haig refused demands from Marshal Foch to continue the Amiens offensive, as that attack was faltering as the troops outran their supplies and artillery, and German reserves were being moved to the sector. Instead, Haig began to plan for an offensive with a new axis, that of the Battle of the Somme in 1916 towards Bapaume, which began on 21 August. The main attack was launched by the British Third Army, with the United States II Corps attached.

The Second Battle of Bapaume developed into an advance which pushed the German Second Army back over a 55km front, from south of Douai to La Fère, south of Saint-Quentin. Albert was captured on 22 August. On 26 August, the British First Army widened the attack by another twelve km, sometimes called the Second Battle of Arras. Bapaume fell on 29 August. The Australian Corps, severely reduced in manpower as the Australian government refused to introduce conscription, crossed the Somme on the night of 31 August, and captured Mont St. Quentin and Péronne. Rawlinson, described the Australian advances of 31 August–4 September as the greatest military achievement of the war.

On the morning of 2 September, after a heavy battle, the Canadian Corps seized control of the Drocourt-Quéant line (representing the west edge of the Hindenburg Line) inflicting heavy casualties but also capturing more than 6,000 unwounded prisoners. The German commander, Ludendorff, had decided to withdraw behind the Canal du Nord.

Once the Hindenburg Line had been reached a number of actions took place in preparation for Foch's final push. These included straightening German salients at Havrincourt and Epehy as well as French attacks by the French First Army in the Battle of Savy-Dallon on 10 September, and the French Tenth Army during the Battle of Vauxaillon on 14 September. The final actions which can be covered by this book are those that took place at the Canal du Nord, the St Quentin Canal and the Battle of Cambrai 1918 all parts of pushing the Germans back from the Hindenburg Line, destroying their communication lines and clearing them from France.

The war came to an end on 11 November 1918 with German troops still occupying parts of France and Belgium. The Peace Treaties signed in the hall of Mirrors at Versailles ended one war and set the groundworks for another.

ORDER OF BATTLE
BATTLES OF THE SOMME 1916

1st CAVALRY DIVISION : Major-General R. L. Mullens
- Battle of Flers-Courcelette 15 Sept (In Reserve to XIV Corps, Fourth Army)

1st Cavalry Brigade : Brigadier-General E. Makins
2nd (Queen's Bays) Dragoon Guards
11th (Prince Albert's Own) Hussars
5th (Princess Charlotte of Wales's) Dragoon Guards
2nd Cavalry Brigade : Brigadier-General D. J. E. Beale-Browne
4th (Royal Irish) Dragoon Guards
18th (Queen Mary's Own) Hussars
9th (Queen's Royal) Lancers
9th Cavalry Brigade : Brigadier-General S. R. Kirby
15th (The King's) Hussars
1st Bedfordshire Yeomanry
19th (Queen Alexandra's Own) Hussars

GUARDS DIVISION : Major-General G. P. T. Feilding
- Battle of Flers-Courcelette 15 - 16 & 20 - 22 Sept (XIV Corps, Fourth Army)
- Battle of Morval 25 - 28 Sept (XIV Corps, Fourth Army)
- Capture of Lesboeufs 25 Sept

1st Guards Brigade : Brigadier-General C. E. Pereira
2nd Grenadier Guards   3rd Coldstream Guards
1st Irish Guards   2nd Coldstream Guards
2nd Guards Brigade : Brigadier-General J. Ponsonby
3rd Grenadier Guards   1st Scots Guards
1st Coldstream Guards   2nd Irish Guards
3rd Guards Brigade : Brigadier-General C. E. Corkran
1st Grenadier Guards   2nd Scots Guards
4th Grenadier Guards   1st Welsh Guards
    Pioneers : 4th Coldstream Guards

1st DIVISION : Major-General E. P. Strickland
- Battle of Bazentin Ridge 14-17 July (III Corps, Fourth Army)
- Battle of Pozieres Ridge 23-26 July & 15 Aug-3 Sept (III Corps, Fourth Army)
- Battle of Flers-Courcelette 15-22 Sept (III Corps, Fourth Army)
- Battle of Morval 25 - 28 Sept (III Corps, Fourth Army)

1st Brigade : Brigadier-General A. J. Reddie
1st Black Watch   10th Gloucesters
1st Cameron Highlanders   8th Royal Berkshires
2nd Brigade : Brigadier-General A. B. Hubback
2nd Royal Sussex   1st Northamptonshires
1st Loyal North Lancashires   2nd King's Royal Rifle Corps
3rd Brigade : Brigadier-General H. R. Davies
1st South Wales Borderers   2nd Welsh
1st Gloucesters   2nd Royal Munster Fusiliers
    Pioneers : 1/6th Welsh

2nd DIVISION : Major-General W. G. Walker, VC
- Battle of Delville Wood 25 July-9 Aug (XIII Corps, Fourth Army)
- Capture and Consolidation of Delville Wood 27 - 28 July
- Attack of Waterlot Farm 8 - 9 Aug
- Battle of the Ancre 13 - 16 Nov (V Corps, Fifth Army)

5th Brigade : Brigadier-General W. Bullen-Smith
17th (Empire) Royal Fusiliers   2nd Highland Light Infantry
2nd Oxford & Bucks Light Infantry
24th (2nd Sportsmens) Royal Fusiliers
6th Brigade : Brigadier-General A. C. Daly
1st King's Liverpool   2nd South Staffordshires
13th (West Ham Pals) Essex
17th (1st Football Pals) Middlesex
99th Brigade : Brigadier-General R. O. Kellett
1st Royal Berkshires   1st King's Royal Rifle Corps
22nd (Kensington) Royal Fusiliers
23rd (1st Sportsmens) Royal Fusiliers
    Pioneers : 10th (Cornwall Pioneers) Duke of Cornwall's Light Infantry

3rd DIVISION : Major-General J. A. L. Haldane to 7 August; Major-General C. J. Deverell
- Battle of Bazentin Ridge 14-25 July (XIII Corps, Fourth Army)
- Battle of Delville Wood 14 - 19 Aug (XIII Corps, Fourth Army to 16 Aug, then XIV Corps, Fourth Army)
- Battle of the Ancre 13-18 Nov (V Corps, Fifth Army)

8th Brigade : Brigadier-General E. G. Williams
2nd Royal Scots   8th East Yorkshires
1st Royal Scots Fusiliers
7th King's Shropshire Light Infantry
9th Brigade : Brigadier-General H. C. Potter to 25 July (wounded 23 July); Brigadier-General H. C. R. Green to 5 August; Brigadier-General H. C. Potter
1st Northumberland Fusiliers   13th King's Liverpool
4th Royal Fusiliers   12th West Yorkshires
76th Brigade : Brigadier-General R. J. Kentish to 1 Oct; Brigadier-General C. L. Porter
2nd South Staffordshires   8th King's Own
1st Gordon Highlanders   10th Royal Welsh Fusiliers
    Pioneers : 20th (British Empire League Pioneers) King's Royal Rifle Corps

4th DIVISION : Major-General Hon. W. Lambton
- Battle of Albert 1 - 2 July (VIII Corps, Fourth Army)
- Battle of The Transloy Ridges 10 - 18 October (XIV Corps, Fourth Army)

10th Brigade : Brigadier-General C. A. Wilding
1st Royal Warwickshires   1st Royal Irish Fusiliers
2nd Seaforth Highlanders   2nd Royal Dublin Fusiliers
11th Brigade : Brigadier-General C. B. Prowse, DSO, to 1 July (killed); Major W. A. T. B. Somerville acting to 3 July; Brigadier-General H. C. Rees
1st Somerset Light Infantry   1st Hampshires
1st East Lancashires   1st Rifle Brigade
12th Brigade : Brigadier-General J. D. Crosbie
1st King's Own   2nd Duke of Wellington's
2nd Lancashire Fusiliers   2nd Essex
    Pioneers : 21st (Wool Textile Pioneers) West Yorkshires

5th DIVISION : Major-General R. B. Stephens
- Attacks on High Wood 20 - 25 July (XV Corps, Fourth Army)
- Battle of Guillemont 3 - 6 Sept (XIV Corps, Fourth Army)
- Battle of Flers-Courcelette 18 - 22 Sept (XIV Corps, Fourth Army)
- Battle of Morval 25 - 26 Sept (XIV Corps, Fourth Army)

13th Brigade : Brigadier-General L. O. W. Jones
2nd King's Own Liverpool   1st Royal West Kents
14th (1st Birmingham Pals) Royal Warwickshires
15th (2nd Birmingham Pals) Royal Warwickshires
15th Brigade : Brigadier-General M. N. Turner
1st Norfolks   1st Cheshires
1st Bedfordshires
16th (3rd Birmingham Pals) Royal Warwickshires
95th Brigade : Brigadier-General C. R. Ballard to 20 July (wounded); Lieutenant-Colonel M. Archer-Shee acting to 21 July; Brigadier-General Lord E. C. Gordon-Lennox
1st Devonshires   1st East Surreys
1st Duke of Cornwall's Light Infantry
12th (Bristol Pals) Gloucesters
 Pioneers : 1/6th (Renfrewshire) Argyll & Sutherland Highlanders

6th DIVISION : Major-General C. Ross
- Battle of Flers-Courcelette 15 - 18 & 21 - 22 Sept (XIV Corps, Fourth Army)
- Battle of Morval 25 - 28 Sept (XIV Corps, Fourth Army)
- Capture of Lesboeufs 25 Sept
- Battle of the Transloy Ridges 9 - 18 Oct (XIV Corps, Fourth Army)

16th Brigade : Brigadier-General W. L. Osborn
1st Buffs   2nd York & Lancasters
1st King's Shropshire Light Infantry
8th Bedfordshires
18th Brigade : Brigadier-General R. J. Bridgford
1st West Yorkshires   2nd Durham Light Infantry
11th Essex   14th Durham Light Infantry
71st Brigade : Brigadier-General J. F. Edwards to 4 Oct (sick); Brigadier-General E. Feetham
1st Leicesters   9th Norfolks
2nd Sherwood Foresters   9th Suffolks
 Pioneers : 11th (Midland Pioneers) Leicesters

7th DIVISION : Major-General H. E. Watts
- Battle of Albert 1 - 5 July (XV Corps, Fourth Army)
- Capture of Mametz 1 July
- Battle of Bazentin Ridge 14 - 17 July (XV Corps, Fourth Army)
- Attacks on High Wood 20 July (XV Corps, Fourth Army)
- Battle of Guillemont 3 - 7 Sept (XV Corps, Fourth Army)

20th Brigade : Brigadier-General C. J. Deverell to 7 Aug; Brigadier-General H. C. R. Green
2nd Border   8th Devonshires
2nd Gordon Highlanders   9th Devonshires
22nd Brigade : Brigadier-General J. McC. Steele
2nd Royal Warwickshires   1st Royal Welsh Fusiliers
2nd Royal Irish
20th (5th Manchester Pals) Manchesters
91st Brigade : Brigadier-General J. R. M. Minshull-Ford
2nd Queen's   1st South Staffordshires
21st (6th Manchester Pals) Manchesters
22nd (7th Manchester Pals) Manchesters
 Pioneers : 24th (Oldham Pals) Manchesters

8th DIVISION : Major-General H. Hudson
- Battle of Albert 1 July (III Corps, Fourth Army)
- Attack on Le Transloy 23 - 30 Oct (XIV Corps, Fourth Army)

23rd Brigade : Brigadier-General H. D. Tuson to 27 Aug; Brigadier-General E. A. Fagan
2nd Devonshires   2nd Cameronians
2nd West Yorkshires   2nd Middlesex
24th Brigade (Transferred to 8th Division on 15 July) Brigadier-General A. J. F. Eden
1st Worcesters   1st Sherwood Foresters
2nd East Lancashires   2nd Northamptonshires
25th Brigade : Brigadier-General J. W. H. Pollard
2nd Lincolns   1st Royal Irish Rifles
2nd Royal Berkshires   2nd Rifle Brigade
70th Brigade (Transferred to 23rd Division on 16 July) Brigadier-General H. Gordon
11th Sherwood Foresters   8th York & Lancasters
8th King's Own Yorkshire Light Infantry
9th York & Lancasters
 Pioneers : 22nd (3rd Durham Pals) Durham Light Infantry (from 2 July)

9th (SCOTTISH) DIVISION : Major-General W. T. Furse
- Battle of Albert 1 - 13 July (In Corps Reserve on 1 July; XIII Corps, Fourth Army)
- Capture of Bernafey Wood (27th Brigade)
- Battle of Bazentin Ridge 14 July (XIII Corps, Fourth Army)
- Attack on Longueval 14 - 18 July (26th & South African Brigades)
- Battle of Delville Wood 15 - 19 July (XIII Corps, Fourth Army)
- Battle of Transloy Ridges 10-18 Oct (III Corps, Fourth Army)
- Attacks on the Butte de Warlencourt 12 - 18 Oct

26th Brigade : Brigadier-General A. B. Ritchie
8th Black Watch   5th Cameron Highlanders
7th Seaforth Highlanders
10th Argyll & Sutherland Highlanders
27th Brigade : Brigadier-General S. W. Scrase-Dickens
11th Royal Scots   12th Royal Scots
6th King's Own Scottish Borderers
9th Cameronians
South African Brigade : Brigadier-General H. T. Lukin
1st South African Infantry   2nd South African Infantry
3rd South African Infantry   4th South African Infantry
 Pioneers : 9th Seaforth Highlanders

11th (NORTHERN) DIVISION : Lieutenant-General Sir C. L. Woollcombe
- Capture of the Wonder Work 14 Sept (32nd Brigade, II Corps, Reserve Army)
- Battle of Flers-Courcelette 15 - 22 Sept (II Corps, Reserve Army)
- Battle of Thiepval Ridge 26 - 28 Sept (II Corps, Reserve Army)

32nd Brigade : Brigadier-General T. H. F. Price
9th West Yorkshires   8th Duke of Wellington's
6th Yorkshires   6th York & Lancasters
33rd Brigade : Brigadier-General J. F. Erskine
6th Lincolns   7th South Staffordshires
6th Border   9th Sherwood Foresters
34th Brigade : Brigadier-General J. Hill
8th Northumberland Fusiliers   5th Dorsets
9th Lancashire Fusiliers   11th Manchesters
 Pioneers : 6th East Yorkshires

12th (EASTERN) DIVISION : Major-General A. B. Scott
- Battle of Albert 2 - 8 July (III Corps, Fourth Army to 5 July then X Corps, Reserve Army)
- Battle of Pozieres Ridge 28 July - 13 Aug (II Corps, Reserve Army)
- Battle of the Transloy Ridges 1 - 18 Oct (XV Corps, Fourth Army)

35th Brigade : Brigadier-General A. Solly-Flood
7th Norfolks	7th Suffolks
9th Essex	5th Royal Berkshires

36th Brigade : Brigadier-General : L. B. Boyd-Moss
8th Royal Fusiliers	7th Royal Sussex
9th Royal Fusiliers	11th Middlesex

37th Brigade : Brigadier-General A. B. E. Cator
6th Queen's	7th East Surreys
6th Buffs	6th Royal West Kents

Pioneers : 5th Northamptonshires

14th (LIGHT) DIVISION : Major-General V. A. Couper
- Battle of Delville Wood 13 - 30 Aug (XV Corps, Fourth Army)
- Battle of Flers- Courcelette 15 - 16 Sept (XV Corps, Fourth Army)

41st Brigade : Brigadier-General P. C. B. Skinner
7th King's Royal Rifle Corps	7th Rifle Brigade
8th King's Royal Rifle Corps	8th Rifle Brigade

42nd Brigade : Brigadier-General F. A. Dudgeon
9th King's Royal Rifle Corps	9th Rifle Brigade
5th King's Shropshire Light Infantry	
5th Oxford & Bucks Light Infantry	

43rd Brigade : Brigadier-General P. R. Wood
6th Somerset Light Infantry	10th Durham Light Infantry
6th King's Own Yorkshire Light Infantry	
6th Duke of Cornwall's Light Infantry	

Pioneers : 11th King's Liverpool

15th (SCOTTISH) DIVISION : Major-General F. W. N. McCracken
- Battle of Pozieres Ridge 8 Aug-3 Sept (III Corps, Fourth Army)
- Battle of Flers-Courcelette 15-18 Sept (III Corps, Fourth Army)
- Capture of Martinpuich 15 Sept
- Battle of Transloy Ridges 18 Oct (III Corps, Fourth Army)

44th Brigade : Brigadier-General F. J. Marshall
9th Black Watch	8th/10th Gordon Highlanders
8th Seaforth Highlanders	7th Cameron Highlanders

45th Brigade : Brigadier-General W. H. L. Allgood
13th Royal Scots	6th Cameron Highlanders
6th/7th Royal Scots Fusiliers	
11th Argyll & Sutherland Highlanders	

46th Brigade : Brigadier-General T. G. Matheson
10th Cameronians	12th Highland Light Infantry
7th/8th King's Own Scottish Borderers	
10th/11th Highland Light Infantry	

Pioneers : 9th Gordon Highlanders

16th (IRISH) DIVISION : Major-General W. B. Hickie
- Battle of Guillemont 3 - 6 Sept (XIV Corps, Fourth Army)
- Battle of Ginchy 9 Sept (XIV Corps, Fourth Army)

47th Brigade : Brigadier-General G. E. Pereira
6th Royal Irish	7th Leinsters
6th Connaught Rangers	8th Royal Munster Fusiliers

48th Brigade : Brigadier-General F. W. Ramsay
1st Royal Munster Fusiliers	7th Royal Irish Rifles
8th Royal Dublin Fusiliers	9th Royal Dublin Fusiliers

49th Brigade : Brigadier-General P. Levenson-Gower
7th Royal Inniskilling Fusiliers	7th Royal Irish Fusiliers
8th Royal Inniskilling Fusiliers	8th Royal Irish Fusiliers

Pioneers : 11th Hampshires

17th (NORTHERN) DIVISION : Major-General T. D. Pilcher to 13 July; Major-General P. R. Robertson
- Battle of Albert 1 - 10 July (XV Corps, Fourth Army)
- Capture of Fricourt 2 July
- Battle of Delville Wood 1 - 12 Aug (XV Corps, Fourth Army)

50th Brigade : Brigadier-General W. J. T. Glasgow
10th West Yorkshires	7th Yorkshires
7th East Yorkshires	6th Dorsets

51st Brigade : Brigadier-General R. B. Fell to 6 July; Brigadier-General G. F. Trotter
7th Lincolns	8th South Staffordshires
7th Border	10th Sherwood Foresters

52nd Brigade : Brigadier-General J. L. J. Clarke
9th Northumberland Fusiliers	9th Duke of Wellington's
10th Lancashire Fusiliers	12th Manchesters

Pioneers : 7th York & Lancasters

18th (EASTERN) DIVISION : Major-General F. I. Maxse
- Battle of Albert 1 - 8 July (XIII Corps, Fourth Army)
- Battle of Bazentin Ridge 14 - 17 July (XIII Corps, Fourth Army)
- Capture of Trones Wood 14 July (54th Brigade)
- Battle of Delville Wood 19 - 21 July (53rd Brigade under 9th Division)
- Battle of Thiepval Ridge 26 - 28 Sept (II Corps, Reserve Army)
- Battle of The Ancre Heights 1 - 5 Oct & 17 Oct - 11 Nov (II Corps, Reserve Army, Fifth Army from 30 Oct)
- Capture of the Schwaben Redoubt 30 Sept - 5 Oct (55th Brigade)
- Capture of Regina Trench 21 Oct
- Battle of the Ancre 13 - 18 Nov (II Corps, Fifth Army)

53rd Brigade : Brigadier-General H. W. Higginson
8th Norfolks	10th Essex
8th Suffolks	6th Royal Berkshires

54th Brigade : Brigadier-General T. H. Shoubridge
11th Royal Fusiliers	6th Northamptonshires
7th Bedfords	12th Middlesex

55th Brigade : Brigadier-General T. D. Jackson to 9 Oct; Brigadier-General F. B. Nugent to 18 Oct; Brigadier-General G. D. Price
7th Queen's	8th East Surreys
7th Buffs	7th Royal West Kents

Pioneers : 8th Royal Sussex

19th (WESTERN) DIVISION : Major-General G. T. M. Bridges
- Battle of Albert 1 - 9 July (III Corps, Fourth Army)
- Capture of La Boiselle 2 - 4 July
- Fighting for High Wood 20 - 22 July (III Corps, Fourth Army)
- Battle of Pozieres Ridge 23 - 31 July (III Corps, Fourth Army)
- Battle of the Ancre Heights 22 Oct - 11 Nov (II Corps, Reserve Army until 31 Oct then Fifth Army)
- Battle of the Ancre 13 - 18 Nov (II Corps, Fifth Army)

56th Brigade : Brigadier-General F. G. M. Rowley
7th King's Own   7th South Lancashires
7th East Lancashires   7th Loyal North Lancashires
57th Brigade : Brigadier-General C. C. Onlsow to 20 July (sick); Lieutenant-Colonel W. Long acting to 22 July; Brigadier-General G. D. Jeffreys
10th Royal Warwickshires   10th Worcesters
8th Gloucesters   8th North Staffordshires
58th Brigade : Brigadier-General A. J. W. Dowell
9th Cheshires   9th Welsh
9th Royal Welsh Fusiliers   6th Wiltshires
  Pioneers : 5th South Wales Borderers

20th (LIGHT) DIVISION : Major-General W. Douglas Smith
- Battle of Delville Wood 21 Aug - 3 Sept (XIV Corps, Fourth Army)
- Battle of Guillemont 3 - 5 Sept (XIV Corps, Fourth Army)
- Battle of Flers-Courcelette 16 - 20 Sept (XIV Corps, Fourth Army)
- Battle of Morval 27 Sept (XIV Corps, Fourth Army)
- Battle of Transloy Ridges 1- 8 Oct (XIV Corps, Fourth Army)

59th Brigade : Brigadier-General C. D. Shute
10th King's Royal Rifle Corps   10th Rifle Brigade
11th King's Royal Rifle Corps   11th Rifle Brigade
60th Brigade : Brigadier-General Hon L. J. P. Butler
12th King's Royal Rifle Corps   12th Rifle Brigade
6th Oxford & Bucks Light Infantry
6th King's Shropshire Light Infantry
61st Brigade : Brigadier-General W. E. Banbury
12th King's Liverpool   7th Somerset Light Infantry
7th Duke of Cornwall's Light Infantry
7th King's Own Yorkshire Light Infantry
  Pioneers : 11th Durham Light Infantry

21st DIVISION : Major-General D. G. M. Campbell
- Battle of Albert 1-3 July & 11-13 July (XV Corps, Fourth Army)
- Battle of Bazentin Ridge 14-17 July (XV Corps, Fourth Army)
- Battle of Flers-Courcelette 17-22 Sept (XV Corps, Fourth Army)
- Battle of Morval 25 - 28 Sept (XV Corps, Fourth Army)
- Capture of Geuedecourt 26 Sept
- Battle of the Transloy Ridges 1 Oct (XV Corps, Fourth Army)

62nd Brigade : Brigadier-General C. G. Rawling
1st Lincolns   10th Yorkshires
12th Northumberland Fusiliers
13th Northumberland Fusiliers
63rd Brigade : (Transferred to 37th Division 8 July) Brigadier-General E. R. Hill
8th Lincolns   4th Middlesex
8th Somerset Light Infantry   10th York & Lancasters
64th Brigade : Brigadier-General H. R. Headlam
1st East Yorkshires   15th Durham Light Infantry
9th King's Own Yorkshire Light Infantry
10th King's Own Yorkshire Light Infantry
110th Brigade : (Transferred from 37th Division 7 July) Brigadier-General W. F. Hessey
6th Leicesters   8th Leicesters
7th Leicesters   9th Leicesters
  Pioneers : 14th Northumberland Fusiliers

23rd DIVISION : Major-General J. M. Babington
- Battle of Albert 4 - 11 July (III Corps, Fourth Army)
- Capture of Contalmaison 10 July
- Battle of Pozieres Ridge 26 July-8 Aug (III Corps, Fourth Army)
- Battle of Flers-Courcelette 15-22 Sept (III Corps, Fourth Army)
- Battle of Morval 25 - 28 Sept (III Corps, Fourth Army)
- Battle of the Transloy Ridges -9 Oct (III Corps, Fourth Army)
- Capture of Le Sars 7 Oct

24th Brigade : (Transferred to 8th Division 15 July) Brigadier-General R. S. Oxley to 11 July; Brigadier-General A. J. F. Eden
1st Worcesters   1st Sherwood Foresters
2nd East Lancashires   2nd Northamptonshires
68th Brigade : Brigadier-General H. Page-Croft
12th Durham Light Infantry   13th Durham Light Infantry
10th Northumberland Fusiliers
11th Northumberland Fusiliers
69th Brigade : Brigadier-General T. S. Lambert
11th West Yorkshires   8th Yorkshires
10th Duke of Wellington's   9th Yorkshires
70th Brigade : (Transferred from 8th Division 17 July) Brigadier-General H. Gordon
8th York & Lancasters   9th York & Lancasters
11th Sherwood Foresters
8th King's Own Yorkshire Light Infantry
  Pioneers : 9th South Staffordshires

24th DIVISION : Major-General J. E. Capper
- Battle of Delville Wood 11 - 22 Aug & 31 Aug - 2 Sept (XIII Corps until 16 August, then XIV Corps to 30 August, then XV Corps from 31 Aug, Fourth Army)
- Battle of Guillemont 3 - 5 Sept (XV Corps, Fourth Army)

17th Brigade : Brigadier-General J. W. V. Carroll
8th Buffs	12th Royal Fusiliers
1st Royal Fusiliers	3rd Rifle Brigade

72nd Brigade : Brigadier-General B. R. Mitford
8th Queen's	8th Royal West Kents
9th East Surreys	1st North Staffordshires

73rd Brigade : Brigadier-General R. G. Jelf
9th Royal Sussex	13th Middlesex
7th Northamptonshires	2nd Leinsters

Pioneers ; 12th Sherwood Foresters

25th DIVISION : Major-General E. G. T. Bainbridge
- Battle of Albert 3 - 16 July (X Corps, Reserve Army)
- Battle of Bazentin Ridge 14 - 16 July (X Corps, Reserve Army)
- Battle of Pozieres Ridge 18 Aug - 3 Sept (II Corps, Reserve Army)
- Fighting for Mouquet Farm 3 Sept
- Battle of the Ancre Heights 1 - 22 Oct (II Corps, Fourth Army)
- Capture of Stuff Redoubt 9 Oct
- Capture of Regina Trench 21 Oct

7th Brigade : Brigadier-General C. E. Heathcote to 30 Aug; Brigadier-General C. C. Onslow
10th Cheshires	8th Loyal North Lancashires
3rd Worcesters	1st Wiltshires

74th Brigade : Brigadier-General G. A. Armytage to 17 Oct (sick); Brigadier-General H. K. Bethell
11th Lancashire Fusiliers	9th Loyal North Lancashires
13th Cheshires	2nd Royal Irish Rifles

75th Brigade : Brigadier-General H. F. Jenkins to 9 July (sick); Lieutenant-Colonel G. S. St. Aubyn acting to 10 July; Brigadier-General E. St. G. Pratt
11th Cheshires	2nd South Lancashires
8th Border	8th South Lancashires

Pioneers : 6th South Wales Borderers

29th DIVISION : Major-General H. de B. de Lisle
- Battle of Albert 1 July (VIII Corps, Fourth Army)
- Battle of the Transloy Ridges 10 - 18 Oct (88th Brigade with 12th Division)

86th Brigade : Brigadier-General W. de L. Williams
2nd Royal Fusiliers	1st Royal Dublin Fusiliers
16th (Public Schools) Middlesex	
1st Lancashire Fusiliers	

87th Brigade : Brigadier-General C. H. T. Lucas
2nd South Wales Borderers	1st Border
1st Royal Inniskilling Fusiliers	
1st King's Own Scottish Borderers	

88th Brigade : Brigadier-General D. E. Cayley
4th Worcesters	2nd Hampshires
1st Essex	
Royal Newfoundland Regiment	

Pioneers : 1/2nd Monmouthshires

30th DIVISION : Major-General J. S. M. Shea
- Battle of Albert 1 - 5 & 7 - 13 July (XIII Corps, Fourth Army) - Capture of Montauban 1 July
- Fighting in Trones Wood 7 - 13 July
- Battle of the Transloy Ridges 10 - 18 Oct (XV Corps, Fourth Army)

21st Brigade : Brigadier-General Hon C. J. Sackville-West to 30 July (wounded); Lieutenant-Colonel W. H. Young acting to 5 Aug; Brigadier-General R. W. Morgan
2nd Wiltshires	2nd Yorkshires
18th (2nd Liverpool Pals) King's Liverpool	
19th (4th Manchester Pals) Manchesters	

89th Brigade : Brigadier-General Hon F. C. Stanley
17th (1st Liverpool Pals) King's Liverpool
20th (4th Liverpool Pals) King's Liverpool
19th (3rd Liverpool Pals) King's Liverpool
2nd Bedfordshires

90th Brigade : Brigadier-General C. J. Steavenson to 20 Aug (sick); Lieutenant-Colonel H. J. Grisewood acting to 28 Aug; Lieutenant-Colonel R. K. Walsh acting to 2 Sept; Brigadier-General C. J. Steavenson to 21 Sept (sick); Lieutenant-Colonel R. K. Walsh acting to 23 Sept; Lieutenant-Colonel J. H. LLoyd acting to 13 Oct; Brigadier-General J. H. LLoyd
2nd Royal Scots Fusiliers
16th (1st Manchester Pals) Manchesters
17th (2nd Manchester Pals) Manchesters
18th (3rd Manchester Pals – Clerks & Warehousemen) Manchesters

Pioneers : 11th (St Helens Pioneers) South Lancashires

31st DIVISION : Major-General R. Wanless O'Gowan
- Battle of Albert 1 July (VIII Corps, Fourth Army)
- Attack on Serre 1 July
- Battle of the Ancre 13 - 18 Nov (XIII Corps, Fifth Army)

92nd Brigade : Brigadier-General O. de L. Williams
10th (Hull Commercials) East Yorkshires
11th (Hull Tradesmen) East Yorkshires
12th (Hull Sportsmen) East Yorkshires
13th (Hull T'Others) East Yorkshires

93rd Brigade : Brigadier-General J. D. Ingles
15th (1st Leeds Pals) West Yorkshires
16th (1st Bradford Pals) West Yorkshires
18th (2nd Bradford Pals) West Yorkshires
18th (1st Durham Pals) Durham Light Infantry

94th Brigade : Brigadier-General H. C. Rees to 2 July; Brigadier-General G. T. C. Carter-Campbell
11th (Accrington Pals) East Lancashires
12th (Sheffield City Battalion) York & Lancasters
13th (1st Barnsley Pals) York & Lancasters
14th (2nd Barnsley Pals) York & Lancasters

Pioneers : 12th (Miners) King's Own Yorkshire Light Infantry

32nd DIVISION : Major-General W. H. Rycroft
- Battle of Albert 1 - 3 July (X Corps, Fourth Army)
- Battle of Bazentin Ridge 14 - 15 July (X Corps, Reserve Army)
- Battle of the Ancre Heights 23 Oct - 11 Nov (In Reserve II Corps, Reserve Army)
- Battle of the Ancre 17 - 19 Nov (V Corps, Fifth Army)

14th Brigade : Brigadier-General C. W. Compton
5th/6th Royal Scots   2nd Manchesters
1st Dorsets
15th (1st Glasgow Pals – Glasgow Tramways) Highland Light Infantry

96th Brigade : Brigadier-General C. Yatman
16th (Newcastle Commercials) Northumberland Fusiliers
2nd Royal Inniskilling Fusiliers
15th (1st Salford Pals) Lancashire Fusiliers
16th (2nd Salford Pals) Lancashire Fusiliers

97th Brigade : Brigadier-General J. B. Jardine
11th (Lonsdale) Border
2nd King's Own Yorkshire Light Infantry
16th (2nd Glasgow Pals – Glasgow Boys Brigade) Highland Light Infantry
17th (3rd Glasgow Pals) Highland Light Infantry
      Pioneers : 17th (North Eastern Railway Pioneers) Northumberland Fusiliers

33rd DIVISION : Major-General H. J. S. Landon to 23 Sept; Major-General R. J. Pinney
- Battle of Albert 12 - 13 July (Corps Reserve, XV Corps, Fourth Army)
- Battle of Bazentin Ridge 14 - 17 July (XV Corps, Fourth Army)
- Attacks on High Wood 18 - 21 July (XV Corps, Fourth Army)
- Capture of Dewdrop & Boritska Trenches 25 Oct - 7 Nov (XIV Corps, Fourth Army)

19th Brigade : Brigadier-General P. R. Robertson to 13 July; Brigadier-General C. R. G. Mayne to 28 Aug; Lieutenant-Colonel J. G. Chaplin acting to 1 Sept; Brigadier-General C. R. G. Mayne
1st Cameronians   5th/6th Cameronians
20th (3rd Public Schools) Royal Fusiliers
2nd Royal Welsh Fusiliers

98th Brigade : Brigadier-General F. M. Carleton to 28 Aug; Brigadier-General C. R. G. Mayne temporary to 1 Sept; Brigadier-General J. D. Heriot-Maitland
4th King's Liverpool   1st Middlesex
1/4th Suffolks
2nd Argyll & Sutherland Highlanders

100th Brigade : Brigadier-General A. W. F. Baird
1st Queen's   2nd Worcesters
16th (Church Lads Brigade) King's Royal Rifle Corps
1/9th (Glasgow Highland) Highland Light Infantry
      Pioneers : 18th (1st Public Works Pioneers) Middlesex

34th DIVISION : Major-General E. C. Ingouville-Williams to 22 July (killed); Brigadier-General R. W. R. Barnes acting to 25 July; Major-General C. L. Nicholson
- Battle of Albert 1 - 3 & 10 - 13 July (III Corps, Fourth Army)
- Capture of Scots & Sausage Redoubts 2 July
- Battle of Bazentin Ridge 14 - 17 July (III Corps, Fourth Army)
- Battle of Pozieres Ridge 31 July - 15 Aug (III Corps, Fourth Army)
- Battle of Flers-Courcelette 15 Sept (103rd Brigade & 18th Northumberland Fusiliers with 15th Division, III Corps, Fourth Army)

101st Brigade : Brigadier-General R. C. Gore
15th (1st Edinburgh City Battalion) Royal Scots
16th (2nd Edinburgh City Battalion) Royal Scots
10th (Grimsby Chums) Lincolns
11th (Cambridge City Battalion) Suffolks

102nd Brigade : (transferred to 37th Division 6 July - 22 Aug) Brigadier-General T. P. B. Ternan
20th (1st Tyneside Scottish) Northumberland Fusiliers
21st (2nd Tyneside Scottish) Northumberland Fusiliers
22nd (3rd Tyneside Scottish) Northumberland Fusiliers
23rd (4th Tyneside Scottish) Northumberland Fusiliers

103rd Brigade : (transferred to 37th Division 6 July - 22 Aug) Brigadier-General N. J. G. Cameron to 1 July (wounded); Lieutenant-Colonel G. R. V. Steward acting to 4 July; Brigadier-General H. E. Trevor
24th (1st Tyneside Irish) Northumberland Fusiliers
25th (2nd Tyneside Irish) Northumberland Fusiliers
26th (3rd Tyneside Irish) Northumberland Fusiliers
27th (4th Tyneside Irish) Northumberland Fusiliers

111th Brigade : (transferred from 37th Division 6 July - 22 Aug) Brigadier-General R. W. R. Barnes
10th Royal Fusiliers   13th King's Royal Rifle Corps
13th Royal Fusiliers   13th Rifle Brigade

112th Brigade : (transferred from 37th Division 6 July - 22 Aug) Brigadier-General P. M. Robinson
11th Royal Warwickshires   8th East Lancashires
6th Bedfordshires   10th Loyal North Lancashires
   Pioneers : 18th (1st Tyneside Pioneers) Northumberland Fusiliers (transferred to 37th Division 6 July - 22 Aug)
9th North Staffordshires (transferred from 37th Division 6 July - 22 Aug)

35th DIVISION : Brigadier-General J. G. Hunter temporary to 5 July; Major-General R. J. Pinney
- Battle of the Bazentin Ridge 15 - 17 July (105th Brigade with 18th Division; 106th Brigade with 9th Division; XIII Corps, Fourth Army)

105th Brigade : Brigadier-General A. H. Marindin
15th (1st Birkenhead Pals) Cheshires
16th (2nd Birkenhead Pals) Cheshires
14th (West of England) Gloucesters
15th (Nottingham Pals) Sherwood Foresters

106th Brigade : Brigadier-General H. O'Donnell
17th (Rosebery) Royal Scots
19th (2nd Durham Pals) Durham Light Infantry
17th (2nd Leeds Pals) West Yorkshires
18th (4th Glasgow Pals) Highland Light Infantry
   Pioneers : 19th (2nd Tyneside Pioneers) Northumberland Fusiliers

36th (ULSTER) DIVISION : Major-General O. S. W. Nugent
- Battle of Albert 1 - 2 July (X Corps, Fourth Army)

107th Brigade : Brigadier-General W. M. Withycombe
8th (East Belfast) Royal Irish Rifles
9th (West Belfast) Royal Irish Rifles
10th (South Belfast) Royal Irish Rifles
15th (North Belfast) Royal Irish Rifles
108th Brigade : Brigadier-General C. R. J. Griffith
11th (South Antrim) Royal Irish Rifles
12th (Central Antrim) Royal Irish Rifles
13th (1st County Down) Royal Irish Rifles
9th (County Armagh) Royal Irish Fusiliers
109th Brigade : Brigadier-General R. G. Shuter
9th (County Tyrone) Royal Inniskilling Fusiliers
10th (Derry) Royal Inniskilling Fusiliers
11th (Donegal and Fermanagh) Royal Inniskilling Fusiliers
14th (Young Citizens) Royal Irish Rifles
  Pioneers : 16th (2nd County Down) Royal Irish Rifles

37th DIVISION : Major-General H. Bruce-Williams
- Battle of the Ancre 13 - 18 Nov (63rd & 111th Brigades with 63rd Division 13 - 15 Nov; 112th Brigade with 2nd Division 13 - 17 Nov; V Corps, Fifth Army)

63rd Brigade : Brigadier-General E. R. Hill
8th Lincolns   4th Middlesex
8th Somerset Light Infantry   10th York & Lancasters
111th Brigade : Brigadier-General R. W. R. Barnes
10th Royal Fusiliers   13th King's Royal Rifle Corps
13th Royal Fusiliers   13th Rifle Brigade
112th Brigade : Brigadier-General P. M. Robinson
11th Royal Warwickshires   8th East Lancashires
6th Bedfordshires   10th Loyal North Lancashires
  Pioneers : 9th North Staffordshires

38th (WELSH) DIVISION: Major-General I. Phillips to 9 July; Major-General H. E. Watts
- Battle of Albert 5 - 11 July (XV Corps, Fourth Army)
- Mametz Wood 7 - 11 July

113th Brigade : Brigadier-General L. A. E. Price-Davies, VC
14th Royal Welsh Fusiliers   16th Royal Welsh Fusiliers
13th (1st North Wales Pals) Royal Welsh Fusiliers
15th (1st London Welsh) Royal Welsh Fusiliers
114th Brigade : Brigadier-General T. O. Marden
10th (1st Rhondda Pals) Welsh
13th (2nd Rhondda Pals) Welsh
14th (Swansea Pals) Welsh
15th (Carmarthenshire Pals) Welsh
115th Brigade : Brigadier-General H. J. Evans
17th (2nd North Wales Pals) Royal Welsh Fusiliers
16th (1st Cardiff Pals) Welsh
10th (1st Gwent Pals) South Wales Borderers
11th (2nd Gwent Pals) South Wales Borderers
  Pioneers : 19th (Glamorgan Pioneers) Welsh

39th DIVISION : Major-General G. J. Cuthbert
- Fighting on the Ancre 3 Sept (V Corps, Reserve Army)
- Battle of Thiepval Ridge 26 - 28 Sept (V Corps, Reserve Army)
- Battle of the Ancre Heights 5 Oct - 11 Nov (II Corps, Reserve Army to 30 Oct then Fifth Army)
- Capture of the Schwaben Redoubt 14 Oct
- Capture of Stuff Trench 21 Oct
- Battle of the Ancre 13 - 14 Nov (II Corps, Fifth Army)

116th Brigade : Brigadier-General M. L. Hornby
11th (1st South Down) Royal Sussex
12th (2nd South Down) Royal Sussex
13th (3rd South Down) Royal Sussex
14th (1st Portsmouth Pals) Hampshires
117th Brigade : Brigadier-General R. D. F. Oldman
16th (Chatsworth Rifles) Sherwood Foresters
17th (Welbeck Rangers) Sherwood Foresters
17th (British Empire League) King's Royal Rifle Corps
16th (St Pancras) Rifle Brigade
118th Brigade : Brigadier-General E. H. Finch-Hatton
1/6th Cheshires   1/1st Cambridgeshires
4th/5th Black Watch   1/1st Hertfordshires
  Pioneers : 13th (Forest of Dean) Gloucesters

40th DIVISION : Major-General H. G. Ruggles-Brice
- Battle of the Ancre 14 - 18 Nov (120th Brigade under 41st Division; XIII Corps, Fifth Army)

120th Brigade : Brigadier-General C. S. Heathcote-Drummond-Willoughby
11th King's Own   14th Highland Light Infantry
13th (Wansdworth) East Surreys
14th Argyll & Sutherland Highlanders

41st DIVISION : Major-General S. T. B. Lawford
- Battle of Flers-Courcelette 15 - 17 Sept (XV Corps, Fourth Army)
- Battle of the Transloy Ridges 4 - 10 Oct (XV Corps, Fourth Army)

122nd Brigade : Brigadier-General F. W. Towsey
12th (Bermondsey) East Surreys
11th (Lewisham) Royal West Kents
15th (2nd Portsmouth Pals) Hampshires
18th (Arts & Crafts) King's Royal Rifle Corps
123rd Brigade : Brigadier-General C. S. Davidson to 23 Sept; Brigadier-General C. W. E. Gordon
11th (Lambeth) Queen's
23rd (2nd Football Pals) Middlesex
10th (Kent County) Royal West Kents
20th (Wearside Pals) Durham Light Infantry
124th Brigade : Brigadier-General W. F. Clemson
10th (Battersea) Queen's
32nd (East Ham) Royal Fusiliers
26th (Bankers) Royal Fusiliers
21st (Yeoman Rifles) King's Royal Rifle Corps
  Pioneers : 19th (2nd Public Works Pioneers) Middlesex

46th (NORTH MIDLAND) DIVISION : Major-General Hon E. J. Montagu-Stuart-Wortley
- Gommecourt 1 July (VIII Corps, Third Army)

137th Brigade : Brigadier-General H. B. Williams
1/5th South Staffordshires   1/6th South Staffordshires
1/5th North Staffordshires   1/6th North Staffordshires
138th Brigade : Brigadier-General G. C. Kemp
1/4th Lincolns   1/5th Lincolns
1/4th Leicesters   1/5th Leicesters
139th Brigade : Brigadier-General C. T. Shipley
1/5th Sherwood Foresters   1/6th Sherwood Foresters
1/7th (Robin Hood) Sherwood Foresters
1/8th Sherwood Foresters
         Pioneers : 1/1st Monmouths

47th (1/2nd LONDON) DIVISION : Major-General C. St. L. Barter to 28 Sept; Brigadier-General W. H. Greenly temporary to 2 Oct; Major-General Sir G. F. Gorridge
- Battle of Flers-Courcelette 15 - 19 Sept (III Corps, Fourth Army)
- Capture of High Wood 15 Sept
- Battle of the Transloy Ridges 1 - 9 Oct (III Corps, Fourth Army)
- Capture of Eaucourt l'Abbaye 1 - 3 Oct
- Attacks on the Butte de Warlencourt 7 - 8 Oct

140th Brigade : Brigadier-General Viscount Hampden
1/6th (Rifles) Londons   1/7th Londons
1/8th (Post Office Rifles) Londons
1/15th (Prince of Wales' Own Civil Service Rifles) Londons
141st Brigade : Brigadier-General R. McDouall
1/17th (Poplar & Stepney Rifles) Londons
1/18th (London Irish Rifles) Londons
1/19th (St Pancras) Londons
1/20th (Blackheath & Woolwich) Londons
142nd Brigade : Brigadier-General F. G. Lewis
1/21st (First Surrey Rifles) Londons
1/22nd (The Queen's) Londons
1/23rd Londons
1/24th (The Queen's) Londons
         Pioneers : 1/4th (Denbighshire) Royal Welsh Fusiliers

48th (SOUTH MIDLAND) DIVISION : Major-General R. Fanshawe
- Battle of Albert 1 July (VIII Corps, Fourth Army)
- Battle of Bazentin Ridge 15 - 17 July (X Corps, Reserve Army)
- Capture of Ovillers 17 July
- Battle of Pozieres Ridge 23 - 27 July & 13 - 28 Aug (X Corps until 24 July, then II Corps, Reserve Army)
- Battle of the Ancre Heights 3 - 11 Nov (III Corps, Fourth Army)
- Battle of the Ancre 13 - 18 Nov (III Corps, Fourth Army)

143rd Brigade : Brigadier-General B. C. Dent to 2 Sept; Brigadier-General G. C. Sladen
1/5th Royal Warwickshires   1/6th Royal Warwickshires
1/7th Royal Warwickshires   1/8th Royal Warwickshires
144th Brigade : Brigadier-General G. H. Nicholson
1/4th (City of Bristol) Gloucesters
1/6th Gloucesters   1/7th Worcesters
1/8th Worcesters
145th Brigade : Brigadier-General H. R. Done
1/5th Gloucesters   1/4th Royal Berkshires
1/4th Oxford & Bucks Light Infantry
1st Bucks Battalion, Oxford & Bucks Light Infantry
         Pioneers : 1/5th (Cinque Ports) Royal Sussex

49th (WEST RIDING) DIVISION : Major-General E. M. Perceval
- Battle of Albert 1 - 3 July (X Corps, Fourth Army)
- Battle of Bazentin Ridge 14 - 17 July (X Corps, Reserve Army)
- Battle of Pozieres Ridge 23 July - 18 Aug & 27 Aug - 3 Sept (X Cps, until 24 July then II Cps, Reserve Army)
- Battle of Flers-Courcelette 15 - 22 Sept (II Corps, Reserve Army)

146th Brigade : Brigadier-General M. D. Goring-Jones
1/5th West Yorkshires   1/6th West Yorkshires
1/7th (Leeds Rifles) West Yorkshires
1/8th (Leeds Rifles) West Yorkshires
147th Brigade : Brigadier-General E. F. Brereton to 13 Oct; Brigadier-General C. G. Lewes
1/4th Duke of Wellington's   1/5th Duke of Wellington's
1/6th Duke of Wellington's   1/7th Duke of Wellington's
148th Brigade : Brigadier-General R. L. Adlercron
1/4th King's Own Yorkshire Light Infantry
1/5th King's Own Yorkshire Light Infantry
1/4th (Hallamshire) York & Lancasters
1/5th York & Lancasters
         Pioneers : 19th (3rd Salford Pals) Lancashire Fusiliers

50th (NORTHUMBRIAN) DIVISION : Major-General P. S. Wilkinson
- Battle of Flers-Courcelette 15 - 22 Sept (III Corps, Fourth Army)
- Battle of Morval 25 - 28 Sept (III Corps, Fourth Army)
- Battle of the Transloy Ridges 1 - 3 Oct (III Corps, Fourth Army)

149th Brigade : Brigadier-General R. M. Ovens
1/4th Northumberland Fusiliers
1/5th Northumberland Fusiliers
1/6th Northumberland Fusiliers
1/7th Northumberland Fusiliers
150th Brigade : Brigadier-General B. G. Price
1/4th East Yorkshires   1/4th Yorkshires
1/5th Durham Light Infantry   1/5th Yorkshires
151st Brigade : Brigadier-General N. J. G. Cameron
1/5th (Cumberland) Border   1/8th Durham Light Infantry
1/6th Durham Light Infantry   1/9th Durham Light Infantry
         Pioneers : 1/7th Durham Light Infantry

51st (HIGHLAND) DIVISION : Major-General G. M. Harper
- Battles of the Somme 21 July - 7 Aug & 4 Oct - 24 Nov
- Attacks on High Wood 21 - 30 July (XV Corps, Fourth Army)
- Battle of the Ancre 13 - 18 Nov (V Corps, Fifth Army)
- Capture of Beaumont Hamel 13 Nov

152nd Brigade : Brigadier-General H. P. Burn
1/5th (Sutherland & Caithness) Seaforth Highlanders
1/6th (Morayshire) Seaforth Highlanders
1/6th (Banff and Donside) Gordon Highlanders
1/8th (The Argyllshire) Argyll & Sutherland Highlanders
153rd Brigade : Brigadier-General D. Campbell
1/6th (Perthshire) Black Watch
1/7th (Fife) Black Watch
1/5th (Buchan and Formartin) Gordon Highlanders
1/7th (Deeside Highland) Gordon Highlanders
154th Brigade : Brigadier-General C. E. Stewart to 14 Sept (killed); Lieutenant-Colonel H. G. Hyslop acting to 17 Sept; Brigadier-General J. G. H. Hamilton
1/9th (Highlanders) Royal Scots
1/4th Gordon Highlanders
1/4th (Ross Highland) Seaforth Highlanders
1/7th Argyll & Sutherland Highlanders
         Pioneers : 1/8th Royal Scots

55th (WEST LANCASHIRE) DIVISION : Major-General H. S. Jeudwine
- Battle of Guillemont 4 - 6 Sept (XV Corps, Fourth Army)
- Battle of Ginchy 9 Sept (XV Corps, Fourth Army)
- Battle of Flers-Courcelette 17 - 22 Sept (XV Corps, Fourth Army)
- Battle of Morval 25 - 28 Sept (XV Corps, Fourth Army)

164th Brigade : Brigadier-General G. T. G. Edwards to 16 Sept (leave); Brigadier-General C. I Stockwell
1/4th King's Own	2/5th Lancashire Fusiliers
1/8th (Irish) King's Liverpool	1/4th Loyal North Lancashires

165th Brigade : Brigadier-General F. J. Duncan
1/5th King's Liverpool	1/6th King's Liverpool (Rifles)
1/7th King's Liverpool	1/9th King's Liverpool

166th Brigade : Brigadier-General Green-Wilkinson
1/5th King's Own	1/5th South Lancashires
1/10th (Scottish) King's Liverpool	
1/5th Loyal North Lancashires	

Pioneers : 1/4th South Lancashires

56th (1st LONDON) DIVISION : Major-General C. P. A. Hull
- Gommecourt 1 July (VIII Corps, Third Army)
- Battle of Ginchy 9 Sept (XIV Corps, Fourth Army)
- Battle of Flers-Courcelette 15 - 22 Sept (XIV Corps, Fourth Army)
- Battle of Morval 25 - 27 Sept (XIV Corps, Fourth Army)
- Capture of Combles 26 Sept
- Battle of the Transloy Ridges 1 - 9 Oct (XIV Corps, Fourth Army)

167th Brigade : Brigadier-General F. H. Nugent to 22 July (sick); Lieutenant-Colonel E. J. King acting to 27 July; Brigadier-General G. H. B. Freeth
1/7th Middlesex	1/8th Middlesex
1/1st (Royal Fusiliers) Londons	
1/3rd (Royal Fusiliers) London	

168th Brigade : Brigadier-General G. G. Loch
1/4th (Royal Fusiliers) Londons
1/12th (The Rangers) Londons
1/13th (Kensington) Londons
1/14th (London Scottish) Londons

169th Brigade : Brigadier-General E. S. de E. Coke
1/2nd (Royal Fusiliers) Londons
1/5th (London Rifle Brigade) Londons
1/9th (Queen Victoria's Rifles) Londons
1/16th (Queen's Westminster Rifles) Londons

Pioneers : 1/5th (Earl of Chester's) Cheshires

63rd (ROYAL NAVAL) DIVISION : Major-General C. D. Shute
- Battle of the Ancre 13 - 15 Nov (V Corps, Fifth Army)

188th Brigade : Brigadier-General R. E. S. Prentice
Howe	Anson
1st Royal Marines Light Infantry	
2nd Royal Marines Light Infantry	

189th Brigade : Brigadier-General L. F. Philips
Drake	Nelson
Hawke	Hood

190th Brigade : Brigadier-General W. C. G. Heneker
7th Royal Fusiliers	4th Bedfordshires
10th Royal Dublin Fusiliers	
1/1st Honourable Artillery Company	

Pioneers : 14th (Severn Valley Pioneers) Worcesters

2nd INDIAN CAVALRY DIVISION : Major-General H J M MacAndrew
- Battle of Bazentin 14-17 July (Fourth Army)
- Battle of Flers-Courcelette 15-22 Sept (Fourth Army)

3rd (Ambala) Cavalry Brigade : Brigadier-General C H Rankin
8th Hussars	9th Hodgson's Horse
18th (King George's Own) Lancers	

9th (Secunderabad) Cavalry Brigade : Brigadier-General C L Gregory
7th (Princess Royal's) Dragoon Guards
20th Deccan Horse
34th (Prince Albert Victor's Own) Poona Horse

Canadian Cavalry Brigade (attached to 2nd Indian Cavalry Division) Brigadier-General J E B Seely
Royal Canadian Dragoons	Fort Garry Horse
Lord Strathcona's Horse	

1st CANADIAN DIVISION : Major General A.W. Currie
- Battle of Flers-Courcelette 15-22 Sept (Canadian Corps, Reserve Army)
- Battle of Thiepval 26-28 Sept (Canadian Corps, Reserve Army)
- Battle of Le Transloy 1-18 Oct (Canadian Corps, Reserve Army)
- Battle of the Ancre Heights 1 Oct – 11 Nov (Canadian Corps, Reserve Army)

1st Brigade : Brigadier-General G B Hughes
1st Battalion (Ontario)	2nd Battalion (East Ontario)
3rd Battalion (Toronto)	4th Battalion

2nd Brigade : Brigadier-General F O W Loomis
5th Battalion (Western Cavalry)
7th Battalion (1st British Columbia)
8th Battalion (90th Rifles)
10th Battalion

3rd Brigade : Brigadier-General G S Tuxford
13th Battalion (Royal Highlanders)
14th Battalion (Royal Montreal)
15th Battalion (48th Highlanders)
16th Battalion (Canadian Scottish)

Pioneers : 1st Canadian Pioneer Battalion

2nd CANADIAN DIVISION : Major General R.E.W. Turner
- Battle of Flers-Courcelette 15-22 Sept (Canadian Corps, Reserve Army)
- Battle of Thiepval 26-28 Sept (Canadian Corps, Reserve Army)
- Battle of Le Transloy 1-18 Oct (Canadian Corps, Reserve Army)
- Battle of the Ancre Heights 1 Oct – 11 Nov (Canadian Corps, Reserve Army)

4th Brigade : Brigadier General R Rennie
18th (West Ontario) Battalion
19th (Central Ontario) Battalion
20th (Central Ontario) Battalion
21st (Eastern Ontario) Battalion

5th Brigade : Brigadier-General A H MacDonnell
22nd (Canadien-Français) Battalion
24th (Victoria Rifles) Battalion
25th (Nova Scotia Rifles) Battalion
26th (New Brunswick) Battalion

6th Brigade : Brigadier-General H D B Ketchen
27th (City of Winnipeg) Battalion
28th (North West) Battalion
29th (Vancouver) Battalion	31st (Alberta) Battalion

Pioneers : 2nd Canadian Pioneer Battalion

3rd CANADIAN DIVISION : Major-General L J Lipsett
- Battle of Flers-Courcelette 15-22 Sept (Canadian Corps, Reserve Army)
- Battle of Thiepval 26-28 Sept (Canadian Corps, Reserve Army)
- Battle of Le Transloy 1-18 Oct (Canadian Corps, Reserve Army)
- Battle of the Ancre Heights 1 Oct – 11 Nov (Canadian Corps, Reserve Army)

7th Brigade : Brigadier-General A C MacDonnell
Princess Patricia's Canadian Light Infantry
42nd (Royal Highlanders) Battalion
Royal Canadian Regiment   49th (Edmonton) Battalion
8th Brigade : Brigadier-General J H Elmsley
1st Battalion, Canadian Mounted Rifles
2nd Battalion, Canadian Mounted Rifles
4th Battalion, Canadian Mounted Rifles
5th Battalion, Canadian Mounted Rifles
9th Brigade : Brigadier-General F W Hill
43rd (Cameron Highlanders) Battalion
52nd (North Ontario) Battalion
58th (Central Ontario) Battalion
60th (Victoria Rifles) Battalion
    Pioneers : 3rd Canadian Pioneer Battalion

4th CANADIAN DIVISION : Major-General D Watson
- Battle of Le Transloy 1-18 Oct (Canadian Corps, Reserve Army)
- Battle of the Ancre Heights 1 Oct – 11 Nov (II Corps, Reserve Army)
- Battle of the Ancre 13-18 Nov (II Corps, Reserve Army)

10th Brigade : Brigadier-General W St. P Hughes
44th Battalion
46th (South Saskatchewan) Battalion
47th (British Columbia) Battalion
50th (Calgary) Battalion
11th Brigade : Brigadier-General V W Odlum
54th (Kootenay) Battalion
75th (Mississauga) Battalion
87th (Canadian Grenadier Guards) Battalion
102nd Battalion
12th Brigade : Brigadier-General J H MacBrien
38th (Ottawa) Battalion
72nd (Seaforth Highlanders) Battalion
73rd (Royal Highlanders) Battalion
78th (Winnipeg Grenadiers) Battalion
    Pioneers : 67th Canadian Pioneer Battalion

NEW ZEALAND DIVISION : Major-General A. H. Russell
- Battle of Flers-Courcelette 15-22 Sept (XV Corps, Fourth Army)
- Battle of Morval 25-28 Sept (XV Corps, Fourth Army)
- Battle of Le Transloy 1-18 Oct (XV Corps, Fourth Army)

1st New Zealand Brigade : Brigadier-General F E Johnston
1st Auckland Battalion   1st Otago Battalion
1st Canterbury Battalion   1st Wellington Battalion
2nd New Zealand Brigade : Brigadier-General W G Braithwaite
2nd Auckland Battalion   2nd Otago Battalion
2nd Canterbury Battalion   2nd Wellington Battalion
3rd New Zealand (Rifles) Brigade : Brigadier-General H T Fulton
1s, NZ Rifle Brigade   2nd NZ Rifle Brigade
3rd NZ Rifle Brigade   4th NZ Rifle Brigade
    Pioneers : New Zealand Pioneer Battalion

1st AUSTRALIAN DIVISION : Major General H. Walker
- Battle of Pozieres 23 July – 3 Sept (I ANZAC Corps, Reserve Army)
- Fighting for Mouquet Farm

1st (New South Wales) Brigade : Brigadier-General N M Smythe
1st Battalion   2nd Battalion
3rd Battalion   4th Battalion
2nd (Victoria) Brigade : Brigadier-General J K Forsythe to 19 Oct; Brigadier-General J M Antill
5th Battalion   6th Battalion
7th Battalion   8th Battalion
3rd Brigade : Brigadier-General E G Sinclair-MacLagan
9th (Queensland) Battalion
10th (South Australia) Battalion
11th (West Australia) Battalion
12th (Tasmania, S and W Australia) Battalion
    Pioneers : 1st Australian Pioneer Battalion

2nd AUSTRALIAN DIVISION : Major General J.G. Legge
- Battle of Pozieres 23 July – 3 Sept (I ANZAC Corps, Reserve Army)
- Fighting for Mouquet Farm

5th (New South Wales) Brigade : Brigadier-General W Holmes
17th Battalion   18th Battalion
19th Battalion   20th Battalion
6th (Victoria) Brigade : Brigadier-General J Gellibrand
21st Battalion   22nd Battalion
23rd Battalion   24th Battalion
7th Brigade : Brigadier-General J Paton
25th (Queensland) Battalion
26th (Queensland & Tasmania) Battalion
27th (South Australia) Battalion
28th (West Australia) Battalion
    Pioneers : 2nd Australian Pioneer Battalion

4th AUSTRALIAN DIVISION : Major General Sir H. Cox
- Battle of Pozieres 23 July – 3 Sept (I ANZAC Corps, Reserve Army)
- Fighting for Mouquet Farm

4th Brigade : Brigadier-General J Monash to 10 August; Brigadier-General C H Brand
13th (New South Wales) Battalion
14th (Victoria) Battalion
15th (Queensland & Tasmania) Battalion
16th (South & West Australia) Battalion
12th Brigade : Brigadier-General D J Glasfurd
45th (New South Wales) Battalion
46th (Victoria) Battalion
47th (Queensland & Tasmania) Battalion
48th (South & West Australia) Battalion
13th Brigade : Brigadier-General T W Glasgow
49th (Queensland) Battalion
50th (South Australia & Tasmania) Battalion
51st (West Australia) Battalion
52nd (West & South Australia, Tasmania) Battalion
    Pioneers : 4th Australian Pioneer Battalion

RETREAT TO THE HINDENBURG LINE

GUARDS DIVISION : Major-General G. P. T. Feilding
- German Retreat to the Hindenburg Line 14 - 24 March (XIV Corps, Fourth Army)

1st Guards Brigade : Brigadier-General G D Jeffreys
2nd Grenadier Guards 3rd Coldstream Guards
2nd Coldstream Guards 1st Irish Guards

2nd Guards Brigade : Brigadier-General Lord H. C. Seymour to 21 March; Brigadier-General J. Ponsonby
3rd Grenadier Guards 1st Scots Guards
1st Coldstream Guards 2nd Irish Guards

3rd Guards Brigade : Brigadier-General C. E. Corkran to 21 March; Brigadier-General Lord H. C. Seymour
1st Grenadier Guards 2nd Scots Guards
4th Grenadier Guards 1st Welsh Guards
Pioneers : 4th Coldstream Guards

1st DIVISION : Major-General E. P. Strickland
- German Retreat to the Hindenburg Line 14 - 21 March (III Corps, Fourth Army)

1st Brigade : Brigadier-General A. J. Reddie
1st Black Watch 10th Gloucesters
1st Cameron Highlanders 8th Royal Berkshires

2nd Brigade : Brigadier-General A. B. Hubback
2nd Royal Sussex 1st Northamptonshires
1st Loyal North Lancashires 2nd King's Royal Rifle Corps

3rd Brigade : Brigadier-General R. C. A. McCalmont to 15 March; Brigadier-General J. L. Clarke to 21 March; Brigadier-General R. C. A. McCalmont
1st South Wales Borderers 2nd Welsh
1st Gloucesters 2nd Royal Munster Fusiliers
Pioneers : 1/6th Welsh

2nd DIVISION : Major-General C. E. Pereira
- Operations on the Ancre 11 Jan - 13 March (II Corps, Fifth Army)
- Actions at Miraumont 17 - 18 February
- Capture of Thilloys 25 Feb - 2 March
- Capture of Grevillers Trench (near Irles) 10 March
- German Retreat to the Hindenburg Line 14 - 19 March (II Corps, Fifth Army)

5th Brigade : Brigadier-General W. Bullen-Smith
17th (Empire) Royal Fusiliers 2nd Highland Light Infantry
2nd Oxford & Bucks Light Infantry
24th (2nd Sportsmens) Royal Fusiliers

6th Brigade : Brigadier-General A. C. Daly to 21 January; Brigadier-General R. K. Walsh
1st King's Liverpool 13th (West Ham Pals) Essex
2nd South Staffordshires
17th (1st Football Pals) Middlesex

99th Brigade : Brigadier-General R. O. Kellett
1st Royal Berkshires 1st King's Royal Rifle Corps
22nd (Kensington) Royal Fusiliers
23rd (1st Sportsmens) Royal Fusiliers
Pioneers : 10th (Cornwall Pioneers) Duke of Cornwall's Light Infantry

7th DIVISION : Major-General G. de S. Barrow to 1 April; Major-General T. H. Shoubridge
- Operations on the Ancre 11 - 15 Jan & 21 Feb - 5 March (V Corps, Fifth Army
- German Retreat to the Hindenburg Line 14 March - 5 April (V Corps, Fifth Army)
- Battle of Bullecourt 3 - 16 May (V Corps, Fifth Army)

20th Brigade : Brigadier-General H. C. R. Green
2nd Border 8th Devonshires
2nd Gordon Highlanders 9th Devonshires

22nd Brigade : Brigadier-General J. McC. Steele
2nd Royal Warwickshires 1st Royal Welsh Fusiliers
2/1st Honourable Artillery Company
20th (5th Manchester Pals) Manchesters

91st Brigade : Brigadier-General H. R. Cumming to 12 May; Colonel W. W. Norman acting to 16 May; Brigadier-General R. T. Pelly
2nd Queen's 1st South Staffordshires
21st (6th Manchester Pals) Manchesters
22nd (7th Manchester Pals) Manchesters
Pioneers : 24th (Oldham Pals) Manchesters

8th DIVISION : Major-General W. C. G. Heneker
- Bouchavesenes 4 March (XV Corps, Fourth Army)
- German Retreat to the Hindenburg Line 14 March - 5 April (XV Corps, Fourth Army)

23rd Brigade : Lieutenant Colonel J. Hamilton-Hall acting to 12 March; Brigadier General G. W. St. G. Grogan
2nd Devonshires 2nd Cameronians
2nd West Yorkshires 2nd Middlesex

24th Brigade : Brigadier General H. W. Cobham
1st Worcesters 1st Sherwood Foresters
2nd East Lancashires 2nd Northamptonshires

25th Brigade : Brigadier-General C. Coffin
2nd Lincolns 1st Royal Irish Rifles
2nd Royal Berkshires 2nd Rifle Brigade
Pioneers : 22nd (3rd Durham Pals) Durham Light Infantry (from 2 July)

11th (NORTHERN) DIVISION : Lieutenant-General A. B. Ritchie
- Operations on the Ancre 11 - 19 Jan (IV Corps, Fifth Army)

32nd Brigade : Brigadier-General T. H. F. Price
9th West Yorkshires 8th Duke of Wellington's
6th Yorkshires 6th York & Lancasters

33rd Brigade : Brigadier-General J. F. Erskine
6th Lincolns 7th South Staffordshires
6th Border 9th Sherwood Foresters

34th Brigade : Brigadier-General J. Hill
8th Northumberland Fusiliers 5th Dorsets
9th Lancashire Fusiliers 11th Manchesters
Pioneers : 6th East Yorkshires

14th (LIGHT) DIVISION : Major-General V. A. Couper
- German Retreat to the Hindenburg Line 14 March - 5 April (VII Corps, Third Army)

41st Brigade : Brigadier-General P. C. B. Skinner
7th King's Royal Rifle Corps   7th Rifle Brigade
8th King's Royal Rifle Corps   8th Rifle Brigade
42nd Brigade : Brigadier-General F. A. Dudgeon
9th King's Royal Rifle Corps   9th Rifle Brigade
5th Oxford & Bucks Light Infantry
5th King's Shropshire Light Infantry
43rd Brigade : Brigadier-General : P. R. Wood
6th Somerset Light Infantry   10th Durham Light Infantry
6th King's Own Yorkshire Light Infantry
6th Duke of Cornwall's Light Infantry
         Pioneers : 11th King's Liverpool

18th (EASTERN) DIVISION : Major-General R. P. Lee
- Operations on the Ancre 16 Jan - 13 March (II Corps, Fifth Army)
- Miraumont 17 - 18 Feb
- Capture of Irles 10 March (53rd Brigade)
- German Retreat to the Hindenburg Line 14 - 20 March (II Corps, Fifth Army)

53rd Brigade : Brigadier-General H. W. Higginson
8th Norfolks   10th Essex
8th Suffolks   6th Royal Berkshires
54th Brigade : Brigadier-General T. H. Shoubridge
11th Royal Fusiliers   6th Northamptonshires
7th Bedfords   12th Middlesex
55th Brigade : Brigadier-General G. D. Price
7th Queen's   8th East Surreys
7th Buffs   7th Royal West Kents
         Pioneers : 8th Royal Sussex

20th (LIGHT) DIVISION : Major-General W. Douglas Smith to 19 March; Maj-Gen T. G. Matheson
- German Retreat to the Hindenburg Line 14 March - 5 April (XIV Corps, to 2 pm on 25 March then XV Corps, Fourth Army)

59th Brigade : Brigadier-General Browne-Clayton
10th King's Royal Rifle Corps   10th Rifle Brigade
11th King's Royal Rifle Corps   11th Rifle Brigade
60th Brigade : Brigadier-General Hon L. J. P. Butler
12th King's Royal Rifle Corps   12th Rifle Brigade
6th King's Shropshire Light Infantry
6th Oxford & Bucks Light Infantry
61st Brigade : Brigadier-General W. E. Banbury
12th King's Liverpool   7th Somerset Light Infantry
7th Duke of Cornwall's Light Infantry
7th King's Own Yorkshire Light Infantry
         Pioneers : 11th Durham Light Infantry

21st DIVISION : Major-General D. G. M. Campbell
- German Retreat to the Hindenburg Line 29 March - 5 April (VII Corps, Third Army)

62nd Brigade : Brigadier-General C. G. Rawling
12th Northumberland Fusiliers   1st Lincolns
13th Northumberland Fusiliers   10th Yorkshires
64th Brigade : Brigadier-General H. R. Headlam
1st East Yorkshires   15th Durham Light Infantry
9th King's Own Yorkshire Light Infantry
10th King's Own Yorkshire Light Infantry
110th Brigade : Brigadier-General W. F. Hessey
6th Leicesters   7th Leicesters
8th Leicesters   9th Leicesters
         Pioneers : 14th Northumberland Fusiliers

29th DIVISION : Major-General H. de B. de Lisle
- Le Transloy 27 Jan (87th Brigade) (XIV Corps, Fourth Army)
- Saillisel 28 Feb (86th Brigade) (XIV Corps, Fourth Army)

86th Brigade : Brigadier-General W. de L. Williams
2nd Royal Fusiliers   1st Lancashire Fusiliers
16th (Public Schools) Middlesex
1st Royal Dublin Fusiliers
87th Brigade : Brigadier-General R. N. Bray to 14 Feb (invalided); Lieutenant Colonel A. J. Welch (acting)
2nd South Wales Borderers   1st Border
1st Royal Inniskilling Fusiliers
1st King's Own Scottish Borderers
         Pioneers : 1/2nd Monmouthshires

30th DIVISION : Major-General J. S. M. Shea
- German Retreat to the Hindenburg Line 14 March - 5 April (VII Corps, Third Army)

21st Brigade : Brigadier-General J. Ponsonby to 17 March (sick); Lieutenant Colonel R. M. T. Gillson acting to 20 March; Brigadier-General D. Goodman
2nd Wiltshires   2nd Yorkshires
18th (2nd Liverpool Pals) King's Liverpool
19th (4th Manchester Pals) Manchesters
89th Brigade : Brigadier-General Hon F. C. Stanley
17th (1st Liverpool Pals) King's Liverpool
19th (3rd Liverpool Pals) King's Liverpool
20th (4th Liverpool Pals) King's Liverpool
2nd Bedfordshires
90th Brigade : Brigadier-General J. H. LLoyd
2nd Royal Scots Fusiliers
16th (1st Manchester Pals) Manchesters
17th (2nd Manchester Pals) Manchesters
18th (3rd Manchester Pals – Clerks & Warehousemen) Manchesters
         Pioneers : 11th (St Helens Pioneers) South Lancashires

31st DIVISION : Major-General R. Wanless O'Gowan
- Operations on the Ancre 22 Feb - 12 March (V Corps, Fifth Army)

92nd Brigade : Brigadier-General O. de. L. Williams
10th (Hull Commercials) East Yorkshires
11th (Hull Tradesmen) East Yorkshires
12th (Hull Sportsmen) East Yorkshires
13th (Hull T'Others) East Yorkshires
93rd Brigade : Brigadier-General J. D. Ingles
15th (1st Leeds Pals) West Yorkshires
16th (1st Bradford Pals) West Yorkshires
18th (2nd Bradford Pals) West Yorkshires
18th (1st Durham Pals) Durham Light Infantry
94th Brigade : Brigadier-General G. T. C. Carter-Campbell
11th (Accrington Pals) East Lancashires
12th (Sheffield City Battalion) York & Lancasters
13th (1st Barnsley Pals) York & Lancasters
14th (2nd Barnsley Pals) York & Lancasters
         Pioneers : 12th (Miners) King's Own Yorkshire Light Infantry

32nd DIVISION : Brigadier-General J. A. Tyler acting to 16 Jan; Major-General R. W. R. Barnes to 29 Jan (sick); Brigadier-General J. A. Tyler acting to 18 Feb; Major-General C. D. Shute
- Operations on the Ancre 11 Jan - 15 Feb (V Corps, Fifth Army)
- German Retreat to the Hindenburg Line 14 March - 5 April (IV Corps, Fourth Army)

14th Brigade : Brigadier-General W. W. Seymour
5th/6th Royal Scots   2nd Manchesters
1st Dorsets
15th (1st Glasgow Pals – Glasgow Tramways) Highland Light Infantry

96th Brigade : Brigadier-General L. F. Ashburner
16th (Newcastle Commercials) Northumberland Fusiliers
2nd Royal Inniskilling Fusiliers
15th (1st Salford Pals) Lancashire Fusiliers
16th (2nd Salford Pals) Lancashire Fusiliers

97th Brigade : Brigadier-General J. B. Jardine to 21 Feb (sick); Lieutenant Colonel C. R. I. Brooke acting to 8 March; Brigadier-General C. A. Blacklock
11th (Lonsdale) Border
2nd King's Own Yorkshire Light Infantry
16th (2nd Glasgow Pals – Glasgow Boys Brigade) Highland Light Infantry
17th (3rd Glasgow Pals) Highland Light Infantry
      Pioneers : 17th (North Eastern Railway Pioneers) Northumberland Fusiliers

35th DIVISION : Major-General H. J. S. Landon
- German Retreat to the Hindenburg Line 14 - 18 March (IV Corps, Fourth Army)

104th Brigade : Brigadier-General J. W. Sandilands
17th (1st South East Lancashire Pals) Lancashire Fusiliers
18th (2nd South East Lancashire Pals) Lancashire Fusiliers
20th (4th Salford Pals) Lancashire Fusiliers
23rd (8th Manchester Pals) Manchesters

105th Brigade : Brigadier-General A. H. Marindin
15th (1st Birkenhead Pals) Cheshires
16th (2nd Birkenhead Pals) Cheshires
14th (West of England) Gloucesters
15th (Nottingham Pals) Sherwood Foresters

106th Brigade : Brigadier-General H. O'Donnell
17th (Rosebery) Royal Scots
19th (2nd Durham Pals) Durham Light Infantry
17th (2nd Leeds Pals) West Yorkshires
18th (4th Glasgow Pals) Highland Light Infantry
      Pioneers : 19th (2nd Tyneside Pioneers) Northumberland Fusiliers

40th DIVISION : Major-General H. G. Ruggles-Brice
- German Retreat to the Hindenburg Line 14 - 25 March (XV Corps, Fourth Army)
- Capture of Fifteen Ravine, Villers-Plouich, Beaucamp and La Vacquerie 21, 24, 25 March & 5 May (XV Corps, Fourth Army)

119th Brigade : Brigadier-General F. P. Crozier
19th Royal Welsh Fusiliers
12th (3rd Gwent Pals) South Wales Borderers
17th (1st Glamorgan Pals) Welsh
18th (2nd Glamorgan Pals) Welsh

120th Brigade : Brigadier-General C. S. Heathcote-Drummond-Willoughby
11th King's Own   14th Highland Light Infantry
13th (Wansdworth) East Surreys
14th Argyll & Sutherland Highlanders

121st Brigade : Brigadier-General J. Campbell
12th (East Anglian) Suffolks   20th (Shoreditch) Middlesex
13th Yorkshires   21st (Islington) Middlesex
      Pioneers : 12th (Teeside Pioneers) Yorkshires

46th (NORTH MIDLAND) DIVISION : Major-General W. Thwaites
- Operations on the Ancre 1 - 13 March (XVIII Corps, Third Army to 7 March then V Corps, Fifth Army)
- Occupation of Gommecourt Defences 4 March (XVIII Corps)
- Attack of Rettemoy Graben 12 March (V Corps)
- German Retreat to the Hindenburg Line 14 - 22 March (V Corps, Fifth Army)

137th Brigade : Brigadier-General J. V. Campbell, VC
1/5th South Staffordshires   1/6th South Staffordshires
1/5th North Staffordshires   1/6th North Staffordshires

138th Brigade : Brigadier-General G. C. Kemp
1/4th Lincolns   1/4th Leicesters
1/5th Lincolns   1/5th Leicesters

139th Brigade : Brigadier-General C. T. Shipley
1/5th Sherwood Foresters   1/6th Sherwood Foresters
1/7th (Robin Hood) Sherwood Foresters
1/8th Sherwood Foresters
      Pioneers : 1/1st Monmouths

48th (SOUTH MIDLAND) DIVISION : Major-General R. Fanshawe
- German Retreat to the Hindenburg Line 14 March - 5 April (III Corps, Fourth Army)
- Occupation of Peronne 18 March (III Corps)

143rd Brigade : Brigadier-General G. C. Sladen
1/5th Royal Warwickshires   1/6th Royal Warwickshires
1/7th Royal Warwickshires   1/8th Royal Warwickshires

144th Brigade : Brigadier-General H. R. Done
1/4th (City of Bristol) Gloucesters
1/6th Gloucesters   1/7th Worcesters
1/8th Worcesters

145th Brigade : Brigadier-General D. M. Watt
1/5th Gloucesters   1/4th Royal Berkshires
1/4th Oxford & Bucks Light Infantry
1st Bucks Battalion, Oxford & Bucks Light Infantry
      Pioneers : 1/5th (Cinque Ports) Royal Sussex

56th (1st LONDON) DIVISION : Major-General C. P. A. Hull
- German Retreat to the Hindenburg Line 14 March - 5 April (VII Corps, Third Army)

167th Brigade : Brigadier-General G. H. B. Freeth
1/7th Middlesex   1/1st (Royal Fusiliers) Londons
1/8th Middlesex   1/3rd (Royal Fusiliers) London
168th Brigade : Brigadier-General G. G. Loch
1/4th (Royal Fusiliers) Londons
1/12th (The Rangers) Londons   1/13th (Kensington) Londons
1/14th (London Scottish) Londons
169th Brigade : Brigadier-General E. S. de E. Coke
1/2nd (Royal Fusiliers) Londons
1/5th (London Rifle Brigade) Londons
1/9th (Queen Victoria's Rifles) Londons
1/16th (Queen's Westminster Rifles) Londons
       Pioneers : 1/5th (Earl of Chester's) Cheshires

58th (2nd/1st LONDON) DIVISION : Maj-Gen H. D. Fanshawe
- German Retreat to the Hindenburg Line 17 - 24 March (XVIII Corps, to 19 March then VII Corps, Third Army)
- Battle of Bullecourt 4 - 17 May (175th Brigade with 2nd Australian Division, I ANZAC Corps from 4 - 12 May; 173rd Brigade with 5th Australian Division, I ANZAC Corps, from 12 - 15 May; and with 58th Division with V Corps, Fifth Army from 16 May)

173rd Brigade : Brigadier-General G. P. S. Hunt to 20 April; Lieutenant Colonel P. W. Beresford acting to 21 April; Brigadier General B. C. Freyburg, VC
2/1st (Royal Fusiliers) Londons
2/2nd (Royal Fusiliers) Londons
2/3rd (Royal Fusiliers) Londons   2/4th (Royal Fusiliers) Londons
174th Brigade : Brigadier-General W. C. G. McGrigor to 21 April; Brigadier-General C. G. Higgins
2/5th (London Rifle Brigade) Londons
2/6th (Rifles) Londons   2/7th Londons
2/8th (Post Office Rifles) Londons
175th Brigade : Brig-Gen H. C. Jackson
2/9th (Queen Victoria's Rifles) Londons
2/10th (Hackney) Londons   2/12th (The Rangers) Londons
2/11th (Finsbury Rifles) Londons

59th (2nd NORTH MIDLAND) DIVISION : Major-General A. E. Sandbach
- German Retreat to the Hindenburg Line 17 March - 5 April (III Corps, Fourth Army)

176th Brigade : Brigadier-General C. V. Humphreys
2/5th South Staffordshires   2/6th South Staffordshires
2/5th North Staffordshires   2/6th North Staffordshires
177th Brigade : Brigadier-General C. H. L. James
2/4th Lincolns   2/4th Leicesters
2/5th Lincolns   2/5th Leicesters
178th Brigade : Brigadier-General E. W. S. K. Maconchy
2/5th Sherwood Foresters   2/6th Sherwood Foresters
2/7th (Robin Hood) Sherwood Foresters
2/8th Sherwood Foresters

61st (2nd SOUTH MIDLAND) DIVISION : Major-General C. J. Mackenzie
- Operations on the Ancre 11 - 15 Jan (IV Corps, Fifth Army)
- German Retreat to the Hindenburg Line 14 March - 5 April (IV Corps, Fourth Army)

182nd Brigade : Brigadier-General F. Burnell-Nugent to 19 Jan (sick); Brigadier-General C. A. Blacklock to 8 March; Lieutenant Colonel J. F. Clyne acting to 12 March; Brigadier-General Hon C. J. Sackville-West
2/5th Royal Warwickshires   2/6th Royal Warwickshires
2/7th Royal Warwickshires   2/8th Royal Warwickshires
183rd Brigade : Brigadier-General A. H. Spooner
2/7th Worcesters   2/8th Worcesters
2/4th (City of Bristol) Gloucesters
2/6th Gloucesters
184th Brigade : Brigadier-General Hon R. White
2/5th Gloucesters   2/4th Royal Berkshires
2/4th Oxford & Bucks Light Infantry
2/1st Bucks Battalion, Oxford & Bucks Light Infantry
       Pioneers : 1/5th Duke of Cornwall's Light Infantry

62nd (2nd WEST RIDING) DIVISION : Major-General W. P. Braithwaite
- Operations on the Ancre 15 Feb - 13 March (V Corps, Fifth Army)
- German Retreat to the Hindenburg Line 14 - 19 March (V Corps, Fifth Army)
- First Attack on Bullecourt 11 April (V Corps, Fifth Army)
- German Attack on Lagnicourt (186th Brigade) (V Corps, Fifth Army)
- Battle of Bullecourt 3 - 17 May (V Corps, Fifth Army)

185th Brigade : Brigadier-General V. Wade Falbe
2/5th West Yorkshires   2/6th West Yorkshires
2/7th (Leeds Rifles) West Yorkshires
2/8th (Leeds Rifles) West Yorkshires
186th Brigade : Brigadier-General F. F. Hill
2/4th Duke of Wellington's   2/5th Duke of Wellington's
2/6th Duke of Wellington's   2/7th Duke of Wellington's
187th Brigade : Brigadier-General R. O'B. Taylor
2/4th King's Own Yorkshire Light Infantry
2/5th King's Own Yorkshire Light Infantry
2/4th (Hallamshire) York & Lancasters
2/5th York & Lancasters

63rd (ROYAL NAVAL) DIVISION : Major-General C. D. Shute to 19 Feb; Major-General C. E. Lawrie
- Operations on the Ancre 20 Jan - 27 Feb (II Corps, Fifth Army)

188th Brigade : Brigadier-General R. E. S. Prentice
Howe   Anson
1st Royal Marines Light Infantry
2nd Royal Marines Light Infantry
189th Brigade : Brigadier-General L. F. Philips
Drake   Nelson
Hawke   Hood
190th Brigade : Brigadier-General H. W. E. Finch
7th Royal Fusiliers   4th Bedfordshires
10th Royal Dublin Fusiliers
1/1st Honourable Artillery Company
       Pioneers : 14th (Severn Valley Pioneers) Worcesters

1st AUSTRALIAN DIVISION : Major General H. Walker
- Operations on the Ancre 11 Jan – 13 March (I ANZAC Corps, Fifth Army)
- Capture of Thilloys 25 Feb – 2 March (I ANZAC Corps, Fifth Army)
- German Attack on Lagnicourt 15 April (I ANZAC Corps, Fifth Army)
- Battle of Bullecourt 3-17 May (I ANZAC Corps, Fifth Army)

1st (New South Wales) Brigade : Brigadier-General W R Lesslie
1st Battalion	2nd Battalion
3rd Battalion	4th Battalion

2nd (Victoria) Brigade : Brigadier-General J Heane
5th Battalion	6th Battalion
7th Battalion	8th Battalion

3rd Brigade : Brigadier-General H G Bennett
9th (Queensland) Battalion
10th (South Australia) Battalion
11th (West Australia) Battalion
12th (Tasmania, S and W Australia) Battalion
    Pioneers : 1st Australian Pioneer Battalion

4th AUSTRALIAN DIVISION : Major General W Holmes
    Operations on the Ancre 11 Jan – 13 March (I ANZAC Corps, Fifth Army)
    Advance to the Hindenburg Line (I ANZAC Corps, Fifth Army)
    First Battle of Bullecourt 11 April (I ANZAC Corps, Fifth Army)

4th Brigade : Brigadier-General C H Brand
13th (New South Wales) Battalion
14th (Victoria) Battalion
15th (Queensland & Tasmania) Battalion
16th (South & West Australia) Battalion

12th Brigade : Brigadier-General J C Robertson
45th (New South Wales) Battalion
46th (Victoria) Battalion
47th (Queensland & Tasmania) Battalion
48th (South & West Australia) Battalion

13th Brigade : Brigadier-General T W Glasgow
49th (Queensland) Battalion
50th (South Australia & Tasmania) Battalion
51st (West Australia) Battalion
52nd (West & South Australia, Tasmania) Battalion
    Pioneers : 4th Australian Pioneer Battalion

2nd AUSTRALIAN DIVISION : Major General N M Smythe; Brigadier General J Gellibrand (temporary in February); Major General N M Smythe from 4 March
- Operations on the Ancre 11 Jan – 13 March (I ANZAC Corps, Fifth Army)
- Capture of Thilloys 25 Feb – 2 March (I ANZAC Corps, Fifth Army)
- Capture of Irles (I ANZAC Corps, Fifth Army)
- Capture of Bapaume (I ANZAC Corps, Fifth Army)
- German Attack on Lagnicourt 15 April (I ANZAC Corps, Fifth Army)
- Battle of Bullecourt 3-17 May (I ANZAC Corps, Fifth Army)

5th (New South Wales) Brigade : Brigadier-General W Holmes to 9 January; Brigadier General R Smith (Lieutenant Colonel until 28 January)
17th Battalion	18th Battalion
19th Battalion	20th Battalion

6th (Victoria) Brigade : Brigadier-General J Gellibrand
21st Battalion	22nd Battalion
23rd Battalion	24th Battalion

7th Brigade : Brigadier-General E A Wisdom
25th (Queensland) Battalion
26th (Queensland & Tasmania) Battalion
27th (South Australia) Battalion
28th (West Australia) Battalion
    Pioneers : 2nd Australian Pioneer Battalion

5th AUSTRALIAN DIVISION : Major General J J T Hobbs
- Capture of Thilloys 25 Feb – 2 March (I ANZAC Corps, Fifth Army)
- Advance to the Hindenburg Line (I ANZAC Corps, Fifth Army)
- Battle of Bullecourt 3-17 May (I ANZAC Corps, Fifth Army)
- Action on the Hindenburg Line 2-26 May (I ANZAC Corps, Fifth Army)

8th Brigade : Brigadier-General E Tivey
29th (Victoria) Battalion
30th (New South Wales) Battalion
31st (Queensland & Victoria) Battalion
32nd (Western Australia & South Australia) Battalion

14th (New South Wales) Brigade : Brigadier-General C J Hobkirk
53rd Battalion
55th Battalion
54th Battalion
56th Battalion

15th (Victoria) Brigade : Brigadier-General H E Elliott
57th (New South Wales) Battalion
59th Battalion
58th Battalion
60th Battalion
    Pioneers : 5th Australian Pioneer Battalion

BATTLES OF THE SOMME 1918

1st CAVALRY DIVISION : Major-General R. L. Mullens
- Battle of St Quentin 21 - 23 March (XIX Corps, Fifth Army)
- First Battle of Bapaume 24 - 25 March (Dismounted Division under Brigadier-General Legard from 24 - 26 March with VIII Corps, Fifth Army)
- Battle of Rosieres 26 - 27 March (Cavalry Corps, Fifth Army)

1st Cavalry Brigade : Brigadier-General E. Makins
2nd (Queen's Bays) Dragoon Guards
5th (Princess Charlotte of Wales's) Dragoon Guards
11th (Prince Albert's Own) Hussars
2nd Cavalry Brigade : Brigadier-General D. J. E. Beale-Browne
4th (Royal Irish) Dragoon Guards
9th (Queen's Royal) Lancers
18th (Queen Mary's Own) Hussars
9th Cavalry Brigade : Brigadier-General D'A. Legard
15th (The King's) Hussars   1st Bedfordshire Yeomanry
19th (Queen Alexandra's Own) Hussars

GUARDS DIVISION : Major-General G. P. T. Feilding
- Battle of St Quentin 21 - 23 March (VI Corps, Third Army)
- First Battle of Bapaume 24 - 25 March (VI Corps, Third Army)

1st Guards Brigade : Brigadier-General C. R. Champion de Crespigny
2nd Grenadier Guards   1st Irish Guards
2nd Coldstream Guards
2nd Guards Brigade : Brigadier-General B. N. Sergison-Brooke to 23 March (wounded); Lieutenant-Colonel G. B. S. Follett acting to 25 March; Brigadier-General G. B. S. Follett
3rd Grenadier Guards   1st Scots Guards
1st Coldstream Guards
3rd Guards Brigade : Brigadier-General Lord H. C. Seymour
1st Grenadier Guards   2nd Scots Guards
1st Welsh Guards
    Pioneers : 4th Coldstream Guards

2nd CAVALRY DIVISION : Major-General W. H. Greenly temporary to 14th Division 22 March; Brigadier-General T. T. pitman acting to 28 March; Major-General W. H. Greenly to 29 March (sick); Brigadier-General T. T. Pitman (acting)
- First Battles of the Somme 21 March - 1 April
- Battle of St Quentin 21 - 23 March (III Corps, Fifth Army)

3rd Cavalry Brigade : Brigadier-General J. A. Bell-Smyth
4th (Queen's Own) Hussars   5th (Royal Irish) Lancers
16th (The Queen's) Lancers
4th Cavalry Brigade : Brigadier-General T. T. Pitman to 25 March; Lieutenant-Colonel S. R. Kirby (acting)
3rd (The King's Own) Hussars
6th (Carabiniers) Dragoon Guards
1st Queen's Own Oxfordshire Hussars
5th Cavalry Brigade : Lieutenant-Colonel W. F. Collins (acting)
2nd (Royal Scots Greys) Dragoons   20th Hussars
12th (Prince of Wales) Lancers

2nd DIVISION : Major-General C. E. Pereira
- Battle of St Quentin 22 - 23 March (V Corps, Third Army)
- First Battle of Bapaume 24 - 25 March (V Corps, Third Army)

5th Brigade : Brigadier-General W. Bullen-Smith to 25 March; Lieutenant-Colonel R. H. Pipon (acting)
2nd Oxford & Bucks Light Infantry
24th (2nd Sportsmens) Royal Fusiliers
2nd Highland Light Infantry
6th Brigade : Brigadier-General R. K. Walsh
1st King's Liverpool   2nd South Staffordshires
17th (1st Football Pals) Middlesex
99th Brigade : Brigadier-General R. B Barker to 24 March (killed); Lieutenant-Colonel E. A. Winter (acting)
1st Royal Berkshires   1st King's Royal Rifle Corps
23rd (1st Sportsmens) Royal Fusiliers
    Pioneers : 10th (Cornwall Pioneers) Duke of Cornwall's Light Infantry

3rd CAVALRY DIVISION : Brigadier-General A. E. W. Harman (acting)
- First Battles of the Somme 21 - 27 March & 1 - 5 April
- Battle of St Quentin 21 - 23 March (III Corps, Fifth Army)
- Actions at the Somme Crossings 24 - 25 March (XVIII Corps, Fifth Army)
- Battle of the Avre 4 - 5 April (XIX Corps, Fourth Army)

6th Cavalry Brigade : Brigadier-General A. G. Seymour
1st Royal Dragoons   3rd Dragoon Guards
10th Hussars
7th Cavalry Brigade : Brigadier-General B. P. Portal
6th (Inniskilling) Dragoons   7th Dragoon Guards
17th Lancers
Canadian Cavalry Brigade : Brigadier-General J. E. B. Seely
Royal Canadian Dragoons   Lord Strathcona's Horse
Fort Garry's Horse

3rd DIVISION : Major-General C. J. Deverell
- Battle of St Quentin 21 - 23 March (VI Corps, Third Army)
- First Battle of Bapaume 24 - 25 March (VI Corps, Third Army)

8th Brigade : Brigadier-General W. E. C. Tanner
2nd Royal Scots   1st Royal Scots Fusiliers
7th King's Shropshire Light Infantry
9th Brigade : Brigadier-General H. C. Potter
1st Northumberland Fusiliers   13th King's Liverpool
4th Royal Fusiliers
76th Brigade : Brigadier-General C. L. Porter
2nd Suffolks   8th King's Own
1st Gordon Highlanders
    Pioneers : 20th (British Empire League Pioneers) King's Royal Rifle Corps

6th DIVISION : Major-General T. O. Marden
- Battle of St Quentin 21 - 22 March (IV Corps, Third Army)

16th Brigade : Brigadier-General H. A. Walker
1st Buffs   2nd York & Lancasters
1st King's Shropshire Light Infantry

18th Brigade : Brigadier-General G. S. G. Cranford
1st West Yorkshires   11th Essex
2nd Durham Light Infantry

71st Brigade : Brigadier-General P. W. Brown
1st Leicesters   9th Norfolks
2nd Sherwood Foresters
        Pioneers : 11th (Midland Pioneers) Leicesters

8th DIVISION : Major-General W. C. G. Heneker
- Battle of St Quentin 23 March (XIX Corps, Fifth Army)
- Actions at the Somme Crossings 24 - 25 March (XIX Corps, Fifth Army)
- Battle of Rosieres 26 - 27 March (XIX Corps, Fifth Army)
- Villers-Bretonneux 24 - 25 April (III Corps, Fourth Army)

23rd Brigade : G. W. St. G. Grogan
2nd Devonshires   2nd Middlesex
2nd West Yorkshires

24th Brigade : Brigadier-General R. Haig
1st Worcesters   1st Sherwood Foresters
2nd Northamptonshires

25th Brigade : Brigadier-General C. Coffin, VC
2nd East Lancashires   2nd Rifle Brigade
2nd Royal Berkshires
    Pioneers : 22nd (3rd Durham Pals) Durham Light Infantry (from 2 July)

9th (SCOTTISH) DIVISION : Brigadier-General H. H. Tudor acting to 25 March; Major-General C. A. Blacklock
- First Battles of the Somme 21 - 27 March
- Battle of St Quentin 21 - 23 March (VII Corps, Fifth Army)
- First Battle of Bapaume 24 - 25 March (VIII Corps, Third Army)

26th Brigade : Brigadier-General J. Kennedy
8th Black Watch   5th Cameron Highlanders
7th Seaforth Highlanders

27th Brigade : Brigadier-General W. D. Croft
11th Royal Scots   12th Royal Scots
6th King's Own Scottish Borderers

South African Brigade : Brigadier-General F. S. Dawson to 24 March (captured); Lieutenant-Colonel B. Young (acting)
1st South African Infantry   2nd South African Infantry
 4th South African Infantry Pioneers : 9th Seaforth Highlanders

12th (EASTERN) DIVISION : Major-General A. B. Scott
- First Battle of Bapaume 25 March (VII Corps, Third Army)
- Battle of the Ancre 5 April (V Corps, Third Army)

35th Brigade : Brigadier-General B. Vincent
7th Norfolks   9th Essex
7th Suffolks

36th Brigade : Brigadier-General : C. S. Owen
9th Royal Fusiliers   7th Royal Sussex
11th Middlesex

37th Brigade : Brigadier-General A. B. Incledon-Webber
6th Queen's   6th Royal West Kents
6th Buffs
        Pioneers : 5th Northamptonshires

14th (LIGHT) DIVISION : Major-General V. A. Couper to 21 March; Major-General W. H. Greenly to 27 March; Major-General Sir V. A. Couper to 31 March; Major-General P. C. B. Skinner
- Battle of St Quentin 21 - 23 March (III Corps, Fifth Army)
- Battle of the Avre 4 April (XIX Corps, Fourth Army)

41st Brigade : Brigadier-General P. C. B. Skinner to 31 March; Lieutenant-Colonel B. J. Curling acting to 3 April; Brigadier-General C. R. P. Winser
7th Rifle Brigade   8th Rifle Brigade
7th King's Royal Rifle Corps

42nd Brigade : Brigadier-General G. N. B. Forster (killed 4 April)
5th Oxford & Bucks Light Infantry
9th King's Royal Rifle Corps
5th King's Shropshire Light Infantry

43rd Brigade : Brigadier-General R. S. Tempest
6th Somerset Light Infantry 7th King's Royal Rifle Corps
9th Cameronians
        Pioneers : 11th King's Liverpool

15th (SCOTTISH) DIVISION : Major-General H. L. Reed, VC
- Battles of the Somme 21 March-5 April (XVII Corps, Third Army)
- Battle of Bapaume 24-25 March (XVII Corps, Third Army)

44th Brigade : Brigadier-General E. Hilliam
8th Seaforth Highlanders   7th Cameron Highlanders
8th/10th Gordon Highlanders

45th Brigade : Brigadier-General W. H. L. Allgood
13th Royal Scots   6th Cameron Highlanders
11th Argyll & Sutherland Highlanders

46th Brigade : Brigadier-General A. F. Lumsden
7th/8th King's Own Scottish Borderers
9th Black Watch   10th Cameronians
        Pioneers : 9th Gordon Highlanders

16th (IRISH) DIVISION : Major-General Sir C. P. A. Hull
- First Battles of the Somme 21 March - 3 April (VII Corps, until 25 March then XIX Corps, Fifth Army until 2 April then Fourth Army)
- Battle of St Quentin 21-23 March (VII Corps, Fifth Army)
- Battle of Rosieres 26 - 27 March (XIX Corps, Fifth Army)

47th Brigade : Brigadier-General H. G. Gregorie
1st Royal Munster Fusiliers 2nd Leinsters
6th Connaught Rangers

48th Brigade : Brigadier-General F. W. Ramsay
1st Royal Dublin Fusiliers   2nd Royal Munster Fusiliers
2nd Royal Dublin Fusiliers

49th Brigade : Brigadier-General P. Levenson-Gower
7th/8th Royal Inniskilling Fusiliers
2nd Royal Irish
7th (South Irish Horse) Royal Irish
        Pioneers : 11th Hampshires

17th (NORTHERN) DIVISION : Major-General P. R. Robertson
- Battle of St Quentin 21 - 23 March (V Corps, Third Army)
- First Battle of Bapaume 24 - 25 March (V Corps, Third Army)

50th Brigade : Brigadier-General C. Yatman
10th West Yorkshires   6th Dorsets
7th East Yorkshires

51st Brigade : Brigadier-General C. E. Bond
7th Lincolns   10th Sherwood Foresters
7th (Westmorland & Cumberland Yeomanry) Border

52nd Brigade : Brigadier-General A. J. F. Eden
10th Lancashire Fusiliers   9th Duke of Wellington's
12th (Duke of Lancaster's Own Yeomanry) Manchesters
        Pioneers : 7th York & Lancasters

18th (EASTERN) DIVISION : Major-General R. P. Lee
- Battle of St Quentin 21 - 23 March (III Corps, Fifth Army)
- Battle of the Avre 4 April (XIX Corps, Fourth Army) Also 1/6th & 1/7th Londons with Division on 4 April
- Villers-Bretonneux 24 - 25 April (III Corps, Fourth Army)

53rd Brigade : Brigadier-General H. W. Higginson to 24 April; Brigadier-General M. G. H. Barker
10th Essex   8th Royal Berkshires
7th Royal West Kents
54th Brigade : Brigadier-General L. W. de V. Sadlier-Jackson
11th Royal Fusiliers   6th Northamptonshires
7th Bedfords
55th Brigade : Brigadier-General E. A. Wood
7th Queen's   8th East Surreys
7th Buffs
        Pioneers : 8th Royal Sussex

19th (WESTERN) DIVISION : Major-General G. D. Jeffreys
- Battle of St Quentin 21 - 23 March (V Corps, to 3 pm on 21 March the IV Corps, Third Army)
- First Battle of Bapaume 24 - 25 March (IV Corps, Third Army)

56th Brigade : Brigadier-General F. G. Willan
9th Cheshires   8th North Staffordshires
1/4th King's Shropshire Light Infantry
57th Brigade : Brigadier-General T. A. Cubitt
10th Royal Warwickshires   10th Worcesters
8th Gloucesters
58th Brigade : Brigadier-General A. E. Glasgow
9th Royal Welsh Fusiliers   9th Welsh
6th(Wiltshire Yeomanry) Wiltshires
        Pioneers : 5th South Wales Borderers

20th (LIGHT) DIVISION : Major-General W. Douglas Smith
- First Battles of the Somme 22 March - 2 April
- Battle of St Quentin 22 - 23 March (XVIII Corps, Fifth Army)
- Actions at the Somme Crossings 24 - 25 March (XVIII Corps, Fifth Army)
- Battle of Rosieres 26 - 27 March (XVIII Corps, Fifth Army)

59th Brigade : Brigadier-General H. H. G. Hyslop
11th King's Royal Rifle Corps   2nd Cameronians
11th Rifle Brigade
60th Brigade : Brigadier-General F. J. Duncan
12th King's Royal Rifle Corps   12th Rifle Brigade
6th King's Shropshire Light Infantry
61st Brigade : Brigadier-General J. K. Cochrane
12th King's Liverpool   7th Somerset Light Infantry
7th Duke of Cornwall's Light Infantry
        Pioneers : 11th Durham Light Infantry

21st DIVISION : Major-General D. G. M. Campbell
- Battle of St Quentin 21-23 March (VII Corps, Fifth Army)
- First Battle of Bapaume 24 March (VII Corps, Fifth Army)

62nd Brigade : Brigadier-General H. Gater
1st Lincolns   2nd Lincolns
12th/13th Northumberland Fusiliers
64th Brigade : Brigadier-General H. R. Headlam
1st East Yorkshires   15th Durham Light Infantry
9th King's Own Yorkshire Light Infantry
110th Brigade : Brigadier-General H. R. Cumming
6th Leicesters   7th Leicesters
8th Leicesters
        Pioneers : 14th Northumberland Fusiliers

24th DIVISION : Major-General A. C. Daly
- Battle of St Quentin 21 - 23 March (XIX Corps, Fifth Army)
- Actions at the Somme Crossings 24 - 25 March (XIX Corps, Fifth Army)
- Battle of Rosieres 26 - 27 March (XIX Corps, Fifth Army)
- Battle of the Avre 4 April (XIX Corps, Fifth Army)

17th Brigade : Brigadier-General P. V. P. Stone
8th Queen's   3rd Rifle Brigade
1st Royal Fusiliers
72nd Brigade : Brigadier-General R. W. Morgan
9th East Surreys   8th Royal West Kents
1st North Staffordshires
73rd Brigade : Brigadier-General W. J. Dugan
9th Royal Sussex   13th Middlesex
7th Northamptonshires
        Pioneers ; 12th Sherwood Foresters

25th DIVISION : Major-General E. G. T. Bainbridge
- Battle of St Quentin 21 - 23 March (IV Corps, Third Army)
- First Battle of Bapaume 24 - 25 March (IV Corps, Third Army)

7th Brigade : Brigadier-General C. J. Griffin
10th Cheshires   1st Wiltshires
4th South Staffordshires
74th Brigade : Brigadier-General H. K. Bethell
11th Lancashire Fusiliers   9th Loyal North Lancashires
3rd Worcesters
75th Brigade : Brigadier-General H. T. Dobbin
11th Cheshires   2nd South Lancashires
8th Border
        Pioneers : 6th South Wales Borderers

30th DIVISION : Major-General W. de L. Williams
- Battle of St Quentin 21 - 23 March (XVIII Corps, Fifth Army)
- Actions at the Somme Crossings 24 - 25 March (XVIII Corps, Fifth Army)
- Battle of Rosieres 26 - 27 March (XVIII Corps, Fifth Army)

21st Brigade : Brigadier-General G. D. Goodman
2nd Yorkshires   2nd Wiltshires
17th (2nd Manchester Pals) Manchesters
89th Brigade : Brigadier-General Hon F. C. Stanley
17th (1st Liverpool Pals) King's Liverpool
18th (Lancashire Hussars) King's Liverpool
20th (4th Liverpool Pals) King's Liverpool
90th Brigade : Lieutenant-Colonel H. S. Poyntz acting to 26 March; Brigadier-General G. A. Stevens
2nd Royal Scots Fusiliers   2nd Bedfordshires
16th (1st Manchester Pals) Manchesters
        Pioneers : 11th (St Helens Pioneers) South Lancashires

31st DIVISION : Major-General R. J. Bridgford
- Battle of St Quentin 23 March (VI Corps, Third Army)
- First Battle of Bapaume 24 - 25 March (VI Corps, Third Army)

4th Guards Brigade : Brigadier-General Lord Ardee
4th Grenadier Guards   2nd Irish Guards
3rd Coldstream Guards
92nd Brigade : Brigadier-General O. de L. Williams
10th (Hull Commercials) East Yorkshires
11th (Hull Tradesmen) East Yorkshires
11th (Accrington Pals) East Lancashires
93rd Brigade : Brigadier-General J. D. Ingles
15th (1st Leeds Pals) West Yorkshires
18th (1st Durham Pals) Durham Light Infantry
13th (1st Barnsley Pals) York & Lancasters
        Pioneers : 12th (Miners) King's Own Yorkshire Light Infantry

32nd DIVISION : Major-General C. D. Shute
- Capture of Ayette 3 April (14th & 96th Brigades) (VI Corps, Third Army)
- Battle of the Ancre 5 April (VI Corps, Third Army)

14th Brigade : Brigadier-General F. W. Lumsden, VC
5th/6th Royal Scots   1st Dorsets
15th (1st Glasgow Pals – Glasgow Tramways) Highland Light Infantry
96th Brigade : Brigadier-General A. C. Girdwood
15th (1st Salford Pals) Lancashire Fusiliers
16th (2nd Salford Pals) Lancashire Fusiliers
2nd Manchesters
97th Brigade : Brigadier-General J. R. M. Minshull-Ford
11th (Lonsdale) Border
2nd King's Own Yorkshire Light Infantry
10th Argyll & Sutherland Highlanders
      Pioneers : 16th Highland Light Infantry

34th DIVISION : Major-General C. L. Nicholson
- Battle of St Quentin 21 - 23 March (VI Corps, Third Army)

101st Brigade : Brigadier-General R. C. Gore
15th (1st Edinburgh City Battalion) Royal Scots
16th (2nd Edinburgh City Battalion) Royal Scots
11th (Cambridge City Battalion) Suffolks
102nd Brigade : Brigadier-General N. A. Thomson
22nd (3rd Tyneside Scottish) Northumberland Fusiliers
23rd (4th Tyneside Scottish) Northumberland Fusiliers
25th (2nd Tyneside Irish) Northumberland Fusiliers
103rd Brigade : Brigadier-General J. G. Chaplin
10th (Grimsby Chums) Lincolns   1st East Lancashires
9th (Northumberland Hussars) Northumberland Fusiliers
    Pioneers : 18th (1st Tyneside Pioneers) Northumberland Fusiliers

35th DIVISION : Major-General G. McK. Franks to 27 March; Brigadier-General A. H. Marindin (acting)
- First Battles of the Somme 24 - 30 March
- First Battle of Bapaume 24 - 25 March (VII Corps, Fifth Army until 24 March then VII Corps, Third Army)
- *Brigadier-General H. R. Cumming's Force (elements of 62nd, 64th & 110th Brigades from 21st Division) served with 35th Division from 4.00pm on 24 March*

104th Brigade : Brigadier-General J. W. Sandilands
17th (1st South East Lancashire) Lancashire Fusiliers
18th (2nd South-East Lancashire) Lancashire Fusiliers
19th (2nd Durham Pals) Durham Light Infantry
105th Brigade : Brigadier-General A. H. Marindin to 26 March; Lieutenant-Colonel W. A. W. Crellin (acting)
15th (1st Birkenhead Pals) Cheshires
1/4th North Staffordshires
15th (Nottingham Pals) Sherwood Foresters
106th Brigade : Brigadier-General J. H. W. Pollard
17th (Rosebery) Royal Scots   12th Highland Light Infantry
18th (Glasgow Yeomanry) Highland Light Infantry
   Pioneers : 19th (2nd Tyneside Pioneers) Northumberland Fusiliers

36th (ULSTER) DIVISION : Major-General O. S. W. Nugent
- Battle of St Quentin 21 - 23 March (XVIII Corps, Fifth Army)
- Actions at the Somme Crossings 24 - 25 March (XVIII Corps, Fifth Army)
- Battle of Rosieres 26 - 27 March (XVIII Corps, Fifth Army)

107th Brigade : Brigadier-General W. M. Withycombe
1st Royal Irish Rifles   2nd Royal Irish Rifles
15th (North Belfast) Royal Irish Rifles
108th Brigade : Brigadier-General C. R. J. Griffith
1st Royal Irish Fusiliers
9th (North Irish Horse) Royal Irish Fusiliers
12th (Central Antrim) Royal Irish Rifles
109th Brigade : Brigadier-General W. F. Hessey
1st Royal Inniskilling Fusiliers   2nd Royal Inniskilling Fusiliers
9th Royal Inniskilling Fusiliers
   Pioneers : 16th (2nd County Down) Royal Irish Rifles

37th DIVISION : Major-General H. Bruce-Williams
- Battle of the Ancre 5 April (IV Corps, Third Army)

63rd Brigade : Brigadier-General E. L. Challenor
8th Lincolns   4th Middlesex
8th Somerset Light Infantry
111th Brigade : Brigadier-General S. G. Francis
10th Royal Fusiliers   13th King's Royal Rifle Corps
13th Rifle Brigade
112th Brigade : Brigadier-General A. E. Irvine
1st Essex   13th Royal Fusiliers
6th Bedfordshires
   Pioneers : 9th North Staffordshires

38th (WELSH) DIVISION: Major-General C. G. Blackadder
- Battle of the Ancre (In Reserve V Corps, Third Army)

113th Brigade : Brigadier-General H. E. ap Rhys Pryce
13th (1st North Wales Pals) Royal Welsh Fusiliers
14th Royal Welsh Fusiliers   16th Royal Welsh Fusiliers
114th Brigade : Brigadier-General A. R. Harman
13th (2nd Rhondda Pals) Welsh
14th (Swansea Pals) Welsh
15th (Carmarthenshire Pals) Welsh
115th Brigade : Lieutenant-Colonel J. B. Cockburn (acting)
17th (2nd North Wales Pals) Royal Welsh Fusiliers
2nd Royal Welsh Fusiliers
10th (1st Gwent Pals) South Wales Borderers
   Pioneers : 19th (Glamorgan Pioneers) Welsh

39th DIVISION : Brigadier-General M. L. Hornby acting to 23 March; Major-General E. Feetham to 29 March (killed); Brigadier-General W. G. H. Thompson acting to 30 March; Major-General C. A. Blacklock
- Battle of St Quentin 22 - 23 March (VII Corps, Fifth Army)
- Actions at the Somme Crossings 24 - 25 March (Less 116th Brigade) (VII Corps until 24 March the XIX Corps, Fifth Army)
- First Battle of Bapaume 24 - 25 March (116th Brigade) (VII Corps until 24 March then XIX Corps, Fifth Army)
- Battle of Rosieres 26 - 27 March (XIX Corps, Fifth Army)

116th Brigade : Lieutenant-Colonel W. C. Millward acting to 23 March; Brigadier-General M. L. Hornby on 23 March (wounded); Lieutenant-Colonel W. C. Millward acting
11th (1st South Down) Royal Sussex
13th (3rd South Down) Royal Sussex
1/1st Hertfordshires
117th Brigade : Brigadier-General G. A. Armytage
16th (Chatsworth Rifles) Sherwood Foresters
17th (British Empire League) King's Royal Rifle Corps
16th (St Pancras) Rifle Brigade
118th Brigade : Brigadier-General E. H. C. P. Bellingham
1/6th Cheshires   1/1st Cambridgeshires
4th/5th Black Watch
    Pioneers : 13th (Forest of Dean) Gloucesters

40th DIVISION : Major-General J. Ponsonby
- Battle of St Quentin 21 - 23 March (VI Corps, Third Army)
- First Battle of Bapaume 24 - 25 March (VI Corps, Third Army)

119th Brigade : Brigadier-General F. P. Crozier
13th (Wandsworth) East Surreys
21st (Islington) Middlesex
18th (2nd Glamorgan Pals) Welsh
120th Brigade : Lieutenant-Colonel R. F. Forbes acting to 23 March; Brigadier-General C. J. Hobkirk
10/11th Highland Light Infantry
14th Highland Light Infantry
14th Argyll & Sutherland Highlanders
121st Brigade : Brigadier-General J. Campbell
12th (East Anglian) Suffolks   20th (Shoreditch) Middlesex
13th Yorkshires
    Pioneers : 12th (Teeside Pioneers) Yorkshires

41st DIVISION : Major-General S. T. B. Lawford
- Battle of St Quentin 22 - 23 March (IV Corps, Third Army)
- First Battle of Bapaume 24 - 25 March (IV Corps, Third Army)

122nd Brigade : Brigadier-General F. W. Towsey
12th (Bermondsey) East Surreys
18th (Arts & Crafts) King's Royal Rifle Corps
15th (Carabiniers) Hampshires
123rd Brigade : Brigadier-General E. Pearce Serocold
11th (Lambeth) Queen's
23rd (2nd Football Pals) Middlesex
10th (Kent County) Royal West Kents
124th Brigade : Brigadier-General W. F. Clemson
10th (Battersea) Queen's   26th (Bankers) Royal Fusiliers
20th (Wearside Pals) Durham Light Infantry
    Pioneers : 19th (2nd Public Works Pioneers) Middlesex

42nd (EAST LANCASHIRE) DIVISION : Major-General A. Solly-Flood
- First Battle of Bapaume 24 - 25 March (VI Corps, Third Army)
- Battle of the Ancre 5 April (IV Corps, Third Army)

125th Brigade : Brigadier-General H. Fargus
1/5th Lancashire Fusiliers   1/7th Lancashire Fusiliers
1/8th Lancashire Fusiliers
126th Brigade : Brigadier-General W. W. Seymour
1/5th East Lancashires   1/8th Manchesters
1/10th Manchesters
127th Brigade : Brigadeier-General Hon A. M. Henley
1/5th Manchesters   1/6th Manchesters
1/7th Manchesters
    Pioneers : 1/7th Northumberland Fusiliers

47th (1/2nd LONDON) DIVISION : Major-General Sir G. F. Gorringe
- Battle of St Quentin 21 - 23 March (V Corps, Third Army)
- First Battle of Bapaume 24 - 25 March (V Corps, Third Army)
- Battle of the Ancre 5 April (V Corps, Third Army)

140th Brigade : Brigadier-General H. B. P. L. Kennedy
1/15th (Prince of Wales Own Civil Service Rifles) Londons
1/17th (Poplar & Stepney Rifles) Londons
1/21st (First Surrey Rifles) Londons
141st Brigade : Brigadier-General W. F. Mildren
1/18th (London Irish Rifles) Londons
1/19th (St Pancras) Londons
1/20th (Blackheath & Woolwich) Londons
142nd Brigade : Brigadier-General V. T. Bailey to 24 March (wounded, captured); Lieutenant-Colonel A. Maxwell acting to 3 April; Brigadier-General R. McDouall
1/22nd (The Queen's) Londons   1/24th (The Queen's) Londons
1/23rd Londons
    Pioneers : 1/4th (Denbighshire) Royal Welsh Fusiliers

50th (NORTHUMBRIAN) DIVISION : Brigadier-General A. V. Stockley acting to 23 March; Major-General H. C. Jackson
- Battle of St Quentin 21 - 23 March (Fifth Army Reserve on 21 March then XIX Corps, Fifth Army)
- Actions at the Somme Crossings 23 March (XIX Corps, Fifth Army)
- Battle of Rosieres 26 - 27 March (XIX Corps, Fifth Army)

149th Brigade : Brigadier-General E. P. A. Riddell
1/4th Northumberland Fusiliers
1/5th Northumberland Fusiliers
1/6th Northumberland Fusiliers
150th Brigade : Brigadier-General H. C. Rees
1/4th Yorkshires   1/5th Yorkshires
1/4th East Yorkshires
151st Brigade : Brigadier-General C. T. Martin
1/5th Durham Light Infantry   1/6th Durham Light Infantry
1/8th Durham Light Infantry
    Pioneers : 1/7th Durham Light Infantry

51st (HIGHLAND) DIVISION : Major-General G. T. C. Carter-Campbell
- Battle of St Quentin 21 - 23 March (VI Corps, Third Army)
- First Battle of Bapaume 24 - 25 March (VI Corps, Third Army)

152nd Brigade : Brigadier-General H. P. Burn
1/5th (Sutherland & Caithness) Seaforth Highlanders
1/6th (Morayshire) Seaforth Highlanders
1/6th (Banff and Donside) Gordon Highlanders
153rd Brigade : Brigadier-General A. T. Beckwith
1/6th (Perthshire) Black Watch   1/7th (Fife) Black Watch
1/7th (Deeside Highland) Gordon Highlanders
154th Brigade : Brigadier-General K. G. Buchanan
1/4th (Ross Highland) Seaforth Highlanders
1/4th Gordon Highlanders
1/7th Argyll & Sutherland Highlanders
          Pioneers : 1/8th Royal Scots

61st (2nd SOUTH MIDLAND) DIVISION : Major-General C. J. Mackenzie
- Battle of St Quentin 21 - 22 March (XVIII Corps, Fifth Army)
- Actions at the Somme Crossings 24 - 25 March (Artillery under 20th Division, Brigades under 30th Division)

182nd Brigade : Brigadier-General W. K. Evans
2/6th Royal Warwickshires   2/7th Royal Warwickshires
2/8th Royal Warwickshires
183rd Brigade : Brigadier-General A. H. Spooner
1/9th (Highlanders) Royal Scots
1/8th (The Argyllshire) Argyll & Sutherland Highlanders
1/5th (Buchan and Formartin) Gordon Highlanders
184th Brigade : Brigadier-General Hon R. White to 22 March (wounded); Lieutenant-Colonel H. de R. Wetherall to 25 March (wounded); Lieutenant-Colonel A. B. Lawson (acting)
2/5th Gloucesters   2/4th Royal Berkshires
2/4th Oxford & Bucks Light Infantry
          Pioneers : 1/5th Duke of Cornwall's Light Infantry

58th (2nd/1st LONDON) DIVISION : Maj-Gen A. B. E. Cator
- First Battles of the Somme 21 March - 3 April (III Corps, Fifth Army to 24 March then 1 French Cavalry Corps, 6th French Army)
- Battle of St Quentin 21 - 23 March (III Corps, Fifth Army)
- Battle of the Avre (6th & &th Londons attached 18th Division)
- Villers-Bretonneux 24 - 25 April (III Corps, Fourth Army)

173rd Brigade : Brigadier-General R. B. Worgan
2/2nd (Royal Fusiliers) Londons
2/3rd (Royal Fusiliers) Londons
2/4th (Royal Fusiliers) Londons
174th Brigade : Brigadier-General C. G. Higgins
2/6th (Rifles) Londons   2/7th Londons
2/8th (Post Office Rifles) Londons
175th Brigade : Brigadier-General M. E. Richardson
2/9th (Queen Victoria's Rifles) Londons
2/10th (Hackney) Londons   2/12th (The Rangers) Londons
          Pioneers : 1/4th Suffolks

62nd (2nd WEST RIDING) DIVISION : Major-General W. P. Braithwaite
- First Battle of Bapaume 25 March (IV Corps, Third Army)

185th Brigade : Brigadier-General Viscount Hampden
2/5th West Yorkshires
2/7th (Leeds Rifles) West Yorkshires
8th (Leeds Rifles) West Yorkshires
186th Brigade : Brigadier-General J. L. G. Burnett
2/4th Duke of Wellington's   5th Duke of Wellington's
2/7th Duke of Wellington's
187th Brigade : Lieutenant-Colonel B. J. Barton (acting)
2/4th King's Own Yorkshire Light Infantry
5th King's Own Yorkshire Light Infantry
2/4th (Hallamshire) York & Lancasters
          Pioneers : 1/9th Durham Light Infantry

59th (2nd NORTH MIDLAND) DIVISION : Major-General C. F. Romer
- Battle of St Quentin 21 - 23 March (VI Corps, Third Army)
- First Battle of Bapaume 24 - 25 March (Divisional Artillery & 177th Brigade under 40th Division, VI Corps, Third Army)

176th Brigade : Brigadier-General T. G. Cope
2/5th South Staffordshires   2/6th South Staffordshires
2/5th North Staffordshires
177th Brigade : Brigadier-General C. H. L. James
2/4th Lincolns   2/5th Lincolns
2/4th Leicesters
178th Brigade : Brigadier-General T. W. Stansfeld
2/5th Sherwood Foresters   2/6th Sherwood Foresters
2/7th (Robin Hood) Sherwood Foresters
          Pioneers : 6/7th Royal Scots Fusiliers

63rd (ROYAL NAVAL) DIVISION Major-General C. E. Lawrie
- Battle of St Quentin 21 - 23 March (V Corps, Third Army)
- First Battle of Bapaume 24 - 25 March (V Corps, Third Army)
- Battle of the Ancre 5 April (V Corps, Third Army)

188th Brigade : Brigadier-General J. F. S. D. Coleridge
Anson
1st Royal Marines Light Infantry
2nd Royal Marines Light Infantry
189th Brigade : Brigadier-General H. D. de Pree
Drake   Hood
Hawke
190th Brigade : Brigadier-General A. R. H. Hutchinson
7th Royal Fusiliers   4th Bedfordshires
1/28th (Artists Rifles) Londons
          Pioneers : 14th (Severn Valley Pioneers) Worcesters

66th (2nd EAST LANCASHIRE) DIVISION Major-General N. Malcolm
- First Battles of the Somme 21 - 30 March
- Battle of St Quentin 21 - 23 March (XIX Corps, Fifth Army)
- Actions at the Somme Crossings 24 - 25 March (XIX Corps, Fifth Army)
- Battle of Rosieres 26 - 27 March (XIX Corps, Fifth Army)

197th Brigade : Brigadier-General O. C. Borrett
2/8th Lancashire Fusiliers   6th Lancashire Fusiliers
2/7th Lancashire Fusiliers
198th Brigade : Brigadier-General A. J. Hunter
4th East Lancashires   2/5th East Lancashires
9th Manchesters
199th Brigade : Brigadier-General G. C. Williams
2/5th Manchesters   2/6th Manchesters
2/7th Manchesters
          Pioneers : 1/5th Border

NEW ZEALAND DIVISION : Major-General A. H. Russell
- Battle of the Ancre 5 April (IV Corps, Third Army)

1st New Zealand Brigade : Brigadier-General C W Melville
1st Auckland Battalion   1st Otago Battalion
1st Canterbury Battalion   1st Wellington Battalion
2nd New Zealand Brigade : Colonel R Young
2nd Auckland Battalion   2nd Otago Battalion
2nd Canterbury Battalion   2nd Wellington Battalion
3rd New Zealand (Rifles) Brigade : Brigadier-General A E Stewart
1st NZ Rifle Brigade   2nd NZ Rifle Brigade
3rd NZ Rifle Brigade   4th NZ Rifle Brigade
          Pioneers : New Zealand Pioneer Battalion

2nd AUSTRALIAN DIVISION : Major General N M Smythe
- Battle of the Avre 4 April (5th Australian Brigade with XIX Corps, Fourth Army)

5th (New South Wales) Brigade : Brigadier-General R Smith
17th Battalion   18th Battalion
19th Battalion   20th Battalion

3rd AUSTRALIAN DIVISION : Major General J Monash
- Battle of the Avre 4 April (9th Australian Brigade with XIX Corps, Fourth Army)

9th Brigade : Brigadier-General C Rosenthal
33rd Battalion   34th Battalion
35th Battalion   36th Battalion

4th AUSTRALIAN DIVISION : Major General E G Sinclair-MacLagan
- Battle of the Ancre 5 April (4th Brigade with IV Corps, 12th & 13th Brigades with VII Corps, Third Army)
- Villers Bretonneux 24-25 April (Australian Corps, Fourth Army)

4th Brigade : Brigadier-General C H Brand
13th (New South Wales) Battalion
14th (Victoria) Battalion
15th (Queensland & Tasmania) Battalion
16th (South & West Australia) Battalion
12th Brigade : Brigadier-General J Gellibrand
45th (New South Wales) Battalion
46th (Victoria) Battalion
47th (Queensland & Tasmania) Battalion
48th (South & West Australia) Battalion
13th Brigade : Brigadier-General T W Glasgow
49th (Queensland) Battalion
50th (South Australia & Tasmania) Battalion
51st (West Australia) Battalion
52nd (West & South Australia, Tasmania) Battalion
          Pioneers : 4th Australian Pioneer Battalion

5th AUSTRALIAN DIVISION : Major General J J T Hobbs
- Battle of the Ancre 5 April (8th & 15th Brigades with XIX Corps, Fourth Army)
- Villers Bretonneux 24-25 April (Australian Corps, Fourth Army)

8th Brigade : Brigadier-General C H Brand
29th (Victoria)Battalion
30th (New South Wales)Battalion
31st (Queensland & Victoria) Battalion
32nd (Western Australia & South Australia)Battalion
14th (New South Wales)Brigade : Brigadier-General J C Stewart
53rd Battalion   54th Battalion
55th Battalion   56th Battalion
15th (Victoria) Brigade : Brigadier-General H E Elliott
57th (New South Wales)Battalion
58th Battalion   59th Battalion
60th Battalion
          Pioneers : 5th Australian Pioneer Battalion

FINAL BREAKOUT 1918 (100 DAYS OFFENSIVE)

1st CAVALRY DIVISION: Major-General R. L. Mullens
- Battle of Amiens 8 - 10 Aug (Cavalry Corps, Fourth Army)
- Battle of Albert 21 Aug (Third Army)

1st Cavalry Brigade: Brigadier-General H. S. Sewell
2nd (Queen's Bays) Dragoon Guards
5th (Princess Charlotte of Wales's) Dragoon Guards
11th (Prince Albert's Own) Hussars

2nd Cavalry Brigade: Brigadier-General A. Lawson
4th (Royal Irish) Dragoon Guards
9th (Queen's Royal) Lancers
18th (Queen Mary's Own) Hussars

9th Cavalry Brigade: Brigadier-General D'A. Legard
15th (The King's) Hussars   1st Bedfordshire Yeomanry
19th (Queen Alexandra's Own) Hussars

2nd CAVALRY DIVISION: Brigadier-General T. T. Pitman (acting)
- Battle of Amiens 8 - 11 Aug (Cavalry Corps, Fourth Army)
- Battle of Albert 21 - 23 Aug (Third Army)
- Second Battle of Bapaume 31 Aug - 3 Sept (4th Cavalry Brigade & part of 5th Cavalry Brigade with Third Army)
- Battle of the Canal du Nord 27 Sept - 1 Oct (3rd & 4th Cavalry Brigade with Third Army)

3rd Cavalry Brigade: Brigadier-General J. A. Bell-Smyth
4th (Queen's Own) Hussars   5th (Royal Irish) Lancers
16th (The Queen's) Lancers

4th Cavalry Brigade: Brigadier-General C. H. Rankin
3rd (The King's Own) Hussars
6th (Carabiniers) Dragoon Guards
1st Queen's Own Oxfordshire Hussars

5th Cavalry Brigade: Brigadier-General N. W. Haig
2nd (Royal Scots Greys) Dragoons
12th (Prince of Wales's) Lancers
20th Hussars

3rd CAVALRY DIVISION: Major-General A. E. W. Harman
- Battle of Amiens (Cavalry Corps, Fourth Army)

6th Cavalry Brigade: Lieutenant-Colonel F. H. D. C. Whitmore (acting)
1st Royal Dragoons   3rd Dragoon Guards
10th Hussars

7th Cavalry Brigade: Lieutenant-Colonel E. Paterson (acting)
6th (Inniskilling) Dragoons   7th Dragoon Guards
17th Lancers

Canadian Cavalry Brigade: Brigadier-General R. W. Paterson
Royal Canadian Dragoons   Lord Strathcona's Horse
Fort Garry's Horse

GUARDS DIVISION: Major-General G. P. T. Feilding
- Battle of Albert 21 - 23 Aug (VI Corps, Third Army)
- Battle of Havrincourt 12 Sept (VI Corps, Third Army)
- Battle of the Canal du Nord 27 Sept (VI Corps, Third Army)

1st Guards Brigade: Brigadier-General C. R. Champion de Crespigny
2nd Grenadier Guards   1st Irish Guards
2nd Coldstream Guards

2nd Guards Brigade: Brigadier-General B. N. Sergison-Brooke
3rd Grenadier Guards   1st Scots Guards
1st Coldstream Guards

3rd Guards Brigade: Brigadier-General G. B. S. Follett (killed 27 Sept)
1st Grenadier Guards   2nd Scots Guards
1st Welsh Guards
   Pioneers: 4th Coldstream Guards

1st DIVISION: Major-General E. P. Strickland
- Battle of Epehy 18 Sept (IX Corps, Fourth Army)

1st Brigade: Brigadier-General W. B. Thornton
1st Black Watch   1st Loyal North Lancashires
1st Cameron Highlanders

2nd Brigade: Brigadier-General G. C. Kelly
2nd Royal Sussex   1st Northamptonshires
2nd King's Royal Rifle Corps

3rd Brigade: Brigadier-General Sir W. A. I. Kay, Bt
1st South Wales Borderers   2nd Welsh
1st Gloucesters
   Pioneers: 1/6th Welsh

2nd DIVISION: Major-General C. E. Pereira
- Battle of Albert 21 - 23 Aug (VI Corps, Third Army)
- Capture of Mory Copse 24 Aug (99th Brigade)
- Capture of Behagnies & Sapignies (5th Brigade)
- Second Battle of Bapaume 3 Sept (VI Corps, Third Army)
- Battle of Havrincourt 11 - 12 Sept (VI Corps, Third Army)
- Battle of the Canal du Nord 27 sept - 1 Oct (VI Corps, Third Army)

5th Brigade: Brigadier-General W. L. Osborn
2nd Oxford & Bucks Light Infantry
24th (2nd Sportsmens) Royal Fusiliers
2nd Highland Light Infantry

6th Brigade: Brigadier-General F. G. Willan
1st King's Liverpool   2nd South Staffordshires
17th (1st Football Pals) Middlesex

99th Brigade: Brigadier-General W. E. Ironside to 7 Sept; Brigadier-General A. E. McNamara
1st Royal Berkshires   1st King's Royal Rifle Corps
23rd (1st Sportsmens) Royal Fusiliers
   Pioneers: 10th (Cornwall Pioneers) Duke of Cornwall's Light Infantry

3rd DIVISION: Major-General C. J. Deverell
- Battle of Albert 21 - 23 Aug (VI Corps, Third Army)
- Second Battle of Bapaume 31 Aug - 2 Sept (VI Corps, Third Army)
- Battle of the Canal du Nord 27 Sept - 1 Oct (VI Corps, Third Army)

8th Brigade: Brigadier-General B. D. Fisher
2nd Royal Scots   1st Royal Scots Fusiliers
7th King's Shropshire Light Infantry

9th Brigade: Brigadier-General H. C. Potter
1st Northumberland Fusiliers   13th King's Liverpool
4th Royal Fusiliers

76th Brigade: Brigadier-General C. L. Porter
2nd Suffolks   8th King's Own
1st Gordon Highlanders
   Pioneers: 20th (British Empire League Pioneers) King's Royal Rifle Corps

4th DIVISION : Major-General L. J. Lipsett
- Battle of the Canal du Nord 27 sept - 1 Oct (XXII Corps, First Army)

10th Brigade : Brigadier-General J. Greene
1st Royal Warwickshires   2nd Duke of Wellington's
2nd Seaforth Highlanders
11th Brigade : Brigadier-General W. J. Webb-Bowen
1st Somerset Light Infantry   1st Hampshires
1st Rifle Brigade
12th Brigade : Brigadier-General E. A. Fagan
1st King's Own   2nd Essex
2nd Lancashire Fusiliers
    Pioneers : 21st (Wool Textile Pioneers) West Yorkshires

5th DIVISION : Major-General J. Ponsonby
- Battle of Albert 21 - 23 Aug (IV Corps, Third Army)
- Second Battle of Bapaume 31 Aug - 3 Sept (IV Corps, Third Army)
- Battle of Epehy 18 Sept (IV Corps, Third Army)
- Battle of the Canal du Nord 27 sept - 30 Sept (IV Corps, Third Army)

13th Brigade : Brigadier-General L. O. W. Jones to 8 Sept (sick, died 14 Sept); Lieutenant-Colonel C. T. Furber acting to 15 Sept; Lieutenant-Colonel J. W. C. Kirk acting to 21 Sept; Brigadier-General A. T. Beckwith
2nd King's Own Scottish Borderer
1st Royal Warwickshires
14th (1st Birmingham Pals) Royal Warwickshires
15th (2nd Birmingham Pals) Royal Warwickshires
15th Brigade : Brigadier-General R. D. F. Oldman
1st Norfolks   1st Cheshires
1st Bedfordshires
16th (3rd Birmingham Pals) Royal Warwickshires
95th Brigade : Brigadier-General C. B. Norton
1st Devonshires   1st East Surreys
1st Duke of Cornwall's Light Infantry
12th (Bristol Pals) Gloucesters
    Pioneers : 1/6th (Renfrewshire) Argyll & Sutherland Highlanders

6th DIVISION : Major-General T. O. Marden
- Battle of Epehy 18 Sept (IX Corps, Fourth Army)

16th Brigade : Brigadier-General H. A. Walker
1st Buffs   2nd York & Lancasters
1st King's Shropshire Light Infantry
18th Brigade : Brigadier-General G. S. G. Cranford
1st West Yorkshires   11th Essex
2nd Durham Light Infantry
71st Brigade : Brigadier-General P. W. Brown
1st Leicesters   9th Norfolks
2nd Sherwood Foresters
    Pioneers : 11th (Midland Pioneers) Leicesters

11th (NORTHERN) DIVISION: Brigadier-General O. de. L'E. Winter (acting)
- Battle of the Canal du Nord 27 Sept - 1 Oct (Canadian Corps, First Army)

32nd Brigade : Brigadier-General W. P. S. Foord
6th York & Lancasters   2nd Yorkshires
9th (Yorkshire Hussars) West Yorkshires
33rd Brigade : Brigadier-General F. G. Spring
6th Lincolns   7th South Staffordshires
9th Sherwood Foresters
34th Brigade : Brigadier-General B. G. Clay
8th Northumberland Fusiliers   5th Dorsets
11th Manchesters
    Pioneers : 6th East Yorkshires

12th (EASTERN) DIVISION: Major-General W. Higginson
- Battle of Amiens 8 - 11 Aug (III Corps, Fourth Army)
- Battle of Albert 22 - 23 Aug (III Corps, Fourth Army)
- Battle of Epehy 18 Sept (III Corps, Fourth Army)

35th Brigade : Brigadier-General B. Vincent to 9 Aug (gassed); Brigadier-General A. T. Beckwith
7th Norfolks   9th Essex
1/1st Cambridgeshires
36th Brigade : Brigadier-General : C. S. Owen
9th Royal Fusiliers   7th Royal Sussex
11th Middlesex
37th Brigade : Brigadier-General A. B. Incledon-Webber
6th Queen's   6th Royal West Kents
6th Buffs
    Pioneers : 5th Northamptonshires

17th (NORTHERN) DIVISION : Major-General P. R. Robertson
- Battle of Albert 21 - 23 Aug (V Corps, Third Army)
- Second Battle of Bapaume 31 Aug - 3 Sept (V Corps, Third Army)
- Battle of Epehy 18 Sept (V Corps, Third Army)

50th Brigade : Brigadier-General G. Gwyn-Thomas to 8 Sept; Lieutenant-Colonel F. E. Metcalfe acting to 9 Sept; Brigadier-General A. R. C. Sanders
10th West Yorkshires   6th Dorsets
7th East Yorkshires
51st Brigade : Brigadier-General R. M. Dudgeon
7th Lincolns   10th Sherwood Foresters
7th (Westmorland & Cumberland Yeomanry) Border
52nd Brigade : Brigadier-General W. Allason
10th Lancashire Fusiliers   9th Duke of Wellington's
12th (Duke of Lancaster's Own Yoemanry) Manchesters
    Pioneers : 7th York & Lancasters

18th (EASTERN) DIVISION : Major-General R. P. Lee
- Battle of Amiens 8 - 9 Aug (III Corps, Fourth Army)
- Battle of Albert 21 - 23 Aug (III Corps, Fourth Army)
- Capture of Usna & Tara Hills 23 Aug
- Capture of Trones Wood 27 Aug
- Second Battle of Bapaume 31 Aug - 3 Sept (III Corps, Fourth Army)
- Battle of Epehy 18 Sept (III Corps, Fourth Army)

53rd Brigade : Brigadier-General M. G. H. Barker
10th Essex   8th Royal Berkshires
7th Royal West Kents
54th Brigade : Brigadier-General L. W. de V. Sadlier-Jackson to 22 Aug (wounded); Lieutenant-Colonel A. E. Percival acting to 23 Aug; Brigadier-General J. A. Tyler
11th Royal Fusiliers   6th Northamptonshires
2nd Bedfords
55th Brigade : Brigadier-General E. A. Wood
7th Queen's   8th East Surreys
7th Buffs
    Pioneers : 8th Royal Sussex

21st DIVISION : Major-General D. G. M. Campbell
- Battle of Albert 21 - 23 Aug (V Corps, Third Army)
- Second Battle of Bapaume 31 Aug - 2 Sept (V Corps, Third Army)
- Battle of Epehy 18 Sept (V Corps, Third Army)

62nd Brigade : Brigadier-General H. Gater
1st Lincolns   2nd Lincolns
12th/13th Northumberland Fusiliers
64th Brigade : Brigadier-General A. J. McCulloch to 24 Aug (wounded); Lieutenant-Colonel C. E. R. Holroyd-Smyth acting to 27 Aug; Brigadier-General C. V. Edwards
1st East Yorkshires   15th Durham Light Infantry
9th King's Own Yorkshire Light Infantry
110th Brigade : Brigadier-General H. R. Cumming
6th Leicesters   7th Leicesters
8th Leicesters
          Pioneers : 14th Northumberland Fusiliers

32nd DIVISION : Major-General T. S. Lambert
- Battle of Amiens 10 - 11 Aug (Canadian Corps, Fourth Army)
- Battle of Albert 21 - 23 Aug (Australian Corps, Fourth Army)
- Second Battle of Bapaume 31 Aug - 3 Sept (Australian Corps, Fourth Army)

14th Brigade : Brigadier-General L. P. Evans, VC
5th/6th Royal Scots   1st Dorsets
15th (1st Glasgow Pals – Glasgow Tramways) Highland Light Infantry
96th Brigade : Brigadier-General A. C. Girdwood
15th (1st Salford Pals) Lancashire Fusiliers
16th (2nd Salford Pals) Lancashire Fusiliers
2nd Manchesters
97th Brigade : Brigadier-General J. R. M. Minshull-Ford
1/5th Border
2nd King's Own Yorkshire Light Infantry
10th Argyll & Sutherland Highlanders
          Pioneers : 16th Highland Light Infantry

33rd DIVISION Major-General R. J. Pinney
- Battle of Epehy 18 Sept (V Corps, Third Army)

19th Brigade : Brigadier-General C. R. G. Mayne
1st Cameronians   1st Queen's
5th/6th Cameronians
98th Brigade : Brigadier-General J. D. Heriot-Maitland
4th King's Liverpool   1st Middlesex
2nd Argyll & Sutherland Highlanders
100th Brigade : Brigadier-General A. W. F. Baird
2nd Worcesters
16th (Church Lads Brigade) King's Royal Rifle Corps
1/9th (Glasgow Highland) Highland Light Infantry
          Pioneers : 18th (1st Public Works Pioneers) Middlesex

37th DIVISION : Major-General H. Bruce-Williams
- Battle of Albert 21 - 23 Aug (IV Corps, Third Army)
- Battle of Havrincourt 12 Sept (IV Corps, Third Army)
- Battle of the Canal du Nord 1 Oct (IV Corps, Third Army)

63rd Brigade : Brigadier-General E. L. Challenor to 26 Sept; Brigadier-General R. Oakley
8th Lincolns   4th Middlesex
8th Somerset Light Infantry
111th Brigade : Brigadier-General S. G. Francis
10th Royal Fusiliers   13th King's Royal Rifle Corps
13th Rifle Brigade
112th Brigade : Brigadier-General A. E. Irvine to 27 Sept; Brigadier-General W. N. Herbert
1st Essex   13th Royal Fusiliers
1/1st Hertfordshires
          Pioneers : 9th North Staffordshires

38th (WELSH) DIVISION: Major-General T. A. Cubitt
- Battle of Albert 21 - 23 Aug (V Corps, Third Army)
- Second Battle of Bapaume 31 Aug - 3 Sept (V Corps, Third Army)
- Battle of Havrincourt 12 Sept (V Corps, Third Army)
- Battle of Epehy 18 Sept (V Corps, Third Army)

113th Brigade : Brigadier-General H. E. ap Rhys Pryce
13th (1st North Wales Pals) Royal Welsh Fusiliers
14th Royal Welsh Fusiliers   16th Royal Welsh Fusiliers
114th Brigade : Brigadier-General T. R. C. Price
13th (2nd Rhondda Pals) Welsh
14th (Swansea Pals) Welsh
15th (Carmarthenshire Pals) Welsh
115th Brigade : Brigadier-General W. B. Hulke to 30 Aug (wounded); Lieutenant-Colonel C. C. Norman acting to 5 Sept; Brigadier-General H. D. de Pree
17th (2nd North Wales Pals) Royal Welsh Fusiliers
2nd Royal Welsh Fusiliers
10th (1st Gwent Pals) South Wales Borderers
          Pioneers : 19th (Glamorgan Pioneers) Welsh

42nd (EAST LANCASHIRE) DIVISION : Major-General A. Solly-Flood
- Battle of Albert 21 - 23 Aug (IV Corps, Third Army)
- Second Battle of Bapaume 31 Aug - 3 Sept (IV Corps, Third Army)
- Battle of the Canal du Nord 27 - 29 Sept (IV Corps, Third Army)

125th Brigade : Brigadier-General H. Fargus
1/5th Lancashire Fusiliers   1/7th Lancashire Fusiliers
1/8th Lancashire Fusiliers
126th Brigade : Brigadier-General G. H. Wedgwood to 1 Sept; Lieutenant-Colonel acting to 5 Sept; Brigadier-General T. H. S. Marchant
1/8th Manchesters   1/10th Manchesters
1/5th East Lancashires
127th Brigade : Brigadeier-General Hon A. M. Henley
1/5th Manchesters   1/6th Manchesters
1/7th Manchesters
          Pioneers : 1/7th Northumberland Fusiliers

47th (1/2nd LONDON) DIVISION : Major-General Sir G. F. Gorringe
- Battle of Albert 22 - 23 Aug (III Corps, Fourth Army)
- Second Battle of Bapaume 31 Aug - 3 Sept (III Corps, Fourth Army)

140th Brigade : Brigadier-General H. B. P. L. Kennedy
1/15th (PoW Own Civil Service Rifles) Londons
1/17th (Poplar & Stepney Rifles) Londons
1/21st (First Surrey Rifles) Londons
141st Brigade : Brigadier-General W. F. Mildren
1/18th (London Irish Rifles) Londons
1/19th (St Pancras) Londons
1/20th (Blackheath & Woolwich) Londons
142nd Brigade : Brigadier-General R. McDouall
1/22nd (The Queen's) Londons
1/23rd Londons
1/24th (The Queen's) Londons
          Pioneers : 1/4th (Denbighshire) Royal Welsh Fusiliers

52nd (LOWLAND) DIVISION : Major-General J. Hill to 23 Sept; Major-General F. J. Marshall
- Battle of Albert 23 Aug (VI Corps, Third Army)
- Battle of the Canal du Nord 27 Sept - 1 Oct (XVIII Corps, Third Army)

155th Brigade : Brigadier-General J. Forbes-Robertson, VC to 23 Sept; Brigadier-General G. H. Harrison
1/4th Royal Scots Fusiliers   1/5th Royal Scots Fusiliers
1/4th (Border) King's Own Scottish Borderers
156th Brigade : Brigadier-General A. H. Leggett
1/7th Cameronians   1/7th Royal Scots
1/ 4th (Queen's Edinburgh Rifles) Royal Scots
157th Brigade : Brigadier-General . D. Hamilton-Moore
1/5th (City of Glasgow) Highland Light Infantry
1/6th (City of Glasgow) Highland Light Infantry
1/7th (Blythswood) Highland Light Infantry
  Pioneers : 17th (North Eastern Railway Pioneers) Northumberland Fusiliers

56th (1st LONDON) DIVISION : Major-General C. P. A. Hull
- Battle of Albert 23 Aug (VI Corps, Third Army)
- Battle of the Canal du Nord 27 Sept - 1 Oct (XXII Corps, First Army)

167th Brigade : Brigadier-General G. H. B. Freeth
1/7th Middlesex   1/8th Middlesex
1/1st (Royal Fusiliers) Londons
168th Brigade : Brigadier-General G. G. Loch
1/4th (Royal Fusiliers) Londons   1/13th (Kensington) Londons
1/14th (London Scottish) Londons
169th Brigade : Brigadier-General E. S. de E. Coke
1/2nd (Royal Fusiliers) Londons
1/5th (London Rifle Brigade) Londons
1/16th (Queen's Westminster Rifles) Londons
  Pioneers : 1/5th (Earl of Chester's) Cheshires

57th (2nd WEST LANCASHIRE) DIVISION : Major-General R. W. R. Barnes
- Battle of the Canal du Nord 27 Sept - 1 Oct (XVII Corps, Third Army)

170th Brigade : Brigadier-General : A. L. Ransome
1/5th Loyal North Lancashires   2/4th Loyal North Lancashires
2/5th King's Own
171st Brigade : Brigadier-General F. C. Long-Browne
2/6th King's Liverpool   2/7th King's Liverpool
8th King's Liverpool
172nd Brigade : Brigadier-General G. C. B. Paynter
9th King's Liverpool   2/4th South Lancashires
1st Royal Munster Fusiliers
  Pioneers : 2/5th Loyal North Lancashires

58th (2nd/1st LONDON) DIVISION : Maj-Gen F. W. Ramsay
- Battle of Amiens 8 - 11 Aug (III Corps, Fourth Army)
- Battle of Albert 22 - 23 Aug (III Corps, Fourth Army)
- Second Battle of Bapaume 31 Aug - 1 Sept (III Corps, Fourth Army)
- Battle of Epehy 18 Sept (III Corps, Fourth Army)

173rd Brigade : Brigadier-General C. E. Corkran
3rd (Royal Fusiliers) Londons   2/4th (Royal Fusiliers) Londons
2/2nd (Royal Fusiliers) Londons
174th Brigade : Brigadier-General A. Maxwell
6th (Rifles) Londons   7th Londons
8th (Post Office Rifles) Londons
175th Brigade : Brigadier-General W. Maxwell-Scott to 10 Aug (temporary); Brigadier-General H. W. Cobham
12th (The Rangers) Londons   2/10th (Hackney) Londons
9th (Queen Victoria's Rifles) Londons
  Pioneers : 1/4th Suffolks

59th (2nd NORTH MIDLAND) DIVISION : Major-General Sir R. D. Whigham
- Battle of Albert 21 - 22 Aug (VI Corps, Third Army)

176th Brigade : Brigadier-General T. G. Cope
25th King's Liverpool   17th Royal Sussex
26th Royal Welsh Fusiliers
177th Brigade : Brigadier-General C. H. L. James
11th Somerset Light Infantry   2/6th Durham Light Infantry
15th Essex
178th Brigade : Brigadier-General T. W. Stansfeld
13th Duke of Wellington's   11th Royal Scots Fusiliers
36th Northumberland Fusiliers
  Pioneers : 25th King's Royal Rifle Corps

62nd (2nd WEST RIDING) DIVISION : Major-General Sir R. D. Whigham
- Battle of Havrincourt 12 Sept (VI Corps, Third Army)
- Battle of the Canal du Nord 27 - 30 Sept (VI Corps, Third Army)

185th Brigade : Brigadier-General Viscount Hampden
1/5th Devonshires
2/20th (Blackheath & Woolwich) Londons
8th (Leeds Rifles) West Yorkshires
186th Brigade : Brigadier-General J. L. G. Burnett
2/4th Duke of Wellington's   2/5th Duke of Wellington's
2/4th Hampshires
187th Brigade : Brigadier-General A. J. Reddie
2/4th King's Own Yorkshire Light Infantry
5th King's Own Yorkshire Light Infantry
2/4th (Hallamshire) York & Lancasters
  Pioneers : 1/9th Durham Light Infantry

63rd (ROYAL NAVAL) DIVISION Major-General C. E. Lawrie
- Battle of Albert 21 - 23 Aug (IV Corps, Third Army)
- Battle of Canal du Nord 27 Sept-1 Oct (XVII Corps, Third Army)

188th Brigade : Brigadier-General J. F. S. D. Coleridge
Anson   2nd Royal Irish
Royal Marines Light Infantry
189th Brigade : Brigadier-General H. D. de Pree to 24 Aug; Commander W. M. Egerton acting to 3 Sept; Brigadier-General B. J. Curling
Drake   Hawke
Hood
190th Brigade : Brigadier-General W. B. Lesslie
7th Royal Fusiliers   4th Bedfordshires
1/28th (Artists Rifles) Londons
  Pioneers : 14th (Severn Valley Pioneers) Worcesters

74th (YEOMANRY) DIVISION Major-General E. S. Girdwood
- Second Battle of Bapaume 2 - 3 Sept (III Corps, Fourth Army)
- Battles of the Hindenburg Line 12 - 24 Sept
- Battle of Epehy 18 Sept (III Corps, Fourth Army)

229th Brigade : Brigadier-General R. Hoare to 9 Sept (wounded); Lieutenant-Colonel C. J. H. Spence acting to 11 Sept; Brigadier-General F. S. Thackeray
16th (Royal 1st Devon and Royal North Devon Yeomanry) Devonshires
14th (Fife and Forfar Yeomanry) Black Watch
12th (West Somerset Yeomanry) Somerset Light Infantry
230th Brigade : Brigadier-General A. A. Kennedy
10th (Royal East Kent and West Kent Yeomanry) Buffs
16th (Sussex Yeomanry) Royal Sussex
15th (Suffolk Yeomanry) Suffolks
231st Brigade : Brigadier-General C. E. Heathcote
25th (Montgomery and Welsh Horse Yeomanry) Royal Welsh Fusiliers
10th (Shropshire and Cheshire Yeomanry) King's Shropshire Light Infantry
24th (Pembroke and Glamorgan Yeomanry) Welsh
Pioneers : 1/12th Loyal North Lancashires

1st CANADIAN DIVISION : Major General A C MacDonnell
- Battle of Amiens 8-11 August (Canadian Corps, Fourth Army)
- Damery 15-17 August (Canadian Corps, Fourth Army)
- Battle of the Canal du Nord 27 Sept – 1 Oct (Canadian Corps, Fourth Army)

1st Brigade : Brigadier-General W A Griesbach
1st Battalion (Ontario)   2nd Battalion (East Ontario)
3rd Battalion (Toronto)   4th Battalion
2nd Brigade : Brigadier-General F O W Loomis
5th Battalion (Western Cavalry)
7th Battalion (1st British Columbia)
8th Battalion (90th Rifles)
10th Battalion
3rd Brigade : Brigadier-General G S Tuxford
13th Battalion (Royal Highlanders)
14th Battalion (Royal Montreal)
15th Battalion (48th Highlanders)
16th Battalion (Canadian Scottish)
Pioneers : 1st Canadian Pioneer Battalion

2nd CANADIAN DIVISION : Major General H E Burstall
- Battle of Amiens 8-11 August (Canadian Corps, Fourth Army)
- Damery 15-17 August (Canadian Corps, Fourth Army)

4th Brigade : Brigadier General R Rennie
18th (West Ontario) Battalion
19th (Central Ontario) Battalion
20th (Central Ontario) Battalion
21st (Eastern Ontario) Battalion
5th Brigade : Brigadier-General J M Ross to 9 August; Brigadier-General T L Tremblay
22nd (Canadien-Français) Battalion
24th (Victoria Rifles) Battalion
25th (Nova Scotia Rifles) Battalion
26th (New Brunswick) Battalion
6th Brigade : Brigadier-General A H Bell
27th (City of Winnipeg) Battalion
28th (North West) Battalion
29th (Vancouver) Battalion
31st (Alberta) Battalion
Pioneers : 2nd Canadian Pioneer Battalion

3rd CANADIAN DIVISION : Major-General L J Lipsett to 12 September' Major-General F O W Loomis
- Battle of Amiens 8-11 August (Canadian Corps, Fourth Army)
- Damery 15-17 August (Canadian Corps, Fourth Army)
- Battle of the Canal du Nord 27 Sept – 1 Oct (Canadian Corps, Fourth Army)

7th Brigade : Brigadier-General H M Dyer to 11 September; Brigadier-General J A Clark
Princess Patricia's Canadian Light Infantry
42nd (Royal Highlanders) Battalion
Royal Canadian Regiment   49th (Edmonton) Battalion
8th Brigade : Brigadier-General D C Draper
1st Battalion, Canadian Mounted Rifles
2nd Battalion, Canadian Mounted Rifles
4th Battalion, Canadian Mounted Rifles
5th Battalion, Canadian Mounted Rifles
9th Brigade : Brigadier-General D M Ormond
43rd (Cameron Highlanders) Battalion
52nd (North Ontario) Battalion   116th Battalion
58th (Central Ontario) Battalion
Pioneers : 3rd Canadian Pioneer Battalion

4th CANADIAN DIVISION : Major-General D Watson
- Battle of Amiens 8-11 August (Canadian Corps, Fourth Army)
- Damery 15-17 August (Canadian Corps, Fourth Army)
- Battle of the Canal du Nord 27 Sept – 1 Oct (Canadian Corps, Fourth Army)

10th Brigade : Brigadier-General R J F Hayter
44th Battalion   50th (Calgary) Battalion
46th (South Saskatchewan) Battalion
47th (British Columbia) Battalion
11th Brigade : Brigadier-General V W Odlum
54th (Kootenay) Battalion   75th (Mississauga) Battalion
87th (Canadian Grenadier Guards) Battalion
102nd Battalion
12th Brigade : Brigadier-General J H MacBrien
38th (Ottawa) Battalion   85th Battalion
72nd (Seaforth Highlanders) Battalion
78th (Winnipeg Grenadiers) Battalion
Pioneers : 67th Canadian Pioneer Battalion

NEW ZEALAND DIVISION : Major-General A. H. Russell
- Battle of Albert 21-23 August (IV Corps, Third Army)
- Second Battle of Bapaume 31 August – 3 Sept (IV Corps, Third Army)
- Battle of Havrincourt 12 September (IV Corps, Third Army)
- Battle of the Canal du Nord 27 Sept – 1 Oct (IV Corps, Third Army)

1st New Zealand Brigade : Brigadier-General C W Melville
1st Auckland Battalion   1st Otago Battalion
1st Canterbury Battalion   1st Wellington Battalion
2nd New Zealand Brigade : Colonel R Young
2nd Auckland Battalion   2nd Otago Battalion
2nd Canterbury Battalion   2nd Wellington Battalion
3rd New Zealand (Rifles) Brigade : Brigadier-General H E Hart
1st NZ Rifle Brigade   2nd NZ Rifle Brigade
3rd NZ Rifle Brigade   4th NZ Rifle Brigade
Pioneers : New Zealand Pioneer Battalion

1st AUSTRALIAN DIVISION : Major General T W Glasgow
- Battle of Amiens 8-11 August (Australian Corps, Fourth Army)
- Battle of Albert 21-23 August (Australian Corps, Fourth Army)
- Capture of Chuignes (Australian Corps, Fourth Army)
- Battle of Epehy 18 Sept (Australian Corps, Fourth Army)

1st (New South Wales) Brigade : Brigadier-General I G Mackay
1st Battalion	2nd Battalion
3rd Battalion	4th Battalion

2nd (Victoria) Brigade : Brigadier-General J Heane
5th Battalion	6th Battalion
7th Battalion	8th Battalion

3rd Brigade : Brigadier-General H G Bennett
9th (Queensland) Battalion
10th (South Australia) Battalion
11th (West Australia) Battalion
12th (Tasmania, S and W Australia) Battalion
    Pioneers : 1st Australian Pioneer Battalion

2nd AUSTRALIAN DIVISION : Major General C Rosenthal
- Second Battle of Bapaume 31 August – 3 September (Australian Corps, Fourth Army)
- Capture of Mont St Quentin (Australian Corps, Fourth Army)
- Battle of the St Quentin Canal 29 Sept – 2 Oct (Australian Corps, Fourth Army)

5th (New South Wales) Brigade : Brigadier-General E F Martin
17th Battalion	18th Battalion
19th Battalion	20th Battalion

6th (Victoria) Brigade : Brigadier-General J Paton to 31 August; Brigadier-General J C Robertson
21st Battalion	22nd Battalion
23rd Battalion	24th Battalion

7th Brigade : Brigadier-General E A Wisdom
25th (Queensland) Battalion
26th (Queensland & Tasmania) Battalion
27th (South Australia) Battalion
28th (West Australia) Battalion
    Pioneers : 2nd Australian Pioneer Battalion

3rd AUSTRALIAN DIVISION : Major General J Gellibrand
- Battle of Albert 21-23 August (Australian Corps, Fourth Army)
- Second Battle of Bapaume 31 August – 3 September (Australian Corps, Fourth Army)
- Battle of the St Quentin Canal 29 Sept – 2 Oct (Australian Corps, Fourth Army)

9th (New South Wales) Brigade : Brigadier-General H A Goddard
33rd Battalion	34th Battalion
35th Battalion	36th Battalion

10th Brigade : Brigadier-General W R McNicoll
37th (Victoria) Battalion	38th (Victoria) Battalion
39th (Victoria) Battalion	40th (Tasmania) Battalion

11th Brigade : Brigadier-General J H Cannan
41st (Queensland) Battalion	42nd (Queensland) Battalion

43rd (South Australia) Battalion
44th (West Australia) Battalion
    Pioneers : 3rd Australian Pioneer Battalion

4th AUSTRALIAN DIVISION : Major General E G Sinclair-Maclagan
- Battle of Amiens 8-11 August (Australian Corps, Fourth Army)
- Battle of Albert 21-23 August (Australian Corps, Fourth Army)
- Battle of Epehy 18 Sept (Australian Corps, Fourth Army)

4th Brigade : Brigadier-General C H Brand
13th (New South Wales) Battalion
14th (Victoria) Battalion
15th (Queensland & Tasmania) Battalion
16th (South & West Australia) Battalion

12th Brigade : Brigadier-General R L Leane
45th (New South Wales) Battalion
46th (Victoria) Battalion
47th (Queensland & Tasmania) Battalion
48th (South & West Australia) Battalion

13th Brigade : Brigadier-General S C E Herring
49th (Queensland) Battalion
50th (South Australia & Tasmania) Battalion
51st (West Australia) Battalion
52nd (West & South Australia, Tasmania) Battalion
    Pioneers : 4th Australian Pioneer Battalion

5th AUSTRALIAN DIVISION : Major General J J T Hobbs
- Battle of Amiens 8-11 August (Australian Corps, Fourth Army)
- Battle of Albert 21-23 August (Australian Corps, Fourth Army)
- Second Battle of Bapaume 31 August – 3 September (Australian Corps, Fourth Army)
- Occupation of Peronne
- Battle of the St Quentin Canal 29 Sept – 2 Oct (Australian Corps, Fourth Army)

8th Brigade : Brigadier-General E Tivey
29th (Victoria)Battalion
30th (New South Wales)Battalion
31st (Queensland & Victoria) Battalion
32nd (Western Australia & South Australia)Battalion

14th (New South Wales)Brigade : Brigadier-General J C Stewart
53rd Battalion	54th Battalion
55th Battalion	56th Battalion

15th (Victoria) Brigade : Brigadier-General H E Elliott
57th (New South Wales)Battalion
58th Battalion	59th Battalion

60th Battalion
    Pioneers : 5th Australian Pioneer Battalion

	UK	Aust	NZ	Can	NF	SAfr	RGLI	BWI	India	Chi	Fr	Ger	Others	Unnamed	KUG	WW2	SM	Total
Ablainzevelle Communal															1			1
Acheux British	179			1														180
Achiet-le-Grand Communal	4																	4
Achiet-le-Grand Communal Extension	1259	61	95	4	1	4						42		200			18	1466
Achiet-le-Petit Communal																7		7
Adanac Military	1973	53	70	1071		5						1		1708	5		13	3178
Adelaide, Villers-Bretonneux	365	519	22											260	48		4	954
Agny Military	407	1										5		118				413
A.I.F. Burial Ground	2815	417	89	67		27					164	3		2262	60		26	3642
Ailly-sur-Noye Churchyard	2																	2
Aizecourt-le-Bas Churchyard	3																	3
Albert Communal Extension	618	39		202				2	3				1	12	1	17	5	883
Allonville Communal	38	40														1		79
Amplier Communal	2																	2
Ancre British	2446		2		42	1						1		1335			59	2492
Andechy Communal				1										1				1
Assevillers New British	647	111		3		16					1			332			37	778
Aubigny British	7	88										1		1				95
Auchonvillers Communal	15																	15
Auchonvillers Military	496		24		8						6			44				534
Authie Churchyard																2		2
Authuile Military	451					3			18			1		38			18	473
Aveluy Communal Extension	549	54		7		1			2					27			3	613
Aveluy Wood (Lancashire Dump)	365	26												172			20	391
Ayette British	53									1							3	54
Ayette Indian & Chinese									52	33		1		17				86
Bac-du-Sud British	640			48								55		4				743
Bailleulmont Communal	33			1														34
Ballieulval Communal	2																	2
Bancourt British	1999	248	176	13	1									1463			44	2437
Bancourt Communal	5	1	1														2	7
Bapaume Australian	12	74							1			23			1			111
Bapaume Communal	2	20	4											2		1		27
Bapaume Post Military	327	18		64		1								181			3	410
Barastre Communal	11		4															15
Bavelincourt Communal	51	3																54
Bazentin-le-Petit Communal	2																	2

349

	UK	Aust	NZ	Can	NF	SAfr	RGLI	BWI	India	Chi	Fr	Ger	Others	Unnamed	KUG	WW2	SM	Total
Bazentin-le-Petit Communal Extension	179	1		5														185
Bazentin-le-Petit Military	116	55				10											58	181
Beacon	575	195	1	1		1								15			4	772
Beacourt British, Beaucourt-en-Santerre	10			77										257				87
Beaulencourt British	599	51	81	3		1								1				750
Beaumetz Communal	4													309			21	4
Beaumetz Cross Roads	207	56	12									4		99			7	279
Beaumetz-les-Cambrai Military No 1	257													182				257
Beaumont-Hamel British	111			1								2		18	63		2	178
Bécourt Military	606	72		31		3								8			1	712
Behencourt Churchyard	2	1																3
Bellacourt Military	259			173					1		117	1		1				550
Berles-au-Bois Churchyard Extension	144										44	9		2			1	197
Berles New Military	167										11			1				178
Berles Position Military	52													1				52
Bernafay Wood British	793	122	2			4			1					417			32	922
Berthaucourt Communal	71													4				71
Bertincourt Château British	47											2		2				47
Bertrancourt Communal		1																1
Bertrancourt Military	416	26	2								3			2	2			449
Beugnatre Communal	5	5																10
Bienvillers Military	1567	25	9	3		1						1		427		16	2	1622
Bihucourt Communal	1		1											1				2
Blairville Churchyard	2																	2
Blangy-Tronville Communal	26	16									1						1	43
Blighty Valley	993	2		1										532			29	996
Boisleux-au-Mont Communal	6															2		8
Bonnay Communal Extension	31	75																106
Bootham	186													71				186
Bouchoir New British	541	6		216		1								231			6	764
Bouvincourt Communal	6																	6
Bouzincourt Communal	33																	33
Bouzincourt Communal Extension	561	8	1	7		2						2		107	8		2	589
Bouzincourt Ridge	667	35	6											313			1	708
Boves East Communal	8	3		4							5							20
Boves West Communal	45	5	1								12		1					64

350

	UK	Aust	NZ	Can	NF	SAfr	RGLI	BWI	India	Chi	Fr	Ger	Others	Unnamed	KUG	WW2	SM	Total
Boves West Communal Extension	38	4		48				1						1			1	92
Boyelles Communal Extension	142											4		5				146
Bray Hill British	102	2												32				104
Bray Military	739	31		3		2			13				8	127	79		18	875
Bray Vale British	258	17		1	3									172	2			281
Bray-sur-Somme Communal	3																	3
Brie British	365	27		1								36		49	1		15	430
Bronfay Farm Military	516	15				1			2					13	1		2	535
Bucquoy Communal	8														2			10
Bucquoy Communal Extension	68													2				68
Bucquoy Road	1453			447					1					169	91	136	44	2128
Buire Communal	2	6																8
Buire-sur-l'Ancre Communal	4	2																6
Bulls Road, Flers	493	155	122											296	2		15	772
Bus-les-Artois Communal	2																	2
Bussy-les-Daours Communal	2																	2
2nd Canadian, Contalmaison				44														44
Cachy Communal		1																1
Cagnicourt British	248	5	1	24	4								1	180		1		284
Cagnicourt Communal																1		1
Caix British	133	13		219										70				365
Caix Communal	1										140							141
Camon Communal	9	8												1		6		23
Carnoy Military	845	1	5	3		1								29			18	855
Caterpillar Valley	5229	100	214	6	2	18							1	3798			38	5570
Cayeux Military	207	1		5		2								114				216
Cerisy-Gailly Military	597	81		65		2			1				1	114			5	746
Chapelle British	621													260			21	621
Cherisy Road East	82													19				82
Chipilly Communal	55										4			2				59
Chipilly Communal Extension	29	2												2				31
Citadel New Military	378													15				378
Clery-sur-Somme Communal		1																1
Cojeul British	349													35				349
Colincamps Communal			9															9
Combles Communal Extension	1462	22		7		11								973			13	1502
Connaught	1286													642			7	1286
Contalmaison Château	264	21		4										45			1	289

351

	UK	Aust	NZ	Can	NF	SAfr	RGLI	BWI	India	Chi	Fr	Ger	Others	Unnamed	KUG	WW2	SM	Total
Contay British	689	29	414	1								40		3			16	1173
Corbie Communal	246					4						15	1				1	266
Corbie Communal Extension	831	58		27								1					2	917
Couin British	397			1		2			1			3					2	404
Couin Communal		1																1
Couin New British	344	14	2									2						362
Courcelette British	673	513	1	783										1176	4		9	1974
Courcelles-au-Bois Communal Extension	105	5	2	3														115
Croisilles British	1165	1		3		2			2			18		647	6		16	1197
Croisilles Railway	181											26		27			1	207
Crucifix Corner	288	296		76							141		2	191	2		2	803
Cuckoo Passage	54																	54
Damery Communal	1													1				11
Dantzig Alley British	2008	13	18	10		3			1					518			87	2053
Daours Communal	2																	2
Daours Communal Extension	760	459	1	2		1			8	2				6	1		4	1233
Dartmoor	633	71	59	4					1									769
Davenescourt Communal																11		11
De Cusine Ravine British	65							2				3						68
Delsaux Farm, Beugny	482	2	6	3										61			32	495
Delville Wood	5242	81	19	29		152								3587	3		29	5526
Demicourt Communal	10																	10
Démuin British	3			40										1				43
Dernancourt Communal	124	3										1					31	261
Dernancourt Communal Extension	1639	425	51	8		33		1	6	3		2	1	177	112			2281
Devonshire	153																	153
Dive Copse British	512	59			18									20	10		10	599
Doingt Communal Extension	342	67	2		5									1	1	2		419
Dominion	17		214											5				231
Domino British	51																	51
Douchy-les-Ayette British	727	5		1		2						1		242			1	736
Doullens Communal																6		6
Doullens Communal Extension No. 1	1146	69	78	40	4	3	1	2	2		479	13	1	16			29	1838
Doullens Communal Extension No. 2	321	1	28	24		2				1		84						461
Dury Communal																1		1
Eclusier Communal	23										126							149

352

	UK	Aust	NZ	Can	NF	SAfr	RGLI	BWI	India	Chi	Fr	Ger	Others	Unnamed	KUG	WW2	SM	Total
Ecoust Military	147	9										71		72			1	227
Ecoust-St Mein British	145			6										7				151
Englebelmer Communal	50		1								6				1			58
Englebelmer Communal Extension	123		27											1	1		2	151
Ennemain Communal Extension	72	4		1										40			2	77
Epéhy Communal	1																	1
Epéhy Wood Farm	996												1	235			31	997
Eppeville Old Churchyard	8										3			3				11
Ervillers Military	66	1												15				67
Eterpigny Communal Extension (Somme)	20	7												9				27
Etreillers Communal	1																	1
Etricourt Communal	5																	5
Euston Road	960	26	302	4		3			1					170	76		34	1369
Favreuil British	347	26	19	1								13		11			5	409
Feuchy Chapel British	1076			26		1								578			20	1103
Fifteen Ravine British	1193		60	1		10						2		740			54	1266
Fins New British	1193	2	3	5		87	1					276		208			10	1567
Five Points	99								1					3				100
Flatiron Copse	1520	17	30			1								416			45	1568
Flesquieres Hill British	810	2	63	10	22		4							332			10	911
Fluquieres Communal	3																	3
Folies Communal	1			1														2
Fonchette Churchyard	1																	1
Foncquevillers Military	625	6	12							2		4	1	53		5	2	655
Forceville Communal & Extension	304		2	1								7		2				314
Foreste Communal	94	3									4			22			23	98
Foucaucourt Communal	8																	8
Fouilly Communal	12	25		1							71							109
Fouquescourt British	139	49		137		2								130	43		6	370
Fouquescourt Old Churchyard				1														1
Framerville Communal	4	1																5
Frankfurt Trench British	161													34				161
Franvillers Communal	4	3		1														8
Franvillers Communal Extension	113	134	1									5						253
Frechencourt Communal	8	49																57
Fresnoy-les-Roye Communal				1														1
Fricourt British (Bray Road)	131		1														1	132

353

	UK	Aust	NZ	Can	NF	SAfr	RGLI	BWI	India	Chi	Fr	Ger	Others	Unnamed	KUG	WW2	SM	Total
Fricourt Communal	208												1			3		210
Fricourt New Military	1	2																1
Frise Communal	48																	48
Gauche Wood	17	3																20
Gentelles Communal	4	3												1			1	8
Glisy Communal	206											27						233
Gomiécourt South	1285	26	46											10			3	1357
Gommecourt British No. 2	692	1	56											682			33	749
Gommecourt Wood New	1													465			10	1296
Gonnelieu Communal	102													1053			34	1
Gonnelieu Communal																		102
Gordon, Mametz	102													5			93	102
Gordon Dump	1582	91	2							1				1053			34	1676
Gouzeaucourt New British	1182		85	2	1	24							2	382			34	1296
Grand Ravine	139													11				139
Grandcourt Road	390		1											108		1		391
Grévillers British	1507	428	153	14		1		2			18	34		189	4	7	20	2135
Grove Town	1365	14	1	12							1			2				1427
Guards', Combles	182			4										15			30	186
Guards', Les Boeufs	2827	202	11	4										1643			88	3045
Guemappe British	169													6				169
Guillemont Road	2259	1		1		1						2		1523		8		2265
H.A.C	1704	176	4	26										1086	145		65	2055
Hailles Communal	1																	1
Halloy Communal														1			2	2
Ham British, Muille-Villette	485													218			53	485
Hamel Military	487		1									4		80			4	492
Hamel British	86	31		1										21			4	118
Hangard Communal Extension	444	47		72								1		294		17		564
Hangard Wood British	58	17		61		5					20			39				161
Hannescamps Churchyard	21																	21
Hannescamps New Military	100							2						19		1		102
Hargicourt British	273	15						22				2		35			1	312
Hargicourt Communal Extension	61	12																73
Harponville Communal	34													1				34
Harponville Communal Extension	138																	138
Hawthorn Ridge No. 1	152			1										71				153
Hawthorn Ridge No. 2	190		6		24									65				214
Heath	859	984	6	9		2								369			47	1860

354

	UK	Aust	NZ	Can	NF	SAfr	RGLI	BWI	India	Chi	Fr	Ger	Others	Unnamed	KUG	WW2	SM	Total
Hébuterne Communal	56	2									54		1	6				113
Hébuterne Military	699		53									5		45			17	757
Hédauville Communal Extension	168	1	9											4		2		180
Heilly Station	2356	401	118	7	8			1				83	1	12			21	2975
Hem Farm Military	368	138		4		88								205			2	598
Henin Communal Extension	192			1										18			2	193
Henin Crucifix	61													2			8	61
Heninel Communal Extension	140													7				140
Heninel-Croisilles Road	297	10										11		104				318
Henu Churchyard	17										88							105
Herbécourt British	8	51																59
Herissart Communal	13																	13
Herleville Churchyard	2																	2
Hermies British	82	27												3			1	109
Hermies Hill British	983	43	7	3										297			37	1036
Hesbecourt Communal	12	2												2				14
Heudicourt Communal	3					1												4
Heudicourt Communal Extension	81			2					2					6				85
Hibers Trench	133			3										6			2	136
Hillside	7			101										3				108
Hourges Orchard	13	4		127										11			1	144
Humbercamps Communal	2																	2
Humbercamps Communal Extension	79												3					79
Hunter's, Beaumont-Hamel	46													5				46
Ignaucourt Churchyard	1																	1
Jeancourt Communal Extension	372	114		6								168		207			2	660
Knightsbridge	490	1	18		39									141	65			613
La Cauchie Communal	8	5																13
La Chapelette British and Indian	207	49	1						320				3	6				580
La Herliere Communal	2															1		3
La Motte-Brebiere Communal	5	4																9
La Neuville British	821	21				24						27		5				893
La Neuville Communal	173	13																186
Lagnicourt Hedge	62	1										15		1				78
Lavieville Communal	1	6														1		8
Le Fermont Military	78									2								80
Le Hamel Communal	1																	1

355

	UK	Aust	NZ	Can	NF	SAfr	RGLI	BWI	India	Chi	Fr	Ger	Others	Unnamed	KUG	WW2	SM	Total
Le Quesnel Communal	3	3									147							153
Le Quesnel Communal Extension	11			54										6		7		72
Le Sars Communal																1		1
Le Verguier Churchyard	1	2																3
Lebucquire Communal Extension	685	66	21									5		266	21	21		779
Lempire Communal	12																	12
L'homme Mort British	126		37	3														166
London & Extension, High Wood, Longueval	3339	300	35	162	33	2					2	2		3114	165	1		4040
London, Neuville-Vitasse	713	11	19	4										318		138		747
Longueau British	72	65	65					2						14	2			206
Longueau Communal	4															1		4
Longueval Communal	185	22	7	1								1		49	3			223
Longueval Road	7		7															
Lonsdale	1538	4									1			816	22			1543
Louvencourt Military	133		17	1							76				3			230
Louverval Military	118	4	2											6				124
Lowrie	251													47				251
Luke Copse British	72													28				72
Mailly Wood	631		28			3						1		60	40	8		702
Mailly-Maillet Communal Extension	122	3		1														126
Manancourt Communal	1																	1
Manchester	67		1											8	3	1		71
Manitoba	2			118										3	8			128
Marieux Communal												1			1			1
Marteville Communal	76										2	1		9		1		79
Martinpuich British	80	34		1												4		115
Martinpuich Communal	5													1		2		5
Martinsart British	383	1	8											156	96	6		488
Meath	125													21		3		125
Méaulte Military	296		1	2				6						21	7	11		312
Meharicourt Communal															41			41
Mercatel Communal														13	20			20
Méricourt-l'Abbé Communal Extension	234	122	5									11		73	51	2		423
Mesnil Communal Extension	262		7	5										94	59	10		333
Mesnil Ridge	94				1													95
Mesnil-St Nicaise Churchyard	1																	1
Metz-en-Couture Communal	415	5	43	1		7						12		44	2	4		486

356

	UK	Aust	NZ	Can	NF	SAfr	RGLI	BWI	India	Chi	Fr	Ger	Others	Unnamed	KUG	WW2	SM	Total
Mézières Communal Extension	95	1		37										63			1	133
Mill Road, Thiepval	1304													815			6	1304
Millencourt Communal Extension	273	50	7	7		1						5		4	2			345
Miraumont Communal	27												1	4			2	30
Moeuvres British	102			1								4		13			4	107
Moeuvres Communal Extension	500	8		22								90	4	262			34	624
Molliens-au-Bois Communal	6																	6
Mondicourt Communal	12															13		26
Mons-en-Chausee Communal	6			1						1								7
Montigny Communal	56													3				56
Montigny Communal Extension	19											3						22
Morchies Australian	41	20										2		3	1			64
Morchies Communal	5	1		2										3				8
Morchies Military	133	17										15		74			18	165
Moreuil Communal Allied Extension	177	3		9					1					96			1	189
Morlancourt British No. 1	74											4		4				75
Morlancourt British No. 2	55	2												2				57
Morval British	54											1						55
Morval Communal																2		2
Mory Abbey Military	616	1	1									230		101			1	848
Mory Street Military	66													5			6	66
Moyenneville (Two Tree)	49													17				49
Munich Trench British	126													28				126
Nesle Communal	135													1				135
Neuville-Bourjonval British	209		5											9			3	214
Neuville-Vitasse Road	86													11				86
New Munich Trench British	146													18				146
Noreuil Australian	62	182				3			1					28			82	244
Norfolk	407	9	1	2										226	126			549
Ontario	182	9	1	144										84			5	336
Orival Wood	281									1		20		10			7	302
Orville Communal	1															1		1
Ovillers Military	3208	57	6	95		13					121			2480			60	3500
Owl Trench	53													10				53
Pargny British	613			6										489			18	619
Pas-en-Artois Communal	1															1		2
Peake Wood	89	7		1													6	97

357

	UK	Aust	NZ	Can	NF	SAfr	RGLI	BWI	India	Chi	Fr	Ger	Others	Unnamed	KUG	WW2	SM	Total
Péronne Communal	1										66							67
Péronne Communal Extension	1065	512	1	6								97		220		5	17	1686
Péronne Road	1299	14		34										366			28	1348
Pigeon Ravine	135													16			2	135
Point 110 New Military	64																	64
Point 110 Old Military	100													3				100
Pommier Communal	26																	26
Pont-Noyelle Communal	3																	3
Pozières British	1809	700		214								1		1382	11		23	2735
Puchevillers British	1132	417	1	213										7				1763
Puisieux Communal																	3	3
Quarry, Marquion	23			45														68
Quarry, Montauban	674	25	36		5									157			24	756
Quarry Wood	14			263										5			1	277
Queant Communal British Extension	159	3		112										6	1			276
Queant Road	1289	995	1	87						2		3		1443	5		82	2382
Quebec	6			189										12				195
Queens, Bucquoy	698		28								5			214			10	731
Queens, Puisieux	311													131				311
Querrieu British	102	84							1		12					1		200
Quesnoy Farm Military	60													1				60
Railway Hollow	107										2			44				109
Railway Cutting	107													16		1		107
Rancourt Military	93											1		12	3	1		96
Raincheval Communal	1													1				1
Red Cross Corney	205	10		4								1		74			1	220
Redan Ridge No. 1	154													74				154
Redan Ridge No. 2	279													124				279
Redan Ridge No. 3	67													34				67
Regina Trench	1667	35	22	563									1	1077			14	2266
Ribecourt British	266											6		18			81	295
Ribecourt Railway	52			1										1				53
Ribecourt Road	255			6										8				261
Ribemont Communal Extension	269	190	4		2			1						33	15		18	481
Riencourt-les-Cagnicourt Communal																1		1
Rocquigny-Equancourt Road British	1764	5	21	12	22	12	2					198	10	21			9	2046

358

	UK	Aust	NZ	Can	NF	SAfr	RGLI	BWI	India	Chi	Fr	Ger	Others	Unnamed	KUG	WW2	SM	Total
Roisel Communal	1																	1
Roisel Communal Extension	721	106		6		29						514		120			15	1376
Ronssoy Communal	38	7										1		7				46
Rookery British	55																	55
Rosières British	60													6				60
Rosières Communal	10										140							150
Rosières Communal Extension	123	66		156						1				157	82		12	428
Rossignol Wood	34		7									70		2				111
Roupy Communal	12													1				12
Rouvrel Communal	1																	1
Rouy-le-Grand Churchyard	1													1				1
Rouy-le-Petit Churchyard	2																	2
Roye New British	350	1		65		6						2		153		43	130	467
Rubempre Communal	3																	3
Ruyaulcourt Military	324	2	20	2										10			2	348
Sailly-au-Bois Military	212	1	24			2						1		1				240
Sailly-Saillisel British	559	12			7									301	185		8	763
Sains-en-Amienois Communal	4			2							52							58
Sains-les-Marquion British	69	1		185										28				255
Sains-les-Marquion Churchyard																1		1
Sanders Keep Military	142											49		7				191
Saulcourt Churchyard Extension	95											7		33			8	102
Sauvillers-Mongival Communal																5		5
Savy British	867					1						1		438			68	868
Savy Communal	3																	3
Senlis Communal Extension	80	23												7			1	104
Serre Road No. 1	2125	147	27	120	1	6								1728			22	2426
Serre Road No. 2	5971	401	73	619	28	34						13		4944			21	7139
Serre Road No. 3	81													49			4	81
Shrine	74	8	7									1		41	1			91
Souastre Churchyard	1																	1
St. Amand British	222		1					1						3				224
St. Fuscien Communal	3																	3
St. Leger British	183					1			1			20		3			6	204
St. Martin Calvaire British	228											3		5				231
St. Pierre, Amiens	563	95	3	10		1			2	1					1	82	1	758
Ste. Emilie Valley	484	25	1	1		2						10		222			21	523
Stump Road	237			24										50	2			263

359

	UK	Aust	NZ	Can	NF	SAfr	RGLI	BWI	India	Chi	Fr	Ger	Others	Unnamed	KUG	WW2	SM	Total
Sucrerie British, Graincourt-lès-Havrincourt	57																	57
Sucrerie Military, Colincamps	965	29	65	13	32									5			1	1104
Summit Trench	74																	74
Sun Quarry	31			160														191
Sunken Road, Boisleux-St. Marc	398		2	14										5				419
Sunken Road, Contalmaison	5			61					1					4			3	214
Sunken Road, Villers-Plouich	51			148														51
Suzanne Communal Extension	141	14												3				155
Suzanne Military No. 3	102	28		8								1		42				139
Talmas Communal	2																2	4
Tank	218			1										25			11	219
Targelle Ravine British	114													7				114
Templeux-le-Guérard British	723	45		1				3						188			16	773
Templeux-le-Guérard Communal Extension	111	20												5			13	131
Terramesnil Communal	1															2		3
Tertry Communal	15																	15
Ten Tree Alley	67													24				67
Thiepval Anglo-French	285	10	1	4							300			239				600
Thilloy Road	230		9						1			10						250
Thistle Dump	122	36	38									7		59	12		4	215
Tigris Lane	86			33										9				119
Tilloy British	1447	91	3	57	4	15						2		610		1	25	1619
Tincourt New British	1562	226		45	2	39	6		20	58		152	1	251	2		33	2111
Tincourt Churchyard	3																	3
Toronto	22	1		74								4		22				101
Toutencourt Communal	22	1						1										23
Trefcon British	282								1					13		1		284
Trescault Communal	7																	7
Triangle	19			69										9	2			90
Ugny-L'Équipée Churchyard	2																	2
Unicorn	689	78	1						4					409	218		18	1008
Upton Wood	9			216								1		9	1		1	226
Vadencourt British	726	11		7					2	4				214		5		750
Vaire-sous-Corbie Communal		4																4
Valley	24	7		37										19			1	68
Varennes Military	1191	2	16	5		4							1					1219

	UK	Aust	NZ	Can	NF	SAfr	RGLI	BWI	India	Chi	Fr	Ger	Others	Unnamed	KUG	WW2	SM	Total
Vaulx Australian Field Ambulance	20	32										61		1				113
Vaulx Hill	658	106	58	1										258			33	823
Vendelles Churchyard	5	1																6
Vermand Communal	42																	42
Villeret Old Churchyard	18								1					5				19
Villers Hill British	702	1	23	5		1						13		350	1		17	746
Villers-Bocage Communal Extension	59	1														2		62
Villers-Bretonneux Communal	2	10									42							54
Villers-Bretonneux Military	1089	779	2	267		4								607		2	20	2143
Villers-Carbonnel Communal										3								3
Villers-Faucon Communal	226								1			90		5				317
Villers-Faucon Communal Extension	432	10	2			1			8			66		144			6	519
Villers-Guislain Communal	51													7			18	51
Villers-les-Cagnicourt Communal																2		2
Villers-Plouich Communal	50				1									8			2	51
Ville-sur-Ancre Communal	20	4									1					4		29
Ville-sur-Ancre Communal Extension	106													54				106
Vis-en-Artois British	1736	6		572	9	2								1461	6		12	2331
Voyennes Communal	1							1										1
Vraignes Communal	7	1												1				8
Vraucourt Copse	66	38												6		2		104
Vrély Communal Extension	4			39										4			2	43
Waggon Road	195													36				195
Wailly Communal																3		3
Wailly Orchard	162			189											15			366
Wancourt British	1026			246										262	566		96	1839
Wancourt Communal																6		6
Warlencourt British	2765	461	79	4		121					2			1825			70	3432
Warloy-Baillon Communal	46										158							204
Warloy-Baillon Communal Extension	857	319		152								18			3	2		1351
Warry Copse	40													2				40
Warvillers Churchyard Extension	13			35										3				48
Windmill British	320			61	4	1						1		17	15		1	402
Wood, Marcelcave	9			41										3				50
Y Ravine	328				38									151			61	427
477	**166410**	**15798**	**3131**	**11393**	**306**	**1048**	**15**	**16**	**525**	**132**	**2767**	**3016**	**46**	**69197**	**2372**	**666**	**3350**	**207720**

361

	UK	Aust	NZ	Can	NF	SAfr	RGLI	BWI	India	Chi	Fr	Ger	Others	Unnamed	KUG	WW2	SM	Total
Bony American Military	2	1											1830					1833
FRENCH NATIONAL CEMETERIES	UK	Aust	NZ	Can	NF	SAfr	RGLI	BWI	India	Chi	French	Ger	Others	Unnamed	KUG	WW2	SM	Total
Albert										1	6290							6291
Beuvraignes											1857							1857
Biaches											1361							1361
Bray-sur-Somme	1										1045							1046
Cerisy-Gailly	342	44	1	4							990			296				1382
Clery-sur-Somme											2332							2332
Cote 80	19	29		1			1				1004			5				1053
Dompierre-Becquincourt											7034	1						7035
Hattencourt											1949		2					1951
Lihons	5			1							6587			2				6593
Marcelcave "Les Buttes"											1610							1610
Maucourt											5302					6		5308
Maurepas											3657		20					3677
Moislains											465							465
Montdidier Communal											745							745
Montdidier											7432		2			24		7458
Rancourt											8567							8567
Serre-Hébuterne											834							834
St. Acheul, Amiens	12										2751		11					2774
St. Pierre, Amiens											1372		25					1397
Villers-Carbonnel											2297							2297
	381	73	2	6	0	0	1	0	0	1	65481	1	1890	303	0	30	0	67866
GERMAN MILITARY CEMETERIES	UK	Aust	NZ	Can	NF	SAfr	RGLI	BWI	India	Chi	French	Ger	Others	Unnamed	KUG	WW2	SM	Total
Achiet-le-Petit												1314						1314
Andechy												2251						2251
Béthencourt-sur-Somme												1242						1242
Bray-sur-Somme												1119						1119
Caix												1264						1264
Fricourt												17027						17027
Ham (Muille-Villette)												1534						1534
Maissemy												30481						30481
Manicourt												7326						7326

362

Montdidier	8051
Morisel	2640
Proyart	4643
Rancourt	11422
Roye-St.Gillies	6535
Sapignies	1550
Vermandovillers	22655
Villers-au-Flos	2449
17	**123503**

VICTORIA CROSS HOLDERS BURIED IN CEMETERIES OR COMMEMORATED ON MEMORIALS INCLUDED IN THIS BOOK

Anderson, William Herbert, Lieutenant Colonel, 12th Highland Light Infantry, awarded the VC for his actions on 25 March 1918 at Bois Favieres, near Maricourt, France. Killed in action 25 March 1918, buried in Peronne Road Cemetery

Beatham, Robert Matthew, Private, 8th Australian Infantry, awarded the VC for his actions at Rosieres on 9-11 August 1918. Killed in action 11 August 1918 buried in Heath Cemetery.

Bell, Eric Norman Frankland, Captain, 9th Royal Inniskilling Fusiliers attached to Light Trench Mortar Battery, awarded the VC for his actions on 1 July 1916 at Thiepval. Killed in action on 1 July 1916 and commemorated on the Thiepval Memorial.

Bell, Donald Simpson, 2nd Lieutenant, 9th Green Howards, awarded the Victoria Cross for his actions on 5 July 1916 at Horseshoe Trench, Somme. Killed in action on 10 July 1916 and buried in Gordon Dump Cemetery. Professional footballer.

Bradford, Roland Boys, MC, Brigadier General, commanding 186th (2/2nd West Riding) Brigade, awarded the VC when Lieutenant Colonel commanding 9th Durham Light Infantry for his actions on 1 October 1916 at Eaucourt L'Abbaye. Killed in action at Cambrai on 30 November 1917, buried in Hermies British Cemetery. His brother won the VC in WW1, they are the only brothers to win the VC in WW1.

Brillant, Jean Baptiste Arthur, MC, Lieutenant, 22nd Canadian Infantry, awarded the VC for his actions on 8-9 August 1918 east of Meharicourt. Died of wounds on 10 August 1918 and buried in Villers-Bretonneux Military Cemetery.

Brodie, Walter Lorrain, MC Lieutenant Colonel, 2nd Highland Light Infantry, awarded the VC when a Lieutenant in 2nd Highland Light Infantry for his actions on 11 November 1914 near Becelaere, Belgium. Killed in action near Moeuvres on 23 August 1918 and buried in Bienvillers Military Cemetery.

Brown, Donald Forrester, Sergeant, 2nd Otago Infantry, NZEF, awarded the VC for his actions on 1 October 1916 in the Battle of Le Transloy near Eaucourt L'Abbaye. Killed in action on 1 October 1916 and buried in Warlencourt British Cemetery.

Buchan, John Crawford, 2nd Lieutenant, 7th attached 8th Argyll and Sutherland Highlanders, awarded the VC for an act he performed on 21 March 1918 east of Marteville. Died of wounds on 22 March 1918 and buried in Roisel Communal Cemetery Extension.

Buckingham, William, Private, 2nd Leicestershires, awarded the Victoria Cross for his actions on 10 and 12 March 1915 at Neuve Chapelle. He was killed at Thiepval on 15 September 1916 and commemorated on the Thiepval Memorial.

Buckley, Alexander Henry, Corporal, 54th Australian Infantry, awarded the VC for his actions on the night of 1-2 September 1918 at Peronne. Killed in action on 1 September 1918 and buried in Peronne Communal Cemetery Extension.

Bushell, Christopher, DSO, Lieutenant Colonel, 7th Queen's (Royal West Surreys), awarded the Victoria Cross for an action on 23 March 1918 west of St. Quentin's Canal and north of Tergnier. Killed in action to the south of Morlancourt on 8 August 1918 and buried at Querrieu British Cemetery.

Castleton, Claud Charles, Sergeant, 5th Machine Gun Company, Australian Machine Gun Corps, awarded the VC for acts on the night of 28-29 July 1916 at Pozieres. Killed in action on 29 July 1916 and buried at Pozières British Military Cemetery.

Cates, George Edward, 2nd Lieutenant, 2nd Rifle Brigade, awarded the VC for his actions on 8 March 1917 at Bouchavesnes. Killed in action on 8 March 1917 and buried in Hem Farm Military Cemetery.

Cather, Geoffrey St. George Shillington, Lieutenant, 9th Royal Irish Fusiliers, awarded the VC for his actions on 1-2 July 1916 near Hamel. Killed in action on 2 July 1916 and commemorated on the Thiepval Memorial.

Cherry, Percy Herbert, MC, Captain, 26th Australian Infantry, awarded the VC for his actions at Lagnicourt on 26-27 March 1918. Killed in action on 27 March 1918 and buried in Queant Road Cemetery.

Clare, George William Burdett, Private, 5th (Royal Irish) Lancers, awarded the Victoria Cross for his actions on 28-29 November 1917 at Bourlon Wood, during the Battle of Cambrai. Killed in action on 29 November 1917 and commemorated on the Cambrai Memorial at Louverval.

Collings-Wells, John Stanhope, DSO, Lieutenant-Colonel, 4th Bedfordshires, awarded the VC for his actions from 22-27 March 1918 near Albert. Killed in action on 27 March 1918 and buried in Bouzincourt Ridge Cemetery.

Columbine, Herbert George, Private, 9th Squadron Machine Gun Corps (Cavalry), awarde the VC for his actions on 22 March 1918 at Hervilly Wood. Killed in action on 22 March 1918 and commemorated on the Pozieres Memorial.

Congreve, William "Billy" La Touche, DSO, MC, Legion d'Honneur, Major, Brigade Major in 76th Brigade, 3rd Divison and Rifle Brigade, awarde the Vc for his actions from 6-20 July 1916. Killed in action on 20 July 1916 and buried at Corbie Communal Cemetery Extension. His father also held the VC.

Cooke, Thomas, Private, 8th Australian Infantry, awarded the VC for his actions at Poziers from 24-25 July 1916. Killed in action at Pozieres on 28 July 1916 and commemorated on the Villers-Bretonneux Memorial.

Croak, John Bernard, Private, 13th Canadian Infantry, awarded the VC for his actions at Hangard Wood on 8 August 1918. Killed in action on 8 August 1918 and buried in Hangard Wood British Cemetery.

Dancox, Frederick George, Private 4th Worcestershires, awarded the VC for his actions at Boesinghe near Ieper on 9 October 1917. Killed in action near Masnieres, France, on 30 November 1917 and is commemorated on the Cambrai Memorial at Louverval.

de Wind, Edmund, 2nd Lieutenant, 15th Royal Irish Rifles, awarded the VC for his actions on 21 March 1918 at Crugies. Killed in action on 21 March 1918 and commemorated on the Pozieres Memorial.

Dimmer, John Henry Stephen, MC, Lieutenant Colonel, 2nd King's Royal Rifle Corps, awarded the VC when a Lieutenant for his actions at Klein Zillebeke, Belgium on 12 November 1914. Killed in action at Marteville, France on 21 March 1918 and buried at Vadencourt British Cemetery in Maissemy.

Dunville, John Spencer, 2nd Lieutenant, 1st Royal Dragoons, awarded the VC for his actions on 24-25 June 1917 near Epehy, France. Died of wounds on 26 June 1917 and buried at Villers-Faucon Communal Cemetery.

Dwyer, Edward, Corporal, 1st East Surreys, awarded the VC as a Private for his actions on 20 April 1915 at Hill 60, Belgium. Killed in action at Guillemont, France on 3 September 1916 and buried in Flatiron Copse Military Cemetery.

Elstob, Wilfrith, DSO, MC, Lieutenant Colonel, 16th Manchesters, awarde the VC for his actions at the Manchestr redoubt on 21 March 1918. Killed in action on 21 March 1918 and commemorated on the Pozieres Memorial.

Emerson, James Samuel, 2nd Lieutenant, 9th (Tyrone Volunteers) Royal Inniskilling Fusiliers, awarded the VC for his actions on 6 December 1917, on the Hindenburg Line north of La Vacquerie, France. Killed in action on 6 December 1917 and is commemorated on the Cambrai Memorial at Louverval.

Forsyth, Samuel, Sergeant, New Zealand Engineers attached 2nd Auckland Infantry, NZEF, awarded the VC for his actions near Grevillers on 24 August 1918. Killed in action on 24 August 1918 and buried in Adanac Military Cemetery.

Gaby, Alfred Edward, Lieutenant, 28th Australian Infantry, awarded the VC for his actions near Villers-Bretonneux on 8 August 1918. Killed in action on 11 August 1918 near Lihons and buried in Heath Cemetery.

Gill, Albert, Sergeant, 1st King's Royal Rifle Corps, awarded the VC for his actions at Delville Wood on 27 July 1916. Killed in action on 27 July 1916 and buried in Delville Wood Cemetery.

Green, John Leslie, Captain, Royal Army Medical Corps, attached to 1/5th Sherwood Foresters (Nottinghamshire and Derbyshire Regiment), awarded the VC for his actions at Gommecourt on 1 July 1916. Killed in action on 1 July 1916 and buried in Foncquevillers Military Cemetery.

Harris, Thomas James, MM, Sergeant, 6th Queen's Own (Royal West Kents), awarded the VC for his actions at Morlancourt, France on 9 August 1918. Killed in action on 9 August 1918 and buried in Dernancourt Communal Cemetery Extension.

Henderson, Arthur, MC, Captain, 4th attached 2nd Argyll and Sutherland Highlanders, awarded the VC for his actions near Fontaine-les-Croisilles, France on 23 April 1917. Died of wounds on 24 April 1917 and buried in Cojeul British Cemetery.

Honey, Samuel Lewis, DCM, MM, Lieutenant, 78th Canadian Infantry, awarded the VC for his actions at Bourlon Wood on 27-29 September 1918. Died of wounds on 30 September 1918 and buried in Queant Communal Cemetery.

Jackson, Harold, Sergeant, 7th East Yorkshires, awarded the VC for his actions at Hermies, France on 22 March 1918. Killed in action at Flers on 24 August 1918 and is buried at the AIF Burial Ground.

Jackson, Thomas Norman, Lance Corporal, 1st Coldstream Guards, awarded the VC for his actions at the Canal du Nord on 27 September 1918. Killed in action on 27 September 1918 and buried in Sanders Keep Military Cemetery.

Johnson, Frederick Henry, Major, Royal Engineers, awarded the VC while a 2nd Lieutenant during the attack on Hill 70 in the Battle of Loos on 25 September 1915. Killed in action in Bourlon Wood on 26 November 1917 and commemorated on the Cambrai Memorial at Louverval.

Jones, David, Sergeant, 12th King's (Liverpools), awarded the VC for his actions at Guillemont, France on 3 September 1916. Killed in action at Bancourt, Somme, on 7 October 1916 and buried in Bancourt British Cemetery.

Knight, Arthur George, Sergeant, 10th Canadian Infantry, awarded the VC for his actions at Villers-les-Cagnicourt, France on 2 September 1918. Died of wounds on 3 September 1918 and buried at Dominion Cemetery.

Lewis, Allan Leonard, Lance-Corporal, 6th Northamptonshires, awarded the VC for his actions at Rossnoy, France on 18 September 1918. Killed in action on 21 September 1918 and commemorated on the Vis-en-Artois Memorial.

Loudoun-Shand, Stewart Walter, Major, 10th Yorkshires, awarded the VC for his actions near Fricourt on 1 July 1916. He was killed in action on 1 July 1916 and is buried in Norfolk Cemetery.

Lumsden, Frederick William, CB, DSO & Three Bars, Brigadier General, commanding 14th Infantry Brigade, awarded the VC for his actions at Francilly, France on 3-4 April 1917. Killed in action at Blairville on 4 June 1918 and buried at Berles New Military Cemetery.

Mactier, Robert, Private, 23rd Australian Infantry, awarded the VC for his actions at Mont St. Quentin near Peronne on 1 September 1918. Killed in action on 1 September 1918 and buried in Hem Farm Military Cemetery.

Mariner, William, Private, 2nd King's Royal Rifle Corps, awarded the VC for his actions near Cambrin on 22 May 1915. Killed in action on 1 July 1916 and commemorated on the Thiepval Memorial.

McFadzean, William Frederick "Billy", Rifleman, 14th Royal Irish Rifles, awarded the VC for his actions at Thiepval Wood on 1 July 1916. Killed in action on 1 July 1916 and commemorated on the Thiepval Memorial.

McIver, Hugh, MM & Bar, Private, 2nd Royal Scots, awarded the VC for his actions east of Courcelle-le Compte, France on 23 August 1918. Killed in action on 2 September 1918 and buried in Vraucourt Copse Cemetery.

McReady-Diarmid, Allastair Malcolm Cluny, Captain, 17th Middlesex, awarded the VC for his actions at Moeuvres on 30 November-1 December 1917. Killed in action on 1 December 1917 and commemorated on the Cambrai Memorial at Louverval.

Miller, James, Private, 7th King's Own (Royal Lancasters), awarded the VC for his actions at Bazentin-le-Petit, France on 30-31 July 1916. Killed in action on 31 July 1916 and buried in Dartmoor Cemetery.

Mynarski, Andrew Charles "Andy", Pilot Officer, No. 419 Squadron, Royal Canadian Air Force, awarded the VC for his actions on 12-13 June 1944. Killed in action on 13 June 1944 and buried in Méharicourt Communal Cemetery. He is the only WW2 VC buried on the Somme.

Parsons, Hardy Falconer, 2nd Lieutenant, 14th Gloucestershires, awarded the VC for his actions near Epehy, France on 20-21 August 1917. Died of wounds on 21 August 1918 and buried in Villers-Faucon Communal Cemetery.

Paton, George Henry Tatham, MC, Captain, 4th Grenadier Guards, awarded the VC for his actions at Gonnelieu, France on 1 December 1917. Died of wounds on 1 December 1917 and buried in Metz-en-Couture Communal Cemetery.

Pope, Charles, Lieutenant, 11th Australian Infantry, awarded the VC for his actions at Louverval, France, during the Battle of Lagnicourt on 15 April 1917. Killed in action on 15 April 1917 and buried in Moeuvres Communal Cemetery Extension.

Prowse, George Henry, DCM, Chief Petty Officer, Drake Battalion, Royal Navy Division, awarded the VC for his actions at Pronville, France on 2 September 1918. Killed in action on 27 September 1918 and commemorated on the Vis-en-Artois Memorial.

Rhodes, John Harold, DCM & Bar, Lance-Sergeant, 3rd Grenadier Guards, awarded the VC for his actions near the Houthulust Forest, Ieper on 9 October 1917. Killed in action at Fontaine-Notre-Dame, France on 27 November 1917 and buried at Rocquigny-Equancourt Road British Cemetery.

Richardson, James (Jimmy) Cleland, Piper, 16th Canadian Infantry, awarded the VC for his actions at Regine Trench on the Somme on 8-9 October 1916. Killed in action on 9 October 1916 and buried in Adanac Cemetery.

Riggs, Frederick Charles, MM, Sergeant, 6th York and Lancasters, awarded the VC for his actions near Epinoy, France on 1 October 1918. Killed in action on 1 October 1918 and commemorated on the Vis-en-Artois Memorial.

Sewell, Cecil Harold, Lieutenant, Queen's Own (Royal West Kents), attached to 3rd (Light) Battalion, Tank Corps, awarded the VC for his actions at Fremicourt, France on 29 August 1918. Killed in action on 29 August 1918 and buried in Vaulx Hill Cemetery.

Short, William Henry, Private, 8th Yorkshires, awarded the VC for his actions at Munster Alley, between Pozieres and Contalmaison on 6 August 1916. Killed in action on 6 August 1916 and buried in Contalmaison Chateau Cemetery.

Stone, Walter Napleton, Captain, 3rd attached 17th Royal Fusiliers, awarded the VC for his actions at Cambrai on 30 November 1917. Killed in action on 30 November 1917 and commemorated on the Cambrai Memorial at Louverval.

Tait, James Edward, MC, Lieutenant, 78th Canadian Infantry, awarded the VC for his actions at Beaucourt Wood from 8-11 August 1918. Killed in action on 11 August 1918 and believed to be buried in Fouquescourt British Cemetery so his grave is represented by a Special Memorial.

Travis, Richard Charles, DCM, MM, Sergeant, 2nd Otago Infantry, NZEF, awarded the VC for his actions at Rossignol Wood on 24 July 1918. Killed in action on 25 July 1918 and buried in Couin New British Cemetery. His birth name was Dickson Cornelius Savage.

Turnbull, James Youll, Sergeant, 17th (Glasgow Commercials) Highland Light Infantry, awarded the VC for his actions at the Leipzig salient near Thiepval on 1 July 1916. Killed in action on 1 July 1916 and buried in Lonsdale Cemetery.

Wain, Richard William Leslie, Captain, 'A' Battalion, Tank Corps, awarded the VC for his actions at Marcoing, near Cambrai on 20 November 1917. Killed in action on 20 November 1917 and commemorated on the Cambrai Memorial at Louverval.

Waller, Horace, Private, 10th King's Own Yorkshire Light Infantry, awarded the VC for his actions near Heninel on 10 April 1917. Killed in action on 10 April 1917 and buried at Cojeul British Cemetery.

Weathers, Lawrence Carthage, Corporal, 43rd Australian Infantry, awarded the VC for his actions as a Private near Peronne on 2 September 1918. Died of wounds on 29 September 1918 and buried in Unicorn Cemetery.

West, Richard Annesley, DSO & Bar, MC, Lieutenant Colonel, North Irish Horse, seconded to 6th Battalion, Tank Corps, awarded the VC for his actions at Courcelles, France on 21 August 1918. Died of wounds on 2 September 1918 and buried in Mory Abbey Military Cemetery.

Wilkinson, Thomas Orde Lawder, Lieutenant, 7th Loyal North Lancashires, awarded the VC for his actions at La Boiselle, France on 5 July 1916. Killed in action on 5 July 1916 and commemorated on the Thiepval Memorial.

Woodcock, Thomas, Corporal, 2nd Irish Guards, awarded the VC for his actions as a Private north of Broenbeek, near Ieper, Belgium on 12-13 September 1917. Killed in action at Bullecourt on 27 March 1918 and is buried in Douchy-les-Ayette British Cemetery.

Young, Alexander "Sandy", Lieutenant, 4th (South African Scottish) South African Infantry, awarded the VC for his actions as a Sergeant-Major in the Cape Police, South African Forces during the Second Boer War on 13 August 1901. Killed in action at the Butte de Warlencourt during the Battle of the Somme on 19 October 1916 and commemorated on the Thiepval Memorial.

Young, Frank Edward, 2nd Lieutenant, 1/1st Hertfordshires, awarded the VC for his actions at Triangle Wood near Havrincourt on 18 September 1918. Killed in action on 18 September 1918 and buried in Hermies Hill British Cemetery.

TERMS AND ABBREVIATIONS

ADS. - Advanced Dressing Station
AIF - Australian Imperial Force
ANZAC - Australian and New Zealand Army Corps
Aust - Australia
BEF - British Expeditionary Force
Bel - Belgian/Belgium
Bt - Baronet
Btn - Battalion
BWI - British West Indies Regiment
Can – Canada
CB – Companion of the Order of the Bath
CCS – Casualty Clearing Station
CMG –Companion of the Order of St. Michael and St. George
CWGC - Commonwealth War Graves Commission
DCLI - Duke of Cornwall's Light Infantry
DCM - Distinguished Conduct Medal
DFC – Distinguished Flying Cross
DS - Dressing Station
DSO - Distinguished Service Order
Fr - France/French
Ger - Germany
HAC - Honourable Artillery Company
Hon - Honourable
IWGC - Imperial War Graves Commission
KCVO - Knight Commander of the Victoria Order
KUG - Known Unto God
MC - Military Cross
MM - Military Medal
NA - New Army
No. - Number
NCO - Non-Commissioned Officer
NF - Newfoundland
NZ - New Zealand
NZEF – New Zealand Expeditionary Force
OBE - Order of the British Empire
RAF – Royal Air Force
RAMC - Royal Army Medical Corps
RE - Royal Engineers
RFC – Royal Flying Corps
S Afr - South Africa
SM - Special Memorial
sq mts - square metres
TF - Territorial Force
UK - United Kingdom (British)
US - United States of America
VC - Victoria Cross
WWII - World War Two
YMCA - Young Men's Christian Association

Regiments

The Argyll and Sutherland Highlanders (Princess Louises's)
The Black Watch (Royal Highlanders)
The Buffs (East Kent Regiment)
The Queen's Own Cameron Highlanders
The Cameronians (Scottish Rifles)
The Duke of Wellington's Regiment (West Riding)
The King's Regiment (Liverpool)
The King's Own Royal (Lancaster) Regiment
The Middlesex Regiment (Duke of Cambridge's Own)
The North Staffordshire Regiment (Prince of Wales's)
The Queen's Royal Regiment (West Surreys)
The Rifle Brigade (The Prince Consort's Own)
The Royal Berkshire Regiment (Princess Charlotte of Wales's)
The Royal Fusiliers (City of London Regiment)
The Royal Irish Fusiliers (Princess Victoria's)
The Royal Scots (Lothian Regiment)
The Queen's Own (Royal West Kent Regiment)
The Seaforth Highlanders (Ross-shire Buffs, The Duke of Albany's)
The Sherwood Foresters (Nottinghamshire and Derbyshire Regiment)
The Somerset Light Infantry (Prince Albert's)
The South Lancashire Regiment (Prince of Wales's Volunteers)
The West Yorkshire Regiment (Prince of Wales's Own)
The Wiltshire Regiment (Duke of Edinburgh's)
The Yorkshire Regiment (Alexandra, Princess of Wales's Own)
For names by which Pals Battalions referred to themselves eg 1st Salford Pals, please refer to the Orders of Battle

Divisions

Guards Division	47th (1/2nd London) Division
9th (Scottish) Division	48th (South Midland) Division
10th (Irish) Division	49th (West Riding) Division
11th (Northern) Division	50th (Northumbrian) Division
12th (Eastern) Division	51st (Highland) Division
13th (Western) Division	52nd (Lowland) Division
14th (Light) Division	53rd (Welsh) Division
15th (Scottish) Division	54th (East Anglian) Division
16th (Irish) Division	55th (West Lancashire) Division
17th (Northern) Division	56th (1/1st London) Division
18th (Eastern) Division	57th (2nd West Lancashire) Division
19th (Western) Division	58th (2/1st London) Division
20th (Light) Division	59th (2nd North Midland) Division
36th (Ulster) Division	60th (2/2nd London) Division
38th (Welsh) Division	61st (2nd South Midland) Division
42nd (East Lancashire) Division	62nd (2nd West Riding) Division
43rd (Wessex) Division	63rd (Royal Naval) Division
44th (Home Counties) Division	66th (2nd East Lancashire) Division
45th (2nd Wessex) Division	74th (Yeomanry) Division
46th (North Midland) Division	

BIBLIOGRAPHY

REFERENCE
The Order of Battle of Divisions, Parts 1, 2A, 2B, 3A & 3B; Major A. F. Becke (H.M.S.O.)
Official History of the Great War in France and Belgium; Brig-Gen. James E. Edmunds (H.M.S.O.)
Commonwealth War Graves Commission Registers
Officers Died in the Great War 1914 - 1919 (J. B. Hayward and Son)
Soldiers Died in the Great War 1914 - 1919 (J. B. Hayward and Son)
British Regiments 1914-1918; Brig-Gen. E. A. James, O.B.E. (Samson Books)
The VC and DSO, Volume II and III; Sir O'Moore Creagh, VC, GCB, GCSI and E M Humphris (Standard Art Book Company)
Register of the VC (This England)
British Battalions on the Somme; Ray Westlake (Pen and Sword)
De Ruvigny's Roll of Honour 1914-18 (Naval and Military Press)

FURTHER READING
Symbol of Courage, A History of the Victoria Cross; Max Arthur (Sidgwick and Jackson)
For the Sake of Example, Anthony Babington (Leo Cooper)
Sir Douglas Haig's Despatches; J H Boraston (J M Dent & Sons)
An Illustrated Companion to the First World War; Anthony Bruce (Michael Joseph)
Armegeddon Road, A V.C.'s Diary 1914 -1916, Billy Congreve, V.C. (William Kimber & Co)
Barnsley Pals; Jon Cooksey (Pen & Sword)
Before Endeavours Fade, A Guide to the Battlefields of the First World War; Rose Coombs, M.B.E. (After the Battle Publications)
One Day on the Somme 1 July 1916; Barry Cuttell (GMS Enterprises
148 Days on the Somme 2 July 1916 to 26 November 1916; Barry Cuttell (GMS Enterprises)
Bloody Red Tabs; Frank Davies and Graham Maddocks (Leo Cooper)
Battles of the Somme; Philip Gibbs (Heinemann)
VC's of the Somme; Gerald Gliddon (Sutton)
Chronical of the First World War, Volumes 1 and 2; Randal Gray and Christopher Argyle (Facts on File Ltd)
The Greater Game; Clive Harris and Julian Whippy (Pen and Sword)
The Sky Their Battlefield; Trevor Henshaw (Grub Street)
Major And Mrs Holt's Battlefield Guide To The Somme; Toni and Valmai Holt; (Pen and Sword)
Serre; Jack Horsfall and Nigel Cave (Pen and Sword)
Visiting the Fallen – Arras South; Peter Hughes (Pen and Sword)
Pozieres; Graham Keech (Pen and Sword)
1914-1918: Voices and Images of the Great War; Lyn Macdonald (Penguin)
Somme; Lyn MacDonald (Papermac)
To the last Man : Spring 1918; Lyn MacDonald (BCA)
The Somme, Day by Day Account; Chris McCarthy (Arms and Armour Press)
Walking with the ANZACs; Mat McLachlan (Hachette)
Slaughter on the Somme : The Complete War Diaries of the British Army's Worst Day; Martin Mace & John Grehan (Pen & Sword)
The First day on the Somme; Martin Middlebrook (Penguin)
The Kaiser's Battle; Martin Middlebrook (Penguin)
The Great War Generals on the Western Front; Robin Neillands (Robinson)
Villers Bretonneux; Peter Pedersen (Pen and Sword)
Murderous Tommies; Julian Putkowski and Mark Dunning (Pen and Sword)
Shot at Dawn, Executions in World War One by Authority of the British Army Act; Julian Putkowski and Julian Sykes (Wharncliffe)
Walking the Somme; Paul Reed (Pen and Sword)
Forgotten Victory; Gary Sheffield (Review)
The Germans at Thiepval; Jack Sheldon (Pen and Sword)
World War One, The Western Front; Peter Simkins (Colour Library Books)
The Old Contemptibles; Keith Simpson (George Allen and Unwin)
Manchester Pals; Michael Stedman (Pen & Sword)
Salford Pals; Michael Stedman (Pen & Sword)
History of World War One; A. J. P. Taylor (Macdonald & Co.)
Accrington Pals; William Turner (Pen & Sword)
Boy Soldiers of the Great War; Richard van Emden (Bloomsbury)
Famous 1914-1918; Richard van Emden and Victor Puik (Pen and Sword)

ADDITIONAL SOURCES
Stand To! The Journal of the Western Front Association
War Diaries of the Battalions CD; Naval and Military Press
WW1 Trench Map Reproductions – Imperial War Museum
Websites –
www.inmemories.com by Pierre Vandervelden
battlefields1418.50megs.com by Paul Reed
www.ww1wargraves.co.uk
www.webmatters.net by Simon Godly
silentwitness.freeservers.com

ACKNOWLEDGMENTS
Commonwealth War Graves Commission
Ibis Richard Pearson
Guild of Battlefield Guides and all members of the Guild, particularly those who have helped, even when they did not know they were helping, with this book and with many other things. But I want to single out Mike Peters for his support of the past few years.
Friends on the battlefield, Jon and Alison Haslock, Avril Williams, Jon Anderson, Myriam Thompson, Robert Gallagher, Peter Smith and many others

INDEX

Australian Imperial Force
Australian Corps, 53, 121, 128
Divisions
1st ANZAC, 133, 138; 1st, 133, 149, 196; 2nd, 6, 20, 102, 190, 265, 270, 289, 300; 3rd, 6, 134, 298; 4th, 6, 118, 132, 171, 267; 5th, 12, 79, 263, 298
Brigades
5th, 128; 6th, 137; 8th, 128; 9th, 263; 12th, 132; 13th, 6, 35, 67, 132, 182, 263; 15th, 6, 35, 67, 263
Infantry
1st, 112, 132, 267, 273; 2nd, 138, 139, 267; 3rd, 132, 138, 267, 273; 4th, 267; 5th, 23, 71, 195; 6th, 23; 7th, 129; 8th, 128, 195, 266; 9th, 71, 129, 154; 10th, 197; 11th, 172, 267; 12th, 183, 277; 13th, 13, 67, 144, 145, 265, 266; 15th, 63; 16th, 266, 267; 17th, 8, 237; 18th, 6, 154, 267, 286; 19th, 190, 248, 265; 20th, 68, 267; 21st, 267, 270; 22nd, 201, 291; 23rd, 134, 262, 267; 24th, 264; 25th, 8, 24; 26th, 72, 89, 201; 27th, 112; 28th, 128; 29th, 129, 132, 267; 31st, 35; 30th, 39; 32nd, 154, 190; 33rd, 71, 190, 310; 34th, 190, 267, 310; 35th, 302, 310; 36th, 33, 128, 263; 37th, 128, 129, 241, 310; 39th, 241; 40th, 41, 301, 310; 41st, 265; 42nd, 35; 43rd, 254, 265; 45th, 196; 46th, 171; 47th, 49, 278; 48th, 210, 262, 266, 267; 49th, 6, 89, 142; 50th, 6, 182, 183, 302; 51st, 6, 142, 182, 183, 263, 264; 52nd, 6, 183; 53rd, 13, 267; 54th, 13, 154, 190; 55th, 71, 137; 56th, 156; 57th, 13; 59th, 71; 60th, 264
Cavalry
1st Light Horse, 13; 6th Light Horse, 137; 11th Light Horse, 72; 2nd Light Horse Divisional Train, 133
Artillery
Royal Australian Garrison Artillery, 259
4th Brigade, Australian Field Artillery, 259; 8th Brigade Australian Field Artillery, 42
10th Brigade, Australian Field Artillery, 297; 11th Brigade, Australian Field Artillery, 102; 13th Brigade, Australian Field Artillery, 265; 14th Brigade, Australian Field Artillery, 190; 13th Battery, Australian Field Artillery, 102; 41st Battery, Australian Field Artillery, 103; 116th Howitzer Battery, Australian Artillery, 265; 272nd Mechanical Transport Company, Heavy Artillery, Australian Corps, 71
5th Battalion, Australian MGC, 195
1st Company, Australian MGC, 183; 7th Company, Australian MGC, 201; 6th Company, Australian Machine Gun Corps, 8
2nd Field Company, Australian Engineers, 200
3rd Australian Pioneers, 310
5th Australian Pioneers, 251
Australian Railway Troops, 267
6th Company, Australian Army Service Corps, 133, 273
7th Company, Australian Army Service Corps, 20
Australian Army Ordnance Corps, 49
Royal Australian Navy, 63
Australian Intelligence Corps, 63
Australian Veterinary Corps, 100
1st ANZAC Corps School, 132
Australian Unknown Warrior, 6

Battles
Albert (1914), 310
Amiens, 185, 299
Ancre, 102, 179, 213, 233, 274
Arras, 261, 275
Artois, 307, 312
Aubers Ridge, 184, 192
Boyne, 43
Cambrai (1917), 36, 92, 93, 94, 96, 105, 110, 139, 140, 157, 159, 164, 172, 185, 210, 213, 220, 223, 234, 240, 246, 250, 256, 261, 268, 269, 290
Cambrai (1918), 185
Canal du Nord, 299
Coronel, 175
Drocourt-Queant Line, 47, 80, 201, 255, 280
Dunes, 212
Epehy, 81, 87, 193
Festubert, 139, 202, 254
First Battle of Villers-Bretonneux, 263
First Battle of Ypres, 125, 175, 213, 239, 294
Flers-Courcelette, 46, 65, 140, 151, 185
Frontiers, 312
Guillemont, 116
Inkerman, 9
Jutland, 118, 155, 253
Langemark, 118
Loos, 7, 36, 48, 63, 66, 139, 150, 152, 165, 184, 187, 220, 258, 294
Mametz Wood, 176
Menin Road, 36, 290
Messines, 83, 167, 190, 214, 294
Moislains, 304
Mount Sorrel, 185, 200
Neuve Chapelle, 94, 256
Passendale, 97, 185
Poelcapelle, 94, 213
Rosieres, 216
Scarpe, 185
Second Battle of Arras, 235
Second Battle of Artois, 130
Second Battle of Bullecourt, 201
Second Battle of Villers-Bretonneux, 263
Second Battle of Ypres, 175, 181, 200, 214, 294
Selle, 214
Third Battle of Ypres, 34, 36, 294, 299
Verdun, 312
Villers-Bretonneux, 176, 231, 308
Vimy Ridge, 185

British Army
Armies
First, 97
Third, 24, 62, 82, 92, 196, 201, 274
Fourth, 89, 99, 126, 191, 197
Fifth, 12, 92, 99, 119, 180, 188, 196, 263, 311
Corps
II, 257, 258
III, 165, 171, 254, 263, 267

V, 10, 11, 16, 38, 101, 102, 111, 126, 127, 154, 159, 164, 170, 177, 179, 182, 203, 204, 206, 208, 221, 226, 229, 242, 274, 281
VI, 91
VII, 45
VIII, 3, 277
IX, 224, 228, 253, 256
XIV, 41, 44, 79
XV, 72, 76
XIX, 302
Cavalry, 150
Divisions
Guards, 16, 66, 82, 105, 114, 115, 147, 164, 177, 178, 221, 223, 240, 261, 269, 312
1st, 134, 256
2nd, 74, 88, 96, 116, 206, 208, 209
3rd, 22, 81, 84, 106, 118, 119, 159, 185, 198, 204, 206, 210, 211, 226, 229, 257, 273, 279, 307
4th, 10, 200, 208, 218, 226, 307
5th, 72, 74, 83, 149, 154, 177, 238
6th, 26, 177, 224, 253
7th, 22, 40, 44, 66, 69, 78, 84, 95, 103, 108, 118, 131, 150, 179, 193, 202, 203, 205, 229, 235, 294
8th, 6, 34, 110, 128, 186, 188, 195, 216, 263
9th, 74, 93, 165, 198
10th, 256
11th, 60, 198
12th, 16, 24, 35, 38, 72, 77, 78, 81, 87, 88, 92, 102, 117, 138, 160, 165, 176, 186, 207, 225, 254, 258
14th, 196, 248, 249, 263
15th, 116, 163
16th, 116, 117, 214, 232
17th, 46, 59, 65, 94, 103, 125, 132, 138, 170, 195, 257
18th, 6, 9, 15, 24, 27, 31, 58, 59, 69, 70, 102, 114, 116, 122, 146, 149, 170, 193, 198, 202, 207, 210, 216, 221, 233, 236, 243, 254, 255, 263
19th, 11, 26, 63, 109, 111, 132, 148, 204, 206, 229
20th, 116, 130
21st, 7, 22, 36, 40, 57, 66, 68, 87, 103, 105, 109, 110, 135, 136, 160, 216
22nd, 45
23rd, 60, 237, 276
24th, 56, 144, 255
25th, 26, 28, 154, 186
29th, 10, 14, 101, 126, 127, 143, 144, 160, 168, 236, 274, 280, 281
30th, 31, 36, 57, 69, 116, 119, 135, 146, 191, 198, 224, 231, 238, 311
31st, 17, 32, 90, 106, 130, 159, 187, 204, 206, 226, 229, 307
32nd, 16, 29, 36, 38, 43, 70, 102, 170, 180, 182, 197, 217, 224, 225, 242, 253
33rd, 40, 77, 81, 136, 151, 164, 193
34th, 21, 38, 60, 95, 108, 124, 143, 167, 186, 197, 230, 237, 278
36th, 7, 10, 51, 58, 59, 111, 168, 170, 172, 197, 209, 224, 233, 239, 245
37th, 21, 32, 33, 44, 91, 95, 203, 205, 206, 229, 230
38th, 16, 21, 22, 38, 39, 51, 59, 60, 61, 74, 75, 95, 110, 116, 125, 154, 170, 176, 177, 186, 187, 221, 225, 237, 257
39th, 11, 128, 144, 170, 190, 232
40th, 13, 93, 190, 230, 300
41st, 7, 46
42nd, 4, 5, 21, 32, 46, 88, 161, 171, 180, 203, 205, 210, 211, 220, 229, 234, 241, 267, 268, 276
46th, 28, 29, 30, 54, 106, 107, 108, 215, 229
47th, 16, 22, 35, 62, 138, 139, 150, 151, 163, 169, 173, 191, 207, 276, 306, 314
48th, 63, 84, 130, 134, 137, 186, 190, 195, 226, 276, 300, 307
49th, 28, 60, 155, 170
50th, 121, 128, 141, 216, 241, 254, 276
51st, 11, 26, 27, 96, 98, 101, 109, 112, 127, 143, 156, 160, 182, 185, 186, 211, 242, 274, 281, 307
52nd, 80, 135, 172, 255
55th, 28, 82, 116, 147, 274
56th, 22, 36, 40, 45, 56, 57, 66, 68, 106, 107, 114, 130, 136, 152, 181, 216, 230, 235, 248, 255
57th, 80, 136, 172
58th, 24, 28, 41, 55, 78, 117, 129, 169, 173, 191, 222, 263, 265
59th, 143, 211, 215, 240, 242, 256
61st, 93, 99, 188, 224
62nd, 91, 98, 106, 110, 139, 145, 159, 177, 194, 203, 205, 228, 229, 230, 234, 242
63rd, 11, 16, 27, 44, 45, 67, 83, 92, 98, 99, 101, 111, 120, 143, 156, 164, 167, 172, 182, 203, 206, 209, 233, 234, 238, 242, 258, 272, 274, 281, 285, 292
66th, 128, 144, 190, 214, 300
74th, 191, 233, 240
Brigades
2nd Mounted, 42; 1st Cavalry, 216; 2nd Cavalry, 142, 257; 2nd Guards, 147; 3rd Guards, 26; 4th Guards, 97; 2nd, 256; 3rd, 256; 6th, 5; 8th, 257; 10th, 234; 11th, 155, 234; 13th, 83; 14th, 29; 21st, 70, 152; 42nd, 196; 50th, 94; 55th, 233; 56th, 63; 60th, 88; 61st, 88; 64th, 57, 115; 70th, 28, 34, 186; 99th, 5, 9; 101st, 21; 102nd, 21; 103rd, 22; 109th, 170; 127th, 268; 137th, 261; 139th, 263; 149th, 9, 128; 169th, 107; 172nd, 136; 186th, 138; 1st Cavalry, 293; 5th Cavalry, 267, 269
Cavalry
Horse Guards, 15
Royal Scots Greys, 63
Dragoons, 1st, 48, 232, 267, 268, 288; 6th, 152, 193, 250
Dragoon Guards, 2nd, 20; 5th, 79; 6th, 51, 75; 7th, 150
Hussars, 3rd, 294; 4th, 257, 258, 288; 7th, 212, 275; 8th, 269; 9th, 175; 10th, 243; 12th, 33, 275; 15th, 38; 18th, 119; 19th, 25
Lancers, 5th, 157, 175, 197, 217; 17th, 50; 21st, 96
14th Regiment of Reserve Cavalry, 88
County of London Yeomanry, 254
Hampshire Yeomanry, 118
King Edward's Horse, 31, 86
Queens Own Oxfordshire Hussars, 121, 169, 241
Queens Own Royal West Kent Yeomanry, 285
North Irish Horse, 177
North Somerset Yeomanry, 141
Northamptonshire Yeomanry, 164
South Irish Horse, 7
Royal 1st Devon Yeomanry, 70
Royal North Devon Hussars, 181

Royal West Kent Hussars, 51
Shropshire Yeomanry, 216
West Kent Yeomanry, 259
Westmoreland & Cumberland Yeomanry, 126
Yorkshire Dragoons, 275
Yorkshire Hussars, 8, 295
Royal Navy, 44, 77, 118, 121, 132, 138, 155, 169, 174, 230, 254, 273, 281
Anson Battalion, 67, 83, 120; Drake Battalion, 156, 258, 272; Hawke Battalion, 45; Hood Battalion, 11, 164, 209, 238; Howe Battalion, 247; Nelson Battalion, 120
Royal Marine Artillery, 29,
Royal Marine Light Infantry, 99, 120; 1st, 234; 2nd, 234
189th Stokes Trench Mortar Battalion, 238,
RNVR, 202, 247; Armoured Car Division, 146
Royal Engineers, 15, 30, 35, 45, 94, 97, 104, 156, 258, 268, 270, 316
4th Company, 30; 7th Company, 172; 11th Company, 56; 59th Company, 184; 61st Company, 226; 73rd Company, 157; 123rd Company, 252, 278; 129th Company, 294; 178th Company, 184; 204th Company, 225; 212th Company, 10; 218th Company, 297; 401st Company, 77; 404th Company, 77; 429th Company, 88; 490th Company, 197; 2/2nd (Highland) Company, 182, 287; Motor Cyclist Section, 211; 2nd Division Signal Company, 291; 29th Division Signal Company, 29; 3rd Special Company, 116; 4th Battalion, Special Brigade, 147; Air Battalion, 189; London Balloon Company, 171; 17th Kite Balloon Company, 258; 312th Road Construction Company, 173 252nd Tunnelling Company, 252; 179th Tunnelling Company, 9, 184; 185th Tunnelling Company, 9, 28, 109; West Lancashire Division, 130;
Royal Artillery, 56, 70, 190, 249
Royal Field Artillery, 3, 29, 35, 42, 87, 119, 120, 149, 158, 196, 215, 288, 294
11th Brigade, 65; 14th Brigade, 199; 15th Brigade, 72; 251st Brigade, 71; 23rd Brigade, 35; 25th Brigade, 31; 32nd Brigade, 28; 34th Brigade, 33; 75th Brigade, 45, 158; 83rd Brigade, 224; 88th Brigade, 83; 104th Brigade, 72, 131; 107th Brigade, 165; 108th Brigade, 294; 110th Brigade, 28, 190; 161st Brigade, 296; 170th Brigade, 130; 181st Brigade, 282; 223rd Brigade, 137; 235th Brigade, 220; 312th Brigade, 89; B/92nd Brigade, 78; XXII Brigade, 132; 12th Battery, 199; 21st Battery, 259; 65th Battery, 8th Brigade, 302; 72nd Battery, 38th Brigade, 212; 82nd Battery, 71; 87th Battery, 14, 147; 186th Battery, 259; 16th (County of London) Battery, 6th London Brigade, 220; P Anti-Aircraft Battery, 84
Royal Garrison Artillery, 10, 58
76th Brigade, 102; 6th Siege Battery, 242; 16th Heavy Battery, 161; 18th Siege Battery, 138; 20th Heavy Battery, 194; 35th Heavy Battery, 125; 41st (Durham) Siege Battery, 9; 102nd Siege Battery, 261; 106th Siege Battery, 198; 112th Siege Battery, 32; 116th Siege Battery, 249; 123rd Siege Battery, 41; 128th Heavy Battery, 121, 169; 135th Heavy Battery, 247; 137th Heavy Battery, 296; 138th Heavy Battery, 124, 125; 141st Heavy Battery, 230; 155th Heavy Battery, 301; 169th Siege Battery, 40; 231st Siege Battery, 249; 267th Siege Battery, 83; 276th Siege Battery, 289; 283rd Siege Battery, 296
Royal Horse Artillery, 13, 31, 45, 84, 158, 160, 289
16th Brigade, RHA, 205, 216; 33rd Battery, RHA, 290; O Battery, RHA, 83; Essex Royal Horse Artillery, 294
III Corps Heavy Artillery, 165
Divisional Ammunition Columns, 252
4th, 142, 252, 296; 26th, 87; 56th, 130
Royal Air Force, 13, 37, 128, 141, 188, 210, 219, 254
No 3 Squadron, 299; No 12 Squadron, 174; No 19 Squadron, 112; No 20 Squadron, 265; No 32 Squadron, 18, 271; No 48 Squadron, 210; No 49 Squadron, 49; No 57 Squadron, 54; No 59 Squadron, 252; No 60 Squadron, 113, 299; No 64 Squadron, 18; No 87 Squadron, 17, 18; No 92 Squadron, 299; No 98 Squadron, 163; No 151 Squadron, 250; No 206 Squadron, 37; No 209 Squadron, 253, 315
Royal Flying Corps, 7, 17, 82, 87, 97, 112, 113, 118, 139, 140, 168, 172, 189, 205, 223, 256, 258, 269, 282, 283, 299, 308
No 3 Squadron, 199; No 4 Squadron, 171, 172, 203, 284; No 5 Squadron, 189; No 6 Squadron, 306; No 7 Squadron, 52; No 8 Squadron, 119, 120; No 11 Squadron, 118, 269; No 12 Squadron, 271; No 13 Squadron, 282, 293; No 18 Squadron, 208, 260; No 19 Squadron, 213, 288; No 22 Squadron, 10, 118, 261; No 24 Squadron, 10, 47, 54, 81; No 27 Squadron, 18, 89; No 29 Squadron, 47, 81; No 35 Squadron, 43; No 44 Squadron, 250; No 45 Squadron, 113, 285; No 48 Squadron, 18, 141; No 54 Squadron, 66; No 55 Squadron, 149; No 56 Squadron, 48, 96; No 59 Squadron, 177; No 60 Squadron, 25, 250, 283; No 70 Squadron, 140; No 78 Squadron, 250; No 79 Squadron, 79; No 1 Army Kite Balloon Section, 64
RNAS, 118, 258, 282
No 8 Squadron, 282
Machine Gun Corps, 5, 58, 118, 122, 126, 140, 143, 246
19th Company, 40; 38th Battalion, 99; 51st Battalion, 130; 59th Battalion, 113; 63rd Battalion, 114; 2nd Company, 12; 103rd Company, 189; 109th Company, 170; 114th Company, 146; 153rd Company, 143; 182nd Company, 296; 9th Squadron (Cavalry), 196
(Royal) Army Service Corps, 9, 98, 252, 284, 288
Labour Corps, 120, 252, 288; 48th Labour Group, 197; 103rd Labour Company, 254; 13th (Civilian) Platelayer Labour Company, Labour Corps, 250; 11th (Civilian) Platelayer Labour Company, Labour Corps, 250; 12th (Civilian) Platelayer Labour Company, Labour Corps, 250; 103rd Auxiliary Petrol Company, 100; 700th Transport Company, 12; 906th Company, 14; 25th Prisoner of War Company, Labour Corps, 235; No 121 Prisoner of War Company, 141
Army Cyclist Corps, 120, 160, 240, 288
Cyclist Battalion, 52nd Division, 240; Cyclist Company, 65th Division, 126; Highland Cyclist Battalion, 182; Huntingdon Cyclist Battalion, 134, 136
Argyll & Sutherland Highlanders, 2nd, 42, 81, 261, 315; 4th, 57; 7th, 139, 214; 1/8th, 27, 187, 214; 1/9th, 92; 11th, 5, 77; 14th, 30, 93
Army Chaplains Department, 201, 241, 247, 268

Bedfordshires, 30; 1st, 45, 72, 147, 158, 221, 233; 2nd, 7, 116; 3rd, 93; 4th, 39; 1/5th, 72; 7th, 3, 72, 263

Black Watch, 45, 277; 1/4th, 23; 1/6th, 77, 143; 1/7th, 26, 143; 8th, 154, 247; 9th, 77, 116; 14th, 191

Borders, 1st, 14, 127; 2nd, 57, 70, 230; 3rd, 230; 6th, 197; 11th, 102, 154, 155, 182, 274, 277; 12th, 57

Buffs (East Kents), 83, 205, 233; 3rd, 83, 92; 6th, 83, 92; 7th, 31, 167, 198, 233, 272

1/1st Cambridgeshires, 24, 87, 176

Cameron Highlanders, 2nd, 192; 7th, 239

Cameronians, 164; 1st, 117, 164; 2nd, 256; 5th/6th, 200; 7th, 200, 202

Cheshires, 4th, 116; 10th, 111, 205; 11th, 38, 122, 246; 13th, 144, 205; 16th, 122, 246, 292

Chinese Labour Corps, 17, 66, 70, 72, 97, 168, 173, 251, 297, 300

Coldstream Guards, 1st, 56, 149, 223; 2nd, 16, 115, 169, 178; 4th, 69

Connaught Rangers, 1st, 50; 2nd, 50; 6th, 50, 215

Devonshires, 28, 203; 8th, 62, 72, 78, 84, 119, 182, 306; 9th, 62, 72, 78, 84, 119, 306; 13th, 86

Dorsets, 1st, 15, 30, 33, 37, 54, 66, 154, 163, 227; 2nd, 291; 3rd, 30; 4th, 46; 5th, 99; 6th, 46, 126, 221; 7th, 221

Duke of Cornwalls Light Infantry, 149, 160, 246; 1st, 98, 117, 194; 6th, 63; 7th, 220

Duke of Wellingtons Regiment, 155, 194; 2nd, 239, 271, 306; 2/5th, 220; 8th, 198; 9th, 252

Durham Light Infantry, 45, 282; 2nd, 19, 134, 138; 3rd, 88, 221; 1/6th, 55, 77, 246,; 1/8th, 181; 1/9th, 78, 246; 10th, 88, 134; 11th, 88, 101; 13th, 246; 14th, 3, 158; 18th, 92, 138, 221; 19th, 149; 20th, 77, 246; 22nd, 6

East Lancashires, 269; 2nd, 58; 1/5th, 180, 181; 7th, 246; 11th, 204, 206

East Surreys, 31, 177; 1st, 95, 238, 269; 5th, 49; 8th, 9, 50; 13th, 93, 238, 269; 1st, 71, 115, 184, 276

East Yorkshires, 1/4th, 121, 175; 7th, 8, 58, 103, 104; 8th, 66; 9th, 189; 10th, 249; 12th, 90; 13th, 90, 246, 266

Essex Regiment, 83, 187, 226; 1st, 8, 31, 90, 91, 127, 144, 281; 2nd, 31, 227; 9th, 87; 10th, 9, 28, 79, 105, 106, 167; 11th, 113; 13th, 227, 286

Gloucestershires, 74; 4th, 268, 280; 1/5th, 149, 254; 1/6th, 130, 131, 172, 268; 8th, 109; 10th, 23, 197; 14th, 268; 2/5th, 94; 2/6th, 243

Gordon Highlanders, 1st, 140, 159, 211; 2nd, 77, 108; 1/5th, 143; 6th, 96; 1/7th, 96, 143

Grenadier Guards, 150, 171, 285; 1st, 15, 46, 97, 150, 192, 284, 285; 2nd, 56, 115, 172, 178, 213, 284, 285; 3rd, 46, 117, 158, 213; 4th, 97, 117, 168; 5th, 28

Guards Trench Mortar Battery, 114

Hampshires, 1st, 121, 209, 234; 1/6th, 47; 14th, 111

1/1st Hertfordshires, 44, 139, 214, 233

Highland Light Infantry, 98, 101, 126, 274, 295; 2nd, 33; 7th, 200; 1/9th, 117, 151, 240, 255; 12th, 125, 126, 191; 14th, 173; 15th, 38, 87; 16th, 32, 102, 182, 274, 295; 17th, 154, 182, 242

Honourable Artillery Company, 11, 42, 57, 203; 1st, 92, 121; 2nd, 118

Irish Guards, 1st, 16, 17, 18, 110, 221, 222; 2nd, 11, 81

Kings (Liverpools), 30, 69, 135, 199; 1st, 136, 178, 195; 2nd, 231; 4th, 136, 247; 1/5th, 116; 1/6th, 279; 1/8th, 192; 1/9th, 231; 1/10th, 82, 117, 247; 12th, 19, 51, 147, 180, 247; 13th, 71, 85, 111, 279; 15th, 216; 17th, 55, 69, 85, 119, 181, 225, 311; 18th, 69, 119, 181, 192, 216, 225, 275, 311; 19th, 69, 119, 181, 225, 311; 20th, 69; 2/10th, 30; Liverpool Pals, 191, 238

Kings Own (Royal Lancasters), 226, 228; 1st, 280; 1/4th, 63, 170; 7th, 72, 278; 8th, 159, 249

Kings Own Scottish Borderers, 150; 1st, 92, 144; 2nd, 50; 3rd, 117; 6th, 93, 250; 7/8th, 91

Kings Own Yorkshire Light Infantry, 2nd, 50, 91, 106, 217; 1/5th, 106, 197, 221; 5th, 106; 7th, 32; 8th, 34; 9th, 109, 183, 250; 10th, 57; 2/5th, 106

Kings Royal Rifle Corps, 43, 147, 224, 225, 230, 249, 256; 1st, 74; 2nd, 31, 63, 244, 256; 3rd, 101, 256; 7th, 141, 156; 8th, 130; 11th, 168; 12th, 118; 13th, 29, 73, 124; 14th, 141; 17th, 11; 18th, 227; 21st, 8, 115

Kings Shropshire Light Infantry, 173; 1st, 93, 246; 1/4th, 93, 246; 6th, 36, 274; 7th, 247, 257

Lancashire Fusiliers, 63; 1st, 14, 27; 1/6th, 3; 1/7th, 32, 211; 8th, 33; 10th, 50, 160; 15th, 32, 205, 225, 244, 291; 16th, 10, 120, 121, 182, 205, 225, 244, 274; 18th, 164, 217

Leicestershires, 283; 1st, 244; 1/2nd, 54; 1/4th, 98, 124; 6th, 7; 7th, 193; 8th, 173, 193; 9th, 124, 167

Leinster Regiment, 257; 1st, 216; 2nd, 44, 214; 5th, 44

Lincolnshire Regiment, 17, 30; 1st, 276; 2nd, 249, 266; 6th, 181; 7th, 105; 10th, 109, 125

London Regiment, 75, 79, 164, 191, 235; 1/1st, 130; 1/2nd, 114, 151, 235; 1/3rd, 137, 230; 1/5th, 247; 1/9th, 55, 102, 107, 230, 247, 263; 1/12th, 113, 284; 1/13th, 117, 118, 247; 1/14th, 46, 49, 147, 158; 1/16th, 36, 239, 259; 1/17th, 169; 1/18th, 266; 1/20th, 233; 1/21st, 41; 1/22nd, 51; 1/23rd, 258; 1/28th (Artist Rifles), 7, 135; 2/1st, 45; 2/2nd, 113; 2/3rd, 194; 2/5th, 51; 2/10th, 22, 284

Loyal North Lancashires, 37; 1st, 251; 1/4th, 81, 254, 285; 7th, 245, 246

Manchesters, 98, 195, 199, 260, 283, 288; 2nd, 3, 58, 205, 228; 4th, 205; 1/5th, 161; 1/6th, 3, 33, 161, 181; 1/7th, 161; 1/8th, 161; 12th, 61, 246; 16th, 55, 197; 17th, 55, 68, 198, 225; 18th, 18, 55, 63, 68, 192, 238; 19th, 55, 135; 20th, 69, 70, 149,; 21st, 67; 22nd, 69, 70, 102; 23rd, 269; 24th, 178, 193; 25th, 158; 2/9th, 260; Manchester Pals, 191, 193, 238

Middlesex, 36, 200; 1st, 200, 261; 2nd, 13, 15, 89, 186, 187; 4th, 157; 1/8th, 95; 11th, 147, 158; 13th, 51; 16th, 14, 27, 126, 127; 17th, 65, 149, 157, 246; 19th, 151; 21st, 190

Monmouthshires, 2nd, 114; 3rd, 219

Norfolks, 1st, 83, 98, 183, 285; 3rd, 285; 1/4th, 83; 5th, 128; 7th, 87, 212; 8th, 50, 183, 184; 9th, 210, 211

Northamptonshires, 187; 1st, 23, 31; 2nd, 6; 6th, 169, 254, 272; 7th, 121

North Staffordshires, 66, 107; 2nd, 152; 1/5th, 98, 107, 218; 1/6th, 73, 218, 260; 2/6th, 84, 85

Northumberland Fusiliers, 54, 60, 237; 1st, 224; 1/5th, 10, 212; 2nd, 3, 35; 8th, 33; 9th, 104; 12th, 95; 13th, 72; 16th, 212, 246; 15th, 198; 20th, 21, 187; 21st, 21, 109, 187; 22nd, 21, 109; 23rd, 21, 85; 24th, 21, 45, 187; 25th, 21, 45; 26th, 21, 45; 27th, 21, 45

Oxford & Bucks Light Infantry, 1/1st, 134; 1/4th, 107; 2nd, 113, 172, 179, 209; 2/1st, 243; 2/4th, 54, 260; 6th, 12

Queens (Royal West Surreys), 164, 187; 1st, 93, 164, 184, 233, 239; 2nd, 69, 150, 184, 192, 203; 3rd, 269; 4th, 40; 1/5th, 217; 6th, 270; 7th, 69, 74, 136, 184, 204, 215, 233, 244

Queens Own (Royal West Kents), 259; 3rd, 149; 6th, 77, 92; 7th, 122, 246; 8th, 126

Rifle Brigade, 1st, 168, 174, 247, 306; 2nd, 101, 110, 133; 3rd, 110, 117, 306; 6th, 228; 7th, 152; 8th, 51; 9th, 228; 11th, 180; 12th, 224; 13th, 21, 64; 14th, 247; 16th, 190, 247

Royal Army Medical Corps, 22, 29, 59, 61, 84, 90, 98, 100, 112, 125, 143, 146, 215, 235, 253, 268, 288

Royal Berkshires, 187; 1st, 182, 258; 2nd, 258; 3rd, 209; 1/5th, 174, 192; 6th, 50, 152; 2/4th, 255, 256, 296, 312

Royal Dublin Fusiliers, 230; 9th, 75, 117, 215

Royal Fusiliers, 149, 187, 254; 2nd, 136; 3rd, 158, 254; 4th, 29, 32, 107, 206; 6th, 254; 7th, 16, 197; 8th, 7, 246, 278; 9th, 15, 187, 246; 10th, 52, 58, 98, 197; 11th, 31, 198; 12th, 7; 13th, 124, 137; 17th, 83, 121, 158, 206; 18th, 171; 20th, 136, 146; 21st, 224; 22nd, 179, 226, 245, 246; 23rd, 246; 24th, 179, 246; 25th, 266; 32nd, 227

1st Royal Guernsey Light Infantry, 158

Royal Inniskilling Fusiliers, 215, 220; 1st, 11, 14, 86, 100, 180; 2nd, 218, 225; 8th, 44, 120; 9th, 59, 157, 170; 10th, 59; 11th, 60, 170

Royal Irish Regiment, 200; 4th, 218; 6th, 50

Royal Irish Fusiliers, 257; 1st, 14, 180; 2nd, 180; 7th, 63; 7th/8th, 231; 9th, 59, 167, 244, 245

Royal Irish Rifles, 28, 50; 5th, 257; 8th, 111; 9th, 43, 235, 245; 10th, 164; 11th, 163, 164, 239; 12th, 51, 59, 245, 257; 13th, 99, 163, 245; 14th, 59, 88, 245; 15th, 161, 196

Royal Munster Fusiliers, 169; 1st, 66, 168, 227, 236; 2nd, 12, 41, 42, 87, 171; 5th, 118; 6th, 118; 9th, 171

Royal Scots, 2nd, 36, 273; 1/4th, 172; 1/5th, 202, 240; 5/6th, 32, 37; 7th, 271; 8th, 52, 182; 11th, 199; 12th, 50, 51, 199; 13th, 92, 271; 14th, 189; 15th, 3, 38, 61

Royal Scots Fusiliers, 1st, 112, 152, 245; 2nd, 55, 152

Royal Sussex, 65, 187; 2nd, 31, 93, 116; 7th, 117, 176; 8th, 15, 237; 11th, 11

Royal Warwickshires, 130, 163, 196, 226, 292; 1st, 63, 234; 2nd, 63, 152; 3rd, 63; 1/5th, 38; 1/6th, 13, 188; 7th, 196, 263; 11th, 28; 16th, 229

Royal Welsh Fusiliers, 253; 1st, 64, 194, 223, 227; 2nd, 141; 3rd, 193; 10th, 75, 141; 13th, 70, 95, 176; 14th, 70, 78, 79, 95, 269; 16th, 50, 70, 79, 95, 187; 17th, 187; 19th, 141; 25th, 80

Scots Guards, 223; 1st, 220

Scottish Rifles, 1st, 117; 2nd, 117; 9th, 51

Seaforth Highlanders, 35; 2nd, 149, 160; 3rd, 123, 199; 1/5th, 91, 186; 7th, 123; 8th, 116

Sherwood Foresters, 107, 297; 1st, 87; 2nd, 113; 3rd, 180; 1/5th, 98, 259; 9th, 75; 10th, 3, 126, 226; 15th, 42, 260; 17th, 11; 2/5th, 181; 2/8th, 180

Somerset Light Infantry, 147; 1st, 66, 99, 155, 208, 227, 228, 235; 7th, 220; 8th, 10, 33; 12th, 191

South Lancashires, 43, 130; 1st, 63, 104; 2nd, 184; 3rd, 63; 1/4th, 63; 7th, 72; 11th, 219

South Staffordshires, 30, 107; 1st, 150; 2nd, 29, 213; 1/5th, 98, 99; 1/6th, 89, 247; 8th, 103, 184

South Wales Borderers, 1st, 171; 2nd, 168, 281; 10th, 114; 12th, 92

Suffolks, 2nd, 85, 159, 199; 1/4th, 239; 7th, 9; 9th, 117; 11th, 109, 239; 15th, 240

Tanks Corps, 46, 105, 113, 128, 148, 158, 164, 165, 176, 185, 186, 196, 211, 219, 240, 261, 269, 273, 279; D Battalion, Tank Corps, 169; E Battalion, Tank Corps, 210, 211; 1st Tank Battalion, 25, 263; 3rd (Light) Battalion, Tank Corps, 259; 4th Tank Battalion, Tank Corps, 46, 123; 6th Battalion, Tank Corps, 33, 177; 8th Battalion, Tank Corps, 193; Machine Gun Corps (Heavy Branch), 46, 58, 196; 4th Section Machine Gun Corps (Heavy Branch), 113; Tanks, 7

Welsh Regiment, 192; 2nd, 95, 162; 5th, 177; 15th, 95; 16th, 95, 247; 17th, 92

1st Welsh Guards, 18, 306

West Yorkshires, 187, 226; 1st, 152, 227, 245; 3rd, 227; 1/5th, 59, 78, 198, 246; 8th, 33; 10th, 3, 46, 70, 104; 12th, 45, 79, 91, 152, 155, 156; 14th, 229; 15th, 178, 187, 221, 226; 16th, 188, 229; 21st, 91; 2/6th, 3, 226; Bradford Pals, 229; Leeds Pals, 229

Wiltshires, 1st, 154; 2nd, 275; 1/4th, 149; 6th, 35

Worcestershires, 1st, 188; 2nd, 193; 3rd, 35, 154, 284; 4th, 94, 157; 1/7th, 155; 1/8th, 184; 10th, 109, 187; 2/7th, 93; 2/8th, 54

York & Lancasters, 178; 2nd, 34, 86; 1/4th, 92; 1/5th, 149, 197; 6th, 272; 7th, 141; 8th, 3, 34, 226; 9th, 28; 10th, 119; 12th, 90, 159, 206, 207, 227, 234; 14th, 130, 159; Barnsley Pals, 207

Yorkshires, 38; 1/4th, 28; 2nd, 35, 135, 249; 3rd, 38; 4th, 214, 215; 7th, 103, 104; 8th, 60, 61, 237; 9th, 60, 61, 214, 237; 10th, 183; 11th, 38

Army Veterinary Corps, 20

No 20 Veterinary Hospital, 20

57th Protection Company, Royal Defence Corps, 118

21st Entrenching Battalion (10th Royal Irish Rifles), 119, 311

Rouen Central Bombing School, 139

Egyptian Labour Corps, 145

21st Infantry Base Depot, 182

Shanghai Light Horse, 199

Carey's Force, 263, 307

9th Trench Mortar Battery, 277

56th Trench Mortar Battery, 130

64th Trench Mortar Battery, 224

109th Light Trench Mortar Battery, 244

Canadian Expeditionary Force

Canadian Corps, 17, 28, 37, 48, 49, 52, 67, 91, 94, 116, 122, 123, 141, 148, 162, 200, 202, 236, 239, 248, 271, 275, 280, 310

Canadian Cavalry Corps, 175

Divisions

1st, 21, 54, 123, 162, 184, 198, 199, 210, 222, 255, 280; 2nd, 25, 48, 65, 196, 209, 216, 237, 273; 3rd, 25, 49, 68, 200, 210; 4th, 210, 254

Brigades
2nd, 48; 3rd, 222; 4th, 65, 153; 5th, 65, 210, 237; 6th, 65; 8th, 36; 10th, 100, 289; Canadian Cavalry, 142

Cavalry
1st Canadian Mounted Rifles, 122; 2nd Canadian Mounted Rifles, 37, 57, 65, 122; 4th Canadian Mounted Rifles, 148; 13th Canadian Mounted Rifles, 199; Canadian Mounted Rifles, 49; Fort Garry Horse, 69, 96, 283; Lord Strathcona's Horse, 140, 175, 223; Royal Canadian Dragoons, 175, 212; Canadian Light Horse, 223; 1st Canadian Division cavalry Squadron, 223; 19th Albert Dragoons, 223

Infantry
1st, 184; 2nd, 47, 54, 184; 3rd, 5, 184, 236, 251, 257; 4th, 184; 5th, 148, 255; 7th, 80, 222; 8th, 162, 200, 227; 9th, 47, 274; 10th, 53, 80, 255; 13th, 10, 123, 306; 14th, 40, 251; 15th, 198, 236; 16th, 5, 76, 80; 17th, 274; 18th, 65, 271; 19th, 48; 20th, 271; 21st, 153; 22nd, 28, 202, 237, 264, 273, 274; 24th, 202, 273, 275; 25th, 273, 274; 26th, 275, 280; 31st, 236, 274; 43rd, 142, 289; 50th, 5, 199, 279; 52nd, 68; 58th, 76, 142; 60th, 141; 72nd, 5, 275; 75th, 141, 148; 78th, 45, 100, 101, 141, 200, 261; 85th, 141; 87th, 5, 21, 257; 95th, 236; 102nd, 199, 306; 127th, 222; 116th, 142; 169th, 142; 192nd, 199; 202nd, 280

9th Brigade, Canadian Field Artillery, 25
Canadian Army Medical Corps, 134
Royal Montreal Regiment, 40
Canadian Motor Machine Gun Service, 188
Canadian Corps Gas Services, 201
Royal Newfoundland Regiment, 8, 11, 50, 127, 144, 281
Princess Patricia's Candian Light Infantry, 61, 65, 184, 185
Royal Canadian Regiment, 65, 162
90th Winnipeg Rifles, 162
2nd Canadian Railway Troops, 222
1st Battalion, Canadian MGC, 249
Royal Military College of Canada, 184, 187

Fench Army
Armies
Sixth, 191, 216, 273; Tenth, 53, 82; Thirty-Second, 314
Corps
XXXI, 175; II, 231, 308; 1st Colonial, 300; XXXII, 306
Divisions
11th, 192; 34th, 224; 72nd, 300
Brigade
33rd, 288; 123rd, 304; 124th, 304
Infantry
61st, 13; 73rd, 114; 110th, 114; 18th Territorial, 115; 153rd, 116, 117; 224th, 192; 26th, 194; 56th Chausseurs a Pied , 300; 58th Chausseurs a Pied , 300; 125th, 305; 1st, 304; 307th, 304; 308th, 304; 325th, 305; 243rd, 306, 307; 233rd, 306, 307; 327th, 306, 307
Legion Etranger (Foreign Legion), 300
94th Lafayette Flying Corps, 305
Tenth Army Casualty Clearing Hospital, 301

German Army
Armies
First, 216, 273; Second, 311

Corps
18th Army, 312; 14th Reserve, 315
Infantry
Prussian Guards, 147, 310; Guards Fusilier Regt, 186; 113rd Infantry Regt, 315; 121st Infantry Regt, 228; 26th Reserve Infantry Regt, 280; 43rd Reserve Infantry Regt, 310; 55th Reserve Infantry Regt, 285; 119th Reserve Infantry Regt, 280; 9th Saxon Infantry Regt, 315; 180th Wurtemberg Infantry Regiment, 170
Royal Bavarian 1st Foot Artillery, 312
Mobile Military Surgical Hospital No 9, 312
Marines, 9

Indian Army
1st Indian Cavalry Division, 269
2nd Lancers, 193, 250
9th Hodson's Horse, 145, 268, 269
18th Lancers, 140
19th Lancers, 7
36th Jacob's Horse, 72
37th Lancers (Baluchi Horse), 69
39th King George's Own Central India Horse, 17
Deccan Horse, 150
3rd Queen Alexandra's Own Gurkha Rifles, 268
28th Punjabi's, 84, 289
45th (Rattrays) Sikhs, 164
26th Battery, Native Mountain Artillery, 102
Queens Own Corps of Guides, 257
Indian Labour Corps, 108, 145

New Zealand Expeditionary Force (NZEF), 8, 11, 64, 72, 78, 83, 96, 112, 168, 299
New Zealand Division, 7, 19, 20, 46, 91, 112, 130, 220, 234, 315
2nd New Zealand Rifle Brigade, 260
3rd New Zealand Rifle Brigade, 51, 83, 90
1st Battalion, 3rd NZ Rifle Brigade, 90
2nd Battalion, 3rd NZ Rifle Brigade, 110, 169
3rd Battalion, 3rd NZ Rifle Brigade, 130
4th Battalion, 3rd NZ Rifle Brigade, 187, 299
1st Auckland Infantry, 78, 96, 188
1st Canterbury Infantry, 8, 32, 112, 287
1st Otago Battalion, 72, 168
2nd Auckland Infantry, 5, 19, 315
2nd Otago Infantry, 64, 112, 276
New Zealand Engineers, 5
New Zealand Unknown Warrior, 51

Nigeria Regiment, 106; 1st, 63; 4th, 178,

South African Brigade, 58, 74, 93, 105, 114
South African Infantry, 1st, 75; 2nd, 290; 3rd, 75; 4th, 158, 192, 245; 6th, 16,
71st Siege Battery, South African Heavy Artillery, 208,
South African Medical Corps, 16,
Cape Auxiliary Horse Transport Corps, 265,

US Army
US II Corps, 254
Divisions
US 1st, 298, 305; US 3rd, 263; US 27th, 241, 261, 298; US 30th, 241, 261, 298; US 33rd, 298; US 80th, 298
Infantry
US 105th, 298; US 107th, 241, 299; US 108th, 241; US 119th, 298
Signal Reserve Corps, US Army, 210
Shaw Air Force Base, NC, USA, 210
US 6th Regiment, 263
US Coastal Artillery, 271
US Marine Corps, 271
US Army Reserve, 299

WW2
British Second Army, 232
50th Division, 9
Guards Armoured Division, 9, 131, 291
British GHQ Reserve, 231
Royal Horse Guards, 62, 291
15th/19th Hussars, 253
Royal Armoured Corps, 293, 294, 297
2nd Armoured Reconnaissance Brigade, Royal Armoured Corps, 297
Royal Army Service Corps, 173
1st Tyneside Scottish, Black watch, 166
Buffs, 173
5th Buffs, 291
2nd Irish Guards, 202
4th Queens Own Cameron Highlanders, 151
Queens Own Royal West Kents, 9, 296; 6th, 83; 7th, 270
7th Royal Sussex, 231
Royal Tank Regiment, 169; 7th, 297
Wiltshires, 297
18th Royal Garhwal Rifles, Indian Army, 169
RAF, 153,
Squadrons
No 4, 253; No 9, 232; No 13, 190; No 15, 293; No 18, 148, 207; No 21, 232; No 35, 305; No 51, 73, 232, 304; No 57, 148; No 59, 289; No 85, 205; No 90, 219; No 106, 295; No 111, 295; No 115, 112; No 157, 306; No 161, 232; No 185, 166; No 253, 294; No 26, 283; No 311 (Czech), 232; No 405, 305; No 412, 166; No 419, 165; No 426, 286; No 427, 98; No 464, 232; No 514, 67; No 550, 282; No 582, 305; No 617, 166, 296; No 635, 219
Royal Australian Air Force, 73
Royal Canadian Air Force, 282
Squadrons
No 6, 286; No 403, 112, 166; No 418, 305
No 487 Squadron, RNZAF, 232, 265
No 129 Squadron, RAFVR, 262
No 25 General Hospital, 232
No 121 General Hospital, 232
Lord Halifax, 71
Battle of Arras (WW2), 297
Bruneval Raid, 232
Operation Jericho, 232, 289
French 4th Colonial Division, 286
German 1st Panzer Division, 231, 289
German 6th Panzer Division, 83

US Marines, 166

Cemeteries
Abbeville Communal Cemetery, 77
Bari War Cemetery, 121, 169
Blankenberge Town Cemetery, 138
Boulogne Eastern, 29
Bully Grenay Communal Cemetery, 122, 246
Cairo War Memorial Cemetery, 72, 240
Dar es Salaam War Cemetery, 266
Duisans British, 138, 281
Etaples Military, 58, 149, 152, 184
Haifa War Cemetery, 14, 149
Harlebeke New British, 181, 225
La Madeleine Cemetery, 232
Le Touret Military, 172
Le Vertannoy British, 63
Leopoldsburg War Cemetery, 202
Lihons French National Cemetery, 12
Maison Blanch German Cemetery, 222
Montdidier French National, 175
Oudenaard Communal, 149
Point du Jour Cemetery, Arras, 306
Ramscappelle Road Military, 212
Royal Irish Rifles, Cemetery, Laventie, 274
St Sever Cemetery, Rouen, 122, 154, 246, 266
St Vaasit Post Military, 92
Terlincthun British, 78, 187, 232, 246
Trois Arbres, 200
Vailly British, 149, 172
Vendresse British, 152
Wimereux Communal, 52

CWGC, 35, 316; IWGC, 10, 21, 65, 130, 171, 277, 289, 294, 316; Directorate of Graves Registration and Enquiries (DGR&E), 86; Graves Registration Units (GRU's), 316; Commission of Grave Registration & Enquiries, 316

Decorations
VC, 5, 8, 9, 11, 19, 29, 30, 33, 38, 39, 57, 59, 60, 61, 62, 64, 72, 74, 75, 77, 80, 81, 95, 97, 98, 100, 101, 109, 117, 118, 121, 123, 128, 133, 134, 138, 139, 151, 154, 155, 157, 158, 160, 165, 166, 168, 169, 170, 172, 173, 177, 183, 184, 188, 190, 191, 193, 195, 196, 197, 200, 201 204 213 214 223 244 245 250 253 254 256 258 259 261 263 264 266 267 268 272 273 276 315
AM, 41, 42, 146, 150
DSO, 6, 8, 9, 11, 15, 22, 26, 28, 29, 30, 33, 34, 35, 36, 38, 40, 42, 45, 48, 50, 56, 63, 64, 77, 79, 81, 83, 84, 87, 92, 93, 94, 95, 97, 98, 99, 102, 104, 112, 113, 114, 117, 120, 121, 127, 128, 130, 132, 133, 136, 140, 149, 150, 151, 152, 153, 155, 156, 162, 173, 177, 178 183 184 185 187 188 192 193 196 197 200 201 204 211 214 219 220 224 225 228 230 232 234 236 237 241 249 250 253 254 256 257 258 259 261 264 266 268 269 271 273 274 275 277 278 282 289 291
MC, 6, 9, 11, 13, 15, 16, 17, 25, 29, 33, 34, 35, 45, 46, 47, 48, 49, 50, 53, 57, 62, 63, 67, 71, 75, 78, 81, 83, 84, 85, 87, 91, 84, 96, 97, 98, 100, 101, 106, 112, 113, 115, 124, 125, 126, 130, 132, 133, 136, 137, 138, 140, 141, 144, 148, 152, 156, 168, 169, 171, 174, 176 177 178

186 188 193 196 197 198 201 202 205 208 214 215 218 223 224 227 228 229 239 246 247 248 250 254 256 258 263 265 268 270 273 279 289 315

DCM, 8, 25, 26, 41, 42, 46, 50, 53, 54, 56, 61, 62, 64, 66, 71, 74, 76, 80, 91, 105, 106, 115, 116, 119, 125, 135, 136, 137, 142, 152, 159, 162, 164, 200, 205, 211, 213, 216, 217, 225, 227, 236, 242, 250, 257, 264, 266, 267, 272

MM, 41, 42, 46, 47, 50, 53, 59, 64, 68, 69, 74, 77, 84, 93, 115, 122, 129, 142, 144, 148, 149, 159, 160, 167, 178, 179, 190, 200, 206, 209, 211, 216, 217, 237, 238, 246, 251, 255, 257, 262, 264, 265, 266, 272, 273, 274, 279, 315

CMG, 45, 56, 63, 83, 94, 136, 155, 190, 192, 196, 200, 201, 224, 225, 232, 256, 258, 277

GCMG, 11

KCB, 11, 62, 263

GCB, 97, 150

CB, 29, 30, 45, 95, 200, 201, 268, 278

KBE, 11

CBE, 97

OBE, 188

MVO, 26, 62, 97, 150, 151, 285

VD, 45

DSC, 62, 132, 133, 164, 273

DFC, 67, 112, 166, 174, 219, 232, 250, 265, 282, 295

DFM, 166, 207, 232, 282, 304

MSM, 131

IDSM, 17, 145, 193, 250

Indian OM, 193, 250

KCMG, 263

Educational Institutions

Aberdeen University, 142; Bristol University, 243; Cambridge University, 28, 31, 66, 68, 127, 171, 218, 224, 294; Durham University, 170; Edinburgh University, 100, 172, 221; Eton College, 150, 164, 224; Glasgow University, 67, 81; Manchester University, 260; Oxford University, 21, 29, 71, 86, 124, 150, 171, 177, 181, 202, 212, 224; Trinity College, Dublin, 174; Uppingham School, 181

Ieper

Artillery Wood Cemetery, 285

Bedford House Cemetery, 107

Belgian Battery Corner ADS Cemetery, 84

Brandhoek Military Cemetery, 226

Essex Farm, 190

Gheluvelt, 256

Godezonne Farm Cemetery, 220

Hedge Row Trench Cemetery, 246

Hill 60, 66, 72, 95

Hooge, 113, 256

Hop Store Cemetery, 14, 230

Klein Zillebeke, 256

Langemark, 230

Lijssenthoek Cemetery, 14, 180, 230, 285

Loker Hospice Cemetery, 225

Mendinghem Military Cemetery, 77

Oostaverne Wood, 72

Passendale, 16, 67, 75, 257

Polygon Wood, 137

Prowse Point Cemetery, 155

Railway Dugouts Cemetery, 45, 158

Ration Farm Cemetery, 8

Ridge Wood Cemetery, 3

St Juliaan, 306

Strand Military Cemetery, 122, 246

Tyne Cot Cemetery, 224, 306

Ypres Reservoir Cemetery, 15, 104

Locations

Accrington, 61; Anglo-Egyptian Nile Expeditionary Force 1895, 112, 196, 277, 278; Battle of Bapaume 1870, 20; Battle of Colenso, 220; Bechuanaland Expedition, 44; Boxer Rebellion, China, 176; Bulgaria, 59; Burma, 45, 236; Burmese Wars, 164; Cameroons, 63, 230; Egypt, 28; Gambia Expedition, 190; German South West Africa, 16; India, 40, 42, 45, 162, 200, 217, 225, 227, 235, 236, 249, 258, 275; Indian Mutiny, 184, 247; Manchester, 61; Mekran Campaign, 102; Mesopotamia, 71, 233; Mohmand Expedition, 225, 227; Newfoundland, 50, 127, 231, 257, 281; North West Frontier, 45, 97, 113, 200, 225, 235, 257; Pilzen, 49; Siege of Lucknow 1857, 247; Sudan, 28, 45, 192, 277; Tirah Campaign, 200; Waziristan (Campaign), 45, 253; Zulu Bambatha Rebellion, 163

Medical Units

Casualty Clearing Stations

1st, 39, 236; 2nd, 201; 3rd, 15, 77, 112, 197; 4th, 257, 299; 5th, 9, 41, 43, 62, 70, 256; 7th, 17; 9th, 15, 61; 11th, 82, 257; 12th, 145; 13th, 53; 18th, 94, 213; 19th, 236; 20th, 17, 45, 79, 131, 236; 21st, 62, 70, 146, 180, 213, 239, 287; 22nd, 45, 236; 28th, 100; 29th, 74, 112; 30th, 45, 236; 33rd, 45; 34th, 70, 112, 113, 145, 287; 35th, 82; 36th, 52, 131; 37th, 70; 38th, 41, 131, 236; 39th, 10, 53, 257; 41st, 70, 79, 82, 214; 43rd, 17, 45, 236, 247; 44th, 197; 45th, 3, 70, 287; 46th, 17, 74, 77; 47th, 43, 77, 256, 257; 48th, 41, 43, 77, 145, 213, 214; 49th, 3, 39, 61, 112, 197; 51st (Highland), 262; 53rd, 70, 100, 145, 214, 219; 55th, 70, 77, 79, 113, 145; 56th (South Midlands), 77, 112, 231; 57th, 201; 58th, 25, 214; 59th, 257; 61st (South Midlands), 70, 119, 256; 1/1st (South Midlands), 70, 77, 287; Lucknow, 70, 145, 287; 2/1st (Northumbrian), 82; 2/1st (South Midlands), 197; 2/2nd (London), 131; 3rd Canadian, 213, 257; 4th Canadian, 39; 3rd Australian, 77, 112,

Corps Main Dressing Station

III, 171; VII, 45; IX, 256; XIV, 41, 44, 79; XV, 72, 76,

Field Ambulances

1st (Royal Navy), 99, 120, 156; 3rd Cavalry, 48, 216; 4th (London), 138; 4th, 266; 7th, 281; 7th Cavalry, 232; 11th, 174; 15th, 228; 17th, 253; 48th, 142; 53rd, 94; 92nd, 99; 107th, 180; 142nd, 174; 6th Canadian, 10; 4th Australian, 287; 12th Australian, 265

Hospitals

41st Stationary, 53, 100, 231; 42nd Stationary, 231; 3rd Canadian Stationary, 82; No 1 Australian Auxiliary, 72; 2nd Australian General, 241; 4th Scottish General, 126; 7th General, 231; New Zealand Stationary, 231; Craiglockhart, 104

4th Canadian Division ADS, 200

Memorials
12th Division, 87, 92
16th Division, 117
17th Division, 103
18th Division, 170
19th Division, 109
20th Division, 117
34th Division, 109
36th Division / Ulster Tower, 59, 102, 170, 182
38th Division, 70, 95
41st Division, 46
47th Division, 151
51st Division, 127
62nd Division, 110
63rd (Royal Naval) Division, 11, 27
1st Australian Division, 196
2nd Australian Division, 190, 300
3rd Australian Division, 167
12th Gloucestershires, 52
12th York & Lancasters, 207, 243
16th Royal Scots, 61
ANZAC's, Amiens, 231, 307
Arras, 51, 83, 134, 186, 196, 200, 254
Arras Flying Services, 48, 175
Australian, Villers-Bretonneux, 89, 154, 190, 195, 196, 201, 266, 316
Australian National War, Canberra, 195
Basra, 289
Cambrai (Louverval), 45, 47, 121, 147, 156, 157
Canadian, Courcelette, 65
Canadian, Le Quesnel, 148
Dar es Salaam, 63
Digger, Bullecourt, 201
Footballers, Longueval, 75
French 132nd Infantry Regiment, 306
French 17th Infantry Regiment, 46
French 18th Infantry Regiment, 46
French 19th Chausseurs a Pied, 305
French 1st Infantry Regiment, 304
French 329th Infantry Regiment, 12
French 363rd Infantry Regiment, 301
General Debeney, Amiens, 231, 307
Grenadier Guards, 115
Guards, 115
Gueudecourt Newfoundland, 7
Halifax, Nova Scotia, 134
Helles, 72
Jerusalem, 83
Kings Royal Rifle Corps, 196
La Ferte-Sous-Jarre, 83
Le Touret, 29, 91, 184, 192
Loos, 152, 184
Manchester & Liverpool Pals, 199
Marshal Foch, 306, 307
Marshal Foch, Amiens, 231, 307
Menin Gate, 3, 15, 35, 77, 78, 92, 133, 226, 244, 246, 266, 273
New Zealand Memorial to the Missing, Grevillers, 112
New Zealand Memorial to the Missing, Longueval, 52

New Zealand, Longueval, 75, 115
Newfoundland, Amiens, 231, 307
Newfoundland, Newfoundland Park, 50,
Nine Brave Men, 23,
Northern Rhodesia, Victoria Falls, 71, 178
Pipers, 75,
Ploegsteert, 57, 58, 92, 190, 202, 255, 266,
Plymouth Naval, 254,
Portsmouth Naval, 76,
Pozieres, 196, 205, 214, 244, 249, 263
Pozieres Windmill, 196,
Raymond Asquith, Amiens, 231, 307
Royal Canadian Dragoons, 231, 307
Sheffield Memorial Park, Serre, 90, 204, 206, 227
Singapore, 169,
South African, Amiens, 231, 307
South African, Delville Wood, 75,
Tank Corps, 196,
Thiepval, 7, 12, 69, 77, 93, 95, 102, 117, 122, 130, 151, 170, 179, 228, 243, 244, 249, 258, 259, 266
Tower Hill, 226, 255
Tyne Cot, 3, 78, 158, 228, 230, 239, 246,
Tyneside Brigade, 109,
US 6th Engineers, Amiens, 231, 307
Vimy, 57, 306
Vis en Artois, 193, 227, 272,

Military Locations
Farms
Cavalry, 239; Falfemont, 114; Malassie, 87; Maltzhorn, 56, 116; Mouquet, 34, 65, 132, 183, 195, 196, 197, 267; Touvent, 306; Vaucelette, 81, 254; Waterlot, 66, 74, 246, 247
Redoubts
Ellis, 54; Engien, 54; Fort Gibraltar Bunker, Pozieres, 196; Harp, 249; Herbercourt, 300; Hohenzollern, 98, 99; Leipzig Salient, 35, 38, 154, 277; Manchester, 197; Quadrilateral, 228, 245; Quentin, 94; Sanders Keep, 223; Schwaben, 43, 54, 59, 136, 144, 170, 258; Stuff, 111
Ridges & Hills
Broodseinde Ridge, 35, 56, 129, 133, 267, 273; Butte de Warlencourt, 123, 181, 201, 276; Hawthorn Ridge, 14, 27, 126; Longueval Ridge, 199; Mont St Quentin, 134, 190, 300; Pozieres Ridge, 195; Redan Ridge, 243; Tara Hill, 21; Usna Hill, 21; Villers Hill, 254; Vimy Ridge, 153, 257
Trenches
Hindenburg Line, 3, 4, 10, 15, 16, 19, 20, 22, 26, 27, 36, 37, 38, 40, 45, 46, 51, 57, 61, 64, 65, 66, 70, 72, 81, 87, 89, 91, 92, 93, 119, 124, 126, 136, 143, 144, 147, 153, 154, 161, 162, 177, 178, 179, 181, 182, 183, 193, 200, 203, 205, 206, 207, 209, 221, 229, 230, 235, 236, 238, 240, 241 247 250 254 258 268 269 270 274 276 306 314 315
Bayreuth, 222; Beaumont, 179; Brook Street, 120; Casement, 192; Central Avenue, 90; Cloudy, 113; Clump, 129; Copse, 191; Dantzig Alley, 69, 70, 95; Desire, 21, 233; Dewdrop, 136; Drocourt-Queant Line, 200; Fabeck Graben, 65; Frankfurt, 101, 102, 179, 182, 242; Gird, 115, 117; Gotha, 222; Grandcourt, 233; Hilt,

380

8; Jean Bart, 90; Lochnagar Street, 109; Longueval Alley, 69; Malt, 201; Mild, 8; Montauban Alley, 198; Munich, 102, 179, 182, 242, 274; Munster Alley, 60, 63; New Munich, 182; Owl, 187; Railway Avenue, 207; Regina, 47, 209, 210, 306; River, 203; Schwaben Hohe, 109; Signal, 275, 276; Snag, 123; Southern Avenue, 90; Straight, 117; Summit, 235; Swan, 203; Switch, 115; Tail, 123; Tara-Usna Line, 21, 109, 186; Tees, 249, 250; Tigris Lane, 249; Tunnel, 231; Valley, 95; Windmill, 115; Y Ravine, 86, 143, 280, 281

Valleys
Blighty, 154, 186, 284; Caterpillar, 79, 96; Mash, 109, 171, 186, 195; Nab, 186, 196; Pigeon Ravine, 88; Sausage, 38, 109, 186

Woods
Abbey, Villers-Bretonneux, 263; Bernafay, 191, 199; Bourlon, 97, 121, 200, 266; Buchanan, 128; Cayeux, 141; Delville, 10, 46, 51, 74, 75, 117, 192, 201, 227, 246, 247, 306; Flatiron Copse, 70; Gauche, 17, 75, 105, 269, 290; Gommecourt, 106; Hangard, 263; Havrincourt, 181; High, 8, 23, 42, 51, 52, 77, 150, 171, 258; Holnon, 54; Leuze, 58, 151, 154; Mametz, 9, 50, 70, 78, 95, 96, 108, 146, 176, 247, 278; Mansel Copse, 78, 306; Moreuil, 175; Savy, 218, 224, 225; Thiepval, 58, 60, 164, 239; Trones, 42, 63, 69, 116, 165, 244;

Broenbeke, Belgium, 81
Bullecourt, 81, 84, 118, 132, 133, 201, 265, 266, 267, 270
Fromelles, 13, 137, 266
Gallipoli, 3, 13, 32, 42, 63, 72, 75, 86, 99, 101, 113, 116, 120, 128, 132, 133, 137, 146, 155, 160, 164, 180, 181, 196, 197, 201, 220, 228, 236, 248, 254, 264, 265, 266, 267, 277, 283, 285, 287, 291
Glory Hole, La Boiselle, 109
Hawthorn Ridge Crater, 126, 127
Lochnagar Crater, 109, 187
Mons, 20, 28, 64, 79, 97, 117, 125, 174, 175, 208, 213, 225
Newfoundland Park, 8, 11, 12, 27, 50, 102, 127, 143, 168, 182, 242, 280, 281
Salonika, 67, 134, 180, 254, 256
Tambour, Fricourt, 104
Verdun, 9, 232, 300, 308
Zeebrugge, Belgium, 133, 138, 156

Misc
2nd Queens (S Afr Wars), 274; 5th Mounted Infantry (S Afr Wars), 115; Amiens Prison, 232; ANZAC, 6; ANZAC Day, 6, 291; Basilica of Notre Dame, Albert, 9; Battle of the Somme Film 1916, 69, 126; Berkshire Mounted Infantry (S Afr Wars), 29; Burma Police, 44; Christmas Truce, 28; Church of Latter Day Saints, 309; City of London imperial Yeomanry (Boer wars), 192; Claims Commission, 232; Egyptian Expeditionary Force, 66; French 4th Regiment (Franco-Prussian War), 286; Imperial Yeomanry (S Afr Wars), 121; Lakota Sioux Nation, 45; Leiling Stollen, 281; Little Big Horn, 45; Natal Carabinieres (S Afr Wars), 163; Naval Brigade (S Afr Wars), 120; Nobel Peace Prize, 151; Notre Dame Cathedral, Amiens, 231, 232, 307; Old Contemptibles, 33; Pagets Horse (S Afr Wars, 121; Quintishill rail Disaster, 271; Ricqueval Bridge, 260; Samoa Expeditionary Force, 83; Somme 1916 Museum, 9; South African Constabulary, 44; Ulster Volunteer Force (UVF), 167; Victoria School, Villers-Bretonneux, 264; Wimbledon Championships, 158; YMCA, 77

Other Wars
Franco Prussian War, 20, 39, 190, 204, 253, 276, 286, 293
Boer War, 36, 56, 77, 115, 130, 177, 192, 237, 271, 277, 278
South African Wars, 9, 28, 29, 38, 44, 62, 63, 71, 79, 102, 106, 112, 113, 117, 118, 120, 121, 162, 163, 173, 175, 176, 181, 187, 190, 192, 196, 200, 209, 220, 224, 230, 235, 249, 254, 256, 257, 258, 259, 269, 274, 275

People
Adams, Bryan, 223
Asquith, Herbert Henry PM, 117
Boelcke, Oswald, 81, 140
Bond, James, 241
Brittain, Vera, 155
Brooke, Rupert, 7, 71, 164
Churchill, Winston, 165
Coombes, Rose MBE, 47
Custer, General George, 45
Dickens, Charles, 117, 247
Duhamel, Georges, 302
Fleming, Ian, 241
Foch, Marshal Ferdinand, 82
French, Field Marshal John Denton Pinkstone, 38, 66, 316
Gladstone, William Ewart PM, 223
Gough, General Sir Hubert de la Poer, 182, 263, 289
Graves, Robert, 64, 70, 193
Haig, Field Marshal Sir Douglas, 50, 82, 157, 216, 264
Henry V, King, 39, 131, 309
Hodgson, Noel, 78
Housman, AE, 246
Immelman, Max, 172
Kitchener, Field Marshal Horatio Herbert, 112, 192, 316
Lauder, Harry, 187
Lichtenstein, Alfred, 315
Lutyens, Sir Edwin, 244
MacKintosh, Ewart Alan, 186
Morpurgo, Michael, 107
Munro, H H 'Saki', 179, 246,
Owen, Wilfred, 53, 126, 179, 228
Peel, Sir Robert, PM, 202
Prince of Wales (David, Edward VIII), 244, 316
Private Peaceful, 107
Queen Victoria, 277
Rathbone, Basil, 30
Rawlinson, General Henry Seymour, 131, 198, 204
Richthofen, Baron Manfred 'Red Baron' von, 263, 269, 311
Salisbury, Lord, PM, 45, 158
Sassoon, Siegfried, 57, 64, 70, 104, 197
Seegar, Alan, 12, 303
Sitting Bull, Chief, 45
Sorge, Reinhard, 315
Streets, John William, 90
Vauban, Marquis de, 54, 190
Verne, Jules, 232
von Kluck, General Alexander Heinrich Rudolph, 116

Ware, Sir Fabian, 237, 316

Sport

Athletics, 41, 247; Australian Rules Football, 100, 132; Boxing, 109, 169, 246; Canadian Gridiron Football, 249; Cricket, 16, 21, 23, 71, 75, 142, 219, 221, 226, 231, 247; Cycling, 112; Football, 5, 14, 16, 28, 50, 51, 61, 65, 69, 70, 83, 105, 109, 111, 197, 246, 315; Hockey, 169; MCC, 21, 226, ; Olympics, 58, 93, 111, 164, 169, 181, 223, 246, 247; Rowing, 29, 164, 223, 247; Rugby Union, 68, 71, 78, 142, 167, 169, 208, 219, 221, 233, 247, 265, 294; Shooting, 247; Swimming, 181; Tennis, 158;

Selected Places

Acheux, 3, 226; Achiet le Grand, 3, 45, 97, 206; Achiet le Petit, 3, 98; Albert, 9, 10, 15, 25, 28, 39, 78, 109, 111, 186, 226, 244; Amiens, 76, 78, 153, 228; Ancre, 11, 15, 25, 27, 34, 37, 60, 144, 203, 243; Armentieres, 8, 133, 187; Arras, 10, 75, 98, 124, 150, 205, 254, 271; Auchonvillers, 27, 90; Authuille, 60, 155, 192, 257; Authuille Wood, 28, 34, 35; Ayette, 205; Bapaume, 19, 20, 25, 177, 234, 244; Bazentin, 52, 71, 72, 75, 79, 96; Beaucourt en Santerre, 48, 101; Beaucourt sur Ancre, 120, 226, 227; Beaulencourt, 7, 19, 91; Beaumont-Hamel, 10, 11, 12, 27, 50, 67, 86, 89, 90, 91, 101, 102, 120, 127, 143, 160, 206, 242, 247, 274, 280, 281; Becourt, 23, 27; Belloy-en-Santerre, 13, 122, 251; Beugny, 4, 74, 91, 207; Blangy Tronville, 153, 265; Bony, 228; Bouchavesnes, 12, 222; Bray sur Somme, 41, 44; Bucquoy, 99, 205, 228; Cachy, 6, 72, 122; Cagnicourt, 118, 202; Cambrai, 16, 17, 118, 193, 202, 234, 249, 275, 298, 306; Carnoy, 70, 192, 245; Cerisy-Gaillet, 129; Cherisy, 36, 152, 228; Clery sur Somme, 54, 134, 228, 251; Colincamps, 89, 90; Combles, 58, 117; Contalmaison, 23, 60, 96, 187, 189, 196, 246, 278; Courcelette, 41, 42, 61, 65, 75, 109, 209, 210, 275; Croisilles, 118, 235; Curlu, 75, 134; Ecoust St Mein, 98, 118, 119; Epehy, 214, 268; Favreuil, 82, 260; Festubert, 271; Ficheux, 166; Flaucourt, 13, 134; Flers, 7, 8, 46, 52, 115, 132, 133, 154, 181, 227, 267; Flesquieres, 96, 185, 186; Foncquevillers, 45, 107; Fricourt, 41, 56, 70, 71, 95, 96, 103, 109, 183, 189, 196; Gentelles, 37, 39, 105, 122; Ginchy, 44, 52, 75, 114, 115, 117, 227, 247, 275; Gomiecourt, 82; Gommecourt, 89, 98, 106, 107, 130, 218, 259; Grandcourt, 15, 60, 65, 111, 203, 209, 210, 233, 246; Grevillers, 5, 25; Gueudecourt, 7, 8, 10, 19, 46, 115, 276, 277; Guillemont, 19, 32, 42, 50, 56, 63, 75, 87, 95, 165, 245, 247, 306; Hangard, 48, 49, 122; Harbonnieres, 71, 129; Havrincourt, 96, 97, 138, 159; Hebuterne, 38, 63, 106, 155, 221; Heudicourt, 110; Inchy en Artois, 118, 185; La Boiselle, 9, 21, 52, 109, 163, 171, 186, 187, 197, 246; Lagnicourt, 201, 202, 259; Le Quesnel, 49, 244; Le Sars, 5, 10, 181, 228, 276; Le Transloy, 113, 117, 239; Le Verguier, 180, 251, 260, 266; Lesboeufs, 19, 52, 56, 117, 136, 221; Longueval, 46, 52, 62, 74, 75, 79, 96, 115, 153, 191; Louverval, 4, 156; Mailly-Maillet, 86, 235; Mametz, 44, 58, 69, 78, 95, 108; Marcelcave, 265, 280; Marcoign, 39, 93, 96, 98; Maricourt, 44, 70, 191, 192; Martinpuich, 52, 76; Masnieres, 96, 98; Maurepas, 58, 75; Meharicourt, 101, 217; Metz-en-Couture, 110; Miraumont, 4, 203, 210; Moeuvres, 121; Monchy le Preux, 91, 271; Montauban, 50, 58, 69, 70, 96, 152, 199, 244; Montdidier, 37, 73, 219; Morchies, 82, 260; Morlancourt, 77, 129, 270; Morval, 58, 222; Nesle, 228; Noreuil, 202; Ovillers, 28, 109, 149, 155, 187, 195, 196, 246, 278; Peronne, 103, 122, 134, 137, 185, 251, 254; Pozieres, 8, 47, 60, 63, 65, 109, 132, 154, 187, 196, 227, 228, 233, 237, 246, 248, 266, 267, 277; Proyart, 129, 216; Puisieux, 203, 227; Pys, 4, 5; Queant, 4, 119; Rancourt, 134; Roisel, 88, 215, 224; Ronssoy, 254, 255; Rosieres, 129; Rouvroy, 37, 217; Rubempre, 32; Sailly Laurette, 22, 25, 129; Sailly le Sec, 25, 35, 79, 265; Sailly Saillisel, 58, 222, 306; Serre, 46, 64, 89, 90, 204, 245; St Pierre Divion, 60, 170; St. Quentin, 43, 54, 197, 228, 244, 256, 293, 298; Thiepval, 35, 38, 42, 43, 51, 52, 53, 58, 60, 65, 111, 149, 170, 196, 197, 243, 244, 246, 258, 277; Tincourt, 185, 251; Vadancourt, 256, ; Vaulx-Vraucourt, 4, 119, 259; Vauvillers, 13, 129; Vermandovillers, 13, 129, 215; Villers Faucon, 131, 241; Villers Plouich, 93, 98, 181, ; Villers-Bretonneux, 6, 13, 34, 67, 68, 196; Villers-Guislain, 17, 110; Vis en Artois, 272; Wailly, 82; Wancourt, 44, 91, 141, 249; Ytres, 151, 213, 228

Printed in Great Britain
by Amazon